THIRD CANADIAN EDITION

PERSONAL FINANCE

Jack R. Kapoor

College of DuPage

Les R. Dlabay

Lake Forest College

Robert J. Hughes

Dallas County Community Colleges

Arshad Ahmad

Concordia University

McGraw-Hill
Ryerson

Toronto   Montréal   Boston   Burr Ridge, IL   Dubuque, IA   Madison, WI   New York
San Francisco   St. Louis   Bangkok   Bogotá   Caracas   Kuala Lumpur   Lisbon   London
Madrid   Mexico City   Milan   New Delhi   Santiago   Seoul   Singapore   Sydney   Taipei

The McGraw·Hill Companies

McGraw-Hill Ryerson

Personal Finance
Third Canadian Edition

Copyright © 2006, 2004, 2001 by McGraw-Hill Ryerson Limited, a Subsidiary of The McGraw-Hill Companies. Copyright © 2004, 2001, 1999, 1996, 1994, 1991, 1988 by the McGraw-Hill Companies, Inc. All rights reserved. No part of this publication may be reproduced or transmitted in any form or by any means, or stored in a data retrieval system, without the prior written permission of McGraw-Hill Ryerson Limited, or in the case of photocopying or other reprographic copying, a licence from The Canadian Copyright Licensing Agency (Access Copyright). For an Access Copyright licence, visit www.accesscopyright.ca or call toll free to 1-800-893-5777.

ISBN-13: 978-0-07-095163-1

ISBN-10: 0-07-095163-2

4 5 6 7 8 9 10   QPD   0 9 8

Printed and bound in the U.S.A.

Care has been taken to trace ownership of copyright material contained in this text; however, the publisher will welcome any information that enables them to rectify any reference or credit for subsequent editions.

Publisher: Lynn Fisher
Senior Marketing Manager: Kelly Smyth
Developmental Editor: Maria Chu
Production Coordinator: Paula Brown
Supervising Editor: Anne Nellis
Copy Editor: Tara Tovell
Editorial Associate: Stephanie Hess
Permissions Editor: Karen Becker
Cover Design: Sharon Lucas
Cover Credits: © FoodPix, Burke/Triolo Productions; The Image Bank, Bernhard Lang
Interior Designer: Sharon Lucas
Composition: Bookman Typesetting Co. Inc.
Printer: China Translation & Printing Services Ltd.

Library and Archives Canada Cataloguing in Publication

Personal finance / Jack R. Kapoor ... [et al.]. — 3rd Canadian ed.

Includes bibliographical references and index.
ISBN 0-07-095163-2

1. Finance, Personal.   I. Kapoor, Jack R.

HG179.P455 2005   332.024   C2005-904352-0

To all our students who make teaching and learning happen.

ABOUT THE AUTHORS

JACK KAPOOR
COLLEGE OF DUPAGE

Jack Kapoor is a Professor of Business and Economics in the Business and Services Division. Dr. Kapoor has taught Business and Economics at College of DuPage since 1969. He received his B.A. and M.S. from San Francisco State College and his Ed.D. from Northern Illinois University. Professor Kapoor was awarded the Business and Services Division's Outstanding Professor Award for 1999–2000.

Dr. Kapoor is known internationally as a co-author of several textbooks including *Business: A Practical Approach* (Rand McNally), *Business* (Houghton Mif-flin), and the forthcoming *Small Business Management* (Richard D. Irwin/McGraw-Hill).

LES DLABAY
LAKE FOREST COLLEGE

Les Dlabay teaches in the Department of Economics and Business at Lake Forest College, Lake Forest, Illinois. Over the past 25 years, he has taught more than 30 different courses in high school, community college, university, adult education, and teacher preparation programs. Dr. Dlabay has developed a wide variety of textbook materials, student activity guides, instructor manuals, testing programs, audio-visual materials, and software packages in the areas of Personal Finance, Consumer Economics, and International Business.

Dr. Dlabay has served as a consultant to corporations, educational institutions, and government agencies. He has presented more than 140 workshops and seminars in over 20 states to encourage teachers to actively involve students in the learning process with video presentations, newsletters, interviews, and Internet research activities.

ROBERT HUGHES
DALLAS COUNTY COMMUNITY COLLEGES

Robert Hughes teaches business, management, and finance courses at Dallas County Community Colleges. In addition to *Personal Finance*, he has written college texts for Introduction to Business, Small Business Management and Entrepreneurship, and Business Math and presently has five books in publication. Dr. Hughes received his bachelor's degree from Southern Nazarene University and his master's and doctorate degrees from the University of North Texas.

ARSHAD AHMAD
CONCORDIA UNIVERSITY

Arshad Ahmad is Associate Professor at the John Molson School of Business at Concordia University. He completed his CGA designation in 1997, received an MBA and Ph.D from McGill University, and was awarded the George L.Geis Dissertation of the Year Award by the Canadian Society for the Study of Higher Education. Dr. Ahmad has received numerous faculty and university teaching awards. He was named a 3M teaching fellow in 1992 by the Society for Teaching and Learning in Higher Education and 3M Canada, and he now serves as Coordinator for the program.

Dr. Ahmad is the author of several texts, including *Canadian Financial Management* (5th Edition), and other pedagogical material, including study guides, case studies, video series, CD-ROMs, and various devices on the World Wide Web. He created and taught the business faculty's first Web-based undergraduate and graduate courses in Personal Finance, which have attracted over 6,000 students since 1999.

BRIEF CONTENTS

CONTENTS

**5   Introduction to Consumer
Credit**   129

Managing Your Credit

**4   The Banking Services of
Financial Institutions**   102

Insuring Your Resources

Investing Your Financial Resources

13 Investing in Mutual Funds

5

Controlling Your Financial Future

14 Retirement Planning

15 Estate Planning

PREFACE

THE TEXTBOOK AS AN ANCHOR

One of the most fulfilling aspects of teaching occurs when past students single out your course or pedagogy as the reason for a profound lifestyle/career change. In one unsolicited letter, Shirley wrote: "Sir, I wish my boyfriend took your course. I have changed my spending habits that I now practise with ease, and I have come to believe that financial problems are challenges disguised as hidden opportunities. There was something about the textbook that made me feel that experts were ever present to guide me to issues that I had either avoided or was most puzzled by...".

Many teachers receive e-mail or letters of this kind. And we can learn a lot from them. In her letter, Shirley is referring to a Web-based course that attracts large numbers of undergraduate students every semester. The course stands out with respect to the convenient access it provides students to the multimedia that have been selected to enhance their learning experience (CD-ROMs, videos, interactive testing, and more).

Despite all of these "extras" in the course, Shirley singled out an aspect of her experience that we often take for granted: the textbook. In this course, the textbook was deliberately used as the centrepiece around which other media and activities were designed. It resonated with the presence of guided expertise, which is a central quality for enabling student learning. The textbook also compelled the learner to attend to difficult issues. Personal testaments such as Shirley's convince us that a well-designed textbook can be the anchor for meaningful learning environments.

VARIETY MAKES FOR A RICH LEARNING ENVIRONMENT

A mosaic becomes functional when its pieces fit together and when the whole exceeds the sum of its parts. We recognize that students have different learning styles and that a textbook can have features that appeal to these differences and help students understand and apply concepts. Beyond informing our readers, in writing this textbook we wanted to encourage them to raise important questions that require further investigation. As well, we decided to limit coverage to 15 chapters grouped under five sections so that we could provide sufficient depth without pretending to give the "last word" on each topic. Thus, we took on the following triple challenge in revising each chapter for this edition. First, each chapter must qualify as being learner centred and provide examples and situations students can easily relate to. Second, multiple perspectives must raise the bar of content so that the learner begins to ask good questions and not simply accept material as prescription. Third, learning depends on the organization of material so that important concepts stand out and are reinforced in as many different contexts as possible.

EXAMPLES

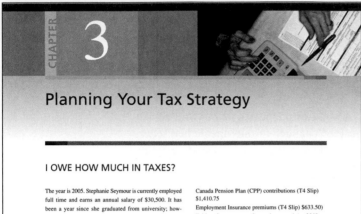

CHAPTER OPENING CASES typically describe a situation that the learner will face or is currently facing. A case begins each chapter's dicussion by presenting a problem, dilemma, or circumstance that clearly needs immediate attention. The questions accompanying the case correspond to the sequence of the chapter's contents and link procedures that may otherwise seem unrelated. For example, Chapter 3 presents the case of Stephanie Seymour, a young graduate planning her tax strategy.

CHAPTER 3

Planning Your Tax Strategy

I OWE HOW MUCH IN TAXES?

The year is 2005. Stephanie Seymour is currently employed full time and earns an annual salary of $30,500. It has been a year since she graduated from university; however, she continues to take a few part-time courses in the evenings. Stephanie is currently paying off her student loan; she makes monthly contributions to her RRSP and has begun to build an income-generating investment portfolio. She recently moved away from her parents' home and into her own apartment in downtown Toronto, which allows her to be 40 km closer to work and school. It should also be noted that Stephanie has made contributions to a few charities over the year. Stephanie is currently preparing to file her 2005 personal income taxes and has gathered the following information:

Canada Pension Plan (CPP) contributions (T4 Slip) $1,410.75
Employment Insurance premiums (T4 Slip) $633.50
Tuition (2 semesters = 8 part-time months)—$565 (T2202A slip)
Interest portion of payments on student loan—$835
Rent—$9,000
Moving expenses—$963.80
Rent on safety deposit box—$30
Investment income (Dividends)—$125 (T5 Slip)
RRSP contributions—$2,050
Charitable contributions—$65

We will follow Stephanie Seymour throughout the chapter as she completes her 2004 federal income tax

---

LEARNING OBJECTIVES structure the chapter, and each objective is repeated in the margin at the appropriate point in the main body of the chapter. The Learning Objectives appear again in the summary at the end of the chapter and are used to organize end-of-chapter questions, problems, and exercises, as well as materials in the Instructor's Manual and the Test Bank.

Ben and Yolanda decided to sort all their cheque stubs, receipts, and credit card statements to see where their money was going. Last year, they spent more than $2,000 in restaurants and charged more than $800 on their vacation.

"I didn't realize we spent that much on those things," commented Ben. "We also had auto maintenance costs of

2 How can knowing where their money goes help Ben and Yolanda plan their spending?

3 What financial goals might Ben and Yolanda consider to address some of their money management concerns?

4 Locate a Web site that would help Ben and Yolanda improve their money management skills.

LEARNING OBJECTIVES

1 Recognize relationships among financial documents and money management activities.
2 Create a system for maintaining personal financial records.
3 Develop a personal balance sheet and cash flow statement.
4 Create and implement a budget.
5 Calculate savings needed to achieve financial goals.

FINANCIAL PLANNING PROBLEMS

1. *Creating Personal Financial Statements.* On the basis of the procedures presented in the chapter, prepare your current personal balance sheet and a cash flow statement for the next month. (Obj. 3)

2. *Calculating Balance Sheet Amounts.* On the basis of the following data, compute the total assets, total liabilities, and net worth: (Obj. 3)

   Liquid assets, $3,670
   Investment assets, $8,340
   Current liabilities, $2,670
   Household assets, $89,890
   Long-term liabilities, $76,230

3. *Preparing a Personal Balance Sheet.* Use the following items to prepare a balance sheet and a cash flow statement. Determine the total assets, total liabilities, net worth, total cash inflows, and total cash outflows. (Obj. 3)

   Rent for the month, $650

Monthly take-home salary, $1,950
Cash in chequing account, $450
Savings account balance, $1,890
Spending for food, $345
Balance of educational loan, $2,160
Current value of automobile, $7,800
Telephone bill paid for month, $65
Credit card balance, $235
Loan payment, $80
Auto insurance, $230
Household possessions, $3,400
Stereo equipment, $2,350
Payment for electricity, $90
Lunches/parking at work, $180
Donations, $70
Home computer, $1,500
Value of stock investment, $860
Clothing purchase, $110
Restaurant spending, $130

56
www.mcgrawhill.ca/college/kapoor

Note: Link to Learning Objectives

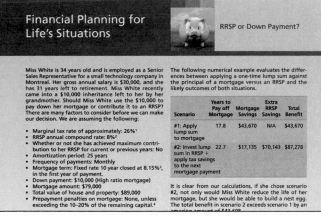

Financial Planning for Life's Situations

RRSP or Down Payment?

Miss White is 34 years old and is employed as a Senior Sales Representative for a small technology company in Montreal. Her gross annual salary is $30,000, and she has 31 years left to retirement. Miss White recently came into a $10,000 inheritance left to her by her grandmother. Should Miss White use the $10,000 to pay down her mortgage or contribute it to an RRSP? There are many factors to consider before we can make our decision. We are assuming the following:

- Marginal tax rate of approximately: 26%[1]
- RRSP annual compound rate: 8%[2]
- Whether or not she has achieved maximum contribution to her RRSP for current or previous years: No
- Amortization period: 25 years
- Frequency of payments: Monthly
- Mortgage term: Fixed rate 10 year closed at 8.15%[3], in the first year of payment.
- Down payment: $10,000 (High ratio mortgage)
- Mortgage amount: $79,000
- Total value of house and property: $89,000
- Prepayment penalties on mortgage: None, unless exceeding the 10–20% of the remaining capital.[4]

The following numerical example evaluates the differences between applying a one-time lump sum against the principal of a mortgage versus an RRSP and the likely outcomes of both situations.

Scenario	Years to Pay off Mortgage	Mortgage Savings	Extra RRSP Savings	Total Benefit
#1: Apply lump sum to mortgage	17.8	$43,670	N/A	$43,670
#2: Invest lump sum in RRSP + apply tax savings to the next mortgage payment	22.7	$17,135	$70,143	$87,278

It is clear from our calculations, if she chose scenario #2, not only would Miss White reduce the life of her mortgage, but she would be able to build a nest egg. The total benefit in scenario 2 exceeds scenario 1 by an amazing amount of $43,608.

STUDENT WORK has been incorporated into the text and depicts how former students have approached a number of decisions relevant to them. These samples serve to model for the students' peers how they tackled difficult questions by highlighting methods of analysis and suggested courses of action.

FINANCIAL PLANNING FOR LIFE'S SITUATIONS offers information that encourages the learner to take action. This feature is based on the principle of active learning; it presents example situations to prompt learners to apply newly acquired concepts and make unique financial planning decisions.

Financial Planning for Life's Situations

Switching to Accelerated Mortgage Payments

There are many ways to reduce the amortization period on your mortgage and, ultimately, the total interest that you will pay. One way involves switching from a regular to an *accelerated* payment. Let's look at an example.

If you took out a $100,000, 25-year mortgage at a rate of 6.5 percent, compounded semi-annually, your monthly mortgage payment would be $670. Total interest costs on the mortgage would amount to approximately $101,000, in addition to the repayment of $100,000 in principal. We calculate this as follows:

$670 × 300 payments = $201,000 in total payments
$201,000 − $100,000 principal = $101,000 in interest charges

If you were offered the opportunity to make accelerated weekly payments, your financial institution would calculate the weekly payment as one-quarter of the monthly payment. In this case, the weekly payment would be $167.50. ($670 ÷ 4). But because there are more than four weeks in each month (except February),

the result of paying $167.50 every week means that you are accelerating the repayment of your mortgage.

Given the same mortgage rate of 6.5 percent compounded semi-annually, and weekly payments of $167.50, the reduced amortization period on your mortgage would be 20 years and 9 months (1,079 weeks). This means you would pay:

$167.50 × 1,079 payments = $180,730 in total payments
$180,730 − $100,000 principal = $80,720 in interest charges

Switching from a monthly to an accelerated weekly mortgage would result in a reduction of 4 years and 3 months in your amortization period and a saving of approximately $20,270 ($101,000 − $80,730) in interest charges!

To explore other options to reduce your mortgage amortization period and interest charges, visit www.tdcanadatrust.com/mortgages/saving.jsp.

Financial Planning Calculations

Ratios for Evaluating Financial Progress

Financial ratios provide guidelines for measuring changes in your financial situation. These relationships can indicate progress toward an improved financial position.

Ratio	Calculation	Example	Interpretation
Debt ratio	Liabilities divided by net worth	$25,000/$50,000 = 0.5	Shows relationship between debt and net worth; a low debt ratio is best.
Current ratio	Liquid assets divided by current liabilities	$4,000/$2,000 = 2	Indicates $2 in liquid assets for every $1 of current liabilities; a high current ratio is desirable to have cash available to pay bills.
Liquidity ratio	Liquid assets divided by monthly expenses	$10,000/$4,000 = 2.5	Indicates the number of months in which living expenses can be paid if an emergency arises; a high liquidity ratio is desirable.
Debt-payments* ratio	Monthly credit payments divided by take-home pay	$540/$3,600 = 0.15	Indicates how much of a person's earnings goes for debt payments (excluding a home mortgage); most financial advisers recommend a debt-payments ratio of less than 20 percent.
Savings ratio	Amount saved each month divided by gross income	$648/$5,400 = 0.12	Financial experts recommend monthly savings of at least 10 percent.

*Unlike the gross debt service (GDS) and total debt service (TDS) ratios explained in Chapter 7, The Finances of Housing, the debt-payments ratio is based on take-home pay, not gross employment income.

FINANCIAL PLANNING CALCULATIONS features approximately 100 mathematical applications that the learner must master. All these calculations are situated in decisions that are typical of what learners encounter but may have shied away from due to the numbers behind these operations. The procedures illustrated in these calculations reinforce concepts introduced in the chapter in an applied setting. They are also tied to end-of-chapter questions and exercises.

ADVICE FROM A PRO is a great example of distributed expertise and multiple perspectives. In this box, industry professionals provide the kind of advice one can take home and internalize in order to make sense of the informational deluge that all of us face.

Advice from a Pro

A Pro's Views on Credit Chaos

According to Jonathan Hoenig, a radio show host and a columnist, "the bubonic plague of personal finance comes in the form of a 17-percent or higher interest rate on your credit card. You'll have to do a lot of bargain shopping and coupon clipping to compensate for your constantly compounding finance charges. Bummer? Yes. Your fault? Yes. Just because you have access to credit doesn't mean you should necessarily partake of the plastic." He cautions that credit cards can be a useful part of personal finance or a painful experience. A good rule to live by: *Don't buy things you can't afford.*

Thankfully, most young people seem to be following the rules these days. Compared with the majority of

cardholders, most of whom carry a balance, young people are demonstrating their financial savvy in record numbers.

Paying cash? You'll still deal with debt. Certain types, like school loans, car payments, and mortgages, are designed to be paid over longer periods of time. This is reflected in a lower interest rate. A credit card bill, and other types of "unsecured" debt, however, should be paid as soon as possible, advises Hoenig.

Various surveys suggest young people are headed in the right direction. Most college/university students recognize the importance of establishing and maintaining a good credit history.

---

important information about your purchases.
- *Review your monthly bank and credit card statements* for any billing errors or unauthorized purchases. Notify your credit card issuer or bank immediately if your credit card or chequebook is lost or stolen.
- *Read the policies of Web sites you visit,* especially the disclosures about a site's security, its refund policies, and its privacy policy on collecting and using your personal information. Some Web sites' disclosures are easier to find than others; look at the bottom of the home page, on order forms, or in the "About" or "FAQ" section of a site. If you can't find a privacy policy, consider shopping elsewhere.
- *Keep your personal information private.* Don't disclose personal information—your address, telephone number, social insurance number, or e-mail address—unless you know who's collecting the information, why they're collecting it, and how they'll use it.
- *Give payment information only to businesses you know and trust,* and only in appropriate places, such as electronic order forms.
- *Never give your password to anyone online,* even your Internet service provider.

DID YOU KNOW?

Sixty-four percent of Canadian households have at least one regular Internet user, and shopping online takes up 18.6 percent of surfing time. When shopping online, the average order cost the Canadian shopper $144.

SOURCE: www.statcan.ca/english/Pgdb/arts01a.htm

137
www.mcgrawhill.ca/college/kapoor

DID YOU KNOW boxes contain up-to-date facts, figures, and answers to frequently asked questions. They are featured several times within each chapter and typically elicit an "a-ha!" from the learner. These are not just catchy but provide well-researched insights that are often quoted by students in discussion forums.

CONCEPT CHECKS are a valuable device to help learners digest conceptual chunks within a section before they proceed further into the chapter. These questions also serve to refocus the student's attention on the learning objective that applies to each section.

[3] Help you assess your spending and saving patterns. Are you directing funds towards the attainment of your goals, or are you spending too much on discretionary items?

The relationship between various personal balance sheet and cash flow items can give an indication of your financial position. The Financial Planning Calculations box, above, explains several commonly used personal financial ratios. These financial ratios and other types of financial analysis provide insight into how well you are managing your cash flows and assets.

CONCEPT CHECK 2–3

1. What are the main purposes of personal financial statements?
2. What does a personal balance sheet tell about your financial situation?
3. How can you use a balance sheet for personal financial planning?
4. What information does a cash flow statement present?

FINANCIAL PLANNING ACTIVITIES

1. *Determining Criteria If a Loan Is Needed.* Survey friends and relatives to find out what criteria they have used to determine the need for credit. (Obj. 1)

2. *Comparing Costs of Loans from Various Lenders.* Prepare a list of sources of inexpensive loans, medium-priced loans, and expensive loans in your area. What are the trade-offs in obtaining a loan from an "easy" lender? (Obj. 1)

3. *Using the Internet to Obtain Information about the Costs of Credit.* As pointed out at the beginning of this chapter, credit costs money; therefore, you must conduct a cost/benefit analysis before making any major purchase. While most people consider credit costs, others simply ignore them and eventually find themselves in financial difficulties. To help consumers avoid this problem, each of the following organizations provides information on a Web site:
   - The Quicken Financial Network, at www.quicken.ca, helps consumers save money when purchasing, financing, or refinancing by keeping them up to date on news, views, and rates.
   - CCC Consumer Credit Counselling, at www.iamdebtfree.com, offers financial counselling and debt consolidation services.

Choose one of the above organizations and visit its Web site. Then, prepare a report that summarizes the information the organization provides. Finally, decide how this information could help you better manage your credit and its costs. (Obj. 2)

4. *Choosing between the Features and Costs of a Loan.* When you choose financing, what are the trade-offs between the features you prefer (term, size of payments, fixed or variable interest, or payment plan) and the cost of your loan? (Obj. 2)

5. *Calculating the Cost of Credit Using Two APR Formulas.* How are the simple interest and simple interest on the declining balance, formulas used in determining the cost of credit? (Obj. 2)

6. *Handling Contacts from Debt Collection Agencies.* Your friend is drowning in a sea of overdue bills and is being harassed by a debt collection agency. Prepare a list of the steps your friend should take if the harassment continues. (Obj. 3)

7. *Seeking Assistance from Consumer Credit Counselling Services.* Visit a local office of a credit counselling service. What assistance can debtors obtain from this office? What is the cost of this assistance, if any? (Obj. 4)

FINANCIAL PLANNING ACTIVITIES provide an opportunity for students to translate learning objectives into research, which in turn feeds into decisions they may be ready to make. A "To Do" list includes various procedures, techniques, and sources of information.

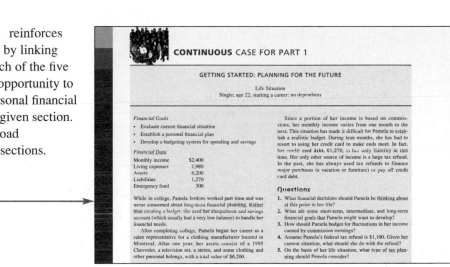

LIFE SITUATION CASE

We Rent, So Why Do We Need Insurance?

"Have you been down in the basement?" Nathan asked his wife, Erin, as he entered their apartment.

"No, what's up?" responded Erin.

"It's flooded because of all that rain we got last weekend!" he exclaimed.

"Oh no! We have the extra furniture my mom gave us stored down there. Is everything ruined?" Erin asked.

"The couch and coffee table are in a foot of water; the loveseat was the only thing that looked okay. Boy, I didn't realize the basement of this building wasn't waterproof. I'm going to call our landlady to complain."

As Erin thought about the situation, she remembered that when they moved in last fall, Kathy, their landlady, had informed them that her insurance policy covered the building but not the property belonging to each tenant. Because of this, they had purchased renter's insurance. "Nathan, I think our renter's insurance will cover the damage. Let me give our agent a call."

When Erin and Nathan purchased their insurance, they had to decide whether they wanted to be insured for cash value or for replacement costs. Replacement was more expensive, but it meant they would collect enough to go out and buy new household items at today's prices. If they had opted for cash value, the couch Erin's mother had paid $1,000 for five years ago would be worth less than $500 today.

Erin made the call and found out their insurance did cover the furniture in the basement, and at replacement value after they paid the deductible. The $300 they had invested in renter's insurance last year was well worth it!

Not every renter has as much foresight as Erin and Nathan. Fewer than four in 10 renters have tenant's insurance. Some aren't even aware they need it. They may assume they are covered by the landlord's insurance, but they aren't. This mistake can be costly.

Think about how much you have invested in your possessions and how much it would cost to replace them. Start with your stereo equipment or the colour television and VCR that you bought last year. Experts suggest that people who rent start thinking about these things as soon as they move into their first apartment. Your policy should cover your personal belongings and provide funds for living expenses if you are dispossessed by a fire or other disaster.

Questions

1. Why is it important for people who rent to have insurance?
2. Does the building owner's property insurance ever cover the tenant's personal property?
3. What is the difference between cash value and replacement value?
4. When shopping for renter's insurance, what coverage features should you look for?

LIFE SITUATION CASES provide opportunities for the learner to understand real-life situations that individuals face. These cases allow the student to assume the role of a consultant who can identify underlying problems, establish a framework for analysis, clarify issues, and propose possible solutions.

THE CONTINUOUS CASE reinforces the benefits of case-based teaching by linking the major concepts presented in each of the five sections in the text. It provides an opportunity to identify and analyze a range of personal financial decisions about several topics in a given section. Students begin to appreciate the broad connections between chapters and sections.

CONTINUOUS CASE FOR PART 1

GETTING STARTED: PLANNING FOR THE FUTURE

Life Situation
Single; age 22; starting a career; no dependants

Financial Goals
- Evaluate current financial situation
- Establish a personal financial plan
- Develop a budgeting system for spending and savings

Financial Data

Monthly income	$2,400
Living expenses	1,980
Assets	6,200
Liabilities	1,270
Emergency fund	300

While in college, Pamela Jenkins worked part time and was never concerned about long-term financial planning. Rather than creating a budget, she used her chequebook and savings account (which usually had a very low balance) to handle her financial needs.

After completing college, Pamela began her career as a sales representative for a clothing manufacturer located in Montreal. After one year, her assets consist of a 1995 Chevrolet, a television set, a stereo, and some clothing and other personal belongs, with a total value of $6,200.

Since a portion of her income is based on commissions, her monthly income varies from one month to the next. This situation has made it difficult for Pamela to establish a realistic budget. During lean months, she has had to resort to using her credit card to make ends meet. In fact, her credit card debt, $1,270, is her only liability at this time. Her only other source of income is a large tax refund. In the past, she has always used tax refunds to finance major purchases (a vacation or furniture) or pay off credit card debt.

Questions

1. What financial decisions should Pamela be thinking about at this point in her life?
2. What are some short-term, intermediate, and long-term financial goals that Pamela might want to develop?
3. How should Pamela budget for fluctuations in her income caused by commission earnings?
4. Assume Pamela's federal tax refund is $1,100. Given her current situation, what should she do with the refund?
5. On the basis of her life situation, what type of tax planning should Pamela consider?

UPDATED CONTENT

In this third edition of *Personal Finance*, we have revised and updated Web sites, facts, and figures, including the Did You Know boxes, using relevant Canadian sources. We have introduced several examples of student work, as well as cases that feature issues important to students. Financial problems have been revised to reflect the new material. We have also illustrated financial calculations throughout the text with the applications used on a Texas Instrument BAII Plus calculator. A tutorial for the TI BAII Plus Calculator can be downloaded at the Kapoor Web site: **www.mcgrawhill.ca/college/kapoor**.

In addition to these features, we have paid special attention to revising several chapters. An improved discussion with respect to analyzing personal financial statements is provided in **Chapter 2**, Money Management Strategy: Financial Statements and Budgeting. **Chapter 3**, Planning Your Tax Strategy, has been rewritten to focus on the federal tax return (the provincial return is now featured in the appendix). We have updated the forms and information to 2004, expanded the section on tax strategy, and provided a better description of the stages involved in calculating the amount of federal taxes due. In **Chapter 6**, Choosing a Source of Credit: The Costs of Credit Alternatives, the Cost of Credit section has been rewritten to reflect the computations used in Canada and to compare the cost of instalment loans versus lines of credit. In **Chapter 7**, The Finances of Housing, we have provided an expanded explanation of mortgage terminology in Canada and re-arranged the steps in the home-buying process to emphasize that home affordability asessement should precede choice of home. **Chapter 11**, Investing in Stocks, has been rewritten to incorporate better numerical measures of shareholder return. We have also introduced a new section on behavioural finance and improved the discussion of various investment techniques. Finally, in **Chapter 15**, Estate Planning, we have expanded and improved the discussion of family law, types of will, and trusts.

We have been mindful of attending to detail, but more importantly, we have made a special effort to put ourselves in the mind of the reader. We are confident that this edition will meet the needs of students so that they can connect with the information, advice, and stories that unfold in the text, and gain the confidence to pursue further mastery of any of the 15 topics presented.

TECHNOLOGY SOLUTIONS

ONLINE LEARNING CENTRE

More and more students are studying online. That is why we offer an Online Learning Centre (OLC) that follows *Personal Finance* chapter by chapter. You don't have to build or maintain anything and it's ready to go the moment you and your students type in the URL:

www.mcgrawhill.ca/college/kapoor

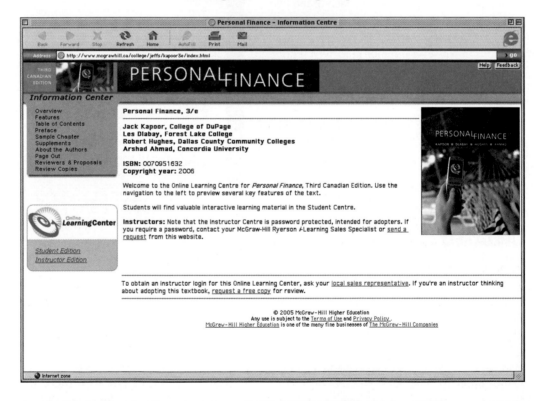

As your students study, they can refer to the OLC Web site for such benefits as:

- Online Quizzes
- Internet Application Questions
- CBC Video
- *The Globe and Mail* Headline Links
- Finance Around the World
- Study to Go

- Glossary and Key Terms
- Summary of Objectives
- TI BA II+ Tutorial
- Interactive Charts
- Flashcards
- Web Links

Remember, the *Personal Finance* OLC content is flexible enough to use with any course management platform currently available. If your department or school is already using a platform, we can help. For information on our course management services, contact your *i*Learning Sales Specialist or see "Superior Service" on page xx.

CLASSROOM PERFORMANCE SYSTEM (CPS)

BRING INTERACTIVITY INTO THE CLASSROOM OR LECTURE HALL

CPS, by eInstruction, is a student response system using wireless connectivity. It gives instructors and students immediate feedback from the entire class. The response pads are remotes that are easy to use and engage students.

- CPS helps you to increase student preparation, interactivity, and active learning so you can receive immediate feedback and know what students understand.
- CPS allows you to administer quizzes and tests, and provide immediate grading.
- With CPS you can create lecture questions that can be multiple-choice, true/false, and subjective. You can even create questions on-the-fly as well as conduct group activities.
- CPS not only allows you to evaluate classroom attendance, activity, and grading for your course as a whole, but CPS Online allows you to provide students with an immediate study guide. All results and scores can easily be imported into Excel and can be used with various classroom management systems.

CPS-ready content is available for use with the book. Please contact your *i*Learning Sales Specialist for more information on how you can integrate CPS into your investments classroom.

MOBILE LEARNING

STUDY TO GO   The businesses and companies of today want their new employees to be adept in all aspects of the changing business environment. They are quick to tell us that they want graduates with the skills of tomorrow . . . today. From laptops to cell phones to PDAs, the new medium is mobility.

As a leader in technology and innovation, McGraw-Hill Ryerson has developed material providing students with optimum flexibility for use anytime, anywhere they need to study— whether with a laptop, PDA, or tablet. These innovations provide instructors with a number of exciting ways to integrate technology into the learning process.

With **Study To Go** we have introduced wireless activities as a part of our Online Learning Centre. Now, whether you are waiting in line, riding on transit, or just filling some spare time, homework and practice are just a click away.

COURSE MANAGEMENT

PAGEOUT   McGraw-Hill Ryerson's course management system, PageOut, is the easiest way to create a Web site for your *Personal Finance* course. There is no need for HTML coding, graphic design, or a thick how-to book. Just fill in a series of boxes in plain English and click on one of our professional designs. In no time, your course is online!

For the integrated instructor, we offer *Personal Finance* content for complete online courses. Whatever your needs, you can customize the *Personal Finance* Online Learning Centre content and author your own online course materials. It is entirely up to you. You can offer online discussion and message boards that will complement your office hours, and reduce the lines outside your door. Content cartridges are also available for course management systems, such as **WebCT** and **Blackboard**. Ask your *i*Learning Sales Specialist for details.

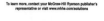

SUPERIOR SERVICE

Service takes on a whole new meaning with McGraw-Hill Ryerson and *Personal Finance*. More than just bringing you the textbook, we have consistently raised the bar in terms of innovation and educational research—both in finance and in education in general. These investments in learning and the education community have helped us to understand the needs of students and educators across the country, and allowed us to foster the growth of truly innovative, integrated learning.

INTEGRATED LEARNING Your Integrated Learning Sales Specialist is a McGraw-Hill Ryerson representative who has the experience, product knowledge, training, and support to help you assess and integrate any of our products, technology, and services into your course for optimum teaching and learning performance. Whether it's helping your students improve their grades, or putting your entire course online, your *i*Learning Sales Specialist is there to help you do it. Contact your *i*Learning Sales Specialist today to learn how to maximize all of McGraw-Hill Ryerson's resources!

*i*LEARNING SERVICES McGraw-Hill Ryerson offers a unique *i*Services package designed for Canadian faculty. Our mission is to equip providers of higher education with superior tools and resources required for excellence in teaching. For additional information, visit *www.mcgrawhill.ca/highereducation/iservices*.

TEACHING, TECHNOLOGY & LEARNING CONFERENCE SERIES The educational environment has changed tremendously in recent years, and McGraw-Hill Ryerson continues to be committed to helping you acquire the skills you need to succeed in this new milieu. Our innovative Teaching, Technology & Learning Conference Series brings faculty together from across Canada with 3M Teaching Excellence award winners to share teaching and learning best practices in a collaborative and stimulating environment. Pre-conference workshops on general topics, such as teaching large classes and technology integration, will also be offered. We will also work with you at your own institution to customize workshops that best suit the needs of your faculty.

RESEARCH REPORTS INTO MOBILE LEARNING AND STUDENT SUCCESS These landmark reports, undertaken in conjunction with academic and private sector advisory boards, are the result of research studies into the challenges professors face in helping students succeed and the opportunities that new technology presents to impact teaching and learning.

COMPREHENSIVE TEACHING AND LEARNING PACKAGE

We have developed a number of supplements for both teaching and learning to accompany this text:

FOR INSTRUCTORS

INSTRUCTOR'S ONLINE LEARNING CENTRE (www.mcgrawhill.ca/college/kapoor)

The Online Learning Centre includes a password-protected Web site for instructors. The site offers downloadable supplements, CBC Video Case Notes, and PageOut, the McGraw-Hill Ryerson course Web site development centre.

INSTRUCTOR'S RESOURCE CD-ROM
The Instructor's Resource CD-ROM contains all the necessary Instructor Supplements, including:

- **Instructor's Manual,** a "Course Planning Guide" with instructional strategies, course projects, and supplementary resource lists. The "Chapter Teaching Materials" section of the Instructor's Manual provides a chapter overview, the chapter objectives with summaries, introductory activities, and detailed lecture outlines with teaching suggestions. This section also includes concluding activities, ready-to-duplicate quizzes, supplementary lecture materials and activities, and answers to concept checks, end-of-chapter questions, problems, and cases.
- **Computerized Test Bank** consists of over 1,000 true-false, multiple choice, and essay questions. These test items are organized by the learning objectives for each chapter, present different levels of difficulty, and are tied to concepts in the text.
- **PowerPoint Presentation,** prepared by Cyndi Hornby of Fanshawe College, contains visual presentations that may be edited and manipulated to fit a particular course format.

CBC VIDEOS AND CASE NOTES

Prepared by Rosemary Vanderhoeven of the University of Guelph. These video segments present CBC broadcasts, selected to assist students in applying personal finance theory to real-world issues. A set of instructor notes for each video segment is available at the Instructor's Online Learning Centre. The video segments are available in DVD format and through video-streaming at the Online Learning Centre.

FOR STUDENTS

STUDENT ONLINE LEARNING CENTRE
(www.mcgrawhill.ca/college/kapoor)
The OLC prepared by Hardeep Gill of the Northern Alberta Institute of Technology, offers a wealth of materials, including online quizzes, CBC video cases, extensive annotated Web resources, Internet Application Questions, and much more. There is also a link to *Finance Around the World*, a tremendous resource that takes students to important and popular finance Web sites from around the globe.

STUDENT CD-ROM
The Student CD-ROM is included with each new text; this rich resource includes:

- **Personal Financial Planner**, a valuable learning tool comprising over 60 interactive worksheets for creating and implementing a personal financial plan.
- **Video Clips**, a series of video interviews produced by the textbook author, Arshad Ahmad.
- Link to the Student Online Learning Centre.

ONE MORE THING ...

Many instructors who have taught the subject of personal finance point out that many students select their elective course simply because the subject matter is intrinsically appealing to them. We agree. Personal finance highlights authentic situations that every student encounters at some point, relating to setting goals, budgeting, taxes, insurance, investment, retirement, and so on. And yet, the subject matter lends itself to decision making that can be terrifying and wonderful at the same time.

Many surveys reveal that a majority of Canadians try to avoid or defer making financial decisions that have a way of popping up frequently, no matter how old we are and no matter what we do. Yet, as mentioned earlier, financial problems are really opportunities in disguise.

We tend to make important lifestyle changes once we falter or when we have to. After taking the first steps in confronting difficult decisions, much of the anxiety dissipates, and alternative courses of action become feasible. We also wonder why we did not tackle these issues earlier. In fact, there is a strong argument for starting to learn about money, choices, and opportunity costs in high school and building on basic concepts during the college and university years and the rest of our careers.

We hope this textbook will help students take these important first steps. We hope it will serve them to build a solid foundation. We also hope that their learning experience will be informative, enjoyable, and lifelong.

ACKNOWLEDGEMENTS

When we consider the efforts of contributors, we are truly humbled by their dedication and professionalism. Former students, friends, colleagues, and family members deserve many thanks and recognition for their sacrifices and especially for giving this textbook its own flavour and character. Some of them are acknowledged below.

We are also indebted and offer special thanks to Penny Ellison, Naz Rahman, and Marlene Osgainian, who did a lot of research updates and more importantly, contributed ideas that has changed the look of this edition. Penny has worked on this project as a peer consultant, contributing the expertise she has achieved as a personal financial planner and lecturer at several universities and the Canadian Institute for Bankers. Her expertise in taxes has resulted in a completely revamped chapter. Naz was first my student, then teaching assistant, and now a part-time instructor. Naz is a perfectionist who has worked miracles with deadlines. Marlene is a final-year student who has been a teaching assistant for our personal finance course; she is always busy designing and grading assignments and is ever willing to embrace a challenge. All have contributed with an eye to quality and have promoted the learner's perspective throughout. A *gros merci* to all!

We also wish to thank the following reviewers, whose constructive suggestions have been incorporated as much as possible into the development of the Third Canadian Edition:

Reviewers of the Third Canadian Edition

Ken Brightling, *Fanshawe College*

Alan Frank, *Southern Alberta Institute of Technology*

Bill Giglio, *Camosun College*

Hardeep Gill, *Northern Alberta Institute of Technology*

Jim Hebert, *Red River College*

Brian Hobson, *Georgian College*

Errol Johnson, *George Brown College*

David Parker, *George Brown College*

Carson Rappell, *Dawson College*

Rosemary Vanderhoeven, *University of Guelph*

Carl Weston, *Mohawk College*

Ellen Wilson, *Northern Alberta Institute of Technology*

We would also like to acknowledge the professional contributions made by McGraw-Hill Higher Education and McGraw-Hill Ryerson. Thanks go to Lynn Fisher, Publisher; Maria Chu, Developmental Editor; Anne Nellis, Supervising Editor; and Tara Tovell, Copy Editor.

Finally, we look forward to teachers' comments, suggestions, and questions. It is our hope that this textbook will make a difference in the lives of your students.

Arshad Ahmad
arshad@jmsb.concordia.ca

Personal Financial Planning: An Introduction

KAREN'S FINANCIAL PLAN

Karen Edwards, 23, completed her Bachelor of Science one year ago. The major cost of her tuition and books was covered by a scholarship. Through wise planning, she was able to save $15,000 from her part-time jobs. Acting on a suggestion from her parents, Karen met with a financial planner, who advised her to invest her money in low-risk bonds and saving certificates.

Karen works in an office in Toronto, Ontario, and she earns $25,000 a year. In approximately three years, she would like to return to school and start her master's degree. Then, she would like to buy a house. Karen wants to live on her salary and invest the $15,000 for her education and future home.

QUESTIONS

1 How did Karen benefit from her parents' advice and her own financial planning?

2 What decisions does Karen need to make regarding her future?

3 How could various personal and economic factors influence Karen's financial planning?

4 What would be the value of Karen's $15,000 in three years if it earned an annual interest rate of 7 percent?

5 Conduct a Web search to obtain information that Karen may find useful.

LEARNING OBJECTIVES

1 Analyze the process for making personal financial decisions.

2 Develop personal financial goals.

3 Assess personal and economic factors that influence personal financial planning.

4 Determine personal and financial opportunity costs associated with personal financial decisions.

5 Identify strategies for achieving personal financial goals for different life situations.

THE FINANCIAL PLANNING PROCESS

Everywhere you turn, someone is talking about money. When it comes to handling your finances, are you an *explorer*, someone who is always searching through uncharted areas? Are you a *passenger*, just along for the ride on the money decision-making trip of life? Or are you a *researcher*, seeking answers to the inevitable money questions of life?

Most people want to handle their finances so that they get full satisfaction from each available dollar. Typical financial goals include such things as a new car, a larger home, advanced career training, extended travel, and self-sufficiency during working and retirement years. To achieve these and other goals, people need to identify and set priorities. Financial and personal satisfaction are the result of an organized process that is commonly referred to as *personal money management* or *personal financial planning*.

Personal financial planning is the process of managing your money to achieve personal economic satisfaction. This planning process allows you to control your financial situation. Every person, family, or household has a unique financial position, and any financial activity, therefore, must also be carefully planned to meet specific needs and goals.

A comprehensive financial plan can enhance the quality of your life and increase your satisfaction by reducing uncertainty about your future needs and resources. The specific advantages of personal financial planning include:

- Increased effectiveness in obtaining, using, and protecting your financial resources throughout your lifetime.
- Increased control of your financial affairs by avoiding excessive debt, bankruptcy, and dependence on others for economic security.
- Improved personal relationships resulting from well-planned and effectively communicated financial decisions.
- A sense of freedom from financial worries obtained by looking to the future, anticipating expenses, and achieving your personal economic goals.

We all make hundreds of decisions each day. Most of these decisions are quite simple and have few consequences. Some are complex and have long-term effects on our personal and financial situations. While everyone makes decisions, few people consider how to make better decisions. As Exhibit 1-1 shows, the financial planning process is a logical, six-step procedure:

1. Determining your current financial situation.
2. Developing financial goals.
3. Identifying alternative courses of action.
4. Evaluating alternatives.
5. Creating and implementing a financial action plan.
6. Re-evaluating and revising the plan.

STEP 1: DETERMINE YOUR CURRENT FINANCIAL SITUATION

In this first step of the financial planning process, you will determine your current financial situation with regard to income, savings, living expenses, and debts. Preparing a list of current asset and debt balances and amounts spent for various items gives you a foundation for financial planning activities. The personal financial statements discussed in Chapter 2 will provide the information you need to match your goals with your current income and potential earning power.

STEP 1 EXAMPLE: Within the next two months, Kent Mullins will complete his undergraduate studies with a major in international studies. He has worked part time in various sales jobs. He has a small savings fund ($1,700) and more than $8,500 in student loans. What additional information should Kent have available when planning his personal finances?

■ OBJECTIVE 1 ■

Analyze the process for making personal financial decisions.

personal financial planning The process of managing your money to achieve personal economic satisfaction.

Visit the Web site
See the Weblinks under Chapter 1 on the online learning centre at www.mcgrawhill.ca/college/kapoor.

Exhibit 1–1

The Financial
Planning Process

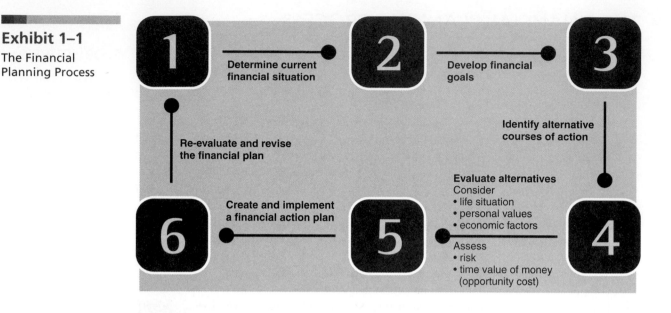

1 Determine current financial situation

2 Develop financial goals

3

Identify alternative courses of action

Re-evaluate and revise the financial plan

Evaluate alternatives
Consider
• life situation
• personal values
• economic factors

Create and implement a financial action plan

6

5

Assess
• risk
• time value of money (opportunity cost)

4

STEP 2: DEVELOP FINANCIAL GOALS

values Ideas and principles that a person considers correct, desirable, and important.

You should periodically analyze your financial values and attitude towards money. They will play a major role in shaping your financial goals.

Analyzing your **values** involves identifying what beliefs you hold with respect to money and how these beliefs lead you to act in certain ways. For example, you may believe that it is wrong to borrow to purchase consumer goods, such as expensive clothes. Because of this belief, you will only shop for clothes once you have saved the money. You will not charge the clothes to a credit card when you know you won't have the funds to pay the bill once it arrives.

You should also be aware of your attitude toward money. Do you view money as a form of security? If so, you are likely to be a good saver. Do you view money as a means by which you can express your appreciation of others? If so, you probably enjoy giving lavish gifts to your friends and family and may risk overspending. Do you view money as a means by which to wield power? People who feel this way may try to manipulate others by dominating all purchase decisions.

Finally, how are financial decisions made in your family? Is there one individual who makes all major financial decisions, such as how much to borrow to buy a home, and who leaves decisions of lesser importance to others? Or are financial decisions a joint effort and responsibility?

An awareness of your values, attitude toward money, and financial decision-making process will help you differentiate your needs from your wants and will lead you to a clearer definition of your financial goals. Financial goals represent what you hope to achieve with your money. They should be realistic, stated in specific dollar terms and time frames, and listed in order of priority. As discussed later in the chapter, they are also closely linked to your life situation and can be influenced by external economic factors as well.

Visit the Web site
See Personal Financial Planning worksheets under Chapter 1 on the online learning centre at www.mcgrawhill.ca/college/kapoor.

STEP 2 EXAMPLE: Kent Mullins has several goals, including obtaining an advanced degree in global business management within five years, paying off his $8,500 student loan within 10 years, and working in Latin America for a multinational company once he completes his education.

STEP 3: IDENTIFY ALTERNATIVE COURSES OF ACTION

Developing alternatives is crucial for making good decisions. Although many factors will influence the available alternatives, possible courses of action usually fall into these categories:

- *Continue the same course of action.* For example, you may determine that the amount you have saved each month is still appropriate.
- *Expand the current situation.* You may choose to save a larger amount each month.
- *Change the current situation.* You may decide to use a money market account instead of a regular savings account.
- *Take a new course of action.* You may decide to use your monthly savings budget to pay off credit card debts.

Not all of these categories will apply to every decision situation; however, they do represent possible courses of action. For example, if you want to stop working full time to go to school, you must generate several alternatives under the category "Take a new course of action."

Creativity in decision making is vital to effective choices. Considering all of the possible alternatives will help you make more effective and satisfying decisions. For instance, most people believe they must own a car to get to work or school. However, they should consider other alternatives, such as public transportation, carpooling, renting a car, shared ownership of a car, or a company car.

Remember, when you decide not to take action, you elect to "do nothing," which can be a dangerous alternative.

STEP 3 EXAMPLE: Kent Mullins has several options available to obtain an advanced degree in global business management. He could go to graduate school full time by taking out an additional loan; or he could go to school part time and work part time. What additional alternatives might he consider?

STEP 4: EVALUATE ALTERNATIVES

You need to evaluate possible courses of action, taking into consideration your life situation, personal values, and current economic conditions. How will the ages of dependants affect your saving goals? How do you like to spend leisure time? How will changes in interest rates affect your financial situation?

CONSEQUENCES OF CHOICES Every decision closes off alternatives. For example, a decision to invest in stocks may mean you cannot take a vacation. A decision to go to school full time may mean you cannot work full time. **Opportunity cost** is what you give up by making a choice. This cost, commonly referred to as the *trade-off* of a decision, cannot always be measured in dollars. It may refer to the money you forgo by attending school rather than working, but it may also refer to the time you spend shopping around to compare brands for a major purchase. In either case, the resources you give up (money or time) have a value that is lost.

opportunity cost
What a person gives up by making a choice.

Decision making will be an ongoing part of your personal and financial situations. Thus, you will need to consider the lost opportunities that will result from your decisions. Since decisions vary on the basis of each person's situation and values, opportunity costs will differ for each person.

EVALUATING RISK Uncertainty is a part of every decision. Selecting a college or university major and choosing a career field involve risk. What if you don't like working in this field or cannot obtain employment in it? Other decisions involve a very low degree of risk, such as putting money in a savings account or purchasing items that cost only a few dollars. Your chances of losing something of great value are low in these situations.

In many financial decisions, identifying and evaluating risk is difficult. Some types of risk can affect everyone, such as interest rate risk or inflation risk. They arise from the financial and economic environment in which we live or from the products and services that we choose. Other risks are personal in nature, such as the risk of premature death or the risk of disability or loss of health. Some different types of risk are explained in Exhibit 1-2. The best way to

Exhibit 1–2
Types of Risk

Economic and Product Risk	Personal Risk
Interest Rate Risk Changing interest rates affect your costs when you borrow and your benefits when you invest.	*Risk of Death* Premature death may cause financial hardship to family members left behind.
Inflation Risk Rising prices cause lost buying power.	*Risk of Income Loss* Your income could stop as a result of job loss or because you fall ill or are hurt in an accident.
Liquidity Risk Some investments may be more difficult to convert to cash or to sell without significant loss in value.	*Health Risk* Poor heath may increase your medical costs. At the same time, it may reduce your working capacity or life expectancy.
Product Risk Products may be flawed or services may not meet your expectations. Retailers may not honour their obligations.	*Asset and Liability Risk* Your assets may be stolen or damaged. Others may sue you for negligence or for damages caused by your actions.

consider risk is to gather information based on your experience and the experiences of others and to seek financial planning expertise by consulting various information sources.

FINANCIAL PLANNING INFORMATION SOURCES When you travel, you often need a road map. Travelling the path of financial planning requires a different kind of map. Relevant information is required at each stage of the decision-making process. This book provides the foundation you need to make personal financial planning decisions. Changing personal, social, and economic conditions will require that you continually supplement and update your knowledge. Exhibit 1–3 offers an overview of the informational resources available when making personal financial decisions. The Financial Planning for Life's Situations box on page 7 and the appendix to this chapter provide additional information.

Exhibit 1–3

Financial Planning
Information Sources

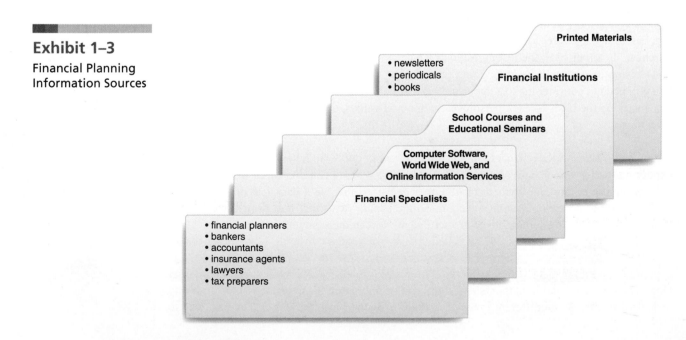

- newsletters
- periodicals
- books

Printed Materials

Financial Institutions

School Courses and
Educational Seminars

Computer Software,
World Wide Web, and
Online Information Services

Financial Specialists

- financial planners
- bankers
- accountants
- insurance agents
- lawyers
- tax preparers

Financial Planning for Life's Situations

Web . . . e-mail . . . URL . . . online banking!

Just a few years ago, these terms made no sense to most people. Even now, many people are still not quite sure about all this stuff. However, most know that good financial planning requires information, and the Internet is the most efficient source of information.

Throughout this book, the financial planning content presented can be expanded and updated using the Internet. The Web sites we suggest, along with others you locate yourself, will allow you to quickly obtain information for making financial decisions appropriate to your life situation. In addition, at the end of each chapter, a feature called "Creating an E-Plan: Financial Decisions Using the Web" will give you an opportunity to plan, research, and implement various components necessary for a comprehensive financial plan.

As you study the personal financial topics discussed in this book, you will find the following Internet topic areas especially useful:

- *Cyber-info for personal financial planning:* With thousands of personal finance Web sites available, where does a person begin? Some of the most useful ones include www.webfin.com, www.quicken.ca, and www.cafp.org.
- *Online banking:* No more lines. No more over-worked bank tellers. No more inhaling exhaust fumes while waiting in the drive-through lane. In addition to existing banks that are online, there are Web-only banks, such as www.ingdirect.ca.

- *Online tax information and advice:* Tax planning should not occur only around April 30. For assistance, go to www.cra-arc.gc.ca and www.kpmg.ca.
- *Applying for a mortgage online:* Instead of waiting days or even weeks, prospective home buyers can now obtain financing online at www.webfin.com and www.scotiabank.ca.
- *Buying a car online:* Information that used to be difficult to get is now available to everyone. More than 70 percent of car buyers research their planned purchases online to obtain information about vehicle features and costs at such Web sites as www.ewheels.ca.
- *Selecting investments online:* As everyone knows, "information is power." This axiom is especially true when investing. You can obtain company information and investment assistance at www.quicken.ca and www.mutualfundsnet.com.
- *Being your own investment broker:* You already know which investments you want to buy? Then it's time to get into the market by going to www.bmoinvestorline.com.
- *Planning for retirement:* Whether you are 40 years or 40 minutes away from retiring, you can get lots of help at www.retireweb.com.

Note: Additional Web sites appear on the end sheets of this book and in the end-of-chapter exercises. Refer to the appendix for this chapter for information on conducting Internet searches. Also, be aware that Web sites may change or no longer be in use.

STEP 4 EXAMPLE: As Kent Mullins evaluates his alternative courses of action, he must consider his income needs for both the short term and the long term. He should also assess career opportunities with his current skills and his potential with advanced training. What risks and trade-offs should Kent consider?

STEP 5: CREATE AND IMPLEMENT A FINANCIAL ACTION PLAN

In this step of the financial planning process, you develop an action plan. This requires choosing ways to achieve your goals. For example, you can increase your savings by reducing your spending or by increasing your income through extra time on the job. If you are concerned about year-end tax payments, you may increase the amount withheld from each paycheque, file quarterly tax payments, or shelter current income in a tax-deferred retirement program. As you achieve your immediate or short-term goals, the goals next in priority will come into focus.

To implement your financial action plan, you may need assistance from others. For example, you may use the services of an insurance agent to purchase property insurance or the

7

services of an investment broker to purchase stocks, bonds, or mutual funds. Your own efforts should be geared toward achieving your financial goals.

STEP 5 EXAMPLE: Kent Mullins has decided to work full time for a few years while he (1) pays off his student loans, (2) saves money for graduate school, and (3) takes a couple of courses in the evenings and on weekends. What are the benefits and drawbacks of this choice?

STEP 6: RE-EVALUATE AND REVISE YOUR PLAN

Financial planning is a dynamic process that does not end when you take a particular action. You need to regularly assess your financial decisions. You should do a complete review of your finances at least once a year. Changing personal, social, and economic factors may require more frequent assessments.

When life events affect your financial needs, this financial planning process will provide a vehicle for adapting to those changes. Regularly reviewing this decision-making process will help you make priority adjustments that will bring your financial goals and activities in line with your current life situation.

> ### DID YOU KNOW ?
>
> Research indicates that people with a financial plan (developed themselves or by a professional) had significantly higher amounts in savings than those who didn't.
>
> (Andrea Rock, "You've Gotta Have a Plan," *Money*, March 1999, pp. 117–20, 123, 125–27.)

STEP 6 EXAMPLE: Over the next six to 12 months, Kent Mullins should reassess his financial, career, and personal situations. What employment opportunities or family circumstances might affect his need or desire to take a different course of action?

CONCEPT CHECK 1–1

1. What steps should we take in developing our financial plan?
2. What are some risks associated with financial decisions?
3. What are some common sources of financial planning information?
4. Why should you re-evaluate your actions after making a personal financial decision?
5. What Web site feature of www.cafp.org or www.canadianfinance.com would provide assistance with your financial decisions?

DEVELOPING PERSONAL FINANCIAL GOALS

■ OBJECTIVE 2 ▌

Develop personal financial goals.

Since Canada is among the richest countries in the world, it is difficult to understand why so many Canadians have money problems. The answer seems to be the result of two main factors. The first is poor planning and weak money management habits in such areas as spending and the use of credit. The other is extensive advertising, selling efforts, and product availability. Achieving personal financial satisfaction starts with clear financial goals.

FACTORS THAT INFLUENCE YOUR FINANCIAL GOALS

Many factors influence your financial aspirations for the future. We have already discussed how your personal values and attitude toward money can shape your financial goals. Additional factors include the time frame in which you would like to achieve your goals, the type of financial need that drives your goals, and your life situation.

TIMING OF GOALS
What would you like to do tomorrow? Believe it or not, that question involves goal setting. *Short-term goals* are goals to be achieved within the next year or so, such as saving for a vacation or paying off small debts. *Intermediate goals* have a time frame of two to five

years. *Long-term goals* involve financial plans that are more than five years off, such as retirement savings, money for children's college/university education, or the purchase of a vacation home.

Long-term goals should be planned in coordination with short-term and intermediate ones. Setting and achieving short-term goals is commonly the basis for moving toward success of long-term goals. For example, saving for a down payment to buy a house is a short- or medium-term goal that can be a foundation for a long-term goal: owning your own home.

Goal frequency is another ingredient in the financial planning process. Some goals, such as vacations or money for gifts, may be set annually. Other goals, such as a higher education, a car, or a house, occur less frequently.

GOALS FOR DIFFERENT FINANCIAL NEEDS A goal of obtaining increased career training is different from a goal of saving money to pay a semi-annual auto insurance premium. *Consumable-product goals* usually occur on a periodic basis and involve items that are used up relatively quickly, such as food, clothing, and entertainment. Such purchases, if made unwisely, can have a negative effect on your financial situation.

Durable-product goals usually involve infrequently purchased, expensive items, such as appliances, cars, and sporting equipment; these consist of tangible items. In contrast, many people overlook *intangible-purchase goals*. These goals may relate to personal relationships, health, education, and leisure. Goal setting for these life circumstances is also necessary for your overall well being.

LIFE SITUATION

People in their 50s spend money differently from those in their 20s. Personal factors, such as age, income, household size, and personal beliefs, influence your spending and saving patterns. Your life situation or lifestyle is created by a combination of factors.

As our society changes, different types of financial needs evolve. Today, people tend to get married at a later age, and more households have two incomes. Many households are headed by single parents. We are also living longer: more than 80 percent of all Canadians now living are expected to live past age 65. The 2002 General Social Survey indicates that approximately one-third of Canadians aged 45 to 64 are not only raising children, but caring for aging parents. Women form the large majority and, in response to these increased demands, report that they have had to reduce their working hours, change schedules, or forgo income.

As Exhibit 1–4 shows, the **adult life cycle**—the stages in the family situation and financial needs of an adult—is an important influence on your financial activities and decisions. Your

adult life cycle The stages in the family situation and financial needs of an adult.

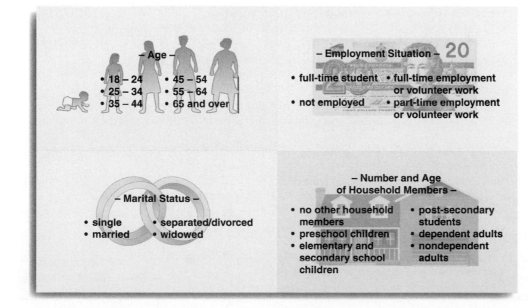

Exhibit 1–4

Life Situation Influences on Your Financial Decisions

life situation is also affected by marital status, household size, and employment, as well as such events as

- Graduation (at various levels of education).
- Engagement and marriage.
- The birth or adoption of a child.
- A career change or a move to a new area.
- Dependent children leaving home.
- Changes in health.
- Divorce.
- Retirement.
- The death of a spouse, family member, or other dependant.

Exhibit 1–5   Financial Goals and Activities for Various Life Situations

COMMON FINANCIAL GOALS AND ACTIVITIES		
• Obtain appropriate career training. • Create an effective financial recordkeeping system. • Develop a regular savings and investment program.	• Accumulate an appropriate emergency fund. • Purchase appropriate types and amounts of insurance coverage. • Create and implement a flexible budget.	• Evaluate and select appropriate investments. • Establish and implement a plan for retirement goals. • Make a will and develop an estate plan.

LIFE SITUATION	SPECIALIZED FINANCIAL ACTIVITIES
Young, single (18–35)	• Establish financial independence. • Obtain disability insurance to replace income during prolonged illness. • Consider home purchase.
Young couple with children under 18	• Carefully manage the increased need for the use of credit. • Obtain an appropriate amount of life insurance for the care of dependants. • Use a will to name a guardian for children.
Single parent with children under 18	• Obtain adequate amounts of health, life, and disability insurances. • Contribute to savings and investment funds for children's higher education. • Name a guardian for children and make other estate plans.
Young dual-income couple, no children	• Coordinate insurance coverage and other benefits. • Develop savings and investment programs for changes in life situation (larger house, children). • Consider tax-deferred contributions to retirement fund.
Older couple (+50), no dependent children at home	• Consolidate financial assets and review estate plans. • Obtain health insurance for post-retirement period. • Plan retirement housing, living expenses, recreational activities, and part-time work.
Mixed-generation household (elderly individuals and children under 18)	• Obtain long-term health care insurance and life/disability income for care of younger dependants. • Use dependent care service, if needed. • Provide arrangements for handling finances of elderly if they become ill. • Consider splitting of investment cost, with elderly getting income while alive and principal going to surviving relatives.
Older (+50), single	• Make arrangements for long-term health care coverage. • Review will and estate plan. • Plan retirement living facilities, living expenses, and activities.

GOAL SETTING GUIDELINES

An old saying goes, "If you don't know where you're going, you might end up somewhere else and not even know it." Goal setting is central to financial decision making. Your financial goals are the basis for planning, implementing, and measuring the progress of your spending, saving, and investing activities. Exhibit 1–5 offers typical goals and financial activities for various life situations.

Your financial goals should be stated to take the following factors into account:

[1] *Financial goals should be realistic.* Financial goals should be based on your income and life situation. For example, it is probably not realistic to expect to buy a new car each year if you are a full-time student.

[2] *Financial goals should be stated in specific, measurable terms.* Knowing exactly what your goals are will help you create a plan designed to achieve them. For example, the goal of "accumulating $5,000 in an investment fund within three years" is a clearer guide to planning than the goal of "putting money into an investment fund."

[3] *Financial goals should have a time frame.* In the preceding example, the goal is to be achieved in three years. A time frame helps you measure your progress toward your financial goals.

[4] *Financial goals should indicate the type of action to be taken.* Your financial goals are the basis for the various financial activities you will undertake.

The Financial Planning for Life's Situations box on page 12 gives you an opportunity to set financial goals.

CONCEPT CHECK 1–2

1. What are examples of long-term goals?
2. What are the four main characteristics of useful financial goals?
3. How does your life situation affect your financial goals?

THE INFLUENCE OF ECONOMIC FACTORS ON PERSONAL FINANCIAL PLANNING

Daily economic activities are another important influence on financial planning. In our society, the forces of supply and demand play an important role in setting prices. **Economics** is the study of how wealth is created and distributed. The economic environment includes various institutions, principally business, labour, and government, that must work together to satisfy our needs and wants.

MARKET FORCES   Prices of goods and services are generally determined by supply and demand. Just as a high demand for a consumer product forces its price up, a high demand for money pushes up interest rates. This price of money reflects the limited supply of money and the demand for it.

At times, the price of an item may seem to be unaffected by the forces of supply and demand, but in fact, at such times, other economic factors may also be influencing its price. Although such factors as production costs and competition influence prices, the market forces of supply and demand remain in operation.

FINANCIAL INSTITUTIONS   Banks, trust companies, credit unions, insurance companies, and investment companies are the financial institutions with which most people do business. Financial institutions provide services that facilitate financial activities in our economy. They accept savings, handle chequing accounts, sell insurance, and make investments on behalf of others.

■ OBJECTIVE 3 ■

Assess economic factors that influence personal financial planning.

economics The study of how wealth is created and distributed.

On the basis of your current situation or expectations for the future, identify two financial goals, one short-term and one long-term, using the following guidelines:

Step 1. Create realistic goals on the basis of your life situation.

A. SHORT-TERM GOAL

_____
_____
_____
_____
_____

B. LONG-TERM GOAL

_____
_____
_____
_____
_____

Step 2. State your goals in specific, measurable terms.

a. _____
_____

b. _____
_____

Step 3. Describe the time frame for accomplishing your goals.

a. _____
_____

b. _____
_____

Step 4. Indicate actions to be taken to achieve your goals.

a. _____
_____

b. _____
_____

While various government agencies regulate financial activities, the Bank of Canada, our nation's central bank, has significant responsibility in our economy. The Bank of Canada is concerned with maintaining an adequate money supply. It achieves this by influencing borrowing, interest rates, and the buying or selling of government securities. The Bank of Canada attempts to make adequate funds available for consumer spending and business expansion while keeping interest rates and consumer prices at an appropriate level.

GLOBAL INFLUENCES The global marketplace also influences financial activities. Our economy is affected by both the financial activities of foreign investors and competition from foreign companies. Canadian businesses compete against foreign companies for the spending dollars of Canadian consumers.

When the level of exports of Canadian-made goods is lower than the level of imported goods, more Canadian dollars leave the country than the dollar value of foreign currency coming into Canada. This reduces the funds available for domestic spending and investment. Also, if foreign companies decide not to invest their dollars in Canada, the domestic money supply is reduced. This reduced money supply may cause higher interest rates.

ECONOMIC CONDITIONS Newspapers and business periodicals regularly publish current economic statistics. Exhibit 1–6 provides an overview of some economic indicators that influence financial decisions. Your personal financial decisions are most heavily influenced by consumer prices, consumer spending, and interest rates.

DID YOU KNOW?

A basket of goods and services that cost $100 in 1914 cost $1,757.75 in 2004.

(www.bankofcanada.ca)

Exhibit 1–6   Changing Economic Conditions and Financial Decisions

Economic Factor	What It Measures	How It Influences Financial Planning
Consumer prices	The value of the dollar; changes in inflation	If consumer prices increase faster than your income, you are unable to purchase the same amount of goods and services; higher consumer prices will also cause higher interest rates.
Consumer spending	The demand for goods and services by individuals and households	Increased consumer spending is likely to create more jobs and higher wages; high levels of consumer spending and borrowing can also push up consumer prices and interest rates.
Interest rates	The cost of money; the cost of credit when you borrow; the return on your money when you save or invest	Higher interest rates make buying on credit more expensive; higher interest rates make saving and investing more attractive and discourage borrowing.
Money supply	The dollars available for spending in our economy	Interest rates tend to decline as more people save and invest; but higher saving (and lower spending) may also reduce job opportunities.
Unemployment	The number of people without employment who are willing and able to work	People who are unemployed should reduce their debt level and have an emergency savings fund for living costs while out of work; high unemployment reduces consumer spending and job opportunities.
Housing starts	The number of new homes being built	Increased home building results in more job opportunities, higher wages, more consumer spending, and overall economic expansion.
Gross domestic product (GDP)	The total value of goods and services produced within a country's borders, including items produced with foreign resources	The GDP provides an indication of a nation's economic viability resulting in employment and opportunities for personal financial wealth.
Trade balance	The difference between a country's exports and its imports	If a country exports more than it imports, interest rates may rise and foreign goods and foreign travel will cost more.
S&P/TSX composite index and other stock market indexes	The relative value of stocks represented by the index	These indexes provide an indication of the general movement of stock prices.

1. Consumer Prices **Inflation** is a rise in the general level of prices. In times of inflation, the buying power of the dollar decreases. For example, if prices increased 5 percent during the last year, items that cost $100 then would now cost $105. This means it now takes more money to buy the same amount of goods and services.

The main cause of inflation is an increase in demand without a comparable increase in supply. For example, if people have more money to spend because of pay increases or borrowing

inflation A rise in the general level of prices.

"Spend less than you earn" is the foundation of long-term financial security, according to financial planner Ellen Rogin.

Although it sounds simple, most people do not follow this basic requirement for financial planning success. Ms. Rogin has been advising people about their money for more than 12 years. While the typical clients of her company range in age from 30 to 50, some are younger or older. Most of her clients are professionals and executives who have a common concern: a secure retirement. But Ms. Rogin is quick to point out that she works with people with a variety of needs, life situations, and investment philosophies. She has even advised a lottery winner, although she doesn't recommend that expectation as a steady path to long-term financial security!

The availability of information, Ms. Rogin believes, is the most significant change in the financial planning marketplace in recent years. With the Internet, television programs, and an extensive number of magazines and books, people can be better informed regarding personal finance topics and investments. However, Ms. Rogin warns that people must assess the validity of the information. She suggests "avoiding specific investment advice from magazines and other sources that may not be appropriate for your individual situation."

When planning your own financial direction, Ms. Rogin recommends three actions:

1. Set specific financial goals.
2. Reduce your debts.
3. Save for retirement.

Even if someone else is managing your finances, Ms. Rogin encourages you to "be involved." Be aware of your personal economic situation and the financial marketplace. Communicate your money views, risk acceptance, and financial priorities. Never let a financial planner, your spouse, or another family member have complete control.

---

but the same amounts of goods and services are available, the increased demand can bid up prices for those goods and services.

Inflation is most harmful to people living on fixed incomes. Due to inflation, retired people and others whose incomes do not change are able to afford smaller amounts of goods and services.

Inflation can also adversely affect lenders of money. Unless an adequate interest rate is charged, amounts repaid by borrowers in times of inflation have less buying power than the money they borrowed. If you pay 10 percent interest on a loan and the inflation rate is 12 percent, the dollars you pay the lender have lost buying power. For this reason, interest rates rise in periods of high inflation.

The rate of inflation varies. During the late 1950s and early 1960s, the annual inflation rate was in the 1 to 3 percent range. During the late 1970s and early 1980s, the cost of living increased 10 to 12 percent annually.

More recently, the annual price increase for most goods and services as measured by the consumer price index has been in the 1 to 3 percent range. The *consumer price index* (CPI), published by Statistics Canada, is a measure of the average change in the prices urban consumers pay for a fixed "basket" of goods and services. For current CPI information, go to www.statcan.ca.

DID YOU KNOW?

To find out how fast prices double, you can use the rule of 72. Just divide 72 by the annual inflation rate (or interest rate). An annual inflation rate of 8 percent, for example, means prices will double in nine years ($72 \div 8 = 9$).

2. Consumer Spending Total demand for goods and services in the economy influences employment opportunities and the potential for income. As consumer purchasing increases, the financial resources of current and prospective employees expand. This situation improves the financial condition of many households.

In contrast, reduced spending causes unemployment, since staff reduction commonly results from a company's reduced financial resources. The financial hardships of unemployment are a major concern of business, labour, and government. Retraining programs, income assistance, and job services can help people adjust.

3. Interest Rates In simple terms, interest rates represent the cost of money. Like everything else, money has a price. The forces of supply and demand influence interest rates. When consumer saving and investing increase the supply of money, interest rates tend to decrease. However, as consumer, business, government, and foreign borrowing increase the demand for money, interest rates tend to rise.

Interest rates affect your financial planning. The earnings you receive as a saver or an investor reflect current interest rates as well as a *risk premium* based on such factors as the length of time your funds will be used by others, expected inflation, and the extent of uncertainty about getting your money back. Risk is also a factor in the interest rate you pay as a borrower. People with poor credit ratings pay a higher interest rate than people with good credit ratings. Finally, we must always take into consideration the role that personal income taxes play with respect to the interest income we earn and the interest expense we pay. Every dollar of interest we earn must be added to our taxable income. Therefore, if our income tax rate is 30 percent, we have only 70 cents of after-tax interest income. On the other hand, we can deduct the interest that we pay on certain types of loans. In that case, the true cost of one dollar of interest paid would be only 70 cents. We will discuss the issue of before and after-tax investment income and borrowing costs in further detail in Chapter 3, Planning Your Tax Strategy.

CONCEPT CHECK 1–3

1. How might the uncertainty of inflation make personal financial planning difficult?
2. What factors influence the level of interest rates?

OPPORTUNITY COSTS AND THE TIME VALUE OF MONEY

Have you noticed that you always give up something when you make choices? In every financial decision, you sacrifice something to obtain something else that you consider more desirable. For example, you might forgo current consumption to invest funds for future purchases or long-term financial security. Or you might gain the use of an expensive item now by making credit payments from future earnings. These *opportunity costs* may be viewed in terms of both personal and financial resources (see Exhibit 1–7).

■ OBJECTIVE 4 ■

Determine personal and financial opportunity costs associated with personal financial decisions.

PERSONAL OPPORTUNITY COSTS

An important personal opportunity cost involves time that when used for one activity cannot be used for other activities. Time used for studying, working, or shopping will not be available for other uses. The allocation of time should be viewed like any decision: Select your use of time to meet your needs, achieve your goals, and satisfy personal values.

Other personal opportunity costs relate to health. Poor eating habits, lack of sleep, or avoiding exercise can result in illness, time away from school or work, increased health care costs, and reduced financial security. Like financial resources, your personal resources (time, energy, health, abilities, knowledge) require management.

Exhibit 1–7

Opportunity Costs
and Financial Results
Should Be Evaluated
When Making
Financial Decisions

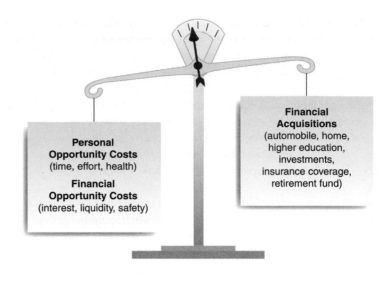

**Personal
Opportunity Costs**
(time, effort, health)

**Financial
Opportunity Costs**
(interest, liquidity, safety)

**Financial
Acquisitions**
(automobile, home,
higher education,
investments,
insurance coverage,
retirement fund)

FINANCIAL OPPORTUNITY COSTS

time value of money
Increases in an amount
of money as a result
of interest earned.

You are constantly making choices among various financial decisions. In making those choices, you must consider the **time value of money**, the increases in an amount of money as a result of interest earned. Saving or investing a dollar instead of spending it today results in a future amount greater than a dollar. Every time you spend, save, invest, or borrow money, you should consider the time value of that money as an opportunity cost. Spending money from your savings account means lost interest earnings; however, what you buy with that money may have a higher priority than those earnings. Borrowing to make a purchase involves the opportunity cost of paying interest on the loan, but your current needs may make this trade-off worthwhile.

The opportunity cost of the time value of money is also present in these financial decisions:

- Setting aside funds in a savings plan with little or no risk has the opportunity cost of potentially higher returns from an investment with greater risk.
- Having extra money withheld from your paycheque in order to receive a tax refund has the opportunity cost of the lost interest the money could earn in a savings account.
- Making annual deposits in a Registered Retirement Savings Plan (RRSP) can help you avoid the opportunity cost of having inadequate funds later in life.
- Purchasing a new automobile or home appliance has the potential benefit of saving you money on future maintenance and energy costs.

INTEREST CALCULATIONS   Three amounts are used to calculate the time value of money for savings in the form of interest earned:

- The amount of the savings (commonly called the *principal*).
- The annual interest rate.
- The length of time the money is on deposit.

simple interest
Interest computed on
the principal, excluding
previously earned
interest.

There are two methods of calculating interest: **simple interest** and compound interest. Simple interest is calculated as follows: $I = P \times r \times T$

| (P)
AMOUNT IN
SAVINGS | × | (R)
ANNUAL
INTEREST RATE | × | (T)
TIME
PERIOD | = | (I)
INTEREST |

For example, $500 on deposit at a 6 percent annual interest rate for two years would earn $60 ($500 × 0.06 × 2).

Compounding refers to interest that is earned on previously earned interest. Each time interest is added to the principal, the next interest amount is computed on the new balance. For example, the $500 on deposit at a 6 percent annual interest rate for two years would earn $61.80. ($500 × 0.06 = $30 the first year and [$500 + $30]× 0.06 = $31.80 the second year, $31.80 + $30 = $61.80)

Since you are earning interest on the principal as well as accumulated interest, the total amount is greater than what you would earn under simple interest ($61.80 > $60).

You can calculate the increased value of your money from interest earned in two ways: You can calculate the total amount that will be available later (future value), or you can determine the current value of an amount desired in the future (present value).

FUTURE VALUE OF A SINGLE AMOUNT Deposited money earns interest that will increase over time. **Future value** is the amount to which current savings will increase on the basis of a certain interest rate and a certain time period. Future value computations typically involve *compounding*, since interest is earned on previously earned interest. Compounding allows the future value of a deposit to grow faster than it would if interest were paid only on the original deposit. For example, $100 deposited in a 6-percent account for two years will grow to $112.36. This amount is computed as follows:

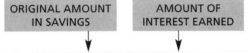

Future value (year 1) = $100 + ($100 × 0.06 × 1 year) = $106

Future value (year 2) = $106 + ($106 × 0.06 × 1 year) = $112.36

The same process could be continued for a third, fourth, and fifth year, but the computations would be time consuming. Future value tables simplify the process (see Exhibit 1–8). To use a future value table, multiply the amount deposited by the factor for the desired interest rate and time period. For example, $650 at 8 percent for 10 years would have a future value of $1,403.35 ($650 × 2.159). The future value of an amount will always be greater than the original amount. As Exhibit 1–8A shows, all the future value factors are larger than 1.

The sooner you make deposits, the greater the future value will be. Depositing $1,000 in a 5-percent account at age 40 will give you $3,387 at age 65. However, making the $1,000 deposit at age 25 would result in an account balance of $7,040 at age 65.

FUTURE VALUE OF A SERIES OF DEPOSITS Quite often, savers and investors make regular deposits. An *annuity* is a series of equal deposits or payments. To determine the future value of equal yearly savings deposits, use Exhibit 1–8B. For this table to be used, the deposits must earn a constant interest rate. If you deposit $50 a year at 7 percent for six years, starting at the end of the first year, you will have $357.65 immediately after the last deposit ($50 × 7.153). The Financial Planning Calculations box on page 20 presents examples of using future value to achieve financial goals.

PRESENT VALUE OF A SINGLE AMOUNT Another aspect of the time value of money involves determining the current value of a desired amount for the future. **Present value** is the current value for a future amount based on a certain interest rate and a certain time period. Present value computations, also called *discounting*, allow you to determine how much to deposit now to obtain a desired total in the future. Present value tables (Exhibit 1–8C) can be used to make the computations. If you want $1,000 five years from now and you earn 5 percent on your savings, you need to deposit $784 ($1,000 × 0.784).

The present value of the amount you want in the future will always be less than the future value, since all of the factors in Exhibit 1–8C are less than 1 and interest earned will increase the present value amount to the desired future amount.

compounding A process that calculates interest based on previously earned interest.

future value The amount to which current savings will increase based on a certain interest rate and a certain time period; typically involves compounding.

present value The current value for a future amount based on a certain interest rate and a certain time period; also referred to as discounting.

Exhibit 1–8

The Value of Money
Tables (condensed)

A. FUTURE VALUE OF $1 (SINGLE AMOUNT)

Year	Percent				
	5%	6%	7%	8%	9%
5	1.276	1.338	1.403	1.469	1.539
6	1.340	1.419	1.501	1.587	1.677
7	1.407	1.504	1.606	1.714	1.828
8	1.477	1.594	1.718	1.851	1.993
9	1.551	1.689	1.838	1.999	2.172
10	1.629	1.791	1.967	2.159	2.367

B. FUTURE VALUE OF A SERIES OF ANNUAL DEPOSITS (ANNUITY)

Year	Percent				
	5%	6%	7%	8%	9%
5	5.526	5.637	5.751	5.867	5.985
6	6.802	6.975	7.153	7.336	7.523
7	8.142	8.394	8.654	8.923	9.200
8	9.549	9.897	10.260	10.637	11.028
9	11.027	11.491	11.978	12.488	13.021
10	12.578	13.181	13.816	14.487	15.193

C. PRESENT VALUE OF $1 (SINGLE AMOUNT)

Year	Percent				
	5%	6%	7%	8%	9%
5	0.784	0.747	0.713	0.681	0.650
6	0.746	0.705	0.666	0.630	0.596
7	0.711	0.665	0.623	0.583	0.547
8	0.677	0.627	0.582	0.540	0.502
9	0.645	0.592	0.544	0.500	0.460
10	0.614	0.558	0.508	0.463	0.422

D. PRESENT VALUE OF A SERIES OF ANNUAL DEPOSITS (ANNUITY)

Year	Percent				
	5%	6%	7%	8%	9%
5	4.329	4.212	4.100	3.993	3.890
6	5.076	4.917	4.767	4.623	4.486
7	5.786	5.582	5.389	5.206	5.033
8	6.463	6.210	5.971	5.747	5.535
9	7.108	6.802	6.515	6.247	5.995
10	7.722	7.360	7.024	6.710	6.418

See Appendix A at the end of the book for more complete future value and present value tables.

PRESENT VALUE OF A SERIES OF DEPOSITS   You can also use present value computations to determine how much you need to deposit so that you can take a certain amount out of the account for a desired number of years. For example, if you want to take $400 out of an investment account each year for nine years and your money is earning an annual rate of 8 percent, you can see from Exhibit 1–8D that you would need to make a current deposit of $2,498.80 ($400 × 6.247).

FINANCIAL CALCULATORS Currently, financial calculators, with time value of money functions built in, are widely used to calculate future value, present values, and annuities. For the following examples, we will use the Texas Instrument BA II Plus financial calculator, which sells for approximately $50 and is recommended by the Canadian Institute of Financial Planning.

When using the BA II Plus calculator to solve time value of money problems, you will be working with the TVM keys that include:

| **CPT** | – Compute key used to initiate financial calculations once all values are inputed. |

| **N** | – Number of periods |

| **I/Y** | – Interest rate per period |

| **PV** | – Present value |

| **PMT** | – Amount of payment, used only for annuities |

| **FV** | – Future value |

Enter values for PV, PMT and FV as negative if they represent cash outflows (for example, investing a sum of money) or as positive if they represent cash inflows (for example, receiving the proceeds of an investment). To convert a positive number to a negative number, enter the number and then press the $+/-$ key.

The examples that are shown in this chapter assume that interest is compounded annually and that there is only one cash flow per period. To reflect this, we must set the number of payments and compounding per period to 1 (the default setting is 12). To do this, press in turn the 2nd button (yellow), the I/Y button (for the P/Y function shown above it), the number 1, the ENTER button, the 2nd button again, and finally the CPT button (for the quit function above it). Before using any financial calculator, we strongly recommend that you consult the instruction manual that accompanies it and attempt the examples shown there.

Now let's try a problem. What is the future value of $100 after three years at a 10 percent annual interest rate? Remember that an investment of money is considered to be an outflow of cash; therefore, the present value of $100 should be entered as a negative number.

First, you must enter the data. Remember that an investment of money is considered to be an outflow of cash; therefore, the $100 should be entered as a negative number.

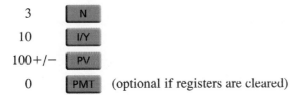

3	**N**	
10	**I/Y**	
100+/−	**PV**	
0	**PMT**	(optional if registers are cleared)

To find the solution, the future value, press CPT FV, and the future value of 133.1 is displayed. The Financial Planning Calculations box on page 20 presents examples of using a financial calculator to solve future value problems.

The formulas for calculating future and present values, as well as tables and the use of the financial calculator covering a wider range of interest rates and time periods, are presented in Appendix A. Computer programs for calculating time value of money are also available.

CONCEPT CHECK 1–4

1. How can you use future value and present value computations to measure the opportunity cost of a financial decision?
2. Use the time value of money tables in Exhibit 1–8 or a financial calculator to calculate the following:
   a. The future value of $100 at 7 percent in 10 years.
   b. The future value of $100 a year for six years earning 6 percent.
   c. The present value of $500 received in eight years with an interest rate of 8 percent.

Achieving specific financial goals often requires regular deposits to a savings or investment account. By using time value of money calculations, you can determine the amount you should save or invest to achieve a specific goal for the future.

EXAMPLE 1

Jonie Emerson has two children who will start college in 10 years. She plans to set aside $1,500 a year for her children's college education during that period and estimates she will earn an annual interest rate of 5 percent on her savings. What amount can Jonie expect to have available for her children's college education when they start college?

Calculation from table:
$1,500 × Future value of a series of deposits,
5%, 10 years
$1,500 × 12.578 = $18,867

With calculator:

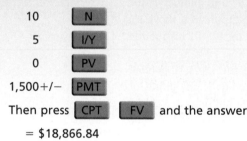

10	N
5	I/Y
0	PV
1,500+/−	PMT

Then press CPT FV and the answer
= $18,866.84

EXAMPLE 2

Don Calder wants to accumulate $50,000 over the next 10 years as a reserve fund for his parents' retirement living expenses and health care. If he earns an average of 8 percent on his investments, what amount must he invest each year to achieve this goal?

Calculation from table:
$50,000 ÷ Future value of a series of deposits,
8%, 10 years
$50,000 ÷ 14.487 = $3,451.37

Don needs to invest approximately $3,450 a year for 10 years at 8 percent to achieve the desired financial goal.

With calculator:

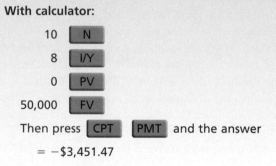

10	N
8	I/Y
0	PV
50,000	FV

Then press CPT PMT and the answer
= −$3,451.47

ACHIEVING FINANCIAL GOALS

■ OBJECTIVE 5 ▮

Identify strategies for achieving personal financial goals for different life situations.

Throughout life, our needs usually can be satisfied with the intelligent use of financial resources. Financial planning involves deciding how to obtain, protect, and use those resources. By using the eight major areas of personal financial planning to organize your financial activities, you can avoid many common money mistakes.

COMPONENTS OF PERSONAL FINANCIAL PLANNING

This book is designed to provide a framework for the study and planning of personal financial decisions. Exhibit 1–9 presents an overview of the eight major personal financial planning areas. To achieve a successful financial situation, you must coordinate these components through an organized plan and wise decision making.

OBTAINING (CHAPTER 1) You obtain financial resources from employment, investments, or ownership of a business. Obtaining financial resources is the foundation of financial planning, since these resources are used for all financial activities.

Key Web Sites for Obtaining: www.quicken.ca   www.monster.ca

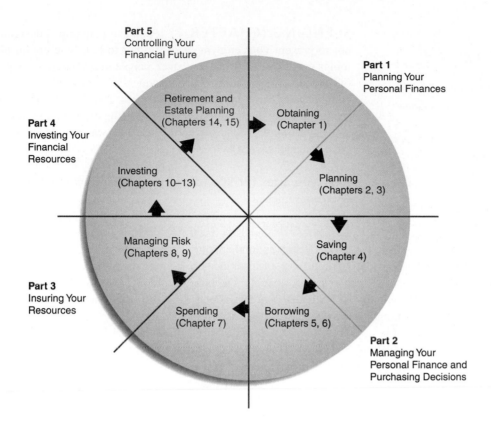

Exhibit 1–9

Components of
Personal Financial
Planning

PLANNING (CHAPTERS 2, 3) Planned spending through budgeting is the key to achieving goals and future financial security. Efforts to anticipate expenses and financial decisions can also help reduce taxes. Paying no more than your fair share of taxes is vital to increasing your financial resources.

Key Web Sites for Planning: www.advocis.ca   www.quicken.ca

SAVING (CHAPTER 4) Long-term financial security starts with a regular savings plan for emergencies, unexpected bills, replacement of major items, and the purchase of special goods and services, such as a higher education, a boat, or a vacation home. Once you have established a basic savings plan, you may use additional money for investments that offer greater financial growth.

An amount of savings must be available to meet current household needs. **Liquidity** refers to the ability to readily convert financial resources into cash without a loss in value. The need for liquidity will vary on the basis of a person's age, health, and family situation. Savings plans, such as interest-earning chequing accounts, money market accounts, and money market funds, earn money on your savings while providing liquidity.

liquidity The ability to readily convert financial resources into cash without a loss in value.

Key Web Sites for Saving: www.ingdirect.ca/en/artofsaving/artofsaving_f.html

BORROWING (CHAPTERS 5, 6) Maintaining control over your credit-buying habits will contribute to your financial goals. The overuse and misuse of credit may cause a situation in which a person's debts far exceed the resources available to pay those debts. **Bankruptcy** is a set of federal laws that allow you to either restructure your debts or remove certain debts. The people who declare bankruptcy each year might have avoided this trauma with wise spending and borrowing decisions. Chapter 6 discusses bankruptcy in detail.

bankruptcy A set of federal laws that allow you to either restructure your debts or remove certain debts.

Key Web Sites for Borrowing: www.cibc.ca   www.scotiabank.ca

SPENDING (CHAPTER 7)   Financial planning is designed not to prevent your enjoyment of life but to help you obtain the things you want. Too often, however, people make purchases without considering the financial consequences. Some people shop compulsively, creating financial difficulties. You should detail your living expenses and your other financial obligations in a spending plan. Spending less than you earn is the only way to achieve long-term financial security.

Key Web Sites for Spending: www.consumerworld.org www.consumer.ca

MANAGING RISK (CHAPTERS 8, 9)   Adequate insurance coverage is another component of personal financial planning. Certain types of insurance are commonly overlooked in financial plans. For example, the number of people who suffer disabling injuries or diseases at age 50 is greater than the number who die at that age, so people may need disability insurance more than they need life insurance. Yet surveys reveal that most people have adequate life insurance but few have disability insurance. The insurance industry is more aggressive in selling life insurance than in selling disability insurance, thus putting the burden of obtaining adequate disability insurance on you.

Many households have excessive or overlapping insurance coverage. Insuring property for more than it is worth may be a waste of money, as may both a husband and a wife having similar health insurance coverage.

Key Web Sites for Managing Risk: www.canadalife.com   www.risksvr.com

INVESTING (CHAPTERS 10–13)   While many types of investment vehicles are available, people invest for two primary reasons. Those interested in current income select investments that pay regular dividends or interest. In contrast, investors who desire long-term growth choose stocks, mutual funds, real estate, and other investments with potential for increased value in the future.

You can achieve investment diversification by including a variety of assets in your portfolio—for example, stocks, bond mutual funds, real estate, and collectibles, such as rare coins. Obtaining general investment advice is easy; however, it is more difficult to obtain specific investment advice to meet your individual needs and goals.

Key Web Sites for Investing: www.canadafinance.com   www.webfin.com

RETIREMENT AND ESTATE PLANNING (CHAPTERS 14, 15)   Most people desire financial security upon completion of full-time employment. But retirement planning also involves thinking about your housing situation, your recreational activities, and possible part-time or volunteer work.

Key Web Sites for Retirement and Estate Planning: www.elderweb.org www.retirenet.com

Transfers of money or property to others should be timed, if possible, to minimize the tax burden and maximize the benefits for those receiving the financial resources. A knowledge of property transfer methods can help you select the best course of action for funding current and future living costs, educational expenses, and retirement needs of dependants.

DEVELOPING A FLEXIBLE FINANCIAL PLAN

A **financial plan** is a formalized report that summarizes your current financial situation, analyzes your financial needs, and recommends future financial activities. You can create this document on your own, seek assistance from a financial planner, or use a money management software package (see the chapter appendix). Exhibit 1–10 offers a framework for developing and implementing a financial plan, along with examples for several life situations. (Also see the Financial Planning for Life's Situations box on pages 24 and 25.)

financial plan A formalized report that summarizes your current financial situation, analyzes your financial needs, and recommends future financial activities.

IMPLEMENTING YOUR FINANCIAL PLAN

You must have a plan before you can implement it. However, once you have clearly assessed your current situation and identified your financial goals, what do you do next?

The most important strategy for success is the development of financial habits that contribute to both short-term satisfaction and long-term financial security, including the following:

[1]   Using a well-conceived spending plan will help you stay within your income while you save and invest for the future. The main source of financial difficulties is overspending.

[2]   Having appropriate insurance protection will help you prevent financial disasters.

Exhibit 1–10   Financial Planning in Action

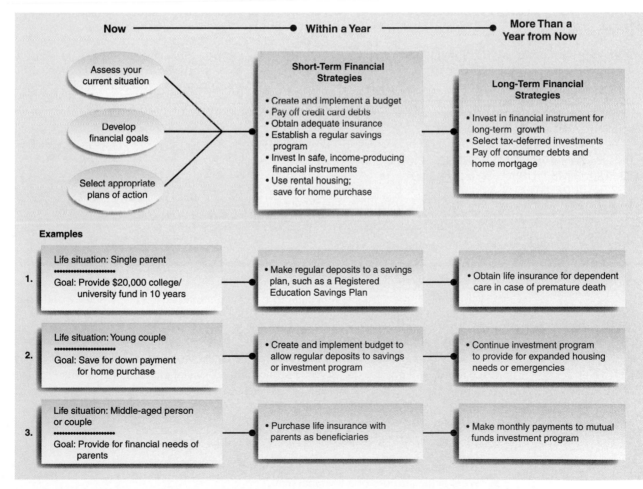

Financial Planning for Life's Situations

I need $20,000 for my education. Should I borrow or work part time?

Jim Stewarts is an Accounting Major at Concordia University; he takes five courses a semester and expects to graduate in three years. Jim came to the Financial Aid Office for help in deciding whether he should borrow money or work part time. Let's look at his situation:

Residential status: Jim lives with his parents and is free of food and board charges.

Potential amount of hours allotted for part-time work: Assuming 35 weeks in a school year and that Jim will be unable to work for four weeks; Jim is left with 31 work weeks. Considering Jim's grades are of primary importance, we advise him to work for a maximum of 15 hours a week.

Potential number of hours allotted for full-time summer employment: Jim will have 17 weeks (52 less 35 weeks) during the summer, when he can work full time for 40 hours a week. We suggest he work only 15 of these weeks so that some time is set aside for a vacation.

Type of job: Assuming an entry level job in his discipline, he will earn roughly $10 an hour.

Personal savings: It is quite common for students to have poor saving habits; therefore, we will assume that Jim currently has no savings.

IF JIM WORKS PART TIME DURING SEMESTERS AND FULL TIME DURING THE SUMMER:

During the school year, Jim can earn $4,650 ($10/hr × 15 hrs × 31 wks = $4,650).

During the summer he can earn $6,000 ($10/hr × 40 hrs × 15 wks = $6,000).

Jim's yearly gross income would be $4,650 + $6,000 = $10,650.

Yet, Jim would not have use of the entire amount. His annual pay—net of taxes, Quebec Pension Plan, and Employment Insurance payments—would be $9,405 (a total of $1,245 would be deducted according to 2003 rates). However, when he files his income tax return, he should receive a refund of any taxes paid ($667 of the total $1,245 deducted).

IF JIM TAKES OUT A STUDENT LOAN FOR $20,000:

There are student loans offered by both the federal and provincial governments; these loans are of greater advantage because they offer lower interest rates than the banks and you are only required to pay them back once you graduate. If Jim were to take out a loan today for $20,000 from the Quebec Government's Aide Financiere aux Etudes program, he would pay an annual interest rate of 4.25 percent. (www.afe.gouv.qc.ca/anglais/renseigner/taux.htm) Since he would want to pay the loan back in six years after graduation, using the Present Value formula, he would make monthly payments of $315.19. (See Appendix A for PV of an Annuity equation).

$$PV = Payments \times \frac{1 - \frac{1}{(1 + i)^n}}{i}$$

Where PV = $20,000, i = Interest Rate = .0425/12, n = # of Monthly Payments = 72.

Visit the Web site
See the Post-Test under Chapter 1 on the online learning centre at www.mcgrawhill.ca/college/kapoor.

[3] Becoming informed about tax and investment alternatives will help you expand your financial resources.

Achieving your financial objectives requires two things: (1) commitment and a willingness to learn, and (2) appropriate information sources. You must provide the first element; the chapters that follow will provide the second. For successful financial planning, know where you are now, know where you want to be, and be persistent in your efforts to get there.

CONCEPT CHECK 1–5

1. What are the main components of personal financial planning?
2. What is the purpose of a financial plan?
3. Identify some common actions taken to achieve financial goals.

Solving for the Payments, obtain $315.19. Jim would be able to make these monthly payments when he graduates, assuming he earns an accountant's starting salary of $33,000. (www.careers-in-accounting.com/ascal.htm). Overall, this loan would cost Jim roughly $22,700 ($315.19 × 72 months).

RECOMMENDATION:

We recommend that Jim work part time during the school year and full time during the summer. We have come to this conclusion on the basis of the following results:

As mentioned above, Jim's net pay after deductions at source will be $9,405. However, when he files his income tax return, all taxes that had been deducted will be reimbursed ($667). He will therefore have use of $9,405 + $667 = $10,072. Furthermore, he will be considered his parents' dependant for Quebec tax purposes and can transfer unused education credits to his parents for Federal tax purposes, which will lower their taxes in turn. They might consider this benefit and reimburse the remaining amounts deducted at source, $224 for Employment Insurance and $354 for the Quebec Pension Plan. With this strategy, Jim actually has full use of the $10,650 he earns. Since he needs $20,000 to finance his education (or $6,666.66 in each of his three years of university), will he still have enough money left over for his additional expenses? The following table suggests that he will:

By working part time, we recognize that Jim will forgo the additional time available for his studies. However, in our experience, students tend to squander additional time and procrastinate in completing their assigned work.

If Jim works instead of taking out a loan, he will earn enough money to finance his education, pay for additional personal expenses, and still save an amount, which he can use toward such expenditures as a car or house. Although one advantage of credit is that you can enjoy a good or service now and only pay for it later, it may be more prudent to avoid loans, if possible. The advantage of working part time is to avoid the cost of borrowed money as well as gain experience in the field. With our recommendation, Jim will be debt free upon graduation and with the money he has saved, he can start building a solid savings foundation (see Chapter 10).

SOURCE: Assignment was written by and reproduced with permission from the following students: Vikram Kotecha, Matthew Berry, Mili De Silva, and Rikesh Shah—Introductory Course in Personal Finance , JMSB, Concordia University, Winter 2002, updated for 2003 tax rates.

EXPENSES OF AN AVERAGE STUDENT WHO LIVES AT HOME:

Expense	Amount (monthly) $	Amount (yearly) $
Clothing	50	600
Entertainment	80	960
Videos & CD's	35	420
Miscellaneous	20	240
Total	185	2,220

$10,650 − $6,666.66 = $3,983.34 (amount of money left over after paying for school)
$3,983.34 − $2,220 = $1,763.34 (balance left over for saving)

SUMMARY OF OBJECTIVES

Objective 1
Analyze the process for making personal financial decisions.
Personal financial planning involves the following process: (1) determine your current financial situation; (2) develop financial goals; (3) identify alternative courses of action; (4) evaluate alternatives; (5) create and implement a financial action plan; and (6) re-evaluate and revise the financial plan.

Objective 2
Develop personal financial goals.
Financial goals should (1) be realistic; (2) be stated in specific, measurable terms; (3) have a time frame; and (4) indicate the type of action to be taken. They are affected by a person's values, attitude toward money, and life situation.

Objective 3
Assess economic factors that influence personal financial planning.
Financial decisions are affected by economic factors such as consumer prices, interest rates, and employment opportunities.

Objective 4
Determine personal and financial opportunity costs associated with personal financial decisions.
Every decision involves a trade-off with things given up. Personal opportunity costs include time, effort, and health. Financial opportunity costs are based on the time value of money. Future value and present value calculations enable you to measure the increased value (or lost interest) that results from a saving, investing, borrowing, or purchasing decision.

Objective 5
Identify strategies for achieving personal financial goals for different life situations.
Successful financial planning requires specific goals combined with spending, saving, investing, and borrowing strategies based on your personal situation and various social and economic factors.

KEY TERMS

FINANCIAL PLANNING PROBLEMS

(Note: Some of these problems require the use of the time value of money tables in Appendix A or a financial calculator.)

1. *Calculating Future Value of Property.* Ben Collins plans to buy a house for $65,000. If that real estate is expected to increase in value by 5 percent each year, what will its approximate value be seven years from now? (Obj. 3)

2. *Using the Rule of 72.* Using the rule of 72, approximate the following amounts: (Obj. 3)

   a. If land in an area is increasing 6 percent a year, how long will it take for property values to double?

   b. If you earn 10 percent on your investments, how long will it take for your money to double?

   c. At an annual interest rate of 5 percent, how long will it take for your savings to double?

3. *Determining the Average Price Increase*: A car that cost $12,000 in 1990 cost $16,000 10 years later. What was the annual increase in the cost of the car over the 10-year period? (Obj. 3)

4. *Determining the Required Deposit*: If you want to have $7,000 in five years, how much would you have to deposit today if your investment earned a rate of 3 percent per annum? (Obj. 3)

5. *Determining the Income Flow*: You have $100,000 to invest today. At 5 percent per year, in 20 years, what sum could you withdraw at the end of each year before your money was exhausted? (Obj. 4)

6. *Other Time Value of Money Applications* Using time value of money tables or a financial calculator, calculate the following: (Obj. 4)

   a. The future value of $450 six years from now at 7 percent.
   b. The future value of $800 saved each year for 10 years at 8 percent.
   c. The amount a person would have to deposit today (present value) at a 6-percent interest rate to have $1,000 five years from now.

   d. The amount a person would have to deposit today to be able to take out $500 a year for 10 years from an account earning 8 percent.

7. *Calculating Future Value of a Series of Amounts.* Elaine Romberg prepares her own income tax return each year. A tax preparer would charge her $60 for this service. Over a period of 10 years, how much does Elaine gain from preparing her own tax return? Assume she can earn 6 percent with a savings certificate. (Obj. 4)

FINANCIAL PLANNING ACTIVITIES

1. *Researching Personal Finance on the Internet.* Using Web sites, such as www.canadianfinance.com, www.cafp.org, or www.quicken.ca, and search engines, obtain information about commonly suggested actions related to various personal financial planning decisions. What are some of the best sources of information on the Internet to assist you with financial planning? (Obj. 1)

2. *Comparing Financial Planning Actions.* Survey friends, relatives, and others to determine the process they use when making financial decisions. How do these people measure risk when making financial decisions? (Obj. 1)

3. *Using Financial Planning Experts.* Prepare a list of financial planning specialists (investment advisers, credit counsellors, insurance agents, real estate brokers, tax preparers) in your community who can assist people with personal financial planning. Prepare a list of questions that might be asked of these financial planning professionals by (a) a young person just starting out on his or her own, (b) a young couple planning for their children's education and for their own retirement, and (c) a person nearing retirement. (Obj. 1, 3)

4. *Setting Financial Goals.* Create one short-term goal and one long-term goal for people in these life situations: (a) a young single person, (b) a single parent with a child aged eight years, (c) a married person with no children, and (d) a retired person. (Obj. 2)

5. *Analyzing Changing Life Situations.* Ask friends, relatives, and others how their spending, saving, and borrowing activities changed when they decided to continue their education, change careers, or have children. (Obj. 3)

6. *Researching Economic Conditions.* Use library resources or Web sites to determine recent trends in interest rates, inflation, and other economic indicators. Information about the consumer price index (measuring changes in the cost of living) may be obtained at www.statcan.com. Report how this economic information might affect your financial planning decisions. (Obj. 3)

7. *Comparing Alternative Financial Actions.* What actions would be necessary to compare a financial planner who advertises "One Low Fee Is Charged to Develop Your Personal Financial Plan" and one that advertises "You Are Not Charged a Fee, My Services Are Covered by the Investment Company for Which I Work"? (Obj. 4, 5)

8. *Determining Opportunity Costs.* What is the relationship between current interest rates and financial opportunity costs? Using time value of money calculations, state one or more goals in terms of an annual savings amount and the future value of this savings fund. (Obj. 2, 4)

9. *Researching Financial Planning Software.* Visit software retailers to obtain information about the features and costs of various personal financial planning activities. Information about such programs as Microsoft Money and Quicken may be obtained on the Internet. (Obj. 5)

CREATING A FINANCIAL PLAN

Starting Your Financial Plan

Planning is the foundation for success in every aspect of life. Assessing your current financial situation along with setting goals is the key to successful financial planning.

Web Sites for Financial Planning

- Investing information at **www.cse.ca** and **www.fpanet.org**.
- Selected articles from Canadian MoneySaver magazine at www.canadianmoneysaver.ca, from MoneySense magazine at **www.moneysense.ca**.
- Information on the banks and their products: **www.td.com, www4.bmo.com, www.rbcroyalbank.ca, www.scotia** bank.ca, www.nbc.ca and www.cba.ca for the Canadian Bankers Association.

- Current consumer price index and inflation information from Statistics Canada at **www.statcan.ca**.
- Information on Bank of Canada activities and publications at **www.bankofcanada.ca**.
- Retirement planning at **www.retirenet.com** and **www.elder web.org**.

(Note: Addresses and content of Web sites change, and new sites are created daily. Use the search engines discussed in the chapter appendix to update and locate Web sites for your current financial planning needs.)

LIFE SITUATION CASE

Triple Trouble for the "Sandwich Generation"

Until recently, Fran and Ed Blake's personal finances ran smoothly. Both have maintained well-paying jobs while raising two children. The Blakes have a daughter who is completing her first year of college and a son three years younger. Currently, they have $22,000 in various savings and investment funds set aside for the children's education. With education costs increasing faster than inflation, they are uncertain whether this amount is adequate.

In recent months, Fran's mother has required extensive medical attention and personal care assistance. Unable to live alone, she is now a resident of a long-term-care facility. The cost of this service is $2,050 a month, with annual increases of about 7 percent. While a major portion of the cost is covered by the Canada Pension Plan and Old Age Security, Fran's mother is unable to cover the entire cost. Their desire to help adds to the Blakes' financial burden.

The Blakes are like many other Canadians who have financial responsibilities for both dependent children and aging parents. Commonly referred to as the "sandwich generation," this group is squeezed on one side by the cost of raising and educating children and on the other side by the financial demands of caring for aging parents.

Finally, the Blakes, ages 47 and 43, are also concerned about saving for their own retirement. While they have consistently made annual deposits to a Registered Retirement Savings Plan (RRSP), various current financial demands may force them to tap into this money.

Questions

1. What actions have the Blakes taken that would be considered wise financial planning choices?
2. What areas of financial concern do the Blakes face? What actions might be appropriate to address these concerns?
3. Using time value of money calculations (tables in the Appendix or a financial calculator), compute the following:
   a. At 12 percent, what would be the value of the $22,000 education funds in three years?
   b. If the cost of long-term care is increasing at 7 percent a year, what will be the approximate monthly cost for Fran's mother eight years from now?
   c. Fran and Ed plan to deposit $1,500 a year to their RRSPs for 35 years. If they earn an average annual return of 9 percent, what will be the value of their RRSPs after 35 years?

1 Financial Planners and Other Financial Planning Information Sources

"ATM fees rise."

"Global currency fluctuations may affect consumer prices."

"Mortgage interest rates remain constant."

These are just a few of the possible influences on personal financial decisions that occur each day. While this book offers the foundation for successful personal financial planning, changing social trends, economic conditions, and technology influence the decision-making environment. Your ability to continually supplement and update your knowledge is a skill that will serve you for a lifetime.

Various resources are available to assist you with personal financial decisions. These resources include printed materials, financial institutions, courses and seminars, the Internet, computer software, and financial planning specialists.

CURRENT PERIODICALS

As Exhibit 1–A shows, a variety of personal-finance periodicals are available to expand and update your knowledge. These periodicals, along with books on various personal-finance topics, can be found in libraries.

FINANCIAL INSTITUTIONS

Some financial advisers, such as insurance agents and investment brokers, are affiliated with companies that sell financial services. Through national marketing efforts or local promotions, banks, trust companies, credit unions, insurance companies, investment brokers, and real estate offices offer suggestions on budgeting, saving, investing, and other aspects of financial planning. These organizations frequently offer booklets, financial planning worksheets, Web sites, and other materials and information.

COURSES AND SEMINARS

Colleges and universities offer courses in investments, real estate, insurance, taxation, and estate planning to enhance your knowledge of personal financial planning.

Civic clubs and community business organizations often schedule free or inexpensive programs featuring speakers and workshops on career planning, small-business management, budgeting, life insurance, tax return preparation, and investments. Financial institutions and financial service trade associations present seminars for current and prospective customers and members.

PERSONAL FINANCE SOFTWARE

Personal computer software is available to help you perform a variety of personal financial planning activities, from selecting a career to writing a will. These programs help you analyze your current financial situation and project your future financial position. Specialized computer

Exhibit 1–A   Personal Financial Planning Periodicals

The area of personal finance is constantly changing. You can keep up with changes by reading the following periodicals. You can subscribe to them, read them at your school or community library, or access them on the Internet.

CA Magazine	**The Globe and Mail**	**MoneySense Magazine**
277 Wellington Street West	444 Front Street West	156 Front Street West
Toronto, ON M5V 3H2	Toronto, ON M5V 2S9	Toronto, ON M5J 2L6
www.camagazine.com	www.globeandmail.com	www.moneysense.ca
Canadian Business	**Maclean's**	**National Post**
777 Bay Street, Fifth Floor	777 Bay Street	300–1450 Don Mills Road
Toronto, ON M5W 1A7	Toronto, ON M5W 1A7	Don Mills, ON M3B 3R5
www.canadianbusiness.com	www.macleans.ca	www.nationalpost.com
Canadian MoneySaver		
P.O. Box 370		
Bath, ON K0H 1G0		
www.canadianmoneysaver.ca		

programs are also available for conducting investment analyses, preparing tax returns, and determining the costs of financing and owning a home. Remember, a personal computer cannot change your saving, spending, and borrowing habits; only *you* can do that. However, your computer can provide fast and current analyses of your financial situation and progress. For information about the latest software, visit a computer store or read the articles and advertisements in magazines, such as *PC Computing*, *PC Magazine*, *Computer Life*, *Windows*, *Family PC*, and *Home PC*.

SPREADSHEETS

A spreadsheet program, such as Excel or Lotus 1-2-3, can assist with various financial planning tasks. Spreadsheet software can store, manipulate, create projections, and report data for such activities as

- Creating budget categories and recording spending patterns.
- Maintaining tax records for different types of expenses, such as mileage, travel expenses, materials and supplies, and business-related costs.
- Calculating the growth potential of savings accounts and investments.
- Monitoring changes in the market value of investments.
- Keeping records of the value of items for a home inventory.
- Projecting needed amounts of life insurance and retirement income.

MONEY MANAGEMENT AND FINANCIAL PLANNING PROGRAMS

Integrated financial planning programs can help you maintain home financial records, create a budget, observe spending patterns, write cheques, keep tax records, select and monitor investments, and project retirement needs. The most popular of these software packages are

Microsoft Money	*Quicken*
Microsoft	Intuit
1-800-668-7975	1-888-829-8684
(www.microsoft.com/money)	(www.quicken.ca)

TAX SOFTWARE

Each year, the software available to prepare tax returns becomes more helpful. Besides preparation and printing of the various forms and schedules, programs include tax-planning tips (with audio and video clips), audit warnings, and the ability to file your tax return electronically. The most readily available tax software includes

Quicktax	*Hometax*
Intuit	CCH Canadian Limited
1-888-829-8684	1-905-624-0303
(www.intuit.com/canada)	(www.hometax.com)

INVESTMENT ANALYSIS PROGRAMS

Software designed for researching, trading, and monitoring an investment portfolio is also available. Most of these programs may be connected to online services to obtain current stock quotes and to buy and sell investments.

THE WORLD WIDE WEB AND PERSONAL FINANCIAL PLANNING

The World Wide Web makes it possible to access more information from your home or office than libraries offer. You may use the Web for a variety of personal financial planning activities, including (1) researching current financial information; (2) obtaining programs to do financial planning calculations; (3) monitoring current stock and investment values; and (4) asking questions of experts and others through help lines, bulletin board services, and discussion forums. Some of the most useful Web sites providing current information on various personal finance topics include:

- *Canadian MoneySaver* magazine at www.canadianmoneysaver.ca; *IE:Money* magazine at www.iemoney.com; and *MoneySense* magazine at www.moneysense.ca.
- Current consumer price index and inflation information from Statistics Canada at www.statcan.ca.
- The Quicken Web site at www.quicken.ca.
- Information on Bank of Canada activities and publications at www.bankofcanada.ca.
- Investing information at www.webfin.com.

Additional Web sites are offered at the end of each chapter in the "Creating a Financial Plan."

USING SEARCH ENGINES

A search engine is a Web site that allows you to locate information related to specific topics. Some of the most commonly used search engines include

www.altavista.ca	www.searchCanada.ca
http://sympatico.msn.insn.ca	www.webcity.ca
www.canada.com	www.webcrawler.com
www.overture.com	www.yahoo.ca

Search engines operate in different ways and provide various features. Some search engines look for topic areas; others seek specific words. When conducting Web searches, be precise with your descriptive words. For example, use "mortgage rates" instead of "interest rates" to obtain information on the cost of borrowing to buy a home. Use "résumés" instead of "career planning" for assistance on developing a personal data sheet.

FINANCIAL PLANNING SPECIALISTS

Various specialists provide specific financial assistance and advice:

- *Accountants* specialize in tax matters and financial documents.
- *Bankers* assist with financial services and trusts.
- *Credit counsellors* suggest ways to reduce spending and eliminate credit problems.
- *Certified financial planners* coordinate financial decisions into a single plan.
- *Insurance agents* sell insurance coverage to protect your wealth and property.
- *Investment brokers* provide information and handle transactions for stocks, bonds, and other investments.
- *Lawyers* help in preparing wills, estate planning, tax problems, and other legal matters.
- *Real estate agents* assist with buying and selling a home or other real estate.
- *Tax preparers* specialize in the completion of income tax returns and other tax matters.

Many of these specialists offer services that include various aspects of financial planning. A financial planner's background or the company he or she represents is a good gauge of the financial planner's principal area of expertise. An accountant is likely to be most knowledgeable about tax laws, while an insurance company representative will probably emphasize how to use insurance for achieving financial goals.

WHO ARE THE FINANCIAL PLANNERS?

Many financial planners represent major insurance companies or investment businesses. Financial planners may also be individuals whose primary profession is tax accounting, real estate, or law. Financial planners are commonly categorized on the basis of three methods of compensation:

[1] **Fee-only planners** charge an hourly rate that may range from $75 to $200, or may charge a fixed fee of between less than $500 and several thousand dollars. Other fee-only planners may charge an annual fee ranging from .04 percent to 1 percent of the value of your assets.

[2] **Fee-and-commission planners** earn commissions from the investment and insurance products purchased and charge a fixed fee (ranging from $250 to $2,000) for a financial plan.

[3] **Commission-only planners** receive their revenue from the commissions on sales of insurance, mutual funds, and other investments.

Consumers must be cautious about the fees charged and how these fees are communicated. A recent study revealed that more than half of financial planners who told "mystery shoppers" that they offer "fee-only" services actually earned commissions or other financial rewards for implementing the recommendations made to their clients.

DO YOU NEED A FINANCIAL PLANNER?

The two main factors that determine whether you need financial planning assistance are (1) your income, and (2) your willingness to make independent decisions. If you earn less than $40,000 a year, you probably do not need a financial planner. Income of less than this amount does not allow for many major financial decisions once you have allocated for the spending, savings, insurance, and tax elements of your personal financial planning.

Taking an active role in your financial affairs can reduce the need for a financial planner. Your willingness to keep up to date on developments related to investments, insurance, and taxes can reduce the amount you spend on financial advisers. This will require an ongoing investment of time and effort; however, it will enable you to control your own financial direction.

When deciding whether to use a financial planner, also consider the services he or she provides. First, the financial planner should assist you in assessing your current financial position with regard to spending, saving, insurance, taxes, and potential investments. Second, the financial planner should offer a clearly written plan with different courses of action. Third, the planner should take time to discuss the components of the plan and help you monitor your financial progress. Finally, the financial planner should guide you to other experts and sources of financial services as needed.

HOW SHOULD YOU SELECT A FINANCIAL PLANNER?

You can locate financial planners by using a telephone directory, contacting financial institutions, or obtaining references from friends, business associates, or professionals with whom you currently deal, such as insurance agents or real estate brokers.

When evaluating a financial planner, ask the following:

- Is financial planning your primary activity, or are other activities primary?
- Are you licensed as an investment broker or as a seller of life insurance?
- What is your educational background and formal training?
- What are your areas of expertise?
- Do you use experts in other areas, such as taxes, law, or insurance, to assist you with financial planning recommendations?
- What professional titles and certifications do you possess?
- Am I allowed a free initial consultation?
- How is the fee determined? (Is this an amount I can afford?)
- Do you have an independent practice, or are you affiliated with a major financial services company?
- What are sample insurance, tax, and investment recommendations you make for clients?
- My major concern is _____. What would you suggest?
- May I see a sample of a written financial plan?
- May I see the contract you use with clients?
- Who are some of your clients whom I might contact?

Also, make sure you are comfortable with the planner and that the planner can clearly communicate. This type of investigation takes time and effort; however, remember that you are considering placing your entire financial future in the hands of one person.

HOW ARE FINANCIAL PLANNERS CERTIFIED?

With the exception of the Province of Quebec, there are currently few regulations governing financial planners in Canada.

Quebec adopted Bill 107 in December 2002 to authorize the creation of the Autorité des marches financiers (AMF) effective February 1, 2004. The AMF certifies and regulates the activities of financial planners, mutual funds representatives, and insurance agents, amongst others. The ongoing training and ethical conduct of financial planners is overseen by the Chambre de la sécurité financière (CSF), while those wishing to enter the profession must pass the licensing exam set by the Institut québécois de la planification financière (IQPF). In order to sit the exam, candidates are required to obtain a 450-hour personal financial planning certificate from one of four authorized educational institutions and two additional undergraduate certificates in a related field (e.g., commerce, law, or economics). In addition, candidates must successfully complete the 45-hour IQPF Professional Training course. Once they have successfully completed the IQPF exam, they are then entitled to use the title *financial planner*. Once certified, 60 hours of continuing education are required every two years.

The code of ethics governing Quebec's financial planners describes the duties and obligations of a financial planner towards the public, clients, and other members of the profession. With respect to clients, a financial planner must act with integrity, objectivity, and independence; avoid conflicts of interest; and put the best interests of his client first. All client information must be kept confidential, and full disclosure of the planner's remuneration must be outlined in the service offer signed by the client and financial planner at the outset.

Elsewhere in Canada, a financial planner may be a professional lawyer, accountant, investment adviser, insurance salesperson, mutual fund specialist, or none of the above. Financial planners are bound by the same statutes and common law that apply to anyone selling services. They must perform their work with due care, and they cannot misrepresent their work or their qualifications. Financial planners should be willing and knowledgeable enough to call on an expert when advanced knowledge or licensing is required to meet the client's needs.

The Financial Planning Standards Council (FPSC) is a non-profit organization established in 1995 to guide the evolution of the financial planning profession across Canada. The FPSC is a self-regulated organization (SRO) and is the only body in Canada authorized to award the CFP (Certified Financial Planner) designation, recognized internationally (although insufficient in the province of Quebec). It also plays a leading role in the development and enforcement of ethical standards amongst financial planning professionals.

In order to sit the CFP exam held twice yearly (June and December), candidates must successfully complete an education program registered directly with the FPSC. Following is a partial list of colleges, universities and organizations registered with the FPSC. For more information, visit the FPSC's website at www.cfp-ca.org:

Advocis	www.advocis.ca
Canadian Institute of Financial Planning	www.ifse.ca
Canadian Securities Institute	www.cse.ca
Institute of Canadian Bankers	www.icb.org
B.C. Institute of Technology	www.bcit.ca
George Brown College	www.gbrownc.ca
Ryerson University	www.ryerson.ca
University of Manitoba	www.umanitoba.ca
Wilfrid Laurier University	www.wlu.ca

Money Management Strategy: Financial Statements and Budgeting

"WE SPENT HOW MUCH ON WHAT?"

"Here we go again," complained Ben. "Every time we try to use a budget, we end up arguing and still don't have enough money."

Yolanda replied, "Maybe if we kept track of everything we spend, we would have some idea of where our money goes."

"No, not that!" Ben exclaimed. "I have a friend who keeps a notebook and lists everything he spends. That would drive me crazy."

"Well, we can't keep going like we have," responded Yolanda. "A year ago, we owed $4,500 on the credit cards. Now it's up to $7,000. And we don't have anything in savings. How will we ever be able to have a down payment for a house?"

Ben and Yolanda decided to sort all their cheque stubs, receipts, and credit card statements to see where their money was going. Last year, they spent more than $2,000 in restaurants and charged more than $800 on their vacation.

"I didn't realize we spent that much on those things," commented Ben. "We also had auto maintenance costs of $1,650 and donated $1,800 to the homeless shelter and church. Those are things we had to do and wanted to do."

Yolanda replied, "But now that we know how we spend our money, what do we do next?"

"Maybe we should get a computerized money management program," Ben suggested.

Yolanda countered, "Maybe we should just start with spending a few dollars on a notebook and file folders to record and sort our receipts."

QUESTIONS

1 What would Ben and Yolanda learn by sorting their expenses into various categories? What categories should they use?

2 How can knowing where their money goes help Ben and Yolanda plan their spending?

3 What financial goals might Ben and Yolanda consider to address some of their money management concerns?

4 Locate a Web site that would help Ben and Yolanda improve their money management skills.

LEARNING OBJECTIVES

1 Recognize relationships among financial documents and money management activities.

2 Create a system for maintaining personal financial records.

3 Develop a personal balance sheet and cash flow statement.

4 Create and implement a budget.

5 Calculate savings needed to achieve financial goals.

PLANNING FOR SUCCESSFUL MONEY MANAGEMENT

■ **OBJECTIVE 1** ■

Recognize
relationships
among financial
documents and
money management
activities.

money management
Day-to-day financial
activities necessary
to manage current
personal economic
resources while working
toward long-term
financial security.

Visit the Web site
See the Pre-Test under
Chapter 2 on the online
learning centre at
www.mcgrawhill.ca/
college/kapoor.

"Each month I have too much month and not enough money. If the month were only 20 days long, budgeting would be easy." Most of us have heard a comment like this when it comes to budgeting and money management.

Your daily spending and saving decisions are at the centre of financial planning. You must coordinate these decisions with your needs, goals, and personal situation. When people watch a baseball or football game, they usually know the score. In financial planning also, knowing the score is important. Maintaining financial records and planning your spending are essential to successful personal financial management. The time and effort you devote to these recordkeeping activities will yield benefits. **Money management** refers to the day-to-day financial activities necessary to manage current personal economic resources while working toward long-term financial security.

OPPORTUNITY COST AND MONEY MANAGEMENT

Consumers can choose from more than 25,000 items in a supermarket, from more than 11,000 periodicals, and from as many as 500 cable television stations. Daily decision making is a fact of life, and trade-offs are associated with each choice made. Selecting an alternative means you give up something else. In terms of money management decisions, examples of trade-off situations, or *opportunity costs*, include the following:

- Spending money on current living expenses reduces the amount you can use for saving and investing for long-term financial security.
- Saving and investing for the future reduces the amount you can spend now.
- Buying on credit results in payments later and a reduction in the amount of future income available for spending.
- Using savings for purchases results in lost interest earnings and an inability to use savings for other purposes.
- Comparison shopping can save you money and improve the quality of your purchases but uses up something of value you cannot replace: your time.

As you develop and implement various money management activities, you need to assess financial and personal costs and benefits associated with financial decisions.

COMPONENTS OF MONEY MANAGEMENT

As Exhibit 2–1 shows, the three major money management activities are interrelated. Personal financial records and documents are the foundation of systematic resource use. They provide

Exhibit 2–1

Money Management
Activities

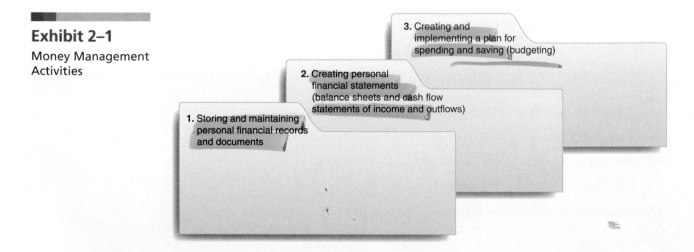

3. Creating and implementing a plan for spending and saving (budgeting)

2. Creating personal financial statements (balance sheets and cash flow statements of income and outflows)

1. Storing and maintaining personal financial records and documents

written evidence of business transactions, ownership of property, and legal matters. Personal financial statements enable you to measure and assess your financial position and progress. Your spending plan, or budget, is the basis for effective money management.

CONCEPT CHECK 2–1

1. What opportunity costs are associated with money management activities?
2. What are the three major money management activities?

A SYSTEM FOR PERSONAL FINANCIAL RECORDS

Experts once predicted that computers would result in fewer paper documents. How wrong they were! Today, computers are generating more paperwork than ever. Much of that paperwork relates to financial matters. Invoices, credit card statements, insurance policies, and tax records are the basis of financial recordkeeping and personal economic choices.

An organized system of financial records provides a basis for:

- Handling daily business affairs, including payment of bills on time.
- Planning and measuring financial progress.
- Completing required tax reports.
- Making effective investment decisions.
- Determining available resources for current and future buying.

As Exhibit 2–2 shows, most financial records are kept in one of three places: a home file, a safety deposit box, or a home computer. A home file should be used to keep records for current needs and documents with limited value. Your home file may be a series of folders, a cabinet with several drawers, or even a cardboard box. Whatever method you use, it is most important that your home file be organized to allow quick access to required documents and information.

Important financial records and valuable articles should be kept in a location that provides better security than a home file. A **safety deposit box** is a private storage area at a financial institution with maximum security for valuables and difficult-to-replace documents. Access to the contents of a safety deposit box requires two keys. One key is issued to you; the other is kept by the financial institution where the safety deposit box is located. Items commonly kept in a safety deposit box include stock certificates, contracts, a list of insurance policies, and valuables, such as rare coins and stamps.

The number of financial records and documents may seem overwhelming; however, they can easily be organized into 10 categories (see Exhibit 2–2). These groups correspond to the major topics covered in this book. You may not need to use all of these records and documents at present. As your financial situation changes, you will add others.

How long should you keep personal finance records? The answer to this question differs for various documents. Such records as birth certificates and wills should be kept permanently. Records on property and investments should be kept as long as you own these items. Federal tax laws dictate the length of time you should keep tax-related information. Copies of tax returns and supporting data should be saved for six years. Normally, an audit will go back only three years; however, under certain circumstances, the Canada Customs and Revenue Agency may request information from six years back. Financial experts recommend keeping documents related to the purchase and sale of real estate indefinitely.

■ OBJECTIVE 2 ■

Create a system for maintaining personal financial records.

safety deposit box
A private storage area at a financial institution with maximum security for valuables.

DID YOU KNOW ?

In Canada, people keep various documents and valuables in safety deposit boxes in banks, trust companies, and credit unions. While these boxes are usually very safe, each year a few people lose the contents of their safety deposit boxes through theft, fire, or natural disasters. Such losses are usually, but not always, covered by the financial institution's insurance.

Exhibit 2–2   Where to Keep Financial Records

Home File

1. **Personal and Employment Records (Chapter 2)** • Current résumé • Employee benefit information • Copy of birth certificates • Social insurance number	2. **Money Management Records (Chapter 2)** • Current budget • Recent personal financial statements (balance sheet, income statement) • List of financial goals • List of safety deposit box contents
3. **Tax Records (Chapter 3)** • Paycheque stubs, T4 slips • Receipts for tax deductible items • Records of taxable income • Past income tax returns and documentation	4. **Financial Services Records (Chapter 4)** • Chequebook, unused cheques • Bank statements, cancelled cheques • Location information and number of safety deposit box
5. **Credit Records (Chapters 5, 6)** • Payment records • Receipts, monthly statements • List of credit account numbers and telephone numbers of issuers	6. **Consumer Purchase & Automobile Records (Chapters 5, 6)** • Warranties • Receipts for major purchases • Owner's manuals for major appliances • Automobile service and repair records • Automobile registration • Automobile owner's manual
7. **Housing Records (Chapter 7)** • Lease (if renting) • Property tax records • Home repair receipts • Copy of mortgage documents	8. **Insurance Records (Chapters 8, 9)** • Original insurance policies • List of insurance premium amounts and due dates • Medical information (health history, prescription drug information) • Claim reports
9. **Investment Records (Chapters 10–13)** • Records of stock, bond, and mutual fund purchases and sales • Brokerage statements • Dividend records	10. **Estate Planning and Retirement Records (Chapters 14–15)** • Will, power of attorney, and living will • Company pension plan information • Canada Pension Plan information • RRSP information • Trust agreements

Safety Deposit Box

• Birth, marriage, and death certificates
• Citizenship papers
• Adoption, custody papers
• Military papers
• Serial numbers of expensive items
• Photographs or video of valuable belongings

• Guaranteed Investment Certificates
• List of chequing and savings account numbers and financial institutions
• Credit contacts
• List of credit card numbers and telephone numbers of issuers

• Mortgage papers, title deed
• Automobile title
• List of insurance policy numbers and company names
• Stock and bond certificates
• Rare coins, stamps, gems, and other collectibles
• Copy of will

Personal Computer System (with back-up)

• Current and past budgets
• Summary of cheques written and other banking transactions
• Past income tax returns prepared with tax preparation software
• Account summaries and performance results of investments
• Computerized version of wills, estate plans, and other documents

CONCEPT CHECK 2–2

1. What are the benefits of an organized system of financial records and documents?
2. What suggestions would you give for creating a system for organizing and storing financial records and documents?
3. What influences the length of time you should keep financial records and documents?

PERSONAL FINANCIAL STATEMENTS FOR MEASURING FINANCIAL PROGRESS

Every journey starts somewhere. You need to know where you are before you can go somewhere else. Personal financial statements tell you the starting point of your financial journey.

Most of the financial documents we have discussed come from financial institutions, other business organizations, or the government. Two documents that you create yourself, the personal balance sheet and the cash flow statement, are called *personal financial statements*. These reports provide information about your current financial position and present a summary of your income and spending. The main purposes of personal financial statements are to

- Summarize the value of the items that you own and the amounts that you owe.
- Track your cash inflows by source and your outflows by type.
- Identify strengths and weaknesses in your current financial situation.
- Measure progress toward your financial goals.
- Provide data for use in filing your income tax return or applying for credit.

■ OBJECTIVE 3 ■

Develop a personal balance sheet and cash flow statement.

THE PERSONAL BALANCE SHEET: WHERE ARE YOU NOW?

The current financial position of an individual or a family is a common starting point for financial planning. A **personal balance sheet**, also called a *net worth statement*, reports what you own and what you owe. You prepare a personal balance sheet to determine your current financial position using the following process:

personal balance sheet A financial statement that reports what an individual or a family owns and owes; also called a *net worth statement*.

ITEMS OF VALUE (WHAT YOU OWN)	−	AMOUNTS OWED (WHAT YOU OWE)	=	NET WORTH (YOUR WEALTH)

For example, if your possessions are worth $4,500 and you owe $800 to others, your net worth is $3,700.

STEP 1: LISTING ITEMS OF VALUE Available cash and money in bank accounts combined with other items of value are the foundation of your current financial position. Assets are cash and other tangible property with a monetary value. The balance sheet for Rose and Edgar Gomez (Exhibit 2–3) lists their assets under four categories.

assets Cash and other property with a monetary value.

[1] **Liquid assets** are cash and items of value that can easily be converted to cash. Money in chequing and savings accounts is liquid and is available to the Gomez family for current spending. The cash value of their life insurance may be borrowed, if needed. While assets other than liquid assets can also be converted into cash, the process is not quite as easy.

[2] *Real estate* includes a home, a condominium, vacation property, or other land that a person or family owns.

[3] *Personal possessions* are a major portion of assets for most people. Included in this category are automobiles and other personal belongings. While these items have value, they may be difficult to convert to cash. You may decide to list your possessions on the balance sheet at their depreciated value (from original cost). However, these values probably need to be revised over time, since a five-year-old television set, for example, is worth less now than when it was new. Alternatively, you may wish to list your possessions at their current resale value (also referred to as *fair market value*). This method takes into account the fact that such things as a home or rare jewellery may increase in value over time, although most assets' resale value drops very rapidly. You can estimate current value by looking at ads for the selling price of

liquid assets Cash and items of value that can easily be converted to cash.

Visit the Web site See Personal Financial Planning worksheets under Chapter 2 on the online learning centre at www.mcgrawhill.ca/college/kapoor.

Exhibit 2–3   Creating a Personal Balance Sheet

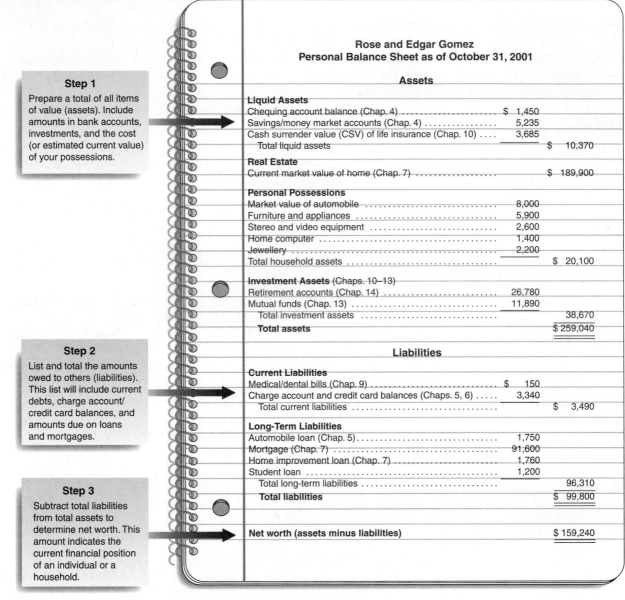

Step 1

Prepare a total of all items of value (assets). Include amounts in bank accounts, investments, and the cost (or estimated current value) of your possessions.

Step 2

List and total the amounts owed to others (liabilities). This list will include current debts, charge account/credit card balances, and amounts due on loans and mortgages.

Step 3

Subtract total liabilities from total assets to determine net worth. This amount indicates the current financial position of an individual or a household.

Rose and Edgar Gomez
Personal Balance Sheet as of October 31, 2001

Assets

Liquid Assets

Chequing account balance (Chap. 4)	$ 1,450	
Savings/money market accounts (Chap. 4)	5,235	
Cash surrender value (CSV) of life insurance (Chap. 10)	3,685	
Total liquid assets		$ 10,370

Real Estate

Current market value of home (Chap. 7)	$ 189,900

Personal Possessions

Market value of automobile	8,000	
Furniture and appliances	5,900	
Stereo and video equipment	2,600	
Home computer	1,400	
Jewellery	2,200	
Total household assets		$ 20,100

Investment Assets (Chaps. 10–13)

Retirement accounts (Chap. 14)	26,780	
Mutual funds (Chap. 13)	11,890	
Total investment assets		38,670
Total assets		**$ 259,040**

Liabilities

Current Liabilities

Medical/dental bills (Chap. 9)	$ 150	
Charge account and credit card balances (Chaps. 5, 6)	3,340	
Total current liabilities		$ 3,490

Long-Term Liabilities

Automobile loan (Chap. 5)	1,750	
Mortgage (Chap. 7)	91,600	
Home improvement loan (Chap. 7)	1,760	
Student loan	1,200	
Total long-term liabilities		96,310
Total liabilities		**$ 99,800**

Net worth (assets minus liabilities)	**$ 159,240**

NOTE: Various asset and liability items are discussed in the chapters listed next to them.

comparable automobiles, homes, or other possessions. Or you may use the services of an appraiser.

[4] *Investment assets* are funds set aside for long-term financial needs. The Gomez family will use their investments for such things as financing their children's education, purchasing a vacation home, and planning for retirement. Since investment assets usually fluctuate in value, the amounts listed should reflect their value at the time the balance sheet is prepared.

STEP 2: DETERMINING AMOUNTS OWED   Looking at the total assets of the Gomez family, you might conclude that they have a strong financial position. However, their debts must also be considered. **Liabilities** are amounts owed to others but do not include items not yet due, such as next month's rent. A liability is a debt you owe now, not something you may owe in the future. Liabilities fall into two categories:

liabilities Amounts owed to others.

[1] **Current liabilities** are debts you must pay within a short time, usually less than a year. These liabilities include such things as medical bills, tax payments, instalment loans, lines of credit, mortgages, student loans, and charge accounts.

[2] **Long-term liabilities** are debts you do not have to pay in full until more than a year from now. Common long-term liabilities include auto loans, educational loans, and mortgages. A *mortgage* is an amount borrowed to buy a house or other real estate that will be repaid over a period of 15, 20, or 25 years. Similarly, a home improvement loan may be repaid to the lender over the next five to 10 years.

The debts listed in the liability section of a balance sheet represent the amount owed at the moment; they do not include future interest payments. However, each debt payment is likely to include a portion of interest. Chapters 5 and 6 discuss the cost of borrowing further.

current liabilities
Debts that must be paid within a short time, usually less than a year.

long-term liabilities
Debts that are not required to be paid in full until more than a year from now.

STEP 3: COMPUTING NET WORTH Your **net worth** is the difference between your total assets and your total liabilities. This relationship can be stated as

$$\text{Assets} - \text{Liabilities} = \text{Net worth}$$

Net worth is the amount you would have if all assets were sold for the listed values and all debts were paid in full. Also, total assets equal total liabilities plus net worth. The balance sheet of a business is commonly expressed as

$$\text{Assets} = \text{Liabilities} + \text{Net worth}$$

As Exhibit 2–3 shows, Rose and Edgar Gomez have a net worth of $159,240. Since very few people, if any, liquidate all assets, the amount of net worth has a more practical purpose: It provides a measurement of your current financial position.

A person may have a high net worth but still have financial difficulties. Having many assets with low liquidity means not having the cash available to pay current expenses. **Insolvency** is the inability to pay debts when they are due; it occurs when a person's liabilities far exceed available assets. Bankruptcy, discussed in Chapter 6, may be an alternative for a person in this position. You can increase your net worth in various ways, including

net worth The difference between total assets and total liabilities.

insolvency The inability to pay debts when they are due because liabilities far exceed the value of assets.

- Increasing your savings.
- Reducing spending.
- Increasing the value of investments and other possessions.
- Reducing the amounts you owe.

Remember, your net worth is *not* money available for use but an indication of your financial position on a given date.

THE CASH FLOW STATEMENT: WHERE DID YOUR MONEY GO?

Each day, financial events can affect your net worth. When you receive a paycheque or pay living expenses, your total assets and liabilities change. **Cash flow** is the actual inflow and outflow of cash during a given time period. Income from employment will probably represent your most important *cash inflow*; however, other income, such as interest earned on a savings account, should also be considered. In contrast, payments for such items as rent, food, and loans are *cash outflows*.

A **cash flow statement**, also called a *personal income and expenditure statement*, (Exhibit 2–4) is a summary of cash receipts and payments for a given period, such as a month or a year. This report provides data on your income and spending patterns, which will be helpful when preparing a budget. A chequing account can provide information for your cash flow statement. Deposits to the account are your *inflows*; cheques written are your *outflows*. Of course, in using this system, when you do not deposit the entire amounts received you must also note the spending of undeposited amounts in your cash flow statement.

cash flow The actual inflow and outflow of cash during a given time period.

cash flow statement A financial statement that summarizes cash receipts and payments for a given period.

Exhibit 2–4   Creating a Cash Flow Statement of Income and Outflows

Step 1

For a set time period (such as a month), record your income from various sources, such as wages, salary, interest, or payments from government.

Step 2

Develop categories and record cash payments for the time period covered by the cash flow statement.

Step 3

Subtract the total outflows from the total inflows. A positive number (surplus) represents the amount available for saving and investing. A negative number (deficit) represents the amount that must be taken out of savings or borrowed.

Lin Ye
Cash Flow Statement for the Month Ended September 30, 2001

Income (cash inflows)

Salary (gross)			$4,350
Less deductions			
Federal income tax	$909		
Provincial income tax	359		
Canada Pension Plan	141		
Employment Insurance	104		
Total deductions		$1,513	$2,837
After-tax investment income			96
Total income			$2,933

Cash Outflows

Fixed Expenses

Rent	$1,150	
Loan payment	216	
Cable television	52	
Monthly train ticket (transit)	196	
Life insurance	32	
Apartment insurance	23	
Total fixed outflows		$1,669

Variable Expenses

Food at home	260	
Food away from home	168	
Clothing	150	
Telephone	52	
Electricity	48	
Personal care (dry cleaning, laundry, cosmetics)	66	
Medical expenses	85	
Recreation/entertainment	100	
Gifts	70	
Donations	80	
Total variable outflows	1,079	
Total outflows		$2,748
Cash surplus + (or deficit –)		+$185

Allocation of Surplus

Emergency fund savings	69
Savings for short-term/intermediate financial goals	33
Savings/investing for long-term financial security	83
Total surplus	$185

The process for preparing a cash flow statement is

TOTAL CASH RECEIVED DURING THE TIME PERIOD	–	CASH OUTFLOWS DURING THE TIME PERIOD	=	CASH SURPLUS OR DEFICIT

STEP 1: RECORD INCOME Creating a cash flow statement starts with identifying the cash received during the time period involved. **Income** is the inflow of cash to an individual or a household. For most people, the main source of income is money received from a job. Other common income sources include

income Inflow of cash to an individual or a household.

- Wages, salaries, and commissions.
- Self-employment business income.
- Savings and investment income (interest, dividends, rent).

- Gifts, grants, scholarships, and educational loans.
- Government payments, such as Canada Pension Plan, welfare, and Employment Insurance benefits.
- Amounts received from pension and retirement programs.
- Alimony and child support payments.

In Exhibit 2–4, note that Lin Ye's monthly salary (or *gross income*) of $4,350 is her main source of income. However, she does not have use of the entire amount. **Take-home pay**, also called *net pay* or *net income*, is a person's earnings after deductions for taxes and other items. Lin's deductions for federal and provincial taxes, Canada Pension Plan contributions, and Employment Insurance are $1,513. Her take-home pay is $2,837. This amount, plus after-tax earnings from investments, is the income she has available for use during the current month.

Take-home pay is also called *disposable income*, the amount a person or household has available to spend. **Discretionary income** is money left over after paying for housing, food, and other necessities. Studies report that discretionary income ranges from less than 5 percent for people under age 25 to more than 40 percent for older people.

take-home pay
Earnings after deductions for taxes and other items; also called *disposable income*.

discretionary income
Money left over after paying for housing, food, and other necessities.

STEP 2: RECORD CASH OUTFLOWS

Cash payments for living expenses and other items make up the second component of a cash flow statement. Lin Ye divides her cash outflows into two major categories: fixed expenses and variable expenses. While every individual and household has different cash outflows, these main categories, along with the subgroupings Lin uses, can be adapted to most situations.

[1] *Fixed expenses* are payments that do not vary from month to month. Rent or mortgage payments, installment loan payments, cable television service fees, and a monthly train ticket for commuting to work are examples of constant or fixed cash outflows.

For Lin, another type of fixed expense is the amount she sets aside each month for payments due once or twice a year. For example, Lin pays $384 every March for life insurance. Each month, she records a fixed outflow of $32 for deposit in a special savings account so that the money will be available when her insurance payment is due.

[2] *Variable expenses* are flexible payments that change from month to month. Common examples of variable cash outflows are food, clothing, utilities (such as electricity, heating and telephone), recreation, medical expenses, gifts, and donations. The use of a chequebook or some other recordkeeping system is necessary for an accurate total of cash outflows.

DID YOU KNOW?

The most common advice from financial planners: "Save more." "Save all you can." "Cut your spending so you can save more."

STEP 3: DETERMINE NET CASH FLOW

The difference between income and outflows can be either a positive (surplus) or a negative (deficit) cash flow. A deficit exists if more cash goes out than comes in during a given month. This amount must be made up by withdrawals from savings or by borrowing. The effect of a net cash flow on net worth is shown in the Financial Planning for Life's Situations feature on page 46.

When you have a cash surplus, as Lin did (Exhibit 2–4), this amount is available for saving, investing, or paying off debts. Each month, Lin sets aside money for her emergency fund in a savings account that she would use for unexpected expenses or to pay living costs if she did not receive her salary. She deposits the rest of the surplus in savings and investment plans that have two purposes. The first is the achievement of short-term and intermediate financial goals, such as a new car, a vacation, or re-enrollment in school; the second is long-term financial security—her retirement.

A cash flow statement provides the foundation for preparing and implementing a spending, saving, and investment plan, discussed in this chapter's Budgeting for Skilled Money Management section.

Exhibit 2–5   The Fraziers Develop and Implement a Monthly Budget

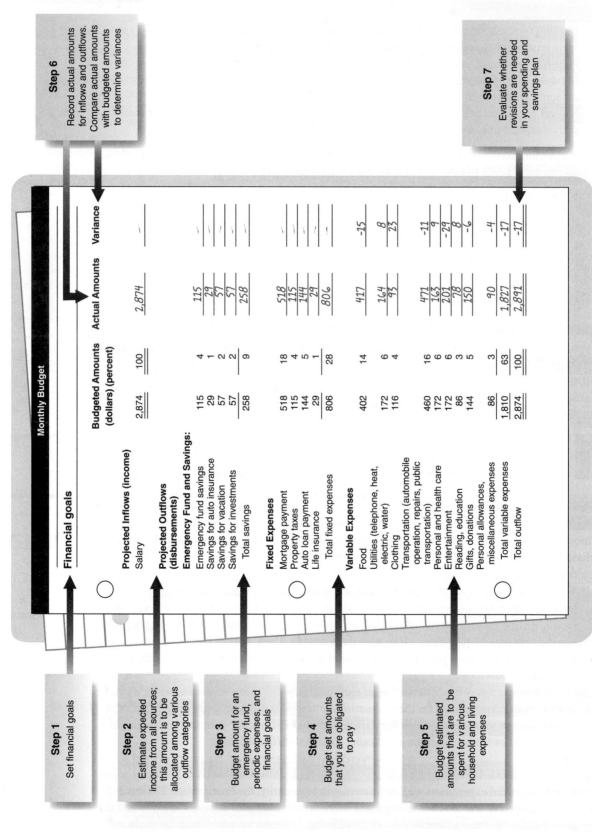

Step 1
Set financial goals

Step 2
Estimate expected income from all sources; this amount is to be allocated among various outflow categories

Step 3
Budget amount for an emergency fund, periodic expenses, and financial goals

Step 4
Budget set amounts that you are obligated to pay

Step 5
Budget estimated amounts that are to be spent for various household and living expenses

Step 6
Record actual amounts for inflows and outflows. Compare actual amounts with budgeted amounts to determine variances

Step 7
Evaluate whether revisions are needed in your spending and savings plan

Monthly Budget

Financial goals	Budgeted Amounts (dollars)	(percent)	Actual Amounts	Variance
Projected Inflows (income)				
Salary	2,874	100	2,874	
Projected Outflows (disbursements)				
Emergency Fund and Savings:				
Emergency fund savings	115	4	115	
Savings for auto insurance	29	1	29	
Savings for vacation	57	2	57	
Savings for investments	57	2	57	
Total savings	258	9	258	
Fixed Expenses				
Mortgage payment	518	18	518	
Property taxes	115	4	115	
Auto loan payment	144	5	144	
Life insurance	29	1	29	
Total fixed expenses	806	28	806	
Variable Expenses				
Food	402	14	417	–15
Utilities (telephone, heat, electric, water)	172	6	164	8
Clothing	116	4	93	23
Transportation (automobile operation, repairs, public transportation)	460	16	471	–11
Personal and health care	172	6	163	9
Entertainment	172	6	201	–29
Reading, education	86	3	78	8
Gifts, donations	144	5	150	–6
Personal allowances, miscellaneous expenses	86	3	90	–4
Total variable expenses	1,810	63	1,827	–17
Total outflow	2,874	100	2,891	–17

situation and employment stability. A three-month emergency fund is probably adequate for a person with a stable income or secure employment, while a person with erratic or seasonal income may need to set aside an emergency fund sufficient for six months or more of living expenses.

The Fraziers also set aside an amount each month for their automobile insurance payment, which is due every six months. Both this amount and the emergency fund are put into a savings account that will earn interest. Savings methods for achieving financial goals are discussed later in this chapter.

A very common budgeting mistake is to save the amount you have left at the end of the month. When you do that, you often have *nothing* left for savings. Since savings are vital to long-term financial security, advisers suggest that an amount be budgeted as a fixed expense.

STEP 4: BUDGETING FIXED EXPENSES

Definite obligations are the basis for this portion of a budget. As Exhibit 2–5 shows, the Fraziers have fixed expenses for housing, taxes, and loan payments. They make a monthly payment of $29 for life insurance. The budgeted total for the Fraziers' fixed expenses is $806, or 28 percent of estimated available income.

Assigning amounts to spending categories requires careful consideration. The amount you budget for various items will depend on your current needs and plans for the future. The following sources can help you plan your spending:

- Your cash flow statement.
- Consumer expenditure data (www.statcan.ca).
- Articles in magazines such as *MoneySaver*.
- Estimates of future income and expenses and anticipated changes in inflation rates.

> **DID YOU KNOW?**
>
> Only 16 percent of Canadian consumers prepare a monthly budget on paper. (Fédération des ACEF du Québec—survey of 1902 Canadians, June 2001)

Exhibit 2–6 provides suggested budget allocations for different life situations. Although this information can be of value when creating budget categories, most financial planners suggest you record and analyze your expenses over a period of one to three months to better understand how you spend your income. Use a simple system, such as a notebook or your chequebook. This "spending diary" will help you know where your money is going. Remember, a budget is an *estimate* for spending and saving intended to help you make better use of your money, not to reduce your enjoyment of life.

STEP 5: BUDGETING VARIABLE EXPENSES

Planning for variable expenses is not as easy as budgeting for savings or fixed expenses. Some variable expenses are repeated every month, such as the cost of entertainment and recreation. Others occur only once a year or every few years, such as the cost of replacing appliances or home renovations. Variable expenses will fluctuate by household situation, time of year, health, economic conditions, and a variety of other factors. A major portion of the Fraziers' planned spending—more than 60 percent of their budgeted income—is for variable living costs.

The Fraziers base their estimates on their needs and desires for the items listed and on expected changes in the cost of living. The *consumer price index (CPI)* is a measure of the general price level of consumer goods and services in Canada. This government statistic indicates changes in the buying power of a dollar. As consumer prices increase due to inflation, people must spend more to buy the same amount. Changes in the cost of living will vary depending on where you live and what you buy.

STEP 6: RECORDING SPENDING AMOUNTS

After you have established your spending plan, you will need to keep records of your actual income and expenses similar to those you keep in preparing an income statement. In Exhibit 2–5, note that the Fraziers estimated specific amounts for income and expenses. These are presented under "Budgeted Amounts." The family's actual spending was not always the same as planned. A **budget variance** is the

budget variance The difference between the amount budgeted and the actual amount received or spent.

Exhibit 2–6   Typical After-Tax Budget Allocations (2002 constant dollars)[1]

	2000	2001	2002
	% Share of Budget	% Share of Budget	% Share of Budget
Total expenditure	100.0	100.0	100.0
Personal taxes	21.6	21.3	20.0
Shelter	18.5	18.7	18.6
Transportation	13.6	13.2	14.0
Food	11.2	11.2	11.1
Recreation	5.7	6.0	5.9
Personal insurance payments and pension contributions	5.6	5.4	5.7
Household operation	4.5	4.6	4.6
Clothing	4.2	4.2	4.1
Household furnishings and equipment	2.8	2.9	3.0
Health care	2.4	2.5	2.6
Tobacco products and alcoholic beverages	2.2	2.3	2.5
Gifts of money and contributions	2.3	2.2	2.4
Education	1.5	1.6	1.5
Miscellaneous expenditures	1.5	1.5	1.5
Personal care	1.3	1.7	1.4
Games of chance (net)	0.5	0.5	0.5
Reading materials and other printed matter	0.5	0.5	0.5

1. The All-items CPI has been used to adjust all 2000 and 2001 spending components.

SOURCE: Statistics Canada (www.statcan.ca/Daily/English/031217/d031217b.htm)

budget deficit The amount by which actual spending exceeds planned spending.

budget surplus The amount by which actual spending is less than planned spending.

difference between the amount budgeted and the actual amount received or spent. The total variance for the Fraziers was a $17 **budget deficit**, since their actual spending exceeded their planned spending by this amount. The Fraziers would have had a **budget surplus** if their actual spending had been less than they had planned.

Variances for income should be viewed as the opposite of variances for expenses. Less income than expected would be a deficit, while more income than expected would be a surplus.

Spending more than planned for an item may be justified by reducing spending for another item or putting less into savings. However, it may be necessary to revise your budget and financial goals.

STEP 7: REVIEWING SPENDING AND SAVING PATTERNS Like most decision-making activities, budgeting is a circular, ongoing process. You will need to review and perhaps revise your spending plan on a regular basis.

Reviewing Your Financial Progress The results of your budget may be obvious: having extra cash in chequing, falling behind in your bill payments, and so on. However, such obvious results may not always be present. Occasionally, you will have to sit down (with other household members, if appropriate) and review areas where spending has been more or less than expected.

As Exhibit 2–7 shows, you can prepare an annual summary to compare actual spending with budgeted amounts. This type of summary may also be prepared every three or six months. A spreadsheet computer program can be useful for this purpose. The summary will help you see areas where changes in your budget may be necessary. This review process is vital to both successful short-term money management and long-term financial security.

Revising Your Goals and Budget Allocations What should you cut first when a budget shortage occurs? This question doesn't have easy answers, and the answers will vary for different household situations. The most common overspending areas are entertainment and food, especially away-from-home meals. Purchasing less expensive brand items, buying quality used products, avoiding credit card purchases, and renting rather than buying are common budget adjustment techniques.

At this point in the budgeting process, you may also revise your financial goals. Are you making progress toward achieving your objectives? Have changes in personal or economic conditions affected the desirability of certain goals? Have new goals surfaced that should be given a higher priority than those that have been your major concern? Addressing these issues while creating an effective saving method will help ensure accomplishment of your financial goals.

> **DID YOU KNOW ?**
>
> Seventeen percent of Canadians aged 18–30 reported not having met some of their monthly payments on bank loans over the preceding 12 months.
>
> (Fédération des ACEF du Québec—survey of 1902 Canadians, June 2001)

CHARACTERISTICS OF SUCCESSFUL BUDGETING

Having a spending plan will not eliminate financial worries. A budget will work only if you follow it. Changes in income, expenses, and goals will require changes in your spending plan. Money management experts advise that a successful budget should be

- *Well planned*. A good budget takes time and effort to prepare. Planning a budget should involve everyone affected by it. Children can learn important money management lessons by helping to develop and use the family budget.
- *Realistic*. If you have a moderate income, don't immediately expect to save enough money for an expensive car or a lavish vacation. A budget is designed not to prevent you from enjoying life but to help you achieve what you want most.
- *Flexible*. Unexpected expenses and changes in your cost of living will require a budget that you can easily revise. Also, special situations, such as two-income families or the arrival of a baby, may require an increase in certain types of expenses.
- *Clearly communicated*. Unless you and others involved are aware of the spending plan, it will not work. The budget should be written and available to all household members. Many variations of written budgets are possible, including a notebook or a computerized system (see the Financial Planning for Life's Situations box on page 53).

CONCEPT CHECK 2–4

1. What are the main purposes of a budget?
2. How does a person's life situation affect goal setting and amounts allocated for various budget categories?
3. What are the main steps in creating a budget?
4. What are commonly recommended qualities of a successful budget?
5. What actions might you take when evaluating your budgeting program?

Exhibit 2–7   An Annual Budget Summary

Item	Monthly Budget	Actual Spending (cash outflows)												Annual Totals	
		Jan.	Feb.	Mar.	Apr.	May	June	July	Aug.	Sept.	Oct.	Nov.	Dec.	Actual	Budgeted*
Income	2,730	2,730	2,730	2,730	2,940	2,750	2,750	2,750	2,750	2,850	2,850	2,850	2,850	33,450	32,760
Savings	150	150	150	200	150	90	50	30	100	250	250	150	40	1,610	1,800
Mortgage/rent	826	826	826	826	826	826	826	826	826	826	826	826	826	9,912	9,912
Housing costs (insurance, utilities)	190	214	238	187	176	185	188	146	178	198	177	201	195	2,283	2,280
Telephone	50	43	45	67	56	54	52	65	45	43	52	49	47	618	600
Food (at home)	280	287	277	245	234	278	267	298	320	301	298	278	324	3,407	3,360
Food (away from home)	80	67	78	84	87	123	109	89	83	67	76	83	143	1,089	960
Clothing	100	98	78	123	156	86	76	111	124	87	95	123	111	1,268	1,200
Transportation (auto operation, public transportation)	340	302	312	333	345	297	287	390	373	299	301	267	301	3,807	4,080
Car loan payments	249	249	249	249	249	249	249	249	249	249	249	249	249	2,988	2,988
Insurance (life, health, other)	45	—	—	135	—	—	135	—	—	135	—	—	135	540	540
Health care	140	176	145	187	122	111	156	186	166	134	189	193	147	1,912	1,680
Recreation	80	67	98	123	98	67	45	87	98	65	87	87	111	1,033	960
Reading, education	40	52	54	44	34	39	54	12	38	54	34	76	45	516	480
Gifts, donations	100	102	110	94	87	123	89	95	94	113	87	99	134	1,227	1,200
Personal miscellaneous expense	60	89	45	67	54	98	59	54	49	71	65	90	56	797	720
Total	2,730	2,702	2,705	2,964	2,674	2,626	2,642	2,638	2,743	2,892	2,786	2,771	2,864	33,007	32,760
Surplus (deficit)		28	25	(234)	266	104	88	92	(13)	(42)	64	79	(14)	443	—

*Monthly budgeted spending times 12.

Although your chequebook will give you a fairly complete record of your expenses, it does not serve the purpose of planning for spending. A budget requires that you outline how you will spend available income. Various types of budgeting systems exist, from informal procedures to computerized spending plans.

A *mental budget* exists only in a person's mind. This simple system may be appropriate if you have limited resources and minimal financial responsibilities. The major drawback of a mental budget is the danger of forgetting what amounts you plan to spend on various items.

A *physical budget* involves the use of envelopes, folders, or containers to hold the money or slips of paper that represent amounts allocated for spending categories. This system allows you to actually see where your money goes. Envelopes would contain the amount of cash or a note listing the amount to be used for "Food," "Rent," "Clothing," "Auto Payment," "Entertainment," and other expenses.

Experienced financial advisers recommend a *written budget*. The exact system and the amount of detail will depend on the time, effort, and information that you put into the budgeting process. A written budget can be kept on notebook paper or in a specialized budgeting book available in office supply stores. A common budget format is a spreadsheet that has several monthly columns for comparing budgeted and actual amounts for various expense items.

The use of *computerized budgeting systems* is increasing. In addition to creating a spreadsheet budget, a home computer is capable of doing other financial recordkeeping tasks, such as writing cheques and projecting the future value of savings accounts. Software packages, such as Microsoft Money (www.microsoft.com/money) and Quicken (www.quicken.ca), can assist you. While it takes time and effort to learn the software and enter data, a computerized budgeting and recordkeeping procedure can yield fast and accurate financial planning data.

SAVING TO ACHIEVE FINANCIAL GOALS

Saving of current income (as well as investing, which is discussed in Part 4) is the basis for an improved financial position and long-term financial security. Common reasons for saving include the following:

- To set aside money for irregular and unexpected expenses.
- To pay for the replacement of expensive items, such as appliances or an automobile, or to have money for a down payment on a house.
- To buy special items, such as home video or recreational equipment, or to pay for a vacation.
- To provide for long-term expenses, such as the education of children or retirement.
- To earn income from the interest on savings for use in paying living expenses.

■ OBJECTIVE 5

Calculate savings needed to achieve financial goals.

SELECTING A SAVING TECHNIQUE

Traditionally, Canada ranks fairly low among industrial nations in savings rate. A low savings rate tends to slow economic growth with fewer funds available for business borrowing and for creation of new jobs. Low savings also affect the personal financial situations of people. Studies reveal that the majority of Canadians do not have an adequate amount set aside for emergencies.

Since most people find saving difficult, financial advisers suggest several methods to make it easier. One method is to arrange an

> ## DID YOU KNOW ?
>
> "Canadians are spending more than ever before, but are richer than they have ever been," claims the Toronto Dominion Bank. Personal wealth increased by 10 percent in 2004—the highest rate in over a decade. The plunging of the savings rate in the 1990s to 0 percent sparked some worry about the spending habits of the average Canadian. Despite this, Canadians are now becoming more cautious of their spending. The TD report says that few Canadians are overburdened by their debt.
>
> SOURCE: "Consumers to Keep on Spending but Slow Their Pace of Debt Accumulation," by Eric Lascelles, for TD Bank. February 14, 2005, www.td.com/economics/special/cp0205.jsp

automatic debit from your bank account and have the funds transferred periodically to an investment account. This savings deposit can be a percentage of income, such as 5 or 10 percent, or a specific dollar amount. Always "pay yourself first." To guarantee setting something aside for savings, view savings as a fixed expense in your spending plan.

Another method is *payroll deduction,* which is available at many places of employment. Under a *direct deposit* system, an amount is automatically deducted from your salary and deposited in a savings or investment account.

Finally, saving coins or spending less on certain items can help you save. Each day, put your change in a container. In a short time, you will have enough money to make a substantial deposit in a savings account. You can also increase your savings by taking a sandwich to work instead of buying lunch or refraining from buying snacks or magazines.

How you save, however, is less important than making regular periodic savings deposits that will help you achieve financial goals. Small amounts of savings can grow faster than most people realize. For example, at 5 percent interest, compounded daily, just $1 a day for 10 years will give you $4,700.

CALCULATING SAVINGS AMOUNTS

To achieve your financial objectives, you should convert your savings goals into specific amounts. While certain saving methods involve keeping money at home, those funds should be deposited in an interest-earning savings plan on a regular basis. To earn interest, you must learn to "hide" money, not in your home but in an account at a financial institution or with an investment company.

Your use of a savings or investment plan is vital to the growth of your money. As Exhibit 2–8 shows, using the time value of money calculations, introduced in Chapter 1, can help you achieve your financial goals.

TWO-INCOME HOUSEHOLDS

Since the 1970s, there has been a large shift in the financial structure of the family from single-earner households to dual-earner households. When women entered the workforce, budgeting

Exhibit 2–8

Using Savings to Achieve Financial Goals

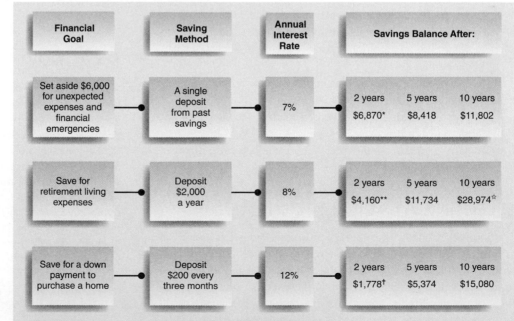

Financial Goal	Saving Method	Annual Interest Rate	Savings Balance After:		
			2 years	5 years	10 years
Set aside $6,000 for unexpected expenses and financial emergencies	A single deposit from past savings	7%	$6,870*	$8,418	$11,802
Save for retirement living expenses	Deposit $2,000 a year	8%	$4,160**	$11,734	$28,974☆
Save for a down payment to purchase a home	Deposit $200 every three months	12%	$1,778†	$5,374	$15,080

* Based on the future value of $1 tables in Chapter 1 and Appendix A.
** Based on the future value of a series of deposits tables in Chapter 1 and Appendix A.
☆ With annual $2,000 deposits, this same retirement account would grow to over $500,000 in 40 years.
† Based on quarterly compounding, explained in Chapter 4.

strategies underwent a significant change. It was no longer reasonable for all resources to be pooled. Here are some suggestions for dual-income households.

[1] *Pooled Income:* Both incomes are combined, and bills are paid from the pool. This method requires trust and shared goals and values.

[2] *Sharing the Bills:* Each person is responsible for paying predetermined bills.

[3] *50/50:* Each person contributes an equal amount into the pool to cover shared expenses.

[4] *Proportionate Contributions:* This method is similar to the 50/50 method; however, each partner contributes a percentage of his/her income. This method is favourable when one partner earns a higher income than the other.

Learning to share financial responsibilities is something many households must face these days. The best solution is the sit down and discuss goals and values in order to make the right decision.

Visit the Web site
See the Post-Test under Chapter 2 on the online learning centre at www.mcgrawhill.ca/college/kapoor.

CONCEPT CHECK 2–5

1. What are some suggested methods to make saving easy?
2. What methods are available to calculate amounts needed to reach savings goals?

SUMMARY OF OBJECTIVES

Objective 1
Recognize relationships among financial documents and money management activities.
Successful money management requires effective coordination of personal financial records, personal financial statements, and budgeting activities.

Objective 2
Create a system for maintaining personal financial records.
An organized system of financial records and documents is the foundation of effective money management. This system should provide ease of access as well as security for financial documents that may be impossible to replace.

Objective 3
Develop a personal balance sheet and cash flow statement.
A personal balance sheet, also known as a net worth statement, is prepared by listing all items of value (assets) and all amounts

owed to others (liabilities). The difference between your total assets and your total liabilities is your net worth. A cash flow statement, also called a personal income and expenditure statement, is a summary of cash receipts and payments for a given period, such as a month or a year. This report provides data on your income and spending patterns.

Objective 4
Create and implement a budget.
Implementing the seven-step budgeting process will help you live within your means and channel your resources toward the attainment of prioritized financial goals.

Objective 5
Calculate savings needed to achieve financial goals.
Future value and present value calculations may be used to compute the increased value of savings for achieving financial goals.

KEY TERMS

assets 39
budget 46
budget deficit 50
budget surplus 50
budget variance 49
cash flow 41
cash flow statement 41

current liabilities 41
discretionary income 43
income 42
insolvency 41
liabilities 40
liquid assets 39

long-term liabilities 41
money management 36
net worth 41
personal balance sheet 39
safety deposit box 37
take-home pay 43

KEY FORMULAS

Page	Topic	Formula
39	Net worth	Net worth = Total assets − Total liabilities *Example:* = $125,000 − $53,000 = $72,000
42	Cash surplus (or deficit)	Cash surplus (or deficit) = Total inflows − Total outflows *Example:* = $5,600 − $4,970 = $630 (surplus)
45	Debt ratio	Debt ratio = Liabilities/Net worth *Example:* = $7,000/$21,000 = 0.33
45	Current ratio	Current ratio = Liquid assets/Current liabilities *Example:* = $8,500/$4,500 = 1.88
45	Liquidity ratio	Liquidity ratio = Liquid assets/Monthly expenses *Example:* = $8,500/$3,500 = 2.4
45	Debt-payments ratio	Debt-payments ratio = Monthly credit payments/Take-home pay *Example:* = $760/$3,800 = 0.20
45	Savings ratio	Savings ratio = Amount saved per month/Gross monthly income *Example:* = $460/$3,800 = 0.12

FINANCIAL PLANNING PROBLEMS

1. *Creating Personal Financial Statements.* On the basis of the procedures presented in the chapter, prepare your current personal balance sheet and a cash flow statement for the next month. (Obj. 3)

2. *Calculating Balance Sheet Amounts.* On the basis of the following data, compute the total assets, total liabilities, and net worth: (Obj. 3)

   Liquid assets, $3,670
   Investment assets, $8,340
   Current liabilities, $2,670
   Household assets, $89,890
   Long-term liabilities, $76,230

3. *Preparing a Personal Balance Sheet.* Use the following items to prepare a balance sheet and a cash flow statement. Determine the total assets, total liabilities, net worth, total cash inflows, and total cash outflows. (Obj. 3)

   Rent for the month, $650

   Monthly take-home salary, $1,950
   Cash in chequing account, $450
   Savings account balance, $1,890
   Spending for food, $345
   Balance of educational loan, $2,160
   Current value of automobile, $7,800
   Telephone bill paid for month, $65
   Credit card balance, $235
   Loan payment, $80
   Auto insurance, $230
   Household possessions, $3,400
   Stereo equipment, $2,350
   Payment for electricity, $90
   Lunches/parking at work, $180
   Donations, $70
   Home computer, $1,500
   Value of stock investment, $860
   Clothing purchase, $110
   Restaurant spending, $130

www.mcgrawhill.ca/college/kapoor

4. *Computing Balance Sheet Amounts.* For each of the following situations, compute the missing amount: (Obj. 3)

   a. Assets $45,000; liabilities $16,000; net worth $_____
   b. Assets $76,500; liabilities $_____; net worth $18,700
   c. Assets $34,280; liabilities $12,965; net worth $_____
   d. Assets $_____; liabilities $38,345; net worth $52,654

5. Renée St. Clair is a 28-year-old occupational therapist living in the Annex district of Toronto. She recently graduated from the University of Toronto and now works as an independent contractor assessing the legitimacy of claims made by victims of car accidents. Like many students, Renée accumulated a large student debt during her years at university and plans to pay it off within the next five years.

   Perform a ratio analysis of Renée's financial statements. What does your analysis reveal? (Obj. 3)

   ### Cash Flow Statement
   ### For the Year Just Ended

Income		
Professional billings	$ 58,205	
Less: Professional expenses		
and taxes	(23,890)	
Professional income net of		
expenses and taxes		$34,315
Dividends (after taxes)		130
Total Income		**$34,445**
Fixed Expenses		
Rent		9,600
Student loan payments		5,800
Total Fixed Expenses		**$15,400**
Variable Expenses		
Utilities, personal, food, clothing		
and dental		$12,785
Moving expenses		225
Credit card interest		1,010
Recreation/entertainment		1,890
Vacations		6,200
Total Variable Expenses		**$22,110**
Total Expenses		**$37,510**
Surplus/(Deficit)		**($ 3,065)**

   ### Personal Balance Sheet
   ### As of Today

Assets	
Liquid Assets	
Bank account	$ 1,540

Personal Possessions	$10,280
Investment Assets	
BCE shares	$ 3,025
Total Assets	**$14,845**
Liabilities	
Current Liabilities	
Credit card balances	$ 7,855
Long-Term Liabilities	
Student loan	20,580
Total Liabilities	**$28,435**
Net Worth	**($13,590)**

6. *Determining Budget Variances.* Fran Bowen created the following budget:

   Food, $350
   Transportation, $320
   Housing, $950
   Clothing, $100
   Personal expenses and recreation, $275

   She actually spent $298 for food, $337 for transportation, $982 for housing, $134 for clothing, and $231 for personal expenses and recreation. Calculate the variance for each of these categories, and indicate whether it was a *budget deficit* or a *budget surplus*. (Obj. 4)

7. *Calculating the Effect of Inflation.* Bill and Sally Kaplan have an annual spending plan that amounts to $36,000. If inflation is 5 percent a year for the next three years, what amount will the Kaplans need for their living expenses three years from now? (Obj. 4)

8. *Computing Time Value of Money for Savings.* Use future value and present value calculations (see examples in Appendix A) to determine the following: (Obj. 5)

   a. The future value of a $500 savings deposit after eight years at an annual interest rate of 7 percent.
   b. The future value of saving $1,500 a year for five years at an annual interest rate of 8 percent.
   c. The present value of a $2,000 savings account that will earn 6 percent interest for four years.

9. *Calculating Present Value of a Savings Fund.* Hal Thomas wants to establish a savings fund from which a community organization could draw $800 a year for 20 years. If the account earns 6 percent, what amount would he have to deposit now to achieve this goal? (Obj. 5)

FINANCIAL PLANNING ACTIVITIES

1. *Researching Money Management Information.* Using Web sites, library sources, friends, relatives, and others, obtain information on common suggestions for successful money management. (Obj. 1)

2. *Developing a Financial Document System.* Working with two or three others in your class, develop a system for filing and maintaining personal financial records. (Obj. 2)

3. *Comparing Financial Record Systems.* Conduct a survey of people of various ages to determine the system they use to keep track of various financial documents and records. (Obj. 2)

4. *Creating Personal Financial Statements.* Prepare a personal balance sheet and cash flow statement. (Obj. 3)

5. *Creating a Student's Personal Budget.* Refer to Exhibit 2-5 and prepare a monthly budget to cover the next six months. Pay particular attention to variable but non-repetitive expenses, such as tuition fees, textbooks, and technology-related costs.

6. *Researching Household Asset Information on the Internet.* Using the World Wide Web or library research, find information about the assets commonly held by households in Canada. How have the values of assets, liabilities, and net worth of Canadian consumers changed in recent years? (Obj. 3)

7. *Researching Money Management Software.* Use the World Wide Web, store visits, or advertisements to determine the software a person might use to prepare personal financial statements, create a budget, and monitor spending, saving, and investing. (Obj. 3, 4)

8. *Analyzing Budgeting Situations* Discuss with several people how the budget in Exhibit 2–5 might be changed on the basis of various budget variances. If the household faced a decline in income, what spending areas might be reduced first? (Obj. 4)

9. *Comparing Budgeting Systems.* Ask two or three friends or relatives about their budgeting systems. Obtain information on how they maintain their spending records. Create a visual presentation (video or slide presentation) that communicates wise budgeting techniques. (Obj. 4)

10. *Analyzing Saving Habits.* Interview a young single person, a young couple, and a middle-aged person about their financial goals and savings habits. What actions do they take to determine and achieve various financial goals? (Obj. 5)

CREATING A FINANCIAL PLAN

Developing Personal Financial Statements and a Spending Plan

Money management activities are the basis for most financial planning activities. Creation of a financial document filing system, a personal balance sheet, a cash flow statement, and a budget provide you with tools for setting, implementing, and achieving financial goals.

Web Sites for Money Management

- Goal-setting and money management information at **www.canadianfinance.com** and **www.quicken.ca**.
- Budgeting and savings information at **www.rbcfunds.com** and **www.webfin.com**.

(Note: Addresses and content of Web sites change, and new sites are created daily. Use search engines to update and locate Web sites for your current financial planning needs.)

LIFE SITUATION CASE

Out of Work but Not Out of Bills

Due to lower sales, the company for which Ed Weston works was cutting back on its workforce. Even though Ed had been with the company for seven years, most of his duties were being performed by new, automated equipment.

After getting the word about losing his job, Ed talked with his wife, Alice, and their two children (ages 12 and 9) about ways they could reduce spending. The Westons started by making up a list of three things: (1) bills they had to pay each month, (2) areas where they could reduce spending, and (3) sources of funds to help them pay current expenses. Each family member had several ideas to help them cope with the difficult financial burden that was likely to occur over the next few weeks and months.

Before Ed was unemployed, the Westons had a monthly take-home income of $3,165. Each month, the money went for the following items: $880 for rent, $180 for utilities, $560 for food, $480 for automobile expenses, $300 for clothing, $280 for insurance, $250 for savings, and $235 for personal and other items. After the loss of Ed's job, the household's monthly income is $1,550, from his wife's wages and his employment insurance (EI). The Westons also have savings accounts, investments, and retirement funds of $28,000.

Questions

1. What budget items might the Westons consider reducing to cope with their financial difficulties?

2. How should the Westons use their savings and retirement funds during this financial crisis? What additional sources of funds might be available to them during this period of unemployment?

3. What other current and future financial actions would you recommend to the Westons?

Planning Your Tax Strategy

I OWE HOW MUCH IN TAXES?

The year is 2005. Stephanie Seymour is currently employed full time and earns an annual salary of $30,500. It has been a year since she graduated from university; however, she continues to take a few part-time courses in the evenings. Stephanie is currently paying off her student loan; she makes monthly contributions to her RRSP and has begun to build an income-generating investment portfolio. She recently moved away from her parents' home and into her own apartment in downtown Toronto, which allows her to be 40 km closer to work and school. It should also be noted that Stephanie has made contributions to a few charities over the year. Stephanie is currently preparing to file her 2005 personal income taxes and has gathered the following information:

Income—$30,500 plus $1,500 bonus (T4 Slip)
Federal Tax paid on income—$3,536 (T4 Slip)
Provincial Tax paid on income—$1,626 (T4 Slip)

Canada Pension Plan (CPP) contributions (T4 Slip) $1,410.75
Employment Insurance premiums (T4 Slip) $633.50)
Tuition (2 semesters = 8 part-time months)—$565 (T2202A slip)
Interest portion of payments on student loan—$835
Rent—$9,000
Moving expenses—$963.80
Rent on safety deposit box—$30
Investment income (Dividends)—$125 (T5 Slip)
RRSP contributions—$2,050
Charitable contributions—$65

We will follow Stephanie Seymour throughout the chapter as she completes her 2004 federal income tax return. All values are taken from this case as well as from Exhibits 3-6a and 3-6b (on pages 72–78) that present her *T1 General 2004 – Income Tax and Benefit Return* and federal *Appendix 1,* respectively.

LEARNING OBJECTIVES

1 Describe the importance of taxes for personal financial planning.

2 Illustrate how federal income taxes are computed by completing a federal income tax return.

3 Select appropriate tax strategies for different financial and personal situations.

4 Identify tax assistance sources.

TAXES AND FINANCIAL PLANNING

■ OBJECTIVE 1 ■

Describe the importance of taxes for personal financial planning.

Visit the Web site
See the Chapter Overview under Chapter 3 on the online learning centre at www.mcgrawhill.ca/college/kapoor.

excise tax A tax imposed on specific goods and services, such as gasoline, cigarettes, alcoholic beverages, tires, and air travel.

Taxes are an everyday financial fact of life. You pay some taxes every time you get a paycheque or make a purchase. However, most people concern themselves with taxes only in April. With about one-third of each dollar you earn going for taxes, an effective tax strategy is vital for successful financial planning. Familiarity with the tax rules and regulations can help you to maximize your after-tax cash flows and net worth.

This financial obligation includes the many types of taxes discussed later in this section. To help you cope with these taxes, common goals related to tax planning include

- Knowing the current tax laws and regulations that affect you.
- Maintaining complete and appropriate tax records.
- Making employment, purchase, and investment decisions that leave you with the greatest after-tax cash flows and net wealth.

Notice that the planning objective is *not* stated as minimizing taxes. While taxes are an important consideration in any financial decision, focusing solely on reducing taxes can lead to undesirable results. Consider, for example, the asset allocation decision. Deposits and other safe investments generate interest income that is 100 percent taxable. Common shares of growing companies often increase in value, resulting in a capital gain when the shares are eventually sold. However, only one-half of capital gains is taxable and so the tax treatment of capital gains is much more favourable than that of interest income. However, shifting your asset allocation toward high-risk common shares solely to reduce taxes may not match your financial goals and risk tolerance. A better approach, encompassing both investment and tax considerations, would be to select an asset allocation based on your goals and risk tolerance and then decide in which account to hold the investments in order to maximize after-tax investment cash flows. This concept will be discussed later in the chapter under tax strategies.

The principal purpose of taxes is to finance government activities. As citizens, we expect the government to provide such services as police and fire protection, schools, road maintenance, parks and libraries, and safety inspection of food, drugs, and other products. Most people pay taxes in four major categories: taxes on purchases, taxes on property, taxes on wealth, and taxes on earnings.

TAXES ON PURCHASES

You probably pay sales tax on many of your purchases—for example, the 7 percent federal goods and services tax, commonly referred to as the GST. Provinces also charge an additional sales tax (with the exception of Alberta). In order to reduce the economic burden of such taxes on the poor, certain goods and services—including most food items and prescription drugs—are exempt from sales taxes, and low-income individuals may be eligible for a refund of a portion of the GST and provincial sales taxes they have paid.

In addition to the sales tax, an **excise tax** may be imposed by the federal and provincial governments on specific goods and services, such as gasoline, cigarettes, alcoholic beverages, tires, air travel, and telephone service.

TAXES ON PROPERTY

Real estate property tax is a major source of revenue for local governments. This tax is based on the assessed value of land and buildings. The increasing amount of real estate property taxes is a major concern of homeowners. Retired people with fixed incomes may encounter financial difficulties when local property taxes increase rapidly.

Some areas also impose personal property taxes. Provincial and municipal governments may assess taxes on the value of automobiles, boats, furniture, and farm equipment.

TAXES ON WEALTH

Currently, the federal and provincial governments impose a tax on the increase in an individual's wealth, called a capital gains tax. With few exceptions, the increase in value of any capital asset that is realized at the time of sale or transfer is subject to capital gains tax. Most exceptions involve transfers to spouses and financially dependent or disabled children. Fifty percent of capital gains, net of any capital losses, are taxable in the year they are incurred.

The sale of an asset, such a stock or bond, can trigger a capital gain (or loss). Transferring ownership of an asset through a gift or inheritance can also trigger capital gains and losses. Although the federal and provincial governments do not impose estate or inheritance taxes, there is a deemed disposition of all capital property by the deceased at the time of death, triggering any accrued capital gains. The executor of the estate must file a "terminal" income tax return for the deceased and include the deemed disposition of all assets. Thus, bequests and property passed on to heirs other than a spouse are received after-tax.

TAXES ON EARNINGS

Income taxes are used by the federal government to support a number of social benefit programs, such as the Canada Pension Plan and Employment Insurance. Income tax is a major financial planning factor for most people. Most workers are subject to federal and provincial income taxes.

Throughout the year, your employer will withhold income tax amounts from your paycheque, and you may be required to make income tax installments if you earn income from other sources, such as a business. Both types of payments are only estimates of your income taxes payable. You may need to pay an additional amount when you file your income tax return, or you may get a tax refund. The following sections will assist you in preparing your federal income tax return and planning your future tax strategies.

FILING YOUR FEDERAL AND PROVINCIAL INCOME TAX RETURN

As you stare at those piles of papers, you know it's time to do your taxes! Submitting your federal income tax return requires several decisions and actions. First, you must determine whether you are required to file a return. Next, you need to identify which basic form you will be required to complete, most often the *T1 General Income Tax and Benefit Return* for a particular province, and any necessary schedules or supplementary forms. Finally, you must decide whether to complete a paper return, file by telephone, or file electronically.

Each taxpayer is personally responsible for the information provided to the government in his income tax return. If any individual or firm has helped you to complete your return, take the time to review it before filing. There is no excuse for being ignorant of your tax situation.

WHO MUST FILE?

All residents of Canada must file a federal income tax return for any year in which they have a balance of taxes owing. A resident is considered to be anyone living in Canada, but also includes non-Canadians who are present 183 days (one-half of a year) or more. Canadian residents are taxed on their worldwide income. Usually, taxes paid to a foreign government can be offset by a foreign tax credit that alleviates potential double taxation of foreign income. In addition, the federal government will tax nonresidents of Canada on certain income earned from Canadian sources, such as investment income.

Your province of residency as of December 31 of the taxation year will determine which provincial income tax return you are required to file. Quebec is the only province that does not "piggyback" on the federal system of personal taxation and, as a result, its residents must file both a federal tax return and a separate Quebec tax return.

While the Quebec *Taxation Act* has a number of similarities with the federal *Income Tax Act*, there are still a number of differences. If you must file a return in the province of Quebec, it is imperative that you contact the Ministère du Revenu du Québec for further information. Quebec tax forms and guides are available in both French and English from the provincial government's Web site at www.gouv.qc.ca.

All other provinces and territories apply a Tax on Income (TONI) system that permits the province to decide its own tax rates to be applied to taxable income, as well as different non-refundable and refundable tax credits.

taxable income The net amount of income, after allowable deductions, on which income tax is computed.

employment income Remuneration received for personal effort.

CONCEPT CHECK 3-1

1. How should you consider taxes in your financial planning?
2. What types of taxes do people frequently overlook when making financial decisions?
3. Who must file an income tax return?

INCOME TAX FUNDAMENTALS

■ OBJECTIVE 2 ▮

Illustrate how federal income taxes are computed by completing a federal income tax return.

Each year, millions of Canadians are required to pay their share of income taxes to the federal government. The process involves computing **taxable income**, determining the amount of income tax owed, and comparing this amount with the income tax payments withheld or made during the year. Exhibit 3-1 outlines the steps required in the calculation of your federal and provincial income tax due for all provinces other than Quebec.

STEP 1: DETERMINING TOTAL INCOME

net business income Net income from an activity that is carried out for profit, after expenses have been deducted.

investment income Income from property, including income in the form of interest, dividends, and rents net of expenses.

taxable capital gains Net gains from the sale of capital assets such as stocks, bonds, and real estate. One-half of net capital gains are taxable.

TYPES OF INCOME With minor exceptions, most income earned by Canadian residents is subject to federal and provincial income tax. Your total income consists of five main components:

1. **Employment income** is remuneration received for personal effort, including salaries, wages, commissions, tips, bonuses, and taxable employee benefits.
2. **Net business income** includes any income from an activity that is carried out for profit, including income from a sole proprietorship, partnership, corporation, or profession, after expenses have been deducted.
3. **Investment income**, or income from property, includes income in the form of interest, dividends, and rental income net of expenses. Dividend income is grossed-up by 25 percent to compute taxable dividends.
4. **Taxable capital gains**, although commonly referred to as investment income, is not defined as such by the *Income Tax Act*. As mentioned earlier, it is a tax on accumulated wealth. Capital gains are generated upon the sale of capital assets such as stocks, bonds, and real estate. Any capital losses incurred in the same calendar year are first subtracted from capital gains, and 50 percent of the resulting amount is taxable.

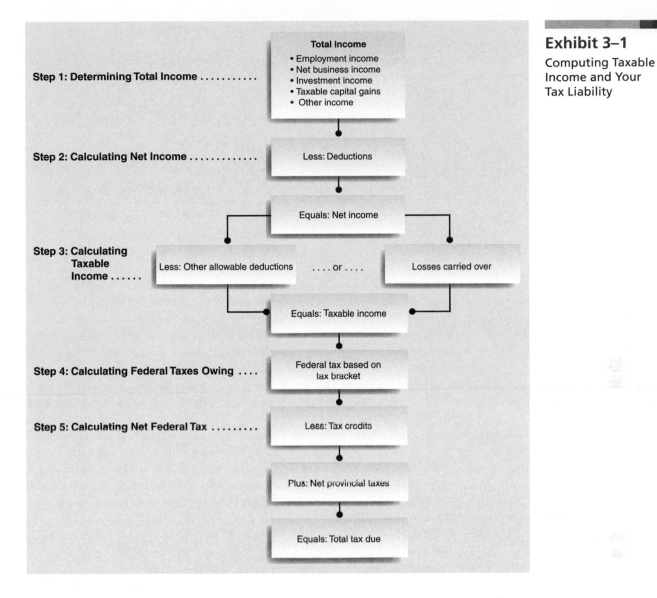

Exhibit 3–1
Computing Taxable Income and Your Tax Liability

5. *Other income* includes retirement income from corporate pension plans and RRSPs; payments from government plans such as the Canada Pension Plan, Employment Insurance, or Old Age Security; spousal and certain child support payments; research grants; and other education-related payments in excess of $3,000.

Income that is not subject to income tax includes lottery winnings, gifts, inheritances, certain child support payments, the GST/HST rebate, and the Canada child tax benefit. Owning a home is one of the best tax shelters available in Canada, primarily because any capital gain realized upon its sale will be exempt from capital gains tax as long as it qualifies as your principal residence. The residence can be a house, a condominium, a share in a co-operative housing corporation, or a summer cottage. The value of the land up to one-half hectare is also included.

STEP 2: CALCULATING NET INCOME

Net income is total income less certain deductions, described below. Its importance lies in the fact that it is often a critical factor in determining the eligibility and size of various federal and provincial income tax deductions, tax credits, and government payments, such as the Guaranteed Income Supplement. In addition, federal payments of Old Age Security must be

net income Total income reduced by certain deductions, such as contributions to an RRSP or RPP.

www.mcgrawhill.ca/college/kapoor

repaid at a rate of 15 percent for every dollar of net income in excess of $59,789 (in 2004). This is referred to as the OAS clawback.

deductions Expenses that can be deducted from total income, such as child care expenses, union dues, disability support payments, investment counselling fees, and certain employment-related expenses.

Deductions are expenses that a taxpayer is allowed to deduct from total income. Common deductions permitted in the calculation of net income include the following:

- *Contributions* to deferred income plans. Common examples of tax-deferred income plans are corporate Registered Pension Plans (RPPs) and Individual Pension Plans (IPPs), as well as personal Registered Retirement Savings Plans (RRSPs). Income from these plans is taxed at a later date, when withdrawals are made.
- *Union and professional dues* are generally deductible although for Quebec provincial taxes they are included under non-refundable tax credits. Union dues are normally withheld at source and reported on the T4 and Québec Relevé 1 you receive from your employer. Dues required to maintain a legally recognized professional status are deductible, even if you do not need to maintain that status for your current job.
- *Child care expenses* can be deducted, usually by the spouse with the lower net income in a two-parent family, subject to various limitations. This is also true for common-law couples who meet certain criteria. Single parents can deduct child care expenses from their own income. These expenses include babysitting, day nursery service, day camps, boarding schools, and camps. The criteria for eligibility are that these services free the parents to work, to carry on business, to attend school full time or part time, or to conduct grant-funded research. In Quebec, the refundable child care tax credit replaces the child care expense deduction and is based on family net income.
- *Disability supports deduction* This deduction includes both attendant care expenses as well as other paid disability expenses that permit the disabled individual to go to school or to earn taxable income.
- *Moving expenses* are largely deductible if you move to start working at a new location, to move closer to school, or to start a business. The move must be to a home that is 40 km closer to your new work location than your old home. The 40-km distance is measured according to the shortest normal route of travel, not as a straight line between points. The deduction is not allowable if you are moving either to or from Canada.
- *Other deductions* that include:
  - Deductible business investment losses, defined as 50 percent of capital losses incurred on investments in Canadian-controlled private corporations.
  - Spousal and child support payments that are made under certain conditions.
  - Interest paid on loans, the proceeds of which are used to earn taxable investment income. This excludes loans for RRSP and RESP contributions. Other costs related to investing, referred to as carrying costs are also deductible.
  - Employment expenses, if the employer requires the employee to pay for his or her own travel and/or other costs of employment by signing form T2200.

Your deductions are subtracted from total income to obtain your net income.

STEP 3: CALCULATING TAXABLE INCOME

Once net income has been determined, additional deductions and losses carried forward from prior years are permitted in the determination of taxable income. These include the following:

- *Security options deduction* that equals one-half of the stock option benefit included under employment income, if certain conditions are met. This deduction effectively renders the taxation of the benefit conferred by exercising a corporate stock option equivalent to that on a capital gain.
- *Capital gains deduction* equal to one-half of the eligible capital gains exemption. Current regulations entitle individuals to a $500,000 lifetime "capital gains exemption" on qualified small business corporation shares and eligible farm property. Taxable

capital gains are included in net income, but then offset by this deduction in order to determine taxable income.

- *Net capital losses of prior years* can be carried forward indefinitely and used to offset any taxable capital gains reported under total income that are not eligible for the capital gains deduction discussed above.
- *Other deductions* that include the employee home relocation loan deduction, special deductions for Northern residents and those employed in the Canadian Forces, and the carry forward of non-capital losses from prior years.

You are required to maintain sufficient records to support tax deductions. Financial advisers recommend a home filing system (see Exhibit 3–2) for storing receipts and other tax documents. Travel expenses can be documented in a daily log with records of mileage, tolls, parking fees, and away-from-home costs.

Generally, you should keep tax records for three years from the date you receive your notice of assessment. However, you may be required to provide backup documentation for up to six years from filing. Certain records, such as housing documents, should be kept indefinitely.

STEP 4: CALCULATING FEDERAL TAXES OWING

Your taxable income is the basis for computing the amount of your income tax owing. Tax rates and the benefits of tax credits are the final phase of the tax computation process. This calculation is performed on CRA Schedule 1, not directly on the *T1 General Income Tax and Benefit Return*. The impact of non-refundable tax credits also appears on Schedule 1.

The four federal tax brackets and corresponding rates in 2004 were:

Taxable Income	Tax Rate
0 – $35,000	16%
$35,001 – $70,000	22%
$70,001 – $113,804	26%
Over $113,804	29%

Exhibit 3–2 A Tax Recordkeeping System

Tax Returns and Tax Filing Information
- Current tax returns and instruction booklets
- Reference books on current tax laws and tax-saving techniques
- Social insurance numbers of household members
- Copies of federal tax returns from previous years

Income Records
- T4 slips reporting salary and taxes withheld at source
- T4 slips reporting pension income
- T5 slips reporting interest, dividends, and capital gains and losses from savings and investments
- Other slips for Employment Insurance benefits, royalty income, retirement, and other support payments

Expense Records
- Receipts for medical, dependant care, charitable donations, and employment-related expenses
- Business, investment, and rental-property expense documents

With the exception of Quebec, all provinces and territories have adopted the Tax on Income also known as the TONI system. TONI is a method of calculating provincial and territorial personal income tax, which parallels the federal calculations with taxable income as the starting point. The TONI system replaces the tax on tax calculations. The province of Quebec continues to administer its own provincial income taxes.

Your **marginal tax rate** is the rate you pay on the next dollar of taxable income earned. For example, suppose you earn $45,000 of taxable income. Your 2004 federal tax liability would be calculated as 16 percent on the first $35,000, while the remaining $10,000 ($45,000 − $35,000) would be taxed at 22 percent. In total, your federal taxes would equal 16 percent of $35,000 = $5,600 and 22 percent of $10,000 = $2,200, for a total of $7,800 before the consideration of any tax credits. Your federal marginal tax rate would be 22 percent, the rate applied to the next dollar of taxable income.

marginal tax rate
The rate of tax paid on the next dollar of taxable income.

average tax rate
Total tax due divided
by total income.

In contrast, the **average tax rate** is based on the total tax due divided by total taxable income. Except for taxpayers in the 16 percent tax bracket, this rate is less than a person's marginal tax rate. To continue our example, your average federal tax rate would be calculated as your total tax bill of $7,800 divided by your taxable income of $45,000, resulting in an average federal tax rate of 17.33 percent.

Exhibit 3–3 shows the combined federal and provincial tax brackets for each province and territory for 2004.

Exhibit 3–3

Province	Combined Income Tax Rate (2004)	
Newfoundland and Labrador	first $29,590	26.57%
	over $29,590 up to $35,000	32.16%
	over $35,000 up to $59,180	38.16%
	over $59,180 up to $70,000	40.02%
	over $70,000 up to $113,804	44.02%
	over $113,804	47.02%
Prince Edward Island	first $30,754	25.80%
	over $30,754 up to $35,000	29.80%
	over $35,000 up to $61,509	35.80%
	over $61,509 up to $70,000	38.70%
	over $70,000 up to $113,804	42.70%
	over $113,804	45.70%
Nova Scotia	first $29,590	24.79%
	over $29,590 up to $35,000	30.95%
	over $35,000 up to $59,180	36.95%
	over $59,180 up to $70,000	38.67%
	over $70,000 up to $93,000	42.67%
	over $93,000 up to $113,804	43.50%
	over $113,804	46.50%
New Brunswick	first $32,183	25.68%
	over $32,183 up to $35,000	30.82%
	over $35,000 up to $64,368	36.82%
	over $64,368 up to $70,000	38.52%
	over $70,000 up to $104,648	42.52%
	over $104,648 up to $113,804	43.84%
	over $113,804	46.84%
Quebec	first $27,635	32.00%
	over $27,635 up to $35,000	36.00%
	over $35,000 up to $55,280	42.00%
	over $55,280 up to $70,000	46.00%
	over $70,000 up to $113,804	50.00%
	over $113,804	53.00%
Ontario	first $33,375	22.05%
	over $33,375 up to $35,000	25.15%
	over $35,000 up to $66,752	31.15%
	over $66,752 up to $70,000	33.16%
	over $70,000 up to $113,804	37.16%
	over $113,804	40.16%

(continued)

Province	Combined Income Tax Rate (2004)	
Manitoba	first $30,544	26.90%
	over $30,544 up to $35,000	30.00%
	over $35,000 up to $65,000	36.00%
	over $65,000 up to $70,000	39.40%
	over $70,000 up to $113,804	43.40%
	over $113,804	46.40%
Saskatchewan	first $35,000	27.00%
	over $35,000 up to $36,155	33.00%
	over $36,155 up to $70,000	35.00%
	over $70,000 up to $103,300	39.00%
	over $103,300 up to $113,804	41.00%
	over $113,804	44.00%
Alberta	first $35,000	26.00%
	over $35,000 up to $70,000	32.00%
	over $70,000 up to $113,804	36.00%
	over $113,804	39.00%
British Columbia	first $32,476	22.05%
	over $32,476 up to $35,000	25.15%
	over $35,000 up to $64,954	31.15%
	over $64,954 up to $70,000	33.70%
	over $70,000 up to $74,575	37.70%
	over $74,575 up to $90,555	39.70%
	over $90,555 up to $113,804	40.70%
	over $113,804	43.70%
Yukon	first $35,000	23.04%
	over $35,000 up to $70,000	31.68%
	over $70,000 up to $113,804	37.44%
	over $113,804	41.76%
Northwest Territories	first $33,245	23.20%
	over $33,245 up to 35,000	25.90%
	over $35,000 up to $66,492	31.90%
	over $66,492 up to $70,000	33.95%
	over $70,000 up to $108,101	37.95%
	over $108,101 up to $113,804	39.55%
	over $113,804	42.55%
Nunavut (only 2003 available)	first $35,000	20.00%
	over $35,000 up to $70,000	29.00%
	over $70,000 up to $113,804	35.00%
	over $113,804	40.50%

Exhibit 3–3
(Continued)

SOURCE: http://www.taxtips.ca/tax_rates.htm

Taxpayers who benefit from the special treatment given to certain income and receive special deductions may be subject to an additional tax. The *alternative minimum tax (AMT)* is designed to ensure that those who receive tax breaks also pay their fair share of taxes. Further discussion of the AMT is beyond the scope of this book; you may obtain information from the Canada Revenue Agency.

STEP 5: NET FEDERAL TAX

tax credit An amount subtracted directly from the amount of taxes owing.

There are two types of **tax credits** that can reduce the amount of tax you owe: non-refundable tax credits and refundable tax credits. The more common are non-refundable tax credits, which are subtracted from the amount of taxes owed but can never reduce net federal tax below zero. (See the Financial Planning Calculations feature above.)

Personal credits, such as the basic, spousal, dependants, age, and disability credits, will reduce your payable income tax directly according to how each may apply to your situation. Some of the other credits that might also be claimed are for charitable or political donations, caregiver and medical expenses, tuition fees, interest on student loans, and dividend tax credits.

The first step in calculating a non-refundable tax credit is to determine the maximum applicable amount. (See Exhibit 3-4 on page 69 for the maximum federal amounts in 2005.) Sometimes, the amount is preset by the government, as is the case for the basic personal amount set at $8,148 for 2005 federal tax purposes (this amount is indexed to inflation every year). In other cases, a calculation is required. The medical amount, for example, is calculated by subtracting 3 percent of your net income to a maximum of $1,813 in 2005 from eligible medical expenses. Once the maximum amounts are determined, the non-refundable tax credit is calculated by multiplying the amount by 16 percent, with the exception of the tax credits for charitable and political contributions, and dividends, where different rates are applied.

At the federal level, there are very few refundable tax credits. These are sums that are refunded to individuals, if they qualify, even if their tax liability is zero. One such credit is the refundable medical expense supplement that can be claimed by individuals who have disproportionately high medical costs with respect to their net income.

Each province and territory has its own refundable and non-refundable tax credits. However, the maximum amounts, calculations, and percentage rates used to convert amounts to credits may be very different. Consult your provincial government's Web site for more details.

Financial Planning Calculations

TAX CREDITS VERSUS TAX DEDUCTIONS

Many people confuse *tax credits* with *tax deductions*. Is one better than the other? A tax *credit*, such as tuition fees or medical expenses, results in a dollar-for-dollar reduction in the amount of taxes owed. A tax *deduction*, such as an RRSP contribution, reduces the taxable income on which your taxes are based.

All non-refundable tax credits reduce taxes payable with the limitation that taxes payable cannot be reduced below zero. Aside from political donations and the dividend tax credit (which require additional procedural calculations), the amount claimed is multiplied by 16 percent to arrive at the tax credit. For example, if $100 is spent on tuition, then about $16 can be claimed as a direct reduction of taxes ($100 × .16).

On the other hand, a deduction of $100 may or may not reduce your taxes by $16 because the tax savings arising from the deduction will depend on your marginal tax rate. Note that tax savings are simply equal to the deduction multiplied by the marginal tax rate.

Thus, it should be apparent that a tax credit of one dollar is worth more than a deduction worth one dollar. However, making a comparison of whether spending on a deductible item is better than spending on an item that generates tax credits requires a careful specification of several variables, including your marginal federal rate, the province you reside in, the rules attributed to the tax credit in question, and so on. Careful financial planning will help you use both tax credits and tax deductions to your maximum advantage.

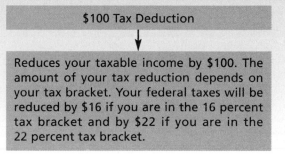

$100 Tax Deduction

Reduces your taxable income by $100. The amount of your tax reduction depends on your tax bracket. Your federal taxes will be reduced by $16 if you are in the 16 percent tax bracket and by $22 if you are in the 22 percent tax bracket.

Exhibit 3–4   2004 Federal Non-Refundable Tax Credit Amounts

Credit Type	Maximum 2004 Federal Base Amounts
Basic personal amount	8,012
Age amount (65 years of age or older)	3,912
—eliminated when taxpayer's net income exceeds	55,204
Spousal/common-law partner/dependant amount	6,803
—eliminated when dependant's net income exceeds	7,484
Infirm dependant amount (over 18 years of age)	3,784
—eliminated when dependant's net income exceeds	9,152
CPP/QPP contributions (employee)	1,831.50
CPP/QPP contributions (self-employed)	3,663
EI premiums	772.20
Pension income amount	1,000
Caregiver amount for in-home care of parent or grandparent over 65 years of age, or of infirm adult relative	3,784
—eliminated when relative's income exceeds	16,705
Disability amount	6,486
Disability amount supplement for taxpayers under 18 years of age	3,784
—eliminated when child/attendant care expenses exceed	6,000
Interest paid on student loan	Amount paid
Tuition and education amount	Tuition paid + $400 per month of full-time attendance
Medical amount	Amount paid in excess of 3% of net income or $1,813, whichever is less

SOURCE: Adapted from www.taxtips.ca/tax_rates.htm

MAKING TAX PAYMENTS

SOURCE WITHHOLDING Source withholding occurs as your employer and others are required to withhold tax at source and remit it to the CRA as well as the Ministère du Revenu du Québec if you live in Quebec. These withholdings will be applied toward all forms of taxable income. Generally, there is no withholding of tax on interest, dividends, rent, or royalties paid to Canadian residents.

Tax withheld from a payment to you is considered to have been paid by you to the tax authorities, even if your employer never remits it. It is also considered to have been paid *to* you in the sense that it forms part of your total income.

After the end of the year, you will receive a federal T4 form (see Exhibit 3–5), which reports your annual earnings and the amounts that have been deducted for income tax, social benefits, and other taxes. A copy of the T4 form is filed with your tax return to document your earnings and the amount you have paid in taxes. The difference between the amount withheld and the tax owed is either the additional amount you must pay or the refund you will receive.

Many taxpayers view an annual tax refund as a "windfall," extra money they can count on each year. However, these taxpayers are forgetting the opportunity cost of withholding excessive amounts. Others view their extra tax withholding as "forced savings." However, a payroll deduction plan for savings could serve the same purpose and would enable them to earn the interest instead of giving the government an interest-free loan.

REDUCTIONS OF SOURCE WITHHOLDINGS It is possible to reduce source withholdings if you prove that you are paying more withholding tax than necessary. In any situation where you expect to receive a refund after filing your return, you can request to have your source withholdings reduced. This type of situation can arise due to personal tax credits, RRSP contributions, charitable donations, medical expenses, and spousal and child support payments. The CRA form used to request this is the TD-1, the Personal Tax Credit Return.

INSTALLMENT PAYMENTS Your tax payments must be paid in installments if the difference between your payable taxes (including provincial tax) and the amount you have

Exhibit 3–5

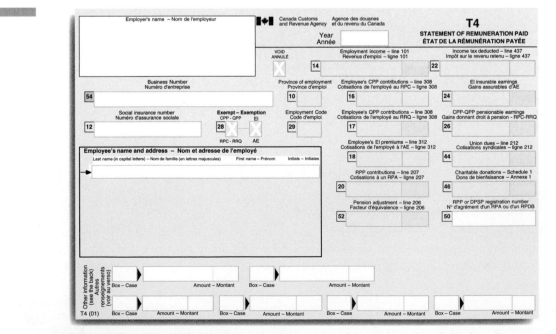

SOURCE: Canada Revenue Agency. Reproduced with permission of the Minister of Public Works and Government Services Canada, 2005.

already had withheld at source is more than $2,000 in both the current year and either of the two preceding years. In Quebec, where the federal government does not collect the provincial tax, the threshold is $1,200 of provincial tax instead of $2,000. The payments, which must be made quarterly, are due on the 15th day of March, June, September, and December.

DEADLINES AND PENALTIES

Most people are required to file their federal and Quebec tax returns by April 30 each year. If you or your spouse (or common-law spouse) has business income, then you have until June 15 to file your return. Note, however, that even though the return is not due until June 15, you will be required to pay any balance of tax owing by April 30. In cases where you have no tax to pay for the year, and neither the CRA nor the Ministère du Revenu du Québec has requested it, you have no obligation to file a return. Despite this, it is often still to your advantage to do so as it may affect your allowable RRSP contribution and other factors in future returns. Note that both parents must file a return to qualify for family support payments and GST and QST refunds.

Your return must be postmarked or transmitted electronically by the due date. Failure to do this will incur an automatic 5-percent penalty on any balance owing. In addition, 1 percent of the unpaid balance will be added for each full month that your return is late, to a maximum of 12 months. If you repeatedly fail to file your returns on time, you may incur even higher penalties.

You should file your return on time even if you are unable to pay the balance owing since doing so will allow you to avoid the 5-percent automatic penalty. (Remember, though, that interest will continue to accrue on your unpaid balance.) Exhibit 3–6a on page 72 recaps the general section of your federal return.

CONCEPT CHECK 3-2

1. What are the five sections of the federal tax return?
2. What information is needed to compute net income?
3. What information is needed to compute taxable income?
4. What is the difference between your marginal tax rate and your average tax rate?
5. How does a tax credit affect the amount owed for federal and provincial income taxes?

STEPHANIE SEYMOUR'S 2004 FEDERAL TAX RETURN

IDENTIFICATION Let's turn now to Stephanie Seymour's *T1 General 2004 - Income Tax and Benefit Return*, shown on the following pages as Exhibit 3–6a. On the first page, Stephanie has filled in the Identification section with her full name, address, province of residence as of December 31, social insurance number, date of birth, and marital status. She has given her consent to the CRA to provide basic personal information to the National Register of Electors. Stephanie has also applied for the GST/HST credit and, at the top of the second page, has indicated that she does not hold foreign property in the amount of $100,000 or more.

Exhibit 3–6a   Stephanie Seymour's *T1 GENERAL Income Tax and Benefit Return for 2004*

Canada Customs and Revenue Agency	Agence des douanes et du revenu du Canada

T1 GENERAL 2004

Income Tax and Benefit Return

Identification

ON **8**

Attach your personal label here. Correct any wrong information.
If you are not attaching a label, print your name and address below.

First name and initial
Stephanie A.

Last name
Seymour

Mailing address: Apt. No. – Street No. Street name
1414 King Street   #6

P.O. Box, R.R.

City   Prov./Terr.   Postal code
Toronto |O,N| |M,6,J|3,B,1|

Information about you

Enter your social insurance number (SIN)
if you are not attaching a label: |6,7,1|2,3,4|5,6,7|

	Year	Month	Day
Enter your date of birth:	1,9,8,0	0,1	0,1

Your language of correspondence: English   Français
Votre langue de correspondance :   [X]

Check the box that applies to your marital status on December 31, 2004:
(see the "Marital status" section in the guide for details)

1 ☐ Married   2 ☐ Living common law   3 ☐ Widowed
4 ☐ Divorced   5 ☐ Separated   6 [X] Single

Information about your spouse or common-law partner (if you checked box 1 or 2 above)

Enter his or her SIN if it is not on the label,
or if you are not attaching a label:

Enter his or her first name:

Enter his or her net income for 2004 to claim
certain credits: (see the guide for details)

Check this box if he or she was self-employed in 2004:   1 ☐

Information about your residence

Enter your province or territory of
residence on **December 31, 2004:**   ONTARIO

Enter the province or territory where you **currently** reside if
it is not the same as that shown
above for your mailing address:

If you were self-employed in 2004,
enter the province or territory of
self-employment:

If you **became** or **ceased** to be a **resident of Canada in 2004**, give the date of:

	Month	Day			Month	Day
entry			or	departure		

	Year	Month	Day
If this return is for a deceased person, enter the date of death:			
Do not use this area			

Elections Canada

THIS SECTION APPLIES ONLY TO CANADIAN CITIZENS.
DO NOT ANSWER THIS QUESTION IF YOU ARE NOT A CANADIAN CITIZEN.

As a Canadian citizen, I authorize the Canada Revenue Agency to provide my name, address
and date of birth to Elections Canada for the National Register of Electors. ....   Yes [X] 1   No ☐ 2
Your authorization is required each year. This information will be used only for purposes permitted
under the *Canada Elections Act*.

Goods and services tax/harmonized sales tax (GST/HST) credit application

See the guide for details.
Are you applying for the GST/HST credit? ....   Yes [X] 1   No ☐ 2

Your guide contains valuable information to help you complete your return.

When you come to a line on the return that applies to you, look up the line number in the guide for more information.

Do not use this area	172				171					

5006-R

Exhibit 3–6a   Stephanie Seymour's *T1 GENERAL Income Tax and Benefit Return for 2004 (Continued)*

2

Please answer the following question

Did you own or hold foreign property at any time in 2004 with a total cost of more than CAN$100,000? (read the "Foreign income" section in the guide for details) .... **266** Yes ☐ 1   No ☒ 2
If *yes*, attach a completed Form T1135.

If you had dealings with a non-resident trust or corporation in 2004, see the "Foreign income" section in the guide.

As a Canadian resident, you have to report your income from all sources both inside and outside Canada.

Total income

Employment income (box 14 on all T4 slips)	**101**	32,000 00	
Commissions included on line 101 (box 42 on all T4 slips)	**102**		
Other employment income	**104 +**		
Old Age Security pension (box 18 on the T4A(OAS) slip)	**113 +**		
CPP or QPP benefits (box 20 on the T4A(P) slip)	**114 +**		
Disability benefits included on line 114 (box 16 on the T4A(P) slip)	**152**		
Other pensions or superannuation	**115 +**		
Employment Insurance and other benefits (box 14 on the T4E slip)	**119 +**		
Taxable amount of dividends from taxable Canadian corporations (see the guide)	**120 +**	156 25	
Interest and other investment income (**attach** Schedule 4)	**121 +**		
Net partnership income: limited or non-active partners only (**attach** Schedule 4)	**122 +**		
Rental income Gross **160** Net	**126 +**		
Taxable capital gains (**attach** Schedule 3)	**127 +**		
Support payments received Total **156** Taxable amount	**128 +**		
RRSP income (from all T4RSP slips)	**129 +**		
Other income Specify:	**130 +**		
Self-employment income (see lines 135 to 143 in the guide)			
Business income Gross **162** Net	**135 +**		
Professional income Gross **164** Net	**137 +**		
Commission income Gross **166** Net	**139 +**		
Farming income Gross **168** Net	**141 +**		
Fishing income Gross **170** Net	**143 +**		
Workers' compensation benefits (box 10 on the T5007 slip)	**144**		
Social assistance payments	**145 +**		
Net federal supplements (box 21 on the T4A(OAS) slip)	**146 +**		
Add lines 144, 145, and 146 (see line 250 in the guide) =	▶ **147 +**		

Add lines 101, 104 to 143, and 147
This is your **total income**. **150** =   32,156 25

Exhibit 3–6a   Stephanie Seymour's *T1 GENERAL Income Tax and Benefit Return for 2004 (Continued)*

↖ **Attach your Schedule 1 (federal tax) and Form 428 (provincial or territorial tax) here. Also attach here any other schedules, information slips, forms, receipts, and documents that you need to include with your return.**   3

Net income

Enter your **total income** from line 150	**150**	32,156 25

Pension adjustment
(box 52 on all T4 slips and box 34 on all T4A slips)   **206**

Registered pension plan deduction (box 20 on all T4 slips and box 32 on all T4A slips)	**207**		
RRSP deduction (see Schedule 7 and **attach** receipts)	**208 +**	2,050	00
Saskatchewan Pension Plan deduction (maximum $600)	**209 +**		
Annual union, professional, or like dues (box 44 on all T4 slips and receipts)	**212 +**		
Child care expenses (**attach** Form T778)	**214 +**		
Disability supports deduction	**215 +**		
Business investment loss Gross **228** Allowable deduction	**217 +**		
Moving expenses	**219 +**	963	80
Support payments made Total **230** Allowable deduction	**220 +**		
Carrying charges and interest expenses (**attach** Schedule 4)	**221 +**	30	00
Deduction for CPP or QPP contributions on self-employment and other earnings (**attach** Schedule 8)	**222 +**	•	
Exploration and development expenses (**attach** Form T1229)	**224 +**		
Other employment expenses	**229 +**		
Clergy residence deduction	**231 +**		
Other deductions Specify:	**232 +**		
Add lines 207 to 224, 229, 231, and 232.	**233 =** ▶ –	3,043	80
Line 150 minus line 233 (if negative, enter "0"). This is your **net income before adjustments**.	**234 =**	29,112	45

Social benefits repayment (if you reported income on line 113, 119, or 146, see line 235 in the guide)   **235 –**   •

Line 234 minus line 235 (if negative, enter "0"). If you have a spouse or common-law partner, see line 236 in the guide. This is your **net income. 236**	29,112	45

Taxable income

Canadian Forces personnel and police deduction (box 43 on all T4 slips)	**244**	
Employee home relocation loan deduction (box 37 on all T4 slips)	**248 +**	
Security options deductions	**249 +**	
Other payments deduction (if you reported income on line 147, see line 250 in the guide)	**250 +**	
Limited partnership losses of other years	**251 +**	
Non-capital losses of other years	**252 +**	
Net capital losses of other years	**253 +**	
Capital gains deduction	**254 +**	
Northern residents deductions (**attach** Form T2222)	**255 +**	
Additional deductions Specify:	**256 +**	
Add lines 244 to 256.	**257 =** ▶ –	

Line 236 minus line 257 (if negative, enter "0") This is your **taxable income. 260 =**	29,112	45

Use your taxable income to calculate your federal tax on Schedule 1 and your provincial or territorial tax on Form 428.

Exhibit 3–6a Stephanie Seymour's *T1 GENERAL Income Tax and Benefit Return for 2004 (Continued)*

Refund or Balance owing   4

Net federal tax: enter the amount from line 19 of Schedule 1 (**attach** Schedule 1, even if the result is "0")	420	2,640	16
CPP contributions payable on self-employment and other earnings (**attach** Schedule 8)	421 +		
Social benefits repayment (enter the amount from line 235)	422 +		
Provincial or territorial tax (**attach** Form 428, even if the result is "0")	428 +	1,135	37

Add lines 420 to 428
This is your **total payable. 435** = 3,775 | 53 ●

Total income tax deducted (from all information slips)	437	5,162	00 ●
Refundable Quebec abatement	440 +		●
CPP overpayment (enter your excess contributions)	448 +		●
Employment Insurance overpayment (enter your excess contributions)	450 +		●
Refundable medical expense supplement	452 +		●
Refund of investment tax credit (**attach** Form T2038(IND))	454 +		●
Part XII.2 trust tax credit (box 38 on all T3 slips)	456 +		●
Employee and partner GST/HST rebate (**attach** Form GST370)	457 +		●
Tax **paid** by instalments	476 +		●
Provincial or territorial credits (**attach** Form 479)	479 +		●

Add lines 437 to 479
These are your **total credits. 482** = 5,162 | 00 ► – 5,162 | 00

Line 435 minus line 482 = –1,386 | 47

If the result is negative, you have a **refund**.
If the result is positive, you have a **balance owing**.
Enter the amount below on whichever line applies.

Generally, we do not charge or refund a difference of $2 or less.

Refund **484** –1,386 | 47 ●   **Balance owing 485** | ●

Amount enclosed **486** | ●

Direct deposit – Start or change (see line 484 in the guide)

You do not have to complete this area every year. Do not complete it this year if your direct deposit information for your refund has not changed.

Refund and GST/HST credit – To start direct deposit or to change account information only, **attach** a "void" cheque or complete lines 460, 461, and 462.

Note: To deposit your **CCTB** payments (including certain related provincial or territorial payments) into the **same** account, also check box 463.

Branch number	Institution number	Account number	CCTB
460	**461**	**462**	**463**
(5 digits)	(3 digits)	(maximum 12 digits)	

Attach to page 1 a **cheque** or **money order** payable to the Receiver General. Your payment is due no later than April 30, 2005.

Ontario Opportunities Fund

You can help reduce Ontario's debt by completing this area to donate some or all of your 2004 refund to the Ontario Opportunities Fund. Please see the provincial pages for details.

Amount from line 484 above			1
Your donation to the Ontario Opportunities Fund	465 –		● 2
Net refund (line 1 minus line 2)	466 =		● 3

I certify that the information given on this return and in any documents attached is correct, complete, and fully discloses all my income.

Sign here

It is a serious offence to make a false return.

Telephone (   )   Date

490 For professional tax preparers only

Name:
Address:

Telephone: (   )

Do not use this area **487** □ **488** □

SOURCE: Canada Revenue Agency. Reproduced with permission of the Minister of Public Works and Government Services Canada, 2005.

TOTAL INCOME Box 14 of Stephanie's T4 slip, provided by her employer, shows that her employment income for the year 2004 was $32,000 ($30,500 salary plus $1,500 bonus). This amount is entered on line 101 on the second page of her federal return.

Stephanie received a T5 slip indicating that she had been paid $125 in Canadian dividends. This amount is "grossed-up" by 25 percent, and the amount of $125 × 1.25 = $156.25 is entered on line 120. See Chapter 10 for more details on the reasoning behind the dividend gross-up and offsetting dividend tax credit calculation.

Stephanie's total income, shown on line 150, is $32,156.25.

NET INCOME Stephanie is able to deduct $2,050 from her total 2004 income on line 208 of the third page of her federal return because she invested this amount in an RRSP before March 1, 2005. This amount is deductible as long as it does not exceed the maximum deduction limit indicated on her *2003 Federal Notice of Assessment* or *Notice of Reassessment*.

Stephanie could not find her *2003 Federal Notice of Assessment*. Luckily the CRA offers a service called "T.I.P.S." (Tax Information Phone Service) which can be reached by telephone at 1-800-267-6999 or online at www.cra.gc.ca/tips. This service provides information on your RRSP deduction limit, as well as any unused contributions. It also allows you to track the status of your refund and offers other useful information. By calling T.I.P.S., Stephanie was able to confirm that the $2,050 RRSP contribution was fully deductible in 2004.

During 2004, Stephanie had moved more than 40 km at a cost of $963.80 in order to start her new job. Stephanie completed Form T1-M (not included here) to determine that her moving expenses are fully deductible on line 219 of her federal return.

Finally, Stephanie is allowed to deduct her safety deposit box fees of $30.00 on line 221. She stores her stock certificate and other valuables in the safety deposit box.

After subtracting all eligible deductions, Stephanie calculates her net income on line 236 as $29,112.45.

TAXABLE INCOME Stephanie's taxable income (line 260, page 3 of the federal return) is equal to her net income of $29,112.45 because she has no additional deductions to claim.

NET FEDERAL TAX The federal Schedule 1 is used to determine an individual's net federal tax by first calculating her federal tax liability and then subtracting non-refundable tax credits. Stephanie's Schedule 1 is presented in Exhibit 3-6b. Her federal tax liability is calculated by multiplying her taxable income of $29,112.45 by the lowest federal tax rate of 16 percent. Before subtracting any tax credits, Stephanie's federal tax liability is $4,657.99.

Under the section "federal non-refundable tax credits," Stephanie is eligible to claim the basic amount (line 300), her CPP contributions (line 308), her Employment Insurance premiums (line 312), the interest paid on her student loan (line 319) and the tuition and education amount (line 323) by completing Schedule 11 (not shown here). The amount of $1,525 entered on line 323 equals her tuition costs of $565, plus an amount of $120 for each month of part-time study (8 × $120 = $960). The total of all amounts to be converted into non-fundable tax credits at the 16 percent rate is $12,416.25 (line 335). Thus far, Stephanie's non-refundable tax credits equal $1,986.60 (line 338).

The first $200 of charitable donations also generate a non-refundable tax credit at a rate of 16 percent. Amounts above $200 that are less than 75 percent of an individual's net income are converted into tax credits at a rate of 29 percent. In Stephanie's case, her charitable donation tax credit equals $10.40 ($65 × 0.16). The amount is calculated on federal Schedule 9 (not shown here) and entered on line 349 of *Schedule 1*.

Her final tax credit, the federal dividend tax credit, is calculated as 13.333 percent of the grossed-up dividends entered on line 120 in the income section of her federal return. Stephanie's dividend tax credit equals $20.83 ($156.25 × 0.1333). This amount is entered on line 425 of Schedule 1.

Exhibit 3–6b Stephanie Seymour's Federal Schedule 1 for 2004

T1-2004	**Federal Tax**	Schedule 1

Complete this schedule to claim your federal non-refundable tax credits and to calculate your net federal tax.

You must attach a copy of this schedule to your return.

Enter your **taxable income** from line 260 of your return _____ 29,112|45 **1**

Use the amount on line 1 to determine which **ONE** of the following columns you have to complete.

If the amount on line 1 is:	$35,000 or less	more than $35,000 but not more than $70,000	more than $70,000 but not more than $113,804	more than $113,804
Enter the amount from line 1 above	29,112|45 **2**	**2**	**2**	**2**
Base amount	00,000|00 **3**	− 35,000|00 **3**	− 70,000|00 **3**	− 113,804|00 **3**
Line 2 minus line 3 (this amount cannot be negative)	= 29,112|45 **4**	= **4**	= **4**	= **4**
Rate	× 16% **5**	× 22% **5**	× 26% **5**	× 29% **5**
Multiply the amount on line 4 by the rate on line 5	= 4,657|99 **6**	= **6**	= **6**	= **6**
Tax on base amount	0,000|00 **7**	+ 5,600|00 **7**	+ 13,300|00 **7**	+ 24,689|00 **7**
Add lines 6 and 7	= 4,657|99 **8**	= **8**	= **8**	= **8**

Federal non-refundable tax credits (Read the guide for details about these credits.)

Basic personal amount	**claim $8,012** **300**	8,012|00	
Age amount (if you were born in 1939 or earlier)	**(maximum $3,912)** **301** +		
Spouse or common-law partner amount:			
Base amount 7,484|00			
Minus: his or her net income (from page 1 of your return) −			
Result: (if negative, enter "0") =	**(maximum $6,803)** ▶ **303** +		
Amount for an eligible dependant (**attach** Schedule 5)	**(maximum $6,803)** **305** +		
Amount for infirm dependants age 18 or older (**attach** Schedule 5)	**306** +		
CPP or QPP contributions:			
through employment from box 16 and box 17 on all T4 slips	**(maximum $1,831.50)** **308** +	1,410|75 •	
on self-employment and other earnings (**attach** Schedule 8)	**310** +	•	
Employment Insurance premiums from box 18 on all T4 slips	**(maximum $772.20)** **312** +	633|50 •	
Pension income amount	**(maximum $1,000)** **314** +		
Caregiver amount (**attach** Schedule 5)	**315** +		
Disability amount	**316** +		
Disability amount transferred from a dependant	**318** +		
Interest paid on your student loans	**319** +	835|00	
Tuition and education amounts (**attach** Schedule 11)	**323** +	1,525|00	
Tuition and education amounts transferred from a child	**324** +		
Amounts transferred from your spouse or common-law partner (**attach** Schedule 2)	**326** +		

Medical expenses for **self, spouse or common-law partner, and your dependent children born in 1987 or later** (see the guide) **330**		
Minus: $1,813 or 3% of line 236, whichever is **less** −		
Subtotal (if negative, enter "0") =	**(A)**	
Allowable amount of medical expenses for **other dependants** (see the calculation at line 331 in the guide and **attach** Schedule 5) **331** +	**(B)**	
Add lines (A) and (B). =	▶ **332** +	
Add lines 300 to 326, and 332. **335** =	12,416|25	

Multiply the amount on line 335 by 16% = **338**	1,986|60	
Donations and gifts (**attach** Schedule 9) **349** +	10|40	
Total federal non-refundable tax credits: Add lines 338 and 349. 350 =	1,977|00	

5000-S1 continue on the back ⟹

Exhibit 3–6b   Stephanie Seymour's Federal Schedule 1 for 2004 *(Continued)*

Net federal tax

Enter the amount from line 8 on the other side		4,657 99	**9**
Federal tax on split income (from line 4 of Form T1206)	**424** +		●**10**
Add lines 9 and 10 =	4,657 99 ▶	4,657 99	**11**

Enter the amount from line 350 on the other side	350	1,997 00	
Federal dividend tax credit (13.3333% of the amount on line 120 of your return)	**425** +	20 83 ●	
Overseas employment tax credit (**attach** Form T626)	**426** +		
Minimum tax carry-over (**attach** Form T691)	**427** +	●	
Add lines 350, 425, 426, and 427 =	2,017 83 ▶ −	2,017 83	**12**

Basic federal tax: Line 11 minus line 12 (if negative, enter "0") **429** =   2,640 16   **13**

Federal foreign tax credit:
Complete the federal foreign tax credit calculation below and enter the amount from
line (i) or line (ii), whichever is **less**   −   **14**

Federal tax: Line 13 minus line 14 (if negative, enter "0") **406** =   2,640 16   **15**

Total federal political contributions (**attach** receipts)	**409**		
Federal political contribution tax credit (see the guide)	**410**	●	
Investment tax credit (**attach** Form T2038(IND))	**412** +	●	
Labour-sponsored funds tax credit			
Net cost **413** Allowable credit **414** +		●	
Add lines 410, 412, and 414. **416** =		▶ −	**16**
Line 15 minus line 16 (if negative, enter "0")			
(if you have an amount on line 424 above, see Form T1206) **417** =			**17**
Additional tax on RESP accumulated income payments (**attach** Form T1172) **418** +			**18**

Net federal tax: Add lines 17 and 18
Enter this amount on line 420 of your return.   **420** =   2,640 16   **19**

─ **Federal foreign tax credit:** (see lines 431 and 433 in the guide) ──────

Make a separate calculation for each foreign country. Enter the result on line 14 above.

Non-business income tax paid to a foreign country   **431**   ●(i)

$$\frac{\text{Net foreign non-business income *} \quad \boxed{433}}{\text{Net income **}} \quad \text{X} \quad \text{Basic federal tax ***} \quad = \quad \text{(ii)}$$

*   Reduce this amount by any income from that foreign country for which you claimed a capital gains deduction, and by any income from that country that was, under a tax treaty, either exempt from tax in that country or deductible as exempt income in Canada (included on line 256). Also reduce this amount by the lesser of lines E and F on Form T626.

**   Line 236 plus the amount on line 3 of Form T1206, minus the total of the amounts on lines 244, 248, 249, 250, 253, 254, and minus any amount included on line 256 for foreign income deductible as exempt income under a tax treaty, income deductible as net employment income from a prescribed international organization, or non-taxable tuition assistance from box 21 of the T4E slip. If the result is less than the amount on line 433, enter your **Basic federal tax***** on line (ii).

***   Line 429 plus the amount on lines 425 and 426, and minus any refundable Quebec abatement (line 440) and any federal refundable First Nations abatement (line 441 on the return for residents of Yukon).

5000-S1

After subtracting her non-refundable tax credits, Stephanie's net federal tax is $2,640.16. This amount is carried forward to line 420 at the top of page 4 of her federal return (see page 75).

REFUND OWING The calculation of Stephanie's Ontario tax of $1,135.37, entered on line 428, is presented in Appendix 1 on page 96 at the end of this chapter.

From box 22 on her 2004 T4 slip, Stephanie determines that the total amount of federal and provincial taxes deducted at source by her employer equals $5,162 ($3,536 for federal income taxes and $1,626 for Ontario provincial taxes). This amount is entered on line 437 of her federal return. As it exceeds her total taxes payable of $3,775.53 (line 435) by $1,386.43, this is the amount of her 2004 tax refund (line 484).

TAX PLANNING STRATEGIES

Most people want to pay no more than their fair share of taxes. They do this by practising **tax planning**, the use of legitimate methods to reduce one's taxes. In contrast, **tax evasion** is the use of illegal actions to reduce one's taxes. To maximize after-tax cash flows, some simple strategies can be investigated:

1. Are you choosing the form of remuneration that is most advantageous to you?
2. Are you taking full advantage of all deductions and credits that are available to you? If you have a legal or common-law spouse, is the right person taking the deduction? Should amounts be accumulated and the tax credit only taken periodically?
3. Are you taking advantage of all possibilities to defer the payment of taxes to a later date?
4. Should you adopt "income-splitting" techniques that permit a lower-income member of your family to declare investment income and pay less tax on it?
5. Have you organized your investment portfolio so that it attracts the lightest tax liability?

We will explore each strategy in turn.

HOW SHOULD YOU RECEIVE INCOME?

If you are an employee, you may be able to arrange your compensation to improve your after-tax income. First, will you be paid a salary or by commission? If you are a salaried employee, in most cases no employment-related deductions are available. If you earn commission income and are required by your employer to travel and/or absorb costs associated with your employment, then these costs may be deductible. This also applies to salaried employees who are required to absorb certain employment-related costs. (Form T-2200 must be signed by the employer.) Second, do you have a choice between receiving employment compensation in the form of a salary or via employee benefits? While most employee benefits are taxable, some, such as the benefit conferred by a stock option, receive more favourable tax treatment than regular income. (A stock option plan permits the employee to acquire shares of the company at a price that is less than the going market price of the stock.) Finally, if part of your remuneration involves a bonus, can the bonus be paid after December 31? The personal taxation year coincides with the calendar year, but some companies have a year-end that differs from December 31. They may be willing to pay your bonus in January of the following year if this still falls within their corporate fiscal year.

One question often asked of a financial planner is whether it is better for a small business owner to pay him- or herself a salary or receive remuneration in the form of dividends. The co-ordination of personal and corporate taxation for small business owners earning less than $250,000 of taxable income means that, in effect, there is very little difference. In the first

■ OBJECTIVE 3 ▮

Select appropriate tax strategies for different financial and personal situations.

tax planning The use of legitimate methods to reduce one's taxes.

tax evasion The use of illegal actions to reduce one's taxes.

instance, the owner would be taxed on his or her salary only. In the second instance, the business would be required to pay corporate taxes before it could declare a dividend. The dividend paid out would then be grossed-up, taxed at the owner's personal tax rate and partially reduced by the dividend tax credit. The combined result of the corporate tax and personal tax on dividends would be very close to the tax levied on the salary alone.

What elements of the tax law would play a role in deciding the salary versus dividend dilemma for the small corporate business owner? First, salaries form part of "earned income" for purposes of calculating an individual's RRSP contribution limit, whereas dividends do not. In 2005, the RRSP contribution maximum is set as $16,500. If a person's maximum RRSP contribution equals 18 percent of his or her prior year's earned income, this implies that receiving a salary of $91,667 in 2004 ($16,500 ÷ 0.18) would bring him or her to the maximum 2005 RRSP contribution. Second, if the business is a Canadian-controlled private corporation and meets certain qualifying criteria, any capital gain earned on the sale or transfer of the common shares in the business would qualify for the $500,000 capital gains exemption discussed on page 81. For the small entrepreneur who plans to grow his or her business by retaining earnings, the resulting increase in the value of the shares of the business, to a maximum of $500,000, could be sheltered from capital gains tax.

Self-employment income from a non-incorporated business or profession is reported on both a gross and net basis and is taxed at the individual's personal tax rate. Any reasonable expense incurred in order to generate taxable income is deducted from gross income to derive net income. This includes the cost of administrative support, leasing or buying an automobile and maintaining it for business purposes, office rent, equipment and supplies, advertising, and utilities. Only 50 percent of entertainment costs, however, are deductible. Of special interest are deductions permitted for maintaining a home office. If you have an office in your home, you can claim a portion of your home expenses as business expenses, subject to certain restrictions. The proportional expenses you can claim include rent or mortgage interest, utilities, maintenance, and home insurance. The portion you will be allowed to claim will depend on the fraction of your home that is used for business purposes.

MAXIMIZING THE BENEFIT OF DEDUCTIONS AND TAX CREDITS

There are a multitude of tax deductions and credits available at both the federal and provincial level. Keeping up to date on the current tax laws and regulations is vital if you wish to ensure that you are taking full advantage of any deductions and credits available to you, your spouse, and your family.

The most common federal income tax deductions were described earlier in this chapter, in the section Income Tax Fundamentals. Contributions to corporate or personal retirement plans result in a tax deduction in the year of contribution, but their most important role is in deferring taxes on income until savings are withdrawn in retirement. With few exceptions, financial planners recommend that you contribute the maximum possible to your RRSP and contribute as early as possible in any taxation year. These plans will be described in the following section, Tax Deferral Techniques.

Other important facts to remember with respect to common deductions are as follows:

- Generally, the lower income spouse is required to take the child care deduction, but there are exceptions to this rule, including situations where one spouse is a full or part-time student.
- Before a ruling on May 1, 1997, alimony, child support and spousal maintenance payments were deductible to the payer and taxable to the recipient. This is no longer the case. Under the new rules, child support payments are not deductible. Assess whether it is prudent to change any legal agreement reached prior to May 1, 1997, as it would then fall under the new tax legislation.

- All or part of the interest charged on funds invested to earn taxable investment income (interest and dividends) is tax deductible. Therefore, it makes better tax sense to use cash flows to acquire personal possessions, such as a car, and borrow to invest. However, as mentioned earlier in the chapter, the financial planning objective is not to *minimize taxes* but to *maximize after-tax cash flows*. Borrowing to invest (commonly referred to as leveraging) entails significant risk if the value of the investment declines, and this strategy should not be adopted merely to reduce one's tax liability.

- If part of your employment remuneration involves a stock option plan, the taxable benefit incurred when the option is exercised must be included in taxable income, unless the shares belong to a Canadian-controlled private corporation (CCPC) or an election has been made to defer the taxable benefit until the shares are ultimately sold. An offsetting deduction, referred to as the security options deduction, can be taken if, at time of issue, the exercise price of the option did not exceed the fair market value of the share (i.e., the employee could not derive an immediate benefit from exercising the option) or, in the case of a CCPC, the employee had owned the shares for two years prior to selling them. This deduction is equal to 50 percent of the taxable benefit included in total income. Care should be taken, therefore, in deciding when to exercise the option and when to sell the shares.

- Capital losses incurred in any year can be subtracted from capital gains earned in the same year to compute net capital gains. Fifty percent of net capital gains will be taxable in the year they are incurred. If capital losses exceed capital gains in any year, then the net capital loss can be carried back three years to offset any capital gains already declared and taxed. However, the window of opportunity is only three years. Once the period of three years has elapsed, the tax paid on the net capital gains can no longer be reclaimed. However, net capital losses can also be carried forward and applied to reduce any capital gains earned at any time in the future. Special care should be taken to track, record, and report capital losses when filing your income tax return. Although they may not be of immediate value, they should not be overlooked in future years when capital gains must be reported.

- Each individual is eligible for a lifetime $500,000 capital gains exemption on shares of qualifying small businesses and eligible farm property. However, several conditions must be met. One of the qualifying criteria is a holding period of two years prior to sale or transfer of the shares. In addition, the firm itself must meet certain criteria over the two-year holding period and at the moment of sale in order that any gain earned on the sale of its shares qualifies for the exemption. Verify that all conditions have been met before you sell shares in a small business.

In addition to various deductions, all individuals qualify for at least the basic personal amount and corresponding income tax credit. The following additional credits can be claimed:

- If you are single, widowed, divorced, or separated and you support another family member (such as a minor or a disabled parent living with you), you will be allowed to claim that person in calculating the amount for an eligible dependent.

- If you paid interest on a student loan made under the *Canada Student Loans Act* or equivalent provincial program, you can claim this credit for any interest paid in the current year and in the five preceding years (after 1997). This credit is not transferable, but it can be carried forward for up to five years.

- If you took post-secondary courses on a full- or part-time basis, your tuition fees and an education amount can be transformed into a tax credit in the current year; transferred to a supporting spouse, parent, or grandparent; or carried forward and used by you in the future.

- If you had medical expenses, you can choose any 12-month period ending in the calendar year and group together expenses incurred by you, your spouse, and minor children. (A separate calculation can be made to claim the medical expenses of dependent adult children 25 years of age or less who are pursuing full-time studies.) The list of eligible expenses is extensive and is updated frequently, so all receipts for any health-related expense should be retained. All amounts in excess of 3 percent of the claimant's net income can be converted into a tax credit. It is best if the lower-income spouse claims the credit.

- If you made charitable contributions, the first $200 of charitable contributions can be converted into a tax credit at the rate of 16 percent. Amounts in excess of $200 that do not exceed 75 percent of an individual's net income are converted at a rate of 29 percent. To maximize the credit, charitable donations for spouses should be taken by one individual. Charitable contributions may be carried forward five years, and it may be beneficial to wait and accumulate contributions before claiming them in order to benefit the most from the 29 percent rate.

Finally, certain unused non-refundable tax credits can be transferred between spouses. These include credits relating to the age amount, pension income amount, tuition and education amount, and disability amount. The transferring spouse must reduce his or her taxable income to zero before transferring any excess amounts.

TAX DEFERRAL TECHNIQUES

Several techniques are available that permit taxpayers to defer the taxation of income until a later date when, presumably, their combined average income tax rate will be lower. Furthermore, during the deferral period, any investment income earned can be reinvested free of tax.

A major tax strategy of benefit to working people is the use of tax-deferred retirement plans, such as RRSPs, RPPs, IPPs, and Deferred Profit Sharing Plans (DPSPs).

RRSP   Registered Retirement Savings Plans are the quintessential tool in the Canadian taxpayer's toolbox. Virtually all taxpayers benefit from having these, and setting them up can be easily done at almost any bank or trust company or through a stockbroker or life insurance agent. The basic concept is simple: If you agree to put some of your salary away and not have immediate access to it, the tax system will tax that income and all proceeds from its investment when it is withdrawn from the RRSP, rather than when it is earned by the taxpayer.

Contributions to an RRSP are deductible for any year in which they are made or for the prior year if made within the first 60 days of the year. The contribution that you are allowed to make will depend on three factors. First, the most that can be contributed in any year has been set at $15,500 for 2004, $16,500 for 2005, $18,000 for 2006, to rise to $20,000 by 2010. Second, you can only contribute up to 18 percent of your prior year's earned income, subject to the above limitations, plus any contribution room that you may have carried forward from prior years. Third is your pension adjustment, defined as the deemed value of your pension earned for the previous year. In other words, the amount you will be allowed to contribute to your RRSP will be diminished by the amount that you and your employer put aside for your retirement pension. The amount of your pension adjustment will be shown on your T4 slip.

An additional advantage offered by RRSPs is that funds can be borrowed from the plan and paid back free of tax under the Home Buyers' Plan and Lifelong Learning Plan. Under the Home Buyers' Plan, you may withdraw up to $20,000 as a loan, if you qualify as a first-time buyer, without it counting as a withdrawal. You must then repay the loan over 15 years. The funds you withdraw must have been in the plan for at least 90 days. This plan will be discussed more fully in later chapters.

The Lifelong Learning Plan permits a maximum tax-free withdrawal of $20,000 to permit you or your spouse to study full-time at a qualifying institution. Withdrawals must be repaid within 10 years, starting in the year after the last year of study. However, a disadvantage of withdrawals under both plans is that repayments are made without interest and the growth potential of your RRSP will be less.

RPP   A Registered Pension Plan is set up for employees by their employers. Larger companies and many smaller ones have such plans, in which your employer contributes an annual amount on your behalf. Occasionally, you will be required or allowed to contribute to the plan and you will be able to deduct your contribution in the year that it is made.

In general, there are two types of registered pension plans: money-purchase and defined benefit. The former, also referred to as a Defined Contribution Pension Plan (DCPP), is much like an RRSP in that the amount of your pension will depend on the contributions made and the growth achieved with those funds. Large corporations and public employers often provide the latter, defined benefit plans (DBPP). Defined Benefit Pension Plans are becoming less common due to the high cost to the employer of administering them. With this type of plan, the amount you will receive as a pension is known in advance and is usually based on a percentage of your actual salary over a specified number of years.

If you are allowed to contribute to a Defined Contribution Pension Plan, consider making your payment to an RRSP instead. Though the benefits in terms of taxes are the same, the amount you hold in your RPP will be locked in and inaccessible.

If you terminate your employment but are not yet eligible to receive pension income, you are allowed to transfer a lump-sum payment from your RPP to a locked-in RRSP or Registered Retirement Income Fund (RRIF). The amount allowed for transfer is limited, however, and you may be required to accept an immediate partial cash payment on which you will be taxed.

IPP   An individual pension plan is a defined-benefit registered pension plan designed and structured for one individual. IPP contributions are made according to the benefit payable at retirement. This type of plan may be to your advantage if you are already in your employer's group RPP but the benefits are not as high as you would want. Generally, this type of plan is optimal for executives or owner-managers, people over 53, or those earning more than $100,000 as a base salary.

DPSP   Deferred Profit Sharing Plans are less common than RPPs but they operate in essentially the same way. Your employer makes contributions, and you are taxed only when you receive the funds. The contributions are based on current or accrued company profits but may have a defined minimum contribution amount. Further, they are limited to no more than 18 percent of your earnings in a year or a set maximum amount. You are not allowed to contribute to this type of plan and the amounts contributed by your employer will be reported as a pension adjustment on your T4, thereby reducing your RRSP contribution allowance.

Additional tax deferral techniques include:

- Investing in capital assets, such as real estate or financial assets, that generate capital gains, as these gains only become taxable in the year of disposition.
- Opening a Registered Education Savings Plan (RESP) or an in-trust investment account to fund your child's higher education. These investment vehicles can be viewed as a means by which to defer taxes, as well as an opportunity to have investment income taxed in the hands of lower-income family members. They will be described in the following section on Income Splitting Techniques.

INCOME SPLITTING TECHNIQUES

Given the Canadian tax system's use of progressive tax rates, with the marginal rate increasing with higher incomes, taxpayers may be tempted to invest in the name of their lower-income spouse or minor children in order to have any investment income taxed in their hands at a lower rate. However, this strategy is not permitted by law. The federal *Income Tax Act* contains a number of "attribution rules" to prevent income splitting in this fashion. In essence, these rules state that if a taxpayer transfers money or assets to a spouse or child under the age of 18, any investment income (interest, dividends, or rents) earned on the amount transferred will be taxed in the hands of the taxpayer, unless the spouse or minor child purchases the asset at its fair market value. In the case of a spouse, future capital gains on any assets transferred are also attributed back to the taxpayer. Attribution of capital gains does not apply to in the situation of a minor.

The assets may be purchased outright with money, but can also be acquired through a swap of assets or loan. The loan can be extended by the taxpayer, as long as interest is charged at a rate at least equal to the CRA prescribed rate and paid by the borrowing spouse or minor by January 31 of the following year.

Other legal means of income splitting include

- Making contributions to a spousal RRSP. Withdrawals are taxed in the hands of the recipient spouse as long as the funds are not withdrawn within two calendar years following the year of contribution.
- Splitting your Canada Pension Plan (CPP) or Quebec Pension Plan (QPP) benefits with your spouse. You may direct that up to half of your CPP/QPP benefits be paid to your spouse, provided that you are both over the age of 60.
- Having the high income spouse pay living expenses, while the lower income spouse invests his income.
- Transferring assets that will be used to generate business income, as business income is not attributable.
- Opening a Registered Education Savings Plan (RESP) for your minor children. RESPs allow you to build an education fund for a child by earning tax-deferred investment income. The contributions are not tax deductible, but all income in the plan grows tax-free until withdrawn and taxed in the hands of the recipient. The maximum lifetime contribution per beneficiary is $42,000 (maximum $4,000 per year). Contributions to an RESP can earn the Canada Education Savings Grant, formerly set at a maximum of $7,200 per beneficiary. However, the limit was increased in the federal budget of March 23, 2004, when it was proposed that the grant on the first $500 of annual contributions for minors be enriched for families with an income of less than $70,000 per year.
- Setting up an in-trust investment account for a minor to acquire capital gains-generating assets, as capital gains earned on funds invested for children under 18 years of age are not attributable.
- Investing the federal Child Tax Benefit in the child's name.
- Transferring assets to an adult child. Transfers to adult children are not subject to the attribution rules as long as they are not made through a loan that charges interest at less than the prescribed rate.

It should be noted that second-generation investment income (i.e., investment income earned on a prior year's reinvested income) is not attributable.

ENSURING THAT YOUR PORTFOLIO IS TAX EFFICIENT

While the taxation of investment income should not affect your choice of asset allocation or specific asset choices, it will play a role in the decision of which investment account should hold which type of asset. Some financial assets pay interest or generate income that is taxed in the same manner as interest—for example, the dividends paid on foreign stocks. Interest income is fully taxable at your marginal tax rate and to minimize the tax burden, such financial assets should be held in registered accounts, such as RRSPs, that defer taxes until withdrawals are made. Other financial assets pay dividends or are expected to appreciate in value and generate a capital gain when sold. Both dividends on Canadian stocks and capital gains are taxed less heavily than interest income, and financial assets that pay dividends and/or generate capital gains should be held in non-registered investment accounts.

Tax efficiency also refers to whether the interest on a loan made for investment purposes can be deducted from taxable income. If the proceeds of a loan are invested in assets that generate taxable dividends, interest, or rents, then the interest paid on the loan is tax deductible, subject to certain conditions.

TAX ISSUES IMPORTANT TO STUDENTS

The CRA has issued a guide called *Students and Income Tax – P105*, which addresses tax issues of special importance to students. This guide can be accessed at the CRA's Web site at www.cra-arc.gc.ca/E/pub/tg/p105/p105-04e.pdf. In brief, the guide describes:

[1] How to report income from scholarships, fellowships, bursaries, grants, and RESPs.

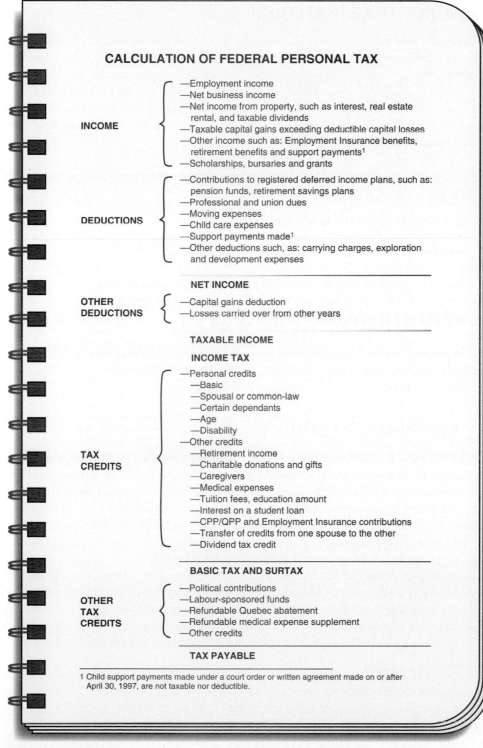

Exhibit 3–7

Five General Sections of Your Federal Tax Return Form

CALCULATION OF FEDERAL PERSONAL TAX

INCOME
—Employment income
—Net business income
—Net income from property, such as interest, real estate rental, and taxable dividends
—Taxable capital gains exceeding deductible capital losses
—Other income such as: Employment Insurance benefits, retirement benefits and support payments[1]
—Scholarships, bursaries and grants

DEDUCTIONS
—Contributions to registered deferred income plans, such as: pension funds, retirement savings plans
—Professional and union dues
—Moving expenses
—Child care expenses
—Support payments made[1]
—Other deductions such, as: carrying charges, exploration and development expenses

NET INCOME

OTHER DEDUCTIONS
—Capital gains deduction
—Losses carried over from other years

TAXABLE INCOME

INCOME TAX

TAX CREDITS
—Personal credits
  —Basic
  —Spousal or common-law
  —Certain dependants
  —Age
  —Disability
—Other credits
  —Retirement income
  —Charitable donations and gifts
  —Caregivers
  —Medical expenses
  —Tuition fees, education amount
  —Interest on a student loan
  —CPP/QPP and Employment Insurance contributions
  —Transfer of credits from one spouse to the other
  —Dividend tax credit

BASIC TAX AND SURTAX

OTHER TAX CREDITS
—Political contributions
—Labour-sponsored funds
—Refundable Quebec abatement
—Refundable medical expense supplement
—Other credits

TAX PAYABLE

1 Child support payments made under a court order or written agreement made on or after April 30, 1997, are not taxable nor deductible.

[2] Common deductions, such as moving expenses, child care expenses and interest paid on a student loan.

[3] Non-refundable tax credits such as the tuition and education amount.

[4] Other tax credits, such as the GST/HST credit and Canada Child Tax Benefit (CCTB).

In addition, most provinces offer tax deductions and credits designed to assist full- and part-time students.

CHANGING TAX STRATEGIES

Someone once said that "death and taxes are the only certainties of life." Changing tax laws seem to be another certainty. Each year, the CRA modifies the tax return and filing procedures. In addition, the government frequently passes legislation that changes the *Income Tax Act*. These changes require that you regularly determine how to best consider the tax laws for personal financial planning. Carefully consider changes in your personal situation and your income level. You should monitor your personal tax strategies to best serve your daily living needs and your long-term financial goals.

CONCEPT CHECK 3–3

1. How does tax avoidance differ from tax evasion?
2. What common tax-planning strategies are available to most individuals and households?

TAX ASSISTANCE AND THE AUDIT PROCESS

▓ OBJECTIVE 4 ▐

Identify tax assistance sources

In the process of completing your federal income tax return, you may seek additional information or assistance. After filing your return, you may be identified for a tax audit. If this happens, several policies and procedures protect your rights.

TAX INFORMATION SOURCES

Visit the Web site
See the Weblinks under Chapter 3 on the online learning centre at www.mcgrawhill.ca/college/kapoor.

As with other aspects of personal financial planning, many resources are available to assist you with your taxes. Both the Canada Revenue Agency and the Ministère du Revenu du Québec offer comprehensive guides to help you plan and complete your tax return. Libraries and bookstores offer books and other publications that are updated yearly and that will help you create a strategy to effectively and legally maximize after-tax wealth and cash flows. In addition, most daily newspapers frequently contain articles related to personal taxes and their various effects. See Exhibit 3–8 for an example of a tax-planning system.

The fastest way to find information on the various rules and regulations for both the CRA and the Ministère du Revenu du Québec is by searching online at their respective Internet sites. The CRA is available at www.cra-arc.gc.ca, while the Ministère du Revenu du Québec site can be found at www.revenu.gouv.qc.ca. Both can also be reached by telephone: you will find the telephone number for the closest service office in the blue pages of your local phone book.

TAX PUBLICATIONS Each year, several personal tax guides are published; most are available either directly from the issuers, in the case of various tax planning companies, or at a bookstore or library in the case of others. Some of the better-known publications from the financial-services sector include Deloitte & Touche's *How to Reduce the Tax You Pay*, KPMG's *Tax Planning for You and Your Family*, and CCH Canadian's *Preparing Your Income Tax Returns*. In various bookstores, you may also find Evelyn Jacks's annual *Jacks on Tax Savings*,

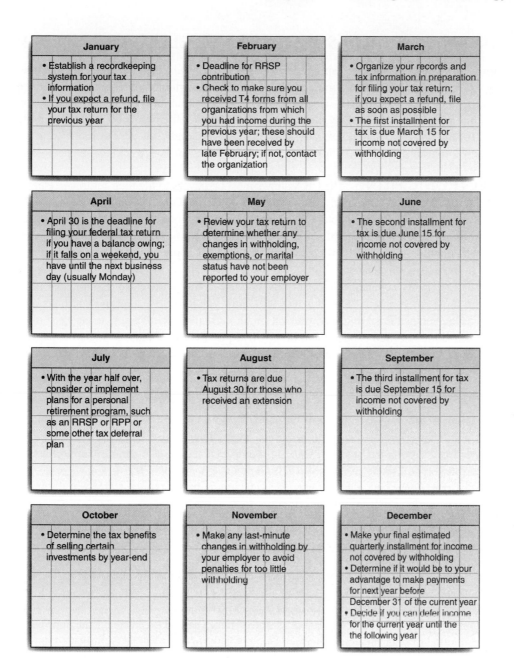

Exhibit 3–8
Tax-Planner
Calendar

January
- Establish a recordkeeping system for your tax information
- If you expect a refund, file your tax return for the previous year

February
- Deadline for RRSP contribution
- Check to make sure you received T4 forms from all organizations from which you had income during the previous year; these should have been received by late February; if not, contact the organization

March
- Organize your records and tax information in preparation for filing your tax return; if you expect a refund, file as soon as possible
- The first installment for tax is due March 15 for income not covered by withholding

April
- April 30 is the deadline for filing your federal tax return if you have a balance owing; if it falls on a weekend, you have until the next business day (usually Monday)

May
- Review your tax return to determine whether any changes in withholding, exemptions, or marital status have not been reported to your employer

June
- The second installment for tax is due June 15 for income not covered by withholding

July
- With the year half over, consider or implement plans for a personal retirement program, such as an RRSP or RPP or some other tax deferral plan

August
- Tax returns are due August 30 for those who received an extension

September
- The third installment for tax is due September 15 for income not covered by withholding

October
- Determine the tax benefits of selling certain investments by year-end

November
- Make any last-minute changes in withholding by your employer to avoid penalties for too little withholding

December
- Make your final estimated quarterly installment for income not covered by withholding
- Determine if it would be to your advantage to make payments for next year before December 31 of the current year
- Decide if you can defer income for the current year until the following year

Prentice Hall Canada's annual *Canadian Guide to Personal Financial Management*, and a number of other books on the topic. Though current taxation rules often change, since the basics usually remain the same you will also find that many non–current-year tax advisory and information publications are very relevant.

THE INTERNET As with other personal finance topics, extensive information may be found on the Internet, especially the World Wide Web. The Web sites for the CRA and the Ministère du Revenu du Québec are great places to start. Both agencies can also be reached by telephone. Such sites as Canoe Webfin at www.webfin.com, the Fraser Institute at www.fraserinstitute.ca, CANTAX at www.cantax.com, and the Canadian Taxpayer Federation at www.taxpayer.com are all excellent sources of Canadian tax information. Two of Canada's largest accounting firms, Ernst & Young and KPMG, provide quality links to many other Internet resources and can be found at www.ey.com and www.kpmg.ca/tax, respectively. In addition, the Web sites of companies that sell tax software and tax-related organizations can be useful (see the Web sites suggested in the next section).

TAX PREPARATION SOFTWARE AND ELECTRONIC FILING

More and more taxpayers are using personal computers for tax recordkeeping and income tax preparation. A spreadsheet program can be very helpful in maintaining and updating tax data on various income and expense categories. There are also a number of different software packages that allow you to complete your return and then either file online or print the completed form for mailing. Popular choices are QuickTax, TaxWiz, and Ufile.ca. For more information on these programs, see www.quicktax.ca, www.taxwiz.ca, and www.ufile.ca, respectively.

ELECTRONIC FILING   The CRA allows most taxpayers to file their returns in electronic form using a personal computer. The system is called EFILE and is available across the country. It permits authorized tax return preparers or transmitters to file returns using tax return preparation and transmission software. The system is not complete, however, and as a result you will incur a small transmission fee charged by EFILE preparers to transmit your return even if you prepare it yourself.

There are many advantages to using this method to file your return. Besides the obvious benefit to the environment, filing this way will allow you to receive a refund within as little as two weeks, versus the six to eight weeks it might normally take. Also, you can keep all your records and are required to send them in only if expressly asked, thus reducing the paper burden. The Ministère du Revenu du Québec offers a similar service, the details of which are available at its Web site.

Under the CRA's TELEFILE program, qualifying wage earners, students, seniors, and credit or benefit filers can file their returns by telephone. If you are eligible for this program you will be sent an invitation to use TELEFILE, and your personalized income tax package will include an access code: you use a touch-tone phone to call the service and enter your information as prompted. As with EFILE, you are not required to send in supporting documents and you will likely receive your refund much sooner. NETFILE is a new service introduced by the CRA which allows you to file your return directly to the CRA over the Internet. Visit www.netfile.gc.ca for more information.

TAX PREPARATION SERVICES

Many Canadian taxpayers pay someone to prepare their income tax returns. The fee for this service can range from $40 at a tax preparation service for a simple return to several thousand dollars to a chartered accountant for a complicated return.

Many people prepare their own tax returns. This experience can help you improve your understanding of your financial situation. Doing your own taxes can be complicated, however, particularly if you have sources of income other than salary. The sources available for professional tax assistance include the following:

- Tax services ranging from local services to national firms with many offices, such as H&R Block.
- Many accountants who offer tax assistance along with other business services. A chartered accountant (CA), a certified general account (CGA), or a certified management account (CMA) with special training in taxes can help with tax planning and the preparation of your annual tax return.
- Tax lawyers usually do not complete tax returns; however, you can use legal services when you are involved in a complicated tax-related transaction or when you have a difference of opinion with the government.

Even if you hire a professional tax preparer, you are responsible for supplying accurate and complete information and for the contents of your income tax return. Hiring a tax preparer will not guarantee that you pay the *correct* amount. A U.S. study conducted by *Money* magazine of 41 tax preparers reported fees ranging from $375 to $3,600, with taxes due ranging from

$31,846 to $74,450 for the same fictional family. If you owe more tax because your return contains errors or you have made entries that are disallowed, it is your responsibility to pay that additional tax, plus any interest and penalties.

Be wary of tax preparers and other businesses that offer your refund in advance. These "refund anticipation loans" frequently charge very high interest rates for this type of consumer credit. Studies reveal that interest rates sometimes exceed 300 percent (on an annualized basis).

WHAT IF YOUR RETURN IS AUDITED?

Canada Revenue Agency (CRA) reviews all returns for completeness and accuracy. If you make an error, your tax is automatically recalculated and you receive either a bill or a refund. If you make an entry that is disallowed, you will be notified by mail. A **tax audit** is a detailed examination of your tax return by the CRA. In most audits, the revenue department requests more information to support the entries on your tax return. Be sure to keep accurate records to support your return. Keep receipts, cancelled cheques, and other evidence to support the amounts that you claim. Avoiding common filing mistakes (see Exhibit 3–9) helps to minimize your chances of an audit.

tax audit A detailed examination of your tax return by the Canada Revenue Agency.

TYPES OF AUDITS   The simplest and most common type of audit is the *desk audit*. This mail inquiry requires you to clarify or document minor questions about your tax return. You usually have 30 days to provide the requested information.

The *field audit* is more complex. An auditing agent visits you at your home, your business, or the office of your accountant so you have access to records. A field audit may be done to verify whether an individual has an office in the home as claimed.

If you use EFILE, TELEFILE, or NETFILE you won't need to file receipts with your return. However, the CRA or the Ministère du Revenu du Québec may later ask to check certain claims, such as donations, RRSP contributions, or tuition fees. This is normally just a formality designed to maintain the integrity of the electronic filing system.

YOUR AUDIT RIGHTS   While most audits of individual taxpayers are desk audits, some are field audits. In either case, you should be aware of your rights. The auditor is not entitled to scrutinize all of your documents at will. He or she may request only specific information, and you have a right to ask why that information is needed. In any situation where you anticipate that you will have problems, you have the right to, and should, seek assistance from

1. Mathematical errors, such as adding or subtracting amounts incorrectly.
2. Forgetting to reduce income by identifying workers' compensation, social assistance payments, and net federal supplements.
3. Calculating and claiming provincial tax credits incorrectly.
4. Not including pension adjustments, which affect RRSP contribution room for the coming year.
5. Claiming GST/HST credits incorrectly by using incorrect spousal income amounts.
6. Entering the wrong amounts on lines referring to Canada Pension Plan, Quebec Pension Plan, and Employment Insurance contribution and overpayments.
7. Claiming incorrect amounts as RRSP contributions.
8. Forgetting to claim the basic personal amount.
9. Claiming the spousal amount incorrectly.
10. Forgetting to claim the age amount, or claiming it incorrectly.

Exhibit 3–9
Top Ten Filing Errors

Any attempt to calculate your investment return must include the least exciting, most annoying financial subject: taxes. Even the word makes me cringe!

The government *will* get their share of your money—no exceptions. Smart tax planning helps you pay less tax legally. The federal government isn't fooling around: Those who use illegitimate techniques to avoid paying taxes get socked with high-priced penalties or jail time. Pay your taxes on time.

Toward the first of the year, you will begin to receive a series of statements from the jobs at which you have worked or financial institutions where you hold accounts. This includes brokerage firms, banks, mutual funds, and other intermediaries. Scrounge up the receipts from any charitable donations you've made and proof of any employment-related expenses you plan on writing off. Keep these materials together: Lost forms waste time and money!

Your tax return has several sections to be aware of. Generally, your income should be added up, including any losses. Figure your taxable income, factor in additional credits or taxes, and write a cheque. *You've just paid your taxes!*

For those with a home business, complicated returns, or sketchy paperwork, some professional tax guidance is highly recommended—*and worth it!* Spending some money on a tax preparer or CA might seem daunting but will ensure that your return is filed accurately and rapidly.

professional advisers. Generally, however, an audit is a simple verification and should not be cause for alarm if you have filed your return in good faith.

If either an audit of your return or an audit of another person's return gives an indication that your tax payable is not what you have calculated and declared, the CRA will issue a reassessment. In cases where this means that you will need to pay more taxes, you will normally be contacted first and given the opportunity to make representations on your behalf. The reassessment cannot be issued if more than three years have passed from the last assessment, except in cases of fraud or misrepresentation stemming from "neglect, carelessness, or wilful default," whereby a reassessment can be issued at any time.

Another situation where the three-year limitation might not apply is where you have signed a waiver regarding a specific disputed issue, as asked by the CRA. You have the right to refuse to sign and can also revoke a signed waiver if you give six months' notice. Refusing to sign may be a sound strategy if the three-year limit is almost up, as it means that the reassessment may not be made if the revenue department does not have adequate time to complete its audit.

If you find yourself unable to pay your taxes or make a tax filing on time due to a natural or human-made disaster, serious illness, or accident, the *Income Tax Act*'s fairness rules give a degree of latitude to the CRA to waive penalties and interest on overdue payments. You should be aware, however, that your past compliance to taxation rules may be considered if you make a fairness-related request.

OBJECTIONS AND APPEALS You have the right to file a Notice of Objection through your local Chief of Appeals in cases where you do not agree with an assessment. Doing so will allow you to have your objection considered by the independent Appeals Officer, but you must file your notice within 90 days of the disputed assessment or one year after the due date of the return.

The Appeals Officer is normally your highest possible level of appeal within the CRA. The next step would be to appeal to the Tax Court of Canada, at which point you would be just two steps and extensive legal wrangling away from the Supreme Court of Canada.

Be aware that it is usually best to pay your full taxes, including items in dispute. Doing so will avoid late charges if you lose your appeal, and interest on your payment will be returned to you if you win. Paying disputed amounts in advance of an appeals decision is not an admission of guilt, but rather a sound financial decision that should have no legal bearing on your dispute.

CONCEPT CHECK 3–4

1. What are the main sources available to help people prepare their taxes?
2. What actions can reduce the chances of an audit?
3. What appeal options do taxpayers have if they disagree with an audit decision?

SUMMARY OF OBJECTIVES

Objective 1
Describe the importance of taxes for personal financial planning.

Tax planning can influence spending, saving, borrowing, and investing decisions. A knowledge of tax laws and maintenance of accurate tax records allows you to take advantage of appropriate tax benefits. An awareness of income taxes, sales taxes, excise taxes, property taxes, estate taxes, and other taxes is vital for successful financial planning.

Objective 2
Illustrate how federal income taxes are computed by completing a federal income tax return.

The major sections of your tax return require you to calculate (1) your filing status, (2) income, (3) deductions, (4) other deductions, (5) tax credits, and (6) your refund or the additional amount you owe.

Objective 3
Select appropriate tax strategies for different financial and personal situations.

You may reduce your tax burden through careful planning and making financial decisions related to consumer purchasing, the use of debt, investments, and retirement planning.

Objective 4
Identify tax assistance sources.

The main sources of tax assistance are CRA services and publications, other publications, the Internet, computer software, and professional tax preparers, such as commercial tax services, accountants, and attorneys.

KEY TERMS

average tax rate 66	**marginal tax rate** 65	**tax evasion** 79
deductions 64	**net business income** 62	**tax planning** 79
employment income 62	**net income** 63	**taxable capital gains** 62
excise tax 60	**tax audit** 89	**taxable income** 62
investment income 62	**tax credit** 68	

Ontario   Provincial Tuition and Education Amounts

Only the student must complete this schedule. Use it to:
- calculate your Ontario tuition and education amounts to claim on line 5856 of your Form ON428;
- determine the provincial amount available to transfer to another designated individual; and
- determine the unused Ontario amount, if any, available for you to carry forward to a future year.

Attach a copy of this schedule to **your** return.

Ontario tuition and education amounts claimed by the student for 2004

Ontario unused tuition and education amounts from your 2003 *Notice of Assessment* or *Notice of Reassessment* *			Ø	**1**
Eligible tuition fees paid for 2004	**5914**	565 00		**2**

Education amount for 2004: Use columns B and C of forms T2202, T2202A and TL11A; (only one claim per month, maximum 12 months)

Enter the number of months from Column **B** (do not include any month that is also included in Column C)	8	× $130 = **5916** +	1,040 00		**3**
Enter the number of months from Column **C**		× $433 = **5918** +			**4**
Add lines 2, 3, and 4	Total 2004 tuition and education amounts	=	►	+	**5**
Add lines 1 and 5	Total available tuition and education amounts	=	1,605 00		**6**

Taxable income from line 1 of your Form ON428		29,112 45	**7**
Total of lines 5804 to 5848 of your Form ON428	–	10,088 25	**8**
Line 7 minus line 8 (if negative, enter "0")	=	18,924 20	**9**
Unused Ontario tuition and education amounts claimed for 2004: Enter the amount from line 1 or line 9, whichever is **less**	– ►	Ø	**10**
Line 9 minus line 10	=	18,924 20	**11**

2004 tuition and education amounts claimed for 2004: Enter the amount from line 5 or line 11, whichever is **less**		+	**12**
Add lines 10 and 12. Enter this amount on line 5856 of your Form ON428.	**Ontario tuition and education amounts claimed by the student for 2004**	= 1,605 00	**13**

Transfer / Carry forward of unused amount

Amount from line 6			**14**
Amount from line 13		–	**15**
Line 14 minus line 15	**Total unused amount**	=	**16**

If you are transferring an amount to another individual, continue on line 17.
Otherwise, enter the amount from line 16 on line 21.

Enter $5,562 or the amount from line 5, whichever is **less**			**17**
Amount from line 12		–	**18**
Line 17 minus line 18 (if negative, enter "0")	**Maximum transferable**	=	**19**

You can transfer all or part of the amount on line 19 to your spouse or common-law partner, to his or her parent or grandparent, or to your parent or grandparent. To do this, you have to **designate** the individual and **specify the provincial amount** that you are transferring to him or her on Form T2202, T2202A or TL11A. Enter the amount on line 20 below.

Note: If you have a spouse or common-law partner, special rules may apply. See line 5856 in the forms book.

Enter the amount you are transferring (cannot be more than line 19)	**Provincial amount transferred** **5920**	–	**20**
Line 16 minus line 20	**Unused provincial amount available to carry forward to a future year**	=	**21**

The person claiming the transfer should not attach this schedule to his or her return.

* If you resided in another province or territory on December 31, 2003, you must enter on line 1 your unused provincial or territorial tuition and education amounts from your 2003 *Notice of Assessment* or *Notice of Reassessment*.
If there are no provincial or territorial amounts, enter your unused federal tuition and education amounts.

5006-S11

Provincial Worksheet *(continued)*

Line 5844 – Disability amount (calculation if you were **under age 18** on December 31, 2004)
(see line 5844 on page 2 of the forms book)

Maximum supplement	3,791 | 00	1

Total child care and attendant care expenses claimed for you by anyone			2
Base amount	–	2,220 | 00	3
Line 2 minus line 3 (if negative, enter "0")	=	▶ –	4
Line 1 minus line 4 (if negative, enter "0")		=	5

Enter, on line 5844 of Form ON428, **the amount on line 5 plus $6,499** (maximum claim $10,290), unless this chart is being completed for the claim on line 5848.

Line 5848 – Disability amount transferred from a dependant

Complete this calculation for each dependant.

Base amount		6,499 | 00	1
If the dependant was **under age 18** on December 31, 2004, enter the amount from line 5 of the chart for line 5844 for the dependant. If the dependant was age **18 or older**, enter "0".	+		2
Add lines 1 and 2	=		3
Total of amounts your dependant can claim on lines 5804 to 5840 of his or her Form ON428	+		4
Add lines 3 and 4	=		5
Dependant's taxable income (from line 260 of his or her return)	–		6
Allowable amount for this dependant: Line 5 minus line 6 (if negative, enter "0") Enter, on line 5848 of Form ON428, the amount on line 3 or line 7, whichever is **less.**	=		7

Enter, on line 5848, the total amount claimed for **all** disabled dependants.

If, at the end of the year, you and your dependant were not residents of the same province or territory, special rules may apply. Call us to determine the amount you can claim.

Line 5872 – Allowable amount of medical expenses for other dependants

Complete this calculation for each dependant.

Medical expenses for other dependant			1
Enter $1,821 or 3% of dependant's net income (from line 236 of his or her return), whichever is **less**	–		2
Line 1 minus line 2 (if negative, enter "0"; if it is more than $5,000, enter $5,000)	=		3

Enter, on line 5872 of Form ON428, the total amount claimed for **all** dependants.

Step 7 – Ontario Health Premium

Enter your **taxable income** from line 260 of your return	29,112 | 45	1

To calculate your Ontario Health Premium, **first go to Part A.**

Part A ⇨	If the amount on line 1 is in one of the income ranges in Part A, enter the corresponding premium amount beside the **OHP box** in Step 7 of Form ON428.	**income range**	**premium amount**
If the amount on line 1 is **not in Part A**, complete the chart in **Part B**.		$20,000 or less.................................zero $25,000 to $36,000............................$300 ← $38,500 to $48,000............................$450 $48,600 to $72,000............................$600 $72,600 to $200,000...........................$750 more than $200,600...........................$900	

Part B ⇨ If line 1 is:	more than **$20,000**, but not more than **$25,000**		more than **$36,000**, but not more than **$38,500**		more than **$48,000**, but not more than **$48,600**		more than **$72,000**, but not more than **$72,600**		more than **$200,000**, but not more than **$200,600**		
Enter the amount from line 1 in the applicable column.											2
Line 2 minus line 3 (cannot be negative)	–	20,000 | 00	–	36,000 | 00	–	48,000 | 00	–	72,000 | 00	–	200,000 | 00	3
	=		=		=		=		=		4
Multiply line 4 by line 5	×	6%	×	6%	×	25%	×	25%	×	25%	5
	=		=		=		=		=		6
Add lines 6 and 7, enter the result beside the **OHP box** in **Step 7** of Form ON428	+	0 | 00	+	300 | 00	+	450 | 00	+	600 | 00	+	750 | 00	7
	=		=		=		=		=		8

5006-D

MANAGING YOUR CREDIT

The Banking Services of Financial Institutions

PRESS ONE TO WITHDRAW CASH . . .
PRESS TWO TO DEPOSIT CASH . . .
PRESS THREE FOR HIGH BANKING FEES!

Chris Carter was visiting the cash machine near his place of work for the third time this week. "Wow! Another cash withdrawal," commented his friend Edwin. "You must have tons of money in that chequing account."

"Well, not really," Chris confessed. "I can use this ATM card to access either my chequing or savings account."

"You mean after you've used up everything in your chequing account, you start taking money out of your savings?" asked Edwin. "Doesn't this machine make it too easy for you to overspend?"

"It's just that I've been very busy at work the last few weeks. I've been eating at restaurants a lot, and my cash is used up quickly," replied Chris.

A couple of weeks later, Chris received his bank statement, which included a couple of surprises. "Oh no!" he exclaimed. "Withdrawing cash from my chequing account made me fall below the minimum balance for the account, so they charged me $8.50. My 11 cash withdrawals resulted in more fees. And what's this? Another charge for an overdraft! All those cash withdrawals and fees really hit me hard! And my savings account is down to $78!"

QUESTIONS

1 What benefits and costs are associated with automated teller machines?

2 How does the use of financial services like ATMs affect a person's overall financial plan?

3 What could Chris do to reduce his banking fees and manage his money more wisely?

4 Locate a Web site that provides information suggesting methods for reducing banking fees.

LEARNING OBJECTIVES

1 Analyze factors that affect selection and use of financial services.

2 Compare the types of financial institutions.

3 Compare the costs and benefits of various savings plans.

4 Identify the factors used to evaluate different savings plans.

5 Compare the costs and benefits of different types of chequing accounts.

A STRATEGY FOR MANAGING CASH

With 53 banks, 55 trust and loan companies, and 2,440 credit unions and *caisses populaires*, an extensive financial services market exists. These organizations provide a variety of services for your daily payment and savings needs. Today, a trip to "the bank" may mean a visit to a credit union, an automated teller machine (or automatic banking machine), or checking an account balance on the Web. In recent years, financial services have expanded. A bank is not the only source of chequing accounts. Mortgages are available from several types of financial institutions.

While some financial decisions relate directly to goals, your daily activities require the use of financial services for various business transactions. Exhibit 4–1 provides an overview of financial services for managing cash flows and moving toward financial goals. In simplest terms, you can increase current savings only by spending less than you take in.

MEETING DAILY MONEY NEEDS

Buying groceries, paying the rent, and other routine spending activities require a cash management plan.

MANAGING CASH Cash, cheque, credit card, or automated teller machine (ATM) card (*debit card*) are the common payment choices. While most people desire ease of payment, they must also consider fees and the potential for impulse buying and overspending. For example, in recent years ATM fees have risen from nothing to as high as $5 per transaction, depending upon the type of transaction, where it takes place, and whether or not ATM transactions are covered under the account's service package.

If you are charged two $1 transaction fees a week and could invest your money at 5 percent, this convenience will cost you more than $570 over a five-year period.

Common mistakes made when managing current cash needs include

- Overspending as a result of impulse buying and using credit cards.
- Having insufficient liquid assets (cash, chequing account) to pay current bills.

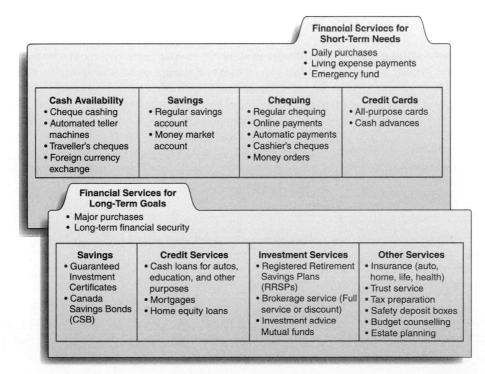

Financial Services for Short-Term Needs
- Daily purchases
- Living expense payments
- Emergency fund

Cash Availability	Savings	Chequing	Credit Cards
• Cheque cashing • Automated teller machines • Traveller's cheques • Foreign currency exchange	• Regular savings account • Money market account	• Regular chequing • Online payments • Automatic payments • Cashier's cheques • Money orders	• All-purpose cards • Cash advances

Financial Services for Long-Term Goals
- Major purchases
- Long-term financial security

Savings	Credit Services	Investment Services	Other Services
• Guaranteed Investment Certificates • Canada Savings Bonds (CSB)	• Cash loans for autos, education, and other purposes • Mortgages • Home equity loans	• Registered Retirement Savings Plans (RRSPs) • Brokerage service (Full service or discount) • Investment advice Mutual funds	• Insurance (auto, home, life, health) • Trust service • Tax preparation • Safety deposit boxes • Budget counselling • Estate planning

■ OBJECTIVE 1 ■

Analyze factors that affect selection and use of financial services.

Exhibit 4–1

Financial Services for Managing Cash Flow

www.mcgrawhill.ca/college/kapoor

- Using savings or borrowing to pay for current expenses.
- Failing to put unneeded funds in an interest-earning savings account or investment plan to achieve long-term goals.

SOURCES OF QUICK CASH　No matter how carefully you manage your money, there may be times when you will need more cash than you currently have available. To cope with that situation, you have two basic choices: liquidate savings or borrow. A savings account, redeemable Guaranteed Investment Certificates, mutual fund, or other investment may be raided when you need funds. Alternatively, a bank overdraft or credit card cash advance may supply funds quickly, but at a very high cost. The best and most efficient source of quick cash would be a personal line of credit, arranged before the need arises. Remember, however, that both using savings and increasing borrowing reduce your net worth and your potential to achieve long-term financial security.

TYPES OF FINANCIAL SERVICES

Banks and other financial institutions offer services to meet a variety of needs. These services fall into four main categories.

1. SAVINGS　Safe storage of funds for future use is a basic need for everyone. These services, commonly referred to as *time deposits*, include money in savings accounts and investment certificates. Selection of a savings plan is commonly based on the interest rate earned, liquidity, safety, and convenience. These factors are discussed later in the chapter.

2. PAYMENT SERVICES　The ability to transfer money to other parties is a necessary part of daily business activities. Chequing accounts and other payment methods, commonly called *demand deposits*, are also covered later in the chapter.

trust　A legal agreement that provides for the management and control of assets by one party for the benefit of another.

3. BORROWING　Most people use credit at some time during their lives. Credit alternatives range from short-term accounts, such as credit cards and cash loans, to long-term borrowing, such as a home mortgage. Chapters 5 and 6 discuss the types and costs of credit.

4. OTHER FINANCIAL SERVICES　Insurance protection, investment for the future, real estate purchases, tax assistance, and financial planning are additional services you may need for successful financial management. With some financial plans, someone else manages your funds. A **trust** is a legal agreement that provides for the management and control of assets by one party for the benefit of another. This type of arrangement is most commonly created through a commercial bank or a lawyer. Parents who want to set aside certain funds for their children's education may use a trust or an RESP (Registered Education Savings Plan). The investments and money in the trust are managed by a bank, and the necessary amounts go to the children for their educational expenses. Trusts are covered in more detail in Chapter 15.

ELECTRONIC BANKING SERVICES

Years ago, people had to conduct banking activities only during set business hours, usually 10 in the morning to three in the afternoon. Today, things are different. Several million Canadians bank or pay bills online. Computerized financial services (see Exhibit 4–2) provide fast, convenient, and efficient systems for recording inflows and outflows of funds.

DID YOU KNOW ?

E-commerce is moving so quickly that it's hard to gather any lasting statistics. While rapid growth continues to be projected, there is no doubt that e-commerce has come of age. Canadians believe almost unanimously that adopting technology and the Internet for business is important, if not critical, to the growth of our economy.

SOURCE: Published by the Canadian Bankers Association, April 2000.

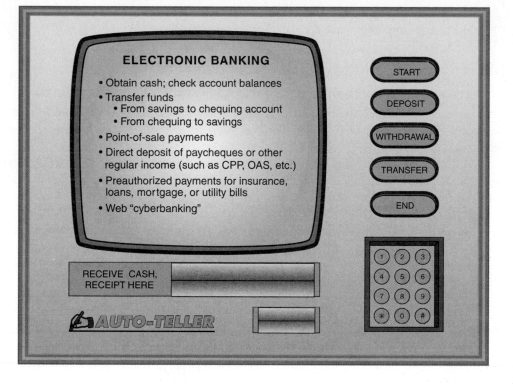

Exhibit 4–2
Electronic Banking Transactions

ELECTRONIC BANKING

- Obtain cash; check account balances
- Transfer funds
  - From savings to chequing account
  - From chequing to savings
- Point-of-sale payments
- Direct deposit of paycheques or other regular income (such as CPP, OAS, etc.)
- Preauthorized payments for insurance, loans, mortgage, or utility bills
- Web "cyberbanking"

START
DEPOSIT
WITHDRAWAL
TRANSFER
END

RECEIVE CASH, RECEIPT HERE

AUTO-TELLER

DIRECT DEPOSIT Each year, more and more workers are receiving only a pay stub on payday. Their earnings are automatically deposited into chequing or savings accounts. This process saves time, effort, and money. Government agencies are also increasing use of direct deposits to reduce costs. Provincial and federal government cheques going to contractors and to Canada Pension Plan, Old Age Security, and welfare recipients are deposited electronically into the payees' bank accounts.

AUTOMATIC PAYMENTS Many utility companies, lenders, and other businesses allow customers to use an automatic payment system, with bills paid through direct withdrawal from a bank account. Experts recommend that you stagger your payments on the basis of when paycheques are received. This allows you to pay bills in an orderly fashion while stabilizing your cash flow. Be sure to check bank statements regularly to ensure that the correct amounts have been deducted from your account. A minor error can result in an overdrawn account and expensive fees.

AUTOMATED TELLER MACHINES **Automated teller machine (ATM)** convenience can be expensive. As the opening case points out, a person who uses an ATM several times a week can incur service charges of several hundred dollars a year.

To reduce ATM fees, experts suggest that you

- Compare ATM fees at different financial institutions before opening an account. Get the fee schedule in writing.
- Use your own bank's ATM, whenever possible, to avoid surcharges imposed when using the ATM of another financial institution.
- Consider purchasing a monthly service package that includes ATM activity.
- Withdraw larger cash amounts, as needed, to avoid fees on several small transactions.

Visit the Web site
See the CBC video exercise under Chapter 4 on the online learning centre at www.mcgraw hill.ca/college/kapoor

automated teller machine (ATM) A computer terminal used to conduct banking transactions.

DID YOU KNOW ?

Canada has the highest rate of debit transactions per inhabitant. There are now over 40,000 Automated Banking Machines located across the country. Of 22 million adult Canadians, 85 percent hold a banking card. In 2004, Canadians used the Interac Direct Payment service 2.819 billion times. December 23, 2004, was the busiest day in the history of debit payments, logging 13 million transactions.

SOURCE: www.interac.org

- Consider using personal cheques, traveller's cheques, credit cards, and prepaid cash cards when away from home if they are more cost effective.

METHODS OF PAYMENT

1. POINT-OF-SALE TRANSACTIONS
Debit cards are routinely accepted in most retail stores and restaurants in major urban centers. Your personal identification number (PIN) is required and the amount is immediately debited to your bank account, reducing your available funds.

Credit cards are also used at the time of sale, but merchandise charges accumulate and appear on the following monthly statement. Credit card transactions only require you to enter your PIN for a cash advance.

2. STORED-VALUE CARDS
Prepaid cards for buying telephone service, transit fares, laundry service, library fees, and school lunches are becoming very common. While some of these access cards, such as phone cards, are disposable (or become collector's items), others are reloadable "stored-value" cards.

3. SMART CARDS
"Smart cards," sometimes called "electronic wallets," look like ATM cards; however, they also include a microchip. This minicomputer stores prepaid amounts for buying goods and services. In addition, the card stores data about a person's account balances, transaction records, insurance information, and medical history. Smart cards are expected to see expanded use in the future as the services they offer increase.

4. ELECTRONIC CASH
SecurNat, offered by the National Bank of Canada (www.nbc.ca) is a payment solution that enables you to safely pay for a Web purchase, from a National Bank–approved merchant, using your credit card.

> **DID YOU KNOW ?**
>
> Generic ATMs are everywhere, with surcharges that are added to the regular transaction fees. These additional fees usually start at $1.50 and can climb much higher. Since the machines warn you about the service charge before your transaction is complete, however, you can cancel your transaction if you think the fee is excessive.

OPPORTUNITY COSTS OF FINANCIAL SERVICES

When making decisions about spending and saving, consider the trade-off between current satisfaction and long-term financial security. In a similar manner, you consider opportunity cost—what you give up—when you evaluate, select, and use financial services. The money you save by shopping around for a low-cost chequing account must be balanced against the value of the time you spend gathering information. Other common trade-offs related to financial services include the following:

- Higher returns of long-term savings and investment plans may be achieved at the cost of *low liquidity*, the inability to obtain your money quickly.
- The convenience of a 24-hour automated teller machine or a bank branch office near your home or place of work must be weighed against service fees.
- The "no fee" chequing account that requires a non–interest-bearing $500 minimum balance means lost interest of nearly $400 at 6 percent compounded over 10 years.

You should evaluate costs and benefits in both monetary and personal terms to choose the financial services that best serve your needs.

FINANCIAL SERVICES AND ECONOMIC CONDITIONS

Changing interest rates, rising consumer prices, and other economic factors also influence financial services. For successful financial planning, be aware of the current trends and future

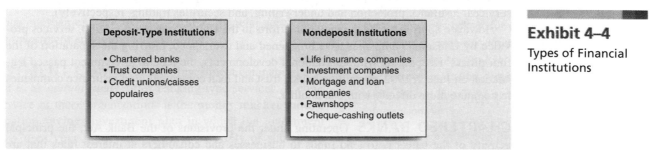

When interest rates are rising...

- Use long-term loans to take advantage of current low rates
- Select short-term savings instruments to take advantage of higher rates when they mature

- Use short-term loans to take advantage of lower rates when you refinance the loans
- Select long-term savings instruments to "lock in" earnings at current high rates

When interest rates are falling...

Exhibit 4–3

Changing Interest Rates and Decisions Related to Financial Services

prospects for interest rates (see Exhibit 4–3, and the Financial Planning for Life's Situations box on page 108). You can learn about these trends and prospects by reading *The Financial Post* (www.canada.com/national/nationalpost/financialpost/index.html), the business section of daily newspapers, and business periodicals such as *Business Week* (www.businessweek.com), and *Fortune* (www.fortune.com).

CONCEPT CHECK 4–1

1. What is the relationship between financial services and overall financial planning?
2. What are the major categories of financial services?
3. What financial services are available through electronic banking systems?
4. Why shouldn't you select financial services on the basis of only monetary factors?
5. How do changing economic conditions affect the use of financial services?

TYPES OF FINANCIAL INSTITUTIONS

Many types of businesses, such as insurance companies, investment brokers, and credit card companies, have become involved in financial services previously limited to banks. Such companies as GM Canada and the Hudson's Bay Company now issue or sponsor credit cards. Banks have also expanded their competitive efforts by opening offices that specialize in financial services, such as investments, insurance, or real estate. Increased competition has brought about the opening of many limited-service offices, sometimes called *nonbanks*. These limited-service offices specialize in a particular banking activity, such as savings or personal loans.

Despite changes in the banking environment, many familiar financial institutions still serve your needs. Most of these institutions have expanded their services. As Exhibit 4–4 shows, financial institutions fall into two major categories: deposit-type institutions and nondeposit institutions.

■ **OBJECTIVE 2**

Compare the types of financial institutions.

Deposit-Type Institutions	Nondeposit Institutions
• Chartered banks • Trust companies • Credit unions/caisses populaires	• Life insurance companies • Investment companies • Mortgage and loan companies • Pawnshops • Cheque-cashing outlets

Exhibit 4–4

Types of Financial Institutions

financial instruments. Your earnings are based on the interest the investment company receives. Unlike accounts at most banks, trust companies, and credit unions, investment company accounts are not covered by federal deposit insurance.

MORTGAGE AND LOAN COMPANIES These companies provide real estate mortgage loans as well as financing opportunities for individuals and small businesses. In general, the loans provided have short and intermediate terms with higher rates than most other lenders charge. Some of these companies have expanded their activities to also offer other financial planning services.

FINANCE AND LEASING COMPANIES Finance and leasing companies extend loans and leases to both individuals and businesses, and are categorized by the type of loan or lease they offer, or the sector they serve. Consumer loan companies offer cash lending services directly to individuals (e.g., Avco Financial Services Canada Ltd.), while finance companies that serve the corporate sector focus on loans or leases to small businesses or new, high-growth companies. Consumer loan companies tend to charge higher administrative fees and rates of interest than do banks, due to their smaller size, high cost of funding, and willingness to accept credit risks that other creditors might refuse.

PAWNSHOPS Pawnshops, which often label themselves *Cash Converters*, make loans based on the value of tangible possessions, such as jewellery or other valuable items. Many low- and moderate-income families use these organizations to obtain cash loans quickly. Pawnshops charge higher fees than other financial institutions.

CHEQUE-CASHING OUTLETS Most financial institutions will not cash a cheque unless the person has an account. Cheque-cashing outlets (CCOs) charge anywhere from 1 to 20 percent of the face value of a cheque; the average cost is between 2 and 3 percent. However, for a low-income family, that can be a significant portion of the total household budget (see the Financial Planning for Life's Situations box on page 111).

CCOs offer a wide variety of services, including electronic tax filing, money orders, and private postal boxes. You can usually obtain most of these services for less expense at other locations.

ONLINE BANKING

The use of online Web portals for personal banking has become very common. Every major Canadian financial institution maintains a Web site where customers can log in and conduct everyday banking transactions, such as verifying account balances, transferring funds, and paying bills and credit card balances. The Web site also permits individuals to apply for loans and provides complete product information. The Bank of Montreal (www.bmo.com) and the TD Canada Trust (www.tdcanadatrust.com) were among the first Canadian banks to do business on the Internet. Citizens Bank of Canada (www.citizensbank.ca) was one of the first Canadian financial institutions to operate exclusively on the Internet. Access to all accounts and transactions is available 24 hours a day, seven days a week. (See the Financial Planning for Life's Situations box on page 113.)

One of the main deterents to banking online is a lack of technical and computer expertise. Most banking transactions require specialized software for securely encrypting data. Do not worry, most financial Web sites show you how and where to download the required software free of charge.

COMPARING FINANCIAL INSTITUTIONS

The basic concerns of a financial services customer are simple:

- Where can I get the best return on my savings?
- How can I minimize the cost of chequing and payments services?

Would you pay $8 to cash a $100 cheque? Or pay $20 to borrow $100 for two weeks? Many people without ready access to financial services (especially low-income consumers) commonly use the services of cheque-cashing outlets, pawnshops, payday loan stores, and rent-to-own centres. Offers of "quick cash" and "low payments" attract consumers without a bank account or credit cards.

PAWNSHOPS

Despite a thriving economy in recent years, thousands of consumers are increasingly in need of small loans—usually $50 to $75, to be repaid in 30 to 45 days. Pawnshops have become the "neighbourhood bankers" and the "local shopping malls," since they provide both lending and retail shopping services, selling items that owners do not redeem.

PAYDAY LOANS

Payday loans are also referred to as *cash advances*, *cheque advance loans*, *postdated cheque loans*, and *delayed deposit loans*. Desperate borrowers pay annual interest rates of as much as 780 percent and more to obtain needed cash from payday loan companies. The most common users of payday loans are workers who have become trapped by debts run up by free spending or who have been driven into debt by misfortune.

In a typical payday loan, a consumer writes a personal cheque for $115 to borrow $100 for 14 days. The payday lender agrees to hold the cheque until the next payday. This $15 finance charge for the 14 days translates into an annual percentage rate of 391 percent. Some consumers "roll over" their loans, paying another $15 for the $100 loan for the next 14 days. After a few rollovers, the finance charge can exceed the amount borrowed.

RENT-TO-OWN CENTRES

Years ago, people who rented furniture and appliances found few deluxe items available. Today, rental businesses offer big-screen televisions, seven-piece cherrywood bedroom sets, and personal computers. The rental-purchase industry—defined as stores that lease products to consumers who can then own the item if they complete a certain number of monthly or weekly payments—is in rapid growth.

Buyer beware, however. The rental agreements drawn up in this industry are not necessarily in the consumer's best interests, and interest rates are often very high.

- Will I be able to borrow money when I need it?

As you use financial services, decide what you want from the organization that will serve your needs. With the financial marketplace constantly changing, you must assess the various services and other factors before selecting an organization (see Exhibit 4–5).

The services the financial institution offers are likely to be a major factor. Personal service is important to many customers. Convenience may be provided by business hours, branch offices, automated teller machines, and online service. Convenience and service have a cost, so be sure to compare fees and other charges at several financial institutions.

Finally, you should consider safety factors and interest rates. Obtain information about earnings you will receive on savings and chequing accounts and the rate you will pay for borrowed funds. Most financial institutions have deposit insurance to protect customers against losses; however, not all of them are insured by federal government programs. Investigate the type of protection you will have.

Your selection of a financial institution should be based on valid information. Never assume that one will provide a better interest rate or service than another. You need to compare banks, trust companies, and credit unions with other providers of financial services.

DID YOU KNOW ?

The stark reality of services offered by cheque-cashing outlets is that the fees you pay are substantially higher than what you might be charged at other financial institutions. Studies reveal that poor consumers (who form the bulk of the outlets' clientele) can spend up to 10 times as much at a cheque-cashing outlet as they would with a basic account. Despite this fact, other studies have proposed that banks often poorly promote the availability of low-cost accounts.

Exhibit 4–5

How Should You Choose a Financial Institution?

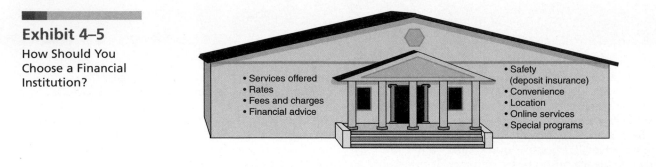

- Services offered
- Rates
- Fees and charges
- Financial advice

- Safety (deposit insurance)
- Convenience
- Location
- Online services
- Special programs

CONCEPT CHECK 4–2

1. What are examples of deposit-type financial institutions?
2. What factors do consumers usually consider when selecting a financial institution to meet their saving and chequing needs?

TYPES OF SAVINGS PLANS

OBJECTIVE 3

Compare the costs and benefits of various savings plans.

As Chapter 2 emphasized, you need a savings program to attain financial goals. Evaluation of various savings plans is the starting point of this process.

Changes in financial services have created a wide choice of savings alternatives (see Exhibit 4–6). While the number of savings plans may seem overwhelming, they can be

Exhibit 4–6   Savings Alternatives

Type of Alternative	Benefits	Drawbacks
Regular savings accounts/ passbook accounts	Low minimum balance Ease of withdrawal Insured to $60,000 per financial institution	Low rate of return
Guaranteed Investment Certificates (GICs)	Guaranteed rate of return for time of GIC Insured	Possible penalty for early withdrawal Minimum deposit
Interest-earning chequing accounts	Chequing privileges Interest earned Insured to $60,000	Possible service charge for going below minimum balance Cost for printing cheques; other fees may apply
Money market accounts	Favourable rate of return (based on current interest rates) Allows some cheque writing	Higher minimum balance than regular savings accounts No interest or service charge, if below a certain balance
Money market funds	Favourable rate of return (based on current interest rates)	Minimum balance Not insured
Canada Savings Bonds (CSBs)	Rate of return varies with current interest rates Low minimum deposit Regular or compound interest Government guaranteed	No interest paid if redeemed before three months

"We never close." "Highest savings rates anywhere." "Lowest chequing account fees ever."

These impressive banking services are now possible with the use of the World Wide Web. Banks, like other businesses and financial service companies, are now online with cyber-versions of their traditional activities.

COMPARING BANKING SERVICES

As you start or expand your use of online banking services, several Web sites provide a wide range of banking information. These include www.royalbank.ca and www.quicken.ca.

ONLINE BANK BRANCHES

Traditional banks are expanding to offer services online. Some examples include www.bmo.com and www.tdcanadatrust.com.

PAYING BILLS ONLINE

It is now possible to receive your bills online through e-mail or by logging into your bank's Web site. One mouse click can pay off your credit card, and another,

your cell phone bill. Paperless billing is fast becoming the new way to settle accounts efficiently using the Internet. For information on paying bills online, go to www.quicken.ca, www.yahoo.com, or www.aol.ca/portal/home/index.adp.

WEB-ONLY BANKS

Many of today's best chequing and savings deals come from branchless banks doing business solely on the Internet. Web banks usually require little or no minimum balance on chequing accounts. Many Internet banks also pay higher interest on chequing accounts than traditional banks. While ATMs are not readily available from Web banks, these online financial companies usually offer banking and customer service over the telephone. Some Internet banks include www.citizensbank.com, President's Choice Financial (www.pcfinancial.ca/), and ING Direct (www.ingdirect.ca).

Be cautious! You may access the Web site of the Canadian Deposit Insurance Corporation (www.cdic.ca) to obtain information on fraudulent cyber-banks. The CDIC can tell you if a Web bank has a legitimate charter to operate as a financial institution.

---

grouped into these main categories: regular savings accounts, term deposits and GICs, interest-earning chequing accounts, and Canada Savings Bonds. Investment vehicles, such as Canadian treasury bills, are discussed in later chapters.

REGULAR SAVINGS ACCOUNTS

Regular savings accounts, traditionally called *passbook accounts*, usually involve a low or no minimum balance. Today, instead of a passbook showing deposits and withdrawals, savers may elect to receive a monthly or quarterly statement with a summary of transactions.

A regular savings account usually allows you to withdraw money as needed. However, *time deposits* may require a waiting period to obtain your funds.

TERM DEPOSITS AND GUARANTEED INVESTMENT CERTIFICATES (GICs)

Higher earnings are commonly available to savers when they leave money on deposit for a set time period.

TERM DEPOSITS Contrary to a savings account, which does not have a guaranteed interest rate of return, **term deposits** guarantee a rate of interest for a specified term. The trade-off is very simply that your money becomes less accessible for a time.

Some term deposits require a minimum deposit, and if you are willing to sacrifice some of the interest you might have earned, you will usually be permitted to withdraw your funds

term deposits A deposit that is made for a specified term in exchange for a higher rate of return. Can be redeemed before maturity by earning a reduced rate of interest (paying a penalty).

113

before maturity. The amount of interest you will earn is inversely related to the term of the investment, which will typically be between 30 and 364 days.

Guaranteed Investment Certificates (GICs)
Term deposits made for a longer period, usually from one to five years.

GUARANTEED INVESTMENT CERTIFICATES (GICs) **Guaranteed Investment Certificates** are essentially term deposits with a longer term, ranging from one to five years. As is the case with term deposits, a minimum deposit is often required. Interest can be fixed-rate, variable, or *indexed-linked*—that is, based on a formula linked to stock market returns. Some GICs are redeemable prior to maturity, but will pay a lower rate of interest if redeemed than GICs of a similar term that are non-redeemable.

MANAGING YOUR TERM DEPOSITS AND GICs When a term deposit or GIC reaches maturity, it is important to assess all earnings and costs. Do not allow your financial institution to automatically roll your money over into another deposit for the same term. If interest rates have dropped, you should consider investing in a term deposit for a shorter term in hopes that rates will rise. Alternatively, if you believe that rates are peaking and you do not think you will need your money for a time, then your best choice will be a longer-term GIC.

Deposit rates will often vary from one financial institution to the next. In addition, their personnel have some flexibility to offer rates higher than those advertised. It is wise to comparison-shop and negotiate the best rate available before locking in your money. Visit www.baystreet.ca/interest_rates/gic_rates.cfm to compare rates by institution and maturity.

INTEREST-EARNING CHEQUING ACCOUNTS

Chequing accounts can also be savings vehicles. These interest-earning accounts, which usually pay a low interest rate, are discussed in the next section.

CANADA SAVINGS BONDS

Historically, Canada Savings Bonds (CSBs) developed from Victory bonds, which were offered between 1940 and 1944 in an effort to raise funds for the Canadian military action of the Second World War. Though crucial at the time and in the half century that followed, CSBs now have a declining role in the federal government's borrowing as the government's need for funds has diminished.

Unlike most investments, CSBs are sold only once a year, for the six-month period starting in October until the following April 1. They have a fixed rate of interest for the first year and, subject to a guaranteed minimum, rates can be adjusted according to market conditions in later years. Starting three months after purchase, CSBs are cashable at any time for their face value plus accrued interest. They are eligible investments for both registered retirement savings plans (RRSPs) and registered retirement income funds (RRIFs). Two types are available: the *regular interest bond* and the *compound interest bond*.

Visit the Web site
See Personal Financial Planning worksheets under Chapter 4 on the online learning centre at www.mcgrawhill.ca/college/kapoor.

REGULAR INTEREST BOND This bond pays regular annual interest by cheque or direct deposit to an investor's account on November 1 of each year. Denominations for this bond range from $300 to $10,000 and they must be purchased with cash.

COMPOUND INTEREST BOND This bond reinvests earned interest automatically until redemption or maturity. It is available in denominations as low as $100 and up to $10,000. Compound interest bonds can be purchased by cash, by a monthly payment plan through a financial institution or through a payroll savings plan.

The Government of Canada also offers The Canada Premium Bond (CPB). The CPB is sold during the same six-month period as the CSB, but offers a slightly higher rate of interest because it can be redeemed only on the anniversary of the issue date and during the thirty days that follow. More information concerning CSBs and CPBs can be found at www.csb.gc.ca.

CONCEPT CHECK 4–3

1. What are the main types of savings plans offered by financial institutions?
2. What are the benefits of Canada Savings Bonds?

EVALUATING SAVINGS PLANS

Your selection of a savings plan will be influenced by the rate of return, inflation, tax considerations, liquidity, safety, and restrictions and fees.

■ OBJECTIVE 4 ▮

Identify the factors used to evaluate different savings plans.

RATE OF RETURN

Earnings on savings can be measured by the **rate of return**, or *yield*: the percentage of increase in the value of your savings from earned interest. For example, a $100 savings account that earned $5 after a year would have a rate of return, or yield, of 5 percent. This rate of return was determined by dividing the interest earned ($5) by the amount in the savings account ($100).

rate of return The percentage of increase in the value of savings as a result of interest earned; also called *yield.*

COMPOUNDING The yield on your savings usually will be greater than the stated interest rate. The more frequent the compounding, the higher your rate of return will be. For example, $100 in a savings account that earns 6 percent compounded annually will increase $6 after a year. But the same $100 in a 6-percent account compounded daily will earn $6.19 for the year. Although this difference may seem slight, large amounts held in savings for long periods of time will result in far higher differences (see Exhibit 4–7).

EFFECTIVE ANNUAL RATE (EAR) To incorporate the compounding effect, the **effective annual rate (EAR)** formula is used. Using the notation that m is the number of periods in a year and k is the rate of return quoted for the year,

$$EAR = \left(1 + \frac{k}{m}\right)^m - 1$$

effective annual rate (EAR) A formula that calculates the effective return, taking compounding into account.

$EAR - \left(1 + \dfrac{k}{m}\right)^m - 1$

m = number of compounding periods in a year

k = rate of return quoted for a year.

It is important to note the effects of compounding. Imagine a simple case where you pay interest on a $100 loan at 12 percent yearly, compounded monthly. Not accounting for the compounding effect will lead you to conclude that you are paying 12 percent, or $12 per year in interest charges.

Shorter compounding periods result in higher yields. This chart shows the growth of $10,000, five-year GICs paying the same nominal rate of 8 percent, but with different compounding methods.

▬▬▬ ▬

Exhibit 4–7

Compounding Frequency Increases the Savings Yield

	COMPOUNDING METHOD			
End of Year	**Daily**	**Monthly**	**Quarterly**	**Annually**
1	$10,832.78	$10,830.00	$10,824.32	$10,800.00
2	11,743.91	11,728.88	11,716.59	11,664.00
3	12,712.17	12,702.37	12,682.41	12,597.12
4	13,770.82	13,756.66	13,727.85	13,604.89
5	14,917.62	14,898.46	14,859.46	14,693.28
Effective rate	8.33%	8.30%	8.24%	8.00%

The reality is that you are paying more. Using the EAR formula, which allows for compounding, will show that you will actually pay 12.68 percent, or $12.68. EAR can also be calculated with a financial calculator; see Appendix A for examples.

INFLATION

The rate of return you earn on your savings should be compared with the inflation rate. When the inflation rate was more than 10 percent, people with money in savings accounts earning 5 or 6 percent were experiencing a real loss in the buying power of that money. The increase (or loss) in purchasing power of an investment is reflected in its *real* rate of return. We can approximate the real rate of return by subtracting the inflation rate from an investment's effective rate of return for the same period. For example, if a deposit pays 6 percent, compounded semi-annually, we have demonstrated that its effective annual interest rate would be 6.09 percent, calculated as $(1 + 0.06/2)^2 - 1$. If inflation over the same year were 3 percent, the investment's real rate of return would be approximately 3.09 percent (6.09 percent − 3 percent). In general, as the inflation rate increases, the interest rates offered to savers must also increase to maintain the real rate of return.

TAX CONSIDERATIONS

Like inflation, taxes reduce interest earned on savings. For example, a 10-percent return for a saver in a 26-percent tax bracket means an after-tax return of 7.4 percent (the Financial Planning Calculations feature on the next page shows how to compute the after-tax savings rate of return). As discussed in Chapter 3 and discussed further in Part 4, several tax-exempt and tax-deferred savings plans and investments can increase your real rate of return.

LIQUIDITY

Liquidity refers to the ease with which you can access cash or convert investments to cash with a minimal loss of principal. Some savings plans impose penalties for early withdrawal or have other restrictions. With certain types of savings certificates and accounts, early withdrawal may be penalized by a loss of interest or a lower earnings rate.

You should consider the degree of liquidity you desire in relation to your savings goals. To achieve long-term financial goals, many people trade off liquidity for a higher return.

SAFETY

Most savings plans at banks, trust companies, and credit unions or caisses populaires are insured by agencies affiliated with the federal government. This protection prevents loss of money due to the failure of the insured institution.

The Canadian Deposit Insurance Corporation (CDIC) will protect eligible deposits up to a maximum of $60,000 per person, including principal and interest, for each different member institution involved. Eligible deposits include savings and chequing accounts, term deposits, Guaranteed Investment Certificates, debentures, and other obligations issued by institutions that are members of the CDIC.

In the event that a member institution becomes insolvent, your insured funds will be secure up to $60,000. In the case of a joint deposit, the funds insured will be $60,000 divided among all the names in the account.

Be aware that deposits in different branches of the same institution will be counted as a single account and will be insured only to $60,000. If you have more than this amount to deposit, it would be wise to spread your money among different members of the CDIC, although chartered banks offer a variety of products that may be insured separately. To find out more about eligible deposits, you can access the CDIC site at www.cdic.ca.

Financial Planning Calculations

After-Tax Savings Rate of Return

The taxability of interest on your savings reduces your after-tax rate of return. In other words, you lose some portion of your interest to taxes. This calculation consists of the following steps:

1. Determine your top tax bracket for federal income taxes.
2. Subtract this rate, expressed as a decimal, from 1.0.
3. Multiply the result by the yield on your savings account.
4. This number, expressed as a percentage, is your after-tax rate of return.

For example,

1. You are in the 26 percent tax bracket (federally).
2. $1.0 - 0.26 = 0.74$.
3. If the yield on your savings account is 6.25 percent, $0.0625 \times 0.74 = 0.046$.
4. Your after-tax rate of return is 4.6 percent.

But what if inflation over the same period is 3 percent? What is your real, after-tax rate of return? It is approximately 4.6 percent less 3 percent, or only 1.6 percent!

Since not all financial institutions have federal deposit insurance, investigate this matter when you are selecting a savings plan.

RESTRICTIONS AND FEES

Other limitations can affect your choice of a savings program. For example, there may be a delay between the time interest is earned and the time it is added to your account. This means it will not be available for your immediate use. Also, some institutions charge a transaction fee for each deposit or withdrawal and pay interest only if you maintain a minimum monthly balance.

In the past, some financial institutions had promotions offering a "free" gift when a certain savings amount was deposited. To receive this gift, you had to leave your money on deposit for a certain time period or you may have received less interest, since some of the earnings were used to cover the cost of the "free" items. Economists tell us that "there is no such thing as a free lunch"; the same holds true for toasters and television sets.

CONCEPT CHECK 4–4

1. When would you prefer a savings plan with high liquidity over one with a high rate of return?
2. What is the relationship between compounding and the future value of an amount?
3. How do inflation and taxes affect earnings on savings?

SELECTING PAYMENT METHODS

With about 90 percent of business transactions conducted by cheque, a chequing account is a necessity for most people.

■ OBJECTIVE 5 ▮

Compare the costs and benefits of different types of chequing accounts.

TYPES OF CHEQUING ACCOUNTS

Chequing accounts fall into three major categories: regular chequing accounts, activity accounts, and interest-earning chequing accounts.

117

REGULAR CHEQUING ACCOUNTS *Regular chequing accounts* usually have a monthly service charge that you may avoid by keeping a minimum balance in the account. Some financial institutions will waive the monthly fee if you keep a certain amount in savings. Avoiding the monthly service charge can be beneficial. For example, a monthly fee of $7.50 results in $90 a year. However, you lose interest on the minimum-balance amount in a non–interest-earning account.

ACTIVITY ACCOUNTS *Activity accounts* charge a fee for each cheque written and sometimes a fee for each deposit, in addition to a monthly service charge. However, you do not have to maintain a minimum balance. An activity account is most appropriate for people who write only a few cheques each month and are unable to maintain the required minimum balance.

INTEREST-EARNING CHEQUING ACCOUNTS *Interest-earning chequing accounts* usually require a minimum balance. If the account balance goes below this amount, you may not earn interest and will likely incur a service charge.

EVALUATING CHEQUING ACCOUNTS

Would you rather have a chequing account that pays interest and requires a $1,000 minimum balance or an account that doesn't pay interest and requires a $300 minimum balance? This decision requires evaluating such factors as restrictions, fees and charges, interest, and special services (see Exhibit 4–8).

RESTRICTIONS The most common limitation on chequing accounts is the amount you must keep on deposit to earn interest or avoid a service charge.

FEES AND CHARGES Nearly all financial institutions require a minimum balance or impose service charges for chequing accounts. When using an interest-bearing chequing account, compare your earnings with any service charge or fee. Also, consider the cost of lost or reduced interest due to the need to maintain the minimum balance.

Chequing account fees have increased in recent years. Such items as cheque printing, overdraft fees, and stop-payment orders have doubled or tripled in price at some financial institutions. Some institutions will try to entice you with fancy cheques at a low price and then charge a much higher price when you reorder. You may be able to purchase cheques at a lower cost from a mail-order company that advertises in magazines or the Sunday newspaper.

INTEREST As discussed earlier, the interest rate, the frequency of compounding, and the interest computation method will affect the earnings on your chequing account.

SPECIAL SERVICES Financial institutions commonly offer chequing account customers services such as 24-hour ATM machines and home banking services. Financial institutions are also attempting to reduce the paper and postage costs associated with chequing accounts. One solution is to not return cancelled cheques to customers. The financial institution then uses microfilm to store cheques and provides customers with detailed statements summarizing the cheques written. If a customer requests a copy of a cancelled cheque, the institution reproduces the copy from its microfilm file for a fee.

DID YOU KNOW ?

"Rubber cheques" mean big money for the banking industry. Every year, banks make billion-dollar profits from bounced-cheque fees. Studies have shown that some institutions charge up to 32 times what it actually costs them to process a cheque that is issued with insufficient funds.

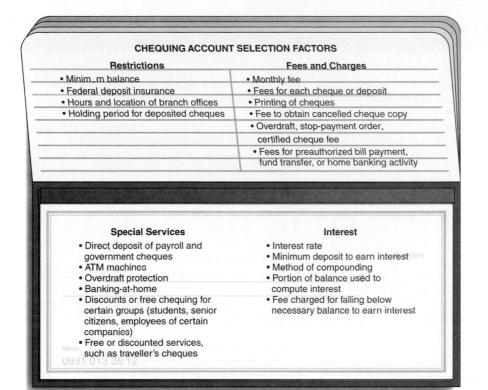

Exhibit 4–8
Chequing Account
Selection Factors

Overdraft protection is an automatic loan made to chequing account customers for cheques written in excess of the available balance. This service is convenient but costly. Most overdraft plans make loans based on $50 or $100 increments. An overdraft of just $1 might trigger a $50 loan and corresponding finance charges of perhaps 18 percent or some minimum fee such as $5 per overdraft. But overdraft protection can be less costly than the fee charged for a cheque you write when you do not have enough money on deposit to cover it. That fee may be $20 or more. Many financial institutions will allow you to cover chequing account overdrafts with an automatic transfer from a savings account for a nominal fee.

overdraft protection
An automatic loan made to chequing account customers to cover the amount of cheques written in excess of the available balance in the account.

Beware of chequing accounts that offer several services (safety deposit box, traveller's cheques, low-rate loans, and travel insurance) for a single monthly fee. This may sound like a good value; however, financial experts observe that such accounts benefit only a small group of people who make constant use of the services offered.

The Financial Planning Calculations box on page 121 offers a method for comparing the costs of various types of chequing accounts.

OTHER PAYMENT METHODS

While personal cheques are the most common payment form, other methods are available. A *certified cheque* is a personal cheque with guaranteed payment. The amount of the cheque is deducted from your balance when the financial institution certifies the cheque. You may purchase a *money order* in a similar manner from financial institutions, post offices, and stores. Certified cheques, cashier's cheques, and money orders allow you to make a payment that the recipient knows is valid.

Traveller's cheques allow you to make payments when you are away from home. This payment form requires you to sign each cheque twice. First, you sign the traveller's cheques when you purchase them. Then, to identify you as the authorized person, you sign them again as you cash them.

Prepaid travel cards are becoming more common. The card allows travellers visiting other nations to get local currency from an ATM.

4 Using a Chequing Account

OPENING A CHEQUING ACCOUNT

Deciding who the owner of the account will be is your starting point for opening a chequing account. Only one person is allowed to write cheques on an *individual account*. A *joint account* has two or more owners, with any authorized person allowed to write cheques if it is specified as an "or" account. In contrast, an "and" account with two owners requires the signatures of both owners on cheques. This arrangement is commonly used by businesses and other organizations.

Both an individual account and a joint account require a signature card. This document is a record of the official signatures of the person or persons authorized to write cheques on the account.

MAKING DEPOSITS

A *deposit form* is used for adding money to your chequing account (see Exhibit 4–A). On this document, you list the amounts of the cash and cheques being deposited. Each cheque you deposit requires an *endorsement*—your signature on the back of the cheque—to authorize the transfer of the funds into your account. The following are three common endorsement forms:

- A *blank endorsement* is your signature. Use this endorsement form only when you are actually depositing or cashing a cheque, since a cheque could be cashed by anyone once its back has been signed.
- A *restrictive endorsement* consists of the words for *deposit only*, followed by your signature. This endorsement form is especially useful when you are depositing cheques by mail.
- A *special endorsement* allows you to transfer a cheque to an organization or another person. On this endorsement form, the words *pay to the order of* are followed by the name of the organization or person and then by your signature.

Exhibit 4-A

Deposit Slip

DEPOSIT				
	CASH	CURRENCY	17	–
		COIN	2	50
	LIST CHECKS SINGLY		16	25
			11	37
Barbara Carter				
7640 Moontree Lane				
Waterloo, ON N2J 2S3				00-0000/0000
	TOTAL FROM OTHER SIDE			
DATE ____ April 10 ___ 19 _2002_	TOTAL		47	12	USE OTHER SIDE FOR ADDITIONAL LISTING
▶	LESS CASH RECEIVED		10	–
_____	NET DEPOSIT		37	12	BE SURE EACH ITEM IS PROPERLY ENDORSED
National Bank of Canada				

⑆00000000⑆ 15 5 303 79⑈ 3323

CHEQUES AND OTHER ITEMS ARE RECEIVED FOR DEPOSIT SUBJECT TO THE PROVISIONS OF THE UNIFORM COMMERCIAL CODE OR ANY APPLICABLE COLLECTION AGREEMENT.

WRITING CHEQUES

Before writing a cheque, record the information in your cheque register and deduct the amount of the cheque from your balance; otherwise, you will think you have more money available than you really do. Many chequing account customers use duplicate cheques to maintain a record of their current balance.

The procedure for proper cheque writing, displayed in Exhibit 4–B, consists of the following steps:

[1] Record the current date.

[2] Write the name of the person or organization receiving the payment.

[3] Record the amount of the cheque in figures.

[4] Write the amount of the cheque in words; cheques for less than a dollar should be written as "only 79 cents," for example, with the word *dollars* on the cheque crossed out.

[5] Sign the cheque in the same way you signed the signature card when you opened your account.

[6] Make a note of the reason for payment to assist with budget and tax preparation.

Cheque-writing software is available as a separate program or as part of a financial planning package, such as Quicken (www.quicken.ca). These programs can easily prepare cheques while maintaining your financial records, such as the cheque register, personal financial statements, and a budget.

A *stop-payment order* may be necessary if a cheque is lost or stolen or if a business transaction was not completed in a satisfactory manner. The fee for a stop-payment commonly ranges from $0 to $20. If several cheques are missing or you lose your chequebook, the bank may suggest closing that account and opening a new one. This action is likely to be less costly than paying several stop-payment fees.

MAINTAINING A CHEQUING ACCOUNT

Each month you can receive a *bank statement*, a summary of the transactions for a chequing account. This document reports deposits made, cheques paid, interest earned, and fees for such items as service charges and printing of cheques. The balance reported on the bank statement probably will differ from the balance in your chequebook. Reasons for a difference are cheques that you have written but have not yet cleared, deposits you have made since the bank statement was prepared, interest added to your account, and deductions for fees and charges.

To determine your true balance, you should prepare a *bank reconciliation*. This report accounts for differences between the bank statement and your chequebook balance. The steps you take in this process, shown in the Financial Planning Calculations box on page 128, are as follows:

Exhibit 4-B

A Personal Cheque

Kenneth Buckley
7828 Carl Drive
Vancouver, BC H4A 2K1

3693

① February 6 20 02

PAY TO THE ORDER OF ② Midland College

③ $ 862.75

④ Eight-hundred sixty-two and 75/100 ———— DOLLARS

BC Employees Credit Union

MEMO ⑥ spring tuition

⑤ Kenneth Buckley

⑈000000000⑈ 1505 303079⑈ 3693

The process of comparing your chequebook balance to the bank statement is vital for determining any errors that may have ocurred. Use the following steps to reconcile your account:

THE BANK STATEMENT		
Balance on current bank statement	$	643.96

	Date	Amount
Step 1.		
Add up outstanding cheques (cheques that you have written but have not yet cleared the banking system) and withdrawals still outstanding.	10-4	70.00
	10-6	130.00
	10-7	111.62
Subtract the total.	$	−311.62
Step 2.	Date	Amount
Add up deposits in transit (deposits that have been made but are not reported on the current statement).	10-2	60.00
	10-5	90.00
Add the total.	$	+150.00
Adjusted bank balance	$	482.34

YOUR CHEQUEBOOK		
Current balance in your chequebook	$	295.91
Step 3.		
Subtract total of fees or other charges listed on bank statement.	$	−15.75
Subtract ATM withdrawals.	$	−100.00
Step 4.		
Add interest earned.	$	+2.18
Add direct deposits.	$	+300.00
Adjusted chequebook balance	$	482.34

[1] Compare the cheques you have written over the past month with those reported as paid on your bank statement. Use the cancelled cheques from the financial institution, or compare your cheque register with the cheque numbers reported on the bank statement (many financial institutions no longer return cancelled cheques to customers). *Subtract* from the *bank statement balance* the total of the cheques written but not yet cleared.

[2] Determine whether any recent deposits are not on the bank statement. If so, *add* the amount of the outstanding deposits to the *bank statement balance*.

[3] *Subtract* any fees or charges on the bank statement and ATM withdrawals from your *chequebook balance*.

[4] *Add* any interest earned to your *chequebook balance*.

At this point, the revised balances for both your chequebook and the bank statement should be the same. If the two do not match, check your math, making sure every cheque and deposit was recorded correctly in your chequebook and on the bank statement.

Many people do not take the time to reconcile their accounts; however, failure to do this could cost you money. If the bank subtracts more for a cheque than the amount for which you wrote it and you don't complain within a year, the bank may not be liable for correcting the error.

www.mcgrawhill.ca/college/kapoor

Introduction to Consumer Credit

A RISING HOUSE OF CARDS? POORER BORROWERS USE MORE PLASTIC

The strong economy of the late 1990s was for the most part a result of the technology boom. However, mid-2000 marked the beginning of a downturn. This mild recession has been different from those in the past; it is primarily driven by the technology slump and a reduction in corporate profits, whereas the consumer has remained very resilient. This downturn has resulted in bankruptcies and excessive use of credit. A recent survey conducted by Leger Marketing showed that three-quarters of Canadians said they had at least one credit card, and cardholders mentioned having an average of 2.5 cards.

Recent trend analyses have shown that as credit card debt has risen, a new class of borrowers has come to the fore. The growing use and convenience of credit cards has facilitated the process of borrowing, and even those who can't really afford to borrow still do. Where at one time credit cards might have been reserved for those with the capacity to handle credit appropriately, they are now available to all.

Recent studies have shown that as ownership of cards has risen, the proportion of cards held by people with lower incomes has gone up. In addition, debt due to credit cards has also risen. A recent study by the Office of Consumer Affairs at Industry Canada showed that credit card debt as a portion of total household debt has risen by more than 50 percent since 1977.

Debt obligations of people seeking credit, debt, and bankruptcy counselling are generally now $13,000 to $14,000, up from $10,000 to $11,000 in 1997. Some consumers are heading for the precipice, perhaps without realizing how close the danger actually is or how sharp the drop might be.

Poorer, riskier borrowers joined the credit card ranks in the 1990s and apparently took on a lot of debt in the process. This group, many of whose members have low-level blue-collar jobs, is highly vulnerable to even a modest cyclical slowdown.

QUESTIONS

1 Why are today's consumers spending and borrowing heavily?

2 Why do some experts suggest that a new class of borrowers may be especially at risk if economic growth slows down?

LEARNING OBJECTIVES

1 Define consumer credit and analyze its advantages and disadvantages.

2 Differentiate among various types of credit.

3 Assess your credit capacity and build your credit rating.

4 Describe the information creditors look for when you apply for credit.

5 Identify the steps you can take to avoid and correct credit mistakes.

WHAT IS CONSUMER CREDIT?

■ **OBJECTIVE 1** ▮

Define consumer credit and analyze its advantages and disadvantages.

credit An arrangement to receive cash, goods, or services now and pay for them in the future.

consumer credit
The use of credit for personal needs (except a home mortgage).

Visit the Web site
See the Pre-Test under Chapter 5 on the online learning centre at www.mcgrawhill.ca/ college/kapoor.

"Charge it!" "Cash or credit?" "Put it on my account." As these phrases indicate, the use of credit is a fact of life in personal and family financial planning. When you use credit, you satisfy needs today and pay for this satisfaction in the future. While the use of credit is often necessary and even advantageous, responsibilities and disadvantages are associated with its use.

Credit is an arrangement to receive cash, goods, or services now and pay for them in the future. **Consumer credit** refers to the use of credit for personal needs (except a home mortgage) by individuals and families, in contrast to credit used for business purposes.

Although Polonius cautioned, "Neither a borrower nor a lender be," using and providing credit have become a way of life for many people and businesses in today's economy. In January, you pay a bill for electricity that you used in December. You write a cheque for $40, a minimum payment on a $300 department store bill. With a bank loan, you purchase a new car. These are all examples of using credit: paying later for goods and services obtained now.

Most consumers have three alternatives in financing current purchases: They can draw on their savings, use their present earnings, or borrow against their expected future income. Each of these alternatives has trade-offs. If you continually deplete your savings, little will be left for emergencies or retirement income. If you spend your current income on luxuries instead of necessities, your well-being will eventually suffer. And if you pledge your future income to make current credit purchases, you will have little or no spendable income in the future.

Consumer credit is based on trust in people's ability and willingness to pay bills when due. It works because people, by and large, are honest and responsible. But how does consumer credit affect our economy, and how is it affected by our economy?

CONSUMER CREDIT IN OUR ECONOMY

Consumer credit dates back to colonial times. While credit was originally a privilege of the affluent, farmers came to use it extensively. No direct finance charges were imposed; instead, the cost of credit was added to the prices of goods. With the advent of the automobile in the early 1900s, installment credit, in which the debt is repaid in equal installments over a specified period of time, exploded on the North American scene.

All economists now recognize consumer credit as a major force in the North American economy. Any forecast or evaluation of the economy includes consumer spending trends and consumer credit as a sustaining force. To paraphrase an old political expression, as the consumer goes, so goes the economy.

The aging of the baby boom generation has added to the growth of consumer credit. This generation currently represents almost 30 percent of the population but holds nearly 60 percent of the outstanding debt. The people in this age group have always been disproportionate users of credit, since consumption is highest as families are formed and homes are purchased and furnished. Thus, while the extensive use of debt by this generation is nothing new, the fact that it has grown rapidly has added to overall debt use.

USES AND MISUSES OF CREDIT

Using credit to purchase goods and services may allow consumers to be more efficient or more productive or to lead more satisfying lives. There are many valid reasons for using credit. A medical emergency may leave a person strapped for funds. A homemaker returning to the workforce may need a car. It may be possible to buy an item now for less money than it will cost later. Borrowing for a higher education is another valid reason. But it probably is not reasonable to borrow for everyday living expenses or to finance a Corvette on credit when a Ford Escort is all your budget allows.

"Shopaholics" and young adults are most vulnerable to misusing credit. Post-secondary students are a prime target for credit card issuers, and issuers make it very easy for students to get credit cards. Tanya Svetlana, a 25-year-old teacher in Victoria, knows this all too well. As a university first-year student, she applied for and got seven credit cards, all bearing at least an 18.9-percent interest rate and a $20 annual fee. Although unemployed, she used the cards freely, buying expensive clothes for herself, extravagant presents for friends and family, and even a one-week vacation in the Bahamas. "It got to a point where I didn't even look at the price tag," she said. By her senior year, Tanya had amassed $9,000 in credit card debt and couldn't make the monthly payments of nearly $200. She eventually turned to her parents to bail her out. "Until my mother sat me down and showed me how much interest I had to pay, I hadn't even given it a thought. I was shocked," Tanya said. "I would have had to pay it off for years."

Using credit increases the amount of money a person can spend to purchase goods and services now. But the trade-off is that it decreases the amount of money that will be available to spend in the future. However, many people expect their incomes to increase and therefore expect to be able to make payments on past credit purchases and still make new purchases.

Here are some questions you should consider before you decide how and when to make a major purchase, for example, a car:

- Do I have the cash I need for the down payment?
- Do I want to use my savings for this purchase?
- Does the purchase fit my budget?
- Could I use the credit I need for this purchase in some better way?
- Could I postpone the purchase?
- What are the opportunity costs of postponing the purchase? (Alternative transportation costs, a possible increase in the price of the car.)
- What are the dollar costs and the psychological costs of using credit? (Interest, other finance charges, being in debt and responsible for making a monthly payment.)

If you decide to use credit, make sure the benefits of making the purchase now (increased efficiency or productivity, a more satisfying life, and so on) outweigh the costs (financial and psychological) of using credit. Thus, credit, when effectively used, can help you have more and enjoy more. When misused, credit can result in default, bankruptcy, and loss of creditworthiness.

> ## DID YOU KNOW ?
>
> The debt-to-income ratio in Canada reached 104 percent in June 2003 and is expected to continue to rise. As debt levels continue to rise faster than personal income, individuals will have a harder time making their debt payments. Only relatively low interest rates in recent years have helped consumers in financial difficulty meet their obligations.
>
> SOURCE: www.canadanewswire.ca/en/releases/archive/February2004/18/c1373.html

ADVANTAGES OF CREDIT

Consumer credit enables people to enjoy goods and services now—a car, a home, an education, help in emergencies—and pay for them through payment plans based on future income.

Credit cards permit the purchase of goods even when funds are low. Customers with previously approved credit may receive other extras, such as advance notice of sales and the right to order by phone or to buy on approval. In addition, many shoppers believe it is easier to return merchandise they have purchased on account. Credit cards also provide shopping convenience and the efficiency of paying for several purchases with one monthly payment.

Credit is more than a substitute for cash. Many of the services it provides are taken for granted. Every time you flick the light switch or telephone a friend, you are using credit.

It is safer to use credit, since charge accounts and credit cards let you shop and travel without carrying a large amount of cash. You need a credit card to make a hotel reservation, rent a car, and shop by phone. You may also use credit cards for identification when cashing cheques, and the use of credit provides you with a record of expenses.

The use of credit cards can provide up to a 30-day "float," the time lag between when you make the purchase and when the lender deducts the balance from your chequing account when the payment is due. This float, offered by many credit card issuers, includes a grace period of 21 to 30 days. During the grace period, no finance charges are assessed on current purchases if the balance is paid in full each month.

Some large corporations, such as General Motors Corporation and Canadian Tire, issue either co-branded or their own Visa and MasterCard and offer rebates on purchases. For example, shopping with a TD Canada Trust/GM Visa allows you to earn 3 percent of every purchase, for a maximum of $1,500 to 3,500, to be applied to the total purchase price or lease down payment of any eligible new GM vehicle. A Canadian Tire Options MasterCard allows you to earn 20 percent more Canadian Tire money per dollar spent at Canadian Tire, and 1 percent earned per dollar spent outside of Canadian Tire. Points can be redeemed instantly at the point of sale in Canadian Tire on all merchandise in the store. Similarly, a Diners/En Route Aeroplan Miles card will give you one Aeroplan mile for each dollar you spend.

Platinum credit cards offered by American Express provide emergency medical evacuation for travellers. In 1994, Nathan Aman of Winnipeg was vacationing in a tiny, isolated town in Brazil. He ate something that made him gravely ill. With no doctor nearby, a friend frantically called Aman's credit card company about its guarantee to arrange emergency medical evacuation and treatment for card users. The company moved fast: It lined up a car to rush Aman to the nearest large town, managed to book a room in a sold-out hotel, and sent a doctor there to make a house call. The physician even accompanied Aman's travel partner, Carlos Piet, to a local pharmacy for medicine. "When we went home to see our doctor, he told us she had saved Nathan's life," recalls Piet. "For the last five years we have been indebted to the company."

Finally, credit indicates stability. The fact that lenders consider you a good risk usually means you are a responsible individual. However, if you do not repay your debts in a timely manner, you will find that credit has many disadvantages.

DISADVANTAGES OF CREDIT

Perhaps the greatest disadvantage of using credit is the temptation to overspend, especially during periods of inflation. It seems easy to buy today and pay tomorrow using cheaper dollars. But continual overspending can lead to serious trouble.

Whether or not credit involves security (something of value to back the loan), failure to repay a loan may result in loss of income, valuable property, and your good reputation. It can even lead to court action and bankruptcy. Misuse of credit can create serious long-term financial problems, damage to family relationships, and a slowing of progress toward financial goals. Therefore, you should approach credit with caution and avoid using it more extensively than your budget permits.

Although credit allows more immediate satisfaction of needs and desires, it does not increase total purchasing power. Credit purchases must be paid for out of future income; therefore, credit ties up the use of future income. Furthermore, if your income does not increase to cover rising costs, your ability to repay credit commitments will diminish. Before buying goods and services on credit, consider whether they will have lasting value, whether they will increase your personal satisfaction during present and future income periods, and whether your current income will continue or increase.

Finally, credit costs money. It is a service for which you must pay. Paying for purchases over a period of time is more costly than paying for them with cash. Purchasing with credit, rather than cash, involves one very obvious trade-off: the fact that it will cost more due to monthly finance charges and the compounding effect of interest on interest.

SUMMARY: ADVANTAGES AND DISADVANTAGES OF CREDIT

The use of credit provides immediate access to goods and services, flexibility in money management, safety and convenience, a cushion in emergencies, a means of increasing resources, and a good credit rating if you pay your debts back in a timely manner. But remember, the use of credit is a two-sided coin. An intelligent decision as to its use demands careful evaluation of your current debt, your future income, the added cost, and the consequences of overspending.

CONCEPT CHECK 5–1

1. How might consumers with credit card debt fare if a cyclical slowdown occurs?
2. What is consumer credit?
3. Why is consumer credit important to our economy?
4. What are the uses and misuses of credit?
5. What are the advantages and disadvantages of credit?

TYPES OF CREDIT

Two basic types of consumer credit exist: closed-end credit and open-end credit. With **closed-end credit**, you pay back one-time loans in a specified period of time with a pre-determined payment schedule. With **open-end credit**, loans are made on a continuous basis and you are billed periodically for at least partial payment. Exhibit 5–1 shows examples of closed-end and open-end credit.

CLOSED-END CREDIT

Closed-end credit is used for a specific purpose and involves a specified amount. Home mortgages and consumer installment loans to purchase an automobile or household furnishings are all types of closed-end credit. Demand loans, where the lender can demand full repayment of the loan at any time, are also classified as closed-end credit.

A written agreement, or contract, lists the repayment terms of closed-end credit for each credit purchase: the number of payments, the payment amount and whether or not the loan rate is floating or fixed. For consumer purchases, a down payment or trade-in may be required, with the remaining cost financed by an installment loan that requires equal periodic payments over a period of time. Demand loans, however, may be interest only for a set period of time. If the

■ OBJECTIVE 2 ┃

Differentiate among various types of credit.

closed-end credit
One-time loans that the borrower pays back in a specified period of time with a pre-determined payment schedule.

open-end credit A line of credit in which loans are made on a continuous basis and the borrower is billed periodically for at least partial payment.

Closed-End Credit	Open-End Credit
• Home mortgages • Automobile loans • Other consumer installment loans • Demand loans	• Credit cards issued by banks (VISA) or stores (Canadian Tire) • Charge cards or Travel and Entertainment cards (Diners' Club) • Lines of credit • Overdraft protection

Exhibit 5–1

Examples of Closed-End and Open-End Credit

loan is secured, the lender will have a legal claim against the security pledged until the loan has been completely paid off.

Exhibit 5–2 shows that consumer credit reached over $258 billion in 2004.

OPEN-END CREDIT

Using a credit card issued by a department store, using a bank credit card (Visa, MasterCard) to make purchases at different stores, charging a meal at a restaurant, and using overdraft protection are examples of open-end or revolving credit. As you will soon see, you do not apply for open-end credit to make a single purchase, as you do with closed-end credit. Rather, you can use open-end credit to make any purchases you wish if you do not exceed your **credit limit**, the maximum dollar amount of credit the lender has made available to you. You may have to pay **interest**, a periodic charge for the use of credit, or other finance charges. Some creditors allow you a grace period to pay a bill in full before you incur any interest charges.

You may have had an appointment with a dentist or chiropractor that you did not pay for until later. Professionals and small businesses often do not demand immediate payment but will charge interest if you do not pay the bill in full within 30 days. *Incidental credit* is a credit arrangement that has no extra costs and no specific repayment plan.

Many retailers use open-end credit. Customers can purchase goods or services up to a fixed dollar limit at any time. Usually, you have the option to pay the bill in full within 30 days without interest charges or to make set monthly installments based on the account balance plus interest.

Many banks extend a **personal line of credit**, a pre-arranged loan for a specified amount that you can use by writing a special cheque. Repayment is made in installments over a set period. The finance charges are based on the amount of credit used during the month and on the outstanding balance.

CREDIT CARDS Credit cards are extremely popular: 83 percent of Canadian households carry one or more credit cards.

One-third of all credit card users generally pay off their balances in full each month. These cardholders are often known as *convenience users*. Others are borrowers; they carry balances beyond the grace period and pay finance charges. Consumers use more than 1.4 billion credit cards to buy clothing, meals, vacations, gasoline, groceries, and other goods and services on credit.

credit limit The dollar amount, which may or may not be borrowed, that a lender makes available to a borrower.

interest A periodic charge for the use of credit.

personal line of credit A prearranged loan from a bank for a maximum specified amount.

Exhibit 5–2

Consumer Credit, Excluding Mortgages, in Billions of Canadian Dollars

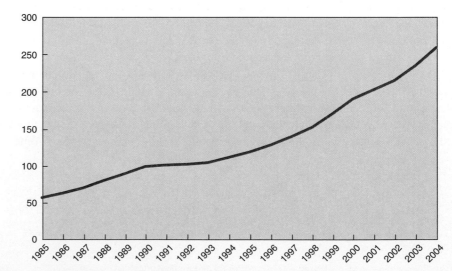

SOURCES: www.economagic.com/em-cgi/data.exe/tmp/65-93-9-219!20050312114054; www.statcan.ca/english/Pgdb/fin20.htm

While cash advances on credit cards can look attractive, remember that interest usually accrues from the moment you accept the cash, and you must also pay a transaction fee. One cash advance could cost you the money you were saving for a birthday gift for that special someone.

Most financial institutions participate in the credit card business, and the vast majority of them are affiliated with Visa International or the Interbank Card Association, which issues MasterCard. The Financial Planning for Life's Situations box on page 136 provides a few helpful hints for choosing a credit card.

Co-branding is the linking of a credit card with a business trade name offering "points" or premiums toward the purchase of a product or service. Co-branding has become increasingly popular since the success of General Motors Corporation's credit card. Co-branded credit cards offer rebates on products and services, such as health clubs, tax preparation services, and gasoline purchases. Banks are realizing that co-branded credit cards help build customer loyalty. *Smart cards*, the ultimate plastic, embedded with a computer chip that can store 500 times the data of a credit card, have been introduced into the market.

A smart card is a plastic card embedded with a computer chip that stores and transacts data between users. The card data is transacted via a reader that is part of a computing system. A single smart card, for example, can be used to buy an airline ticket, store it digitally, and track frequent-flyer miles. In the near future, smart cards will provide a crucial link between the World Wide Web and the physical world. In 1997, Visa Canada and Scotiabank launched Canada's first field trial of a reloadable chip-based Visa Cash card in Barrie, Ontario. The card's "take-up rate" in the first three months of the trial exceeded all expectations, and to date, over 130,000 purchase transactions have been made totalling over CND$380,000 and more than 500 merchants are participating in the trial. In addition, Visa announced a multifunction chip card, which was introduced at Georgian College campuses in Barrie, Orillia, and Owen Sound, Ontario.

DID YOU KNOW ?

Thirty years after its introduction in Canada as Chargex, the Visa brand remains the credit card of choice among Canadians. Approximately 25 million cards are in circulation in Canada, and they can be used to make purchases at more than 20 million locations or to draw down cash at close to 1 million ATMs in more than 150 countries worldwide.
In 2004, Canadians charged a record US$99.5 billion to their Visa cards and conducted about 1 billion transactions.

SOURCES: http://corporate.visa.com/ut/getacard.jsp
www.visa.ca/en/about/mc_products.cfm

PROTECTING YOURSELF AGAINST DEBIT/CREDIT CARD FRAUD

Credit fraud losses, when compared against the total debt owned by consumers on their credit cards, represents less than one-hundredth of 1 percent of the total owed. As a result, fraud losses related to credit may not seem all that terrible. But it *is* terrible for victims of fraud. Though they may be protected financially, they are forced to endure major inconvenience. Many fraud victims are devastated emotionally. The negative effects can linger for years. Moreover, all of us pay the costs of credit card fraud through higher prices, higher interest rates, and increased inconvenience.

How can you protect yourself against credit card fraud? You can take several measures:

- Sign your new card as soon as it arrives.
- Treat your card like money. Store it in a secure place.
- Shred anything with your account number before throwing it away.
- Don't give your card number over the phone or online unless you initiate the call.
- Don't write your card number on a postcard or on the outside of an envelope.

DID YOU KNOW ?

At least 71 percent of Canadians surveyed in January 2005 say they carry a credit card balance, with 30 percent carrying an unpaid balance of $1,000 or more.

SOURCE: www.newswire.ca/en/releases/archive/
January2005/17/c3248.html

Financial Planning for Life's Situations

Should I Lease or Borrow-to-Buy My Car?

The decision whether to buy or lease a car is one which requires a lot of thought and financial consideration. Besides monetary discrepancies, personal preferences also come into the decision process. Many drivers prefer to own their automobiles, while many drivers must lease the cars they cannot presently afford. In addition, many people lease because they would rather switch cars every few years for added variety.

To compare the pure financial cost of buying a car versus that of leasing a car, we will first compute the monthly payment, then the present value of all the cash flows under each scenario.

Borrow-to-buy

Retail price	$26,995
Cost with taxes at 15.025%	$31,951
Down payment	$ 8,000
Loan amount	$23,951
Resale value in 4 years	$13,500
Financing rate (APR, compounded monthly)	5.25%, or 0.4375% per month
Loan term	48 months

The monthly loan payment would be calculated as:

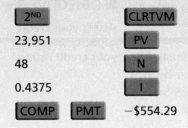

2ND	CLRTVM
23,951	PV
48	N
0.4375	I
COMP PMT	−$554.29

(Refer to the Appendix on the time value of money (at the end of this book) for an explanation of the time value of money calculations and calculator keystrokes. Ensure the I/Y button is set to 1.)

The present value of all cash flows of the purchase decision would equal:

2ND	CLRTVM
554.29+/−	PMT
13,500	FV
0.4375	I
48	N
COMP PMT	$13,003 + $8,000 = $21,003

Leasing

Capital cost reduction ($8,000 ÷ 1.15025) ($8,000 − $6,955 = $1,045 to pay the associated sales tax)	$ 6,955
Net capitalized value ($26,995 − $6,955)	$20,040
Residual value	$13,500
Lease term	48 months
Dealer interest rate (APR, compounded monthly)	5.25%

Lease payments are made at the beginning of the month and would equal:

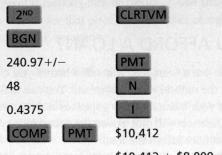

2ND	CLRTVM
BGN	
20,040	PV
13,500+/−	FV
0.4375	I
48	N
COMP PMT	$209.50

Taxes at 15.015 percent (in Quebec) would be added to the lease payment for a total of $240.97.

The present value of all cash flows of the leasing decision would equal:

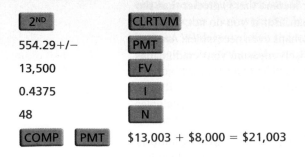

2ND	CLRTVM
BGN	
240.97+/−	PMT
48	N
0.4375	I
COMP PMT	$10,412
	$10,412 + $8,000 = $18,412

There is a small financial advantage to leasing the car, largely the result of the fact that taxes are not paid on the residual value in a lease, whereas taxes on the full listed price are charged if the vehicle is purchased, but are not recovered at time of resale.

For more information concerning the buy-versus-lease decision with respect to automobiles, visit http://strategis. ic.gc.ca/epic/internet/inoca-bc.nsf/en/ca01852e.html.

20 percent of your net (after-tax) income on consumer credit payments. Thus, as Exhibit 5–3 shows, a person making $1,068 per month after taxes should spend no more than $213 on credit payments per month.

The 20 percent estimate is the maximum; however, 15 percent is much better. The 20 percent estimate is based on the average family, with average expenses; it does not take major emergencies into account. If you are just beginning to use credit, you should not consider yourself safe if you are spending 20 percent of your net income on credit payments.

Some financial institutions do not take the actual monthly credit card or personal line of credit payment into account when calculating the debt-payments-to-income ratio. Instead, they factor in the minimum payment on the card or line assuming that the balance had reached the maximum. This implies that even if a card or personal line of credit is not used, the credit potential that it provides is factored into the ratio. For this reason, some financial planners will recommend that an individual carry, at most, two credit cards.

DEBT-TO-EQUITY RATIO   The debt-to-equity ratio is calculated by dividing your total liabilities by your net worth. In calculating this ratio, do not include the value of your home and the amount of its mortgage. If your debt-to-equity ratio is about 1—that is, if your consumer installment debt roughly equals your net worth (not including your home or the mortgage)—you have probably reached the upper limit of debt obligations.

The debt-to-equity ratio for business firms in general ranges between 0.33 and 0.50. The larger this ratio, the riskier the situation for lenders and borrowers. Of course, you can lower the debt-to-equity ratio by paying off debts.

None of the above methods is perfect for everyone; the limits given are only guidelines. Only you, on the basis of the money you earn, your current obligations, and your financial plans for the future, can determine the exact amount of credit you need and can afford. You must be your own credit manager.

Keep in mind that you adversely affect your credit capacity if you co-sign a loan for a friend or a relative.

Visit the Web site
See Personal Financial Planning worksheets under Chapter 5 on the online learning centre at www.mcgrawhill.ca/college/kapoor.

CO-SIGNING A LOAN

What would you do if a friend or a relative asked you to co-sign a loan? Before you give your answer, make sure you understand what co-signing involves.

You are being asked to guarantee a debt. Think carefully before you do. If the borrower doesn't pay the debt, you will have to. Be sure you can afford to pay if you have to and that you want to accept this responsibility.

Exhibit 5–3

How to Calculate Debt-Payments-to-Income Ratio

Spend no more than 20 percent of your net (after-tax) income on credit payments.

Monthly gross income	$1,500
Less:	
All taxes	270
Canada Pension Plan contribution	112
Monthly RRSP contribution	50
Monthly net income	$1,068
Monthly installment credit payments:	
Visa	25
MasterCard	20
Diners/En Route card	15
Education loan	—
Personal bank loan	—
Auto loan	153
Total monthly payments	$ 213
Debt-payments-to-income ratio ($213/$1,068)	19.94%

You may have to pay up to the full amount of the debt if the borrower does not pay. You may also have to pay late fees or collection costs, which increase this amount.

The creditor can use the same collection methods against you that can be used against the borrower, such as suing you, garnishing your wages, and so on. If this debt is ever in default, that fact may become a part of your credit record.[3]

CO-SIGNERS OFTEN PAY   Some studies of certain types of lenders show that as many as three of four co-signers are asked to wholly or partially repay the loan. That statistic should not surprise you. When you are asked to co-sign, you are being asked to take a risk that a professional lender will not take. The lender would not require a co-signer if the borrower met the lender's criteria for making a loan.

If you do co-sign and your friend or relative misses a payment, the lender can collect the entire debt from you immediately without pursuing the borrower first. Also, the amount you owe may increase if the lender decides to sue to collect. If the lender wins the case, it may be able to take your wages and property.

IF YOU DO CO-SIGN   Despite the risks, at times you may decide to co-sign. Perhaps your child needs a first loan or a close friend needs help. Here are a few things to consider before you co-sign:

[1] Be sure you can afford to pay the loan. If you are asked to pay and cannot, you could be sued or your credit rating could be damaged.
[2] Consider that even if you are not asked to repay the debt, your liability for this loan may keep you from getting other credit you want.
[3] Before you pledge property, such as your automobile or furniture, to secure the loan, make sure you understand the consequences. If the borrower defaults, you could lose the property you pledge.
[4] Check your provincial law. Some provinces have laws giving you additional rights as a co-signer.
[5] Request that a copy of overdue-payment notices be sent to you so that you can take action to protect your credit history.

BUILDING AND MAINTAINING YOUR CREDIT RATING

If you apply for a charge account, credit card, car loan, personal loan, or mortgage, your credit experience, or lack of it, will be a major consideration for the creditor. Your credit experience may even affect your ability to get a job or buy life insurance. A good credit rating is a valuable asset that should be nurtured and protected. If you want a good rating, you must use credit with discretion: Limit your borrowing to your capacity to repay, and live up to the terms of your contracts. The quality of your credit rating is entirely up to you.

In reviewing your creditworthiness, a creditor seeks information from a credit bureau. Most creditors rely heavily on credit reports in considering loan applications.

credit bureau A reporting agency that assembles credit and other information about consumers.

CREDIT BUREAUS   **Credit bureaus** collect credit and other information about consumers. There are two main credit bureaus in Canada: Equifax Canada (www.equifax.ca, 1-866-525-0262) and Trans Union of Canada (www.tuc.ca, 1-800-663-9980). In addition, several thousand regional credit bureaus collect credit information about consumers. These firms sell the data to creditors that evaluate credit applications.

WHO PROVIDES DATA TO CREDIT BUREAUS?   Credit bureaus obtain their data from banks, finance companies, merchants, credit card companies, and other creditors.

---

[3] *Cosigning Loan: Facts for Consumers* (Washington, DC: Federal Trade Commission, Bureau of Consumer Protection, January 1988), p. 1.

These sources regularly send reports to credit bureaus containing information about the kinds of credit they extend to customers, the amounts and terms of that credit, and customers' paying habits. Credit bureaus also collect some information from other sources, such as court records.

WHAT IS IN YOUR CREDIT FILES? As the sample credit report in Exhibit 5–4a shows, the credit bureau file contains your name, address, social insurance number, and birthdate. It may also include the following information:

- Your employer and position.
- Your former address.
- Your former employer.
- Your spouse's name, social insurance number, and employer.
- Public records and information.
- Cheques returned for insufficient funds.

Exhibit 5–4a
Sample Credit Report

All credit reports contain your name, address, social insurance number, and birthdate.

SOURCE: Sample Credit Report. Used with permission of Equifax Canada Inc.

EQUIFAX
Consumer Services Canada

Equifax Credit Report

Personal Information

Personal Data

		Other Names	
Name:	RICHARD DENTON	Also Known as: C RICHARD DENTON	
SIN:	899XXX157		
Date of Birth:	1967-04-XX		

CurrentAddress

		Previous Address	
Address:	11TH AVE WILLOW ST TORONTO, ON	Address:	WILLOW ST TORONTO, ON
Date Reported:	2001-12	Date Reported:	2000-12
		Address:	WESTMARR RD REGINA, SK
		Date Reported:	1999-06

Current Employment

		Previous Employment	
Employer:	MCDOUGLAS HAULAGE	Employer:	PRIORITY TRUCKING
Occupation:	SUPERVISOR	Occupation:	DRIVER
		Employer:	MIDTOWN CATERING
		Occupation:	SUPERVISOR

Consumer Statement

Date Reported:	2002-02	Date to Be Removed: 2009-09	
Statement:	CONSUMER STATES SLOW PAYMENTS ON ACCOUNT ARE DUE TO BEING UNEMPLOYED		

Credit Information

This section contains information on each account that you've opened in the past. It is retained in our database for not more than 6 years from the date of last activity.

An installment loan is a fixed-payment loan in which the monthly payment does not change from month to month. Examples of such loans are a mortgage, car loan or a student loan. A revolving loan is a loan in which the balance or amount owed changes from month to month, such as a credit card.

Note: The account numbers have been partially masked for your security.

HUDSONS BAY

Phone Number:	Not Available	High Credit/Credit Limit:	$4,500.00
Account Number:	XXX...890	Payment Amount:	$910.00
Association to Account:	Individual account	Balance:	$6,700.00
Type of Account:	Revolving	Past Due:	$6,700.00
Date Opened:	1999-01	Date of Last Activity:	2002-03
Status:		Date Reported:	2002-05
Months Reviewed:	36		
Payment History:	No payment 30 days late No payment 60 days late No payment 90 days late		
Prior Paying History:	Meaning two payments past due(2002-05) Meaning one payment past due(2002-02) Meaning at least 120 days past due(2001-12)		
Comments:	Subject disputes this account Employee account		

Exhibit 5–4a

(Continued)

Banking Information
Bank Account Information

Date Reported:	2002-03	Account Number:	423156
Financial Institution:	BQE NATIONALE	Account Type:	Savings Account
Date Opened:	2000-01	Balance:	$5,255.00
Telephone Number:	Not Available	# of NSF:	2 NSF IN 2001
Status:			
Comments:	Overdraft		

Public Records and Other Information

This section includes bankruptcies, judgments, voluntary repayment programs and secured loans. Public record information is retained in our database for a maximum of 7 years from the date filed, except in the case of multiple bankruptcies, which results in retention of bankruptcy information for 14 years. P.E.I is an exception to this and displays Public Records for 7 to 10 years and Bankruptcies for 14 years.

Bankruptcy

Date Filed:	1998-03
Name of Court:	MIN OF ATTORNEY GEN
Case Number and Trustee:	456789 ABC ASSOCIATES
Assets:	$1,500.00
Liabilities:	$55,000.00
Type:	Individual
Filer:	Subject
Date Discharged:	1999-12
Comments:	

Legal Item

Date Filed:	1998-12	Legal Item Status:	
Case Number:	321245	Date Verified:	
Court Name:	COLL MTL	Satisfied Date:	1998-12
Amount:	$255.00	Lawyer:	
Plaintiff:	CITY OF TORONTO		
Defendant:	RICHARD DENTON		
Comments:			

Secured Loans

Court Name:	COLL MTL	Date Filed:	1998-09
Industry Class:	Credit Unions	Creditor's Name and Amount:	TRANS CANADA CREDIT 9 ELLIS AVE TOR 3600
Maturity Date:	2002-04		
Comments:			

Collections

The following accounts have been turned over to an agency for collection. Collection information stays on file for a maximum period of 6 years from date of last payment to the creditor, or if none, 5 years from the date assigned to the collection agency.

32145 TIM HORTON

Date Assigned:	1998-05	Account Number:	32415678
Collection Agency:	COLL MTL	Reason:	Unknown
Amount:	$1,260.00	Balance:	$1,260.00
Date of Last Payment:	1998-12	Date Paid:	
Date Verified:			
Comments:			

Credit Inquiries

The following inquiries were generated because the listed company requested a copy of your credit report.

2002-02-15	FIRST DATA RESOURCES (402)777-9729
2001-04-27	FUTURE MORTGAGE CORP (416)783-1808
2001-03-24	BANK OF MONTREAL (Phone Number Not Available)

The following "soft" inquiries were also generated. These soft inquiries do not appear when lenders look at your file; they are only displayed to you and do not affect your credit score.

2002-06-11	EQUIFAX CONS SERV CP (Phone Number Not Available)
2002-06-10	EQUIFAX CONS SERV CP (Phone Number Not Available)
2002-06-07	EQUIFAX CONS SERV CP (Phone Number Not Available)

Investigate your File

Your confirmation number is 0010627347. Please keep this number in your records for future communication with us.

To launch an investigation of information contained in your credit report, you will need to complete a Consumer Credit Report Update Form.

Your credit file may also contain detailed credit information. Each time you buy from a reporting store on credit or take out a loan at a bank, a finance company, or some other reporting creditor, a credit bureau is informed of your account number and the date, amount, terms, and type of credit. As you make payments, your file is updated to show the outstanding balance, the number and amounts of payments past due, and the frequency of 30-, 60-, or 90-day delinquencies. Any suits, judgments, or tax liens against you may appear as well. However, a federal law protects your rights if the information in your credit file is erroneous. Exhibit 5–4b shows the consumer update form; you can use this form to make changes or inquiries to your credit report.

CREDIT BUREAU REGULATION IN CANADA   Besides Alberta, New Brunswick, and the territories, each province has legislation regarding consumer reporting agencies, such as credit bureaus. The principal concerns of these regulations are the protection of consumer privacy with respect to credit information and the consumer's right not to suffer from false credit and personal information.

Exhibit 5–4b
Consumer Update Form

Form used to make changes or inquiries to your credit report.

SOURCE: Consumer Credit Report Update Form. Used with permission of Equifax Canada Inc.

Consumer Credit Report Update Form

Upon review of your personal credit report should you wish to make corrections you will need to complete the form below. **All required fields are in bold.**

Personal Identification

First Name [   ]   Middle Name [   ]
Last Name [   ]   Suffix [▼]

Month Day Year
Date of Birth [▼][▼][   ]

Social insurance Number [   ]–[   ]–[   ]

Current Address
Street Address [   ]
City [   ]   Province [▼]
Postal Code [   ]–[   ]

Previous Address
Street Address [   ]
City [   ]   Province [▼]
Postal Code [   ]–[   ]

Current Employment [   ]

E-mail Address [   ]
Please note: Equifax will not provide the personal information you supply to any non-affiliated third party.

Public Record Items, Bankruptcy and Collections Information

Courthouse Name or Agency   Case # /Account / Plaintiff
[   ]   [   ]

Reason for Investigation
[▼]

If other, please explain
[   ]

Credit Account Information

Company Name   Account Number
[   ]   [   ]

Reason for Investigation
[▼]

If other, please explain
[   ]

credit reporting legislation

Fair Credit Reporting Act—Applicable in British Columbia, Ontario, Nova Scotia, and Prince Edward Island

Credit Reporting Agencies Act—Applicable in Saskatchewan and Newfoundland

Personal Investigations Act—Applicable in Manitoba

Consumer Protection Act—Applicable in Quebec

In addition, **credit reporting legislation** stipulates the nature of the information that can be used in a credit report; a distinction is made between consumer information and personal data. While the former might include such details as your name, address, occupation, income, paying habits, and a number of other pertinent issues, personal information, such as character, reputation, and other characteristics, may not be included in a credit report.

ACCESS TO CREDIT REPORTS

While you have a right to know the contents of your credit bureau file at any time, others may view your file only if you have given written consent or if you have been sent a written notice that your report has been obtained. Generally, you will find that a request for permission to access your report is included in a credit application.

In the event that you do not apply for credit but a request for information is made, the credit bureau must inform you of the request and provide you with the name and address of the requestor.

Though access to information is well legislated and despite the claims to the contrary by credit bureaus, many consumer organizations have expressed concerns that credit bureau files are less than secure. The relatively recent shift to electronic files has created a whole new level of vulnerability in terms of privacy and consumer groups are worried that anyone with a computer and a modem will be able to access confidential files.

TIME LIMITS ON ADVERSE DATA

There are limitations to the inclusion of detrimental information in a credit report. As an example, in Ontario, a first bankruptcy can be reported only within seven years of its occurrence. In the event of a second bankruptcy, however, that information is never deleted from the file. In Saskatchewan, the limit is 14 years for bankruptcy and seven years for any other adverse data. The actual limits may vary slightly from province to province, but the common goal is to limit the credit-damaging effect of past events.

There are also rules in place to protect the consumer's privacy, including restrictions on the situations in which a credit report agency may make a report. Your data can be divulged only in the event of a court order or a legitimate request from a person or organization concerned with extending credit, employment, or insurance to you.

INCORRECT INFORMATION IN YOUR CREDIT FILE

Credit bureaus are required to follow reasonable procedures to ensure that subscribing creditors report information accurately. However, mistakes may occur. Your file may contain erroneous data or records of someone with a name similar to yours. When you notify the credit bureau that you dispute the accuracy of its information, it must reinvestigate and modify or remove inaccurate data. You should give the credit bureau any pertinent data you have concerning an error. If you contest an item on your credit report, the reporting agency must remove the item unless the creditor verifies that the information is accurate (see Exhibit 5–5).

DID YOU KNOW ?

Consumers are given one of the following ratings in their credit report. This ranking can be arrived at in many ways.

RATING	WHAT IT MEANS
R0	Too new to rate; approved but not used
R1	Pays (or paid) within 30 days of payment due date or not over one payment past due
R2	Pays (or paid) in more than 30 days from payment due date, but not more than 60 days, or not more than two payments past due
R3	Pays (or paid) in more than 60 days from payment due date, but not more than 90 days, or not more than three payments past due
R4	Pays (or paid) in more than 90 days from payment due date, but not more than 120 days, or four payments past due
R5	Account is at least 120 days overdue, but is not yet rated "9"
R7	Making regular payments through a special arrangement to settle your debts
R8	Repossession (voluntary or involuntary return of merchandise)
R9	Bad debt; placed for collection; moved without giving a new address

R = Revolving credit (includes line of credits, overdraft, credit cards, charge cards, etc.)

SOURCE: www.equifax.com Used with permission of Equifax Canada Inc.

Date
Your Name
Your Address
Your City, Province, Postal Code

Complaint Department
Name of Credit Reporting Agency
Address
City, Province, Postal Code

Dear Sir or Madam:

I am writing to dispute the following information in my file. The items I dispute are also encircled on the attached copy of the report I received. (Identify item(s) disputed by name of source, such as creditor or tax court, and identify type of item, such as credit account, judgment, etc.)

This item is (inaccurate or incomplete) because (describe what is inaccurate or incomplete and why). I am requesting that the item be deleted (or request another specific change) to correct the information.

Enclosed are copies of (use this sentence if applicable and describe any enclosed documentation, such as payment records, court documents) supporting my position. Please reinvestigate this (these) matter(s) and (delete or correct) the disputed item(s) as soon as possible.

Sincerely,
Your name

Enclosures: (List what you are enclosing)

Exhibit 5–5
Sample Dispute Letter

The law requires credit card companies to correct inaccurate or incomplete information in your credit report.

SOURCE: U.S. Federal Trade Commission, June 1999.

You should review your credit files every few years even if you are not planning to apply for a big loan. Married women and young adults should make sure that all accounts for which they are individually and jointly liable are listed in their credit files. Exhibit 5–6 shows how you can obtain a copy of your credit report.

CREDIT SCORING Credit scoring is a system used by lenders and others to assess the credit risk of prospective borrowers, most often when they apply for credit cards, automobile loans, and, more recently, home mortgages. Information about the applicant and his or her credit history is collected from the credit application and the individual's credit bureau report. Data contained in the credit report is summarized in a credit score, such as a *FICO* score (derived from statistical models developed by Fair Isaac Corporation), which awards points for each factor that helps predict the applicant's creditworthiness. The higher the score, the more likely the individual is to pay his or her bills on time.

FICO scores assign different weightings, or importance, to five categories of data contained in a credit report: payment history, length of credit history, amounts owed, types of credit used, and number of recent applications for credit. However, they do not consider such factors as age, race, colour, religion, nationality, sex, marital status, or employment data.

A strong credit score will enable you to obtain credit faster and at more advantageous rates. So how can you improve your credit score? The answer is simple: by managing your debt responsibly. Establish a credit history as soon as possible, pay your bills on time, limit the amount of credit you use or have access to, and avoid certain types of credit, such as loans from finance companies. Don't apply for too much new credit at one time—frequent applications will have a negative impact on your credit score.

Exhibit 5–6

Obtaining Your Credit Report

Equifax Canada Inc. (www.equifax.ca) is a recognized leader in the consumer and commercial credit reporting and information services industry. Equifax also delivers sophisticated decisioning, data, fraud, and e-commerce solutions to the business community. It is a subsidiary of Atlanta-based Equifax Inc. (NYSE: EFX), a worldwide leader in enabling and securing global commerce.

SOURCE: Your Credit Report. Used with permission of Equifax Canada Inc.

EQUIFAX
Consumer Services Canada

YOUR CREDIT REPORT AS OF 04/09/2001

This Credit Report is available for you to view for 30 days. If you would like a current Credit Report, you may order another from MyEquifax.

Personal Data

John Q. Public
2351 N 85th Ave
Phoenix, AZ 85037

Social Security Number: 022-22-2222
Date of Birth: 1/11/1960

Previous Address(es):
133 Third Avenue
Phoenix, AZ 85037

Employment History

Cendant Hospitality FR

Location: Employment Date: Verified Date:
Phoenix, AZ   2/1/1989   1/3/2001

Previous Employment(s):
SOFTWARE Support Hospitality Franch

Location: Employment Date: Verified Date:
Atlanta, GA   01/3/2001   01/3/2001

Public Records
No bankruptcies on file
No liens on file
No judgements on file
No garnishments on file
No secured loans on file
No marital statuses on file
No financial counseling on file
No foreclosures on file
No non-responsibility entries on file

Collection Accounts
No collections on file.

Credit Information

Company Name	Account Number and Whose Account	Date Opened	Last Activity	Type of Account and Status	High Credit	Items as of Terms	Date Reported Balance	Past Due	Date Reported
Americredit Financial Services	40404XXXX JOINT ACCOUNT	03/1999	03/2000	Installment REPOSSESION	$16933	$430	$9077	$128	2/2000

Prior Paying History
30 days past due 07 times; 60 days past due 05 times; 90+ days past due 03 times

INVOLUNTARY REPOSSESION AUTO

Capital One	412174147128XXXX INDIVIDUAL ACCOUNT	10/1997	01/2001	Revolving PAYS AS AGREED	$777	15	$514		01/2001

Prior Paying History
30 days past due 02 times; 60 days past due 1 times; 90+ days past due 00 times
CREDIT CARD

Credit Inquiries

Companies that Requested your Credit File

04/29/2001 EFX Credit Profile Online
06/30/2001 Automotive
06/16/2000 AR-Associates National Bank

THE FOLLOWING INQUIRIES ARE NOT REPORTED TO BUSINESSES:
PRM - This is a promotional inquiry in which only your name and address were given to a credit grantor so you could be solicited you with an offer such as a credit card. (PRM inquiries remain on file for 12 months.)
AM or AR - These inquiries indicate a periodic review of your credit history by one of your creditors (AM and AR inquiries remain on file for 12 months.)
EQUIFAX, ACIS or UPDATE - These inquiries indicate Equifax's activity in response to your contact with us for either a copy of your credit file or a request for research.
PRM, AM, AR, INQ, EQUIFAX, ACIS and UPDATE inquiries do not show on credit files that businesses receive, only on copies provided to you.

Your confirmation number is 109933931. Please keep this number in your records for future communication with us.

CONCEPT CHECK 5–3

1. What are the general rules for measuring credit capacity?
2. What can happen if you co-sign a loan?
3. What can you do to build and maintain your credit rating?
4. How do you correct erroneous information in your credit file?
5. What is credit scoring?

APPLYING FOR CREDIT

A SCENARIO FROM THE PAST

Marie and Jerome Mangan have a joint income that is more than enough for them to make payments on their dream house, yet they are turned down for a mortgage loan. The lender says Marie might become pregnant and leave her job.

■ OBJECTIVE 4 ■

Describe the information creditors look for when you apply for credit.

In fact, however, it is illegal for a creditor to ask or assume anything about a woman's childbearing plans. It is even illegal to discourage the Mangans from applying for a loan because Marie is of childbearing age. Also, the lender must fully acknowledge Marie's income.

When you are ready to apply for credit, you should know what creditors think is important in deciding whether you are creditworthy. You should also know what they cannot legally consider in their decisions. By law, race, colour, age, gender, marital status, and certain other factors may not be used to discriminate against you in any part of a credit dealing. All individuals should build and protect their own credit histories, using the checklist shown in the Financial Planning for Life's Situations box on page 153.

WHAT CREDITORS LOOK FOR: THE FIVE C'S OF CREDIT MANAGEMENT[4]

When a lender extends credit to its customers, it recognizes that some customers will be unable or unwilling to pay for their purchases. Therefore, lenders must establish policies for determining who will receive credit. Most lenders build their credit policies around the five Cs of credit: character, capacity, capital, collateral, and conditions (see the Financial Planning for Life's Situations box on page 154).

Character is the borrower's attitude toward credit obligations. Most credit managers consider character the most important factor in predicting whether you will make timely payments and ultimately repay your loan.

character The borrower's attitude toward credit obligations.

Capacity is your financial ability to meet credit obligations—that is, to make regular loan payments as scheduled in the credit agreement. Therefore, the lender checks your salary statements and other sources of income, such as dividends and interest. Your other financial obligations and monthly expenses are also considered before credit is approved. Typically, the gross debt service (GDS) ratio is approximately 30 percent and the total debt service (TDS) ratio 40 percent. See Chapter 7 for more information on GDS and TDS ratios.

capacity The borrower's financial ability to meet credit obligations.

Capital refers to your assets or net worth. Generally, the greater your capital, the greater your ability to repay a loan. The lender determines your net worth by requiring you to complete a credit application (see Exhibit 5–7). You must authorize your employer and financial institutions to release information to confirm the claims made in the credit application.

capital The borrower's assets or net worth.

---

[4] Adapted from William M. Pride, Robert J. Hughes, and Jack R. Kapoor, *Business*, 6th ed. (Boston: Houghton Mifflin, 1999), pp. 498–500.

Exhibit 5–9

Steps in the Process of Resolving a Billing Dispute

The Consumers' Association of Canada (www.consumer.ca) offers advice about effective complaining in *Don't Be a Puppet in the Marketplace— Complain Effectively!*

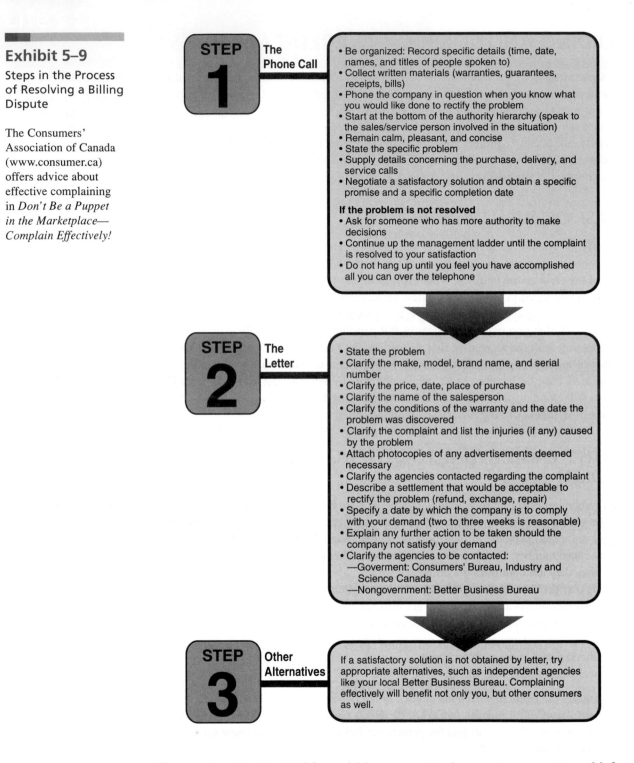

STEP 1 — The Phone Call

- Be organized: Record specific details (time, date, names, and titles of people spoken to)
- Collect written materials (warranties, guarantees, receipts, bills)
- Phone the company in question when you know what you would like done to rectify the problem
- Start at the bottom of the authority hierarchy (speak to the sales/service person involved in the situation)
- Remain calm, pleasant, and concise
- State the specific problem
- Supply details concerning the purchase, delivery, and service calls
- Negotiate a satisfactory solution and obtain a specific promise and a specific completion date

If the problem is not resolved
- Ask for someone who has more authority to make decisions
- Continue up the management ladder until the complaint is resolved to your satisfaction
- Do not hang up until you feel you have accomplished all you can over the telephone

STEP 2 — The Letter

- State the problem
- Clarify the make, model, brand name, and serial number
- Clarify the price, date, place of purchase
- Clarify the name of the salesperson
- Clarify the conditions of the warranty and the date the problem was discovered
- Clarify the complaint and list the injuries (if any) caused by the problem
- Attach photocopies of any advertisements deemed necessary
- Clarify the agencies contacted regarding the complaint
- Describe a settlement that would be acceptable to rectify the problem (refund, exchange, repair)
- Specify a date by which the company is to comply with your demand (two to three weeks is reasonable)
- Explain any further action to be taken should the company not satisfy your demand
- Clarify the agencies to be contacted:
  —Goverment: Consumers' Bureau, Industry and Science Canada
  —Nongovernment: Better Business Bureau

STEP 3 — Other Alternatives

If a satisfactory solution is not obtained by letter, try appropriate alternatives, such as independent agencies like your local Better Business Bureau. Complaining effectively will benefit not only you, but other consumers as well.

To prevent an identity thief from picking up your trash to capture your personal information, tear or shred your charge receipts, copies of credit applications, insurance forms, bank cheques and statements, expired charge cards, and credit offers you get in the mail.

If you believe an unauthorized person has accessed your bank accounts, chequing account, or ATM card, close the accounts immediately. When you open new accounts, insist on password-only access. If your cheques have been stolen or misused, stop payment. If your ATM card has been lost, stolen, or otherwise compromised, cancel the card and get another with a new personal identification number (PIN).

If, after taking all these steps, you are still having identity problems, stay alert to new instances of identity theft. Notify the company or creditor immediately and follow up in writing.

CONCEPT CHECK 5–5

1. What should you do to protect your rights if a billing error occurs?
2. What can you do if your identity is stolen?

SUMMARY OF OBJECTIVES

Objective 1
Define consumer credit and analyze its advantages and disadvantages.

Consumer credit is borrowing money to obtain goods or services by individuals and families for personal needs. Among the advantages of using credit are the ability to purchase goods when needed and pay for them gradually, the ability to deal with financial emergencies, convenience in shopping, and establishment of a credit rating. Disadvantages are that credit costs money, encourages overspending, and ties up future income.

Objective 2
Differentiate among various types of credit.

Closed-end (installment) and open-end (revolving) credit are two types of consumer credit. With closed-end credit, the borrower pays back a one-time loan in a stated period of time and with a specified number of payments. With open-end credit, the borrower is permitted to take loans on a continuous basis and is billed for partial payments periodically.

Objective 3
Assess your credit capacity and build your credit rating.

Two general rules for measuring credit capacity are the debt-payments-to-income ratio and the debt-to-equity ratio. In reviewing your creditworthiness, a creditor seeks information from one of the two national credit bureaus or a regional credit bureau.

Objective 4
Describe the information creditors look for when you apply for credit.

Creditors determine creditworthiness on the basis of the five Cs: character, capacity, capital, collateral, and conditions.

Objective 5
Identify the steps you can take to avoid and correct credit mistakes.

If a billing error occurs on your account, notify the creditor in writing within 60 days. If the dispute is not settled in your favour, you can place your version of it in your credit file. You may also withhold payment on any defective goods or services you have purchased with a credit card as long as you have attempted to resolve the problem with the merchant.

KEY TERMS

capacity 151	**conditions** 152	**credit reporting legislation** 148
capital 151	**consumer credit** 130	**home equity line of credit** 138
character 151	**credit** 130	**interest** 134
closed-end credit 133	**credit bureau** 144	**open-end credit** 133
collateral 152	**credit limit** 134	**personal line of credit** 134

FINANCIAL PLANNING PROBLEMS

1. *Calculating the Amount for a Home Equity Loan.* A few years ago, Misha Azim purchased a home for $100,000. Today, the home is worth $150,000. His remaining mortgage balance is $50,000. Assuming Misha can borrow up to 80 percent of the market value of his home, what is the maximum amount he can borrow? (Obj. 2)

2. *Determining the Debt-Payments-to-Income Ratio.* Louise Gendron's monthly gross income is $2,000. Her employer withholds $400 in federal and provincial income taxes and $160 in Canada Pension Plan contributions per month. Louise contributes $80 per month for her RRSP. Her monthly credit payments for Visa, MasterCard, and Diners/

En Route cards are $35, $30, and $20, respectively. Her monthly payment on an automobile loan is $285. What is Louise's debt-payments-to-income ratio? Is Louise living within her means? Explain. (Obj. 3)

3. *Calculating the Debt-to-Equity Ratio.* Robert Thomas owns a $140,000 townhouse and still has an unpaid mortgage of $110,000. In addition to his mortgage, he has the following liabilities:

Visa	$ 565
MasterCard	480
Diners/En Route card	395
Student loan	920
Personal bank loan	800
Auto loan	4,250
Total	$7,410

Robert's net worth (not including his home) is about $21,000. This equity is in mutual funds, an automobile, a coin collection, furniture, and other personal property. What is Robert's debt-to-equity ratio? Has he reached the upper limit of debt obligations? Explain. (Obj. 3)

4. Calculating Net Worth and Determining a Safe Credit Limit.

   a. Calculate your net worth on the basis of your present assets and liabilities.
   b. Refer to your net worth statement and determine your safe credit limit. Use the debt-payments-to-income and debt-to-equity formulas. (Obj. 3)

5. *Using Credit Cards as Identification.* Dinesh Dani flew to Toronto to attend his brother's wedding. Knowing that his family would be busy, he did not ask anyone to meet him at the airport. Instead, he planned to rent a car to use while in Toronto. He has no nationally known credit cards but is prepared to pay cash for the rental car. The car rental agency refuses to rent him a car, even though it has several cars available. Why do you think Dinesh is unable to rent a car? (Obj. 4)

6. *Determining What Creditors Look for in Approving Loans.* Juan Villavera, a recent college graduate, has accepted a teaching position at Brockville High School. Jim moved to Brockville and applied for a car loan at the Royal Bank. He had never used credit or obtained a loan. The bank notified him that it will not approve the loan unless he has a co-signer. On what basis has the bank denied Juan credit? (Obj. 4)

7. *Analyzing Feasibility of a Loan.* Friedrich Reine has had a student loan, two auto loans, and three credit cards. He has always made timely payments on all obligations. He has a savings account of $2,400 and an annual income of $25,000. His current payments for rent, insurance, and utilities are about $1,100 per month. Friedrich has accumulated $12,800 in an individual retirement account. Friedrich's loan application asks for $10,000 to start up a small restaurant with some friends. Friedrich will not be an active manager; his partner will run the restaurant. Will he get the loan? Explain your answer. (Obj. 4)

FINANCIAL PLANNING ACTIVITIES

1. *Determining Whether or Not to Use Credit.* Survey friends and relatives to determine the process they used in deciding whether or not to use credit to purchase an automobile or a major appliance. What risks and opportunity costs did they consider? (Obj. 1)

2. *Analyzing Opportunity Costs Using Credit.* Think about the last three major purchases you made. (Obj. 1)

   a. Did you pay cash? If so, why?
   b. If you paid cash, what opportunity costs were associated with the purchase?
   c. Did you use credit? If so, why?
   d. What were the financial and psychological opportunity costs of using credit?

3. *Comparing Reasons for Using Credit.* Prepare a list of similarities and differences in the reasons the following individuals might have for using credit. (Obj. 2)

   a. A teenager.
   b. A young adult.
   c. A growing family of four.
   d. A retired couple.

4. *Using the Internet to Obtain Information about Credit Cards.* Choose one of the following organizations and visit its Web site. Then prepare a report that summarizes the information the organization provides. How could this information help you in choosing your credit card?

   a. Canoe Webfin provides information on credit card rates. (www.webfin.com)
   b. The Canadian Broadcasting Corporation provides information on how to regain financial health, uses and misuses of credit cards, and many other related topics. (www. cbc.ca/consumers) (Obj. 2)

5. *Using Your Home Equity to Obtain a Loan.* Visit your local financial institutions, such as banks, trust companies, and credit unions, to obtain information about getting a home equity loan. Compare their requirements for the loan. (Obj. 2)

6. *Determining Whether to Co-sign a Loan.* Talk to a person who has co-signed a loan or to a representative from a financial institution. What experiences did this person have as a co-signer? (Obj. 3)

7. *Determining Net Worth and Credit Capacity.* What changes might take place in your personal net worth during different stages of your life? How might these changes affect your credit capacity? (Obj. 4)

8. *Assessing How Lenders Determine Creditworthiness.* Survey credit representatives, such as bankers, managers of credit departments in retail stores, managers of finance companies, credit union officers, managers of credit bureaus, and loan officers. Ask what procedures they follow in granting or refusing a loan. Write a report of your survey. (Obj. 4)

9. *Analyzing Credit-Related Problems.* Bring to class examples of credit-related problems of individuals or families. Suggest ways in which these problems might be solved. (Obj. 5)

10. *Evaluating Creditors and Seeking Help with Credit-Related Problems.* Compile a list of places a person can call to report dishonest credit practices, get advice and help with credit problems, and check out a creditor's reputation before signing a contract. (Obj. 6)

CREATING A FINANCIAL PLAN

Establishing and Maintaining A Credit Record

The wise use of credit requires a knowledge of the process for establishing credit. In addition, you should develop an awareness of credit reports and the legal rights associated with using consumer credit.

Web Sites for Wise Use of Credit

- The Canadian Broadcasting Corporation provides a great site at **http://cbc.ca/consumers**. Surf here for the latest consumer news and issues, including credit, credit fraud, and strategies for consumer protection.

- The BankruptcyCanada.com site (**www.bankruptcycanada.com**) provides information on all aspects of insolvency,

including business, personal bankruptcy, consumer proposals, and choosing a trustee.

- Information on credit reports is available from Equifax Canada at **www.equifax.ca**.

- Canoe Webfin, at **www.webfin.com**, has a credit quiz that can help you assess your credit situation and find out if it is time to get help.

- Finally, Industry Canada, at **www.strategis.ic.gc.ca/oca**, offers a calculator that helps you determine the real rate you are being charged on your credit cards so you can differentiate between good cards and bad ones.

(Note: Addresses and content of Web sites change, and new sites are created daily. Use search engines to update and locate Web sites for your current financial planning needs.)

LIFE SITUATION CASE

A Hard Lesson on Credit Cards

Parents of post-secondary students, beware: The empty-nest syndrome you're experiencing may end up as empty-wallet syndrome. The moment your kids step on campus, they become highly-sought-after credit card customers. To establish relationships they hope will extend well beyond the post-secondary years, card marketers are offering students everything from free T-shirts to chances to win airline tickets as enticements to sign up. As a result, some students now have heavy credit card debts.

"Students who have no history with credit are being handed it on a silver platter," say Gina Orente, education adviser for a consumer advocacy group in Hull, Quebec. As long as they are over 18, students can get a card without asking mom or dad to co-sign. But when they get into trouble, they often go running

to their folks for help. Huan Kwo did—and then some. Now 21 and in his final year at McGill University in Montreal, Kwo racked up $21,000 in debt on 16 cards over four years. "When I first started, my attitude was: 'I'll get a job after college to pay off all my debt,'" he says. He realized he dug himself into a hole when he couldn't meet the minimum monthly payments. Now he works three part-time jobs, and his parents are helping him pay his tuition and loans.

Questions

1. Why should parents of students be wary?
2. How do credit card marketers entice students?
3. Where do students turn for help when they get into debt trouble?

0·6%

Instant Access

Choosing a Source of Credit:
The Costs of Credit Alternatives

THE PERILS OF TEASER RATES

Remember Huan Kwo from the previous chapter, who racked up $21,000 in credit card debt? Having educated himself on the pitfalls of credit, Kwo now speaks to student groups on the issue. Since card issuers' pitches may be confusing, he and other experts offer this advice: Beware of teaser rates. Credit card marketers may advertise a low annual percentage rate (APR), but it often jumps substantially after three to nine months. One group that is often targeted by marketers is the student population. The incentive offered is a discounted rate for the first few months, which then leaps upward afterwards. Many students, eager for credit and receptive to the notion of "fast cash," will sign up without fully understanding the risks involved.

Because students move often and may not get their mail forwarded quickly, bills can get lost. Then, the students fall prey to late-payment fees. Some cards have late fees as high as $30. If one or two payments are overdue, many cards bump interest rates up as well.

Students are often unaware that rates on cash advances are much higher than those on card balances. Some cards also impose a fee of as much as 4 percent of the advance.

The moral? *Don't ask for extra credit.* Instead, find a card that has a restrictive credit line. Another option: Get a secured credit card. Its credit limit depends on your savings at the issuing bank. Debt advisers say students should hold only a credit card on which they can carry a small balance and a charge card they must pay off monthly. They should pay more than the minimum on credit cards. And they should not charge purchases they can pay for in cash, such as pizza and gas.

If you are a parent, talk to your kids about responsible credit card use. Make sure your kids know a card isn't a way of getting items they can't afford.

QUESTIONS

1 What is Huan Kwo's advice to student groups?

2 Are teaser rates unique to student credit cards?

3 Should you get a secured credit card? Why, or why not?

LEARNING OBJECTIVES

1   Analyze the major sources of consumer credit.

2   Determine the effective cost of borrowing by considering the quoted rate, the number of compounding periods, the timing of the interest payments, and any other service charges.

3   Develop a plan to manage your debts.

4   Evaluate various private and governmental sources that assist consumers with debt problems.

5   Assess the choices in declaring personal bankruptcy.

SOURCES OF CONSUMER CREDIT

Credit costs got you down? Well, you are not alone. Credit costs money; therefore, always weigh the benefits of buying an item on credit now versus waiting until you have saved enough money to pay cash. We can all get into credit difficulties if we do not understand how and when to use credit.

Financial and other institutions, the sources of credit, come in all shapes and sizes. They play an important role in our economy, and they offer a broad range of financial services. By evaluating your credit options, you can reduce your finance charges. You can reconsider your decision to borrow money, discover a less expensive type of loan, or find a lender that charges a lower interest rate.

Before deciding whether to borrow money, ask yourself these three questions: Do I need a loan? Can I afford a loan? Can I qualify for a loan? We discussed the affordability of loans and the qualifications required to obtain loans in the last chapter. Here we wrestle with the first question.

You should avoid credit in two situations. The first situation is one in which you do not need or really want a product that will require financing. Easy access to installment loans or possession of credit cards sometimes encourages consumers to make expensive purchases they later regret. The solution to this problem is simple: After you have selected a product, resist any sales pressure to buy immediately and take a day to think it over.

The second situation is one in which you can afford to pay cash. Consider the trade-offs and opportunity costs involved. Paying cash is almost always cheaper than using credit. In fact, some stores even offer a discount for payment in cash.

■ OBJECTIVE 1 ▮

Analyze the major sources of consumer credit.

WHAT KIND OF LOAN SHOULD YOU SEEK?

As discussed in the last chapter, two types of credit exist: closed-end and open-end credit. Because installment loans may carry a lower interest rate, they are the less expensive credit option for loans that are repaid over a period of many months or years. However, because credit cards usually provide a float period—a certain number of days during which no interest is charged—they represent the cheaper way to make credit purchases that are paid off in a month or two. Also, once you have a credit card, using it is always easier than taking out an installment loan. An alternative to a credit card is a travel and entertainment (T&E) card, such as an American Express or Diners/En Route card. A T&E card usually requires full payment of the balance due each month and does not impose a finance charge, although some cards, such as American Express, offer the option to pay over time. Annual fees on T&E cards can be high.

In seeking an installment loan, you may think first of borrowing from a bank or a credit union. However, less expensive credit sources are available.

INEXPENSIVE LOANS Parents or family members are often the source of the least expensive loans. They may charge you only the interest they would have earned had they not made the loan—as little as the percentage they would have earned on a passbook account. In order to avoid the income tax attribution rules described in Chapter 3, family members should charge a rate equal to or greater than the CRA's prescribed rate, set quarterly. Such loans, however, can complicate family relationships. All loans to or from family members should be in writing and state the interest rate, if any, repayment schedule, and the final payment date.

Also relatively inexpensive is money borrowed on financial assets held by a lending institution—for example, a bank guaranteed investment certificate or the cash value of a whole life insurance policy. The interest rate on such loans typically ranges from 7 to 10 percent. But the trade-off is that your assets are tied up until you have repaid the loan.

MEDIUM-PRICED LOANS Often, you can obtain medium-priced loans from banks, trust companies, and credit unions. New-car loans, for example, may cost 8 to 12 percent; used-car loans and home improvement loans may cost slightly more.

Borrowing from credit unions has several advantages. These institutions provide credit life insurance, are generally sympathetic to borrowers with legitimate payment problems, and provide personalized service. Credit unions can now offer the same range of consumer loans that banks and other financial institutions do. More than 10 million Canadians belong to credit unions, and the number of credit union members has been growing steadily. About 800 credit unions exist in Canada today.

EXPENSIVE LOANS Though convenient to obtain, the most expensive loans available are from finance companies, retailers, and banks through credit cards. Finance companies often lend to people who cannot obtain credit from banks or credit unions. Typically, the interest ranges from 12 to 25 percent, although a card from The Bay or Canadian Tire can cost up to 29 percent. Other organizations, such as Money Mart, provide cheque cashing and related financing services that can cost up to 1 percent per week. By law, no lender in Canada can charge a rate higher than 60 percent per annum. If you are denied credit by a bank or a credit union, you should question your ability to afford the higher rate a loan company charges.

Borrowing from car dealers, appliance stores, department stores, and other retailers is also relatively expensive. The interest rates retailers charge are usually similar to those charged by finance companies, frequently 20 percent or more.

Banks lend funds not only through installment loans but also through cash advances on MasterCard or Visa cards. Credit card co-branding has become increasingly popular with banks and industries. Co-branded credit cards, such as the Yahoo! Visa card, will make shopping over the Internet easier and faster. Yahoo! will designate Visa as its "preferred card" and will promote Visa throughout its Web sites and to online merchants worldwide.

One type of loan from finance companies is currently less expensive than most other credit. Loans of this kind, which often can be obtained at a rate of under 8 percent, are available from the finance companies of major automakers. But a car dealer that offers you such a rate may be less willing to discount the price of the car or throw in free options.

CONCEPT CHECK 6–1

1. Why do students fall prey to late-payment fees?
2. What are the major sources of consumer credit?
3. What are some advantages and disadvantages of securing a loan from a credit union? from a finance company?

THE COST OF CREDIT

If you are thinking of borrowing money or opening a credit account, your first step should be to figure out how much it will cost you and whether you can afford it. Then, you should shop for the best terms. Two key concepts that you should remember are the finance charge and the annual percentage rate.

THE EFFECTIVE COST OF BORROWING

Credit costs vary. The effective annual interest rate charged on a loan will depend upon the quoted annual percentage rate, how frequently interest is compounded, whether interest is charged on a discount basis (upfront) and whether any other charges are incurred, such as service charges, credit-related insurance premiums, or appraisal fees.

The **annual percentage rate** (APR) is the yearly interest rate quoted by the financial institution on a loan. However, interest may be charged more frequently than once a year—for example, on a monthly basis. In this case, we say that the loan is compounded monthly. The higher the compounding frequency, the higher is the effective annual rate (EAR) of the loan, as demonstrated in the table below. Effective annual rates were discussed in Chapter 4, The Banking Services of Financial Institutions, on page 115. Financial institutions are obliged to disclose both the APR and the EAR to the borrower at the time the loan contract is signed.

Let's look at an example. Suppose you wish to borrow $100 for a year and your bank quotes you an annual interest rate of 6 percent, compounded semi-annually. The quoted rate of 6 percent is the APR. Compounding semi-annually means that the bank will charge you 3 percent interest on the loan after six months (6 percent ÷ 2) and another 3 percent after the remaining six months. When you repay the loan after one year, you will owe $3 of interest for the first semi-annual period ($100 × 3 percent) and, as this interest is not actually paid but added to the amount you owe, the interest charged for the second six months of the year will be $3.09 ($103 × 3 percent). The total interest charge will equal $6.09 ($3 + $3.09) and the effective annual interest rate of your loan will be 6.09 percent ($6.09 ÷ $100 × 100).

We can calculate the effective annual interest rate on the loan using the following formula, where m equals the number of times a year the interest is compounded:

$$EAR = (1 + APR/m)^m - 1$$

$$EAR = (1 + 0.06/2)^2 - 1 = 0.0609 \times 100 = 6.09\%$$

■ OBJECTIVE 2 ■

Determine the effective cost of borrowing by considering the quoted rate, the number of compounding periods, the timing of the interest payments, and any other service charges.

annual percentage rate (APR) The yearly interest rate quoted by a financial institution on a loan. The APR may be compounded more frequently than once a year, in which case the effective annual rate on the loan will be higher than the APR.

	EAR IF COMPOUNDING FREQUENCY IS			
Quoted APR	**Semi-annual**	**Monthly**	**Weekly**	**Daily**
5	5.0625	5.1162	5.1246	5.1267
6	6.0900	6.1678	6.1800	6.1831
7	7.1225	7.2290	7.2458	7.2501
8	8.1600	8.3000	8.3220	8.3278
9	9.2025	9.3807	9.4089	9.4162
10	10.2500	10.4713	10.5065	10.5156

If the financial institution charges interest upfront, we say that the loan is made on a discount basis. Interest that is prepaid will increase the effective annual cost of the loan. For example, assume that a bank quotes a loan rate of 5 percent, compounded monthly. We can see from the above table that the effective annual rate charged on the loan would be 5.1162 percent. This would be the effective annual cost of the loan if the interest and principal are repaid after one year. However, if you pay the $5.1162 in interest up front, the actual dollar amount you will be able to use over the year will equal $94.8838. This means that the effective annual cost of borrowing will be 5.3921 percent ($5.1162 ÷ $94.8838 × 100). Discounting interest results in a higher annual cost of borrowing.

What if the financial institution charges you an upfront administrative fee of $5 on your loan, but interest is repaid after one year? At an APR of 5 percent, compounded monthly, the effective annual interest rate on the loan would be 5.1162 percent. However, the $5 fee would reduce the funds available to you over the year. You would be paying $5.1162 for the use of $95 ($100 less $5). As is the case with discount interest, the administrative fee would increase the effective annual cost of your loan, this time to 5.3855 percent ($5.1162 ÷ $95 × 100).

TACKLING THE TRADE-OFFS

When you choose your financing, there are trade-offs between the features you prefer (term, size of payments, fixed or variable interest, or payment plan) and the cost of your loan. Here are some of the major trade-offs you should consider.

TERM VERSUS INTEREST COSTS   Many people choose longer-term financing because they want smaller monthly payments. But the longer the term for a loan at a given interest rate, the greater is the amount you must pay in interest charges. Consider the following analysis of the relationship between the term and interest costs.

Even when you understand the terms a creditor is offering, it's easy to underestimate the difference in dollars that different terms can make. Suppose you're buying a $7,500 used car. You put $1,500 down, and you need to borrow $6,000. Compare the following three credit arrangements:

	APR, Compounded Monthly	Term of Loan	Monthly Payment	Total Amount Repaid	Total Interest Cost
Creditor A	14%	36 months	$205.07	$7,382.52	$1,382.52
Creditor B	14%	48 months	$163.96	$7,870.08	$1,870.08
Creditor C	15%	48 months	$166.98	$8,015.04	$2,015.04

How do these choices compare? The answer depends partly on what you need. The lowest-cost loan is available from creditor A. If you are looking for lower monthly payments, you could repay the loan over a longer period of time. However, you would have to pay more in total costs. A loan from creditor B—also at a 14 percent APR, but for four years—would add about $488 to your finance charge.

If that four-year loan were available only from creditor C, the APR of 15 percent would add another $145 to your total interest cost. Other terms, such as the size of the down payment, will also make a difference. Be sure to look at all the terms before you make your choice.

LENDER RISK VERSUS INTEREST RATE   You may prefer financing that requires low fixed payments with a large final payment or only a minimum of upfront cash. But both of these requirements can increase your cost of borrowing because they create more risk for your lender.

If you want to minimize your borrowing costs, you may need to accept conditions that reduce your lender's risk. Here are a few possibilities.

VARIABLE INTEREST RATE   A variable interest rate is based on fluctuating rates in the banking system, such as the prime rate. With this type of loan, you share the interest rate

Financial Planning for Life's Situations

Bank of Canada Rate and Credit Card interest Rates

In Canada, from 1980 to 1995, credit card interest rates generally moved up and down with the Bank rate, with a time lag. However, this trend has not been evident in the past few years. Generally, the interest rates on standard cards have not moved along with the Bank rate since 1995, and low-rate cards have not followed suit since 1999. Moreover, retail credit card rates have not changed in the last 18 years (see chart below).

THE BANK OF CANADA RATE AND CREDIT CARD INTEREST RATES

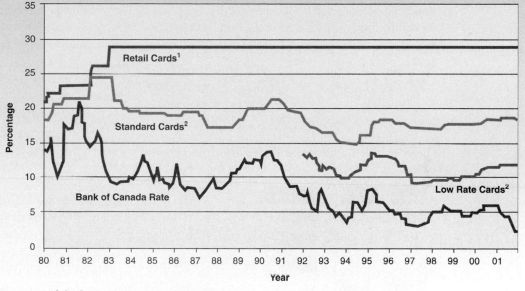

[1] Based on the average of the Sears card and the Hudson's Bay card
[2] Based on the average of the six major banks (for purchases)

SOURCE: Federal Consumer Agency of Canada (FCAC), "Credit Cards and You." Quarterly Credit Card Cost Report, December 2001. www.fcac-acfc.gc.ca.

---

risks with the lender. Therefore, the lender may offer you a lower initial interest rate than it would with a fixed-rate loan.

A SECURED LOAN If you pledge property or other assets as collateral, you'll probably receive a lower interest rate on your loan.

UPFRONT CASH Many lenders believe you have a higher stake in repaying a loan if you pay cash for a large portion of what you are financing. Doing so may give you a better chance of getting the other terms you want. Of course, by making a large down payment, you forgo interest that you might earn in a savings account.

A SHORTER TERM As you have learned, the shorter the period of time for which you borrow, the smaller the chance that something will prevent you from repaying and the lower the risk to the lender. Therefore, you may be able to borrow at a lower interest rate if you accept a shorter-term loan, but your payments will be higher.

In the next section, you will see how the above-mentioned trade-offs can affect the cost of closed-end and open-end credit.

Visit the Web site
See Personal Financial Planning worksheets under Chapter 6 on the online learning centre at www.mcgrawhill.ca/ college/kapoor.

CALCULATING YOUR LOAN PAYMENTS

In this section, we will examine how your loan payments are determined for two typical forms of consumer credit—a fixed-rate installment loan and a floating rate personal line of credit—and will highlight the advantages and disadvantages of each.

FIXED-RATE INSTALLMENT LOAN   Peter MacLellan wants to buy a used car. The car's price is listed as $10,000 and a sales tax of 15 percent will apply, bringing the total cost of the car to $11,500 ($10,000 × 1.15). Peter has $6,500 for a down payment and has approached his bank for a $5,000 loan to be repaid in equal monthly installments over one year. The bank has quoted a fixed rate of 9 percent, compounded monthly, meaning that Peter's monthly interest rate will be 0.75 percent (9 percent ÷ 12). The monthly payment on Peter's car loan will be fixed over the term of the loan and can be calculated as follows (Refer to the Time Value of Money discussion in Chapter 1 and the formula given in Exhibit A-4 on page 464):

$$\$5,000 = PMT \frac{[1 - (1 \div 1.0075)^{12}]}{0.0075}$$

$$\$5,000 = PMT\,[11.4349]$$

$$PMT = \$5,000 \div 11.4349 = \$437.26$$

or by using the BAII calculator as follows (remember to set the I/Y button to 1, as explained in Chapter1):

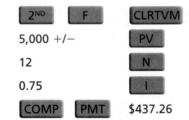

Peter's loan will be amortized over 12 months; this means that the monthly payments he makes will gradually reduce the loan balance. Each payment will be composed of interest and principal repayments, with the interest component higher in the earlier payments and reducing over time. As his loan approaches maturity, more of the monthly payment will be used to pay off the principal than to pay the interest. See the following loan amortization chart.

Month	Beginning Loan Balance	Monthly Payment	Interest Component	Principal Component	Ending Loan Balance
1	$5,000.00	$437.26	$37.50	$399.76	$4,600.24
2	$4,600.24	$437.26	$34.50	$402.76	$4,197.49
3	$4,197.49	$437.26	$31.48	$405.78	$3,791.71
4	$3,791.79	$437.26	$28.44	$408.82	$3,382.89
5	$3,382.89	$437.26	$25.37	$411.89	$2,971.01
6	$2,971.01	$437.26	$22.28	$414.98	$2,556.03
7	$2,556.03	$437.26	$19.17	$418.09	$2,137.94
8	$2,137.94	$437.26	$16.03	$421.22	$1,716.72
9	$1,761.72	$437.26	$12.88	$424.38	$1,292.34
10	$1,292.34	$437.26	$ 9.69	$427.56	$ 864.77
11	$ 864.77	$437.26	$ 6.49	$430.77	$ 434.00
12	$ 434.00	$437.26	$ 3.26	$434.00	$ 0

Installment loans impose financial responsibility as they are designed to pay off the loan over a pre-determined period of time. Each payment represents a blend of interest and principal. With blended payments, interest owing is satisfied first and the remaining portion of the payment is applied to the principal.

FLOATING RATE PERSONAL LINE OF CREDIT Had Peter made arrangements with his bank to set up a personal line of credit, he could have drawn down the required $5,000 loan when he purchased the car. Lines of credit usually charge a variable interest rate tied to the lender's prime rate. Interest is compounded daily. In view of Peter's credit risk, let's assume that his bank charges him a rate of prime plus 3 percent. The line of credit payment may be interest only, but borrowers are often required to repay a minimum 3 to 5 percent of the outstanding loan balance on a periodic basis. We will assume that Peter must pay at least 5 percent of the outstanding loan balance each month.

If the prime rate is 6 percent and he pays 3 percent above prime, then the daily interest rate charged on Peter's line of credit would be 0.0246575 percent (9 percent ÷ 365). Assuming 30 days in each month, his first three loan payments would be:

Month	Beginning Loan Balance	Interest Charge	Principal Reduction	Total Payment	Ending Loan Balance
1	$5,000.00	$36.99*	$250.00	$286.99	$4,750.00
2	$4,750.00	$35.14	$237.50	$272.64	$4,512.50
3	$4,512.50	$33.76	$225.63	$259.39	$4,250.03

*Calculated as: $5,000 × 0.000246575 × 30

If the prime rate rises to 7 percent, the interest rate on Peter's loan would rise to 10 percent (7 percent + 3 percent). His daily interest rate would be 0.0273973 percent (10 percent ÷ 365) and his fourth loan payment would be:

Month	Beginning Loan Balance	Interest Charge	Principal Reduction	Total Payment	Ending Loan Balance
4	$4,250.03	$34.93	$212.50	$247.43	$4,037.53

Notice that Peter's total loan payment drops to $247.43 from $259.39 because he is required to pay a lesser amount against the principal each month. However, the interest component of his fourth payment has risen because the bank's prime rate rose 1 percent. Peter's loan payments are not fixed and are subject to the risk that interest rates could rise (unless he has the option to lock in the current rate). However, if interest rates fall, the interest component of his total payment would fall as well. In this way, a floating interest rate can be either an advantage or a disadvantage to the borrower.

The principal disadvantage of using an interest only line of credit, or one with a very low minimum principal repayment, is the considerably longer time it takes to repay the loan compared to a traditional consumer installment loan. If Peter only makes the minimum required principal payment each month, it will take him almost eight years to reimburse the principal of $5,000 on his line of credit!

FINANCIAL PLANNING CALCULATIONS

When you apply to a financial institution for a consumer installment loan, the loan officer can provide you with a complete amortization schedule, as described above. However, there is a shorter way to determine your loan balance at any point in time, or what the interest and principal components of any payment might be.

The balance of a loan will equal the present value of the remaining payments. Referring to Peter's automobile loan, what would be his loan balance after three payments?

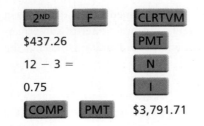

$437.26

12 − 3 =

0.75

$3,791.71

Once we have determined his loan balance at any point in time, we can then calculate the interest and principal components of the following payment, in this instance the fourth payment:

| Interest | $3,791.71 × 0.75 ÷ 100 | = $ 28.44 |
| Principal | $ 437.26 − $28.44 | = $408.82 |

adjusted balance method The assessment of finance charges after payments made during the billing period have been subtracted.

previous balance method A method of computing finance charges that gives no credit for payments made during the billing period.

average daily balance method A method of computing finance charges that uses a weighted average of the account balance throughout the current billing period.

COST OF CARRYING CREDIT CARD BALANCES Open-end credit includes not only personal lines of credit, but also credit cards, store cards, and overdraft protection. During the month, all purchases made with a credit card are tallied and appear on the bill issued on the card's billing date. This delay in billing can be viewed as a period during which you benefit from an interest-free loan. In addition, creditors must tell you when finance charges on your credit account begin so that you know how much time you have to pay your bills before a finance charge is added. Some creditors, for example, give you a 20- to 25-day grace period, from the billing date, to pay your balance in full before imposing a finance charge. But in most cases, the grace period applies only if you have no outstanding balance on your card.

When you do not pay off the balance on your bank or store credit card each month, an interest charged will appear on your following monthly statement. Creditors use various methods to calculate the balance on which they will apply interest charges. Some creditors add interest after subtracting payments made during the billing period; this is called the **adjusted balance method**. Other creditors give you no credit for payments made during the billing period; this is called the **previous balance method**. Under the third—and the fairest—method, the **average daily balance method**, creditors add your balances for each day in the billing period and then divide by the number of days in the period. The average daily balance may include or exclude new purchases during the billing period.

Here is how these different methods of calculating the interest on unpaid credit card balances affects the cost of credit:

	Average Daily Balance (*including* new purchases)	Average Daily Balance (*excluding* new purchases)
Monthly rate	1½%	1½%
APR	18%	18%
Previous balance	$400	$400
New purchases	$50 on 18th day	$50 on 18th day
Payments	$300 on 15th day (new balance = $100)	$300 on 15th day (new balance = $100)
Average daily balance	$270*	$250**
Finance charge	$4.05 (1½% × $270)	$3.75 (1½% × $250)

*To figure average daily balance (*including* new purchases):
($400 × 15 days) + ($100 × 3 days) + ($150 × 12 days) ÷ 30 days
= ($6,000 + $300 + $1,800) ÷ 30 or, $8,100 ÷ 30 days = $270
**To figure average daily balance (*excluding* new purchases):
[($400 × 15 days) + ($100 × 15 days)] ÷ 30 days = $7,500 ÷ 30 days = $250

	Adjusted Balance	Previous Balance
Monthly rate	1½%	1½%
APR	18%	18%
Previous balance	$400	$400
Payments	$300	$300
Average daily balance	N/A	N/A
Finance charge	$1.50 (1½% × $100)	$6 (1½% × $400)

As the example shows, the interest charge varies for the same pattern of purchases and payments. Therefore, you only benefit from an interest-free period on your card if you pay the bill in full every month.

COST OF CREDIT AND EXPECTED INFLATION As you have seen, interest rates dictate when you must pay future dollars to receive current dollars. Borrowers and lenders, however, are less concerned about dollars, present or future, than about the goods and services those dollars can buy—that is, their purchasing power.

Inflation erodes the purchasing power of money. Each percentage point increase in inflation means a decrease of approximately 1 percent in the quantity of goods and services you can purchase with a given quantity of dollars. As a result, lenders, seeking to protect their purchasing power, add the expected rate of inflation to the interest rate they charge. You are willing to pay this higher rate because you expect inflation to enable you to repay the loan with cheaper dollars.

For example, if a lender expects a 4-percent inflation rate for the coming year and desires an 8-percent return on its loan, it will probably charge you a 12-percent nominal or stated rate (a 4-percent inflation premium plus an 8-percent "real" rate).

For another example, assume you borrowed $1,000 from your relative at the bargain rate of 5 percent for one year. If the inflation rate was 4 percent during that year, your relative's real rate of return was only 1 percent (5 percent stated interest minus 4 percent inflation rate) and your "real" cost was not $50 but only $10 ($50 minus $40 inflation premium).

AVOID THE MINIMUM MONTHLY PAYMENT TRAP The "minimum monthly payment" is the smallest amount you can pay and still be a cardholder in good standing. Banks often encourage you to make the minimum payment, such as 3–5 percent of your outstanding balance or a minimum of $10. Some statements refer to the minimum as the "cardholder amount due." But that is not the total amount you owe.

Consider the following examples. In each example, the minimum payment is based on $\frac{1}{36}$ of the outstanding balance or $20, whichever is greater.

Example 1 You are buying new books for your courses. If you spend $500 on textbooks using a credit card charging 19.8 percent interest and make only the minimum payment, it will take you more than 2½ years to pay off the loan, adding $150 in interest charges to the cost of your purchase. The same purchase on a credit card charging 12 percent interest will cost only $78 extra.

Example 2 You purchase a $2,000 stereo system using a credit card with 19 percent interest and a 2-percent minimum payment. If you pay just the minimum every month, it will take you 265 months—more than 22 years—to pay off the debt and will cost you nearly $4,800 in interest payments. Doubling the amount paid each month to 4 percent of the balance owed would allow you to shorten the payment time to 88 months from 265 months—or 7 years as opposed to 22 years—and save you about $3,680.

Many bank cards offer added value through enhancements, such as discounts on merchandise, rebates on purchases, travel and accident insurance, frequent-flyer points, emergency card replacement, donations to non-profit groups, and 24-hour customer service. The trick to finding the bank card that's right for you is to balance the benefits with the right price. You should consider interest rates and fees on the basis of how you plan to use the card.

- *Annual fee.* If you plan to pay your balance in full each month, shop for a card that has a grace period and carries no annual fee, or a low annual fee, even if the trade-off is a higher interest rate. You plan to pay little or no interest anyway. Gold or platinum cards often charge $100 or more in annual fees.
- *Low rates.* If you prefer to stretch out repayment, aim for a card with a lower interest rate. In general, lower-interest-rate cards tend to have tougher credit approval requirements, may not offer a grace period, and often have slightly higher annual fees. But if you qualify, the money you save on interest is likely to offset a higher fee.
- *Variable rates.* Some credit cards promote variable interest rates tied to the prime rate. You may benefit from lower interest rates when the rate is low, but remember that when the rate rises, you'll pay the higher rate even on purchases you've already made.
- *Grace period.* Not all credit cards offer a grace period. When you use such a card, the bank begins charging you interest on the day you make the purchase or the day the purchase is recorded on your account. Try to pay off your balance in full each month to maintain the grace period and avoid paying interest.

- *Other fees.* Most credit cards charge a special fee when you take a cash advance. Usually, the fee is about 2 or 3 percent of the amount borrowed.

Many banks impose late fees even when payment arrives a day after the due date. Some banks charge a set fee, such as $25 or $30, while others charge a percentage, such as 5 percent, of the minimum payment due.

Most cards assess an over-credit-limit fee. For instance, if you charge $400 over your limit and the penalty is 5 percent, you will pay a $20 fee in addition to interest charges. A few companies charge lost-card replacement fees, usually $5 or $10.

Some credit card issuers allow you to skip a payment without a penalty. While this sounds like the bank is giving you a break, you will be charged interest during this period and will owe more in interest than you did before.

Once you decide on the right combination of features and price, you can begin shopping. Federal law requires that every mail solicitation, "take one" application, and application brochure carry a special box listing the interest rate, annual fee, length of grace period, and other fees. This will allow you to easily compare the costs of different card plans.

SOURCES: American Bankers Association; *Understanding Credit Card Costs* (San Francisco: Consumer Action, March 1994); *Choosing and Using Credit Cards* (Washington, DC: Federal Trade Commission, January 1999). © American Bankers Association. Reprinted with permission.

Example 3 You charge $2,000 in tuition and fees on a credit card charging 18.5 percent interest. If you pay off the balance by making the minimum payment each month, it will take you more than 11 years to repay the debt. By the time you have paid off the loan, you will have spent an extra $1,934 in interest alone—almost the actual cost of your tuition and fees. Again, to be prudent, pay off the balance as quickly as possible.

See the Financial Planning for Life's Situations feature above for guidance in choosing the card that is right for you.

CREDIT INSURANCE

credit insurance Any type of insurance that ensures repayment of a loan in the event the borrower is unable to repay it.

Credit insurance ensures the repayment of your loan in the event of death, disability, or loss of property. The lender is named the beneficiary and directly receives any payments made on submitted claims.

There are three types of credit insurance: credit life, credit accident and health, and credit property. The most commonly purchased type of credit insurance is credit life insurance, which provides for the repayment of the loan if the borrower dies. According to many consumer organizations, most borrowers don't need credit life insurance. Those who don't have life insurance can buy term life insurance for less. Term life insurance is discussed in Chapter 9.

Credit accident and health insurance, also called *credit disability insurance*, repays your loan in the event of a loss of income due to illness or injury. Credit property insurance provides coverage for personal property purchased with a loan. It may also insure collateral property, such as a car or furniture. However, premiums for such coverage are quite high and the coverage may be substandard.

CONCEPT CHECK 6–2

1. Distinguish between the APR and the EAR.
2. What can you learn from a loan amortization schedule?
3. Distinguish among the adjusted balance, previous balance, and average daily balance methods of calculating the cost of open-end credit.

MANAGING YOUR DEBTS

A sudden illness or the loss of your job may make it impossible for you to pay your bills on time. If you find you cannot make your payments, contact your creditors at once and try to work out a modified payment plan with them. If you have paid your bills promptly in the past, they may be willing to work with you. Do not wait until your account is turned over to a debt collector. At that point, the creditor has given up on you.

OBJECTIVE 3

Develop a plan to manage your debts.

Automobile loans present special problems. Most automobile financing agreements permit your creditor to repossess your car anytime you are in default on your payments. No advance notice is required. If your car is repossessed and sold, you will still owe the difference between the selling price and the unpaid debt, plus any legal, towing, and storage charges. Try to solve the problem with your creditor when you realize you will not be able to meet your payments. It may be better to sell the car yourself and pay off your debt than to incur the added costs of repossession.

If you are having trouble paying your bills, you may be tempted to turn to a company that claims to offer assistance in solving debt problems. Such companies may offer debt consolidation loans, debt counselling, or debt reorganization plans that are "guaranteed" to stop creditors' collection efforts. Before signing with such a company, investigate it. Be sure you understand what services the company provides and what they will cost you. Do not rely on verbal promises that do not appear in your contract. Also, check with the Better Business Bureau and your provincial or local consumer protection office. It may be able to tell you whether other consumers have registered complaints about the company.

WARNING SIGNS OF DEBT PROBLEMS

Jerome Olsen, in his early 30s, has a steady job with an annual income of $40,000. Jerome, his wife, and their two children enjoy a comfortable life. A new car is parked in the driveway of their home, which is furnished with such modern conveniences as a new microwave oven, a new freezer, an electric washer and dryer, a DVD player, and a large-screen colour television set.

However, Jerome Olsen is in debt. He is drowning in a sea of bills, with most of his income tied up in repaying debts. Foreclosure proceedings on his home have been instituted, and several

DID YOU KNOW ?

The Royal Bank of Canada offers eight booklets on personal money management as part of its *Your Money Matters* series. Call 1-800-769-2511 or visit your local branch office for your free copies.

stores have court orders to repossess practically every major appliance in it. His current car payment is overdue, and three charge accounts at local stores are several months delinquent.

This case is neither exaggerated nor isolated. Unfortunately, a large number of people are in the same floundering state. These people's problem is immaturity. Mature consumers have certain information; they demonstrate self-discipline, control their impulses, and use sound judgment; they accept responsibility for money management; and they are able to postpone and govern expenditures when overextension of credit appears likely.

Referring to overindebtedness as one of the nation's main family financial problems, an expert on consumer affairs lists the following as frequent reasons for indebtedness:[1]

[1] *Emotional problems*, such as the need for instant gratification, as in the case of a man who can't resist buying a costly suit or a woman who impulsively purchases an expensive dress in a trendy department store.

[2] *The use of money to punish*, such as a husband who buys a new car without consulting his wife, who, in turn, buys a diamond watch to get even.

[3] *The expectation of instant comfort* among those who assume that by use of the installment plan, they can immediately have the possessions their parents acquired after years of work.

[4] *Keeping up with the Joneses*, which is more apparent than ever, not only among prosperous families but also among limited-income families.

[5] *Overindulgence of children*, often because of the parents' own emotional needs, competition with each other, or inadequate communication regarding expenditures for the children.

[6] *Misunderstanding or lack of communication among family members.* For example, a salesperson visited a Calgary family to sell them an expensive freezer. Although the freezer was beyond the means of this already overindebted family and too large for their needs anyway, the husband thought his wife wanted it. Not until later, in an interview with a debt counsellor, did the wife relate her concern when she signed the contract; she had wanted her husband to say no.

[7] *The amount of the finance charges*, which can push a family over the edge of their ability to pay, especially when they borrow from one company to pay another and these charges pyramid.

Exhibit 6–1 lists some danger signals of potential debt problems.

THE SERIOUS CONSEQUENCES OF DEBT

Just as the causes of indebtedness vary, so too does a mixture of other personal and family problems that frequently result from overextension of credit.

Loss of a job because of garnishment proceedings may occur in a family that has a disproportionate amount of income tied up in debts. Another possibility is that such a family is forced to neglect vital areas. In the frantic effort to rob Peter to pay Paul, skimping may seriously affect the family's health and neglect the educational needs of children. Excessive indebtedness may also result in heavy drinking, neglect of children, marital difficulties, and drug abuse. But help is available to those debtors who seek it.

See the Financial Planning for Life's Situations feature on page 173 to find out where you can obtain free credit information on the Internet.

---

[1] Judy Hammond, "Consumer Credit Counselors Say Debt Recovery Can Take Three to Five Years," *Knight-Ridder/Tribune Business News*, February 16, 1999.

Whether you're developing a plan for reaching your financial goals or searching for a low-interest credit card, you can look to the Internet for a world of free information. Many Web sites provide interactive worksheets that allow you to plug in personal information and obtain customized reports. Here are some suggestions.

FinanCenter, at www.financenter.com, provides nifty payment calculators that help you figure out the actual dollars paid in interest over the period of a credit card debt or the maximum amount you should borrow at your current income. If your payments have been piling up, take a deep breath before travelling here.

Canoe Webfin, at www.webfin.com, provides you with everything you need to successfully manage your personal finances. News and reference materials allow you stay up to date on money matters. You can also use analytical tools to track your investments and plan your finances, and there are discussion groups and real-time chats with experts.

Industry Canada's Java calculator at http://strategis.ic.gc.ca/SSG/ca00491e.html will identify the cards that will cost you least in interest and other charges based on the way you have used your credit card recently. All you need to do is to identify your average monthly outstanding balance from recent credit card statements.

The Canadian Association of Financial Planners, at www.cafp.org, offers consumer information on what to expect from a financial planner, as well as how and why to choose one. A handy search tool lets you pinpoint an adviser close to home.

The Quicken Financial Network, at www.quicken.ca, is the developer of the popular software programs Quicken and QuickTax, which encompass a financial fitness test, expert advice, investment tracking, and other financial help.

The National Foundation for Consumer Credit at www.nfcc.org is a Web site for a network of local nonprofit organizations that provide consumer credit education and services.

CONCEPT CHECK 6–3

1. What are the most frequent reasons for indebtedness?
2. What are common danger signals of potential debt problems?

According to the the Government of Canada's Office of the Superintendent of Bankruptcy, in its December 1998 publication "Dealing with Debt: A Consumer's Guide," you have—or are going to have—a debt problem if:

- You continually go over your spending limit or you use your credit cards as a necessity, rather than a convenience;
- You are always borrowing money to make it from one payday to the next;
- Your wages have been garnisheed or appropriated to pay for outstanding debts;
- You pay only interest or service charges monthly and do not reduce your total debt over many months;
- Creditors pressure you for payment, threaten to sue or repossess your car, furniture or television, or hire a collection agency to recover the money for them; or
- Utility companies cut off service because your bills have gone unpaid.

SOURCE: Based on "Dealing with Debt: A Consumer's Guide," Office of the Superintendent of Bankruptcy, December 1998.

Exhibit 6–1

Danger Signals of Potential Debt Problems

Seek help from a consumer credit counselling service if you experience these danger signals.

CONSUMER CREDIT COUNSELLING SERVICES

■ OBJECTIVE 4 ■

Evaluate various private and governmental sources that assist consumers with debt problems.

If you are having problems paying your bills and need help, you have several options. You can contact your creditors and try to work out an adjusted repayment plan yourself, or you can check your telephone directory for a nonprofit financial counselling program to get help.

Various provincial authorities provide debt counselling services for families and individuals with financial problems. For example, the Government of Alberta's Web site provides a consumer tip sheet www3.gov.ab.ca/gs/information/publications/. Links to other provincial consumer tip sheets and services can be found at www.cbc.ca/consumers/consumertips/tips_creditrating.html.

Credit counsellors are aware that most people who are in debt over their heads are basically honest people who want to clear up their indebtedness. Too often, the problems of such people arise from a lack of planning or a miscalculation of what they earn. Therefore, the counsellor is as concerned with preventing the problems as with solving them. As a result, credit counselling activities are divided into two parts:

[1] Aiding families with serious debt problems by helping them manage their money better and setting up a realistic budget and plan for expenditures.

[2] Helping people prevent debt problems by teaching them the necessity of family budget planning, providing education to people of all ages regarding the pitfalls of unwise credit buying, suggesting techniques for family budgeting, and encouraging credit institutions to provide full information about the costs and terms of credit and to withhold credit from those who cannot afford to repay it.

Universities, military bases, credit unions, some employers and provincial and federal housing authorities sometimes provide nonprofit counselling services. These organizations usually charge little or nothing for such assistance. You can also check with your local bank or consumer protection office to see whether it has a listing of reputable, low-cost financial counselling services.

But what if a debtor suffers from an extreme case of financial woes? Is there any relief? The answer is yes: bankruptcy proceedings.

CONCEPT CHECK 6–4

1. What is a credit counselling service?
2. What are the two major activities of credit counselling services?
3. What options do consumers have for financial counselling?

DECLARING PERSONAL BANKRUPTCY

■ OBJECTIVE 5 ■

Assess the choices in declaring personal bankruptcy.

Janine Leclaire typifies the new face of bankruptcy. A 43-year-old freelance commercial photographer from Victoria, British Columbia, she was never in serious financial trouble until she began incurring big dental costs last year and reached for her credit cards to pay the bills. Since Janine didn't have dental insurance, her debt quickly mounted. It was too much for her to pay off with her $25,000-a-year freelance income. Her solution: Declare personal bankruptcy for the immediate freedom it would bring from creditors' demands.

Ms. Leclaire's move put her in familiar company, demographically speaking. An increasing number of bankruptcy filers are well-educated, middle-class baby boomers with an overwhelming level of credit card debt. These baby boomers make up 44 percent of the adult population, but they account for 59 percent of personal bankruptcies. In that group, the people most likely to be in bankruptcy are between 40 and 44 years old, an age group that is usually

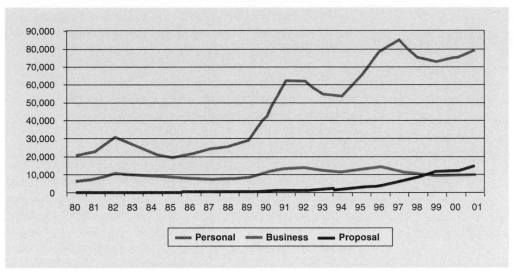

Exhibit 6–2
Canadian
Bankruptcies
and Proposals
1980–2001

SOURCE: As reproduced on the Bankruptcy Canada Web site at www.bankruptcy canada.com/bankstats1.htm and as adapted from Industry Canada statistics. Reproduced with permission of the Minister of Public Works and Government Services, 2002.

assumed to be economically established. Increasingly, too, the bankruptcy debtor is likely to be female.

Unfortunately for some debtors, bankruptcy has become an acceptable tool of credit management. During the last nine years, the personal bankruptcy rate has increased almost 8 percent annually (see Exhibit 6–2).

FENDING OFF BANKRUPTCY: CONSOLIDATION LOANS

Visit the Web site
See the Weblinks under Chapter 6 on the online learning centre at www.mcgrawhill.ca/college/kapoor.

It may sometimes be possible to avoid declaring bankruptcy. If you are under an excessive debt load and would like to regularize and control your payments, you may be able to obtain a consolidation loan. This is a new loan that is used to discharge a collection of existing debts and it may have different advantages and disadvantages.

The advantages of a consolidation loan are that it will have a single interest rate on the full amount of your selected debts and you may be able to extend the term of the loan beyond that of your initial debts, allowing you to make smaller payments as you repay your loan.

The disadvantages of this type of loan are twofold: cost and term. In general, you will be asked to pay a higher interest rate because you are considered to be a higher risk for the lender. In addition, as you extend the term of the loan you will find that the total of what you pay might be considerably higher than the sum of your debt load.

If you do decide to use a consolidation loan, it is best to limit it to paying off only your highest interest debts. It would be unwise to use this option to pay off any debt that is low– or non–interest-bearing.

BANKRUPTCY AND INSOLVENCY ACT

The decision to declare bankruptcy is a hard one, but each year sees at least 100,000 Canadian consumers choosing this route when all else fails. The *Bankruptcy and Insolvency Act*, a federal law initiated in 1992 and amended in 1997, regulates bankruptcy (a straight declaration of insolvency) and proposal (a wage earner plan) proceedings in Canada. It falls under the responsibility of the Office of the Superintendent of Bankruptcy at Industry Canada. By this Act you are allowed to declare insolvency either through a consumer proposal or through an assignment in bankruptcy.

consumer proposal
A maximum five-year plan for paying creditors all or a portion of a debt owed.

CONSUMER PROPOSALS   A **consumer proposal** is a maximum five-year plan for paying creditors all or a portion of the total debt owed. To be eligible for this type of insolvency protection application, you must be insolvent and be less than $75,000 in debt (excluding a mortgage on your principal residence). Initiating the process involves applying to an administrator of consumer proposals, who may be a trustee in bankruptcy or another person appointed to the task. The administrator will provide you with counselling and guidance and will disburse paid funds to your creditors.

Both the court and your creditors must approve a consumer proposal. Once approved, it becomes binding for both you and your creditors. While, in general, this type of agreement will not release you from certain obligations, such as fines, alimony, or co-signer responsibilities, what it will do is protect you from a number of types of harassment or abuse. Your creditors will be restricted from demanding accelerated payments; any pre-existing wage-garnishment arrangements will be annulled; and your employer cannot subject you to any type of disciplinary action resulting from your consumer proposal. When all the conditions of your consumer proposal have been met, you will be issued a "certificate of performance."

The advantage of a consumer proposal is that it will save you from bankruptcy if it is approved. If it is not approved, either by the court or by your creditors, you may then need to seek a trustee in bankruptcy. This person will be a federally licensed individual (generally a chartered accountant) who will carry out the insolvency process.

BANKRUPTCY   Approximately 90 percent of all bankruptcies in Canada are by consumers, rather than businesses. If you are forced to take this choice, the first step will be the assignment of your assets to a licensed trustee. From this time until you are released from your debt by the courts, you will be considered an undischarged bankrupt.

A meeting will then be held among your creditors, who will need to prove their claim against your estate. Your secured creditors, such as your mortgage and your car-loan lenders, will be paid first, as their claims will be against specific assets. After that, your remaining assets will be distributed by specified order with the costs of the bankruptcy administration taking precedence over all other claims. Once this process is complete, the court can grant you a discharge. This document will free you from all claims from creditors, with some exceptions, such as court costs, alimony or support payments, and certain debts incurred through fraud.

PROTECTED ASSETS   It is important to realize that not all of your assets will be seized or considered in a bankruptcy proceeding. Some of your property will be protected from creditors by provincial law. Typically, items that you may require to live and earn a living will be exempt from the tally of your assets.

EFFECTS OF BANKRUPTCY ON FUTURE CREDIT

Different people have different experiences in obtaining credit after they file bankruptcy. Some find obtaining credit more difficult. Others find obtaining credit easier because they have relieved themselves of their prior debts or because creditors know they cannot file another bankruptcy case for a period of time. Obtaining credit may be easier for people who file a consumer proposal and repay some of their debts than for people who file a straight bankruptcy and make no effort to repay. The bankruptcy law prohibits your employer from discharging you simply because you have filed a bankruptcy case.

WHAT ARE THE COSTS?   According to the Office of the Superintendent of Bankruptcy (http://strategis.ic.gc.ca/sc_mrksv/bankrupt/engdoc/superint.html), the costs associated

CREDIT-ABILITY SCORECARD

Test your credit IQ. For each question, circle the letter that best describes your credit habits.

1. I pay my bills when they are due.
   (A) Always   (B) Almost always   (C) Sometimes

2. After paying my regular bills each month, I have money left from my income.
   (A) Yes   (B) Sometimes   (C) Never

3. I know how much I owe on my credit cards each month before I receive my bills.
   (A) Yes   (B) Sometimes   (C) No

4. When I get behind in my payments, I ignore the past-due notices.
   (A) Never or not applicable   (B) Sometimes
   (C) Always

5. When I need more money for my regular living expenses, I take out a loan or use my line of credit on my credit card or chequing account.
   (A) Never   (B) Sometimes   (C) Often

6. If I wanted to see a copy of my credit report, I would contact . . .
   (A) A credit reporting agency   (B) My lenders
   (C) My lawyer

7. My credit record shows that I am current on all my loans and charge accounts.
   (A) Yes   (B) Don't know   (C) No

8. I pay more than the minimum balance due on my credit card accounts.
   (A) Always   (B) Sometimes   (C) Never

9. To pay off my current credit and charge card accounts, it would take me . . .
   (A) 4 months or less   (B) 5 to 8 months
   (C) More than 8 months

10. My consumer loans (including auto loans, but not mortgage payment) and credit card bills each month average more than 20 percent of my take-home pay.
    (A) No   (B) Sometimes   (C) Always

11. If I had serious credit problems, I would contact my creditors to explain the problem.
    (A) Yes   (B) Probably   (C) No

12. If I default (don't repay) on a loan, that fact can stay on my credit report for . . .
    (A) 7 years   (B) 3 years   (C) 1 year

Assign a score of 3 for each "A" answer, 2 for each "B" answer, and 1 for each "C" answer. Total the score.

If you scored:

31–36   You have an excellent knowledge of credit and its responsible use.

24–30   You should take steps toward a better understanding of your personal finances and of the credit process.

18–23   You probably need to take a serious look at your personal finances; consider controlling your spending and staying on a tight budget.

12–17   You may be heading for serious trouble; consider seeking help, such as nonprofit consumer credit counselling services.

SOURCE: *How to Be Credit Smart*, AFSA Education Foundation, 1997.

---

with submitting a consumer proposal are a basic fee of $1,500, a filing fee of $100, plus an additional 20 percent of the amount of your assets that are distributed to creditors. In addition, there is a fee of $170 for budget counselling. In the case of bankruptcy, the trustee may charge 100 percent of the first $975 of receipts plus 35 percent of receipts between $975 and $2,000 plus 50 percent of receipts in excess of $2,000. The filing fee is $75, and there is a fee of $170 for budget counselling.

There are also intangible costs to bankruptcy. For example, obtaining credit in the future may be difficult, since bankruptcy reports are retained in credit bureaus for six years. Therefore, you should take the extreme step of declaring personal bankruptcy only when no other options for solving your financial problems exist.

For a quick test of your credit IQ, read the above Financial Planning for Life's Situations feature.

Visit the Web site
See the Post-Test under Chapter 6 on the online learning centre at www.mcgrawhill.ca/college/kapoor.

CONCEPT CHECK 6–5

1. What is the purpose of a consumer proposal?
2. What is the difference between a consumer proposal and bankruptcy?
3. How does bankruptcy affect your job and future credit?
4. What are the costs of declaring bankruptcy?

SUMMARY OF OBJECTIVES

Objective 1
Analyze the major sources of consumer credit.
The major sources of consumer credit are banks, trust companies, credit unions, finance companies, life insurance companies, and family and friends. Each of these sources has unique advantages and disadvantages.

Parents or family members are often the source of the least expensive loans. They may charge you only the interest they would have earned had they not made the loan. Such loans, however, can complicate family relationships.

Objective 2
Determine the effective cost of borrowing by considering the quoted rate, the number of compounding periods, the timing of the interest payments, and any other service charges.
Financial institutions quote an annual percentage rate (APR) on installment loans and lines of credit, but the effective cost of borrowing will rise if this rate is compounded more frequently than once a year, or if the loan is made on a discount basis with service fees added.

Objective 3
Develop a plan to manage your debts.
Debt has serious consequences if a proper plan for managing it is not implemented.

Most experts agree that emotional problems, the use of money to punish, the expectation of instant comfort, keeping up with the Joneses, overindulgence of children, misunderstanding or lack of communication among family members, and the amount of finance charges are common reasons for indebtedness.

Objective 4
Evaluate various private and governmental sources that assist consumers with debt problems.
If you cannot meet your obligations, contact your creditors immediately. Before signing up with a debt consolidation company, investigate it thoroughly. Better yet, contact a credit counselling service or other debt counselling organization.

Such organizations help people manage their money better by setting up a realistic budget and planning for expenditures. These organizations also help people prevent debt problems by teaching them the necessity of family budget planning and providing education to people of all ages.

Objective 5
Assess the choices in declaring personal bankruptcy.
A debtor's last resort is to declare bankruptcy. Consider the financial and other costs of bankruptcy before taking this extreme step. A debtor can declare insolvency either through a consumer proposal or through an assignment in bankruptcy.

Some people find obtaining credit more difficult after filing bankruptcy. Others find obtaining credit easier because they have relieved themselves of their prior debts or because creditors know they cannot file another bankruptcy case for a period of time.

KEY TERMS

adjusted balance method 168	**average daily balance method** 168	**credit insurance** 170
annual percentage rate (APR) 163	**consumer proposal** 176	**previous balance method** 168

KEY FORMULAS

Page	Topic	Formula
163	Calculating the EAR	$(1 + APR/m)^m - 1$
		Example:
		APR $= 6\%$
		m $= 4$, for quarterly compounding
		EAR $= (1 + 0.06/4)^4 - 1 = 0.06136.$ or 6.14%
166	Calculating an installment loan payment	$PMT = PV \div \dfrac{\{1 - [1 \div (1 + i)^n]\}}{i}$
		Example:
		PV $= \$10,000$ (loan amount)
		n $= 48$ months
		i $= 0.5\%$ per month
		$PMT = \$10,000 \div \left\{ 1 - \dfrac{1 \div (1.005)^{48}}{0.005} \right\}$
		PMT $= \$10,000 \div 42.58$
		$= \$234.85$
167	Calculating monthly interest on a line of credit	Interest $= B \times APR \times (n/365)$
		Example:
		B $= \$10,000$ (loan balance)
		APR $= 9\%$
		N $= 30$ days
		Interest $= \$10,000 \times 0.09 \times (30/365)$
		$= \$73.97$

FINANCIAL PLANNING PROBLEMS

1. *Calculating the Effective Cost of Borrowing.* Dave borrowed $500 and paid $50 in interest when he repaid the principal after one year. The bank also charged him a $5 service fee on a discount basis. What was the effective cost of his loan? (Obj. 2)

2. *Calculating the Effective Annual Interest Rate.* If the 5 percent interest rate quoted on Dave's loan had been compounded monthly, what would have been the effective annual interest rate charged on the loan? (Obj. 2)

3. *Calculating Installment Loan Payments, Interest, and Principal*: If Dave had borrowed the $500 for one year at an APR of 5 percent, compounded monthly, what would have been his monthly loan payment? What would have been the breakdown between interest and principal of the fifth payment? (Obj. 2)

4. *Calculating the Payment on a Line of Credit*: Assume Dave borrowed the $500 on his personal line of credit. Interest is charged at a rate of 5 percent, but calculated on a daily basis. Dave is required to pay a minimum of 5 percent of the remaining loan balance every month. What would be Dave's first monthly loan payment? Assume a 30-day month. (Obj. 2)

5. *Comparing the Costs of Credit Cards.* Bobby is trying to decide between two credit cards. One has no annual fee and an 18-percent interest rate, and the other has a $40-annual fee and an 8.9-percent interest rate. Should he take the card that's free or the one that costs $40? (Obj. 2)

6. *Calculating Cash Advance Fee and the Dollar Amount of Interest.* Sidney took a $200 cash advance by using cheques linked to her credit card account. The bank charges a 2-percent cash advance fee on the amount borrowed and offers

OREA Ontario Real Estate Association

Agreement to Lease
Residential

Form **400**
for use in the Province of Ontario

TENANT (Lessee),..
(Full legal names of all Tenants)

LANDLORD (Lessor),...
(Full legal name of Landlord)

The Tenant hereby offers to lease from the Landlord the premises as described herein on the terms and subject to the conditions as set out in this Agreement.

1. **PREMISES:** Having inspected the premises and provided the present tenant vacates, I/we, the Tenant hereby offer to lease, premises known as:

   ....

2. **TERM OF LEASE:** The lease shall be for a term of ....commencing...

3. **RENT:** The Tenant will pay to the said Landlord monthly and every month during the said term of the lease the sum of ....

   ....Canadian Dollars(CDN$..................................),
   payable in advance on the first day of each and every month during the currency of the said term. First and last months' rent to be paid in advance upon completion or date of occupancy, whichever comes first.

4. **DEPOSIT AND PREPAID RENT:** The Tenant delivers...by negotiable cheque payable to.....................................
   (herewith/upon acceptance)

   ....

   in the amount of..

   Canadian Dollars (CDN$...) as a deposit to be held in trust without interest as security for the faithful performance by the Tenant of all terms, covenants and conditions of the Agreement and to be applied by the Landlord against the.....................................
   and............................month's rent. If the Agreement is not accepted, the deposit is to be returned to the Tenant without interest or deduction.

5. **USE:** The Tenant and Landlord agree that unless otherwise agreed to herein, only the Tenant named above and any person named in a Rental Application completed prior to this Agreement will occupy the premises.

   Premises to be used only for:..

   ....

   ....

   ....

6. **SERVICES AND COSTS:** The cost of the following services applicable to the premises shall be paid as follows:

	LANDLORD	TENANT		LANDLORD	TENANT
Gas			Cable TV		
Oil			Condominium/Cooperative fees		
Electricity			Other:............................		
Hot water heater rental			Other:............................		
Water and Sewerage Charges			Other:............................		

The Landlord will pay the property taxes, but if the Tenant is assessed as a Separate School Supporter, Tenant will pay to the Landlord a sum sufficient to cover the excess of the Separate School Tax over the Public School Tax, if any, for a full calendar year, said sum to be estimated on the tax rate for the current year, and to be payable in equal monthly installments in addition to the above mentioned rental, provided however, that the full amount shall become due and be payable on demand on the Tenant.

INITIALS OF TENANT(S): ( )   **INITIALS OF LANDLORD(S):** ( )

OREA Standard Form: Do not alter when printing or reproducing the standard pre-set portion.   **Form 400**   01/2005   **Page 1 of 3**

7. **PARKING:**...
....
....

8. **ADDITIONAL TERMS:**...
....
....
....
....
....
....
....
....
....

9. **SCHEDULES:** The schedules attached hereto shall form an integral part of this Agreement to Lease and consist of: Schedule(s)...............................
....

10 **IRREVOCABILITY:** This offer shall be irrevocable by.............................until.............................p.m. on the...............................
                                                            (Landlord/Tenant)

day of...,20.......................after which time if not accepted, this Agreement shall be null and void and all monies paid thereon shall be returned to the Tenant without interest or deduction.

11. **NOTICES:** Landlord hereby appoints the Listing Broker as Agent for the purpose of giving and receiving notices pursuant to this agreement. **Only if the Co-operating Broker represents the interests of the Tenant in this transaction,** the Tenant hereby appoints the Co-operating Broker as Agent for the purpose of giving and receiving notices pursuant to this Agreement. Any notice relating hereto or provided for herein shall be in writing. This offer, any counter offer, notice of acceptance thereof, or any notice shall be deemed given and received, when hand delivered to the address for service provided in the Acknowledgement below, or where a facsimile number is provided herein, when transmitted electronically to that facsimile number.

FAX No...(For delivery of notices to Landlord) FAX No...(For delivery of notices to Tenant)

12. **EXECUTION OF LEASE:** Lease shall be drawn by the Landlord pursuant to the Short Form of Leases Act, shall include the provisions as contained herein and in any attached schedule, and shall be executed by both parties before possession of the premises is given.

13. **ACCESS:** The Landlord shall have the right, at reasonable times to enter and show the demised premises to prospective tenants, purchasers or others. The Landlord or anyone on the Landlord's behalf shall also have the right, at reasonable times, to enter and inspect the demised premises.

14. **USE AND DISTRIBUTION OF PERSONAL INFORMATION:** The Tenant consents to the collection, use and disclosure of the Tenant's personal information by the Landlord and/or agent of the Landlord, from time to time, for the purpose of determining the creditworthiness of the Tenant for the leasing, selling or financing of the premises or the real property, or making such other use of the personal information as the Landlord and/or agent of the Landlord deems appropriate.

15. **CONFLICT OR DISCREPANCY:** If there is any conflict or discrepancy between any provision added to this Agreement (including any Schedule attached hereto) and any provision in the standard pre-set portion hereof, the added provision shall supersede the standard pre-set provision to the extent of such conflict or discrepancy. This Agreement, including any Schedule attached hereto, shall constitute the entire Agreement between Landlord and Tenant. There is no representation, warranty, collateral agreement or condition, which affects this Agreement other than as expressed herein. This Agreement shall be read with all changes of gender or number required by the context.

16. **AGENCY:** It is understood that the brokers involved in the transaction represent the parties as set out in the Representation section below.

17. **CONSUMER REPORTS: The Tenant is hereby notified that a consumer report containing credit and/or personal information may be referred to in connection with this transaction.**

INITIALS OF TENANT(S): ( )   **INITIALS OF LANDLORD(S):** ( )

18. **BINDING AGREEMENT:** This Agreement and acceptance thereof shall constitute a binding agreement by the parties to enter into the Lease of the Premises and to abide by the terms and conditions herein contained.

DATED at...this............................ day of..., 20.........

SIGNED, SEALED AND DELIVERED in the presence of: IN WITNESS whereof I have hereunto set my hand and seal:

....   (Seal) DATE.................................
(Witness)   (Tenant or Authorized Representative)

....   (Seal) DATE.................................
(Witness)   (Tenant or Authorized Representative)

....   (Seal) DATE.................................
(Witness)   (Guarantor)

We/I the Landlord hereby accept the above Offer, and agree that the commission together with applicable Goods and Services Tax (and any other tax as may hereafter be applicable) may be deducted from the deposit and further agree to pay any remaining balance of commission forthwith.

DATED at...this............................ day of..., 20.........

SIGNED, SEALED AND DELIVERED in the presence of: IN WITNESS whereof I have hereunto set my hand and seal:

....   (Seal) DATE.................................
(Witness)   (Landlord or Authorized Representative)

....   (Seal) DATE.................................
(Witness)   (Landlord or Authorized Representative)

CONFIRMATION OF EXECUTION: Notwithstanding anything contained herein to the contrary, I confirm this Agreement with all changes both typed and

written was finally executed by all parties at............a.m./p.m. this..............day of............................., 20......... ....
(Signature of Landlord or Tenant)

REPRESENTATION

Listing Broker... Tel. No. (..........)........................ Represents..............................

....

Co-op/Tenant Broker.. Tel. No. (..........)........................ Represents..............................

....

I acknowledge receipt of my signed copy of this accepted Agreement to Lease and I authorize the Agent to forward a copy to my lawyer.   I acknowledge receipt of my signed copy of this accepted Agreement to Lease and I authorize the Agent to forward a copy to my lawyer.

.... DATE....................   .... DATE....................
(Landlord)   (Tenant)

.... DATE....................   .... DATE....................
(Landlord)   (Tenant)

Address for Service...   Address for Service...

......................................Tel.No.(..........)..........   ....Tel.No.(..........)..........

Landlord's Lawyer..   Tenant's Lawyer..

Address..   Address..

(..........)............................ (..........).......   (..........)............................ (..........).......
          Tel.No.   FAX No.   Tel.No.   FAX No.

FOR OFFICE USE ONLY   **COMMISSION TRUST AGREEMENT**

To: Co-operating Broker shown on the foregoing Agreement to Lease:
In consideration for the Co-operating Broker procuring the foregoing Agreement to Lease, I hereby declare that all moneys received or receivable by me in connection with the Transaction as contemplated in the MLS Rules and Regulations of my Real Estate Board shall be receivable and held in trust. This agreement shall constitute a Commission Trust Agreement as defined in the MLS Rules and shall be subject to and governed by the MLS Rules pertaining to Commission Trust.

DATED as of the date and time of the acceptance of the foregoing Agreement to Lease.   Acknowledged by:

....
Signature of Listing Broker or authorized representative   Signature of Co-operating Broker or authorized representative

R   **OREA Standard Form: Do not alter when printing or reproducing the standard pre-set portion.**   **Form 400**   01/2005   **Page 3 of 3**
REALTOR

SOURCE: Ontario Real Estate Association. Used by permission.

PART 3

INSURING YOUR RESOURCES

Home and Automobile Insurance

ROAD TRIPS ARE FUN, BUT ARE YOU INSURED?

José and Marty are excited about their spring break trip to the Rocky Mountains. They decided to rent a car because Marty drives an old car and José doesn't want to put kilometres on the Honda his parents gave him as a graduation gift. When they go to pick up the car, the sales agent asks them if they want a loss-damage and collision-damage waiver, which would cost them $10 per day. They don't want to spend an extra $70 on this trip, but neither one knows if his personal insurance covers rental cars. What should they do?

Motorists usually decline trip insurance. They get the same or better protection from their personal auto insurance. However, sometimes there are gaps in personal coverage. If you don't know the rules and decline the rental agency's offer, you may be driving uninsured. For example, Marty may not have comprehensive and collision coverage on his old car because he knows it isn't worth the additional coverage. This means he also won't be covered on the rental car.

If Marty's or José's auto policy doesn't cover collision or theft when driving a rental car, they have another option. Certain credit cards will protect them against damage or theft if the card is used when paying for the rental. But again, there may be limitations.

If José and Marty don't know their rental car insurance rules, they should check with their auto insurer or credit card company before signing the rental agreement. Otherwise, the safest thing might be to pay the additional $10 per day.

QUESTIONS

1 Why do most motorists decline additional coverage when they rent a car? What are the limitations of this strategy?

2 What other option do Marty and José have if their personal auto insurance does not cover rental cars?

3 What Web research could they do before they rent a car again?

LEARNING OBJECTIVES

1 Develop a risk management plan using insurance.

2 Discuss the importance of property and liability insurance.

3 Explain the insurance coverages and policy types available to homeowners and renters.

4 Analyze factors that influence the amount of coverage and cost of home insurance.

5 Identify the important types of automobile insurance coverages.

6 Evaluate factors that affect the cost of automobile insurance.

INSURANCE AND RISK MANAGEMENT: AN INTRODUCTION

You purchase insurance to control the effects of uncontrollable financial risk inherent to life and living (and for that matter even death). The idea is that certain bad things will happen, but you have no idea when or what, so your best bet is to be ready for them at all times. You do this by buying insurance, and the amount of insurance you buy should reflect the potential financial impact of the loss or partial loss of what you are insuring.

■ OBJECTIVE 1 ┃

Develop a risk management plan using insurance.

WHAT IS INSURANCE?

Insurance is protection against possible financial loss. Although many types of insurance exist, they all have one thing in common: They give you the peace of mind that comes from knowing that money will be available to meet the needs of your survivors, pay medical expenses, protect your home and belongings, and cover personal or property damage.

Life insurance replaces income that would be lost if the policyholder died. Health insurance helps meet medical expenses when the policyholder becomes ill. Automobile insurance helps cover property and personal damage caused by the policyholder's car. Home insurance covers the policyholder's place of residence and its associated financial risks, such as damage to personal property and injuries to others.

An **insurance company**, or **insurer**, is a risk-sharing firm that agrees to assume financial responsibility for losses that may result from an insured risk. A person joins the risk-sharing group (the insurance company) by purchasing a **policy** (a contract). Under the policy, the insurance company agrees to assume the risk for a fee (the **premium**) that the person (the **insured**, or the **policyholder**) pays periodically.

Insurance mitigates the risks of financial uncertainty and unexpected losses. The financial consequences of failing to obtain the right amount and type of insurance can be disastrous.

insurance Protection against possible financial loss.

insurance company A risk-sharing firm that assumes financial responsibility for losses that may result from an insured risk.

insurer An insurance company

policy A written contract for insurance.

premium The amount of money a policyholder is charged for an insurance policy.

insured A person covered by an insurance policy.

policyholder A person who owns an insurance policy.

risk Chance or uncertainty of loss; may also mean "the insured."

peril The cause of a possible loss.

hazard A factor that increases the likelihood of loss through some peril.

TYPES OF RISKS

You face risks every day. You can't cross the street without some danger that you'll be hit by a car. You can't own property without taking the chance that it will be lost, stolen, damaged, or destroyed. Insurance companies offer financial protection against such dangers and losses by promising to compensate the insured for a relatively large loss in return for the payment of a much smaller but certain expense called the *premium*.

Risk, *peril*, and *hazard* are important terms in insurance. Each has a distinct, technical meaning in insurance terminology.

Risk is the chance that something may be lost. When someone buys insurance, they assume that even if the associated risk happens, they will not be overly affected. For example, many people insure their car for loss and damage because they know the odds are good that risk may occur, and they know that repair or replacement costs could be very large. By buying insurance, they minimize the potential impact of a risk.

Peril is the cause of a possible loss. It is the event that causes someone to take out insurance. People buy policies for financial protection against such perils as fire, windstorms, explosions, robbery, accidents, and premature death.

Hazard increases the likelihood of loss through some peril. For example, defective house wiring is a hazard that increases the likelihood of the peril of fire.

The most common risks are classified as personal risks, property risks, and liability risks. *Personal risks* are the uncertainties surrounding loss of income or life due to premature death, illness, disability, old age, or unemployment. *Property risks* are the uncertainties of direct or indirect losses to property due to fire, windstorms, accidents, theft, and other hazards. *Liability risks* are loss possibilities due to negligence resulting in bodily harm or property damage to others. Such harm or damage could be caused by an automobile, professional misconduct, injury suffered on one's property, and so on.

Personal risks, property risks, and liability risks are types of **pure risk**, or *insurable risk*, since there would be a chance of loss only if the specified events occurred. Pure risks are accidental and unintentional risks for which the nature and financial cost of the loss can be predicted.

A **speculative risk** is a risk that carries a chance of either loss or gain. Starting a small business that may or may not succeed is an example of speculative risk. So is gambling. Speculative risks are legally defined as uninsurable.

pure risk A risk in which there is only a chance of loss; also called *insurable risk*.

speculative risk A risk in which there is a chance of either loss or gain.

RISK MANAGEMENT METHODS

Risk management is an organized strategy for protecting assets and people. It controls financial losses caused by destructive events. Risk management is a long-range planning process. People's risk management needs change at various points in their lives. If you understand risks and how to manage them, you can provide better protection for yourself and your family. You can reduce your financial losses and thereby improve your chances for economic, social, physical, and emotional well-being. Since you will probably be unable to afford to cover all risks, you need to understand how to obtain the best protection you can afford.

Most people think of risk management as buying insurance. However, insurance is not the only method of dealing with risk; in certain situations, other methods may be less costly. Four general risk management techniques are commonly used.

1. RISK AVOIDANCE You can avoid the risk of an automobile accident by not driving to work. General Motors can avoid the risk of product failure by not introducing new cars. Risk avoidance would be practised in both instances, but at a very high cost. You might have to give up your job, and General Motors might lose out to competitors that introduce new models.

In some situations, however, risk avoidance is practical. At the personal level, people avoid risks by not smoking or by not walking through high-crime neighbourhoods. At the business level, jewellery stores avoid losses through robbery by locking their merchandise in vaults. Obviously, no person or business can avoid all risks.

> **DID YOU KNOW ?**
>
> Alien abduction protection, pet insurance, and coverage if you turn into a werewolf are some of the strange but real-life policies available for a price. Wedding disaster insurance paid for an entire wedding party to reassemble at the original location—Hawaii—to recreate the scene for new photos when all the negatives were stolen from the photographer's car. One life insurance company gives fast runners discounts off their policies by submitting a certified race time for an event that's 5K or longer.
>
> (Kimberly Lankford, "Weird Insurance," *Kiplinger's Personal Finance Magazine*, October, 1998, pp. 113–116.)

2. RISK REDUCTION While avoiding risks completely may not be possible, reducing risks may be a cause of action. You can reduce the risk of injury in an auto accident by wearing a seat belt. You can install smoke alarms and fire extinguishers to protect life and reduce potential fire damage. You can reduce the risk of illness by eating a balanced diet and exercising.

3. RISK ASSUMPTION Risk assumption means taking on responsibility for the loss or injury that may result from a risk. Generally, it makes sense to assume a risk when the potential loss is small, when risk management has reduced the risk, when insurance coverage is expensive, and when there is no other way to obtain protection. For instance, you might decide not to purchase collision insurance on an older car. Then, if an accident occurs, you will bear the costs of fixing the car.

self-insurance The process of establishing a monetary fund to cover the cost of a loss.

Self-insurance is the process of establishing a monetary fund to cover the cost of a loss. Self-insurance does not eliminate risks; it only provides means for covering losses. Many people self-insure by default, not by choice. Others take on as much insurance as they can afford and then self-insure the rest.

4. RISK SHIFTING The most common method of dealing with risk is to shift, or transfer, it to an insurance company or some other organization. Insurance is the protection against loss afforded by the purchase of an insurance policy from an insurance company. Insurers, in their turn, usually insure themselves through what is known as re-insuring. By re-insuring the risks they have assumed by insuring your risk, they are acting very much like you: they are controlling the potential effects should risks actualize.

Exhibit 8–1 summarizes various risks and appropriate strategies for managing them.

> **DID YOU KNOW ?**
>
> Deductibles are a combination of risk assumption and risk shifting. The insured person assumes part of the risk, paying the first $100, $250, or $500 of a claim. The majority of the risk for a large claim is shifted to another party, the insurance company.

PLANNING AN INSURANCE PROGRAM

Because all people have their own needs and goals, many of which change over the years, a personal insurance program should be tailored to those changes. In the early years of marriage, when the family is growing, most families need certain kinds of insurance protection. This protection may include property insurance on an apartment or a house, life and disability

Exhibit 8–1 Examples of Risks and Risk Management Strategies

RISKS		STRATEGIES FOR REDUCING FINANCIAL IMPACT		
Personal Events	**Financial Impact**	**Personal Resources**	**Private Sector**	**Public Sector**
Disability	Loss of one income Loss of services Increased expenses	Savings, investments Family observing safety precautions	Disability insurance	Disability insurance
Illness	Loss of one income Medical expenses	Health-enhancing behaviour	Health insurance	Medicare

Death	Loss of one income
	Loss of services
	Funeral expenses
		Estate planning
		Risk reduction
			Life insurance	Veteran's life
				  insurance
				Government
				  programs
				  survivor's benefits

Retirement	Decreased income
	Unplanned living
	  expenses
		Savings
		Investments
		Hobbies, skills
			Retirement and/or
			  pensions
				Public pensions
				Pension plan for
				  government
				  employees

Property loss	Catastrophic storm
	  damage to property
	Repair or replacement
	  cost of theft
		Property repair
		  and upkeep
		Security plans
			Automobile
			  insurance
			Homeowner's
			  insurance
			Tenant's insurance
				Basic disaster
				  relief

Liability	Claims and settlement
	  costs
	Lawsuits and legal
	  expenses
	Loss of personal assets
	  and income
		Observing safety
		  precautions
		Maintaining
		  property
			Homeowner's
			  insurance
			Automobile
			  insurance	

One pro, a fee-only insurance consultant, states that North Americans make thousands of costly decisions about life insurance. He advises that when you are in doubt about which life insurance to purchase, buy term. It is the least expensive, easy to understand, and a good start. If you want a whole life policy, buy a low-load cash-value policy. These policies are sold directly to the public or through fee-for-service advisers. Ask your agent to explain plausible risk in writing. Review annual statements and ask your agent for an in-force illustration every few years to determine if the current premium is still adequate.

NAMING YOUR BENEFICIARY

beneficiary A person designated to receive something, such as life insurance proceeds, from the insured.

An important provision in every life insurance policy is the right to name your beneficiary. A **beneficiary** is a person who is designated to receive something, such as life insurance proceeds, from the insured. In your policy, you can name one or more persons as contingent beneficiaries who will receive your policy proceeds if the primary beneficiary dies before you do. It is essential to name a beneficiary of your life insurance policy if you do not wish the death benefit of the policy to form part of your estate and be subject to a probate fee that is often calculated as a percent of your estate's value.

THE GRACE PERIOD

When you buy a life insurance policy, the insurance company agrees to pay a certain sum of money under specified circumstances and you agree to pay a certain premium regularly. The *grace period* is applicable in situations where the premium is due but not yet paid. It allows 28 to 31 days to elapse, during which time you may pay the premium without penalty. After that time, the policy lapses if you have not paid the premium.

POLICY REINSTATEMENT

A lapsed policy can be put back in force, or reinstated, if it has not been turned in for cash. To reinstate the policy, you must again qualify as an acceptable risk, and you must pay overdue premiums with interest. There is a time limit on reinstatement, usually one or two years.

NONFORFEITURE CLAUSE

nonforfeiture clause A provision that allows the insured not to forfeit all accrued benefits.

One important feature of the whole life policy is the **nonforfeiture clause**. This provision prevents the forfeiture of accrued benefits if you choose to drop the policy. For example, if you decide not to continue paying premiums, you can exercise specified options with your cash value.

INCONTESTABILITY CLAUSE

incontestability clause A provision stating that the insurer cannot dispute the validity of a policy after a specified period.

The **incontestability clause** stipulates that after the policy has been in force for a specified period (usually two years), the insurance company cannot dispute its validity during the lifetime of the insured for any reason, including fraud. One reason for this provision is that the beneficiaries, who cannot defend the company's contesting of the claim, should not be forced to suffer because of the acts of the insured.

SUICIDE CLAUSE

The **suicide clause** provides that if the insured dies by suicide during the first two years the policy is in force, the death benefit will equal the amount of the premium paid. Generally, after two years, the suicide becomes a risk covered by the policy and the b━━━ aries of a suicide receive the same benefit that is payable for death fro━

AUTOM━━

suicide clause A provision stating that if the insured dies by suicide during the first two years the policy is in force, the death benefit will equal the amount of the premium paid.

...hin the grace
...e if that cash
...allowing the

...as incor-
...ad been
...herwise

...been
...per-
...pan

rider A document attached to a policy that modifies its coverage.

A━
is ━
ifie━
pre━ ... a waiver of

WA━ ━ ━ ᴅISABILITY BENEFIT Under this provision, the company ━ ━ premiums that are due after the onset of total and permanent disability. In effect, the company pays the premiums. The disability must occur before you reach a certain age, usually 60.

The waiver of premium rider is sometimes desirable. Don't buy it, however, if the added cost will prevent you from carrying needed basic life insurance. Some insurance companies include this rider automatically in all policies issued through age 55.

ACCIDENTAL DEATH BENEFIT Under this provision, the insurance company pays twice the face amount of the policy if the insured's death results from an accident. The accidental death benefit is often called **double indemnity**. Accidental death must occur within a certain time period after the injury, usually 90 days, and before the insured reaches a certain age, usually 60 or 65.

The accidental death benefit is expensive. Moreover, your chances of dying in the exact manner stated in the policy are very small, as are the chances that your beneficiary will collect the double payment.

double indemnity A benefit under which the company pays twice the face value of the policy if the insured's death results from an accident.

GUARANTEED INSURABILITY OPTION This option, also refered to as future increase option, allows you to buy additional amounts of life insurance without proof of insurability. Thus, even if you do not remain in good health, you can increase the amount of your insurance as your income rises. This option is desirable if you anticipate the need for additional life insurance in the future.

CRITICAL ILLNESS *Critical illness* benefits are life insurance policy proceeds paid to a terminally ill policyholder *before* he or she dies. The benefits may be provided for directly in the policies, but more often, they are added by riders or attachments to new or existing policies.

JOINT, LAST TO DIE A *joint, last to die life insurance* policy, also called *survivorship life*, insures two lives, usually husband and wife. The death benefit is paid when the second spouse dies. Usually, a second-to-die policy is intended to pay estate taxes when both spouses die. However, some attorneys claim that with the right legal advice, you can minimize or avoid estate taxes completely.

Now that you know the various types of life insurance policies and the major provisions of and riders to such policies, you are ready to make your buying decisions.

CONCEPT CHECK 9–4

1. What are the most common provisions in life insurance contracts?
2. What is a beneficiary?
3. What is a rider?
4. What is the concept of double indemnity?

BUYING LIFE INSURANCE

■ OBJECTIVE 5 ▮

Create a plan to buy life insurance.

You should consider a number of factors before buying life insurance. As discussed earlier in this chapter, these factors include your present and future sources of income, other savings and income protection, group life insurance, group annuities (or other pension benefits), government benefits, and, of course, the financial strength of the company.

FROM WHOM TO BUY?

Look for insurance coverage from financially strong companies with professionally qualified representatives. It is not unusual for a relationship with an insurance company to extend over a period of 20, 30, or even 50 years. For that reason alone, you should choose carefully when deciding on an insurance company or an insurance agent. Fortunately, you have a choice of sources.

SOURCES Protection is available from a wide range of private and public sources, including insurance companies and their representatives; private groups, such as employers, labour unions, and professional or fraternal organizations; and financial institutions and manufacturers offering credit insurance.

RATING INSURANCE COMPANIES Some of the strongest, most reputable insurance companies in the nation provide excellent insurance coverage at reasonable costs. In fact, the financial strength of an insurance company may be a major factor in holding down premium costs for consumers.

DID YOU KNOW ?

In 2003, Canadians purchased:

Individual life insurance	$ 167.5 billion
Group life insurance	90.5 billion
Total life insurance	$258.0 billion

SOURCE: www.clhia.ca/e3i_FactBook.htm

Locate an insurance company by checking the reputations of local agencies. Ask members of your family, friends, or colleagues about the insurers they prefer.

CHOOSING YOUR INSURANCE PROVIDER Before you purchase your insurance, you'll need to consider whether you want to buy through a "direct" insurer, an agent, a broker, or a group plan. Agents and direct insurers represent one insurance company and offer only the products of that company. If that company has a range of products, then your needs will likely be met. It does, however, require that you have some knowledge of the products available in the marketplace so you can compare.

A broker, considered by most to be the better option, contracts with a limited number of insurance companies and can offer the products of those companies with which the broker has a contract.

A group plan can function either through an agent or a broker system. In some cases, while the plan may be serviced by a broker, the broker may use one insurance company almost exclusively for that plan. In this sense, the broker is really functioning more as an agent. Group plans may be offered through an employer, an alumni association, or another group affiliation.

Once you have found a provider, you must decide which policy is right for you. The best way to do this is to talk to your agent, which does not obligate you to buy insurance.

The Canadian Life and Health Insurance Association (www.clhia.ca) suggests you ask about the professional qualifications and training the agent has had. Agents with a CLU Chartered Life Underwriter) or CH.F.C. (Chartered Financial Consultant) demonstrate commitment to their profession. These programs require several years of study and examinations.

COMPARING POLICY COSTS

Each life insurance company designs the policies it sells to make them attractive and useful to many policyholders. One policy may have features another policy doesn't; one company may be more selective than another company; one company may get better returns on its investments than another company. These and other factors affect the prices of life insurance policies.

In brief, five factors affect the price a company charges for a life insurance policy: the company's cost of doing business, the returns on its investments, the mortality rate it expects among its policyholders, the features the policy contains, and competition among companies with comparable policies.

The prices of life insurance policies, therefore, vary considerably among life insurance companies. Moreover, a particular company will not be equally competitive for all policies. Thus, one company might have a competitively priced policy for 24-year-olds but not for 35-year-olds.

Ask your agent to give you interest-adjusted indexes. An **interest-adjusted index** is a method of evaluating the cost of life insurance by taking into account the time value of money. Highly complex mathematical calculations and formulas combine premium payments, dividends, cash-value buildup, and present value analysis into an index number that makes possible a fairly accurate cost comparison among insurance companies. The lower the index number, the lower the cost of the policy. The Financial Planning Calculations feature on page 259 shows how to use an interest-adjusted index to compare the costs of insurance.

interest-adjusted index A method of evaluating the cost of life insurance by taking into account the time value of money.

OBTAINING A POLICY

A life insurance policy is issued after you submit an application for insurance and the insurance company accepts the application. The application usually has two parts. In the first part, you state your name, age, and gender, what type of policy you desire, how much insurance you want, your occupation, and so forth. In the second part, you give your medical history. While a medical examination is frequently required for ordinary policies, usually no examination is required for group insurance.

Financial Planning for Life's Situations

Life Insurance Checklist

Top 10 questions to ask your insurance provider BEFORE you purchase or renew your insurance:

1. What kind of homeowner's policy do I have, and who/what is covered under it?
2. How do I know if I am adequately insured?
3. What is NOT covered in my homeowner's policy? (What are the "exclusions"?)
4. Do I have replacement cost? guaranteed replacement cost?
5. What are the limitations on valuables, like jewellery, silverware, and computers?
6. What does my policy cover me for in terms of water damage?
7. What optional coverages should I consider?
8. What is my deductible? How much money can I save on my premium by choosing a higher deductible?
9. What safety features can I install that will help me save money and increase my protection?
10. Does the company offer 24-hour claims service?

When you have a claim . . .

1. Am I covered? For how much? (If not, why not? Show me where in the policy it explains that.)
2. Is there a deductible? How much?
3. Can I get assistance right now to make temporary repairs? How do I go about arranging the repairs?
4. What do I need to do to file my claim as soon as possible?
5. How long will it take to settle my claim?

(The preceding questions are intended as a guideline only and are not meant to be exhaustive.)

SOURCE: Homeowner's Insurance Checklist. Used with permission of Insurance Canada.
http://www.insurance-canada.ca/

The company determines your insurability by means of the information on your application, the results of the medical examination, and the inspection report. Of all applicants, 98 percent are found to be insurable, though some may have to pay higher premiums because of an existing medical condition.

EXAMINING A POLICY

BEFORE THE PURCHASE When you buy a life insurance policy, read every word of the contract and, if necessary, ask your agent for a point-by-point explanation of the language. Many insurance companies have rewritten their contracts to make them more understandable. These are legal documents, and you should be familiar with what they promise, even though they use technical terms. Above all, ensure that your policy stipulates that your insurance provider will allow you some time to examine the policy properly and will allow you to cancel it without cost within a certain time limit, usually 10 days.

AFTER THE PURCHASE After you buy new life insurance, you have a 10-day "free-look" period during which you can change your mind. If you do so, the company will return your premium without penalty.

It's a good idea to give your beneficiaries and your lawyer a photocopy of your policy. Your beneficiaries should know where the policy is kept because to obtain the insurance proceeds, they will have to send it to the company upon your death, along with a copy of the death certificate.

CHOOSING SETTLEMENT OPTIONS

A well-planned life insurance program should cover the immediate expenses resulting from the death of the insured. However, that is only one of its purposes. In most instances, the primary purpose of life insurance is to protect dependants against a loss of income resulting from

In determining the cost of insurance, don't overlook the time value of money. You must include as part of that cost the interest (opportunity cost) you would earn on money if you did not use it to pay insurance premiums. For many years, insurers did not assign a time value to money in making their sales presentations. Only recently has the insurance industry widely adopted interest-adjusted cost estimates.

If you fail to consider the time value of money, you may get the false impression that the insurance company is giving you something for nothing. Here is an example. Suppose you are 35 and have a $10,000 face amount, 20-year, limited-payment, participating policy. Your annual premium is $210, or $4,200 over the 20-year period. Your dividends over the 20-year payment period total $1,700, so your total net premium is $2,500 ($4,200 − $1,700). Yet the cash value of your policy at the end of 20 years is $4,600. If you disregard the interest your premiums could otherwise have earned, you might get the impression that the insurance company is giving you $2,100 more than you paid ($4,600 − $2,500). But if you consider the time value of money (or

its opportunity cost), the insurance company is not giving you $2,100. What if you had invested the annual premiums in a conservative-stock mutual fund? At an 8-percent annual yield, your account would have accumulated to $6,180 in 20 years. Therefore, instead of having received $2,100 from the insurance company, you have paid the company $1,580 for 20 years of insurance protection:

Premiums you paid over	
20 years	$4,200
Time value of money	1,980 ($6,180 − $4,200)
Total cost	6,180
Cash value	4,600
Net cost of insurance	1,580 ($6,180 − $4,600)

Be sure to request interest-adjusted indexes from your agent; if he or she doesn't give them to you, look for another agent. As you have seen in the example, you can compare the costs among insurance companies by combining premium payments, dividends, cash value buildup, and present value analysis into an index number.

the premature death of the primary wage earner. Thus, selecting the appropriate settlement option is an important part of designing a life insurance program. The most common settlement options are lump-sum payment, limited installment payment, life income option, and proceeds left with the company.

LUMP-SUM PAYMENT The insurance company pays the face amount of the policy in one installment to the beneficiary or to the estate of the insured. This form of settlement is the most widely used option.

LIMITED INSTALLMENT PAYMENT This option provides for payment of the life insurance proceeds in equal periodic installments for a specified number of years after your death.

LIFE INCOME OPTION Under the life income option, payments are made to the beneficiary for as long as she or he lives. The amount of each payment is based primarily on the gender and attained age of the beneficiary at the time of the insured's death.

PROCEEDS LEFT WITH THE COMPANY The life insurance proceeds are left with the insurance company at a specified rate of interest. The company acts as trustee and pays the interest to the beneficiary. The guaranteed minimum interest rate paid on the proceeds varies among companies.

SWITCHING POLICIES

Think twice if your agent suggests that you replace the whole life or universal life insurance you already own. Consumers lose millions of dollars each year because they don't hold onto their cash life insurance policies long enough or because they purchase the wrong policies. Half of those who buy whole or universal life policies drop them within 10 years.

Before you give up this protection, make sure you are still insurable (check medical and any other qualification requirements). Remember that you are now older than you were when you purchased your policy, and a new policy will therefore cost more. Moreover, the older policy may have provisions that are not duplicated in some of the new policies. This does not mean you should reject the idea of replacing your present policy; rather, you should proceed with caution. We recommend that you ask your agent or company for an opinion about the new proposal to get both sides of the argument.

The Financial Planning for Life's Situations feature on page 261 presents important guidelines for purchasing life insurance.

CONCEPT CHECK 9–5

1. How do insurance companies price their products?
2. How do insurance companies determine your insurability?
3. What should you do in examining a policy before and after the purchase?
4. What are the four most common settlement options?
5. Should you switch life insurance policies?

HEALTH INSURANCE AND FINANCIAL PLANNING

■ OBJECTIVE 6 ▮

Define *health insurance* and explain its importance in financial planning.

In Canada, most basic medical procedures are provided for under provincial government health-care plans. This publicly financed health-care system is refered to as Medicare. You are assured of proper treatment that will not affect your financial situation to an overly large extent.

Because such items as semi-private or private hospital rooms, prescription drugs, eyeglasses, and dental care are either not covered or only partially covered by provincial insurance plans, you may want to supplement your health insurance through private medical insurance companies, such as Blue Cross, Greenshield Canada, Maritime Life, or Liberty Health.

When travelling outside Canada, it is important to remember that health-care costs outside the country can be very high and may not be fully covered by provincial health-care plans. In such cases, it is imperative to have adequate insurance protection.

WHAT IS HEALTH INSURANCE?

Health insurance, like other forms of insurance, reduces the financial burden of risk by dividing losses among many individuals. It works in the same way as life insurance, homeowner's insurance, and automobile insurance. You pay the insurance company a specified premium, and the company guarantees you some degree of financial protection. Like the premiums and benefits of other types of insurance, the premiums and benefits of health insurance are figured on the basis of average experience. To establish rates and benefits, insurance company actuaries rely on general statistics that tell them how many people in a certain population group will become ill and how much their illnesses will cost.

Medical expense insurance and disability income insurance, discussed in the next section, are an important part of your financial planning. To safeguard your family's economic security, both protections should be a part of your overall insurance program.

THE NEED FOR SUPPLEMENTAL HEALTH INSURANCE

While the bulk of financial risks related to medical costs are minimized by the various provincial health-care insurance programs, you should establish your capacity to pay any costs that are not

Remember that your need for life insurance coverage will change over time. Your income may go up or down, or your family size might change. Therefore, it is wise to review your coverage periodically to ensure that it keeps up with your changing needs.

Follow these rules when buying life insurance:	Done
1. Understand and know what your life insurance needs are before you make any purchase, and make sure the company you choose can meet those needs.	☐
2. Buy your life insurance from a company that is licensed in your province.	☐
3. Select an agent who is competent, knowledgeable, and trustworthy.	☐
4. Shop around and compare costs.	☐
5. Buy only the amount of life insurance you need and can afford.	☐
6. Ask about lower premium rates for nonsmokers.	☐
7. Read your policy and make sure you understand it.	☐
8. Inform your beneficiaries about the kinds and amount of life insurance you own.	☐
9. Keep your policy in a safe place at home, and keep your insurance company's name and your policy number in a safety deposit box.	☐
10. Check your coverage periodically, or whenever your situation changes, to ensure that it meets your current needs.	☐

SOURCE: American Council of Life Insurance, 1001 Pennsylvania Avenue, NW, Washington, DC 20004-2599.

covered. Consider, for example, your willingness to share a room should you fall ill and require hospitalization. Basic provincial medical coverage will provide you with a room that will hold at least three other beds besides your own. This means that—at a time when you may be feeling less than sociable—you will be required to make concessions to the noise and occasional indiscretions of your roommates and their visitors. If this proposition is unappealing, you will want to request a private or at the least a semi-private room. Financially, this is where a problem can arise.

Since provincial medical coverage will not pay for the additional costs of a semi-private or private room, you will be asked to defray these costs yourself. For extended stays, this could translate to thousands of dollars. Similarly, once you leave the hospital, you will be required to assume either some or all of the costs for your medications. Again, this could prove costly.

Having thought out a few scenarios in which you might incur similar charges, you may choose to purchase supplemental medical coverage. Especially in cases where your personal wealth is small and might possibly be rapidly exhausted by the incidental costs of ill health, dental maintenance, and vision correction, buying supplemental medical coverage can be a sound financial planning decision.

GROUP HEALTH INSURANCE

Group plans comprise about 60 percent of all the health insurance issued by health and life insurance companies. Most of these plans are employer sponsored, and the employer often pays part or most of their cost. Group insurance will cover you and your immediate family. Group insurance seldom requires evidence that you are insurable if you enroll when you first become eligible for coverage.

The protection group insurance provides varies from plan to plan. The plan may not cover all of your health insurance needs; therefore, you will have to consider supplementing it with individual health insurance. Most universities offer health insurance coverage to full-time students. One of the leading providers for student health and dental plans in Canada is studentcare.net/work (aseq.com in Quebec).

Two factors to examine with group insurance are transferability and how the coverage is paid for. Many group plans do not allow for transfer of an insurance policy to the individual when an employee leaves the group. This is because underwriting for a group policy does not transfer well to individuals, but the consequence is that the departing employee loses both his or her benefits and coverage. He or she will need to replace his or her coverage privately and may find such factors as being older or having a degraded health status leading to heavy costs.

In the case of premium payments in a group plan, it matters who pays for what. Tax consequences will vary depending on payment source. With disability insurance, for example, if the premium is paid for by the employer, then the benefit received is taxed. If, instead, the individual makes the payments, then the benefit is not taxed. Be sure to discuss this with your plan administrator.

INDIVIDUAL HEALTH INSURANCE

Individual health insurance covers either one person or a family. If the kind of health insurance you need is not available through a group or if you need coverage in addition to the coverage a group provides, you should obtain an individual policy—a policy tailored to your particular needs—from the company of your choice. This requires careful shopping because coverage and cost vary from company to company.

Find out what your group insurance will pay for and what it won't. Make sure you have enough insurance, but don't waste money by overinsuring.

SUPPLEMENTING YOUR GROUP INSURANCE

A sign that your group coverage needs supplementing would be its failure to provide benefits for the major portion of your medical care bills. If, for example, your group policy will pay only $50 per day toward a hospital room and the cost in your area is $100, you should look for an individual policy that covers most of the remaining amount. In supplementing your group health insurance, also consider the health insurance benefits your employer-sponsored plan provides for family members.

If you have any questions about your group plan, you should be able to get answers from your employer, union, or association. If you have questions about an individual policy, talk with your insurance company representative.

CONCEPT CHECK 9–6

1. What is health insurance, and what is its purpose?

DISABILITY INCOME INSURANCE

◼ OBJECTIVE 7 ◼

Recognize the need for disability income insurance.

Because you feel healthy, you may overlook the very real need for disability income insurance. Disability income insurance protects your most valuable asset: your ability to earn income. Most people are more likely to lose their incomes due to disability than to death. The fact is that for all age groups, disability is more likely than death.

Disability income insurance provides regular cash earnings lost by individuals as the result of an accident or illness. Disability income insurance is probably the most neglected form of insurance protection. Many people who insure their houses, cars, and other property fail to insure their most valuable resource: their earning power. Disability can cause much greater financial problems than death. In fact, disability is often called "the living death." Disabled persons lose earning power while expenses continue to rise. They often face huge expenses for the medical treatment and special care their disabilities require.

disability income insurance Provides payments to replace income when an insured person is unable to work.

If you are between ages 35 and 65, your chances of being unable to work for 90 days or more due to a disabling illness or injury are about equal to your chances of dying. To be more specific, at age 40 you face a 12-percent chance of dying before reaching age 65 and a 19-percent chance of having at least one disability lasting 90 days or longer.[1] If you have no disability income protection, you are betting that you will not become disabled, and that could be a very costly bet.

The probability of a male becoming temporarily or permanently disabled between ages 20 and 30 is 1.3 percent, but between ages 20 and 60, it increases to 19.1 percent. Females have only a 15.3 percent chance of becoming disabled between 20 and 60 years of age.[2]

DEFINITION OF DISABILITY

Disability has several definitions. The *own occupation* definition refers to the inability to perform the duties of your ordinary occupation, and full benefits will be provided even if you return to work in some other capacity. Under a *regular occupation* definition, you are insured if you cannot perform the duties of your ordinary occupation, but benefits will be reduced if you return to an alternative occupation. Under an *any occupation* definition, full benefits are paid only if you cannot perform the duties of any occupation for which your experience or education qualifies you. *Total disability* occurs if you are unable to work at all, while *residual or partial disability* benefits apply of you are able to work, but at a reduced workload.

Good disability plans pay when you are unable to work at your regular job; poor disability plans pay only when you are unable to work at any job. A good disability plan will also make partial disability payments when you return to work on a part-time basis.

DISABILITY INSURANCE TRADE-OFFS

Following are some important trade-offs you should consider in purchasing disability income insurance.

WAITING OR ELIMINATION PERIOD Benefits don't
begin on the first day you become disabled. Usually, there is a waiting or elimination period of between 30 and 90 days. Some waiting periods may be as long as 180 days. Generally, disability income policies with longer waiting periods have lower premiums. If you have substantial savings to cover three to six months of expenses, the reduced premiums of a policy with a long waiting period may be attractive. But if you need every paycheque to cover your bills, you are probably better off paying the higher premium for a short waiting period. Short waiting periods, however, are very expensive.

> **DID YOU KNOW ?**
>
> In 2004, some 3,601,000 Canadians were disabled—that's one in eight. A third of all people now aged 35 will be unable to work for six months before reaching age 65.
>
> SOURCE: www.sdc.gc.ca/en/hip/odi/documents/research Bulletin04/researchBulletin04.pdf; www.insurance-canada.ca "Shopping for Disability Insurance" by Jim Bullock, 1997.

---

[1] *The Consumer's Guide to Disability Insurance* (Washington, DC: Health Insurance Association of America, September 1991), p. 1.

[2] *Source Book of Health Data* (Washington, DC: Health Insurance Association of America, 1991), pp. 95–96.

DURATION OF BENEFITS The maximum time a disability income policy will pay benefits may be a few years, to age 65, or for life. You should seek a policy that pays benefits for life. If you became permanently disabled, it would be financially disastrous if your benefits ended at age 55 or 65.

AMOUNT OF BENEFITS You should aim for a benefit amount that, when added to your other income, will equal 60 to 70 percent of your gross pay. Of course, the greater the benefits, the greater the cost.

ACCIDENT AND SICKNESS COVERAGE Consider both accident and sickness coverage. Some disability income policies will pay only for accidents, but you want to be insured for illness, too.

GUARANTEED RENEWABILITY Ask for noncancellable and guaranteed renewable coverage. Either coverage will protect you against your insurance company dropping you if your health becomes poor. The premium for these coverages is higher, but the coverages are well worth the extra cost. Furthermore, look for a disability income policy that waives premium payments while you are disabled.

SOURCES OF DISABILITY INCOME

Before you buy disability income insurance, remember that you may already have some form of such insurance. This coverage may come to you through your employer, government benefits, or worker's compensation. Use Exhibit 9–8 to determine how much income you will have available if you become disabled.

EMPLOYER Many, but not all, employers provide disability income protection for their employees through group insurance plans. Your employer may have some form of wage continuation policy that lasts a few months or an employee group disability plan that provides long-term protection. In most cases, your employer will pay part or all of the cost of this plan.

PRIVATE Most medical insurance policies offered by insurance companies will include coverage for disability. The exact details of coverage will depend on the cost of your premium, the company, and your policy details.

Exhibit 9–8

Disability Income Worksheet

How much income will you have available if you become disabled?

	Monthly Amount	After Waiting:	For a Period of:
Sick leave or short-term disability	_____	_____	_____
Group long-term disability	_____	_____	_____
Employment Insurance	_____	_____	_____
Other government programs	_____	_____	_____
Individual disability insurance	_____	_____	_____
Credit disability insurance	_____	_____	_____
Other income:	_____	_____	_____
Savings	_____	_____	_____
Spouse's income	_____	_____	_____
Total monthly income while disabled:	$_____		

PUBLIC The provincial governments have established various social programs to provide some insurance against disability. The protection available may vary from one province to another, and eligibility requirements might include your having previously contributed to the program or your having suffered your injury either at work or during military service. The major social supports available to the disabled in Canada are outlined briefly below.

Employment Insurance This is a federal program that will provide short-term benefits to those who have previously contributed. While very helpful for short-term health issues, its benefits are limited by the relatively short term in which payments will be made.

> ### DID YOU KNOW ?
>
> In 2004, the average Canada Pension Plan disability benefit was $749.08 per month.
>
> www.sdc.gc.ca/en/isp/pub/factsheets/rates.shtml

Canada and Quebec Pension Plans Both these plans include a disability pension for contributors with a severe or prolonged disability. The funds can also be used in compensation for dependants and survivors. Again, however, the payments obtained from these plans are inadequate to maintain a decent standard of living. The Canada Pension Plan, for example, provides a disability pension of up to a maximum of $1,013.23 monthly to age 65 (rate as of April 2005), after which a regular pension is paid. Furthermore, the rules and restrictions regarding these plans are very strict, and many disabilities do not qualify, particularly if they are only partial.

Worker's Compensation These are provincial plans that provide medical, financial, and rehabilitative assistance to workers who suffer disability as a result of accidents or illness related to their work.

Short-Term or Long-Term Welfare Provided at a municipal and provincial level, these programs are geared toward those with extremely limited alternative financial resources.

Whatever the form of social support you receive, it is virtually certain to be insufficient for your needs. At best, these government programs should be viewed as a supplement to your disability insurance coverage, rather than as a replacement.

DETERMINING YOUR DISABILITY INCOME INSURANCE REQUIREMENTS

When considering the amount of benefits available, several separate calculations should be made, depending on different levels of disability (severe to mild) and based on how long your current resources, all mentioned above (e.g., employer-provided sick leave, workers' compensation, non-salary income from investments) would last in the event that a disability occured. If the sum of your disability benefits approaches your after-tax income, you can safely assume that should disability strike, you'll be in good shape to pay your day-to-day bills while recuperating.

You should know how long you would have to wait before the benefits begin (the waiting or elimination period) and how long they would be paid (the benefit period).

What if, as is often the case, your disability benefits are not sufficient to support your family? In that case, you may want to consider buying disability income insurance to make up the difference.

Don't expect to insure yourself for your full salary. Most insurers limit benefits from all sources to no more than 70 to 80 percent of your take-home pay. For example, if you earn $400 a week, you could be eligible for disability insurance of about $280 to $320 a week. You will not need $400 because while you are disabled, your work-related expenses will be eliminated and your taxes will be far lower or may be even zero.

The Financial Planning for Life's Situations box on the next page shows you how to compare different features among disability income policies.

Clearly, anticipating the costs of long-term care by considering insurance is sound financial planning, but there are various factors to consider. The cost of LTC insurance itself can be prohibitive, depending on your age and policy options.

The annual premium for LTC policies can range depending on your age and the choices you make. The older you are when you enroll, the higher your annual premium. Typically, individual insurance plans are sold to the 50-to-80 age group, pay benefits for a maximum of two to six years, and carry a dollar limit on the total benefits they will pay.

The Financial Planning for Life's Situations box on page 269 can help you compare the features of long-term-care policies.

An insurance company usually allows you a minimum of 10 days to review your health insurance policy, so be sure to check the major provisions that affect your coverage. Other major provisions are described in the following sections.

MAJOR PROVISIONS IN A HEALTH INSURANCE POLICY

All health insurance policies have certain provisions in common. Be sure you understand what your policy covers. Even the most comprehensive policy may be of little value if a provision in small print limits or denies benefits.

ELIGIBILITY   The eligibility provision defines who is entitled to benefits under the policy. Age, marital status, and dependency requirements are usually specified in this provision. For example, foster children usually are not automatically covered under the family contract, but stepchildren may be. Check with your insurance company to be sure.

ASSIGNED BENEFITS   When you assign benefits, you sign a paper allowing your insurance company to make payments to your hospital or doctor. Otherwise, the payments will be made to you when you turn in your bills and claim forms to the company.

INTERNAL LIMITS   A policy with internal limits will pay only a fixed amount for your hospital, room no matter what the actual rate is. For example, if your policy has an internal limit of $200 per hospital day and you are in a $300-a-day hospital room, you will have to pay the difference.

co-payment A provision under which the insured pays a flat dollar amount each time a covered medical service is received after the deductible has been met.

CO-PAYMENT   **Co-payment** is a type of cost sharing. Most major medical plans define co-payment as the amount the patient must pay for medical services after the deductible has been met. You pay a flat dollar amount each time you receive a covered medical service. Co-payments for prescriptions are common. The amount of co-payment does not vary with the cost of service.

BENEFIT LIMITS   The benefit limits provision defines the maximum benefits possible, in terms of either a dollar amount or a number of days in the hospital. Many policies today have benefit limits.

EXCLUSIONS AND LIMITATIONS   The exclusions and limitations provision specifies the conditions or circumstances for which the policy does not provide benefits. For example, the policy may exclude coverage for pre-existing conditions or cosmetic surgery.

COORDINATION OF BENEFITS   As discussed earlier, the coordination of benefits provision prevents you from collecting benefits from two or more group policies that would in total exceed the actual charges. Under this provision, the benefits from your own and your spouse's policies are coordinated to allow up to 100 percent payment of your covered charges.

www.gov.on.ca/health is a site of the Ontario Ministry of Health and Long-Term Care that educates users about mental health, women's health, long-term care, drug programs, medical insurance, and health care professional regulations.

www.clhia.ca/ is the site for the Canadian Life & Health Insurance Association, which represents the majority of life and health insurance companies in Canada. Check here for facts and figures about insurance in Canada. They also provide a list of insurance companies that offer disability insurance.

www.compcorp.ca is the site of COMPCORP, the Canadian Life and Health Insurance Compensation Corporation, which was created by the life and health insurance industry in Canada to provide Canadian policyholders with protection, within limits, against loss of policy benefits in the event of the insolvency of their insurance company. Check here to discover the extent of protection afforded to you should your insurance company dissolve.

www.hc-sc.gc.ca/medicare is Health Canada's site to provide information about medicare and the Canada Health Act.

GUARANTEED RENEWABLE With this policy provision, the insurance company cannot cancel a policy unless you fail to pay premiums when due. Also, it cannot raise premiums unless a rate increase occurs for all policyholders in that group.

CANCELLATION AND TERMINATION This provision explains the circumstances under which the insurance company can terminate your health insurance policy. It also explains your right to convert a group contract into an individual contract.

HEALTH INSURANCE TRADE-OFFS

The benefits of health insurance policies differ, and the differences can have a significant impact on your premiums. Consider the following trade-offs:

REIMBURSEMENT VERSUS INDEMNITY A reimbursement policy provides benefits based on the actual expenses you incur. An indemnity policy provides specified benefits, regardless of whether the actual expenses are greater or less than the benefits.

INTERNAL LIMITS VERSUS AGGREGATE LIMITS A policy with internal limits stipulates maximum benefits for specific expenses, such as the maximum reimbursement for daily hospital room and board. Other policies may limit only the total amount of coverage, such as $1 million major expense benefits, or may have no limits.

DEDUCTIBLES AND CO-INSURANCE The cost of a health insurance policy can be greatly affected by the size of the deductible (the amount you must pay toward medical expenses before the insurance company pays), the degree of co-insurance, and the share of medical expenses you must pay (for example, 20 percent).

OUT-OF-POCKET LIMIT A policy that limits the total of the co-insurance and deductibles you must pay (for example, $2,000) will limit or eliminate your financial risk, but it will also increase the premium.

1. If you pay your own premiums directly, try to arrange to pay them on an annual or quarterly basis, rather than a monthly basis. It is cheaper.
2. Policies should be delivered to you within 30 days. If not, contact your insurer and find out, in writing, why.
3. When you receive a policy, take advantage of the free-look provision. You have 10 days to look it over and obtain a refund if you decide it is not for you.
4. Unless you have a policy with no internal limits, read over your contract every year to see whether its benefits are still in line with medical costs.
5. Don't replace a policy because you think it is out of date. Switching may subject you to new waiting periods and new exclusions. Rather, add to what you have, if necessary.
6. On the other hand, don't keep a policy because you've had it a long time. You don't get any special credit from the company for being an old customer.
7. Don't try to make a profit on your insurance by carrying overlapping coverages. Duplicate coverage is expensive. Besides, most group policies now contain a coordination of benefits clause limiting benefits to 100 percent.
8. Use your health emergency fund to cover small expenses.
9. If you're considering the purchase of a critical illness policy, such as cancer insurance, understand that it is supplementary and will pay for only certain diseases. You should have full coverage before you consider it. Otherwise, it's a gamble.
10. Don't lie on your insurance application. If you fail to mention a pre-existing condition, you may not get paid. You can usually get paid even for that condition after one or two years have elapsed if you have had no treatment for the condition during that period.
11. Keep your insurance up to date. Some policies adjust to inflation better than others. Some insurers check that benefits have not been outdistanced by inflation. Review your policies annually.
12. Never sign a health insurance application (such applications are lengthy and detailed for individually written policies) until you have recorded full and complete answers to every question.

SOURCE: Health Insurance Association of America.

Visit the Web site
See the Post-Test under Chapter 9 on the online learning centre at www.mcgrawhill.ca/college/kapoor.

HEALTH INFORMATION ONLINE

Recent studies indicate that consumers are seeking information on health and health care online to supplement traditional medical counsel. Many legitimate providers of reliable health and medical information, including Health Canada, offer brochures and in-depth information on specific topics at their Web sites. The Financial Planning for Life's Situations feature on page 271 lists some good health care Web sites, and the feature above provides some tips for consumers.

CONCEPT CHECK 9–8

1. What are several types of health insurance coverage available under group and individual policies?
2. What are the major provisions of a health insurance policy?
3. How do you decide which coverage to choose?
4. How can you analyze the costs and benefits of your health insurance policy?

SUMMARY OF OBJECTIVES

Objective 1
Define *life insurance* and describe its purpose and principle.

Life insurance is a contract between an insurance company and a policyholder under which the company agrees to pay a specified sum to a beneficiary upon the insured's death. Most people buy life insurance to protect someone who depends on them from financial loss caused by their death. Fundamental to the life insurance principle is the predictable mortality experience of a large group of individuals.

Objective 2
Determine your life insurance needs.

In determining your life insurance needs, you must first determine your insurance objectives and then use the income replacement method, or the family need method to calculate the amount of insurance needed. The family need method is recommended. You should consider a number of factors before you buy insurance, including your present and future sources of income, other savings and income protection, group life insurance, group annuities (or other pension benefits), and government benefits.

Objective 3
Distinguish between the two types of life insurance policies and analyze various types of life insurance.

The two types of life insurance policies are term life or permanent life. In general, term insurance provides protection against a specified financial risk for a finite period of time, often 10 or 20 years. Permanent life insurance is purchased to cover lifelong needs, such as funeral expenses and supplementing a survivor's income. Many variations of these two types of life insurance policies are available. Term life insurance is available with a renewability option, conversion option, or a decreasing option. Permanent life insurance is available in the following forms: whole life, universal life, and variable insurance. There are many additional options; therefore, you should check with your insurance company to determine which type offers the best policy for your particular needs at the lowest price.

As with other forms of insurance, price should not be your only consideration in choosing a life insurance policy. You should also consider the financial stability, reliability, and service the insurance company provides.

Objective 4
Select important provisions in life insurance contracts.

The naming of the beneficiary, the grace period, policy reinstatement, the incontestability clause, the suicide clause, automatic premium loans, the misstatement of age provision, and the policy loan provision are important provisions in most life insurance policies. Common riders in life insurance policies

are the waiver of premium disability benefit, the accidental death benefit, the guaranteed insurability option, cost of living protection, and accelerated benefits.

Objective 5
Create a plan to buy life insurance.

Before buying life insurance, consider your present and future sources of income, group life insurance, group annuities (or other pension benefits), and government benefits. Then compare the costs of several life insurance policies. Examine your policy before and after the purchase, and choose appropriate settlement options. The most common settlement options are lump-sum payment, limited installment payment, life income option, and proceeds left with the company. Online services provide a wealth of information about all topics related to life insurance.

Objective 6
Define *health insurance* and explain its importance in financial planning.

Health insurance is protection that provides payment of benefits for a covered sickness or injury. Disability income insurance protects a person's most valuable asset: the ability to earn income. Critical illness insurance protects against the most common critical illness

Health insurance, critical illness, and disability income insurance are three protections against economic losses due to illness, accident, or disability. These should be a part of your overall insurance program to safeguard your family's economic security.

Disability can cause even greater financial problems than death. In fact, disability is often called "the living death." Disabled persons lose their earning power while continuing to incur normal expenses. In addition, they often face huge expenses for the medical treatment and special care their disabilities require.

Objective 7
Recognize the need for disability income insurance.

Disability income insurance provides regular cash income lost by employees as the result of an accident or illness. Sources of disability income insurance include the employer, government benefits, unions, and private insurance.

Objective 8
Understand the value of supplemental health insurance.

Supplemental health insurance is coverage that you can purchase in addition to the coverage available to you from the government, your employer, and other policies. Types of supplemental health insurance include dental expense insurance, vision care insurance, and long-term-care insurance.

KEY TERMS

beneficiary 254

cash value 250

co-payment 270

disability income insurance 263

double indemnity 255

incontestability clause 254

interest-adjusted index 257

long-term care 268

nonforfeiture clause 254

nonparticipating policy 250

participating policy 250

rider 255

suicide clause 255

term insurance 246

universal life 251

whole life policy 248

FINANCIAL PLANNING PROBLEMS

1. *Illustrating the Principle of Life Insurance.* A group of 100,000 males, age 30, wish to contribute each year an amount to a common fund sufficient to pay $1,000 to the dependants of each group member who dies during the year. Use the mortality table in Exhibit 9–1 to determine the following: (Obj. 1)

   a. How many members of the group can be expected to die during the year?

   b. What amount must each of the 100,000 members contribute at the beginning of the year to provide $1,000 for the dependants of those who die before the end of the year?

2. *Calculating the Amount of Life Insurance Needed Using the Income Replacement Method.* You are the wage earner in a "typical family," with $30,000 gross annual income. Use the income replacement method to determine how much life insurance you should carry. (Obj. 2)

3. *Comparing the Methods of Determining Life Insurance Requirements.* Analyze the two methods of determining life insurance requirements. Which method is best, and why? (Obj. 2)

4. *Estimating Life Insurance Needs Using the Family Need Method.* You and your spouse are in good health and have reasonably secure careers. You make about $35,000 annually and have opted for life insurance coverage of three times your salary through your employer. With your spouse's income, you are able to absorb ongoing living costs of $45,000 a year. You own a home with an $80,000 mortgage. Other debts include a $10,000 car loan, $5,000 student loan, and $3,000 charged to credit cards. In the event of your death, you wish to leave your family debt-free. One of your most important financial goals involves building an education fund of $50,000 to cover the cost of a three-year university program for your two-year-old child. To date, you have accumulated $15,000 toward this goal. Should you die, your beneficiaries would receive a $2,500 lump sum payment from the Canada Pension Plan and $10,000 from your corporate pension plan. Your other financial assets are as follows:

Bank accounts	$2,100
Term deposits (3 months)	3,000
Canada Savings Bonds	1,000
Stock investment account	2,500

   Use the Family Need Method to determine your life insurance needs. (Obj. 2)

5. *Comparing the Costs of Life Insurance and Various Provisions in a Life Insurance Policy.* Obtain premium rates for $25,000 whole life, universal life, and term life policies from local insurance agents. Compare the costs and provisions of these policies. (Obj. 3)

6. *Calculating Your Life Insurance Needs.* Use Exhibit 9–2 to calculate your life insurance needs. (Obj. 3)

7. *Calculating the Amount of Disability Benefits.* Georgia Braxton, a widow, has take-home pay of $600 a week. Her disability insurance coverage replaces 70 percent of her earnings after a four-week waiting period. However, depending on who is making the premium payments, the replacement earnings may be taxable. What amount would she receive in disability benefits if an illness kept Georgia off work for 16 weeks? (Obj. 7)

FINANCIAL PLANNING ACTIVITIES

1. *Assessing the Need for Life Insurance.* Interview relatives and friends to determine why they purchased life insurance. Prepare an essay summarizing your findings. (Obj. 1)

2. *Comparing Premiums for Life Insurance Policies.* Choose one stock company and one mutual life insurance company. Obtain and compare premiums for

   a. Term life insurance for $50,000.

   b. Whole life insurance for $50,000.

   c. Universal life insurance for $50,000.

   Prepare a summary table indicating which policy you would consider and why. (Obj. 3)

3. *Reviewing an Employer's Health Benefit Package.* List the benefits included in your employee benefit package, such as health insurance, disability income insurance, and life insurance. Discuss the importance of such a benefit package to the consumer. (Obj. 6)

4. *Comparing Major Provisions in a Health-Care Insurance Policy.* Obtain sample health insurance policies from insurance agents or brokers, and analyze the policies for definitions, coverages, exclusions, limitations on coverage, and amounts of coverage. In what ways are the policies similar? In what ways do they differ? (Obj. 7)

CREATING A FINANCIAL PLAN

Comparing Health Insurance Plans

Changing programs and regulations influence your ability to be properly covered for health care and disability insurance coverage. Awareness of policy types, coverages, and limitations will help you plan this phase of your financial plan.

Web Sites for Life Insurance

- Find out more about the insurance industry by visiting the Canadian Life & Health Insurance Association at **www.clhia.ca**.
- Find out about the protection afforded to Canadian Insurance product buyers at **www.compcorp.ca/**, the site for COMPCORP (the Canadian Life and Health Insurance Compen-sation Corporation).
- Robert Barney has written a number of articles strongly in favour of term insurance over whole life and universal life insurance for *Canadian MoneySaver* magazine. You can view these articles as well as contributions by other authors at **www.canadianmoneysaver.ca**.

Web Sites for Health and Disability Insurance

- Visit the Health Canada site at **www.hc-sc.gc.ca/medicare** to learn more about medicare and the Canada Health Act.

- The Life and Health Insurance Foundation for Education (LIFE), at **www.life-line.org**, is an American nonprofit organization that provides information and education on life, health, and disability insurance. They also have a "disability needs" calculator to help you establish how much disability insurance you may need. Much of the information is applicable to Canada.
- You can visit the Blue Cross's Canadian site at **www.blue cross.ca** to find out about the health and disability insurance products it offers.

(Note: Addresses and content of Web sites change, and new sites are created daily. Use search engines to update and locate Web sites for your current financial planning needs.)

Short-Term Financial Planning Activities

1. Analyze current health insurance coverage in relation to family and household needs.
2. Compare the cost of health insurance programs available from various sources.

Long-Term Financial Planning Activities

1. Develop a plan for reducing health-care and disability insurance costs.

LIFE SITUATION CASE

How Much Is Enough?

Joanne and Glenn Kitsos recently had their second child and decided to make a change to their life insurance. "We've got two kids now, and we have to start thinking about the future." Joanne said.

The Kitsoses and other new parents are among the people experts say ought to have life insurance. Anyone who has someone financially dependent on them or anyone whose death would cause someone to lose money should be insured.

"Term life insurance is extraordinarily cheap when people are in their 20s and 30s, so people with children should purchase a sufficient amount," says Elliot S. Lipson, a financial planner. "All too often, people buy expensive policies that offer savings or investment components but lack a basic benefit that is large enough to provide for their needs."

The amount you need isn't easy to determine because the total can be as little as five times and as much as 10 times your annual salary.

Jim Hunt, consultant to a major insurance group, says the total need for an average couple with two young children is close to six to eight times their salary. For example, the Kitsoses' combined income is $100,000, so they probably need a minimum of $600,000 in insurance and maybe a little more if they have no group life insurance at work.

Here are a few questions to ask when figuring how much life insurance you need:

- How much income will your dependants need every year if you die?
- How much income will your dependants have from other sources, such as investments, pensions, or savings, if you die?
- How much income will your dependants have access to from sources, such as your spouse's salary or government benefits?

Once you've come up with a total, you have to decide whether you want term, whole life, or some hybrid variation.

Your goal, Hunt says, is to buy as much insurance as you need. But because of the costs of whole life insurance, that often means term. While whole life costs more in the early years, it guarantees that you will pay the same premium 10, 15, or even 20 years down the road.

The Kitsoses started out with whole life insurance, but they have decided to switch to term insurance that will last until their kids graduate from college. They want to have enough insurance to cover their funeral costs and the cost of their children's college educations. But rather than using their insurance as an investment, they plan to invest more in mutual funds.

Questions

1. What is the advantage of buying life insurance when you are younger, and what is a good reason for having it?
2. What would be the total coverage needed for an average couple with two children and a combined income of $45,000?
3. What is one advantage of whole life insurance?
4. Is term insurance the right choice for the Kitsoses? Why, or why not?

SOURCES: Earl C. Gottschalk Jr., "Avoiding the Big Mistakes along Life's Path," *The Wall Street Journal*, May 27, 1997, p. C1; Candy McCampbell, "How Much Insurance to Carry Is a Question Not Easily Answered," *Gannett News Service*, July 9, 1997, p. S12.

CONTINUOUS CASE FOR PART 3

MANAGING RISKS FOR EFFECTIVE FINANCIAL PLANNING

Life Situation
Pamela, 36; Isaac, 38; three children, ages 9, 7, and 4

Financial Goals

- Evaluate property and liability insurance needs
- Assess the need for disability insurance
- Determine additional life insurance needs

Financial Data

Monthly income	$ 4,300
Living expenses	4,075
Assets	150,850
Liabilities	99,520

Both Pamela and Isaac Mortimer are comfortable. They now have three children, are happy with their home, and are more financially secure than they were six years ago. In fact, everything seems to be right on track. Yet the Mortimers still have financial needs they must address. Several changes have affected their financial planning:

- The value of their home has increased due to inflation and home improvements.

- They have purchased a used car to meet additional transportation needs.
- Isaac's current employer offers him only 30 days of sick leave.
- Pamela's life insurance policy is for only $2,000. Isaac has life insurance coverage equal to approximately eight times his annual salary.

Questions

1. How should the Mortimers determine whether they have enough insurance coverage for their home?
2. What factors should the Mortimers consider in deciding whether to purchase collision insurance coverage for their used car?
3. When considering disability income insurance, what length of waiting period and duration of benefits should the Mortimers consider?
4. Do you think Pamela and Isaac Mortimer have enough life insurance? If not, what changes would you recommend? Explain your answer.

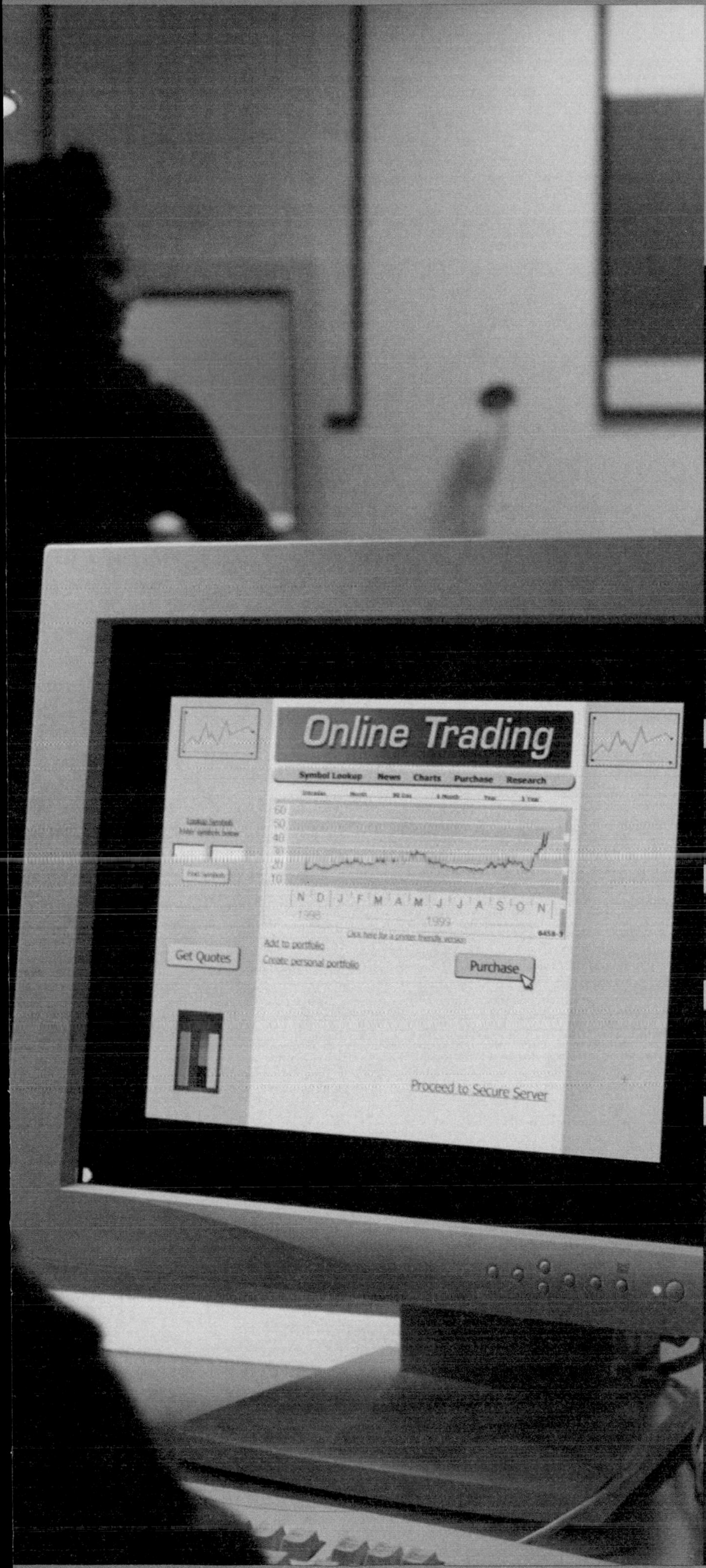

PART 4

INVESTING YOUR FINANCIAL RESOURCES

10

Fundamentals of Investing

THE MONEYSENSE PERSONAL FINANCE WEB SITE: HELP YOU CAN USE

Need some help establishing an investment program? Why not go to the Internet? That's what Jane and Brian Seward did. Six months ago, they purchased a computer for their two kids to use for schoolwork. Little did they realize how the computer would affect their investment planning and other financial decisions.

One afternoon, Jane was helping one of the kids with a homework assignment to determine the effect of compounding on savings. After looking at a number of different sites, they found the Moneysense personal finance Web site. As they wandered around through the site, they soon forgot about the assignment. The site, beyond offering current rates and various types of calculators, was a gold mine of personal finance information. There were no "get rich quick" schemes, but instead some solid financial advice and analysis that would help the Seward family with their finances.

Today, more and more Canadians are using the Internet to help plan their financial future, evaluate investment alternatives, and monitor the value of their investments. Although just one of many, the Moneysense Web site (www.moneysense.ca) is an excellent choice not only for beginning investors like Jane and Brian but also for more experienced investors. Within the site, the Sewards found information on credit, investing, tax planning, home mortgages, and a number of other important topics.

After reading the material on the Web site, both Jane and Brian decided it was time to take charge of their family's finances. They began by paying off some high-interest credit card bills and saving some money they could use for emergencies. Then, they started saving the money needed to finance an investment program. During this time, they also continued to learn. They studied additional material in the Moneysense Web site, visited other financial planning Web sites, and began to read *MoneySaver* and *IE:Money* magazines. They even began tracking some potential stock and mutual fund investments in anticipation of when they could actually purchase their first investments. According to Brian, their financial planning was not only rewarding but also fun. For the first time since they got married, they were getting their financial affairs in order.

QUESTIONS

1 How important is an investment program for financial planning?

2 Jane and Brian Seward began their search for investment information by examining the Moneysense Web site. If you were seeking help to establish an investment program, where would you obtain the needed information?

LEARNING OBJECTIVES

1   Explain why you should establish an investment program.

2   Describe how safety, risk, income, growth, and liquidity affect your investment decisions.

3   Identify the major types of investment alternatives.

4   Recognize the role of the professional financial planner and your role in a personal investment program.

5   Use various sources of financial information that can reduce risks and increase investment returns.

PREPARING FOR AN INVESTMENT PROGRAM

The old saying goes "I've been rich and I've been poor, but believe me, rich is better." While being rich doesn't guarantee happiness, the accumulation of money does provide financial security and is a worthy goal. Jane and Brian Seward, the couple in the opening case, began their financial planning and investment program by examining the material in the Moneysense site. Why not take a look and see the type of financial and investment information that it offers? View the material that the Sewards used to create their financial plan. Type in the following Web address: www.moneysense.ca. Within this page, you will find information on investments, stocks, and money management.

By studying the material contained in this Web site and following the basic investment principles presented in this chapter, along with the information on stocks, bonds, mutual funds, real estate, and other investments in the remaining chapters in Part 4, you can create an investment plan that is custom-made for you.

The decision to establish an investment plan is an important first step to accomplishing your long-term financial goals. Like other decisions, the decision to start an investment plan is one you must make for yourself. No one is going to make you save the money you need to fund an investment plan. These things won't be done unless you want to do them. In fact, the *specific* goals you want to accomplish must be the driving force behind your investment plan.

■ OBJECTIVE 1 ■

Explain why you should establish an investment program.

ESTABLISHING INVESTMENT GOALS

Some people say they want to be rich. Others say they want to be financially secure. But it takes more than just wishing. While it would be nice if you could magically accumulate wealth, it takes careful planning and discipline to achieve the financial freedom you desire. For most people, the first step is to establish investment goals. Without investment goals, you cannot know what you want to accomplish.

To be useful, investment goals must be specific and measurable. They must be tailored to your particular financial needs. Some financial planners suggest that investment goals be stated in terms of money: By December 31, 2008, I will have total assets of $120,000. Other financial planners believe investors are more motivated to work toward goals that are stated in terms of the particular things they desire: By January 1, 2008, I will have accumulated enough money to purchase a second home in the mountains. The following questions will help you establish valid investment goals:

[1]   What will you use the money for?
[2]   How much money do you need to satisfy your investment goals?
[3]   How will you obtain the money?
[4]   How long will it take you to obtain the money?
[5]   How much risk are you willing to assume in an investment program?

[6]   What possible economic or personal conditions could alter your investment goals?

[7]   Considering your economic circumstances, are your investment goals reasonable?

[8]   Are you willing to make the sacrifices necessary to ensure that you meet your investment goals?

[9]   What will the consequences be if you don't reach your investment goals?

Your investment goals are always oriented toward the future. In Chapter 1, we classified goals as short term (less than two years), intermediate (two to five years), or long term (more than five years). These same classifications are also useful in planning your investment program. For example, you may establish a short-term goal of accumulating $3,000 in a savings account over the next 18 months. You may then use the $3,000 to purchase stocks or mutual funds to help you obtain your intermediate or long-term investment goals.

PERFORMING A FINANCIAL CHECKUP

Before beginning an investment program, your personal financial affairs should be in good shape. In this section, we examine several factors you should consider before making your first investment.

WORK AND LEARN TO SAVE TO BALANCE YOUR BUDGET Most often, people must learn to live within their means before they begin investing. Many individuals regularly spend more than they make. They purchase items on credit and then must make monthly installment payments and pay finance charges ranging between 0 and 28 percent or higher (some retail cards can charge up to 28.8 percent interest). With this situation, it makes no sense to start an investment program until credit card and installment purchases, along with the accompanying finance charges, are reduced or eliminated. Therefore, you should limit credit purchases to only the necessities or to purchases required to meet emergencies. A good rule of thumb is to limit installment payments to 10 percent of your monthly pay after taxes. Eventually, the amount of cash remaining after the bills are paid will increase and can be used to start a savings program or finance investments. A word of caution: Corrective measures take time, and it is impossible to improve a bad situation overnight.

OBTAIN ADEQUATE INSURANCE PROTECTION We discussed insurance in detail in Part 3 and will not cover that topic again here. However, it is essential that you consider insurance needs before beginning an investment program. The types of insurance and the amount of coverage will vary from one person to the next. Before you start investing, examine the amount of your insurance coverage for life insurance, hospitalization, your home and other real estate holdings, automobiles, and any other assets that may need coverage.

emergency fund An amount of money you can obtain quickly in case of immediate need.

START AN EMERGENCY FUND Most financial planners suggest that an investment program should begin with the accumulation of an emergency fund. An **emergency fund** is an amount of money you can obtain quickly in case of immediate need. This money should be deposited in a savings account paying the highest available interest rate or in a money market mutual fund that provides immediate access to cash, if needed.

The amount of money to be put away in the emergency fund varies from person to person. However, most financial planners agree that an amount equal to three to nine months' living expenses is reasonable. For example, Della Martinez earns $30,000 a year. Her monthly expenses total $1,600. Before Della can begin investing, she must save at least $4,800 ($1,600 × 3 months = $4,800) in a savings account or other near-cash investments to meet emergencies.

HAVE ACCESS TO OTHER SOURCES OF CASH FOR EMERGENCY NEEDS You may also want to establish a line of credit, which is an arrangement between a financial institution (usually a bank) and a customer establishing a maximum loan balance that the bank will permit the borrower to maintain. The advantage of a line of credit compared to a regular loan is that you usually don't pay interest on the part of the loan that you don't use. Because the paperwork has already been completed and the loan has been pre-approved, you can later obtain the money as soon as you need it. The cash advance provision offered by major credit card companies can also be used in an emergency.

However, both lines of credit and credit cards have a ceiling, or maximum dollar amount, that limits the amount of available credit. If you have already exhausted both these sources of credit on everyday expenses, they will not be available in an emergency.

GETTING THE MONEY NEEDED TO START AN INVESTMENT PROGRAM

Once you have established your investment goals and completed your personal financial checkup, it's time to start investing—assuming you have enough money to finance your investments. Unfortunately, the money doesn't automatically appear. In today's world, you must work to accumulate the money you need to start any type of investment program.

PRIORITY OF INVESTMENT GOALS   How badly do you
want to achieve your investment goals? Are you willing to sacrifice some purchases to provide financing for your investments? The answers to both questions are extremely important. Take Rita Plouffe, a 32-year-old nurse in a large Vancouver hospital. As part of a divorce settlement in 2003, she received a cash payment of almost $55,000. At first, she was tempted to spend this money on a trip to Europe, a new BMW, and new furniture. But after some careful planning, she decided to save $35,000 in a Guaranteed Investment Certificate (GIC) and invest the remainder in a conservative mutual fund.

> **DID YOU KNOW ?**
>
> In 2003, polling showed that most Canadians traditionally favour safer places to invest—particularly their homes, RRSPs, RESPs, and investment real estate.
>
> SOURCE: www.manulife.com/corporate/corporate2.nsf/ Public/canada040303.html

As pointed out earlier in this chapter, no one can make you save money to finance your investment program. You have to *want* to do it.

And *you* may be the most important part of a successful investment program. What is important to you? What do you value? Each of these questions affects your investment goals. At one extreme are people who save or invest as much of each paycheque as they can. Their savings and investment program and the satisfaction they get from attaining their intermediate and long-term financial goals are more important than the more immediate satisfaction of spending a large part of their paycheques on new clothes, a meal at an expensive restaurant, or a weekend getaway. At the other extreme are people who spend everything they make and run out of money before their next paycheque. Most people find either extreme unacceptable and take a more middle-of-the-road approach. These people often spend money on the items that make their life more enjoyable and still save enough to fund an investment program. As you will see later in this section, even a small amount of money saved or invested on a regular basis can amount to a large sum over a period of time.

Here are some suggestions to help you obtain the money you need.

[1] *Pay yourself first.* Too often, people save or invest what is left over after they have paid everything else. As you might guess, nothing is left over in many cases, and the investment program is put on hold for another month. A second and much better approach is to (1) pay your monthly bills, (2) save a reasonable amount of money, and (3) use whatever money is left over for personal expenses, such as new clothes or entertainment.

[2] *Participate in an elective savings program.* You can elect to have money withheld from your paycheque each payday and automatically deposited in a savings account. It is much easier to put money into the account than it is to get money out of it. You can also make investing easier by arranging with a mutual fund or brokerage firm to take a fixed sum from your bank account automatically every month and invest it. An elective savings program is an excellent way to fund an RRSP or RESP (both topics are discussed in Chapters 3 and 14).

FACTORS AFFECTING THE CHOICE OF INVESTMENTS

▮ OBJECTIVE 2 ▮

Describe how safety, risk, income, growth, and liquidity affect your investment decisions.

Millions of Canadians buy stocks, bonds, or mutual funds, purchase gold and silver, or make similar investments. And they all have reasons for investing their money. Some people want to supplement their retirement income when they reach age 65, while others want to become millionaires before age 40. Although each investor may have specific, individual goals for investing, all investors must consider a number of factors before choosing an investment alternative.

SAFETY AND RISK

The safety and risk factors are two sides of the same coin. You cannot evaluate any investment without assessing how safety relates to risk. Safety in an investment means minimal risk of loss. On the other hand, risk in an investment means a measure of uncertainty about the outcome. Investments range from very safe to very risky. At one end of the investment spectrum are very safe investments that attract conservative investors. Investments in this category include government savings bonds, savings accounts, term deposits, guaranteed investment certificates, and certain negotiable government and corporate bonds. Investors pick such investments because they know there is very little chance that investments of this kind will fluctuate in value or become worthless. Many investors choose conservative investments because of the individual life situations in which they find themselves. As people approach retirement, for example, they usually choose more conservative investments with less chance of losing a large part of the nest egg they have built up over the years. Today, one interesting change in investment philosophy is that most financial planners recommend that retirees still invest a small portion of their money in investments that will increase in value. The reason is simple: People are living longer, and they need more money for their retirement years. Some people choose to invest one-time windfalls or inheritances in a conservative investment because they know it may be impossible to replace the money if it is lost. Finally, some investors simply dislike taking chances.

speculative investment A high-risk investment made in the hope of earning a relatively large profit in a short time.

At the other end of the investment spectrum are speculative investments. A **speculative investment** is a high-risk investment made in the hope of earning a relatively large profit in a short time. Such investments offer the possibility of a larger dollar return, but if they are unsuccessful, you may lose most or all of your initial investment. Speculative stocks, certain bonds, real estate, derivatives, commodities, options, precious metals, precious stones, and collectibles are risk-oriented investments. Although many of these investments are discussed in detail in later chapters, they are often considered too risky for beginning investors.

By now, you probably realize that the safety and risk factors are more complex than the simple definitions just presented. From an investor's standpoint, one basic rule sums up the relationship between the factors of safety and risk: *The potential return on any investment should be directly related to the risk the investor assumes.* For example, Anne Landry was injured in a work-related accident three years ago. After a lengthy investigation, she received an insurance settlement totalling $420,000. As a result of the injury, she was no longer qualified to perform her old job as an assembler for an electronics manufacturer. When she thought about the future, she knew she needed to get a job but realized she would be forced to acquire new employment skills. She also realized she had received a great deal of money that could be invested to provide a steady source of income not only for the next two years while she obtained job training but also for the remainder of her life. Having never invested before, she quickly realized her tolerance for risk was minimal. She had to conserve her $420,000 settlement. Eventually, after much discussion with professionals and her own research, she chose to save about half her money in GICs. For the remaining half, she chose three stocks that offered a 4-percent average dividend, a potential for growth, and a high degree of safety because of the financial stability of the corporations that issued the stocks.

A more risk-oriented investor might have criticized Anne's decisions as too conservative. In fact, this second type of investor might have chosen to invest in more speculative stocks that offer a greater potential for growth and increase in market value even though the corporations issuing the stocks are not paying dividends at the present time. Often, beginning investors are afraid of the risk associated with many investments. But it helps to remember that without the risk, it is impossible to obtain the larger returns that really make an investment program grow. The key is to determine how much risk you are willing to assume and then choose quality investments that offer higher returns without an unacceptably high risk. The bottom line is this: What is right for one investor may not be right for another.

The problem of assessing safety and risk is further complicated by the large number of potential investments from which to choose. You must determine how much risk you are willing to assume. Once you have determined the amount of risk you are comfortable with, you can choose different investments that hopefully will provide the expected return.

RISK TOLERANCE

Risk tolerance is the amount of psychological pain you're willing to suffer from your investments. There are risks associated with investing: you could lose part or all of your principal, the purchasing power of your investment can decrease, and you may not receive the returns you expected. In addition, unlike GICs, the money you invest in securities, mutual funds, and other similar investments are not insured by the Canada Deposit Insurance Corporation (CDIC). Therefore, it is important to determine your risk tolerance before you start investing your money. Since you have already determined your investment goals, you already have an idea of how much risk you can tolerate. For example, if you are saving for a short-term goal, you should choose a less risky investment because you need to guarantee that the cash will be available when you need it; you don't want to have to wait if the investment has decreased in value. Some financial advisors may tell you that regardless of age, you must always look towards long-term investing. This is false and is often used as an excuse by investment companies to cover up poor performance. To help you determine how much risk you are willing to assume, take the test for risk tolerance presented in the Financial Planning for Life's Situations feature on the next page. In addition, see the Advice from a Pro feature from Merrill Lynch on page 287.

COMPONENTS OF THE RISK FACTOR

The risk factor associated with a specific investment does change from time to time. For example, the stock of Computer-Tabulating-Recording Company was once considered a high-risk investment. Then, this company changed its name to IBM and eventually became a leader in the computer industry. By the early 1980s, many conservative investors were purchasing IBM stock because of its safety and earnings potential. But in the early 1990s, many of these same investors sold their IBM stock because changes in the computer industry had brought financial problems for IBM. IBM was once again considered too risky for many investors. Now, as a result of solving many of its financial problems, IBM is once again considered a good choice for many investors.

When choosing an investment, you must carefully evaluate changes in the risk factor. We can differentiate different types of risk according to their source, be it the company or its business sector, the economy as a whole, or international factors.

BUSINESS RISK   Business risk is associated with investments in common stock, preferred stock, and corporate bonds. With each of these investments, you face the possibility that bad management, unsuccessful products, competition, or a host of other factors will cause the business to be less profitable than originally anticipated. Lower profits usually mean lower dividends or no dividends at all. If the business continues to operate at a loss, even interest payments and repayment of bond principal may become difficult. The business may even fail and be forced to file for bankruptcy, in which case your investment may become totally worthless.

For example, the owner of real estate may have to lower the asking price to find a buyer. And it may be difficult to find a buyer for investments in collectibles, such as antiques and paintings.

CONCEPT CHECK 10–2

1. Why are safety and risk two sides of the same coin?
2. What are the five components of the risk factor?
3. How do income, growth, and liquidity affect the choice of an investment?

AN OVERVIEW OF INVESTMENT ALTERNATIVES

▌ OBJECTIVE 3 ▐

Identify the major types of investment alternatives.

Once you have considered the risks involved, established your emergency fund, and have some money accumulated for investment purposes, it's time to consider the investment alternatives most people choose. you should begin by gathering as much information as possible about investment alternatives. Then you will be able to decide whether purchasing stocks, bonds, real estate, or mutual funds investing in any of these is a better use of your money than putting it in the bank. The remainder of this section provides a brief overview of different investment alternatives. The remaining chapters of Part 4 provide more detailed information on stocks, bonds, mutual funds, real estate, and other investment alternatives.

STOCK OR EQUITY FINANCING

equity capital Money that a business obtains from its owners.

Equity capital is money that a business obtains from its owners. If a business is a sole proprietorship or a partnership, it acquires equity capital when the owners invest their own money in the business. For a corporation, equity capital is provided by shareholders, who buy shares of its stock. Since all shareholders are owners, they share in the success of the corporation. This can make buying stock an attractive investment opportunity.

However, you should consider at least two factors before investing in stocks. First, a corporation is not required to repay the money obtained from the sale of stocks or to repurchase the stocks at a later date. Assume you purchased 100 shares of Google stock. Later, you decide to sell your Google stock. Your stocks are sold to another investor, not back to the company. In many cases, a shareholder sells his or her stocks because he or she thinks their price is going to decrease in value. The purchaser, on the other hand, buys those stocks because he or she thinks their price is going to increase. This creates a situation in which either the seller or the buyer earns a profit while the other party to the transaction experiences a loss.

dividend A distribution of money, stocks, or other property that a corporation pays to shareholders.

Second, a corporation is under no legal obligation to pay dividends to shareholders. A **dividend** is a distribution of money, stocks, or other property that a corporation pays to shareholders. Dividends are paid out of earnings, but if a corporation that usually pays dividends has a bad year, its board of directors can vote to omit dividend payments to help pay necessary business expenses. Corporations may also retain earnings to make additional financing available for expansion, research and product development, or other business activities.

There are two basic types of stocks: *common stocks* and *preferred stocks*. Both types have advantages and disadvantages that you should consider before deciding which to use for an investment program. A share of common stocks represents the most basic form of corporate ownership. People often purchase common stocks because this type of investment can provide (1) a source of income if the company pays dividends, (2) growth potential if the dollar value of the stocks increases, and (3) growth potential if the company splits its common stocks. And because it is a popular type of investment, most large corporations sell common stocks to satisfy a large part of their financing needs.

The most important priority an investor in preferred stocks enjoys is receiving cash dividends before common shareholders are paid any cash dividends. This factor is especially

Stocks have historically produced the highest average returns over the long-term. Fixed-income investments, like bonds, have historically earned lower long-term returns than stocks, while safe cash investments like treasury bills have generated the lowest returns.

From 1990 to 2000, no single type of asset has been the top performer for more than two consecutive years.

Top-performing asset types vary almost year to year.

Year	Canadian Equities	Canadian Bonds	Canadian T-bills
1990	−14.8%	7.5%	13.5%
1991	12.0%	22.1%	9.8%
1992	−1.4%	9.9%	7.1%
1993	32.6%	18.1%	5.5%
1994	−0.2%	−4.3%	5.4%
1995	14.5%	20.7%	7.4%
1996	28.4%	12.3%	5.0%
1997	15.0%	9.7%	3.2%
1998	−1.6%	9.2%	4.7%
1999	37.7%	−1.2%	4.7%
2000	7.4%	10.3%	5.5%
2001	−12.6%	8.1%	4.7%
2002	−12.4%	8.7%	2.5%
2003	26.7%	6.7%	2.9%

SOURCE: Standard & Poor's Micropal ®© Micropal, Inc. (2000); "Diversify your investments for portfolio success" Table provided by Royal Mutual Funds Inc., www.royalbank.com/investments

---

important when a corporation is experiencing financial problems and cannot pay cash dividends to both preferred and common shareholders. Other factors you should consider before purchasing both common or preferred stocks are discussed in Chapter 11.

CORPORATE AND GOVERNMENT BONDS

There are two types of bonds an investor should consider. A **corporate bond** is a corporation's written pledge to repay a specified amount of money, along with interest. A **government bond** is the written pledge of a government or a municipality to repay a specified sum of money, along with interest. Thus, when you buy a bond, you are lending a corporation or government entity money for a period of time. Regardless of who issues the bond, you need to consider two major questions before investing in bonds. First, will the bond be repaid at maturity? The maturity dates for most bonds range between one and 30 years. An investor who purchases a bond has two options: keep the bond until maturity and then redeem it, or sell the bond to another investor. In either case, the value of the bond is closely tied to the ability of the corporation or government agency to repay the bond at maturity. Second, will the corporation or government agency be able to maintain interest payments to bondholders? Bondholders normally receive interest payments every six months. Again, if a corporation or government agency cannot pay the interest on its bonds, the value of those bonds will decrease.

Receiving periodic interest payments until maturity is one method of making money on a bond investment. Investors also use two other methods that can provide more liberal returns on bond investments. Chapter 12 discusses each of these methods.

corporate bond A corporation's written pledge to repay a specified amount of money, along with interest.

government bond The written pledge of a government or a municipality to repay a specified sum of money, along with interest.

MUTUAL FUNDS

mutual fund An investment alternative chosen by people who pool their money to buy stocks, bonds, and other securities selected by professional managers employed by an investment company.

A **mutual fund** is an investment alternative chosen by people who pool their money to buy specific quantities of stocks, bonds, and other securities selected by professional managers employed by an investment company. Professional management is an especially important factor for investors with little or no previous experience in financial matters. Another reason investors choose mutual funds is *diversification*. Since mutual funds invest in a number of different securities, an occasional loss in one security is often offset by gains in other securities. As a result, the diversification provided by a mutual fund reduces risk.

The goals of one investor often differ from those of another. The managers of mutual funds realize this and tailor their funds to meet individual needs and objectives. Some invest in Canadian companies, while others invest in stocks and bonds issued by companies in foreign countries. As a result of all the different investment alternatives, mutual funds range from very conservative to extremely speculative investments.

Although investing money in a mutual fund provides professional management, even the best managers can make errors in judgment. The responsibility for choosing the right mutual fund is still based on the investor's evaluation of a mutual fund investment. Chapter 13 presents more information on the different types of mutual funds, the costs involved, and techniques for evaluating these investments.

SEGREGATED FUNDS

segregated fund An investment alternative in the form of an annuity that is similar to a mutual fund but that is less risky as it provides a certain degree of insurance to the investor.

A **segregated fund** is a type of annuity that combines the growth and diversification potential of mutual funds with the security of insurance. These funds are sold only by life insurance companies, and have maturities of at least 10 years. It is like buying an insurance contract, using the money from each contract to invest in an underlying mutual fund. You don't actually own the mutual fund; however, your investment closely tracks its performance. Segregated funds are especially attractive because they come with guarantees designed to protect your money from market instability. You are guaranteed to receive back up to 70 to 100 percent of your initial investment, regardless of how markets perform. Once the annuity matures, the investor is entitled to 100 percent of the initial investment minus any withdrawals. Furthermore, upon maturity, the payment can be passed directly to any beneficiaries without any probate fees. Similar to mutual funds, segregated funds can be bought or sold at any time. If you sell prior to maturity, the fund is sold at market value, which may be less than the initial investment.

REAL ESTATE

As a rule, real estate increases in value and eventually sells at a profit, but there are no guarantees. Although many beginning investors believe real estate values increase by 10 or 15 percent a year, in reality the nationwide average annual increase is about 3 percent. This growth rate makes real estate a long-term investment and not a get-rich-quick scheme.

Success in real estate investments depends on how well you evaluate alternatives. Experts often tell would-be investors that the three most important factors when evaluating a potential real estate investment are *location*, *location*, and *location*. While location may be the most important factor, other factors may determine whether or not a piece of real estate is a good investment. For example, you should answer the following questions before making a decision to purchase any property:

[1] Is the property priced competitively with similar properties?
[2] What type of financing is available, if any? What are the current interest rates?
[3] How much are the taxes?
[4] What is the condition of the buildings and houses in the immediate area?
[5] Why are the present owners selling the property?
[6] Is there a chance that the property will decrease in value?

Any investment has disadvantages, and real estate is no exception. Many people were "taken" by unscrupulous promoters who sold inaccessible land in the Florida Everglades. Poor location can cause a piece of property to decrease in value. Also, to sell your property, you must find an interested buyer who is able to obtain enough money or financing to complete the transaction. Finding a buyer can be difficult if loan money is scarce, the real estate market is in a decline, or you overpaid for the property. If you are forced to hold your investment longer than you originally planned, you must also consider taxes and loan payments.

OTHER INVESTMENT ALTERNATIVES

As defined earlier in this chapter, a speculative investment is a high-risk investment made in the hope of earning a relatively large profit in a short time. By its very nature, any investment may be speculative; that is, it may be quite risky. However, a true speculative investment is speculative because of the methods investors use to earn a quick profit. Typical speculative investments include:

- Call options
- Put options
- Derivatives
- Commodities
- Hedge funds
- Income trusts
- Precious metals

- Gemstones
- Coins
- Stamps
- Antiques and collectibles

Without exception, investments of this kind are normally referred to as speculative for one reason or another. The gold market has many unscrupulous dealers who sell worthless gold-plated lead coins to unsuspecting, uninformed investors. Call and put options are a risky way to make money without investing too much of your own. The risk lies in the position you take as the buyer, for example, you need to decide whether you think the underlying stock price will fall or rise and, based on that, purchase an option. It is risky in that you are only speculating and, without insider information (which is illegal!), it is hard to ensure that your position will be the profitable choice. Derivatives are securities such as options and forward and futures contracts, whose value depends on the performance of an underlying security. Hedge funds are considered derivative investments. The basic idea behind a hedge fund is to take two simultaneous positions in two different investments in order to reduce risk. An example is buying long/selling short, where managers will buy securities they believe are under priced and then sell them once they appreciate in price, thus making a profit for their clients. Concurrently, the manager sells securities that the fund does not own, from investment dealers, intending to buy them back once the price of the stock drops, then paying back the borrowed money to the broker and pocketing the difference. Since the market is guaranteed to go up or down, the position you hold can be considered hedged to a certain degree against risk. Income trusts are issued in the stock market and are designed to pay out cash flow generated from a business or set of investments through cash disbursements to unit holders. Income trusts are desirable due to their ability to produce constant cash flows for investors. One of the most popular income trusts are Real Estate Investment Trusts (REITs). With any speculative investment, it is extremely important to deal with reputable dealers and recognized investment firms. It pays to be careful. While investments in this category can lead to large dollar gains, they should not be used by anyone who does not fully understand the risks involved. Chapter 11 presents more information on options.

SUMMARY OF FACTORS THAT AFFECT INVESTMENT CHOICES

Earlier in this chapter, we examined how safety, risk, income, growth, and liquidity affect your investment choices. In the preceding section, we looked at available investment alternatives.

met. The Canadian Association of Financial Planners (CAFP) requires that all Registered Financial Planners (RFP) achieve an academic or professional standing recognized by the Association. The Member must be sponsored by other planners in the industry, be currently engaged in the profession, and have demonstrated competence in financial planning. A minimum of two years' experience in the practice of financial planning is required. CAFP members must abide by the CAFP Code of Professional Ethics and make an ongoing commitment to maintaining professional standards through continuing education. The Financial Planners Standards Council (FPSC) believes that it is important that Canada participate in the international movement trying to globalize the financial planning profession, through the Certified Financial Planning (CFP) designation. There are four steps, similar to the RFP, which must be completed in order to be awarded the internationally recognized CFP designation. The Canadian Institute of Financial Planning offers six correspondence courses to be completed as part of its requirements for the Chartered Financial Planner designation. Finally, the Canadian Securities Institute (CSI) and the Institute of Canadian Bankers (ICB) both offer a number of investment and personal finance courses.

In selecting a financial adviser, you will need to be aware of how they are being paid as well as how this might influence the advice you are given. Salaried employees of such institutions as banks or trust companies are sometimes designated as financial planners and will provide advice either free of charge or for a nominal fee. Commission planners receive their compensation from the sellers of the services and products that they recommend. In general, it would be a safe bet to assume that any advice you get from either of these types of planners will be biased in some way.

More objective advice might be available from fee-based planners and fee-only or fee-for-service planners. Fee-based planners receive their compensation partly in the form of fees paid by you and partly in the form of commissions from the institutions. Fee-only or fee-for-service planners will charge you directly on an hourly basis (typically from $50 to $250 per hour), and that will be their sole source of income for the service that they provide to you.

YOUR ROLE IN THE INVESTMENT PROCESS

Successful investors continually evaluate their investments. They never sit back and let their investments manage themselves. Obviously, different types of investments will require different methods of evaluation. Some factors to consider when choosing different investments are described next.

EVALUATE POTENTIAL INVESTMENTS Let's assume you have $25,000 to invest. Also assume your investment will earn a 10-percent return the first year. At the end of one year, you will have earned $2,500 and your investment will be worth $27,500. Not a bad return on your original investment! Now ask yourself: How long would it take to earn $2,500 if I had to work for this amount of money at a job? For some people, it might take a month; for others, it might take longer. The point is that if you want this type of return, you should be willing to work for it, but the work takes a different form than a job. When choosing an investment, the work you invest is the time it takes to research different investments so that you can make an informed decision.

Some people invest large sums of money and never research the investments they purchase. Obviously, this is a flawed approach that can lead to large dollar losses. On the other hand, an informed investor has a much better chance of choosing the types of investments that will increase in value. In fact, much of the information in the remainder of Part 4 will help you learn how to evaluate different investment opportunities. But you have to be willing to work and learn if you want to be a successful investor. As you will see in the next section, evaluation doesn't stop once you make a decision to purchase an investment. It continues as long as you own the investment.

To monitor the value of their investments, many investors use a simple chart like the one illustrated here. To construct a chart like this one, place the original purchase price of your investment in the middle on the side of the chart. Then use price increments of a logical amount to show increases and decreases in dollar value.

Place individual dates along the bottom of the chart. For stocks, bonds, mutual funds, and similar investments, you may want to graph every two weeks and chart current values on, say, a Friday. For longer-term investments, such as real estate, you can chart current values every six months.

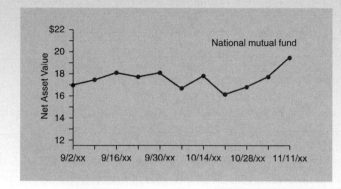

A WORD OF CAUTION

If an investment is beginning to have a large increase or decrease in value, you should watch that investment more closely. You can still continue to chart at regular intervals, but you may want to check dollar values more frequently—in some cases, daily.

MONITOR THE VALUE OF YOUR INVESTMENTS Would you believe that some people invest large sums of money and don't know what their investments are worth? They don't know if their investments have increased or decreased in value. They don't know if they should sell their investments or continue to hold them. A much better approach is to monitor the value of your investments. If you choose to invest in stocks, bonds, mutual funds, commodities, or options, you can determine the value of your holdings by looking at the price quotations reported on the Internet, on financial news television and radio programs, and in newspapers. Your real estate holdings may be compared with similar properties currently for sale in the surrounding area. Finally, you can determine the value of your precious metals, gemstones, and collectibles by checking with reputable dealers and investment firms. Regardless of which type of investment you choose, close surveillance will keep you informed of whether your investment increases or decreases in value. The Financial Planning Calculations box above presents further information on monitoring the value of your investments.

KEEP ACCURATE AND CURRENT RECORDS Accurate recordkeeping can help you spot opportunities to maximize profits or reduce dollar losses when you sell your investments. Accurate recordkeeping can also help you decide whether you want to invest additional funds in a particular investment. At the very least, you should keep purchase records for each of your investments that include the actual dollar cost of the investment, plus any commissions or fees you paid. It is also useful to keep a list of the sources of information (Internet addresses, business periodicals, research publications, and so on), along with copies of the material you used to evaluate each investment. Then, when it is time to re-evaluate an existing investment, you will know where to begin your search for current information. As you will see in the next section, accurate recordkeeping is also necessary for tax purposes.

TAX CONSIDERATIONS

As discussed in Chapter 3, one aspect of a personal tax strategy is to build a tax-efficient portfolio. Dividends, interest, rental income, and capital gains are taxed in different ways by the

CRA and provincial governments. Interest and rental income, net of expenses, is fully taxed. Dividends and capital gains receive more favourable tax treatment, as described below. Therefore, in order to ensure the most favourable tax treatment of your investment portfolio, it is best to hold interest-generating assets inside registered accounts, such as RRSPs and RESPS, and dividend and capital-gains generating assets in non-registered accounts. Rental property is a real asset, not a financial asset, and therefore cannot be held in registered accounts.

As always in personal financial planning, it is important to realize all the consequences of your investment and tax decisions. Areas of concern for the former might include decisions about dividends, interest, rental income, and capital gains and losses. As for taxes, it's important to keep in mind the tax effect of all your sources of income, as some income may be more advantageous.

DIVIDENDS, INTEREST INCOME, AND RENTAL INCOME As defined earlier in this chapter, a dividend is a distribution of money, stocks, or other property that a corporation pays to shareholders. Dividends are taxed in a peculiar way that is designed to reflect that the corporation paying you a dividend has already paid taxes on its profits (which it is sharing with you in the form of dividend payments). The total of the amount you receive in this form is "grossed-up" by 25 percent. This means that if you receive $100 in dividends, you will declare it as $125 in income. You are then taxed at your marginal rate minus a dividend tax credit at the rate of 13.33 percent. Capital dividends, or dividends derived from a corporation's capital gains, are the exception to this rule and will not be taxed.

Exhibit 10–7 demonstrates how dividends are taxed and the differences between marginal and effective rates depending on an individual's tax bracket.

Interest from banks, credit unions, and savings and loan associations is subject to federal taxation. Interest that you receive from promissory notes, loans, bonds, and Canadian securities must also be reported as income. You must report the total of such income as ordinary income on your tax return.

Exhibit 10–7

Calculation of Tax Rates on Dividend Income

| | FEDERAL TAX RATES | | | |
	16%	22%	26%	29%
Dividends received	$1,000.00	$1,000.00	$1,000.00	$1,000.00
Gross-up (25 percent)	250.00	250.00	250.00	250.00
Grossed-up dividends	1,250.00	1,250.00	1,250.00	1,250.00
Federal tax	200.00	275.00	325.00	362.50
Less dividend tax credit (16.67% of dividends received)	(166.67)	(166.67)	(166.67)	(166.67)
Net federal tax	33.33	108.33	158.88	195.83
Add provincial tax (assume a provincial rate of 42.75%)	14.25	46.31	67.69	83.72
Total tax	47.58	154.64	226.57	279.55
Dividend after taxes	952.42	845.36	773.43	720.45
Effective tax rate (total tax ÷ dividends received)	4.76%	15.46%	22.66%	27.96%
Total marginal tax rate (federal rate)(1 + provincial rate)	22.84%	31.41%	37.12%	41.39%

Note: Note that although the effective tax rate on dividend income is lower than the total marginal tax rate in each income category, because the dividend tax credit remains constant, the marginal benefit of receiving dividend income reduces as the income tax bracket increases.

Net income from rental property is also subject to federal taxation and is treated as ordinary income like wages or salaries. Generally, you must report all income and expenses on rental property.

CAPITAL GAINS AND CAPITAL LOSSES   Under current laws, profit resulting from the sale of stocks, mutual funds, bonds, land, and some personal property is considered a capital gain. For owners of certain small businesses and farm property, there is a $500,000 capital gains exemption. However, these two types of investments are defined very specifically, and you should check in advance to verify that your investment qualifies for the deduction. You will be taxed on 50 percent of all other capital gains you receive, minus any losses you may have incurred on nondepreciable assets, considered capital losses.

For example, assume Cody Shaw sold 100 shares of Ballard Power stocks for a profit of $1,000. If he is in the 26-percent tax bracket, the total tax he will pay on his profit will be $130 (26% × $500 = $130). Now suppose that he also incurred a capital loss of $200 upon selling 100 shares of Bid.com. Now his total taxes will be $104 (26% × (500 − 100)).

Under current taxation laws, an allowable capital loss is 50 percent of a capital loss; this amount can be used to offset taxable capital gains. Note, however, that if you do not have capital gains, then you will not be allowed to use your capital loss to offset other income.

Visit the Web site
See the Weblinks under Chapter 10 on the online learning centre at www.mcgrawhill.ca/college/kapoor.

CONCEPT CHECK 10–4

1. What type of training does a qualified financial planner have?
2. What is your role in the investment process?
3. How do dividends, interest, and rental income differ from capital gains and losses?

SOURCES OF INVESTMENT INFORMATION

With most investments, more information is available than you can read and comprehend. Therefore, you must be selective in the type of information you use for evaluation purposes. With some investments, however, only a limited amount of information is available. For example, a wealth of information is available on individual stocks and mutual funds, whereas the amount of information on a metal, such as cobalt or manganese, may be limited to one source. Regardless of the number or availability of sources, always determine how reliable and accurate the information is. Following are sources of information you can use to evaluate present and future investments.

■ OBJECTIVE 5 ■

Use various sources of financial information that can reduce risks and increase investment returns.

THE INTERNET AND ONLINE COMPUTER SERVICES

While no one knows the exact number, experts estimate that there are more than 605 million Internet users worldwide.[1] Today, more people have access to information provided by computers located in their homes or at libraries, universities, or businesses than ever before, and this number is growing. More importantly, a wealth of information is available on most personal finance topics and different investment alternatives. For example, you can obtain interest rates for guaranteed investment certificates; current price information for stocks, bonds, and mutual funds; and brokers' recommendations to buy, hold, or sell a corporation's stocks. You can even trade securities online just by pushing the right button on your computer keyboard. You can also use computers and financial planning software to develop a personal financial plan.

---

[1] www.nua.ie/surveys/how_many_online/www.mcgrawhill.ca/college/kapoor

To use your computer to generate information you really need, you must be selective. One of the best ways to access needed information is to use a search engine. Search engines, such as Yahoo Canada, AltaVista Canada, Google.ca, and Canada.com, allow you to do a keyword search for either the personal finance topic or investment alternative that you want to explore. Federal, provincial, and local governments and most corporations also have Web sites where you can obtain valuable information.

Today, thousands of Internet service providers allow users to connect to the Internet and use search engines, newsgroups, mailing lists, and e-mail. If you're a beginner, you may find it easier to use one of the commercial online companies, such as Canada.com, AOLCanada, Bell Sympatico, and MSN.com. These companies usually provide subscribers with access to a broad range of information on a variety of topics, as well as a connection to the Internet. While it is impossible to list all of the Internet sites related to personal finance, those listed in Exhibit 10–8 will get you started. We will examine other specific Internet sites in the remaining chapters in Part 4. Also, read the appendix at the end of Chapter 1 for information on how to use the Internet for personal financial planning.

Exhibit 10–8

Useful Internet Sites for Personal Financial Planning

The following six Internet sites provide information that you can use to establish a financial plan and begin an investment program.

Sponsor and Description	Web Address
The **Canoe Webfin** Web site provides current financial news and material that can help both beginning and experienced investors sharpen their investment skills.	www.Webfin.com
The **Quicken** Web site provides information about investments, home mortgages, insurance, taxes, banking and credit, and different types of retirement programs.	www.quicken.ca
About Canada has an Investing: Canada link under its Business/Careers section. Click here to find a tremendous array of personal finance facts, advice, articles, and more. There's also an Investing for Beginners section.	http://home.about.com/index.htm
Canadian Financial Network (CFN) has well over 6,000 international online financial resources gathered and saves time for investors by describing these resources in sufficient detail to allow you to stop surfing and start targeting the information that you want.	http://canadianfinance.com
Bell Sympatico has a section entitled Personal Finance that offers everything from family finance to current business and finance news to information on borrowing, budgeting, and more.	www.sympatico.ca
The Investor Learning Centre of Canada makes learning about investing easier than it has ever been before. Whether you're an absolute beginner or a seasoned investor, you'll find what you need.	www.investorlearning.ca
The **Investopedia** Web site provides an online investment dictionary, various articles, investing tutorials, stock ideas, simulators, as well as many different free tools to aid in investment decisions.	www.investopedia.com

NEWSPAPERS AND NEWS PROGRAMS

One of the most readily available sources of information for the average investor is the financial page of a national newspaper or *The Financial Post*. There you will find a summary of the day's trading on the Montreal Stock Exchange, the TSX Venture Exchange, the Toronto Stock Exchange, and the two main U.S. exchanges, the NASDAQ Stock Market and the New York Stock Exchange. In addition to stock coverage, most newspapers provide information on stocks traded in the over-the-counter markets, mutual funds, corporate and government bonds, commodities and options, and general economic news. Detailed information on how to read price quotations for stocks, bonds, mutual funds, and other investments is presented in the remaining chapters of Part 4.

It is also possible to obtain economic and investment information on radio or television. Many stations broadcast investment market summaries and economic information as part of their regular news programs. See Exhibit 10–9 for publications and news programs used by successful investors.

BUSINESS PERIODICALS AND GOVERNMENT PUBLICATIONS

Most business periodicals are published weekly, twice a month, or monthly. *The Globe and Mail*'s *Report on Business*, *Business Week*, *Canadian Business*, *Fortune*, and similar business periodicals provide not only general news about the overall economy but also detailed financial information about individual corporations. Some business periodicals—for example, *Business 2.0* and *Canadian Banker*—focus on information about firms in a specific industry. In addition to business periodicals, more general magazines, such as *The Economist*, *Time*, and *Newsweek*, provide investment information as a regular feature. Finally, *Money*, *MoneySaver*,

---

While individual investors have their favourite sources for investment information, it is quite likely that most successful investors use some of the following newspapers, periodicals, and news programs on a regular basis.

Exhibit 10–9
A Personal Reading List for Successful Investing

Newspapers
- Larger local newspapers
- *The National Post*
- *The Globe and Mail*

Television
- CBC Business News, ROBtv, Business Television

Business Periodicals
- *The Globe and Mail's Report on Business* (ROB)
- *Business Week*
- *Canadian Business*
- *Fortune*
- *The Economist*
- *Newsweek*

Personal Financial Publications
- *Canadian MoneySaver*
- *IE:Money*
- *Money*
- *MoneySaver*
- *Maclean's Guide to Personal Finance*

Canadian MoneySaver, *IE:Money*, and similar periodicals provide information and advice designed to improve your investment skills.

The Canadian government is an excellent source of information that is often free or offered at low cost. Statistics Canada provides information compiled both nationally and regionally. Industry Canada's Strategis is also an excellent resource for businesses and consumers alike.

CORPORATE REPORTS

The federal government requires corporations selling new issues of securities to disclose information about corporate earnings, assets and liabilities, products or services, and the qualifications of top management in a *prospectus* that they must give to investors. In addition to the prospectuses, all publicly owned corporations send their shareholders annual reports and quarterly reports that contain detailed financial data. Included in annual and quarterly corporate reports are statements of financial position, which describe changes in assets, liabilities, and owners' equity. Also included in these reports are income statements, which provide dollar amounts for sales, expenses, and profits or losses.

STATISTICAL AVERAGES

Investors often gauge the value of their investments by following one or more widely recognized statistical averages. Such an average is a statistical measure that indicates whether a broad investment category (stocks, bonds, mutual funds, and so on) is increasing or decreasing in value.

How much importance should you attach to statistical averages? These averages show trends and direction, but they do not pinpoint the actual value of a specific investment. The remaining chapters of Part 4 describe many of these averages.

INVESTOR SERVICES AND NEWSLETTERS

Many stockbrokers and financial planners mail a free monthly or quarterly newsletter to their clients. In addition, investors can subscribe to services that provide investment information. The fees for investor services generally range from $30 to $750 a year.

Five widely used services are available for investors who specialize in stocks, bonds, and mutual funds:

[1] *SEDAR*. The System for Electronic Document Analysis and Retrieval (SEDAR) is used for electronically filing securities information in Canada. Since January 1, 1997, it has been mandatory for Canadian companies to file electronically. SEDAR, therefore, provides access to all Canadian public companies and mutual fund filings, including annual reports, prospectuses, financial statements, press releases, and continuous disclosure documents. (See www.sedar.com.)

[2] *Stockhouse Canada*. Located at www.stockhouse.ca, this site offers free access to a number of newsletters, as well as quotes, charts, chats, and news.

[3] *The Fund Library*. The Fund Library, at www.fundlibrary.com, tracks more than 2,000 mutual funds and offers a number of tools and advice to help you compare them.

[4] *Value Line*. This service provides reports supplying detailed information, such as earnings, dividends, sales, liabilities, and other financial data, about major corporations. While the focus is the U.S. market, more than 100 Canadian corporations are also examined. (See www.valueline.com.)

Other investment publications that may help you evaluate potential investments are the Canadian Bond Rating Service's (CBRS) *Guide to Conservative Fixed-Income Investing*; the *Blue Book of CBS Stock Reports*; the *Investor's Digest of Canada* from MPL Communications; and publications by the International Monetary Fund.

In addition to the preceding publications, each of the following securities exchanges provides information through printed materials and the Internet:

- Toronto Stock Exchange (www.tse-cdnx.com)
- TSX Venture Exchange (www.tse-cdnx.com)
- Montreal Stock Exchange (www.m-x.ca)
- New York Stock Exchange (www.nyse.com)
- NASDAQ Stock Market (www.nasdaq.com)
- International Federation of Stock Exchanges (www.fibv.com)

Each of these Web sites provides basic information about the exchange, offers educational material and a glossary of important terms, and describes how investors can profit from transactions through the exchange.

The preceding discussion of investor services and newsletters is not exhaustive, but it gives you some idea of the amount and scope of information available to serious investors. Although most small investors find many of the services and newsletters described here too expensive for personal subscriptions, this information may be available from stockbrokers or financial planners. This type of information is also available at many public libraries.

DESKTOP INFORMATION SERVICES

Recently introduced into the financial services industry are desktop information services such as Bloomberg Professional service (http://about.bloomberg.com/), 3000 Xtra, and Reuters (http://about.reuters.com/), which provide instantaneous access to real-time historical financial data, news, and many other services. These desktop information services have transformed the securities business and levelled the playing field between buyers and sellers.

CONCEPT CHECK 10–5

1. What do you think is the most readily available source of information for the average investor? Explain your answer.
2. What type of information can you obtain using the Internet?
3. Briefly describe the additional sources of information you can use to evaluate a potential investment and lessen risk.

SUMMARY OF OBJECTIVES

Objective 1
Explain why you should establish an investment program.
Investment goals must be specific and measurable and should be classified as short-term, intermediate, and long-term. Before beginning an investment program, you must make sure your personal financial affairs are in order. This process begins with learning to live within your means and obtaining adequate insurance protection. The next step is the accumulation of an emergency fund equal to three to nine months' living expenses. Then, and only then, is it time to save the money needed to establish an investment program.

Objective 2
Describe how safety, risk, income, growth, and liquidity affect your investment decisions.
Although each investor may have specific, individual reasons for investing, all investors must consider the factors of safety, risk, income, growth, and liquidity. Especially important is the relationship between safety and risk. Basically, this concept can be summarized as follows: The potential return for any investment should be directly related to the risk the investor assumes. The risk factor can be broken down into five components: inflation risk, interest rate risk, business failure risk, market risk, and global investment risk.

Exhibit 11–1

S&P/TSX Composite Portfolio Characteristics as of June, 2005

Portfilio Characteristics	S&P/TSX Composite
No. of Companies	222
Adjusted Market Capitalization (C$ bill)	987.11
Company size (Adjusted C$ bill):	
Average	4.45
Largest	49.06
Smallest	0.21
Median	1.46
% Weight Largest Company	4.97%
Top 10 Holdings (% Market Capitalization Share)	35.31%

Sector Weights	S&P/TSX Composite
Consumer Discretionary	6.85%
Consumer Staples	2.80%
Energy	23.88%
Financials	32.41%
Health Care	1.38%
Industrials	6.87%
Information Technology	5.22%
Materials	14.28%
Telecommunication Services	4.81%
Utilities	1.50%

SOURCE: Standard & Poors, www2.standardandpoors.com

DOW JONES INDUSTRIAL AVERAGE DJIA, often referred to as the Dow, is the best known and most widely reported indicator of the stock market's performance. The Dow tracks the price changes of 30 significant industrial stocks traded on the New York Stock Exchange.

NYSE COMPOSITE INDEX An index that covers the price movements of all stocks listed on the New York Stock Exchange.

Exhibit 11–2

The S&P/TSX Composite Index since 1985.

Copyright 2005 Yahoo! Inc.
SOURCE: http://finance.yahoo.com/

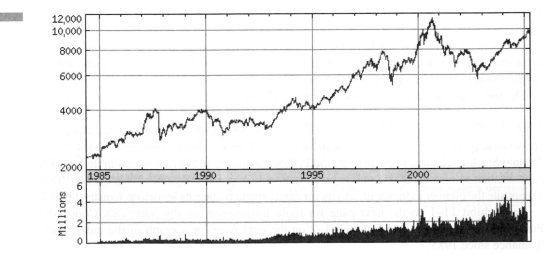

NASDAQ COMPOSITE INDEX An index that covers the price movements of all stocks traded on the NASDAQ stock market. The NASDAQ Composite is heavily weighted in technology and Internet stocks. As such, the companies listed in the composite are considered to have high growth potential.

STANDARD & POOR'S 500 STOCK INDEX The S&P 500 is one of the best benchmarks in the world for large-cap stocks. By containing 500 companies, it has great *diversification*, and is considered one of the best overall indicators of market performance.

WHY CORPORATIONS ISSUE COMMON STOCKS

Corporations issue common stocks to finance their business start-up costs and to help pay for their ongoing business activities. Today, corporations are classified as either private corporations or public corporations. A *private corporation* is a corporation whose stocks owned by relatively few people and not traded openly in stock markets. A *public corporation* is a corporation whose stocks traded openly in stock markets and may be purchased by individuals. Public corporations may have thousands or even millions of shareholders. Corporate managers prefer selling common stocks as a method of financing for several reasons.

A FORM OF EQUITY Corporations don't have to repay the money a shareholder pays for stocks. Generally, a shareholder in a public corporation may sell his or her stocks to another individual. The selling price is determined by how much a buyer is willing to pay for the stocks. Simply put, if the demand for a particular stock increases, the market value of the stock will increase. If the demand for a particular stock decreases, the market value of the stock will decrease. Demand for a stock changes when information about the firm or its future prospects is released to the general public. For example, information about expected sales revenues, earnings, expansions or mergers, or other important developments within the firm can increase or decrease the demand for, and ultimately the market value of, the firm's stocks.

DIVIDENDS NOT MANDATORY Dividends are paid out of profits, and dividend payments must be approved by the corporation's board of directors. Dividend policies vary among corporations, but most firms distribute between 30 and 70 percent of their earnings to shareholders. However, some corporations follow a policy of smaller or no dividend distributions to shareholders. In general, these are rapidly growing firms, such as Chapters (including Chapters Online), Gildan Activwear (Activwear), and Office Depot (office supplies), that retain a large share of their earnings for research and development, expansion, or major projects. On the other hand, utility companies and other financially secure enterprises may distribute 80 to 90 percent of their earnings. Always remember that if a corporation has had a bad year, dividend payments may be reduced or omitted. Although board members may vote to continue paying dividends when a corporation is operating at a loss, they often vote to completely omit dividend payments to shareholders.

VOTING RIGHTS AND CONTROL OF THE COMPANY In return for the financing provided by selling common stocks, management must make concessions to shareholders that may restrict corporate policies. For example, corporations are required by law to have an annual meeting at which shareholders have a right to vote, usually casting one vote per share of stock. Shareholders may vote in person or by proxy. A **proxy** is a legal form that lists the issues to be decided at a shareholders' meeting and requests that shareholders transfer their voting rights to some individual or individuals. The common shareholders elect the board of directors and must approve major changes in corporate policies. Typical changes in corporate policy include (1) an amendment of the corporate charter, (2) the sale of certain assets, (3) possible mergers, (4) the issuance of preferred stocks or corporate bonds, and (5) changes in the amount of common stocks.

proxy A legal form that lists the issues to be decided at a shareholders' meeting and requests that shareholders transfer their voting rights to some individual or individuals.

pre-emptive right
The right of current shareholders to purchase any new stocks the corporation issues before it is offered to the general public.

Legally, a corporation may include a provision for pre-emptive rights in its corporate charter. A **pre-emptive right** is the right of current shareholders to purchase any new stock the corporation issues before it is offered to the general public. By exercising their pre-emptive rights, shareholders are able to maintain their current proportion of corporate ownership. This may be important when the corporation is small and management control is a matter of concern to shareholders.

Finally, corporations are required by law to distribute annual and quarterly reports to shareholders. These reports contain details about sales, earnings, and other vital information.

WHY INVESTORS PURCHASE COMMON STOCKS

How do you make money by buying common stocks? Basically, common stock investments can increase your wealth in two ways: income from dividends and dollar appreciation of stock value.

INCOME FROM DIVIDENDS
While the corporation's board members are under no legal obligation to pay dividends, most board members like to keep shareholders happy (and prosperous). Few things will unite shareholders into a powerful opposition force more rapidly than omitted or lowered dividends. Therefore, board members usually declare dividends if the corporation's after-tax profits are sufficient for them to do so. Since dividends are a distribution of profits, investors must be concerned about future after-tax profits. In short, how secure is the dividend?

Corporate dividends for common stocks may take the form of cash, additional stocks, or company products. However, the last type of dividend is extremely unusual. If the board of directors declares a cash dividend, each common shareholder receives an equal amount per share. Although dividend policies vary, most corporations pay dividends on a quarterly basis. Some corporations, particularly those experiencing large swings in earnings, declare special year-end or extra dividends in addition to their regular quarterly dividends.

record date The date on which a shareholder must be registered on the corporation's books in order to receive dividend payments.

Note in Exhibit 11–3 that Sobeys Inc. has declared a quarterly dividend of $0.06 per share to shareholders who own the stock on the record date of July 14. The **record date** is the date on which a shareholder must be registered on the corporation's books in order to receive dividend payments. When a stock is traded around the record date, the company must determine whether the buyer or the seller is entitled to the dividend. To solve this problem, this rule is followed: *Dividends remain with the stock until two business days before the record date*. On the second day before the record date, the stock begins selling ex-dividend. An investor who purchases an ex-dividend stock is not entitled to receive dividends for that quarter, and the dividend is paid to the previous owner of the stock.

For example, Sobeys Inc. declared a quarterly dividend of $0.06 per share to shareholders who owned stocks on Friday, July 14. The stocks went ex-dividend on Wednesday, July 12, 2000, two *business* days before the July 14 date. A shareholder who purchased the stock on July 12 or after was not entitled to this quarterly dividend payment. Sobeys Inc. made the actual dividend payment on July 28 to shareholders who owned stocks on the record date.

Exhibit 11–3

Typical Information on Corporation Dividends as Presented in *The Montreal Gazette*

SOURCE: Adapted from *The Montreal Gazette*, Thursday, June 29, 2000.

DIVIDENDS
Corporate dividends declared Wednesday (quarterly unless otherwise indicated): **Sobeys Inc.**: Common, $0.06. Payable July 28. Record July 14.

Investors are generally very conscious of the date on which a stock goes ex-dividend, and the dollar value of the stock may go down by the value of the quarterly dividend.

CHANGES IN STOCK VALUE
In most cases, you purchase stocks and then hold on to them for a period of time. If the market value of the stocks increases, you must decide whether to sell them at the higher price or continue to hold them. If you decide to sell, the dollar amount of difference between the purchase price and the selling price represents your profit. Of course, the market value of the stock can also decline, in which case the decision is the same—to sell and trigger a loss or continue to hold in the expectation that the stock price will rise.

Let's assume that on June 4, 1999, you purchased 100 shares of Indigo Books and Music Inc. on the TSE at a cost of $13 a share. Your cost for the stocks was $1,300 plus $29 commission charges, for a total investment of $1,329. (Note: Commissions, a topic covered later in this chapter, are charged when you purchase stocks *and* when you sell stocks.) Let's also assume you held your 100 shares until June 4, 2002, and then sold them for $38 a share. Each year of the two-year period you owned Indigo Books and Music Inc., the company paid an annual dividend totalling $2.20 a share. Exhibit 11–4 shows your return on the investment. In this case, you made money because of quarterly dividend distributions and through an increase in stock value from $13 to $38 per share. Exhibit 11–4 shows the cash flows of your transaction. Of course, if the stock's value should decrease, or if the firm's board of directors reduces or votes to omit dividends, your return may be less than the original investment. For help in deciding if it's time to sell stocks, read the Financial Planning for Life's Situations box on page 319.

POSSIBILITY OF INCREASED VALUE FROM STOCK SPLITS
Investors can also increase potential profits through a stock split. A **stock split** is a procedure in which the shares of stock owned by existing shareholders are divided into a larger number of shares. In 2001, for example, Gildan Activwear's board of directors approved a 2-for-1 stock split. After the stock split, a shareholder who had previously owned 100 shares now owned 200 shares. The most common stock splits are 2-for-1, 3-for-1, and 4-for-1.

Why do corporations split their stocks? In many cases, a firm's management has a theoretical ideal price range for the firm's stocks. If the market value of the stocks rises above the ideal range, a stock split brings the market value back in line. In the case of Gildan Activwear, the 2-for-1 stock split reduced the market value to about one-half of the stock's previous market value. The lower market value for each share of stock was the result of dividing the dollar value of the company by a larger number of shares of common stocks. Also, a decision to split a company's stocks and the resulting lower market value makes the stocks more attractive to

Visit the Web site
See Personal Financial Planning worksheets under Chapter 11 on the online learning centre at www.mcgrawhill.ca/ college/kapoor.

stock split A procedure in which the shares of common stocks owned by existing shareholders are divided into a larger number of shares.

Assumptions			
100 shares of common stocks purchased June 4, 1999, sold June 4, 2002; dividends of $4 per share for the two-year period.			
Cost when purchased		**Proceeds when sold**	
100 shares @ $13 =	$1,300	100 shares @ $38 =	$3,800
Plus commission	29	Minus commission	29
Total cost	$1,329	Net proceeds	$3,771
Transaction summary			
Net proceeds	$ 3,771		
Minus total cost	−1,329		
Profit from stock sale	$ 2,442		
Annual dividend	+ 220		

Exhibit 11–4

Sample Stock Transaction for Indigo Books and Music Inc.

the investing public. This attraction is based on the belief that most corporations split their stocks only when their financial future is improving and on the upswing. As a result, investors have an expectation of future financial growth. This expectation of future growth can mean increases in the firm's sales and profits *and* increases in the market value of the firm's stocks. *Be warned: There are no guarantees that a stock's market value will go up after a split.*

CONCEPT CHECK 11–1

1. If you needed information about a stock investment, would you go the the library or the Internet? Why?
2. Why do corporations issue common stocks?
3. What are the typical issues on which shareholders vote?
4. Describe two reasons shareholders purchase common stocks.

PREFERRED STOCKS

■ OBJECTIVE 2 ▮

Discuss the most important features of preferred stocks.

In addition to or instead of purchasing common stocks, you may purchase preferred stocks. The most important priority an investor in preferred stocks enjoys is receiving cash dividends before common shareholders are paid any cash dividends. This factor is especially important when a corporation is experiencing financial problems and cannot pay cash dividends to both preferred and common shareholders. Unlike the amount of the dividend on common stocks, the dollar amount of the dividend on preferred stocks is known before the stocks are purchased. The dividend amount is a stated amount of money for each share of preferred stock.

Preferred stocks are often referred to as "middle" investments because they represent an investment midway between common stocks (an ownership position) and corporate bonds (a creditor position). When compared with corporate bonds, the yield on preferred stocks is often smaller than the yield on bonds. When compared with common stocks, preferred stocks are safer investments that offer more secure dividends. They are often purchased by conservative investors wanting preferential tax treatment on the dividend and possible capital gains. They are also purchased by other corporations because corporations receive a tax break on the dividend income from preferred stocks.

While preferred stocks do not represent a legal debt that must be repaid, if the firm is dissolved or declares bankruptcy, preferred shareholders do have first claim to the corporation's assets after creditors (including bondholders).

callable preferred stocks Stocks that a corporation may exchange, at its option, for a specified amount of money.

Generally, preferred stocks are callable. **Callable preferred stocks** are stocks that a corporation may exchange, at its option, for a specified amount of money. To understand why a corporation would call in a preferred stock issue, you must first realize that dividend rates paid by similar investments increase and decrease. If dividends are decreasing and similar investments provide a smaller return than the corporation's preferred stock issue, management may decide to call in their existing preferred issue and substitute new preferred stocks that pay a lower dividend. Management may also decide to call in the preferred stocks and issue common stocks with no specified dividend. The dividend amount paid on a preferred issue can also affect the market value of the stock. For example, the preferred stock issue in the last example paid a 6-percent dividend. When the corporation issued preferred stocks, the 6-percent dividend was competitive with the dividends paid by corporations issuing preferred stocks at that time. If dividend rates on similar investments decrease, the market value of the 6-percent preferred stock issue will go up due to its higher dividend. On the other hand, if dividends paid on similar investments increase, the market value of the 6-percent preferred stock issue will fall due to its lower dividend rate.

Assume that in January 2000, Marina Stahl purchased 100 shares of Royal Bank of Canada, one of Canada's big-six banks, for $21.37 a share. According to Marina, all the financial information about the Royal Bank of Canada looked good. Two years later, when the value of Royal Bank of Canada had increased to $32.57 a share, Marina decided to sell the stocks for a profit. During that two-year period, she had thought about selling her stocks at least four times. But she just couldn't make the decision to sell.

According to financial experts, the value of a share of stock may go up or down, but investors like Marina Stahl always have trouble deciding when to sell. Generally, most investors have a reason for buying a stock, but when it is time to sell that same stock, they are often blinded by a sense of loyalty to "their" investments, whether deserved or not. Although no sure cures for this problem exist, the following suggestions may help:

1. *Follow your stock's value.* Too often, investors purchase a stock and then forget about it. They assume everything is okay and the stock will magically increase in value. A much better approach is to graph the dollar value of your stock on a weekly basis.
2. *Watch the company's financials.* Smart investors evaluate a stock investment before they make it. The smartest investors use all the available information to continuously evaluate their stocks. If the amounts reported or projected for sales,

profits, or other important financial measures are declining or are well below industry averages, it may be time to sell the stocks. If you would not buy the same investment today, it's time to sell it no matter how much you have gained or lost.
3. *Track the firm's product line.* Simply put, if the firm's products become obsolete and the company fails to introduce state-of-the-art new products, its sales—and ultimately profits—may take a nosedive. The failure to introduce new products may destroy the firm's ability to compete.
4. *Monitor economic developments.* An economic recession or an economic recovery may cause the value of a stock investment to increase or decrease. For example, most consumers who are unemployed don't buy new cars. Therefore, manufacturing firms, such as General Motors or Ford, may experience lower sales, lower profits, and lower stock values until the employment outlook brightens. Also, watch the inflation rate, interest rates, productivity rates, and similar economic indicators that may be a red flag.
5. *Be patient.* The secret of success for making money with stocks is time. As pointed out earlier in this chapter, stocks have returned over 10 percent before adjusting for inflation each year for over a 40-year period and, assuming you purchased good stocks, your investments will eventually increase in value.

When compared with corporations selling common stocks, preferred stocks are used less often and by only a few corporations, yet it is an alternative method of financing that may attract investors who do not wish to buy common stocks. Preferred stocks, like common stocks, are equity financing that does not have to be repaid. And dividends on preferred stocks, as on common stocks, may be omitted by action of the board of directors.

Many small investors consider preferred stocks to be as safe as corporate bonds. Generally, however, they are less safe because corporate bonds represent borrowed money that must be repaid. Bondholders are more likely to receive interest payments until maturity and eventual repayment of their initial investment than preferred shareholders are to continue receiving dividends or recover their initial investment in the stocks. To make preferred stock issues more attractive, some corporations may offer three additional features.

THE CUMULATIVE FEATURE OF PREFERRED STOCKS

If the corporation's board of directors believes that omitting dividends is justified, it can vote to omit both the dividends paid to common shareholders and the dividends paid to preferred shareholders. One way preferred shareholders can protect themselves against omitted dividends

cumulative pre-ferred stocks Stocks with unpaid dividends that accumulate and must be paid before any cash dividend is paid to common shareholders.

is to purchase cumulative preferred stocks. **Cumulative preferred stocks** are stocks with unpaid dividends that accumulate and must be paid before any cash dividend is paid to the common shareholders. If a corporation does not pay dividends to the cumulative preferred shareholders during one dividend period, the amount of the missed dividends is added to the following period's preferred dividends. If you own noncumulative preferred stocks, an omitted dividend will not be made up later.

THE PARTICIPATION FEATURE OF PREFERRED STOCKS

To make a preferred stock issue more attractive, corporations sometimes add a *participation feature*. This feature allows preferred shareholders to share with the common shareholders in the corporation's earnings. Participating preferred stocks are rare; this feature is used only when special measures are necessary to attract investors.

The participation feature of preferred stocks works like this: (1) The required dividend is paid to preferred shareholders; (2) a stated dividend, usually equal to the dividend amount paid to preferred shareholders, is paid to common shareholders; and (3) the remainder of the earnings available for distribution is shared by both preferred and common shareholders.

THE CONVERSION FEATURE OF PREFERRED STOCKS

Convertible preferred stocks can be exchanged, at the shareholder's option, for a specified number of shares of common stocks. The conversion feature provides the investor with the added safety of preferred stocks and the possibility of greater speculative gain through conversion to common stocks.

All the information relating to the number of shares of common stocks that may be obtained through conversion of preferred stocks is stated in the corporate records and is usually printed on the preferred stock certificate. For example, assume Martin & Martin Manufacturing Corporation has issued convertible preferred stocks. Each share of preferred stocks in this issue is convertible into two shares of common stocks. Assume the market price of Martin & Martin's convertible preferred stocks is $24 and the stocks pay an annual dividend of $1.60 a share. Also assume the market price of the company's common stocks is $9 and the common stocks currently pays an annual dividend of $0.54 a share. Under these circumstances, you would keep the preferred stocks. If the market price of the common stocks increased to above $12 a share, however, you would have an incentive to exercise the conversion option.

The decision to convert preferred stocks to common stocks is complicated by three factors. First, the dividends paid on preferred stocks are more secure than the dividends paid on common stocks. Second, the amount of the dividend for preferred stocks is generally higher than the amount of the dividend for common stocks. Third, because of the conversion option, the market value of convertible preferred stocks usually increases as the market value of common stocks increases.

The next section discusses additional factors you should evaluate before purchasing either preferred stocks or common stocks.

CONCEPT CHECK 11–2

1. What is the most important priority a preferred shareholder has compared with common shareholders?
2. Why would a corporation call in preferred stocks?
3. Why do corporations issue preferred stocks?
4. Describe three features corporations can offer to make preferred stocks more attractive.

EVALUATION OF A STOCK ISSUE

Many investors expect to earn a 10-percent or higher return on their investments, yet they are unwilling to spend the time required to become a good investor. In fact, many people purchase investments without doing *any* research. They wouldn't buy a car without a test drive or purchase a residence without comparing different houses, but for some unknown reason they invest without doing their homework. The truth is that there is no substitute for a few hours of detective work when choosing an investment. This section explains how to evaluate a potential stock investment.

A wealth of information is available to stock investors. Sources of this information include newspapers, the Internet, business periodicals, corporate reports, and investor services. Most local newspapers carry several pages of business news. *The Financial Post* and *Canadian Business* are devoted almost entirely to financial and economic news. And following the economic upturn, more people are using the Internet to evaluate or monitor the value of their investments. Obviously, different types of investments require different methods of evaluation, but a logical place to start the evaluation process for stock is with the classification of different types of stocks investments.

CLASSIFICATION OF STOCK INVESTMENTS

When evaluating a stock investment, stockbrokers, financial planners, and investors often classify stocks into different categories. We describe eight commonly used classifications.

A **blue-chip stock** is a safe investment that generally attracts conservative investors. Stocks of this kind are issued by the strongest and most respected companies, such as Bell Canada Enterprise, Royal Bank, and Power Corporation. Characteristics to watch for when evaluating this type of stock include leadership in an industrial group, a history of stable earnings, and consistency in paying dividends.

An **income stock** pays higher-than-average dividends. To be able to pay above-average dividends, a corporation must have a steady, predictable source of income. Stocks issued by electric, gas, telephone, and other utility companies are generally classified as income stocks. Many investors seeking income may also include quality preferred stock issues in their portfolios.

A **growth stock** is issued by a corporation that has the potential to earn profits above the average profits of all firms in the economy. Key factors to evaluate when choosing a growth stock include an expanding product line of quality merchandise and an effective research and development department. Retail expansion, state-of-the-art manufacturing facilities, and expansion into international markets are also characteristic of growth stocks. In fact, most growth companies retain a large part of their earnings to pay for their research and development efforts. As a result, such companies generally pay out less than 30 percent of their earnings in dividends to their shareholders. In the late 1990s, typical growth stocks included Adobe Systems, Southwest Airlines, and Home Depot.

A **cyclical stock** follows the business cycle of advances and declines in the economy. When the economy expands, the market value of a cyclical stock increases; when the economy declines, the market value decreases. Most cyclical stocks are in basic industries, such as automobiles, steel, paper, and heavy manufacturing. Investors try to buy cyclical stocks just before the economy expands and sell them just before it declines. Typical cyclical stocks include Ford Motor Company, Caterpillar Inc., and Deere and Company.

A **defensive stock** remains stable during declines in the economy. Generally, companies that issue such stocks have a history of stable earnings and are able to maintain dividend payments to

blue-chip stock A safe investment that generally attracts conservative investors.

income stock A stock that pays higher-than-average dividends.

growth stock A stock issued by a corporation that has the potential to earn profits above the average profits of all firms in the economy.

cyclical stock A stock that follows the business cycle of advances and declines in the economy.

defensive stock A stock that remains stable during declines in the economy.

■ OBJECTIVE 3 ■

Explain how you can evaluate stock investments.

DID YOU KNOW ?

Blue chips are named after the blue chip in poker, which is the chip that carries the highest value.

shareholders during periods of economic decline. Many stocks that are classified as income stocks or blue-chip stocks are also classified as defensive stocks because of their stable earnings and consistent dividend policies. Stocks in this classification include Procter & Gamble, Kellogg, and stocks issued by utility companies.

large-cap stock A stock issued by a large corporation that has a large amount of stocks outstanding and a large amount of capitalization.

capitalization The total amount of securities—stocks and bonds—issued by a corporation.

small-cap stock A stock issued by a company that has a capitalization of $150 million or less.

penny stock A stock that typically sells for less than $1 per share.

Stocks may also be classified as large cap or small cap. A **large-cap stock** is issued by a large corporation that has a large amount of stocks outstanding and a large amount of capitalization. In financial circles, **capitalization** is usually defined as the total amount of securities—stocks and bonds—issued by a corporation. Typically, the companies listed in the Dow Jones averages are considered large caps. Because many large-cap stocks are often considered much more secure than small-cap stocks, they may appeal to more conservative investors. A **small-cap stock** is generally defined as a stock issued by a company that has a capitalization of $150 million or less. Since these stocks are issued by smaller companies, they tend to be more speculative and are often purchased by speculators hoping to make a quick profit.

A **penny stock** typically sells for less than $1 a share. These are stocks issued by new companies or companies with erratic sales and earnings. Therefore, penny stocks are more volatile than more conservative stocks. These stocks are classified as high-risk investments and are more difficult to research because information about them is hard to find. They are also more difficult to track, and dramatic increases and decreases in market value are common. Unfortunately, when the bubble bursts, these stocks can become worthless. As a result, penny stocks should be purchased only by investors who understand *all* the risks.

HOW TO READ THE FINANCIAL SECTION OF THE NEWSPAPER

Most metropolitan newspapers contain information about stocks listed on the Toronto Stock Exchange, the TSX Venture Exchange, and other major stock exchanges, and stocks of local interest. Although not all newspapers print exactly the same information, they usually provide the basic information. Stocks are listed alphabetically, so your first task is to move down the table to find the stocks you're interested in. Then, to read the stock quotation, you simply read across the table. The first row in Exhibit 11–5 gives detailed information about Finning International Inc. (Each numbered entry in the list below the enlarged stock table refers to a column of the stock table.)

If a corporation has more than one stock issue, the common stock issues are always listed first. Then the preferred stock issues are listed and are indicated by the letters *pf* behind the firm's name.

THE INTERNET

Today, most corporations have a Web site, and the information these pages provide is especially useful. First, it is easily accessible. All you have to do is use a search engine to locate the corporation's site. Second, the information on the site may be more up to date than printed material obtained from the corporation or outside sources. Finally, this information may be more complete than that in the corporation's annual report, quarterly report, or other publications.

You can also use such Web sites as Canada.com and other search engines to obtain information about stock investments. Each site will provide links that provide additional information, updates, and advice on specific types of investments, such as stocks, bonds, and mutual funds. At most sites, you can also obtain current stock quotes, track individually chosen securities, and receive updates on news releases and industry events.

STOCK ADVISORY SERVICES

In addition to newspapers and the Internet, sources of information you can use to evaluate potential stock investments are the printed materials provided by stock advisory services. In

THE FINANCIAL POST, SATURDAY, JULY 1, 2000

52W high	52W low	Stock	Ticker	Div	Yield %	P/E	Vol 00s	Friday High /ask	Low /bid	Net chg	Earnings data fiscal	Interim EPS	12 mth EPS	Vol 00s	Week High	Low	Cls/ last	Net chg
15.40	11.50	Finning◇	FTT	0.20	1.6	14.9	413	12.75	12.50	–0.05	Ma 3M	0.17	0.84	8333	12.95	12.50	12.50	
n 10.50	8.00	FirmCap	FC	p0.67	7.3		nt	9.80	9.30					31	9.50	9.25	9.25	–0.25
5.95	4.20	1stAsia un	FAI	p0.52	10.2	14.7	26	5.20	5.10		Ma 3M	0.35	0.35	899	5.35	5.05	5.10	–0.10
9.90	7.10	1stAustPr	FAP	0.84	10.7	10.0	255	7.95	7.75	+0.05	Ja 3M	0.18	0.78	2065	8.00	7.75	7.85	–0.10
0.35	0.05	1stAust wt					z85	0.055	0.055					47	0.055	0.055	0.055	
2.70	0.35	1stCalg	FCP				648	0.85	0.82	–0.01	Ma 3M	d0.01	d0.22	13766	1.21	0.82	0.85	–0.13

1. Highest price paid for one share of Finning International during the past 52 weeks: $15.40
2. Lowest price paid for one share of Finning International in the past 52 weeks: $11.50
3. Name of the company: Finning International Inc.
4. Ticker symbol or letters that identify a stock for trading: FTT
5. Projected annual dividend for next year based on the amount of the firm's last dividend: $0.20
6. Yield percentage, or the percentage of return based on the dividend and current price of the stock: $0.20 ÷ $12.50 = 0.016 = 1.6%
7. Price–earnings (PE) ratio—the price of a share of stock divided by the corporation's earnings per share of stock outstanding over the last 12 months: 12.50 ÷ .84 = 14.9
8. Number of shares of Finning International traded during the previous business day, expressed in hundreds of shares: 413
9. Highest price paid for one share of Finning International during the previous business day: $12.75
10. Lowest price paid for one share of Finning International during the previous business day: $12.50
11. Price paid for the last transaction of the day: $12.50
12. Difference between the price paid for the last share today and the price paid for the last share on the previous day: minus $0.05 (in Bay Street terms, Finning International "closed down 0.05" on this day)
13. Fiscal year-end for reporting earnings: March (3 months)
14. Interim earnings per share: $0.17
15. Annual earnings per share: $0.84
16. Number of shares traded during the week, expressed in hundreds: 8,333
17. Highest price paid for one share during the week: $12.95
18. Lowest price paid for one share during the week: $12.50
19. Price paid for last transaction for the week: $12.50
20. Difference between the price paid for the last trading day and the price paid one week ago: $0

Exhibit 11–5

Financial Information about Common Stock Given in *The Financial Post*

SOURCE: Adapted from *The Financial Post.* "FP Investing," Saturday, July 1, 2000.

choosing among the hundreds of stock advisory services that charge fees for their information, you must consider both the quality and the quantity of the information they provide. The information ranges from simple alphabetical listings to detailed financial reports.

SEDAR, Standard & Poor's reports, and Value Line are briefly described in Chapter 10. A useful online service is found at www.zacks.com. Here we will examine a company report for BCE, Canada's largest communications company.

The report shown in Exhibit 11–6 on the next page is a document issued by Zacks Investment Research. The top section lists the company name and symbol on an exchange (here the New York Stock Exchange) and identifies the industry that BCE participates in.

Exhibit 11–6

Zacks Investment
Research Report
for BCE

SOURCE: Zacks
Investment Research
Inc., Company Reports,
June 7, 2002.

Zacks Investment
Research, Inc.
-Company Reports-   **BCE INC**   June 7, 2002

Ticker	BCE	Shares/ Outstanding	808.4 MM
Exchange	NYSE		
Industry	UTIL-TELEPHONE	Institutions	
Type	Large	Insiders	16.69%

Rec Price	P/E	Mkt Rate	Cap	Div (12Mo)	Yield Gr	Sales Gr	Sls Gr	EPS Rank	Div	Zacks
$18.51	18.5	$14963 MM	$1.20	6.5%	$14138	MM	–14%	1%	–6%	Hold

Price/Volume Data

52 Week High	$27.23
52 Week Low	$14.60
Price Change: Year to Date	–19%
Year to Date (Relative to S & P 500)	–13%
Average Daily Volume	784 000s
Beta	1.12

Zacks Company Profile

BCE Inc. is Canada's largest communications company. Through their operations in communications services, they provide residence and business customers in Canada with wireline and wireless communications products and applications, satellite communications and direct-to-home television services, systems integration expertise, electronic commerce solutions, Internet access, and high-speed data services and directories. Their shares are listed in Canada, the United States, and Europe. (press release)

Symbol
BCE

Previous Close
18.81

Yesterday's Volume
537500

Yesterday's Hi
19.03

Yesterday's Low
18.4

Numbers of Brokers Recommending
(06/02/02)

Strong Buy	1
Moderate Buy	6
Hold	1
Moderate Sell	0
Strong Sell	0
Current Average Recommendation (1.0=Strong Buy, 5.0=Strong Sell)	2
Last Weeks Average Recommendation	1.9
Change In Average Recommendation	–.1

Earnings Estimates and Actuals

Actual Earnings Last Quarter	$0.24
EPS Surprise Last Quarter	4 %
Consensus Estimate for Current Quarter	$0.28
Consensus Estimate for Current Fiscal Year	$1.09
Consensus Estimate for Next Fiscal Year	$1.28

Industry Information

Company Industry Group	UTIL-TELEPHONE
Rank Within Industry Group	N/A of 158

Below the market information, such as the most recent price, price–earnings ratio (P/E), and dividend and capitalization values is a brief description of the company. This description displays the company's most prominent products and identifies its clientele.

BCE Inc. shares trading on the New York Stock Exchange have been bought or sold for as little as $14.60 and as high as $27.23, at an average rate of 784,000 shares per day. To date,

BCE INC. COMPANY SNAPSHOT

| BCE-T: | Last: C$ 27.91 | Net Change: C$ −0.340 | % Change: -1.20 | Volume: 1,170,800 |

Symbol:	Annual Income Statement	Annual Balance Sheet	Annual Cash Flow Statement
BCE-T	Annual Ratios	Quarterly Income Statement	Quarterly Balance Sheet
	Quarterly Cash Flow Statement		

Bottom of Form BCE INC. is a communications company. The company provides connections through wireline, wireless, data/Internet, and satellite services, largely under the Bell brand. BCE leverages those connections with extensive content creation capabilities through Bell Globemedia, which features CTV, *The Globe and Mail*, and Sympatico-Lycos.

Industry: Utilities (Telephone Utilities)
Symbol: BCE
Exchange(s):   Toronto Stock Exchange, New York Stock Exchange

ANNUAL FINANCIALS

	Dec 31, 2001 12 Months C$	Dec 31, 2000 12 Months C$	Dec 31, 1999 12 Months C$	3Yr. Growth
Total Revenue ($000):	25,795,000	17,451,000	14,625,000	-7.41
Earnings before Interest & Tax ($000):	5,574,000	3,075,000	2,479,000	-8.54
Profit/Loss ($000):	523,000	4,651,000	5,459,000	-51.55
Earnings per Share:	0.57	7.43	8.35	-85.80
Total Assets ($000):	54,335,000	51,383,000	35,960,000	19.09
Dividends Per Share:	1.20	1.24	1.35	
Return on Com. Equity:	2.66	29.55	38.14	
Employees:	75,000	75,000	55,000	

Trailing 12 Month Results

	12 Months ended Sep 30, 2002, C$	12 Months ended Sep 30, 2001, C$	%Change
Total Revenue ($000):	21,063,000	23,816,000	-11.46
Profit/Loss ($000):	411,000	786,000	-47.71
Earnings per Share:	0.41	0.89	-53.93
Dividends Per Share:	1.20	1.20	
Number of Shares:	905,025,009	808,143,000	

COMPANY INFORMATION
Report on Business Magazine Top 1000 Ranking
Profit: 0030   Revenue: 0003   Assets: 0013

Key Personnel
CEO: Michael J. Sabia, President and CEO
CFO: Siim A. Vanaselja, Chief Financial Officer

Contact Information

Address:	1000 rue de La Gauchetiere O., Bureau 3700, Montreal, QC, H3B 4Y7	**Phone:**	514-870-8777
		Fax:	514-786-3970
		Web Address:	www.bce.ca
		E-Mail:	bcecomms@bce.ca
Investor Relations:	Maarika Paul, 800 3396363		
Company Type:	Public	**Company Status:**	Active
Auditors:	Deloitte & Touche		
Transfer Agent:	Computershare Trust Co. Of Can Montreal		
Incorporation:	Canada, Feb 25, 1970		

Securities: BCE.N BCE.T BCE.PR.A-T BCE.PR.P-T BCE.PR.R-T BCE.PR.S-T BCE.PR.Y-T

Top Companies in Telephone Utilities (Selected by Assets)

Bell Canada	TELUS	TELUS Communications
Aliant Inc.	Manitoba Telecom Services	Call-Net Enterprises
Bell Nordiq Group		

Exhibit 11–7
Globeinvestor GOLD Stock Report for BCE

SOURCE: http://gold.globeinvestor.com/home1.html 2002 BCE Inc, Company snapshot. globeinvestgold.com

the share value has dropped by 19 percent and the earnings per share (EPS) have grown at a rate of 1 percent.

Exhibit 11–7 presents a detailed four-page report on BCE issued by Globeinvestor GOLD. While other stock advisory services provide basically the same types of information as in Exhibits 11–6 and 11–7, it is the investor's job to interpret such information and decide whether the company's stocks are a good investment.

CORPORATE NEWS

As mentioned in Chapter 10, the federal government requires corporations selling new issues of securities to disclose information about corporate earnings, assets and liabilities, products

Advice from a Pro

How to Spot Online Investment Scams

There are signs that you can look out for before you invest in a company which is being promoted.

Beware of any stocks that you learn about on a bulletin board, chat room, newsgroup, or e-mail. Promoters usually use these to promote stocks.

- Be on guard for high pressure tactics to buy from people you don't know. Promoters make their money from inflating the prices of stocks in order to allow them and insiders to sell their cheap stocks at higher prices. This is called pump and dump, and it is a favourite tactic of promoters who are improperly promoting stocks.
- Watch out for information that you see in online newsletters. Such information might appear to be unbiased and independent, but usually, such information is being provided by individuals paid to recommend the stocks.
- Look out for information contained in publications that contain good investment information along with recommendations or stories about praiseworthy stocks. These publications are veiled attempts to advertise a company; even though the articles appear to be unbiased commentary, the publishers, in fact, have been paid to promote a stock.
- Beware of promises of high profits and the sale relating to products of a new company. It takes time for businesses to become successful and usually the path to success is a gradual increase and not an overnight success. Be realistic when reviewing promises made by companies.
- Never be fooled by press releases or announcements of pending or imminent acquisitions. Unless such acquisitions become reality, this is a warning sign that there is nothing behind the announcement but an attempt to fool you into buying stocks.
- If the company has weak fundamentals, then its low stock price is a reflection of what it's worth and not what a promoter tells you it's worth. Review the financials of a company and rely on only what you see and not on what you are promised.
- Be on the lookout for small-cap companies that pay a generous executive salary or compensation package. This is a telltale sign that any money that the

company is raising is going into the pockets of insiders and not into the company itself.

- Be leery of small-cap companies that are investing in projects unrelated to their businesses. Small-cap companies should not be changing their businesses when they have been created to pursue their original line of business.
- Beware of mining companies that change their focus, especially after another company has announced a large discovery. For example, you will have noticed that in the early 1990s, diamond stocks were very popular. Mining companies that were looking for gold suddenly started hinting in their news releases that they also had properties that could contain diamonds. This was an effort to fool investors into believing that their companies could be the ones to make the next big diamond find.
- Watch out for reverse splits. For example, a company that is trading at $2 per share consolidates its stocks, say on a 3-to-1 basis. Consequently, if you had 300 shares at $2, after the reverse split you would have 100 shares at $6. While the value of the stock seems to be the same, $600, you will begin to notice that the price of your stock will fall probably back to $2 and the value of your stock would be only $200. If the stock does not fall, it could be a sign that the company is trying to make its stocks look more attractive by making them appear that they are worth more. A good company with high profits doesn't need to consolidate its stocks to increase the value of its shares.
- Beware of companies that have been previously suspended or have had delinquent filings. This is an indication that the company is not well managed.
- Be leery of stocks that are thinly traded but have sporadic volume surges. This is an indication that heavy promotion is going on.
- Finally, if you think you have been scammed, report the scam to our *Complaint Centre* and your local *Better Business Bureau*. You may also want to contact your local Enforcement Agency to assist you in investigating the scam.

SOURCE: Based on www.fraudbureau.com/

---

or services, and the qualifications of top management in a prospectus that they must give to investors. In addition to a prospectus, all publicly owned corporations send their shareholders an annual report and quarterly reports that contain detailed financial data. Even if you're not a shareholder, you can obtain an annual report from the corporation. For most corporations, all it takes is a call to a toll-free telephone number. A written request to the corporation's headquarters can also help you obtain an annual report. To see how the information contained in an

One of the best resources you can use to determine the soundness of a stock investment is a corporation's annual report. These reports are an excellent tool for learning about a company, its management, its past performance, and its goals. But while thumbing through these glossy publications, you must always keep in mind that corporations use this medium to "toot their own horns." The letter from the chair of the board, the upbeat, smiling faces of the employees, and the artistic layout and beautiful photographs are nice to look at, but it's the accounting statements and footnotes that give the true picture of the financial health of a corporation. Understanding the items presented on these pages tucked away in the back of the report is the real key to determining if a company is making a profit. Once you know the basics of reading annual reports, you will be in a better position to evaluate different investment opportunities.

Experts recommend that before investing, you review and compare the annual reports a corporation has

published over the last three years. Read the shareholders' letters to see if they met their goals each year. Are any areas of concern mentioned? Are the facts presented in a straightforward manner, or do you have to struggle to interpret their meaning? Learn to read between the lines to separate the hype from the truth. And watch for words like *except for*, *challenges*, and *contingencies*.

Next, turn to the statement of financial position (sometimes called the balance sheet). This is where you can compare the corporation's financial position by noting changes in its current assets, current liabilities, inventories, total liabilities, and owners' equity. Information on the income statement will enable you to determine if the corporation earned a profit. Be sure to look at the amounts reported for sales, expenses, and profit or loss figures.

Finally, don't overlook the footnotes: They contain (and sometimes hide) important information.

---

annual report can help you choose stock investments, read the Financial Planning for Life's Situations feature above.

In addition to corporate publications, many periodicals can help you evaluate a corporation and its stock issues. *Report on Business*, *Canadian Business*, and *Business Week* provide not only general economic news but detailed financial information about individual corporations. Magazines, such as *MoneySense*, *MoneySaver*, and *Consumer Reports*, provide information to help you make informed investment decisions. Trade or industry publications, such as *Canadian Banker*, provide information about firms within a specific industry. Finally, news magazines, such as *The Economist*, *Maclean's*, and *Newsweek*, feature financial news on a regular basis.

FACTORS THAT INFLUENCE THE PRICE OF A STOCK

A **bull market** occurs when investors are optimistic about the nation's economy and buy stocks. In a bull market, the fact that more investors are buying stocks causes the value of both individual stocks and the stock market as a whole to increase. A **bear market** occurs when investors are pessimistic about the nation's economy and sell their stocks. Because more investors are selling their stocks, the value of both individual stocks and the stock market as a whole declines.

How do you determine whether it is the right time to buy or sell a particular stock? Many factors affect the market value of a stock. Therefore, you must also consider potential sales revenues, profits or losses, cash flow, and other important fundamentals when determining whether a stock will increase or decrease in value. In the remainder of this section, we examine some numerical measures that indicate corporate performance and shareholder returns, psychological traps when investing, and analytical techniques that help us to overcome some common investing mistakes and determine whether a stock is priced correctly.

bull market Occurs when investors are optimistic about a nation's economy and buy stocks.

bear market Occurs when investors are pessimistic about a nation's economy and sell their stocks.

MEASURES OF CORPORATE RISK, PERFORMANCE, AND SHAREHOLDERS' RETURNS

Investors should track an investment's return over time to see if it is performing well. As mentioned earlier in the chapter, shareholders purchase stocks to earn dividend income and see the value of their investment increase over time, generating a capital gain.

Let's use the example of an investment in BCE Enterprises Inc. to track an investor's return over the years of 2003 and 2004, given the information below that was taken from the company's 2004 Annual Report:

Year	2004	2003	2002
Dividends per share	$ 1.20	$ 1.20	$ 1.20
Market value at year-end	$28.92	$28.90	$28.50

The cost of acquiring BCE stock at the end of 2002 was $28.50. Over the year, the investor would have earned a $1.20 dividend, and the value of the stock would have risen 40 cents ($28.90 − $28.50). In total, if the investor chose to sell the stock, then he or she would have made $1.20 + $0.40 = $1.60 on an investment of $28.50. The annual return would have been:

annual shareholder return A stock's annual dividend and increase in value divided by its beginning-of-year stock price.

$$\text{Annual shareholder return} = \frac{\text{Annual dividend} + \text{Appreciation in value}}{\text{Initial stock investment}}$$

$$= \frac{\$1.20 + (\$28.90 - \$28.50)}{\$28.50}$$

$$= 0.056 \text{ or } 5.6 \text{ percent}$$

This return could be broken down into two parts: the dividend yield and the capital gains yield. These two components of the total shareholder return are calculated as follows:

dividend yield A stock's annual dividend divided by its beginning-of-year stock price. If the dividend is divided by the end-of-year stock price, it is referred to as its *trailing* dividend yield.

$$\text{Annual dividend yield} = \frac{\text{Annual dividend}}{\text{Initial stock investment}}$$

$$= \frac{\$1.20}{\$28.50}$$

$$= 0.042 \text{ or } 4.2 \text{ percent}$$

capital gains yield A stock's increase in value divided by its beginning-of-year stock price.

$$\text{Capital gains yield} = \frac{\text{Appreciation in value}}{\text{Initial stock investment}}$$

$$= \frac{(\$28.90 - \$28.50)}{\$28.50}$$

$$= 0.014 \text{ or } 1.4 \text{ percent}$$

Investors looking for income will choose stocks that they expect will pay a high dividend. BCE's dividend yield in 2004 was over 4 percent, while that of the S&P/TSX Composite Index was under 2 percent. Investors looking for growth will choose stocks that are expected to appreciate in value.

If we perform the same calculations using the 2004 dividend and increase in stock value from the end of 2003 to the end of 2004, BCE's 2004 total return was 4.2 percent. An investor who had purchased the stock at the end of 2002 and sold it at the end of 2004 (over a period of two years) would have earned an average annual compound return of:

Annual average compound return = $[(1.056)(1.042)]^{1/2} - 1 = 0.049$ or 4.9 percent

While it is easy to calculate historical returns where all the facts are known, we must be careful not to presume that historical returns will indicate what will happen in the future. For

The scandalous collapse of the Enron Corporation has alerted Americans (one would hope) to the inherent dangers of deregulating vital industries, such as energy. However, while the mainstream media focus on the question of whether corporate accounting firms should be held more accountable, they naturally miss the most important issue. Enron was more than just a corrupt corporation; it was functioning as part of the U.S. government.

Enron collapsed like a house of cards just when Wall Street was proclaiming it to be the very model of corporate perfection. Enron stocks were selling at over $80 a share at their peak last fall, and now those shares are worth less than a dollar. If there were justice in the world, we could all sit back and relax, knowing that Enron executives got what they deserved for their corruption and mismanagement. The problem is, Enron's collapse has put thousands of innocent Americans out of work and wiped out the retirement portfolios of thousands more.

When Enron stocks took a nosedive last fall, its corporate captains decided not to go down with the ship.

They and their top investors sold their stocks while hiding the true financial condition of the company from everyone else. In fact, Ken Lay, Enron's chairman, lied to Enron's small investors, telling them that the company's future had never looked brighter. As if that's not bad enough, after years of encouraging their employees to invest their retirement savings almost exclusively in Enron stocks, Enron's pension administrators blocked trading for those same employees for 90 days even as the prices plummeted. By the time investors knew that the company was bankrupt, it was too late. Their stocks were worthless and their bosses had dumped and run. Enron employees weren't the only ones harmed. At least half a dozen state governments throughout the U.S. had also invested their employees' retirement savings in Enron stocks. Those portfolios, too, have lost nearly all their value. Thousands of Americans lost their life savings virtually overnight. Enron employees lost their jobs and their life savings.

SOURCE: The Email Activist, at www.theemail activist.org/

---

example, the investor who purchased the stock at the end of 2002 could not be certain as to the level of the dividend or whether or not the stock would appreciate in value.

Earnings per share (EPS) are a corporation's after-tax earnings divided by the number of outstanding common shares. For example, BCE's 2004 and 2003 earnings per share were $1.65 and $1.90, respectively. Most shareholders consider the level of a firm's earnings per share to be an important measure of the company's profitability. No meaningful average for this measure exists, mainly because the number of common shares issued at any point in time may vary. As a general rule, an increase in earnings per share is a healthy sign for the corporation and its shareholders. However, potential investors should be aware of what specific factors have caused changes in a firm's EPS over time.

> **earnings per share (EPS)** A corporation's after-tax earnings divided by the number of outstanding shares of common stocks.

The **price–earnings (P/E) ratio** is calculated by dividing a company's year-end stock price by its earnings per share. (This ratio would be referred to as the *trailing* P/E ratio because the earnings per share are taken from the year just ended.) Using the BCE example, its end-of-year 2004 price-earnings ratio was 17.52 ($28.92 ÷ $1.65) versus a ratio of 15.2 ($28.90 ÷ $1.90) in 2003. The price-earnings ratio tells us what investors are willing to pay for $1 of current earnings. It is useful to identify the trend in a company's P/E ratio over time or to compare it to the P/E ratios of other firms in the same industry or market in general. Ideally, investors should try to identify firms with relatively low P/E ratios that they expect will outperform in the future. They would expect the firm's share price to rise eventually, driving its P/E ratio up. Although P/E ratios vary by industry, they range between 5 and 35 for most corporations. By May 2005, the S&P/TSX Composite Index average price-earnings ratio was 17.2.

> **price–earnings (P/E) ratio** The price of a share of stock divided by the corporation's earnings per share of stocks outstanding over the last 12 months.

The **beta** is an index reported in many financial publications that compares the risk associated with a specific stock issue with the risk of the stock market in general. The beta for the stock market in general (or the "average" stock) is 1.0. The majority of stocks have betas between 0.5 and 2.0. Generally, conservative stocks have low betas and speculative stocks have high betas.

> **beta** An index that compares the risk associated with a specific stock issue with the risk of the stock market in general.

Before completing this section, you may want to examine the Financial Planning Calculations box on the next page.

Exhibit 11–9

Dollar Cost Averaging

Year	Investment	Stock Price	Shares Purchased
1998	$2,000	$50	40.0
1999	2,000	65	30.8
2000	2,000	60	33.3
Total	$6,000		104.1

Investors use dollar cost averaging to avoid the common pitfall of buying high and selling low. In the situation shown in Exhibit 11–9, you would lose money only if you sold your stocks at less than the average cost of $57.64. Thus, with dollar cost averaging, you can make money if the stocks are sold at a price higher than the average purchase price.

DIRECT INVESTMENT AND DIVIDEND REINVESTMENT PLANS Today, a large number of corporations offer direct investment plans. A **direct investment plan** allows you to purchase stocks directly from a corporation without having to use an account executive or a brokerage firm. Similarly, a **dividend reinvestment plan** allows you the option to reinvest your cash dividends to purchase stocks of the corporation. For shareholders, the chief advantage of both types of plans is that these plans enable them to purchase stocks without paying a commission charge to a brokerage firm. (Note: A few companies may charge a small fee for dividend reinvestment, but the charge is less than what most brokerage firms charge.) As an added incentive, some corporations even offer their stocks at a small discount to encourage the use of their direct investment and dividend reinvestment plans. Also, with the dividend reinvestment plan, you can take advantage of dollar cost averaging, discussed in the previous section. For corporations, the chief advantage of both types of plans is that they provide an additional source of capital. As an added bonus, they are providing a service to their shareholders.

SHORT-TERM TECHNIQUES

In addition to the long-term techniques presented in the preceding section, investors sometimes use more speculative, short-term techniques. In this section, we discuss buying stock on margin, selling short, and trading in options. *Be warned:* The methods presented in this section are quite risky; do not use them unless you fully understand the underlying risks. Also, you should not use them until you have experienced success using the more traditional long-term techniques described above.

BUYING STOCK ON MARGIN When buying stocks on **margin**, you borrow part of the money needed to buy a particular stock. The margin requirements are set by the exchanges and are subject to periodic change. Although margin rules are regulated by the exchanges, margin requirements and the interest charged on the loans used to fund margin transactions may vary among brokers and dealers. Usually, the brokerage firm either lends the money or arranges the loan with another financial institution. Investors buy on margin because doing so offers them the potential for greater profits. Exhibit 11–10 gives an example of buying stocks on margin.

As Exhibit 11–10 shows, it is more profitable to use margin. In effect, the financial leverage (often defined as the use of borrowed funds to increase the return on an investment) allowed William Oliver, who is single and 32 years old, to purchase a larger number of stocks. Since the dollar value of each share increased, William obtained a larger profit by buying the stocks on margin.

In this example, William's stocks did exactly what they were supposed to do: They increased in market value. His stocks increased $4 per share, and he made $4,000 because he owned

direct investment plan A plan that allows shareholders to purchase stocks directly from a corporation without having to use an account executive or a brokerage firm.

dividend reinvestment plan A plan that allows current shareholders the option to reinvest or use their cash dividends to purchase stocks of the corporation.

margin A speculative technique whereby an investor borrows part of the money needed to buy a particular stock.

Visit the Web site See the CBC video exercises under Chapter 11 on the online learning centre at www.mcgrawhill.ca/ college/kapoor.

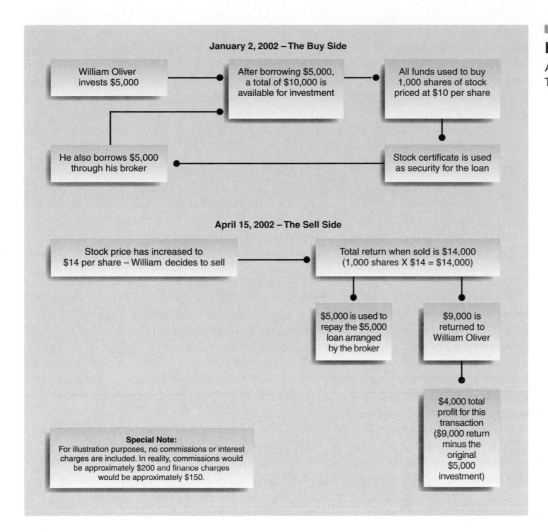

Exhibit 11–10
A Typical Margin
Transction

January 2, 2002 – The Buy Side

William Oliver invests $5,000

After borrowing $5,000, a total of $10,000 is available for investment

All funds used to buy 1,000 shares of stock priced at $10 per share

He also borrows $5,000 through his broker

Stock certificate is used as security for the loan

April 15, 2002 – The Sell Side

Stock price has increased to $14 per share – William decides to sell

Total return when sold is $14,000 (1,000 shares X $14 = $14,000)

$5,000 is used to repay the $5,000 loan arranged by the broker

$9,000 is returned to William Oliver

$4,000 total profit for this transaction ($9,000 return minus the original $5,000 investment)

Special Note:
For illustration purposes, no commissions or interest charges are included. In reality, commissions would be approximately $200 and finance charges would be approximately $150.

1,000 shares. His actual profit would be reduced by commissions and the amount of interest his broker would charge for the margin transaction. Had the value of the stocks gone down, buying on margin would have increased his loss. For example, William would have lost $3,000 if the price of the stocks had dropped from $10 a share (the original purchase price) to $7 a share.

If the market value of a margined stocks decreases to approximately one-half of the original price, you will receive a *margin call* from the brokerage firm. After the margin call, you must pledge additional cash or securities to serve as collateral for the loan. If you don't have acceptable collateral or cash, the margined stocks are sold and the proceeds are used to repay the loan. The exact price at which the brokerage firm issues the margin call is determined by the amount of money you borrowed when you purchased the stocks. Generally, the more money you borrow, the sooner you will receive a margin call if the market value of the margined stocks drops.

In addition to facing the possibility of larger dollar losses, you must pay interest on the money borrowed to purchase stocks on margin. Most brokerage firms charge 1 to 3 percent above the prime rate. Normally, economists define the prime rate as the interest rate that the best business customers pay. Interest charges can absorb the potential profits if the value of margined stocks does not increase rapidly enough and the margined stocks must be held for long periods of time.

SELLING SHORT Your ability to make money by buying and selling securities is related to how well you can predict whether a certain stock will increase or decrease in market value. Normally, you buy stocks and assume they will increase in value, a procedure referred to as *buying long*. But not all stocks increase in value. In fact, the value of a stock may decrease for many reasons, including lower sales, lower profits, reduced dividends, product failures, increased competition, and product liability lawsuits. With this fact in mind, you may use a procedure called *selling short* to make money when the value of a stock is expected to decrease in value. **Selling short** is selling stock that has been borrowed from a brokerage firm and must be replaced at a later date. When you sell short, you sell today, knowing you must buy or *cover* your short transaction at a later date. To make money in a short transaction, you must take these steps:

selling short Selling stocks that have been borrowed from a brokerage firm and must be replaced at a later date.

[1] Arrange to *borrow a stock certificate* for a certain number of shares of a particular stock from a brokerage firm.

[2] *Sell the borrowed stocks*, assuming it will drop in value in a reasonably short period of time.

[3] *Buy the stocks at a lower price* than the price sold for in step 2.

[4] Use the stocks purchased in step 3 to *replace the stocks borrowed from the brokerage firm* in step 1.

For example, Beatrice Maly, who is 28 years old, believes a dot-com stock is overpriced because of increased competition among dot-com companies and numerous other factors. As a result, she decides to sell short 100 shares of the dot-com company (Exhibit 11–11).

As Exhibit 11–11 shows, Beatrice's total return for this short transaction was $700 because the stocks did what they were supposed to do in a short transaction: decrease in value. A price decrease is especially important when selling short because you must replace the stocks borrowed from the brokerage firm with stocks purchased (hopefully at a lower market value) at a later date. If the stocks increase in value, you will lose money because you must replace the borrowed stocks with stocks purchased at a higher price. If the price of the dot-com stocks in Exhibit 11–11 had increased from $90 to $97, Beatrice would have lost $700.

There is usually no special or extra brokerage charge for selling short, since the brokerage firm receives its regular commission when the stocks are bought and sold. Before selling short,

Exhibit 11–11

An Example of Selling Short

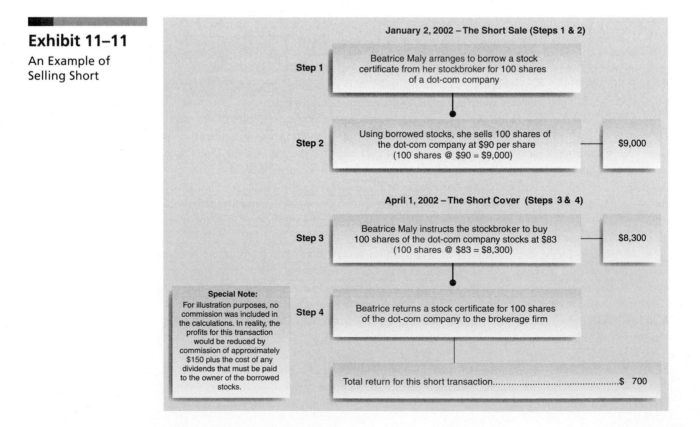

January 2, 2002 – The Short Sale (Steps 1 & 2)

Step 1 Beatrice Maly arranges to borrow a stock certificate from her stockbroker for 100 shares of a dot-com company

Step 2 Using borrowed stocks, she sells 100 shares of the dot-com company at $90 per share (100 shares @ $90 = $9,000) — $9,000

April 1, 2002 – The Short Cover (Steps 3 & 4)

Step 3 Beatrice Maly instructs the stockbroker to buy 100 shares of the dot-com company stocks at $83 (100 shares @ $83 = $8,300) — $8,300

Special Note:
For illustration purposes, no commission was included in the calculations. In reality, the profits for this transaction would be reduced by commission of approximately $150 plus the cost of any dividends that must be paid to the owner of the borrowed stocks.

Step 4 Beatrice returns a stock certificate for 100 shares of the dot-com company to the brokerage firm

Total return for this short transaction...$ 700

consider two factors. First, since the stocks you borrow from your broker are actually owned by another investor, you must pay any dividends the stocks earn before you replace the stocks. After all, you borrowed the stocks and then sold the borrowed stocks. Eventually, dividends can absorb the profits from your short transaction if the price of the stocks does not decrease rapidly enough. Second, to make money selling short, you must be correct in predicting that the stocks will decrease in value. If the value of the stocks increases, you lose.

TRADING IN OPTIONS An **option** gives you the right to buy or sell stocks at a pre-determined price during a specified period of time. Options are usually available for three-, six-, or nine-month periods. If you think the market price of a stock will increase during a short period of time, you may decide to purchase a call option. A *call option* is sold by a shareholder and gives the purchaser the right to *buy* 100 shares at a guaranteed price before a specified expiration date.

It is also possible to purchase a put option. A *put option* is the right to *sell* 100 shares at a guaranteed price before a specified expiration date. With both call and put options (see Exhibit 11–12), you are betting that the price of the stocks will increase or decrease in value before the expiration date. If this price movement does not occur before the expiration date, you lose the money you paid for your option.

Because of the increased risk involved in option trading, a more detailed discussion of how you profit or lose money with options is beyond the scope of this book. *Be warned:* Amateurs and beginning investors should stay away from options unless they fully understand all of the risks involved. For the rookie, the lure of large profits over a short period of time may be tempting, but the risks are real.

option The right to buy or sell stocks at a predetermined price during a specified period of time.

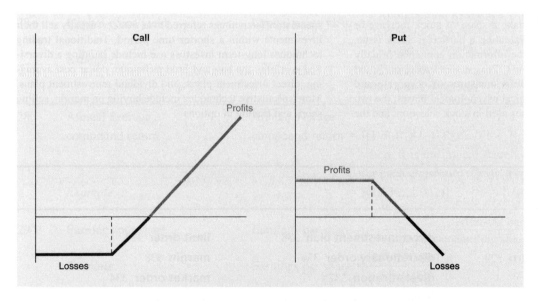

Exhibit 11–12
Payoff for Call and Put Options

CONCEPT CHECK 11–5

1. Why is it better for investors to diversify their stock portfolios?
2. How can an investor make money using the buy-and-hold technique?
3. What is the advantage of using dollar cost averaging?
4. Explain the difference between direct investment plans and dividend reinvestment plans.
5. Why would an investor buy stocks on margin?
6. Why would an investor use the selling-short technique?

LEARNING OBJECTIVES

1 Describe the characteristics of corporate bonds.

2 Discuss why corporations issue bonds.

3 Explain why investors purchase corporate bonds.

4 Discuss why federal, provincial, and municipal governments issue bonds and why investors purchase government bonds.

5 Evaluate bonds when making an investment.

Visit the Web site
See the Pre-Test under Chapter 12 on the online learning centre at www.mcgrawhill.ca/college/kapoor.

Opportunity costs! Bethan Jackson, the woman in the opening case, took a chance when she purchased 12 corporate bonds issued by a utility company. Her investment, which cost more than $12,000, could decrease in value. But because she took the time to evaluate the investment using reliable sources, she could be reasonably certain she would receive interest payments each year and eventual repayment when this bond issue reaches maturity in 2010.

The company that issued the bond also took advantage of the concept of opportunity costs when it sold bonds. It agreed to pay bondholders 7 percent interest until the bonds mature in 2010. It also agreed to repay Jackson's original investment when the bonds mature. In return, the company obtained the money it needed to provide telecommunications services to its customers, provide more jobs, and ultimately earn larger profits.

We begin this chapter by describing the basic characteristics of corporate bonds that define the relationship between investors, like Bethan Jackson, and corporations that sell bonds to obtain financing.

CHARACTERISTICS OF CORPORATE BONDS

■ OBJECTIVE 1 ■

Describe the characteristics of corporate bonds.

corporate bond A corporation's written pledge to repay a specified amount of money, along with interest.

face value The dollar amount the bondholder will receive at the bond's maturity.

maturity date For a corporate bond, the date on which the corporation is to repay the borrowed money.

A **corporate bond** is a corporation's written pledge to repay a specified amount of money with interest. Exhibit 12–1 shows a typical corporate bond. Note that it states the dollar amount of the bond, the interest rate, and the maturity date. The **face value** is the dollar amount the bondholder will receive at the bond's maturity. The usual face value of a corporate bond is $1,000, but the face value of some corporate bonds may be as high as $50,000. The total face value of all the bonds in an issue usually runs into millions of dollars (see Exhibit 12–2). Between the time of purchase and the maturity date, the corporation pays interest to the bondholder, usually every six months, at the stated interest rate (refered to as the coupon rate of the bond). For example, assume you purchase the bond shown in Exhibit 12–1, and the coupon rate for this bond is 8.5 percent. Using the following formula, you can calculate the annual interest amount for this bond:

$$
\begin{aligned}
\text{Dollar amount of annual interest} &= \text{Face value} \times \text{Interest rate} \\
&= \$1{,}000 \times 8.5 \text{ percent} \\
&= \$1{,}000 \times 0.085 \\
&= \$85
\end{aligned}
$$

In this situation, you receive interest of $85 a year from the corporation. The interest is paid semi-annually, or every six months, in $42.50 ($85 ÷ 2 = $42.50) installments until the bond matures.

The **maturity date** of a corporate bond is the last date on which the corporation is to repay the borrowed money. At the maturity date, the bondholder returns the bond to the corporation and receives cash equal to the bond's face value. Maturity dates for bonds generally range from 1 to 30 years after the date of issue. Maturities for corporate bonds may also be classified as short term (under 5 years), intermediate term (5 to 15 years), and long term (over 15 years).

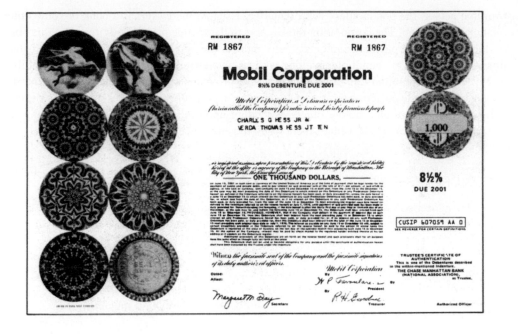

Exhibit 12–1
A Typical Corporate Bond

The actual legal conditions for a corporate bond are described in a bond indenture. A **bond indenture** is a legal document that details all of the conditions relating to a bond issue. Often containing over 100 pages of complicated legal wording, the bond indenture remains in effect until the bonds reach maturity or are redeemed by the corporation.

Since corporate bond indentures are very difficult for the average person to read and understand, a corporation issuing bonds appoints a trustee. The **trustee** is a financially independent

bond indenture A legal document that details all the conditions relating to a bond issue.

trustee A financially independent firm that acts as the bondholders' representative.

Exhibit 12–2
Advertisement for a 7½-Percent Convertible Debenture Issued by Meditrust (Meditrust was renamed La Quinta in 2001)

firm that acts as the bondholders' representative. Usually, the trustee is a bank or some other financial institution. The corporation must report to the trustee periodically regarding its ability to make interest payments and eventually redeem the bonds. In turn, the trustee transmits this information to the bondholders along with its own evaluation of the corporation's ability to pay. If the corporation fails to live up to all the provisions in the indenture agreement, the trustee may bring legal action to protect the bondholders' interests. In cases of bankruptcy, certain bondholders are paid before others depending upon the class or type of bond; they are always paid after Canada Revenue Agency and the employee payroll.

CONCEPT CHECK 12–1

1. If you needed information about a bond issue, would you go to the library or use the Internet?
2. What is the usual face value for a corporate bond?
3. What is the annual interest amount for a $1,000 bond issued by Power Corporation of Canada that pays 6.5 percent interest?
4. In your own words, define *maturity date* and *bond indenture*.
5. How does a trustee evaluate the provisions contained in a bond indenture?

WHY CORPORATIONS SELL CORPORATE BONDS

■ OBJECTIVE 2 ■

Discuss why corporations issue bonds.

Let's begin this section with some basics of why corporations sell bonds. Corporations, such as Meditrust (see Exhibit 12–2), borrow when they don't have enough money to pay for major purchases—much as individuals do. Bonds can also be used to finance a corporation's ongoing business activities. In addition, corporations often sell bonds when it is difficult or impossible to sell stocks. The sale of bonds can also improve a corporation's financial leverage—the use of borrowed funds to increase the corporation's return on investment. Finally, the interest paid to bond owners is a tax-deductible expense and, thus, can be used to reduce the taxes the corporation must pay to the federal and provincial governments.

While a corporation may use both bonds and stocks to finance its activities, there are important distinctions between the two. The issuance of corporate bonds are a form of *debt financing*, whereas the issuance of stocks is a form of *equity financing*. Bond owners must be repaid at a future date; shareholders do not have to be repaid. Interest payments on bonds are required; dividends are paid to shareholders at the discretion of the board of directors. Finally, in the event of bankruptcy, bondholders have a claim to the assets of the corporation prior to that of shareholders.

Before issuing bonds, a corporation must decide what type of bond to issue and how the bond issue will be repaid.

TYPES OF BONDS

debenture A bond that is backed only by the reputation of the issuing corporation.

Most corporate bonds are debentures. A **debenture** is a bond that is backed only by the reputation of the issuing corporation. If the corporation fails to make either interest payments or repayment at maturity, debenture bondholders become general creditors, much like the firm's suppliers. In the event of corporate bankruptcy, general creditors, including debenture bondholders, can claim any asset not specifically used as collateral for a loan or other financial obligations.

mortgage bond A corporate bond secured by various assets of the issuing firm.

To make a bond issue more appealing to conservative investors, a corporation may issue a mortgage bond. A **mortgage bond** is a corporate bond secured by various assets of the firm. This type of bond pledges land, buildings, or equipment as security for the loan and entitles the trustee to take ownership of these assets on behalf of bondholders if interest and principal payments are defaulted. A first mortgage bond is the most secure that a corporation can offer and is considered foremost of all obligations a company may have. Often, this type of mortgage will apply against both current and future assets. A general mortgage bond is secured by all the fixed assets of the firm that have not been pledged as collateral for other financial obligations. A *collateral trust bond* is secured by a pledge of securities and is often issued by companies that do not own many fixed assets but do own other securities.

A secured bond is safer than a debenture, as the issuing company offers to pay back the loan but does not require any claim on assets or property to secure the loan. A **subordinated debenture** is an unsecured bond that gives bondholders a claim secondary to that of other designated bondholders with respect to interest payments, repayment, and assets. Investors who purchase subordinated debentures usually enjoy higher interest rates than other bondholders because of the increased risk associated with this type of bond.

subordinated debenture An unsecured bond that gives bondholders a claim secondary to that of other designated bondholders with respect to both interest payments and assets.

CONVERTIBLE BONDS AND BONDS WITH WARRANTS

A special type of bond a corporation may issue is a convertible bond. A **convertible bond** can be exchanged, at the owner's option, for a specified number of shares of the corporation's common stocks. This conversion feature allows investors to enjoy the lower risk of a corporate bond but also take advantage of the speculative nature of common stocks. For example, Noranda's $1,000 bond issue with a 2007 maturity date is convertible. Each bond can be converted to 28.9 shares of the company's common stocks. This means you could convert the bond to common stocks whenever the price of the company's common stocks is $34.60 ($1,000 ÷ 28.9 = $34.60) or higher.

convertible bond A bond that can be exchanged, at the owner's option, for a specified number of shares of the corporation's common stocks.

In reality, there is no guarantee that Noranda bondholders will convert to common stocks even if the market value of the common stocks does increase to $34.60 or higher. The reason for choosing not to exercise the conversion feature in this example is quite simple. As the market value of the common stocks increases, the market value of the convertible bond also increases. By not converting to common stocks, bondholders enjoy the added safety of the bond and interest income in addition to the increased market value of the bond caused by the price movement of the common stocks.

The corporation gains three advantages by issuing convertible bonds. First, the interest rate on a convertible bond is often 1 to 2 percent lower than that on traditional bonds. Second, the conversion feature attracts investors who are interested in the possible gain that conversion to common stocks may provide. Third, if the bondholder converts to common stocks, the corporation no longer has to redeem the bond at maturity.

Some bonds are issued with warrants. A *warrant* is an option that is detachable from the associated bond that gives the holder the right to purchase the firm's common shares at a set price for a pre-determined period, usually a number of years. Warrants are attached to newly issued bonds to make them more attractive to potential investors.

PROVISIONS FOR REPAYMENT

Today, most corporate bonds are callable. A **call feature** allows the corporation to call in or buy outstanding bonds from current bondholders before the maturity date. In the 1990s, investors saw a large number of bonds called because corporations could replace high-interest bond issues with new bond issues that have lower interest rates. The money needed to call a bond may come from the firm's profits, the sale of additional stocks, or the sale of a new bond issue that has a lower interest rate.

call feature A feature that allows the corporation to call in or buy outstanding bonds from current bondholders before the maturity date.

In most cases, corporations issuing callable bonds agree not to call them for the first 5 to 10 years after the bonds have been issued. When a call feature is used, the corporation may have to pay the bondholders a *premium*, an additional amount above the face value of the bond. The amount of the premium is specified in the bond indenture; a $10 to $50 premium over the bond's face value is common.

The federal government sells bonds and securities to finance both the national debt and the government's ongoing activities. The main reason investors choose Canadian government securities is that most investors consider them risk free. In fact, some financial planners refer to them as the ultimate safe investment because their quality is considered to be higher than that of any other investment. Because they are backed by the full faith and credit of the Canadian government and carry a decreased risk of default, they offer lower interest rates than corporate bonds.

TYPES OF BONDS

GOVERNMENT OF CANADA SECURITIES
The government of Canada issues three main types of securities in the form of marketable bonds, treasury bills, and Canada Savings Bonds. It is also the largest single issuer in the Canadian bond market, having direct marketable debt in the hundreds of billions of dollars. Government of Canada bonds are also classified as debentures for the simple reason that they do not have any assets pledged to them; they are only backed by the government's reputation (which generally is good enough).

MARKETABLE BONDS
These issues are referred to as marketable bonds because in addition to having a specific maturity date and interest rate, they are also transferable and, as a result, can be traded in the bond market. They are generally noncallable, which means that the government does not have the option of calling them in to be redeemed before maturity. As of 1991, there was also an issue of Government of Canada Real Return Bonds, which had their nominal return tied to the Consumer Price Index, a measure of inflation. With this type of bond, the maturity value is calculated by multiplying the original face value of the bond times the total inflation since the date of issue.

TREASURY BILLS
A *treasury bill*, sometimes called a *T-bill*, is sold in a minimum unit of $1,000 with additional increments of $1,000 above the minimum. Treasury bills with terms to maturity of 91, 186, or 364 days are currently auctioned on a bi-weekly basis, generally on Tuesday for delivery on Thursday. See Exhibit 12–4 for an example of a treasury bill.

> **DID YOU KNOW ?**
>
> Canadian Government Bond Yields
>
>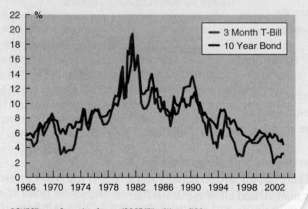
>
> — 3 Month T-Bill
> — 10 Year Bond
>
> SOURCE: www.fitt.ca/conference/2003/Files/Warren%20 Jestin%2003-06-09%20FITT%200ttawa.ppt

T-bills are discounted securities, and the actual purchase price you pay is less than the maturity value of the T-bill. Let's assume you purchased a 91-day T-bill with a purchase price of $990.13 and a face value of $1,000. This means that the discounted amount is $9.87 ($1,000 − $990.13). The convention in Canada is to quote T-bills in yield terms. In this example, you receive $9.87 on a $990.13 investment which produces an annualized rate of return equal to 4 percent, computed as follows:

$$Y = [(F - P)/P] \times (365/T)$$

where

Y = Current yield for a T-Bill	$Y = [(\$1,000 - \$990.13)/\$990.13] \times [365/91]$
F = Face value of the T-Bill	$Y = [\$9.87 / \$990.13] \times 4$
P = Purchase price	$Y = .03987$ or approximately 4%
T = Term	

The price of the T-bill can be determined by rearranging the above equation and solving for (F − P)/P and then given F, solving for P.

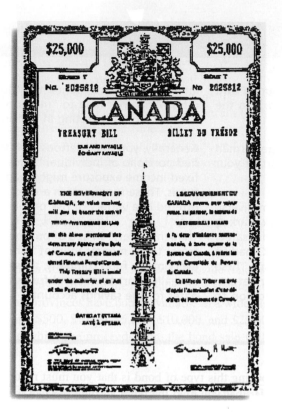

CANADA SAVINGS BONDS (CSBs)

These bonds first went on sale in the fall of 1946 and were developed from Victory bonds, which were issued between 1940 and 1944 to help Canada fight in World War II. Over the past half century or so, they have played an important role in the federal government's borrowing, though less so in recent times. The year 2002 marked the issue of Series 74. See Exhibit 12–5 for a sample CSB.

Since 1977, CSBs have been available as either a regular interest bond or a compound interest bond. The *regular interest bond* pays annual interest either by cheque or direct deposit to the holder's bank account on November 1 of each year. It is available in denominations of $300, $500, $1,000, $5,000, and $10,000, with a maximum of five each of the $300 and $500 bonds per registered owner. Interest is paid only on bonds held longer than three months from the date of issue. Should you choose to do so, you may also exchange your regular interest bond for a compound interest bond of the same series up to August 31 of the year following the issue.

The *compound interest bond* allows you to forfeit receipt of annual interest to allow the unpaid interest to compound annually and earn interest on the accumulated interest. This bond is available in denominations of $100, $300, $500, $1,000, $5,000, and $10,000, with a limit of five each of the $100, $300, and $500 bonds per registered owner. You may also exchange your compound interest bond for a regular interest bond of the same series at any time until maturity.

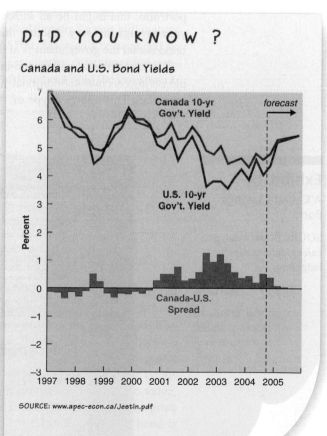

DID YOU KNOW ?

Canada and U.S. Bond Yields

SOURCE: www.apec-econ.ca/Jestin.pdf

Exhibit 12–6

Financial Information about Corporate Bonds Available in *The Financial Post*

SOURCE: *The Financial Post*, Saturday, July 1, 2000, p. C17.

BONDS

Supplied by RBC Dominion Securities Inc., International from Reuters

RBC DS Index	Index level	Total ret	Price ret	MTD tot.ret
Market	336.89	0.07	0.05	1.43
Short	287.97	0.02	0.00	1.08
Intermed	339.97	0.12	0.10	1.60
Long	413.73	0.07	0.05	1.82
Govts	335.36	0.05	0.03	1.46
Canadas	327.06	0.04	0.02	1.36
Provs	357.06	0.08	0.06	1.71
Munis	122.89	0.07	0.05	1.77
Corps	355.93	0.12	0.10	1.34

	Coupon	Mat. date	Bid $	Yld%
Canada	7.000	Sep 01/01	101.05	6.04
Canada	9.500	Oct 01/01	104.10	6.01
Canada	9.750	Dec 01/01	104.97	6.01
Canada	5.250	Dec 01/01	98.98	6.01
Canada	8.750	Feb 01/02	104.05	6.01
Canada	8.500	Apr 01/02	104.05	6.00
Canada	10.000	May 01/02	106.75	6.02
Canada	5.750	Jun 01/02	99.64	5.95
Canada	5.500	Sep 01/02	98.98	6.01
Canada	11.250	Dec 15/02	111.66	6.05
Canada	11.750	Feb 01/03	113.38	6.05
Canada	7.250	Jun 01/03	103.24	6.01
Canada	5.250	Sep 01/03	97.80	6.02
Canada	9.500	Oct 01/03	110.00	6.05
Canada	7.500	Dec 01/03	104.47	6.03
Canada	10.250	Feb 01/04	113.22	6.07
Canada	6.500	Jun 01/04	101.67	6.01
Canada	5.000	Sep 01/04	96.45	5.98
Canada	10.500	Oct 01/04	116.35	6.06
Canada	9.000	Dec 01/04	111.40	6.01
Canada	12.000	Mar 01/05	123.75	6.06
Canada	6.000	Sep 01/05	100.38	5.91

	Coupon	Mat. date	Bid $	Yld%
B C	9.000	Jan 09/02	104.07	6.13
B C	7.750	Jun 16/03	104.19	6.17
B C	9.000	Jun 21/04	109.67	6.21
B C	8.000	Aug 23/05	107.68	6.23
B C	5.250	Dec 01/06	94.92	6.22
B C	6.000	Jun 09/08	98.22	6.29
B C	6.250	Dec 01/09	99.63	6.30
B C	9.500	Jan 09/12	125.28	6.37
B C	8.500	Aug 23/13	118.83	6.36
B C	7.500	Jun 09/14	110.30	6.37
B C	9.950	May 15/21	139.49	6.47
B C	8.750	Aug 19/22	126.72	6.46
B C	8.000	Sep 08/23	118.54	6.45
B C	6.150	Nov 19/27	96.94	6.39
B C	5.700	Jun 18/29	91.69	6.33
B C MF	7.750	Dec 01/05	106.57	6.30
B C MF	5.500	Mar 24/08	94.73	6.37
HydQue	10.875	Jul25/01	104.76	6.13
HydQue	5.750	Feb 15/02	102.25	6.23
HydQue	5.500	May 15/03	98.15	6.21
HydQue	7.000	Jun01/04	102.58	6.24
HydQue	8.500	Aug 15/05	109.57	6.28
HydQue	13.250	Sep 30/05	101.56	6.27
HydQue	7.000	Feb 15/07	103.50	6.34
HydQue	6.000	Jul 15/09	97.20	6.41
HydQue	10.000	Sep 26/11	127.85	6.47
HydQue	10.250	Jul 16/12	131.15	6.48
HydQue	11.000	Aug 15/20	148.05	6.64
HydQue	10.500	Oct 15/21	143.90	6.62
HydQue	9.625	Jul 15/22	134.80	6.60
HydQue	6.000	Aug 15/31	94.00	6.45
Manit	6.500	Sep 04/01	100.41	6.12
Manit	9.750	Sep 03/02	107.12	6.17
Manit	7.875	Apr 07/03	104.27	6.16
Manit	5.650	Jul 15/04	98.02	6.21

	Coupon	Mat. date	Bid $	Yld%
Ontario	7.500	Jan 19/06	106.03	6.20
Ontario	7.750	Jul 24/06	107.71	6.20
Ontario	6.125	Sep 12/07	99.60	6.19
Ontario	5.700	Dec 01/08	96.45	6.25
Ontario	6.150	Apr 01/09	97.78	6.48
Ontario	6.200	Nov 19/09	99.63	6.25
Ontario	9.500	Jul 13/22	136.23	6.41
Ontario	8.100	Sep 08/23	120.56	6.39
Ontario	7.500	Feb 07/24	113.53	6.38
Ontario	8.500	Dec 02/25	126.60	6.37
Ontario	8.000	Jun 02/26	120.65	6.36
Ontario	8.000	Dec 02/26	120.59	6.38
Ontario	7.600	Jun 02/27	116.49	6.32
Ontario	6.250	Aug 25/28	99.11	6.32
Ontario	6.500	Mar 08/29	103.14	6.26
Ontario	6.200	Jun 02/31	99.69	6.22
OntHyd	8.625	Feb 06/02	103.70	6.13
OntHyd	9.000	Apr 16/02	104.75	6.13
OntHyd	9.000	Jun 24/02	105.23	6.13
OntHyd	12.500	Nov 30/02	102.49	6.03
OntHyd	5.375	Jun 02/03	97.95	6.15
OntHyd	7.750	Nov 03/05	106.93	6.20
OntHyd	14.250	Apr 21/06	106.12	6.18
OntHyd	5.600	Jun 02/08	95.94	6.26
OntHyd	10.000	May 10/09	103.00	6.28
OntHyd	10.500	Jan 15/10	116.22	6.32
OntHyd	13.250	May 14/10	117.73	6.35
OntHyd	13.000	Jan 29/11	120.63	6.43
OntHyd	10.000	Oct 17/14	133.96	6.35
OntHyd	10.125	Oct 15/21	142.69	6.42
OntHyd	8.900	Aug 18/22	129.25	6.41
OntHyd	9.000	May 26/25	132.50	6.38
OntHyd	8.500	May 26/25	126.37	6.37
OntHyd	8.250	Jun 22/26	123.83	6.36
Quebec	10.250	Oct 15/01	104.90	6.18
Quebec	5.250	Apr 01/02	98.55	6.14
Quebec	9.250	Apr 01/02	105.00	6.16
Quebec	13.000	Apr 07/03	116.85	6.24
Quebec	9.000	May 01/03	107.05	6.23

1. The first line of the first column shows information for a Government of Canada bond issue bearing a coupon value of 7 percent of the face value. It pays $1,000 × 0.07 = $70 per year and matures on September 1, 2001.
2. The current yield, or return, based on today's price is 6.04%.
3. The current bid to purchase a bond from this issue is for $101.05.

page 366. Finally, column three indicates that BCTel will mature on June 19, 2021. For the remainder of this section, we examine methods you can use to evaluate bond investments.

ANNUAL REPORTS

As pointed out earlier in this chapter, bondholders must be concerned about the financial health of the corporation or government unit that issues bonds. To understand how important financial information is when evaluating a bond issue, consider the following two questions:

- Will the bond be repaid at maturity?
- Will you receive interest payments until maturity?

While it may be difficult to answer these questions with 100 percent accuracy, the information contained in a firm's annual report is the logical starting point. Today, there are three ways to obtain a corporation's annual report. First, you can either write or telephone the corporation and request an annual report. (Hint: Many corporations have toll-free telephone numbers for your use.) Second, as mentioned in the next section, most corporations maintain a Web site that contains detailed information about their financial performance. Third, some financial publications provide a reader's service that allows you to use a toll-free telephone number or a postcard to obtain an annual report.

Regardless of how you obtain an annual report, you should look for signs of financial strength or weakness. Is the firm profitable? Are sales revenues increasing? Are the firm's long-term liabilities increasing? In fact, there are many questions you should ask before making a decision to buy a bond. To help you determine the right questions to ask when evaluating a bond issue, examine the Financial Planning Calculations feature on page 367. Also, you may want to examine the bond's rating and perform the calculations described on pp. 366–369 before investing your money.

THE INTERNET

Just as you can use the Internet to evaluate a stock investment, you can use much of the same financial information to evaluate a bond investment. By accessing a corporation's Web page and locating the topics "financial information," "annual report," or "investor relations," you can find many of the answers to the questions discussed in the last section. As an added bonus, a corporation may provide more than one year's annual report on its Web site, so you can make comparisons from one year to another.

When investing in bonds, you can use the Internet in three other ways. First, you can obtain price information on specific bond issues to track your investments. Especially, if you live in an area without access to newspapers that provide bond coverage, the Internet can be a welcome source of current bond prices. Second, it is possible to trade bonds online and pay lower commissions than you would pay a full-service or discount brokerage firm. Third, you can get research about a corporation and its bond issues (including recommendations to buy or sell) by accessing specific bond Web sites. *Be warned:* Bond Web sites are not as numerous as Web sites that provide information on stocks, mutual funds, or personal financial planning. And many of the better bond Web sites charge a fee for their research and recommendations. Each of the following Web sites provides information and educational materials designed to make you a better bond investor:

www.cbrs.com   www.dbrs.com
www.bondcan.com   www.webfin.com
www.bondsonline.com   www.investinginbonds.com
www.moodys.com   www.standardpoor.com

junk bond A type of bond that offers a very high return but is very risky as the bond is nearing or currently in default.

BOND RATINGS

To determine the quality and risk associated with bond issues, investors rely on the bond ratings provided by the CBRS and the DBRS. Both companies rank thousands of corporate and municipal bonds.

As Exhibit 12–7 on the next page illustrates, bond ratings generally range from AAA (the highest) to D (the lowest). The first four individual categories represent investment-grade securities. Investment-grade securities are suitable for conservative investors who want a safe investment that provides a predictable source of income. Bonds in the next two categories are considered speculative in nature. Finally, the C and D categories are used to rank bonds that may be in default due to poor prospects of repayment or even continued payment of interest. Bonds that fall in those categories can be termed **junk bonds**, which offer a very high return but with an unreasonable amount of risk, thus making them undesirable to the average investor. Although bond ratings may be flawed or inaccurate, most investors regard the work of both the CBRS and the DBRS as highly reliable.

Generally, government securities are not graded because they are risk-free for practical purposes. The rating of long-term municipal bonds is similar to that of corporate bonds.

DID YOU KNOW ?

GOVERNMENT OF CANADA LONG-TERM CREDIT RATINGS

	Domestic debt Trend	Foreign debt Trend
Standard & Poor's Current	AAA Stable	AA+ Stable
Moody's Investors Service Current	Aa1 Stable	Aa1 Stable
Canadian Bond Rating Service Current	AA+ Stable	AA+ Stable
Dominion Bond Rating Service Current	AAA Stable	AA (high) Stable

SOURCE: Canada Savings Bonds Web site at www.csb.gc.ca.

Exhibit 12–7   Description of Bond Ratings Provided by the Dominion Bond Rating Service (DBRS)

Quality	Rating by DBRS	Description
Highest credit quality	AAA	Exceptionally strong protection for the timely repayment of principal and interest.
Superior credit quality	AA	Protection of interest and principal is considered high.
Satisfactory credit quality	A	Considered to be more susceptible to adverse economic conditions and have greater cyclical tendencies.
Adequate credit quality	BBB	Entity is more susceptible to adverse changes in financial and economic conditions, or there may be other adversities present.
Speculative	BB	The protection afforded interest and principal is uncertain. Small size or lack of competitive strength may be additional negative considerations.
Highly speculative	B	Reasonably high level of uncertainty as to ability of the entity to pay interest and principal on a continuing basis in the future, especially in periods of economic recession or industry adversity.
Very highly speculative	CCC	Bonds rated CCC often have characteristics which, if not remedied, may lead to default.
Extremely speculative	CC	Bonds rated CC have characteristics which, if not remedied, will lead to default.
Extremely speculative	C	In immediate danger of default. This is the lowest rating category provided to long-term instruments that are not in default.
In default of principal, interest, or both	D	Currently in default of interest, principal, or both.

SOURCE: Dominion Bond Rating Service, 2002.

BOND YIELD CALCULATIONS

yield The rate of return earned by an investor who holds a bond for a stated period of time.

For a bond investment, the **yield** is the rate of return earned by an investor who holds a bond for a stated period of time. In the section A Typical Bond Transaction, on page 357, we discussed the calculation to determine the average annual compound return from holding a bond investment when all the cash flows from the investment are known with certainty. Two additional methods are used to measure the expected yield on a bond investment when the cash flows are not known for certain, but anticipated.

current yield Determined by dividing the dollar amount of annual interest from an investment by its current market value.

The **current yield** is determined by dividing the dollar amount of annual interest from an investment by its current market value. For bonds, the following formula may help you complete this calculation:

$$\text{Current yield on a corporate bond} = \frac{\text{Dollar amount of annual interest}}{\text{Current market value}}$$

For example, assume you own a Rogers Telecom corporate bond that pays 7.5 percent interest on an annual basis. This means that each year you will receive $75 ($1,000 × 7.5% = $75). Also assume the current market price of the Rogers Telecom bond is $960. Because the current market value is less than the bond's face value, the current yield increases to 7.8 percent, as follows:

No checklist can serve as a foolproof guide for choosing a corporate or government bond. However, the following questions will help you evaluate a potential bond investment. (Usual sources of information include CBRS and DBRS.)

CATEGORY 1: INFORMATION ABOUT THE CORPORATION

1. What is the corporation's name? _____
2. What are the corporation's address and telephone number? _____
3. What type of products or services does this firm provide? _____
4. Briefly describe the prospects for this company. (Include significant factors, such as product development, plans for expansion, plans for mergers, etc.)

_____
_____
_____

CATEGORY 2: BOND BASICS

5. What type of bond is this? _____
6. What is the face value for this bond? _____
7. What is the interest rate for this bond? _____
8. What is the annual interest amount for this bond? _____
9. When are interest payments made to bondholders? _____
10. Is the corporation currently paying interest as scheduled? ☐ Yes ☐ No
11. What is the maturity date for this bond? _____
12. What is the CBRS rating for this bond? _____
13. What is the DBRS rating for this bond? _____
14. What do these ratings mean? _____

_____
_____

15. What was the original issue date? _____
16. Who is the trustee for this bond issue? _____

_____

17. Is the bond callable? If so, when? _____
18. Is the bond secured with collateral? If so, what? ☐ Yes ☐ No
19. How did the corporation use the money from this bond issue?

_____

CATEGORY 3: FINANCIAL PERFORMANCE

20. Has the firm's total debt increased over the last three years? ☐ Yes ☐ No
21. Is the corporation profitable? If so, how profitable? ☐ Yes ☐ No $ _____
22. Have profits increased over the last seven years? ☐ Yes ☐ No
23. Are this year's sales higher than last year's sales? ☐ Yes ☐ No _____
24. Have sales increased over the last seven years? ☐ Yes ☐ No _____
25. Briefly describe any other information that you obtained from Moody's, Standard & Poor's, or other advisory services. _____

_____
_____
_____
_____

A WORD OF CAUTION

When you use a checklist, there is always a danger of overlooking important relevant information. The above checklist is not a cure-all, but it does provide some very sound questions that you should answer before making a decision to invest in bonds. Quite simply, it is a place to start. If you need other information, *you* are responsible for obtaining it and for determining how it affects your potential investment.

$$\text{Current yield} = \frac{\$75}{\$960}$$
$$= 0.078, \text{ or } 7.8 \text{ percent}$$

This calculation allows you to compare the yield on a bond investment with the yields of other investment alternatives, which include Guaranteed Investment Certificates, common stocks, preferred stocks, and mutual funds. Naturally, the higher the current yield, the better it is! A current yield of 10 percent is better than a current yield of 7.8 percent.

yield to maturity
A yield calculation that takes into account the relationships among a bond's maturity value, the time to maturity, the current price, and the dollar amount of interest.

The **yield to maturity** takes into account the relationships among a bond's maturity value, the time to maturity, the current price, and the dollar amount of interest. A formula for calculating the approximate yield to maturity is as follows:

$$\text{Yield to maturity} = \frac{\text{Dollar amount of annual interest} + \dfrac{\text{Face value} - \text{Market value}}{\text{Number of periods}}}{\dfrac{\text{Market value} + \text{Face value}}{2}}$$

For example, assume that on January 1, 1995, you purchased at the current market price of $830 a corporate bond with a $1,000 face value issued by Fruit of the Loom. The bond pays 7 percent annual interest, and its maturity date is 2011. The yield to maturity is 8.7 percent, as follows:

$$\text{Yield to maturity} = \frac{\$70 + \dfrac{\$1,000 - \$830}{17}}{\dfrac{\$830 + \$1,000}{2}}$$

$$= \frac{\$80}{\$915}$$

$$= 0.087, \text{ or } 8.7 \text{ percent}$$

In this situation, the yield to maturity takes into account two types of return on the bond. First, you will receive interest income from the purchase date until the maturity date. Second, at maturity you will receive a payment for the face value of the bond. If you purchased the bond at a price below the face value, the yield to maturity will be greater than the stated interest rate. If you purchased the bond at a price above the face value, the yield to maturity will be less than the stated interest rate. (Remember, the actual price you pay for a bond may be higher or lower than the face value because of many factors, including changes in the economy, increases or decreases in comparable interest rates on other investments, and the financial condition of the company.) The precise yield to maturiy (YTM) can be calculated using the time value of money concepts from Chapter 1, where the bond price is equated to the present value of coupon plus principal payments discounted at the YTM.

CALCULATOR

2ND	CLR TVM
830+/−	PV
1,000	FV
70	PMT
17	N
COMP	I 8.98%

The yield to maturity is the annual yield an investor expects when purchasing a bond. However, it is based on two assumptions. First, it assumes that the bondholder will hold the bond to its maturity and receive the face value of $1,000. Second, it assumes that the interest received on an annual or semi-annual basis will be reinvested at the bond's yield to maturity. If either of these assumptions does not hold, then the investment's average annual compound return may be more or less than the expected yield to maturity.

After evaluating a Canadian telecommunications utility, Bethan Jackson, the investor in the opening case, wanted to purchase the firm's corporate debentures. But she was concerned about the corporation's ability to make future interest payments. To determine the utility's ability to pay interest, she calculated a formula called the *times interest earned* ratio, illustrated below:

$$\text{Times interest earned} = \frac{\text{Operating income before interest and taxes}}{\text{Interest expense}}$$

Assume that the utility had interest expense of $837 million and operating income before interest and taxes of $6,588 million in 2001. The times interest earned ratio for the utility is 7.87 to 1, as follows:

$$\text{Times interest earned} = \frac{\$6,588 \text{ million}}{\$837 \text{ million}}$$
$$= 7.87 \text{ to } 1$$

Although the average for the times interest earned ratio varies from industry to industry, a higher number is better than a lower number. The utility is earning slightly over 7.87 times the amount required to pay the annual interest on its long-term notes, bonds, and other financial obligations. With a times interest earned ratio of 7.87 to 1, the utility could experience a "significant" drop in earnings and still meet its financial obligations.

One additional calculation, times interest earned, is described in the Financial Planning Calculations box above.

OTHER SOURCES OF INFORMATION

Investors can use two additional sources of information to evaluate potential bond investments. First, business periodicals can provide information about the economy and interest rates and detailed financial information about a corporation or government entity that issues bonds. You can locate many of these periodicals at your school or public library or on the Internet.

Second, a number of federal agencies provide information that may be useful to bond investors in either printed form or on the Internet. Reports and research published by the Bank of Canada and Department of Finance may be used to assess the nation's economy. You can also obtain information that corporations have reported to SEDAR by accessing the SEDAR Web site (www.sedar.com). Finally, provincial and municipal governments will provide information about specific provincial and municipal bond issues.

Visit the Web site See the Post-Test under Chapter 12 on the online learning centre at www.mcgrawhill.ca/college/kapoor.

CONCEPT CHECK 12–5

1. What is the market value for a bond with a face value of $1,000 and a newspaper quotation of 77.25?
2. What type of information is contained in a corporation's annual report? On a corporation's Web site? How could this information be used to evaluate a bond issue?
3. How important are bond ratings when evaluating a bond issue?
4. Why should you calculate the current yield and yield to maturity on a bond investment?
5. How can business periodicals and government publications help you evaluate a bond issue?

Mackenzie Universal Fund

Value of investment as of June 2004 is $8,983

Calendar Year Returns		Calendar Year Returns	
2004	2.5%	1999	48.7%
2003	22.7%	1998	5.9%
2002	−20.3%	1997	14.4%
2001	−7.6%	1996	16.3%
2000	−0.8%	1995	18.3%

Source: www.mackenziefinancial.com/

QUESTIONS

1   Although Bryan Nations doubled his original investment in three years, he now admits that he made a mistake during the first three years he owned shares in the Mackenzie Universal Future mutual fund. In your own words, what did he do wrong?

2   If you owned shares in the Mackenzie Universal Future mutual fund, would you use published materials available in the library or sources found on the Internet to monitor your investment? Explain your answer.

LEARNING OBJECTIVES

1   Describe the characteristics of mutual fund investments.

2   Classify mutual funds by investment objective.

3   Evaluate mutual funds for investment purposes.

4   Describe how and why mutual funds are bought and sold.

If you ever thought about buying stocks or bonds but decided not to, your reasons were probably like most other people's: You didn't know enough to make a good decision, and you lacked enough money to diversify your investments among several choices. These same two reasons explain why people invest in mutual funds. By pooling your money with money from other investors, a mutual fund can do for you what you can't do on your own. Specifically, a **mutual fund** is an investment chosen by people who pool their money to buy stocks, bonds, and other financial securities selected by professional managers who work for investment companies. Every person who invests in a mutual fund has the right to his or her proportional share of the assets of the fund and any income that the fund earns. Mutual funds are an excellent choice for many individuals. In many cases, they can also be used for retirement accounts.

mutual fund An investment chosen by people who pool their money to buy stocks, bonds, and other financial securities selected by professional managers who work for an investment company.

Bryan Nations, the investor in the opening case, did his homework before purchasing shares in the Mackenzie Universal Future mutual fund. But like many investors, he just assumed his investment would increase in value. Thus, he made a critical mistake. He didn't continue to monitor the value of his investment after his initial purchase. Fortunately for Nations, his mutual fund did earn exceptional returns over the first three years, and his investment doubled in value. While he was lucky, you may not be so fortunate. Make no mistake about this: *Good investors evaluate an investment before purchase. The best investors continue to evaluate their investments after the purchase.*

An investment in mutual funds is based on the concept of opportunity costs, which we have discussed throughout this text. Simply put, you have to be willing to take some chances if you want to get larger returns on your investments. Before deciding whether mutual funds are the right investment for you, read the material presented in the next section.

WHY INVESTORS PURCHASE MUTUAL FUNDS

Investors like—no, love—their mutual fund investments. The following statistics illustrate how important mutual fund investments are to both individuals and the nation's economy:

■ OBJECTIVE 1 ■

Describe the characteristics of mutual fund investments.

[1] Although the mutual fund concept originated in Europe and then spread to North America in the late 1800s, mutual funds didn't gain real popularity until the last 25 years.

[2] As of February 2002, the Investment Funds Institute of Canada (IFIC), the national trade association for the Canadian mutual fund industry, had a membership of 82 fund management companies sponsoring 1,864 mutual funds, 111 dealer firms selling mutual funds, and 65 affiliates. Its member funds manage nearly $427 billion in assets.

[3] The value of assets under management in the industry has increased from $3.5 billion in 1981 to nearly $427 billion—making mutual funds the fastest-growing sector of the Canadian financial services industry.

No doubt about it, the mutual fund industry is big business. And yet, you may be wondering why so many people invest in mutual funds.

The major reasons investors purchase mutual funds are *professional management* and *diversification*. Most investment companies do everything possible to convince you that they can do a better job of picking securities than you can. Sometimes, these claims are true, and sometimes, they are just so much hot air. Still, investment companies do have professional fund managers with years of experience who devote large amounts of time to picking just the "right" securities for their funds' portfolios. *Be warned:* Even the best portfolio managers make mistakes. So you, the investor, must be careful!

The diversification mutual funds offer spells safety because an occasional loss incurred with one investment contained in a mutual fund is usually offset by gains from other investments in the fund. With a mutual fund, you can diversify your holdings in two ways. (1) by buying a mutual fund that owns stock in hundreds of different companies or (2) across asset classes by buying a mutual fund that owns stocks, bonds, as well as other securities. For example, consider the diversification provided in the portfolio of the Royal Canadian Value Fund, shown in Exhibit 13–1 on the next page. With more than $48 million in assets, this fund contains almost 45 different stock investments spread over 14 different industrial areas. Note that the information contained in Exhibit 13–1 is from the Royal Mutual Funds 2002 Annual Report. If you want more up-to-date information on the composition of investments within the fund or other information about the fund, visit the Royal Mutual Funds Web site at www.royalbank.com/rmf.

DID YOU KNOW ?

INDUSTRY STATISTICS

Net sales of all funds: $65.1 million

Net new sales (excl.reinv.distr.): $263 million

Reinvested distributions: $197.5 million

Assets under administration: $436.3 billion

Unitholder accounts: 53.5 million

May 2002 Estimate

SOURCE: www.ific.ca/

However, regardless of professional management and diversification, investing in mutual funds does have its risks, which should not be overlooked. The risks presented by mutual funds are based on the investments they hold. For example, a bond fund faces interest rate risk and income risk. Bond values are inversely related to interest rates. If interest rates go up, bond values will go down and vice versa. Similarly, a sector stock fund (which invests in a single industry, such as oil) may surrender to industry risk, where its price will decline due to new

Exhibit 13–1

Types of Securities
Included in the
Portfolio of the
Royal Canadian
Value Fund

SOURCE: Royal Mutual
Funds Report 2002,
www.royalbank.com/rmf

Royal Mutual Funds RBC

APRIL 30, 2002

Royal Canadian Value Fund

Ina van Berkel, CFA, MBA
Vice-President and Portfolio Manager
Industry Experience: Since 1972

COMMENTARY

- The Royal Canadian Value Fund was down 1.7% in April compared to the TSE 300 Capped Total Return Index, which was down 2.3% in the month.
- The fund's performance in April was again largely due to individual stock selection, as the rise in the Index in April was led by Golds, Pipelines and Merchandising, but the fund is significantly underweight in golds and merchandising (although well overweight in pipelines).
- During April, the fund liquidated its position in Fairmont Hotels, as the shares had reached fair valuation. Other positions in the portfolio were fine-tuned. Further purchases will occur as individual stocks come into value range.

Fund Inception Date	March 1998
Net Assets	$49.4MM
NAV	$11.81
MER	2.15%

Distribution Policy
Income: Annually (Dec.)
Capital Gains: Annually (Dec.)

RRSP Eligibility
Fully eligible for registered plans

Benchmark
100% TSE 300 Capped Total Return Index

Investment Objectives
To provide long-term capital growth by investing primarily in equity securities of Canadian companies attractively priced below their intrinsic value.

PORTFOLIO COMPOSITION

Asset Mix

- 70.3% Canadian Equities
- 12.7% U.S. Equities
- 3.8% Foreign Equities
- 13.2% Cash

Top Sector Mix (%)	Jan '02	Apr. '02
Financial Services	23.1	24.0
Industrial Products	13.9	13.0
Oil and Gas	7.8	8.9
Metals and Mines	5.5	6.1
Pipelines	4.6	4.7
Communication and Media	4.5	4.6
Utilities	2.9	3.3
Gold and Precious Minerals	1.8	2.2
Conglomerates	1.6	1.6
Transportation and Environment	1.0	1.0

TOP 10 HOLDINGS

Company	Sector	%
Bank of Nova Scotia	Financial Services	4.4
Toronto-Dominion Bank	Financial Services	4.4
Suncor Energy Inc.	Oil & Gas	4.2
Canadian Natural Resources Ltd.	Oil & Gas	3.4
BCE Inc.	Utilities	3.3
CIBC	Financial Services	3.2
Alcan Inc.	Metals & Minerals	3.2
United Technologies Corp.	Industrials	3.1
Bank of Montreal	Financial Services	3.0
Inditex	Information Technology	2.8
% Assets in Top 10		35.0
Total Number of Holdings		57

FUND CODE

Series A — RBF 554
Series F — RBF 608

PERFORMANCE

Compound Annual Returns	6 mo.	1 yr.	3 yr.	5 yr.	10 yr.	Inception
	10.6%	3.3%	8.8%	–	–	4.4%

Calendar Fund Data	YTD	2001	2000	1999	1998	1997
Calendar Return (%)	2.8	0.8	13.5	16.0	-12.9	–
MER (%)	–	2.15	2.15	2.14	2.14	–
Total Distributions	0.00	0.00	0.00	0.02	0.04	–
Investment Income	0.00	0.00	0.00	0.02	0.04	–
Capital Gains	0.00	0.00	0.00	0.00	0.00	–

VOLATILITY RATING

Low	Av-	Av	Av+	High

ADDITIONAL INFORMATION

	Registered	Non-Registered
Minimum Investment		
Initial Investment	$ 500	$ 1,000
Additional Investment	$ 25	$ 25
Pre-Authorized Contribution	$ 25	$ 25

Royal Mutual Funds are offered by RBC Funds Inc. and distributed through authorized dealers. There may be commissions, trailing commissions, management fees and expenses associated with mutual fund investments. Please read the prospectus before investing. The indicated rates of return are the historical annual compounded total returns for the period ended April 30, 2002 including changes in unit value, assume reinvestment of all distributions and do not take into account sales, redemption, distribution or optional charges or income taxes payable by any unitholders that would have reduced returns. Mutual funds are not guaranteed, their values change frequently and past performance may not be repeated.

---

developments within its industry. A stock fund that invests across many industries is better protected from this risk, although it may succumb to other forms of risk, such as market risk, which affects the market as a whole and cannot be diversified away.

CHARACTERISTICS OF MUTUAL FUNDS

investment company
A firm that, for a management fee, invests the pooled funds of small investors in securities appropriate to its stated investment objectives.

An **investment company** is a firm that, for a management fee, invests the pooled funds of small investors in securities appropriate to its stated investment objectives. Today, mutual funds sponsored by investment companies may be classified as either closed-end funds or open-end mutual funds.

closed-end fund
A mutual fund whose shares are issued by an investment company only when the fund is originally set up.

CLOSED-END FUNDS OR OPEN-END MUTUAL FUNDS
A **closed-end fund** is a fund of finite size. Its shares are issued by an investment company only when the fund is originally set up. Once that's done, the fund size remains more or less static. The fund neither issues nor redeems shares. Since a closed-end fund does not ever have to buy back shares from investors like an open-end mutual fund, it does not have to maintain a percentage

of its asset in cash; therefore 100 percent of the fund's assets can be invested at all times. After all the shares originally issued have been sold, an investor can purchase shares only from another investor who is willing to sell. Shares of closed-end funds are traded on the floors of stock exchanges or in the over-the-counter market. Like the prices of stocks, the prices of shares for closed-end funds are determined by the factors of supply and demand, by the value of stocks and other investments contained in the fund's portfolio, and by investor expectations.

An **open-end fund** is a mutual fund whose shares are issued and redeemed by the investment company at the request of investors. Investors are free to buy and sell shares at the net asset value. The **net asset value (NAV)** per share is equal to the current market value of securities contained in the mutual fund's portfolio minus the mutual fund's liabilities divided by the number of shares outstanding:

$$\text{Net asset value per share} = \frac{\text{Current market value of the fund's portfolio} - \text{Liabilities}}{\text{Number of shares outstanding}}$$

For example, assume the portfolio of all investments contained in the Scotia Canadian Income Fund has a current market value of $124 million. The fund also has liabilities totalling $4 million. If this mutual fund has 6 million shares outstanding, the net asset value per share is $20:

$$\text{Net asset value} = \frac{\text{Current market value of the fund's portfolio} - \text{Liabilities}}{\text{Number of shares outstanding}}$$

$$= \frac{\$124 \text{ million} - \$4 \text{ million}}{6 \text{ million shares}}$$

$$= \$20 \text{ per share}$$

For most mutual funds, the net asset value is calculated at the close of trading each day. In addition to buying and selling shares on request, most open-end funds provide their investors with a wide variety of services, including payroll deduction programs, automatic reinvestment programs, automatic withdrawal programs, and the option to change shares in one fund to another fund within the same fund family—all topics discussed later in this chapter. Two "new" types of funds have emerged in the last five years: exchange traded funds (ETFs) and index funds. ETFs and index funds are similar to conventional mutual funds in that they provide investors with an affordable way to invest in a diversified basket of securities. However, unlike conventional mutual funds, which can only be bought or sold at a fixed price at the end of each trading day, ETFs funds can be traded throughout the day at changing market prices on the stock exchange, and index funds are bought at end-of-day prices. The big banks are the main suppliers of index funds, whereas you have to buy an ETF through a broker, as you would buy a stock, and pay a commission. In addition, you can buy ETFs on margin, as well as sell them short. ETFs also have lower management expenses than their conventional mutual fund cousins and are more tax efficient.

LOAD FUNDS AND NO-LOAD FUNDS

Before investing in mutual funds, you should compare the cost of this type of investment with the cost of other investment alternatives, such as stocks or bonds. With regard to cost, mutual funds are classified as load funds or no-load funds. A **load fund** is a mutual fund in which investors pay a commission every time they buy (front-end load) or sell (back-end load) shares. The commission charge, sometimes referred to as the *sales fee*, may be as high as 8.5 percent of the price for investments under $10,000. (Typically, this fee declines for investments over $10,000.)

While many exceptions exist, the average load charge for mutual funds is between 3 and 5 percent. Let's assume you decide to invest $10,000 in the Standard Life Growth Equity Fund. This fund charges a sales load of 5 percent that you must pay when you purchase shares. The dollar amount of the sales charge on your $10,000 investment is $500 ($10,000 × 5% = $500). After paying the $500, the amount available for investment is reduced to $9,500 ($10,000 − $500 = $9,500). The "stated" advantage of a load fund is that the fund's sales

open-end fund A mutual fund whose shares are issued and redeemed by the investment company at the request of investors.

net asset value (NAV) The current market value of the securities contained in the mutual fund's portfolio minus the mutual fund's liabilities divided by the number of shares outstanding.

Visit the Web site
See Personal Financial Planning worksheets under Chapter 13 on the online learning centre at www.mcgrawhill.ca/college/kapoor.

load fund A mutual fund in which investors pay a commission (as high as 8.5 percent) every time they purchase or sell shares.

Exhibit 13–2   Comparison of Various Financial Instruments

Characteristics	ETFs	Equity funds	Index certificates	Futures	Shares
Financial instrument	Stock indices	Equity funds	Bonds	Derivatives	Shares
Market liquidity	Very high	No exchange	Medium trading	High	High
Maturity	No	No	Yes	Yes	No
Reinvestment risk	No	No	Yes	Yes	No
Short sales	Yes	No	No	Yes	Yes
Costs for purchase/sale	Exchange fees	Issuance and redemption commissions	Purchase and reinvestment costs	Initial and variation margin payments and rollover costs	Exchange fees

SOURCE: www.virt-x.com

contingent deferred sales load A 1- to 6-percent charge that shareholders pay when they withdraw their investment from a mutual fund.

no-load fund A mutual fund in which the individual investor pays no sales charge.

force (account executives, financial planners, or brokerage divisions of banks and other financial institutions) will explain the mutual fund to investors and offer advice as to when shares of the fund should be bought or sold.

Instead of charging investors a fee when they purchase shares in a mutual fund, some mutual funds charge a **contingent deferred sales load** (sometimes referred to as a *back-end load*). These fees range from 1 to 6 percent, depending on how long you own the mutual fund before making a withdrawal. For example, assume you withdraw $5,000 from shares that you own in the Greenline Balanced Growth mutual fund within a year of your original purchase date. You must pay a 5-percent contingent deferred sales fee. Your fee is $250 ($5,000 × 5% = $250). After the fee is deducted from your $5,000 withdrawal, you will receive $4,750 ($5,000 − $250 = $4,750). Generally, the deferred charge declines until there is no withdrawal charge if you own the shares in the fund for more than five to seven years. Unlike a front-end load, however, your entire $5,000 goes to work for you immediately. There is no deduction when you purchase. Choosing the back-end load allows all of your investment dollars to go to work for you immediately. Keep in mind, however, that although you don't pay a fee directly to your sales representative at the time of purchase, the mutual fund company does. This, of course, increases its costs. As a result, you may be paying a higher MER (see discussion on page 381). In addition, if the fund does not perform as well as expected, due to a change in management or other circumstances, you may be reluctant to switch because of the high penalty. If all other factors are equal, a fund that doesn't charge a contingent deferral sales load is superior to a fund that does.

A **no-load fund** is a mutual fund in which the individual investor pays no sales charge. No-load funds don't charge commissions when you buy or sell shares because they have no salespeople. If you want to buy shares of a no-load fund, you must deal directly with the investment company. The usual means of contact is by

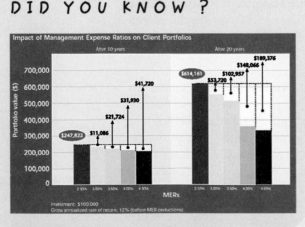

SOURCE: Courtesy Standard Life, www.standardlife.ca/eng/dealers/pdf/4356.pdf

telephone, the Internet, or mail. You can also purchase shares in a no-load fund from many discount brokers, such as TD Waterhouse.

As an investor, you must decide whether to invest in a load fund or a no-load fund. Some investment salespeople have claimed that load funds outperform no-load funds. But many financial analysts suggest there is no significant difference between mutual funds that charge commissions and those that do not. *Since no-load funds offer the same investment opportunities load funds offer, you should investigate them further before deciding which type of mutual fund is best for you.* Although the sales commission should not be the decisive factor, the possibility of saving an 8.5 percent load charge is a factor to consider. For example, suppose Marianne Lowen invests $10,000 in a mutual fund that charges an 8.5 percent sales fee. Since this fee is deducted in advance, her initial $10,000 investment is reduced by $850. Simply put, she now has $9,150 that she can use to buy shares in this load fund. By comparison, Jane Edwards decides to invest $10,000 in a no-load mutual fund. Since there is no sales fee, she can use the entire $10,000 to purchase shares in this no-load fund. Depending on the load fund's performance, it may take Marianne a year or more to "catch up" and cover the cost of the sales fee.

MANAGEMENT FEES AND OTHER CHARGES

In evaluating a specific mutual fund, you should consider management fees and other charges. The investment companies that sponsor mutual funds charge management fees. This fee, which is disclosed in the fund's prospectus, is a fixed percentage of the fund's asset value. Today, annual management fees range between 0.5 and 4 percent of the fund's asset value. While fees vary considerably, the average is between two and three percent of the fund's assets.

Generally, all mutual funds have management expenses that are deducted from the fund. The management fee pays for such things as the mutual fund company's investment management and marketing and administrative costs. Each fund also pays its own operating costs, such as brokerage fees on securities trading, audit fees, and unitholder communications.

MANAGEMENT EXPENSE RATIO

The fund will report the management fee and direct costs it pays each year as a management expense ratio (MER) that relates those costs to the fund's value. If a $100-million fund has $2 million in costs, its MER is 2 percent. The costs are deducted before the fund's performance returns are calculated. If your fund made 13 percent and the MER was 2 percent, the reported return for the year would be 11 percent.

SPECIAL FEES

Unlike management expenses, which apply to all unitholders, special fees apply to individual situations. You pay them directly or through specific deductions. Some examples include:

- Annual RRSP, RRIF, or RESP trustee fee—this covers the cost of operating the plan.
- Account setup fee—some dealers levy a one-time charge for new clients.
- Short-term trading fee—mutual fund companies are allowed to deduct an amount, generally 2 percent from any redemption that occurs within 90 days of purchase; however, many don't.
- Transfer fee—at the discretion of the individual adviser, dealers can levy a charge of up to 2 percent when you switch among funds in the same family.
- Processing fees—your fund company may levy a fee if you require transactions that require special processing.

SERVICE FEES Also called *trailers*, these are ongoing commissions to pay advisers and dealers for ongoing service. The adviser or dealer gets a yearly amount that equals a certain percentage of your account's value. That's often about 1 percent on front-load accounts and 0.5 percent on deferred sales load accounts. No-load companies may also pay trailers to dealers. You do not pay service fees directly. They're paid by the mutual fund company—in most cases, from its management fee. As with commissions, funds that carry low trailers or none at all may or may not have lower management expense ratios.

There are no easy answers, but your professional financial adviser or broker can help you determine which particular mutual fund best suits your financial needs. You can also do your own research to determine which fund is right for you. Factors to consider include whether you want to invest in a load fund or no-load fund, as well as the fund's management fees and expense ratios. As you will see later in this chapter, a number of sources of information can help you make your investment decisions.

The investment company's prospectus must provide all details relating to management fees, contingent deferred sales fees, and other expenses. Exhibit 13–3 shows a sample report on the AGF Canadian Growth Equity Fund, as presented by Yahoo mutual Fund Centre at http://mutualfunds.yahoo.ca. Here, you'll see a reported MER of 2.5 percent, the objective of the mutual fund, and the proportional investment by industry. It even provides information, on the NAVPS, or net asset value per share.

Exhibit 13–4 on page 384 summarizes load charges and no-load charges. In addition, it reports management fees, contingent deferred sales loads, and other charges.

CONCEPT CHECK 13–1

1. What type of information about a mutual fund can be found on the Internet?
2. What are two major reasons investors purchase mutual funds?
3. How do a closed-end fund and an open-end fund differ?
4. What are the typical fees charged for a load and no-load mutual fund?
5. What are the typical management fees, and front and back load fees?

CLASSIFICATIONS OF MUTUAL FUNDS

■ **OBJECTIVE 2** ┃

Classify mutual funds by investment objective.

The managers of mutual funds tailor their investment portfolios to the investment objectives of their customers. Usually, a fund's objectives are plainly disclosed in its prospectus. For example, the objectives of the Royal Balanced Growth Fund are as follows:

> The Royal Balanced Growth Fund is considered a "one-decision" fund, for growth-oriented investors investing in a diversified portfolio of Canadian, U.S., and International equities, and Canadian bonds, and short-term debt securities. The fund employs a more aggressive asset allocation strategy and invests in a more focused list of securities than the Royal Balanced Fund, in order to achieve the highest possible total return consistent with a moderate level of risk. The percentage of assets held in each asset class will vary according to the outlook for the economy and financial markets, and the fund intends to maximize its foreign content. The fund may also invest in derivative instruments.

While it may be helpful to categorize the 1,400-plus mutual funds into different categories, note that different sources of investment information may use different categories for the same

Fund Background

Category	Canadian Small-Cap Equity
Fund Family	AGF Group of Funds
Total Assets in $millions (2002-05-31)	964.650
Year-to-Date Return	8.8800%
NAVPS (2002-06-14)	$ 35.6000
Daily Change	$ −0.2200
52 week high	$ 38.0600
52 week low	$ 28.5400

Objective

The fund's objective is to provide capital growth. It invests primarily in shares of small and medium Canadian companies that are expected to profit from future economic growth.

Strategy

Stock selection begins with an evaluation of companies that have demonstrated or have potential to achieve above-average growth in earnings and cash flow. Companies are evaluated through internal and street research. Interviews with corporate managers are crucial to determine their business plans and growth strategies. Successful investment candidates are then evaluated on the basis of a determination of a reasonable price to pay for that company's growth.

Fund Operations

Inception:	30-September-1994
Management Company:	AGF Funds Inc.
Managing Company since:	1-January-1972
Lead Manager:	Robert Farquharson
Manager Since:	30-September-1994
Manager Tenure:	7 years

Returns (%)

	3 mo	1 yr avg	3 yr avg	5 yr avg
AGC*GEQ.TO	4.0750	2.1800	11.1180	5.9170

Investment Information

New Investment	Open
Currency	CAD
Min Initial Investment	$ 1000
Min Subsequent Investment	$ 100
RRSP Eligible	Yes
RESP Eligible	Yes
Min. Initial Investment (RRSP)	$ 100
Min. Subsequent Investment (RRSP)	$ 25
Availability	AB,BC,MB,NB,NF,NU,NS,NT,ON,PE,PQ,SK,YT

Fees & Expenses

Management Fee	2.50%
Load or No-Load	Load
Choice of Front- or Back-End Load	Yes
Max Front-End Load	6.00%
Max Back-End Load	5.50%

Sector Weightings (%) 30-April-2002

Sector	%
Oil & Gas	19.02
Industrial/Capital Goods	12.87
Not Reported - Sector	8.97
Consumer Staples (Non Cyc)	7.32
Gold & Precious Metals	5.86
Pharmaceuticals & Biotechnology	5.27
Consumer Discretionary (Cyclical)	4.89
Financial	4.47
Merchandising	4.25
Commerical Services	3.82
Technology	2.91
Metals & Minerals	2.37
Health-Care Equipment & Services	2.30
Communications	2.20
Funds - Sector	1.80
Venture Capital	1.78
Transportation & Environment	1.64
Basic Materials	1.61
Software & Services	1.55
Real Estate - Sector	1.52
Paper & Forest Products	0.84
Utilities	0.65
Cash Equivalent - Sector	0.51
Energy	0.37
Insurance	0.33
Conglomerates	0.33
Supranational	0.25
Media	0.22
Index - Sector	0.08

Exhibit 13–3

Sample Mutual Fund Report on the AGF Growth Equity Fund, from Yahoo Mutual Fund Centre

SOURCE: Yahoo mutual fund centre at http://mutualfunds.yahoo.ca

Exhibit 13–4

Typical Fees Associated with Mutual Fund Investments

Type of Fee or Charge	Definition and Rate
Load fund	Either a front-end or back-end sales charge
No-load fund	No sales charge
Front-end load	A sales fee charged with each purchase; reduces the funds actually invested. Most fund companies have lowered the maximum front-end load on their funds to around 6 percent.
Back-end load	Also referred to as a contingent deferred sales load. One to six percent of withdrawals on a sliding scale decreasing with time held, then zero if selling after a set number of years.
Management fee	Expressed as a fixed percentage of the fund's total value, called the Management Expense Ratio (MER). Ranges from 0.25 percent (rare) to 4 percent, to cover investment company's costs. Fee is up to 0.5 percent higher for back-end load funds.

mutual fund. In most cases, the name of the category gives a pretty good clue as to the types of investments included within the category. The *major* fund categories are described as follows:

- *Money market funds* seek to achieve a high level of income and liquidity through investment in short-term money market instruments, such as T-bills, commercial paper, and short-term government bonds. These are relatively low risk.
- *Mortgage funds* aim for income and safety. Investors in mortgage funds hold a group of mortgages, rather than a single property title. These have a lower risk than bond funds.
- *Bond funds* aim for safety of principal and income but are subject to capital gains and losses, which have tax implications. Bond funds are generally invested in good quality, high-yielding government and corporate debt securities. The risk here is related to changes in interest rates.
- *Dividend funds* aim for tax-advantaged income with some possibility of capital growth, and invest in preferred shares as well as high quality common shares that have a history of consistently paying dividends.
- *Balanced* and *asset allocation funds* are similar in that they both aim to provide a mixture of safety, income, and capital appreciation. Where they differ is in the fact that only balanced funds need respect a stated minimum investment in given classes of aggressive or defensive types of investments.
- *Equity* or *common stock funds* aim for capital gains and, as such, are invested almost entirely in common shares. These will tend to fluctuate in price much more than any of the previously listed funds.
- *Specialty funds* sacrifice diversification in an effort to build capital gains. They concentrate portfolio holdings on shares of a group of

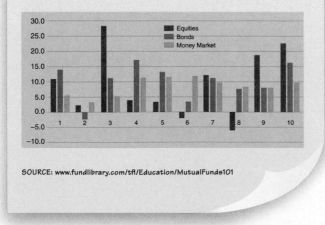

DID YOU KNOW ?

No single fund type is best all the time. Performance varies from year to year.

SOURCE: www.fundlibrary.com/tfl/Education/MutualFunds101

Mutual fund investing provides a good way to get started with small amounts of money, at the same time affording the investor professional management. By investing in mutual funds you can diversify your investments to fit your personal goals and objectives. However, the most important advantage is still the ability to get professional management.

When choosing a mutual fund, the pros recommend that investors rely on research. Research gives investors an understanding of the kind of investment they are making, whether or not they feel comfortable with the choice, and lets them know what the track record for a specific mutual fund is. While research may not be foolproof, it does provide a guide as to what can be expected of a particular fund in the future. Only after an investor has researched a potential investment is it possible to find a mutual fund that fits the investor's needs, had good management, and has a successful long-term track record.

According to a pro, many investors are always changing funds and chasing funds that were hot last year. Consequently, they incur more fees, sales charges, and so on. This can make mutual fund investing more expensive, and in most cases, investors end up with smaller total returns. This is not to say that changes cannot be made in the mutual funds an investor owns. However, it is best to give a well-managed fund time to work.

companies in one industry, geographical area, or segment of the capital market. They can be susceptible to fluctuations within industries and to currency value fluctuations as well.

- *International* or *global funds* are often considered a subset of specialty funds in that they are focused investments, with portfolios holding investments in the markets that offer the best prospects, regardless of location.
- *Real estate funds* aim for long-term growth through capital appreciation and the reinvestment of income by investing in income-producing real property. These are generally the least liquid of all the types of mutual funds.
- *Ethical funds* seek to make investment decisions that are guided by moral criteria that can vary from fund to fund. Each investment made is examined from the perspective of obeying certain requirements.
- *Segregated funds* are offered by insurance companies as an alternative to conventional mutual funds and offer a range of investment objectives and categories of securities. They are unique in that they guarantee that a portion (usually 75 percent or more) of your principal will be returned to you at maturity, regardless of the performance of the fund.
- *Labour-sponsored venture capital corporations (LSVCCs)* are sponsored by labour organizations, and their specific mandate is to invest in small to medium-sized businesses. LSVCCs have the advantage of being eligible for generous federal and provincial tax credits but entail higher risks.

A **family of funds** exists when one investment company manages a group of mutual funds. Each fund within the family has a different financial objective. For instance, one fund may be a government bond fund and another a growth fund. Most investment companies offer exchange privileges that enable shareholders to switch among the mutual funds in a fund family. For example, if you own shares in the Desjardins growth fund, you may, at your discretion, switch to the Desjardins ethical income fund. Generally, investors may give instructions to switch from one fund to another within the same family either in writing, over the telephone, or via the Internet. The family-of-funds concept makes it convenient for shareholders to switch their investments among funds as different funds offer more potential, financial reward, or security. Charges for exchanges, if any, generally are small for each transaction. For funds that do charge, the fee may be as low as $5 per transaction. **Managed Asset Programs (MAP)** are becoming more and more prevalent amongst mutual fund investors. These programs are

family of funds
A group of mutual funds managed by one investment company.

Managed Asset Program (MAP)
A program allowing an investor to invest in portfolios grouping together many different mutual funds.

designed for investors who want to invest in a selection of mutual funds rather then in just one. Each portfolio consists of several, separate mutual funds packaged together. This allows you to have several individual, skilled fund managers managing your assets. MAPs are attempting to optimize asset allocation, through the selection of several different funds, as well as to adequately diversify the portfolio for the investor based on their time horizon and tolerance for risk.

Many financial analysts suggest that the true mark of a quality mutual fund investment is the fund's ability to increase the investor's return during good times and maintain that return during bad times. To help accomplish this task, a large number of investors have turned to market timers. A **market timer** is an individual who helps investors decide when to switch their investments from one fund to another fund, usually within the same family of funds. Market timers usually charge an annual fee of 1.5 to 3 percent of the dollar value of the funds they manage. When evaluating market timers, keep in mind that the services they offer are a relatively recent innovation. Thus, it may be hard to judge their long-term track record accurately. Early research indicates that market timers must be evaluated on their individual investment philosophy and their past performance, and it is impossible to pass judgment on *all* market timers as a group.

market timer An individual who helps investors decide when to switch their investments from one fund to another fund, usually within the same family of funds.

CONCEPT CHECK 13–2

1. How important is the investment objective as stated in a fund's prospectus?
2. Why do you think fund managers offer so many different kinds of funds?
3. What is a family of funds? How is it related to shareholder exchanges?
4. How does a market timer help people manage their mutual fund investments?

HOW TO MAKE A DECISION TO BUY OR SELL MUTUAL FUNDS

■ OBJECTIVE 3 ▐

Evaluate mutual funds for investment purposes.

Often, the decision to buy or sell shares in mutual funds is "too easy" because investors assume they do not need to evaluate these investments. Why question what the professional portfolio managers decide to do? Yet, professionals do make mistakes. The responsibility for choosing the right mutual fund rests with *you*. After all, you are the only one who knows how much risk you are willing to assume and how a particular mutual fund can help you achieve your goals.

If you think there are mutual funds designed to meet just about any conceivable investment objective, you are probably right. Hundreds of mutual funds trade daily under the headings "aggressive growth," "small-cap," and "growth-income." Fortunately, a lot of information is available to help you evaluate a specific mutual fund. Unfortunately, you can get lost in all the facts and figures and forget your ultimate goal: to choose a mutual fund that will help you achieve your financial goals. To help you sort out all the research, statistics, and information about mutual funds and give you some direction as to what to do first, we have provided the checklist in Exhibit 13–5. Don't forget, when evaluating the funds, that past performance may not necessarily be indicative of future returns. The remainder of this section explains the types of information you can obtain from each source listed in the exhibit.

HOW TO READ THE MUTUAL FUNDS SECTION OF THE NEWSPAPER

The Financial Post and *The Globe and Mail* provide information about mutual funds. Exhibit 13–6 is a guide to reading mutual fund tables as presented by *The Financial Post*. Other newspapers have similar reporting schemes, and in general, all provide the fund name, family, and current price. In addition, the 52-week highest and lowest paid prices will be shown, as well as the net asset value per share (NAVPS) and the percent change in price. Much of this same information is also available on the Internet.

Exhibit 13–5

Common Steps
Used by Investors
to Evaluate
Mutual Funds

☐ **Step 1: Perform a financial checkup to make sure you are ready to invest.**
For more information, review the material presented in Chapter 10.

☐ **Step 2: Obtain the money you need to purchase mutual funds.**
Although the amount will vary, $250 to $2,500 is usually required to open an account with a brokerage firm or an investment company.

☐ **Step 3: Determine your investment objectives.**
For more information, review the material presented in Chapter 10.

☐ **Step 4: Find a fund with an objective that matches your objective.**
The Financial Post, The Globe and Mail's Report on Business, and *IE:Money* may help you identify funds with objectives that match your investment objectives. Also, you can contact the investment company and ask for a prospectus and an annual report for a specific mutual fund. Finally, you can use the Internet to screen mutual funds that are compatible with your investment objectives.

☐ **Step 5: Evaluate, evaluate, and evaluate any mutual fund before buying or selling.**
Complete the Evaluation of a Mutual Fund form on p. 397 before making a decision to buy or sell a mutual fund. Possible sources of information include newspapers, the fund's prospectus, the fund's annual report, financial publications, the Internet, and professional advisory services—all sources described in this chapter. Be sure to evaluate the fund manager's background and how long the manager has been managing the fund.

The letters beside the name of a specific fund can be very informative. You can find out what they mean by looking at the footnotes that accompany the newspaper's mutual fund quotations. Generally, "N" means no-load, "U" means U.S. currency, "F" is front load or fee, and "B" signifies both front- and back-end fees.

In many cases, the search for a no-load fund starts with a newspaper quotation. Therefore, the N footnote is especially important. As pointed out earlier, no-load mutual funds do not charge sales fees. Since no-load funds offer the same investment opportunities that load funds do, financial experts often recommend these funds.

The newspaper coverage described in this section is a good means of monitoring the value of your mutual fund investments. However, other sources of information provide a more complete basis for evaluating mutual fund investments.

Exhibit 13–6

Financial
Information
about Mutual
Funds Available in
the Mutual Funds
Section of *The
Financial Post*

SOURCE: *The Financial
Post* (as part of *National
Post*), Saturday, July 1
2000, p. C7.

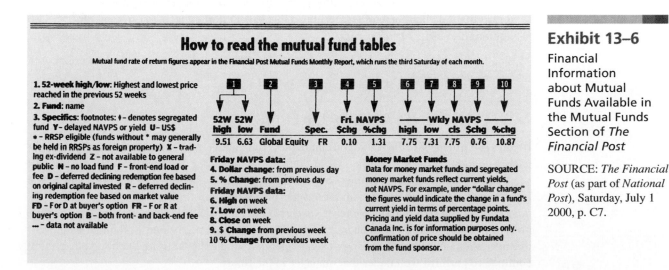

How to read the mutual fund tables

Mutual fund rate of return figures appear in the Financial Post Mutual Funds Monthly Report, which runs the third Saturday of each month.

1. **52-week high/low:** Highest and lowest price reached in the previous 52 weeks
2. **Fund:** name
3. **Specifics:** footnotes: ⬥ – denotes segregated fund **Y** – delayed NAVPS or yield **U** – US$ ∗ – RRSP eligible (funds without ∗ may generally be held in RRSPs as foreign property) **X** – trading ex-dividend **Z** – not available to general public **N** – no load fund **F** – front-end load or fee **D** – deferred declining redemption fee based on original capital invested **R** – deferred declining redemption fee based on market value **FD** – For D at buyer's option **FR** – For R at buyer's option **B** – both front- and back-end fee ⋯ – data not available

1		2	3	4	5	6	7	8	9	10
52W high	**52W low**	**Fund**	**Spec.**	**Fri. NAVPS $chg**	**%chg**	**Wkly NAVPS high**	**low**	**cls**	**$chg**	**%chg**
9.51	6.63	Global Equity	FR	0.10	1.31	7.75	7.31	7.75	0.76	10.87

Friday NAVPS data:
4. **Dollar change:** from previous day
5. **% Change:** from previous day
Friday NAVPS data:
6. **High** on week
7. **Low** on week
8. **Close** on week
9. **$ Change** from previous week
10 **% Change** from previous week

Money Market Funds
Data for money market funds and segregated money market funds reflect current yields, not NAVPS. For example, under "dollar change" the figures would indicate the change in a fund's current yield in terms of percentage points. Pricing and yield data supplied by Fundata Canada Inc. is for information purposes only. Confirmation of price should be obtained from the fund sponsor.

FINANCIAL OBJECTIVES—AGAIN

In Chapter 10, we talked about establishing investment goals and objectives. In this chapter, we have looked at the investment objectives of mutual funds. Here, our aim is to point out the relationship between the two. In establishing your own investment goals and objectives, you must evaluate the personal factors of age, family situation, risk tolerance, income, and future earning power. Only then can you establish short-term, intermediate, and long-term objectives. Now, you must find a mutual fund whose investment objectives match your own.

You may want to look at *The Financial Post*, which spotlights a different fund investment category, along with the top performers in each category, every week. You can also use the mutual fund filter on the Fund Library Web site (www. fundlibrary.com) to identify funds whose objective matches your objective. Finally, as mentioned earlier in this chapter, a mutual fund's prospectus provides a detailed description of the fund's investment objective. *Be warned:* Many mutual funds have developed objectives that sound good but don't really describe the investment philosophy. While the fund's objective is a place to start, you still need to gather as much information as possible about the fund and the investment company that sponsors it.

MUTUAL FUND PROSPECTUS

An investment company sponsoring a mutual fund must give potential investors a prospectus. According to financial experts, the prospectus is usually the first piece of information investors receive, and they should read it completely before investing. Although it may look intimidating, a common-sense approach to reading a fund's prospectus can provide valuable insights. In fact, most investors find that a fund's prospectus can provide a wealth of information. As pointed out earlier, the prospectus summarizes the fund's objective. Also, the fee table provides a summary of the fees a fund charges. In addition to information about objectives and fees, the prospectus should provide the following:

- A statement describing the risk factor associated with the fund.
- A description of the fund's past performance.
- A statement describing the type of investments contained in the fund's portfolio.
- Information about dividends, distributions, and taxes.
- Information about the fund's management.
- Information on limitations or requirements the fund must honour when choosing investments.
- The process investors can use to buy or sell shares in the fund.
- A description of services provided to investors and fees for services, if any.
- Information about how often the fund's investment portfolio changes (sometimes referred to as its *turnover ratio*).

Finally, the prospectus provides information about how to open a mutual fund account with the investment company.

MUTUAL FUND ANNUAL REPORT

If you are a prospective investor, you can request an annual report through the mail, a toll-free telephone number, or the Internet. Once you are a shareholder, the investment company will send you an annual report. A fund's annual report contains a letter from the president of the investment company, from the fund manager, or both. *Caution: Don't forget the role of the fund manager in determining a fund's success.* One important question is, how long has the present fund manager been managing the fund? If a fund has performed well under its present manager over a five-year, 10-year, or even longer period, there is a strong likelihood that it will continue to perform well under that manager in the future.

The annual report also contains detailed financial information about the fund's assets and liabilities, statement of operations, and statement of changes in net assets. Next, the annual report includes a schedule of investments. (Take a second look at the schedule of investments for the Royal Canadian Value Mutual Fund in Exhibit 13–1.) Finally, the fund's annual report should include a letter from the fund's independent auditors that provides an opinion as to the accuracy of the fund's financial statements.

FINANCIAL PUBLICATIONS

Investment-oriented magazines, such as *IE:Money*, *Canadian Business*, and *Report on Business*, are another source of information about mutual funds. Each of these publications provides an annual survey of mutual funds and ranks them on a number of important investment criteria.

In addition, a number of mutual fund guidebooks are available at your local bookstore or public library. Some of the more popular publications are:

[1] Gordon Williamson, *The 100 Best Mutual Funds You Can Buy, 2003*
[2] Bruce McDougall, Wilfred Vos, *The Best of the Best 2000: Mutual Funds and Blue-Chip Stocks for Canadians*
[3] Newsome, *Canadian Mutual Fund Bible*
[4] Stephen Gadsen, *The Canadian Mutual Funds Handbook*
[5] Eric Kirzner, Gordon Pape, *Gordon Pape's 2002 Buyer's Guide to Mutual Funds*
[6] Jim Yih, Neil Sawers, *Mutual Fundamentals: Canada's Guide to Quality Mutual Funds*

A great deal of information is also available online. A sample of the information provided on the Fund Library Web site for All-Canadian Capital Fund is illustrated in Exhibit 13–7 on the next page.

THE INTERNET

Many investors have found a wealth of information about mutual fund investments on the Internet. Basically, there are three ways to access information. First, you can obtain current market values for mutual funds by using one of the Internet search engines, such as Canada.com. The Canada.com finance page (http://finance.canada.com) has a box where you can enter the symbol of the mutual fund you want to research. In addition to current market values, you can obtain a price history for a mutual fund and a profile that includes specific holdings that the fund owns.

Second, most investment companies that sponsor mutual funds have Web pages. To obtain information, all you have to do is access one of the Internet search engines and type in the name of the fund. Before reading on, take a look at Exhibit 13–8 on the next page, the opening page for Acuity Funds Ltd. Generally, statistical information about individual funds, procedures for opening an account, available literature (including a prospectus and an annual report), and different investor services are provided. *Be warned:* Investment companies want you to become a shareholder. As a result, the Web sites for *some* investment companies read like a sales pitch. Read between the glowing descriptions and look at the facts before investing your money.

Note that information about the fund symbol, current NAV, adviser and portfolio manager, and minimum investment amounts is provided. It is also possible to obtain a current quote, chart, and information on returns, risk, holdings, and news by clicking on the appropriate button of the Web site. Also, read the Financial Planning for Life's Situations feature on page 392 to see why one couple invested in Altamira Asia Pacific Fund.

For more information on the evaluation process, study the checklist provided in the Financial Planning Calculations feature on page 393.

Visit the Web site
See the Weblinks under Chapter 13 on the online learning centre at www.mcgrawhill.ca/college/kapoor.

Exhibit 13–7

Online FundCARD for All-Canadian Capital Fund

SOURCE: www.fundlibrary.com

FundCARD™
The Fund Library

All-Canadian CapitalFund

FundCARD

| Details | Charting | Fund News | Company News | Profile | Distribution

Fund Overview

Fund Company:	All-Canadian Management Inc.
Fund Type:	AB - Canadian Equity
Inception Date:	October 1954
RRSP Eligible:	Y - Yes
Assets:	$ 8.75 million
Mgmt Expense Ratio:	2.00 %
Portfolio Manager:	Paul A. Gratton, Michael A. Parente, J.L. Michele Spicer, J.C. Stefan Spicer
Advisor:	All-Canadian Management Inc.
Sales Codes:	F - Initial sales charge (Front-end load)
Primary Investments:	Invests in common shares although treasury bills, bonds and preferred shares may be held.

Fund Price $ 8.4200 (up 0.0700) as of December 20, 2000

Net Asset Values for the last week:

Price Date		Price	Net Change	% Change
20-Dec-2000	↑	$ 8.4200	0.0700	0.8383
19-Dec-2000	-	$ 8.3500	-	-
18-Dec-2000	↓	$ 8.3500	(0.0400)	(0.4768)
15-Dec-2000	-	$ 8.3900	-	-
14-Dec-2000	↓	$ 8.3900	(0.0600)	(0.7101)
13-Dec-2000	↓	$ 8.4500	(0.0500)	(0.5882)

Fund Performance

Annual compound return as of: November 30, 2000

Period	Performance(1)	Rank(2)
1 month	1.19%	5 / 310
3 month	-2.08%	35 / 305
6 month	-0.24%	132 / 300
1 year	-3.37%	273 / 281
2 year	-5.84%	186 / 191
3 year	-4.63%	144 / 148
4 year	-3.17%	109 / 111
5 year	-1.03%	85 / 88
7 year	1.75%	73 / 76
10 year	4.54%	57 / 59
15 year	4.47%	30 / 31
20 year	6.64%	23 / 24
YTD	-2.64%	252 / 281
Since Inception	6.39%	244 / 310

(1) Returns for one year or less are expressed as simple rates of return.
(2) Rankings are based on the last complete comparitive ranking calculation, usually done during the first week after the previous month-end performance figures are determined.

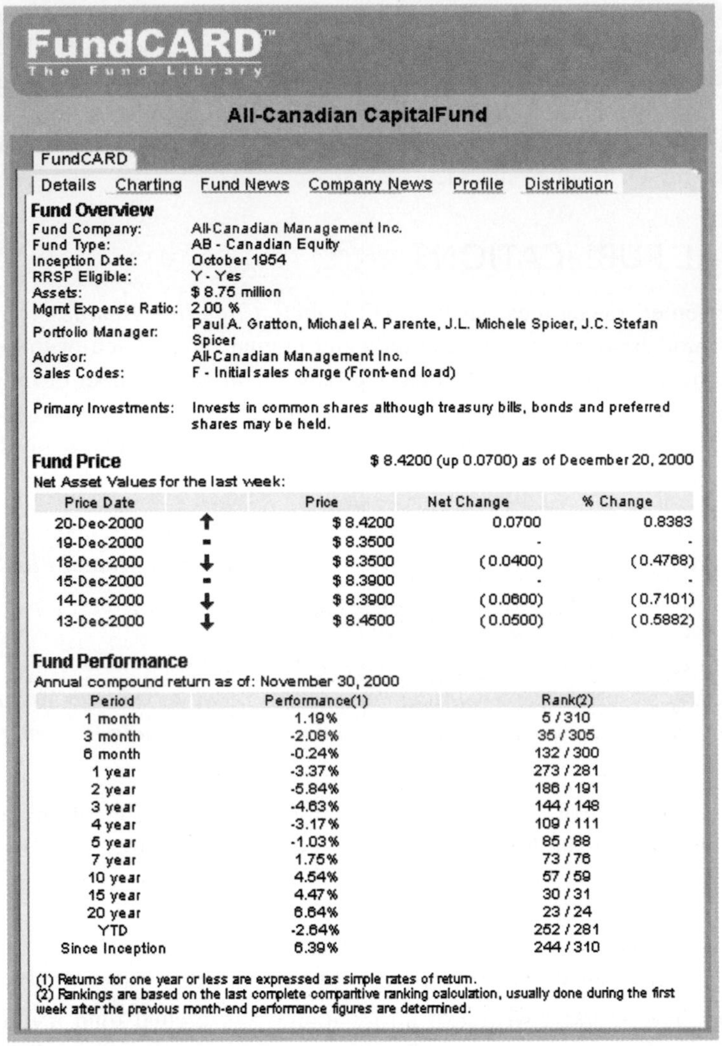

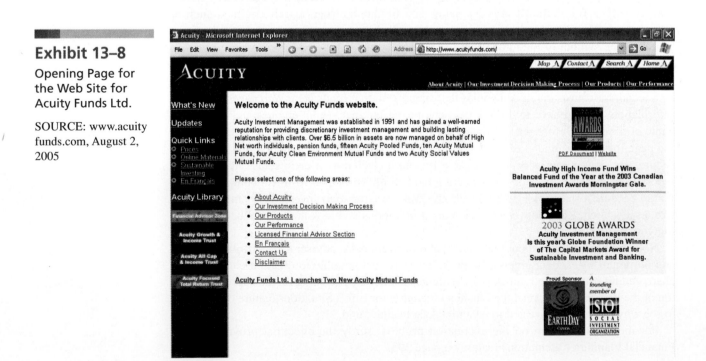

Exhibit 13–8

Opening Page for the Web Site for Acuity Funds Ltd.

SOURCE: www.acuityfunds.com, August 2, 2005

CONCEPT CHECK 13–3

1. Many financial experts say that purchasing a mutual fund is "too easy." Do you think this statement is true or false? Explain.
2. How can the following help you evaluate a mutual fund?
   a. Newspapers
   b. The fund's objective
   c. The prospectus
   d. The annual report
   e. Financial publications
   f. The Internet

THE MECHANICS OF A MUTUAL FUND TRANSACTION

For many investors, mutual funds have become the investment of choice. In fact, you probably either own shares or know someone who owns shares in a mutual fund—they're that popular! They may be part of a retirement savings plan or owned outright by purchasing shares through a brokerage firm or an investment company that sponsors a mutual fund. As you will see later in this section, it's easy to purchase shares in a mutual fund. For $250 to $2,500, you can open an account and begin investing. And there are other advantages that encourage investors to purchase shares in funds. Unfortunately, there are also disadvantages. Exhibit 13–9 summarizes the advantages and disadvantages of mutual fund investments.

One advantage of any investment is the opportunity to make money on it. In the next section, we examine how you can make money by investing in closed-end funds or open-end funds. We consider how taxes affect your mutual fund investments. Then, we look at the options used to purchase shares in a mutual fund. Finally, we examine the options used to withdraw money from a mutual fund.

■ OBJECTIVE 4 ▮

Describe how and why mutual funds are bought and sold.

Advantages
• Diversification
• Professional management
• Ease of buying and selling shares
• Smaller amount of money often required to open a mutual fund account
• Multiple withdrawal options
• Distribution or reinvestment of income and capital gains
• Switching privileges within the same fund family
• Services that include toll-free telephone numbers, complete records of all transactions, and savings and chequing accounts

Disadvantages
• Purchase/withdrawal costs
• Ongoing management fees
• Poor performance that does not match the TSE 300 Stock Index or some other index
• Inability to control when capital gain distributions occur and complicated tax-reporting issues
• Potential market risk associated with all investments
• Some sales personnel are aggressive

Exhibit 13–9

Advantages and Disadvantages of Investing in Mutual Funds

Financial Planning for Life's Situations

A Dream Come True for the Adamses

For Mike and Kathy Adams, both in their 30s, the last three years have been like a roller-coaster ride. In late 1996, they invested $11,500 in the Altamira Asia Pacific mutual fund. When they made their investment, just about everyone was talking about global investments. The fund seemed to be one of the best and was definitely a high flyer until October 1997. Then, the economies in Hong Kong, Indonesia, and other Pacific Rim countries began to experience financial troubles, and investors got scared. The Adamses' Altamira fund, like many other global investments in stocks and mutual funds, took a real hit. At that point, they considered selling their Altamira Asia Pacific shares, but they didn't want to lose some of their initial investment.

The Adamses had decided to purchase the fund on the basis of research they did in the library and on the Internet. Both admitted they were overwhelmed with the amount of information they found on mutual fund investments. Some of the more interesting articles stressed the need to diversify and place 10 to 30 percent of one's assets in global investments. According to another article, global investors enjoyed two major advantages. First, global investments provide investors with diversification. Second, economies in many nations around the globe are expanding faster than the Canadian economy.

On the basis of their research, the Adamses decided to go global, but then they had to decide if they wanted to invest in individual stocks issued by foreign companies or global mutual funds. Much of the research they read pointed out that purchasing individual, global stocks was a road full of potholes. For starters, evaluating foreign firms may be more difficult than evaluating Canadian firms because reliable accounting informa-

tion is often scarce. It was easier to get reliable information about global mutual funds. By calling a toll-free phone number, they could obtain a prospectus, an annual report, and information about the fund manager. *Report on Business*, *Canadian Business*, *The Financial Post*, and other financial publications also provided information about global mutual fund investments. For these reasons, most financial planners recommended global mutual funds for people with less than $200,000 to invest.

Now, the Adamses are glad they didn't sell their shares in Altamira Asia Pacific. By the end of 1997, just a little over two months after the big downturn in October 1997, their fund had recovered and was worth more than they had paid for it. In late 1999, three years after their purchase of shares in Altamira Asia Pacific, they had averaged between 21 and 22 percent every year, and the value of their investment had increased to almost $20,000.

The Adamses continue to monitor their investment.

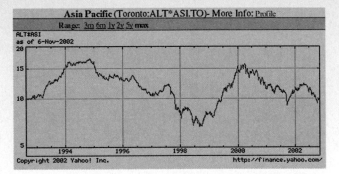

SOURCE: http://ca.finance.yahoo.com

RETURN ON INVESTMENT

income dividends
The earnings a fund pays to shareholders after it has deducted expenses from its dividend and interest income.

capital gain distributions The payments made to a fund's shareholders that result from the sale of securities in the fund's portfolio.

As with other investments, the purpose of investing in a closed-end fund or an open-end fund is to earn a financial return. Shareholders in such funds can receive a return in one of three ways. First, both types of funds pay income dividends. **Income dividends** are the earnings a fund pays to shareholders after it has deducted expenses from its dividend and interest income. Mutual fund dividends are usually paid once or twice a year. Second, investors may receive capital gain distributions. **Capital gain distributions** are the payments made to a fund's shareholders that result from the sale of securities in the fund's portfolio. These amounts generally are paid once a year. Third, as with stock and bond investments, you can buy shares in both types of funds at a low price and then sell them after the price has increased. For example, assume you purchased shares in the Royal Dividend Mutual Fund at $22.50 per share and sold your shares two years later at $25 per share. In this case, you made $2.50 ($25 selling price

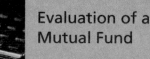
No checklist can serve as a foolproof guide for choosing a mutual fund. However, the following questions will help you evaluate a potential investment in such a fund.

CATEGORY 1: FUND CHARACTERISTICS

1. What is the value of the assets of this fund?

   _____

2. What is this fund's CBRS rating? _____
3. What is the minimum investment? _____
4. Does the fund allow telephone exchanges?
   ☐ Yes   ☐ No
5. Is there a fee for telephone exchanges?
   ☐ Yes   ☐ No

CATEGORY 2: COSTS

6. Is there a front-end load charge? If so, how much is it? _____

7. Is there a redemption fee? If so, how much is it?

   _____

8. How much is the annual management fee?

   _____

9. What is the fund's expense ratio? _____

CATEGORY 3: DIVERSIFICATION

10. What is the fund's objective? _____
11. What types of securities does the fund's portfolio include? _____
12. How many securities does the fund's portfolio include? _____
13. How many types of industries does the fund's portfolio include? _____

CATEGORY 4: FUND PERFORMANCE

14. How long has the fund manager been with the fund? _____
15. How would you describe the fund's performance over the past 12 months? _____

    _____

16. How would you describe the fund's performance over the past five years? _____

    _____

17. How would you describe the fund's performance over the past 10 years? _____

    _____

CATEGORY 5: CONCLUSION

18. On the basis of the above information, do you think an investment in this fund will help you achieve your investment goals?
    ☐ Yes   ☐ No
19. Explain your answer to question 18.

    _____

    _____

    _____

    _____

A WORD OF CAUTION

When you use a checklist, there is always a danger of overlooking important relevant information. The above checklist is not a cure-all, but it does provide some very sound questions that you should answer before making a mutual fund investment decision. Quite simply, it is a place to start. If you need other information, *you* are responsible for obtaining it and for determining how it affects your potential investment.

minus $22.50 purchase price) per share. With this financial information and dollar amounts for income dividends and capital gain distributions, you can calculate a total return for your mutual fund investment.

When shares in a mutual fund are sold, the profit that results from an increase in value is referred to as a *capital gain*. Note the difference between a capital gain distribution and a capital gain. A capital gain distribution occurs when *the fund* distributes profits that result from *the fund* selling securities in the portfolio at a profit. On the other hand, a capital gain is the profit that results when *you* sell your shares in the mutual fund for more than you paid for them. Of course, if the price of a fund's shares goes down between the time of your purchase and the time of sale, you incur a loss.

TAXES AND MUTUAL FUNDS

Income dividends, capital gain distributions, and financial gains and losses from the sale of closed-end or open-end funds are subject to taxation. At the end of each year, investment companies are required to send each shareholder a statement specifying how much he or she received in dividends and capital gain distributions. Investment companies may provide this information as part of their year-end statement.

Income passed through a mutual fund to its shareholders retains its nature; in other words, it retains its character as interest, foreign or Canadian dividends, or capital gains. As discussed in Chapter 3, Planning Your Tax Strategy, interest and foreign dividend income are 100 percent taxable at the investor's marginal tax rate, while Canadian dividends are grossed-up by 25 percent and offset by a dividend tax credit that is equal to 16.67 percent of the dollar dividend received. Fifty percent of capital gains are taxable.

Three specific problems develop with taxation of mutual funds. First, almost all investment companies allow you to reinvest income distributions and capital gain distributions from the fund in additional shares instead of receiving cash. Even though you didn't receive cash because you chose to reinvest such distributions, they are still taxable and must be reported on your federal and provincial tax returns as current income. Second, when you purchase shares of stock, corporate bonds, or other investments and use the buy-and-hold technique described in Chapter 11, you decide when you sell. Thus, you can pick the tax year when you pay tax on capital gains or deduct capital losses. Mutual funds, on the other hand, buy and sell securities within the fund's portfolio on a regular basis during any 12-month period. At the end of the year, profits that result from the mutual fund's buying and selling activities are paid to shareholders in the form of capital gain distributions. Unlike with investments that you manage, you have no control over when the mutual fund sells securities and when you will be taxed on capital gain distributions. Finally, if you purchase a mutual fund toward the end of the year, but before distributions are paid, you will be subject to tax on the entire distribution as if you had owned the mutual fund for the entire year. This may result in an unfair tax burden for the investor, when a successful mutual fund sells stocks at year-end that have grown throughout the year.

To ensure having all of the documentation you need for tax reporting purposes, it is essential that *you* keep accurate records. For example, additional shares of a mutual fund can be purchased by reinvesting interest, dividends, and capital gains distributions. However, these distributions have already been reported by you for tax purposes and you would not want to be taxed on the same amount twice. Therefore, it's up to you to keep track of their adjusted cost base, which is equal to the amounts reinvested. When these shares are eventually redeemed, their adjusted cost base is subtracted from their net redemption value to determine the capital gain (or loss). The same records will help you monitor the value of your mutual fund investments and make more intelligent decisions with regard to buying and selling these investments.

PURCHASE OPTIONS

You can buy shares of a closed-end fund through various stock exchanges or in the over-the-counter market. You can purchase shares of an open-end, no-load fund by contacting the investment company that sponsors the fund. You can purchase shares of an open-end, load fund through a salesperson who is authorized to sell them, through an account executive of a brokerage firm, or directly from the investment company that sponsors the fund.

You can also purchase both no-load and load funds from mutual fund supermarkets, available through discount brokerage firms. A

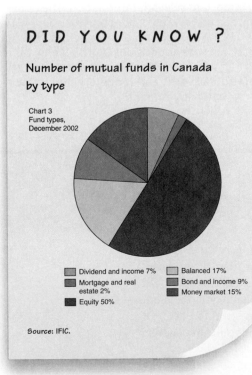

D I D   Y O U   K N O W ?

Number of mutual funds in Canada by type

Chart 3
Fund types,
December 2002

- Dividend and income 7%
- Mortgage and real estate 2%
- Equity 50%
- Balanced 17%
- Bond and income 9%
- Money market 15%

Source: IFIC.

mutual fund supermarket offers at least two advantages. First, instead of dealing with numerous investment companies that sponsor mutual funds, you can make one toll-free phone call to obtain information, purchase shares, and sell shares in a large number of mutual funds. Second, you receive one statement from the discount brokerage firm instead of receiving a statement from each investment company you deal with. One statement can be a real plus because it provides the information you need to monitor the value of your investments in one place and in the same format.

Because of the unique nature of open-end fund transactions, we will examine how investors buy and sell shares in this type of mutual fund from an investment company.

To purchase shares in an open-end mutual fund from an investment company, you may use four options: regular account transactions, voluntary savings plans (pre-authorized contribution [PAC]), contractual savings plans, and reinvestment plans. The most popular and least complicated method of purchasing shares in an open-end fund is through a regular account transaction. When you use a regular account transaction, you decide how much money you want to invest and when you want to invest and simply buy as many shares as possible.

The chief advantage of the voluntary savings plan is that it allows you to make smaller purchases than the minimum purchases required by the regular account method described above. At the time of the initial purchase, you declare an intent to make regular minimum purchases of the fund's shares. Although there is no penalty for not making purchases, most investors feel an "obligation" to make purchases on a periodic basis, and, as noted throughout this text, small monthly investments are a great way to save for long-term objectives. For most voluntary savings plans, the minimum purchase ranges from $25 to $100 for each purchase after the initial investment. Funds try to make investing as easy as possible. Most offer payroll deduction plans, and many will deduct, upon proper shareholder authorization, a specified amount from a shareholder's bank account. Also, many investors can choose mutual funds as a vehicle to invest money that is contributed to an RRSP account. Chapter 14 provides more information on the tax advantages of different types of retirement accounts.

Contractual savings plans require you to make regular purchases over a specified period of time, usually 10 to 15 years. These plans are sometimes referred to as *front end load funds* because almost all of the commissions are paid in the first few years of the contract period. You will incur penalties if you do not fulfill the purchase requirements. For example, if you drop out of a contractual savings plan before completing the purchase requirements, you sacrifice the prepaid commissions. Many financial experts and government regulatory agencies are critical of contractual savings plans.

You may also purchase shares in an open-end fund by using the fund's reinvestment plan. A **reinvestment plan** is a service provided by an investment company in which income dividends and capital gain distributions are automatically reinvested to purchase additional shares of the fund. Most reinvestment plans allow shareholders to use reinvested money to purchase shares without having to pay additional sales charges or commissions. *Reminder:* When your dividends or capital gain distributions are reinvested, you must still report these transactions as taxable income.

All four purchase options allow you to buy shares over a long period of time. As a result, you can use the principle of *dollar cost averaging*, which was introduced in Chapter 11. Dollar cost averaging allows you to average many individual purchase prices over a long period of time. This method helps you avoid the problem of buying high and selling low. With dollar cost averaging, you can make money if you sell your mutual fund shares at a price higher than their *average* purchase price.

reinvestment plan
A service provided by an investment company in which shareholder income dividends and capital gain distributions are automatically reinvested to purchase additional shares of the fund.

WITHDRAWAL OPTIONS

Because closed-end funds are listed on securities exchanges or traded in the over-the-counter market, it is possible to sell shares in such a fund to another investor. Shares in an open-end fund can be sold on any business day to the investment company that sponsors the fund. In this case, the shares are redeemed at their net asset value. All you have to do is give proper notification, and the fund will send you a cheque. With some funds, you can even write cheques to withdraw money from the fund.

In addition, most funds have provisions that allow investors with shares that have a minimum net asset value of at least $5,000 to use four options to systematically withdraw money. First, you may withdraw a specified, fixed dollar amount each investment period until your fund has been exhausted. Normally, an investment period is three months, and most funds require investors to withdraw a minimum amount, usually $50, each investment period.

A second option allows you to liquidate or "sell off" a certain number of shares each investment period. Since the net asset value of shares in a fund varies from one period to the next, the amount of money you receive will also vary. Once the specified number of shares has been sold, a cheque is mailed directly to you.

A third option allows you to withdraw a fixed percentage of asset growth. For example, assume you arrange to receive 60 percent of the asset growth of your investment, and the asset growth of your investment amounts to $800 in a particular investment period. For that period, you will receive a cheque for $480 ($800 × 60% = $480). If no asset growth occurs, no payment is made to you. Under this option, your principal remains untouched.

A final option allows you to withdraw all asset growth that results from income dividends and capital gains earned by the fund during an investment period. Under this option, your principal remains untouched.

Visit the Web site
See the Post-Test under Chapter 13 on the online learning centre at www.mcgrawhill.ca/ college/kapoor.

CONCEPT CHECK 13–4

1. How can you make money when investing in mutual funds?
2. What is the difference among income dividends, capital gain distributions, and capital gains?
3. How are income dividends, capital gain distributions, and capital gains reported on your federal tax return?
4. Whom would you contact to purchase a closed-end fund? An open-end fund?
5. What options can you use to purchase shares in a mutual fund from an investment company?
6. What options can you use to withdraw money from a mutual fund?

SUMMARY OF OBJECTIVES

Objective 1
Describe the characteristics of mutual fund investments.
The major reasons investors choose mutual funds are professional management and diversification. Mutual funds are also a convenient way to invest money. There are two types of mutual funds. A closed-end fund is a mutual fund whose shares are issued only when the fund is originally set up. An open-end fund is a mutual fund whose shares are sold and redeemed by the investment company at the net asset value (NAV) at the request of investors. Mutual funds are also classified as load or no-load funds. A load fund charges a commission every time you purchase shares. No commission is charged to purchase shares in a no-load fund. Mutual funds can also be front-end load or back-end load. Other possible fees include management fees and contingent deferred sales loads.

Objective 2
Classify mutual funds by investment objective.
The managers of mutual funds tailor their investment portfolios to the investment objectives of their customers. The major fund categories includes money market funds, mortgage funds, bond funds, dividend funds, balanced and asset allocation funds, equity or common stock funds, specialty funds, international or global funds, real estate funds, ethical funds, segregated funds, and labour-sponsored venture capital corporations (LSVCCs). Today, many investment companies use a family of funds concept, which allows shareholders to switch their investments among funds as different funds offer more potential, financial reward, or security.

Objective 3
Evaluate mutual funds for investment purposes.
The responsibility for choosing the "right" mutual fund rests with you, the investor. The information in newspapers, the financial objectives of the fund, the information in the prospectus and annual reports, financial publications, professional advisory services, and the Internet can all help you evaluate a mutual fund.

Objective 4
Describe how and why mutual funds are bought and sold.
The advantages and disadvantages of mutual funds have made mutual funds the investment of choice for many investors. For

$250 to $2,500, you can open an account and begin investing. The shares of a closed-end fund are bought and sold on organized stock exchanges. The shares of an open-end fund may be purchased through a salesperson who is authorized to sell them, through an account executive of a brokerage firm, from a mutual fund supermarket, or from the investment company that sponsors the fund. The shares in an open-end fund can be sold to the investment company that sponsors the fund. Shareholders in mutual funds can receive a return in one of three ways: income dividends, capital gain distributions when the fund buys and sells securities in the fund's portfolio at a profit, and capital gains when shares in the mutual fund are sold at a higher price than the price paid. A number of purchase and withdrawal options are available.

KEY TERMS

capital gain distributions 392	**investment company** 378	**mutual fund** 376
closed-end fund 378	**load fund** 379	**net asset value (NAV)** 379
contingent deferred sales load 380	**Managed Asset Program (MAP)** 385	**no-load fund** 380
family of funds 385	**market timer** 386	**open-end fund** 379
income dividends 392		**reinvestment plan** 395

KEY FORMULA

Page	Topic	Formula
379	Net asset value	$$\text{Net asset value} = \frac{\text{Current market value of a funds portfolio} - \text{Liabilities}}{\text{Number of shares outstanding}}$$
	Example:	$$\text{Net asset value} = \frac{\$24,500,000 - \$2,000,000}{1,800,000}$$ $$= \$12.50 \text{ per share}$$

FINANCIAL PLANNING PROBLEMS

1. *Calculating Net Asset Value.* Given the following information, calculate the net asset value for the Altamira Bond mutual fund. (Obj. 1)

Total assets	$225,000,000
Total liabilities	$ 5,000,000
Total number of shares	4,400,000

2. *Calculating Net Asset Value.* Given the following information, calculate the net asset value for the New Empire small-cap mutual fund. (Obj. 1)

Total assets	$350,000,000
Total liabilities	$ 10,000,000
Total number of shares	17,000,000

3. *Calculating Sales Fees.* Jane Tong invested $15,000 in the ADA Diversified Futures Mutual Fund. The fund charges a 5.5 percent commission when shares are purchased. Calculate the amount of commission Jane must pay. (Obj. 1)

4. *Calculating Sales Fees.* Tony Matteo invested $9,800 in the CI Harbour Growth growth and income fund. The fund charges a 5.3 percent commission when shares are purchased. Calculate the amount of commission Tony must pay. (Obj. 1)

5. *Determining Management Fees.* Chris Lavigne invested a total of $8,500 in the AIC Diversified Canada Mutual Fund. The management fee for this particular fund is 2.38 percent of the total investment amount. Calculate the management fee Chris must pay this year. (Obj. 1)

6. *Calculating Contingent Deferred Sales Loads.* Mary Canfield purchased the All-Canadian Compound bond fund. While this fund doesn't charge a front-end load, it does charge a contingent deferred sales load of 4 percent for any withdrawals in the first five years. If Mary withdraws $6,000 during the second year, how much is the contingent deferred sales load? (Obj. 1)

7. *Matching Mutual Funds with Investor Needs.* This chapter classified mutual funds into different categories based on the nature of their investments. Using the following information, pick a mutual fund category that you consider suitable for each investor described and justify your choice. (Obj. 2)

   a. A 25-year-old single investor with a new job that pays $30,000 a year.

Mutual fund category _____
Why? _____

   b. A single parent with two children who has just received a $100,000 divorce settlement, has no job, and has not worked outside the home for the past five years.
   Mutual fund category _____
   Why? _____

   c. A husband and wife who are both in their early 60s and retired.
   Mutual fund category _____
   Why? _____

8. *Using Dollar Cost Averaging.* Over a four-year period, Matt Ewing purchased shares in the Barreau du Quebec Canadian Equity Fund. Using the following information, answer the questions that follow. You may want to review the concept of dollar cost averaging in Chapter 11 before completing this problem. (Obj. 4)

Year	Investment Amount	Price per Share
1999	$3,000	$40 per share
2000	$3,000	$50 per share
2001	$3,000	$60 per share
2002	$3,000	$45 per share

   a. At the end of four years, what is the total amount invested?
   b. At the end of four years, what is the total number of mutual fund shares purchased?
   c. At the end of four years, what is the average cost for each mutual fund share?

FINANCIAL PLANNING ACTIVITIES

1. *Deciding If Mutual Funds Are Right for You.* Assume you are 35, are divorced, and have just received a $120,000 legal settlement. Prepare a two-page report on the major reasons you want to invest in mutual funds. (Obj. 1)

2. *Applying Terms to Mutual Fund Investments.* Using recent newspapers, magazines, mutual fund reports, or the Internet, find examples of the following concepts: (Obj. 1)

   a. The net asset value for a mutual fund.
   b. An example of a load fund.
   c. An example of a no-load fund.
   d. The management fee for a specific mutual fund.
   e. A fund that charges a contingent deferred sales load.

3. *Understanding Fees Associated with Mutual Fund Investments.* Assume you are single, are 28 years old, and have decided to invest $8,000 in mutual funds. (Obj. 1)

   a. Prepare a chart that shows the typical charges for load funds, no-load funds, and management fees.
   b. Calculate the following fees for your $8,000 mutual fund investment: (1) a 5-percent load charge, and (2) an annual 0.50-percent management fee.

4. *Matching Mutual Funds with Investor Needs.* This chapter explored a number of different classifications of mutual funds. (Obj. 2)

   a. On the basis of your age and current financial situation, which type of mutual fund seems appropriate for your investment needs? Explain your answer.
   b. As people get closer to retirement, their investment goals often change. Assume you are now 45 and have accumulated $110,000 in a retirement account. In this situation, what type of mutual fund would you choose? Why?
   c. Assume you are now 60 years of age and have accumulated $400,000 in a retirement account. Also, assume you would like to retire when you are 65. What type of mutual funds would you choose to help you reach your investment goals? Why?

5. *Using Information to Evaluate Mutual Funds.* Obtain specific information on either the Fidelity Disciplined Equity Class mutual fund or the Fidelity Canadian Short Term Bond-A fund. Then, describe how each of the following sources of information could help you evaluate one of these mutual funds: (Obj. 3)

   a. Newspapers.
   b. The fund's investment objective.
   c. The fund's prospectus.
   d. The fund's annual report.
   e. Financial publications.
   f. The Internet.

After researching one of the Fidelity funds, would you invest in the fund? Why or why not?

6. *Evaluating Mutual Funds.* Choose one of the following mutual funds and use information from newspapers, magazines, mutual fund reports, or the Internet to complete the mutual fund evaluation form presented in the Financial Planning Calculations feature on page 393. Then, answer the following questions: (Obj. 3)

Name of Fund	Type of Fund
AIM Canadian Premier	large-cap equity
Altamira Health Sciences	specialty
Dynamic APEX Balances	balanced
BMO Emerging Markets	emerging markets
AIC Diversified Canada	Canadian equity

a. Which fund did you choose?
b. Why did you choose this fund?
c. Do you think this fund could help you achieve your investment objectives? Explain your answer.

7. *Applying the Concept of Dollar Cost Averaging.* In a one-page report, explain how the concept of dollar cost averaging applies to the options used to purchase mutual funds. (Obj. 4)

8. *Reading a Prospectus.* Obtain a mutual fund prospectus to determine the options you can use to purchase and redeem shares. Then, prepare a chart that illustrates which options can be used to purchase and redeem shares in the fund, and answer the following questions: (Obj. 4)

a. Which purchase option would appeal to you?
b. Assuming you are now of retirement age, which withdrawal option would appeal to you?

CREATING A FINANCIAL PLAN

Investing in Mutual Funds

Diversification through the use of mutual funds provides investors with convenience and professional management. The variety of mutual funds contributes to your ability to achieve various financial goals.

Web Sites for Mutual Funds

- The Fund Library at **www.fundlibrary.com**
- Investor Canada at **www.canadian-investor.com**
- Webfin Money mutual funds at **www.webfin.com/en/funds/**
- Fundata Canada Inc. at **www.fundata.com**
- Fundwatch at **www.fundwatch.ca**
- GLOBEfund at **www.globefund.com**
- The Investment Funds Institute of Canada at **www.ific.ca**
- Canadian Mutual Fund **www.investcom.com/page/mutual.html**
- SEDAR at **www.sedar.com**
- Morningstar Canada at **www.morningstar.ca**

- The Canadian Financial Network at **www.canadian finance.com**
- Yahoo mutual fund centre at **http://mutualfunds.yahoo.ca**
- Mutual funds investor centre at **www.mfea.com**

(Note: Addresses and content of Web sites change, and new sites are created daily. Use search engines to update and locate Web sites for your current financial planning needs.)

Short-Term Financial Planning Activities

1. Identify types of mutual funds that might be appropriate for your various financial goals and life situations.
2. Research the recent performance records and costs of various mutual funds that could be appropriate investments for you.

Long-Term Financial Planning Activities

1. Identify types of mutual funds that you might use for your long-term financial goals.
2. Develop a plan for selecting and monitoring your mutual fund portfolio.

LIFE SITUATION CASE

The Wrong Mutual Fund?

According to Mike and Lorraine Racine, an Edmonton couple in their middle 30s, mutual funds were one of the biggest disappointments in their lives. In 1996, they invested $11,500 in the All-Canadian Resources mutual fund. Three years later, their original investment had lost over 20 percent, or about $2,500, during a period when most mutual funds were posting huge profits. What went wrong?

Three years after their investment, the Racines admitted they had invested money without researching the All-Canadian fund. They made their investment choice because Mike had heard a "high-powered" financial planner on a radio talk show raving about gold as the "ultimate" safe investment. Over the next two days, Mike had convinced Lorraine that gold was an investment that could be trusted. The Racines would have purchased the gold coins the talk show host was selling, but Mike lost the phone number. For lack of some other way to invest in gold, they decided to purchase shares in the All-Canadian Resources mutual fund. Besides, they reasoned, shares in a mutual fund would be a better investment than purchasing individual coins because mutual funds provided diversification and professional management. Both thought they were choosing the right investment. What could be better than a mutual fund that "specialized" in gold? Their investment would be a safe choice even if other investments went down in value.

The Racines also thought that since everybody was investing in mutual funds, they had to be the perfect investment. After all, there were thousands of different funds to choose from. Indeed, it seemed almost fashionable to invest in mutual funds. Because of professional management and diversification, there was no need to evaluate a mutual fund. Certainly, the fund manager knew more about picking the investments contained in the fund's portfolio than they did. It seemed mutual funds were almost guaranteed to increase in value. But after losing over 20 percent in three years, they realized that "almost guaranteed" was not the same thing as "guaranteed."

At the time of their investment, both had heard good things about All-Canadian mutual funds. A number of their friends had opened accounts with All-Canadian and had done well. And All-Canadian made it so easy! Just fill out an application, send the money, and let the professional managers make all the decisions. In fact, the Racines didn't realize that All-Canadian, the nation's largest mutual fund family, offered funds ranging from very conservative to very speculative investments. Simply put, they chose the wrong All-Canadian mutual fund.

Questions

1. Often, investors indicate that diversification and professional management are the two main reasons they choose mutual fund investments. How important do you consider these two factors? Why?

2. According to the Racines, everybody was investing in mutual funds—indeed, it seemed almost fashionable to invest in mutual funds. In your own words, what did the Racines do wrong?

3. Obtain information about a reputable mutual fund at the library or via the Internet. Then, complete a mutual fund evaluation form (see the Financial Planning Calculations feature on page 393) for this fund and answer the following questions:

   a. What sources of information did you use to evaluate the fund?

   b. What fees must investors pay to invest in the fund?

   c. What is the investment objective for the fund?

   d. How would you describe the fund's financial performance over the past 12 months? The past three years? The past five years?

   e. How would you rate the risk associated with the fund?

   f. Would you invest your money in this fund? Justify your answer.

CONTINUOUS CASE FOR PART 4

BUILDING AN INVESTMENT PROGRAM

Life Situation
Pamela, 43; Isaac, 45; three children, ages 16, 14, and 11

Financial Goals

- Evaluate current financial condition
- Build an investment portfolio that considers various risk factors

Financial Data

Monthly income	$ 4,900
Living expenses	4,450
Assets	262,700
Liabilities	84,600
Emergency fund	5,000

With approximately 20 years to retirement, Pamela and Isaac Mortimer want to establish a more aggressive investment program to accumulate funds for their long-term financial needs. Isaac does have a retirement program at work. This money, about $110,000, is invested in various conservative mutual funds. In addition, the Mortimers established their own investment program about four years ago, and today, they have about $36,000 invested in conservative stocks and mutual funds.

In addition to their investment program, the Mortimers have accumulated $11,000 to help pay for the children's education. Also, they have $5,000 tucked away in a savings account that serves as the family's emergency fund. Finally, both will qualify for the Canada Pension Plan when they reach retirement age.

Questions

1. How would you rate the Mortimers' financial condition at this stage in their lives?
2. Given the fact that Pamela is 43 and Isaac is 45 and they have three children who will soon begin their post-secondary education, what investment goals would be most appropriate for this middle-aged couple?
3. According to Pamela, "We both know we should have started our investment program sooner, but we always seemed to have 'emergencies' that took what extra money we had." Many investors feel the same way and, to compensate for a late start, often invest in highly speculative investments that promise large returns. Would you recommend such investments to a couple like the Mortimers? Explain your answer.
4. Describe the investment portfolio you would recommend for the Mortimers. Be sure to include *specific* types of investments (stocks, bonds, mutual funds, and so on), as well as information about the risk factor(s) associated with each investment alternative.

CONTROLLING YOUR FINANCIAL FUTURE

Retirement Planning

SCOPE OUT YOUR SOCIAL SECURITY BENEFITS

When Meg Hansen and her husband, Andrew Belanger, checked their CPP retirement benefits four years ago, they confirmed a nagging suspicion: They would have to play catchup to have a comfortable retirement. As a result, they closed their home renovation business in Red Deer, Alberta, and switched to careers that would provide steadier incomes. Hansen became a certified massage therapist, and Belanger returned to his previous occupation as a social worker.

The document that supplied the couple's wake-up call was the Canada Pension Plan (CPP) statement of contributions. This document provides you with a tally of your CPP contributions as well as estimates of the benefits you are eligible to receive. "When I got the statement, I realized I would get only about $300 a month in CPP benefits unless I did something about it," says Hanson, now 54. Belanger, now 65, would have been entitled to about $600, but his career switch enabled him to draw $763 monthly when he began collecting his CPP benefits.

When making retirement plans for clients, Marilyn, a personal finance adviser in Alberta, starts with the CPP personal contributor statement. She suggests that clients look at the benefit level and see if they can live on it. Often, they say they can't. "That serves as a motivator to make sure savings are moving in the right direction," she says.

The amount of the benefits you will receive is based on your earnings and your contributions to the plan. CPP covers virtually all working Canadians, except those who live in Quebec; Quebec workers come under the Quebec Pension Plan (QPP). These two plans are closely coordinated so that you are protected wherever you live in Canada. Whether in Canada or abroad at the time of retirement, you will receive your benefits in Canadian dollars.

Every year, if you are 30 years old or older, the CPP sends you a statement of your contributions along with an estimate of the monthly benefit you can expect to receive when you retire at age 65. You may also apply for your personal statement of contributions once in any 12-month period.

It is important to check that the personal information that appears on your statement is accurate and complete. All Canada Pension Plan benefits you may be eligible for in the future will be based on this information. If your name, birthdate, social insurance number, or earnings and contributions information is incorrect or missing you should request that it be corrected.

Next, you need to determine whether you can live on your benefits. Keep in mind that the Canadian Pension Plan was designed to replace only 25 percent of the salary from which you made your CPP contributions. There are also restrictions regarding when you actually retire. For example, if you start your pension at age 60, your monthly payment will be 30 percent lower than if you wait to age 65, but by starting it sooner you are likely to get the pension for a longer period of time. If you start your pension at age 70, your monthly payment will be 30 percent higher than if you took it at age 65.

The CPP statement of contributions is an important personal finance tool. Make sure you carefully consider how the information it holds may affect your retirement plans and goals. It could be a real eye-opener.

QUESTIONS

1 What were Meg Hansen's and Andrew Belanger's concerns about retirement income?

2 Why did they close their home renovation business?

3 What document served as the couple's wake-up call?

4 How can the Internet assist you in retirement planning?

LEARNING OBJECTIVES

1 Recognize the importance of retirement planning.

2 Analyze your current assets and liabilities for retirement.

3 Estimate your retirement spending needs.

4 Identify your retirement housing needs.

5 Determine your planned retirement income.

6 Develop a balanced budget based on your retirement income.

WHY RETIREMENT PLANNING?

Retirement can be a rewarding phase of your life. However, a successful, happy retirement doesn't just happen; it takes planning and continual evaluation. Thinking about retirement in advance can help you anticipate future changes and gain a sense of control over the future.

The ground rules for retirement planning are changing rapidly. Re-examine your retirement plans if you hold any of these misconceptions:

- My expenses will drop when I retire.
- My retirement will last only 15 years.
- I can depend on the government and my company pension to pay for my basic living expenses.
- My pension benefits will increase to keep pace with inflation.
- My employer's health insurance plan and medicare will cover my medical expenses.
- There's plenty of time for me to start saving for retirement.
- Saving just a little bit won't help.

It is vital to engage in basic retirement planning activities throughout your working years and to update your retirement plans periodically. While it is never too late to begin sound financial planning, you can avoid many unnecessary and serious difficulties by starting this planning early. Saving now for the future requires tackling the trade-offs between spending and saving, thus taking advantage of the time value of money.

TACKLING THE TRADE-OFFS

Although exceptions exist, the old adage "You can't have your cake and eat it, too" is particularly true in planning for retirement. For example, if you buy state-of-the-art home entertainment systems, drive expensive cars, and take extravagant vacations now, don't expect to retire with plenty of money.

Only by saving now and curtailing current spending can you ensure a comfortable retirement later. Yet, saving money doesn't come naturally to many young people. Ironically, although the time to begin saving is when you are young, the people who are in the best position to save are middle-aged.

THE IMPORTANCE OF STARTING EARLY

Consider this: If from age 25 to 65 you invest $300 per month and earn an average of 9 percent interest a year, you'll have $1.4 million in your retirement fund. Waiting just 10 years until age 35 to begin your $300-a-month investing will yield about $550,000, while if you wait 20 years to begin this investment, you will have only $201,000 at age 65. Exhibit 14–1 on the next page shows how even a $2,000 annual investment earning just 4 percent will grow.

■ OBJECTIVE 1 ▮

Recognize the importance of retirement planning.

Visit the Web site
See the Post-Test under Chapter 14 on the online learning centre at www.mcgrawhill.ca/college/kapoor.

DID YOU KNOW ?

You could retire a millionaire at age 65 if you contribute monthly to a fund that closely tracks the S&P 500, based on its historical annual average of 11.2 percent since 1926.

Your Age	Number of Years to Invest	Monthly Contribution	Accumulated Value
25	40	$127.09	$1,000,050
30	35	$218.49	$1,000,024
40	25	$ 663.99	$1,000,008
50	15	$2,243.50	$1,000,001

Calculations do not consider fees or taxes and are based on monthly payments at the beginning of the month with annual compounding. This is for illustrative purposes only and is not representative of any actual investment. The S&P 500 is an index. Indexes are not managed funds, have no identifiable objectives, and cannot be purchased. They do not provide an indicator of how individual investments performed in the past or how they will perform in the future. Past performance of indexes does not guarantee the future performance of any investment.

SOURCE: Investment Digest, VALIC, an American General Company, Summer 1999, p. 4.

For 40 years, your life, and probably your family's life, revolves around your job. One day, you retire, and practically every aspect of your life changes. There's less money, more time, and no daily structure.

You can expect to spend about 16 to 20 years in retirement—too many years to be bored, lonely, and broke. You want your retirement years to be rewarding, active, and rich in new experiences. It's never too early to begin planning for retirement; some experts even suggest starting while you are in school. Be certain you don't let your 45th birthday roll by without a comprehensive retirement plan. Remember, the longer you wait, the less you will be able to shape your life in retirement.

Retirement planning has both emotional and financial components. Emotional planning for retirement involves identifying your personal goals and setting out to meet them. Financial planning for retirement involves assessing your post-retirement needs and income and plugging any gaps you find. Financial planning for retirement is critical for several reasons:

[1] You can expect to live in retirement for up to 20 years. At age 65, the average life expectancy is 14 years for a man and 19 years for a woman.

[2] Government benefits and a private pension, if you have one, are most often insufficient to cover the cost of living.

[3] Inflation may diminish the purchasing power of your retirement savings. Even a 3-percent rate of inflation will cause prices to double every 24 years.

You should anticipate your retirement years by analyzing your long-range goals. What does retirement mean to you? Does it mean an opportunity to stop work and relax, or does it mean time to travel, develop a

Exhibit 14–1

It's Never Too Late to Start Planning for Retirement

Start young. A look at the performance of $2,000 per year of retirement plan investments over time even at 4 percent shows the value of starting early.

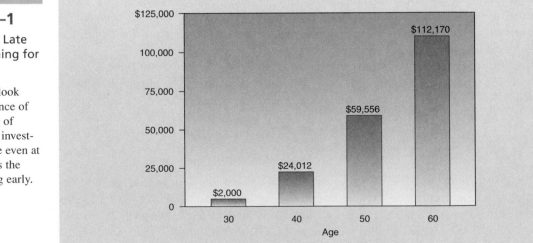

Exhibit 14–2
Using a Personal
Computer for
Retirement Planning

General Web Sites
Canadian Bankers Association (www.cba.ca; see the Publications link)
Bell's Sympatico-Lycos (www.sympatico.ca; see the Personal Finance link)
Webfin (http://argent.canoe.com; Canoe Money)
Human Resources and Development Canada (www.hrsdc.gc.ca/en/home.shtml)
CARP, Canada's Association for the Fifty-Plus (www.fifty-plus.net)
Software Packages
QuickWealth Planner 2nd Edition (www.intuit.com/canada/quickwealth)
RRIFmetic, Personal Use Edition, by Fimetrics (www.fimetrics.com)
RetireWare (www.retireware.com)

hobby, or start a second career? Where and how do you want to live during your retirement? Once you have considered your retirement goals, you are ready to evaluate their cost and assess whether you can afford them.

THE BASICS OF RETIREMENT PLANNING

Before you decide where you want to be financially, you have to find out where you are. Your first step, therefore, is to analyze your current assets and liabilities. Then estimate your spending needs and adjust them for inflation. Next, evaluate your planned retirement income. Finally, increase your income by working part time, if necessary. Recent articles and other retirement information may be accessed through online computer services. Exhibit 14–2 shows some good online sources for retirement planning using a personal computer. Also, read the Financial Planning for Life's Situations features on the next page and on page 427.

CONCEPT CHECK 14–1

1. Why is retirement planning important?
2. What are the four basic steps in retirement planning?

CONDUCTING A FINANCIAL ANALYSIS

As you learned in Chapter 2, your assets include everything you own that has value: cash on hand and in chequing and savings accounts; the current value of your stocks, bonds, and other investments; the current value of your house, car, jewellery, and furnishings; and the current value of your life insurance and pensions. Your liabilities are everything you owe: your mortgage, car payments, credit card balances, taxes due, and so forth. The difference between the two totals is your *net worth*, a figure you should increase each year as you move toward retirement. Use Exhibit 14–3 on page 409 to calculate your net worth now and at retirement.

OBJECTIVE 2

Analyze your current assets and liabilities for retirement.

REVIEW YOUR ASSETS

Reviewing your assets to ensure they are sufficient for retirement is a sound idea. Make any necessary adjustments in your investments and holdings to fit your circumstances. In reviewing your assets, consider the following factors:

If you can manipulate a mouse, you can develop a retirement plan. That's the message from Web sites and software publishers eager to tap aging baby boomers' financial anxieties and Gen-Xers' fascination with the market. Planning tools are, indeed, better than ever at crunching numbers, projecting risks, and handling, or at least spotlighting, tricky tax and pension problems. No PC can deliver complete peace of mind about your old age. So, even do-it-yourself investors turn to financial advisers for guidance and reassurance. "Eventually, you'll need a higher level of sophistication than you can get from software," says U.S. Institute of Certified Financial Planners president Elissa Buie.

Web-based planners are starting to provide services you would expect from personal finance software. Intuit's Quicken.ca features a retirement planner that users can link to an online portfolio tracker.

The newest calculators have their roots in casinos. They use the Monte Carlo method, a mathematical technique for testing thousands of possible investment outcomes to assess your portfolio for worst-case results. While two asset mixes might have the same average return, one may keep you solvent in 90 percent of all possible market forecasts, while with the other you would go broke in 40 percent of the cases. When your retirement's on the line, you need to shoot for the 9-to-1 odds. The best-known Monte Carlo calculator is offered by Financial Engines, founded by economics Nobel laureate William F. Sharpe. Nonmathematicians may be baffled by the Monte Carlo calculators' odds-based output. When you master the charts, however, the results are eye opening—and they are closer to reality than what-if scenarios run on a traditional calculator.

Whatever their algorithms, software planning tools still have one weakness: No program will look you in the eye and say, "Are you following that budget? Have you bought that insurance?" You must find the discipline within yourself to plan and follow through—or hire a human adviser to provide it.

SOURCE: Adapted from Mike McNamee, "Building the Best Retirement Plan," *Business Week*, July 19, 1999, pp. 108–16. Reprinted from the July 19, 1999 issue of *Business Week* by special permission. © 1999 McGraw-Hill Companies, Inc.

HOUSING If you own your house, it is probably your biggest single asset. The amount tied up in your house, however, may be out of line with your retirement income. You might consider selling your house and buying a less expensive one. The selection of a smaller, more easily maintained house can also decrease your maintenance costs. The difference saved can be put into a savings account or GICs or other income-producing investments.

If you wish to remain in your existing home, programs are available to assist homeowners with significant home equity but a need for cash. Reverse mortgages provide elderly homeowners with tax-free income in the form of a loan that is paid back (with interest) when the home is sold or the homeowner dies.

In a term or straight reverse mortgage, a financial institution provides the homeowner with a lump-sum amount or monthly income based on the current market value of the home, the loan's interest rate, and its term. At the end of the term, the loan and accrued interest must be repaid from the homeowner's estate, or by selling the house if the homeowner is still living.

It is quite possible, however, that the money lost to compound interest could well be greater than the "disposable" cash received by the homeowner, given a situation where the person lives for many years. This is something that must be given the proper consideration before opting for a reverse mortgage.

reverse annuity mortgage (RAM)
A loan based on the equity in a home that provides elderly homeowners with tax-free income and is paid back with interest when the home is sold or the homeowner dies.

Reverse annuity mortgages (RAM) are used to buy a life annuity from an insurance company that pays out a given sum of money on a regular basis for as long as the homeowner lives. When the homeowner dies or the house is sold, the mortgage and accrued interest must be repaid. The amount you can borrow increases as you grow older, usually in the range of 15 to 45 percent of the equity in your home. The minimum age to undertake a RAM is 62, based on the criteria for the Canadian Home Income Plan (CHIP).

	Sample Figures	Your Figures
Assets: What We Own		
Cash:		
Chequing account	$ 800	_____
Savings account	4,500	_____
Investments:		
Canada Savings Bonds (current cash-in value)	5,000	_____
Stocks, mutual funds	4,500	_____
Life insurance:		
Cash value, accumulated dividends	10,000	_____
Company pension rights:		
Accrued pension benefit	20,000	_____
Property:		
House (resale value)	50,000	_____
Furniture and appliances	8,000	_____
Collections and jewellery	2,000	_____
Vehicle	3,000	_____
Other:		
Loan to brother	1,000	_____
Gross assets	$108,800	_____
Liabilities: What We Owe		
Current unpaid bills	600	_____
Home mortgage (remaining balance)	9,700	_____
Vehicle loan	1,200	_____
Property taxes	1,100	_____
Home improvement loan	3,700	_____
Total liabilities	$ 16,300	_____

Exhibit 14–3

Review Your Assets, Liabilities, and Net Worth

Net worth: Assets of $108,800 minus liabilities of $16,300 equals $92,500.

With a reverse annuity mortgage the lender will then hold a mortgage on your house, but as the owner, you will not be required to either move or sell the house. Another advantage is that this revenue will not be taxed since the income you receive is generated from your equity in your home. Also, you will be protected against a decline in real estate values because if the value of your home falls beneath the mortgage amount, you will be accountable only for the actual value of the home.

There are two disadvantages to this arrangement, though both are essentially the same. First, a reverse annuity mortgage is essentially a choice to *spend your equity*. You are choosing to reduce your net worth. Second—the other side of the same coin—is that the remainder owing on your mortgage at the time of your death will be paid by your estate, thereby reducing the amount of inheritance available to your family.

LIFE INSURANCE You may have set up your life insurance to provide support and education for your children. Now you may want to convert some of this asset into cash or income (an annuity). Another possibility is to reduce premium payments by decreasing the face value of your insurance. This will give you extra money to spend on living expenses or invest for additional income.

OTHER INVESTMENTS Evaluate any other investments you have. When you chose them, you may have been more interested in making your money grow than in getting an early return. Has the time come to take the income from your investments? You may now want to take dividends rather than reinvest them.

After thoroughly reviewing your assets, estimate your spending needs during your retirement years.

CONCEPT CHECK 4–2

1. How can you calculate your net worth today and at retirement?

RETIREMENT LIVING EXPENSES

■ OBJECTIVE 3 ■

Estimate your retirement spending needs.

The exact amount of money you will need in retirement is impossible to predict. However, you can estimate the amount you will need by considering the changes you anticipate in your spending patterns and in where and how you live.

Your spending patterns will probably change. Although no two families adjust their spending patterns to changes in the life cycle in the same manner, the tabulation in Exhibit 14–4 can guide you in anticipating your own future spending patterns.

The following expenses may be lowered or eliminated:

- *Work expenses.* You will no longer make payments into your retirement fund. You will not be buying gas and oil for the drive back and forth to work or for train or bus fares. You may be buying fewer lunches away from home.
- *Clothing expenses.* You will probably need fewer clothes after you retire, and your dress may be more casual.
- *Housing expenses.* If you have paid off your house mortgage by the time you retire, your cost of housing may decrease (although increases in property taxes and insurance may offset this gain).
- *Federal income taxes.* Your federal income taxes will probably be lower. No federal tax has to be paid on some forms of income, such as Guaranteed Income Supplement (GIS) benefits, trading down on your home, or getting a reverse mortgage. You will probably pay taxes at a lower rate because your taxable income will be lower.

You can also estimate which of the following expenses may increase:

- *Insurance.* The loss of your employer's contribution to health and life insurance will increase your own payments.
- *Medical expenses.* Although medical expenses vary from person to person, they tend to increase with age.
- *Expenses for leisure activities.* With more free time, many retirees spend more money on leisure activities. You may want to put aside extra money for a retirement trip or other large recreational expenses.
- *Gifts and contributions.* Many retirees who continue to spend the same amount of money on gifts and contributions find their spending in this area takes a larger share of their smaller income. Therefore, you may want to re-evaluate such spending.

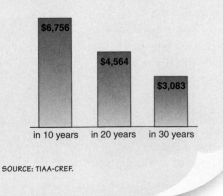

DID YOU KNOW ?

THE EFFECTS OF INFLATION OVER TIME
This chart shows you what $10,000 will be worth in 10, 20, and 30 years assuming a fairly conservative 4-percent rate of inflation.

$6,756 — in 10 years
$4,564 — in 20 years
$3,083 — in 30 years

SOURCE: TIAA-CREF.

Using the worksheet in Exhibit 14–5 on page 412, list your present expenses and estimate what these expenses would be if you were retired. To make a realistic comparison, list your major spending categories, starting with fixed expenses, such as rent or mortgage payments, utilities, insurance premiums, and taxes. Then, list variable expenses—food, clothing,

Exhibit 14–4   Average Household Expeditures, Canada and Provinces

Household characteristics	2000					
	Canada[1]		Quebec		Ontario	
Number of households in sample	14,250		1,828		1,857	
Estimated number of households	11,361,810		2,930,590		4,210,680	
Average household size	2.57		2.40		2.68	
	Average expenditure per household $	Households reporting expenditures %	Average expenditure per household $	Households reporting expenditures %	Average expenditure per household $	Households reporting expenditures %
Total expenditures	55,834	100.0	48,318	100.0	62,738	100.0
Total current consumption	39,385	100.0	33,758	100.0	43,645	100.0
Food	6,217	100.0	6,073	100.0	6,556	100.0
Shelter	10,498	99.7	8,533	99.8	12,224	99.9
Household operation	2,516	100.0	2,034	99.9	2,834	99.9
Household furnishings and equipment	1,557	93.4	1,218	88.3	1,811	95.3
Clothing	2,351	99.1	2,123	98.7	2,675	99.4
Transportation	7,576	98.0	6,164	96.8	8,476	98.6
Health care	1,357	97.1	1,359	96.8	1,194	96.9
Personal care	740	99.3	722	98.8	810	99.5
Recreation	3,165	97.7	2,553	96.4	3,430	98.1
Reading materials and other printed matter	275	86.3	239	79.8	310	87.9
Education	826	42.5	487	40.5	1,031	40.7
Tobacco products and alcoholic beverages	1,218	84.3	1,302	88.6	1,186	82.9
Games of chance (net amount)	261	74.2	285	80.1	263	72.2
Miscellaneous	827	90.4	665	88.8	843	91.4
Personal income taxes	12,012	90.4	11,131	87.2	13,782	93.3
Personal insurance payments and pension contributions	3,125	80.0	2,690	80.6	3,719	79.6
Gifts of money and contributions	1,302	73.4	739	60.6	1,592	78.8

[1] The Canada total excludes data for the Yukon, the Northwest Territories, and Nunavut.
SOURCE: Statistics Canada, CANSIM II, table 203-001. Last modified: December 4, 2001. For more information on the concepts, methods and quality of the data contained in this table, consult the Statistical data documentation. This table was created from CANSIM II, Statistics Canada's online statistical database: Adapted from the Statistics Canada Website http://www.statcan.ca/english/Pgdb/People/Families/famil16c.htm

Exhibit 14–5

Your Present Monthly Expenses and Your Estimated Monthly Retirement Expenses

Item	MONTHLY EXPENSES Present	Retirement
Fixed expenses:		
Rent or mortgage payment	$_____	$_____
Taxes	_____	_____
Insurance	_____	_____
Savings	_____	_____
Debt payment	_____	_____
Other	_____	_____
Total fixed expenses	_____	_____
Variable expenses:		
Food and beverages	_____	_____
Household operation and maintenance	_____	_____
Furnishings and equipment	_____	_____
Clothing	_____	_____
Personal	_____	_____
Transportation	_____	_____
Medical expenses	_____	_____
Recreation and education	_____	_____
Gifts and contributions	_____	_____
Other	_____	_____
Total variable expenses	_____	_____
Total expenses	_____	_____

DID YOU KNOW ?

Many financial planners say that you will need about 70 percent of your current (pre-tax) earnings to maintain your standard of living in retirement. For example, if you earn $40,000 now, you might aim for $28,000 of income in retirement. However, this is only a general rule. You'll need to look at your own circumstances to decide what level of income is right for you.

SOURCE: Human Resources and Development Canada, at www.hrdc-drhc.gc.ca/

transportation, and so on, as well as miscellaneous expenditures, such as medical expenses, entertainment, vacations, gifts, contributions, and unforeseen expenses.

Be sure you have an emergency fund for unforeseen expenses. Even when you are living a tranquil life, unexpected events can occur.

ADJUST YOUR EXPENSES FOR INFLATION

You now have a list of your likely monthly (and annual) expenses if you were to retire today. With inflation, however, those expenses will not be fixed. The potential loss of buying power due to inflation is what makes planning ahead so important. During the 1970s and the early 1980s, the cost of living increased an average of 6.1 percent a year, though the annual increase slowed to less than 3 percent between 1983 and 1999.

To help you plan for this likely increase in your expenses, use the inflation factor table in the Financial Planning Calculations feature on page 415.

CONCEPT CHECK 14–3

1. How can you estimate the amount of money you will need during retirement?
2. What expenses are likely to increase or decrease during retirement?
3. How might you adjust your expenses for inflation?

Retirement? Ah, yes: *retirement*. Better to save now and avoid the deprivation later. You know the spiel: government pensions, a joke; corporate pensions, all but eliminated; job security, gone; the 30-minute-pizza guarantee, abolished. With such an uncertain future, it is best one be prepared.

There are monetary returns, although the pros contend that the psychological feeling of safety that regular investing provides trumps all. While the boomers freak about not having saved enough for retirement, young people have time to spare. With a long-term horizon, investing is safe, easy, and relatively hassle free. Mutual funds have made retirement investing more convenient than sleeping through that 9 a.m. class. Automatic investment plans can deduct as little as $25 a month from bank accounts or pay-cheques. Even pocket cash can get things rockin': Take that double tall latte ($2.39) and raisin cinnamon scone ($1.70) you snag each morning and put it in an index fund. You'll have over $20,000 before your first midlife crisis. Keep it up until your second, and you'll have accumulated over $110,000—more than enough to pay for intensive therapy and a week in Boca. Systematic investing is the fiscal equivalent of a tetanus shot: a regular bummer that doesn't hurt as bad as one initially believes.

If you are frightened of investing, worried that a crash or prolonged bear market will turn your retirement into an episode of Good Times, *you must chill!* Don't waste the Xanax worrying about the market because the fact is that over a long period of time, stocks go up. Over a two-year time horizon, the market's *worst* performance has been about 2 percent. While it might seem you can't afford to invest, the unfortunate reality is that you can't afford not to. With inflation humming along, common stocks are the only asset class that will consistently keep you ahead, the pros advise.

RRSPs, RPPs, pension plans—stock 'em full of quality mutual funds and chill. "Home runs" look great on the cover of *Money* magazine, but real wealth is born over time. Compound interest, or the titillating phenomenon of earning interest on interest, provides hefty gains to patient investors. This "get-rich-slowly" scheme won't get your picture in *Barron's*, but it will provide for an adequate retirement.

PLANNING YOUR RETIREMENT HOUSING

Think about where you will want to live. If you think you will want to live in another city, it's a good idea to plan vacations now in areas you might enjoy later. When you find one that appeals to you, visit that area during various times of the year to experience the year-round climate. Meet the people. Check into available activities, transportation, and taxes. Be realistic about what you will have to give up and what you will gain.

Where you live in retirement can influence your financial needs. You must make some important decisions about whether to stay in your present community and in your current home. Everyone has unique needs and preferences; only *you* can determine the location and housing that are best for you.

Consider what moving involves. Moving is expensive, and if you are not satisfied with your new location, returning to your former home may be impossible. Consider the social aspects of moving. Will you want to be near your children, other relatives, and good friends? Are you prepared for new circumstances?

■ OBJECTIVE 4 ■

Identify your retirement housing needs.

TYPE OF HOUSING

Housing needs often change as people grow older. The ease and cost of maintenance and nearness to public transportation, shopping, church/synagogue, and entertainment often become more important to people when they retire.

Many housing alternatives exist, several of which were discussed in Chapter 7. Staying in their present homes, whether a single-family dwelling, a condominium, or an apartment, is the alternative preferred by most people approaching retirement. That's what Mike and Abby

Wootton decided to do after Mike took early retirement at age 47 from his job as a service manager of a Saskatoon Ford dealership in the late 1970s. Even though the couple had already paid off the mortgage on their small, three-bedroom ranch house and could have moved up into a bigger or fancier place, all Mike wanted to do was tinker in the garage and dabble in the stock market. A recent U.S. survey of over 5,000 men and women revealed that 92 percent wanted to own their homes in retirement.[1]

Diane Forrest of Grenville, Ontario, has seen the future, and she wants to be prepared. Diane, 69, has osteoporosis, just as her mother did. Although she's not having difficulty now, she knows the debilitating bone condition eventually could make it difficult, if not impossible, to navigate steep stairs, cramped bathrooms, and narrow doorways. So, two years ago, she and her husband Carl, a 72-year-old retired sales executive, moved into a novel type of home, one that can comfortably accommodate them no matter what disabilities old age may bring. Called a "universal design home," their residence is on the cutting edge of an architectural concept that an aging population may well embrace. The only house of its kind in the neighbourhood, it has wide doors, pull-out cabinet shelves, easy-to-reach electrical switches, and dozens of other features useful for elderly persons or those with disabilities. Yet, these features are incorporated into the design unobtrusively.

This new setup suits the Forrests just fine. Unlike their peers who are moving into continuing-care communities, they want to stay where they have always lived, near their three children and around people of all ages. They now have a home that can accommodate a wheelchair and even has a room for a nurse, if the need arises. "We hope to be able to live here for the rest of our lives," says Diane—in comfort and with all the touches they need to ease their daily tasks.

Whatever retirement housing alternative you choose, make sure you know what you are signing and understand what you are buying.

AVOIDING RETIREMENT HOUSING TRAPS

Visit the Web site
See Personal Financial Planning worksheets under Chapter 14 on the online learning centre at www.mcgrawhill.ca/college/kapoor.

Too many people make the move without doing enough research, and invariably it's a mistake. How can retirees avoid being surprised by hidden tax and financial traps when they move?

Here are some tips from retirement specialists on how to uncover hidden taxes and other costs of a retirement area before moving:

- Write or call the local chamber of commerce to get an economic profile and details on area property taxes.
- Contact the province's tax department to find out provincial income, sales, and inheritance taxes and special exemptions for retirees. If your pension will be taxed by the province you're leaving, check whether the new province will give you credit for those taxes.
- Subscribe to the weekend edition of a local newspaper.
- Call a local accountant to find out which taxes are rising.
- Check with local utilities to estimate your energy costs. Visit the area in as many seasons as possible. Talk to retirees and other local residents about costs of health care, auto insurance, food, and clothing.
- Rent for a while instead of buying immediately.

CONCEPT CHECK 14–4

1. What are some housing options for retirees?
2. How can retirees avoid retirement housing traps?

---

[1] Jeanette A. Brandt, "Housing and Community Preferences: Will They Change in Retirement?" *Family Economics Review*, U.S. Department of Agriculture, May 1989, p.7.

ESTIMATED ANNUAL RATE OF INFLATION BETWEEN NOW AND RETIREMENT										
Years to Retirement	3%	4%	5%	6%	7%	8%	9%	10%	11%	12%
5	1.2	1.2	1.3	1.3	1.4	1.5	1.5	1.6	1.7	1.8
8	1.3	1.4	1.5	1.6	1.7	1.8	2.0	2.1	2.3	2.5
10	1.4	1.5	1.6	1.8	2.0	2.2	2.4	2.6	2.8	3.1
12	1.5	1.6	1.8	2.0	2.3	2.5	2.8	3.1	3.5	3.9
15	1.6	1.8	2.1	2.4	2.8	3.2	3.6	4.2	4.8	5.5
18	1.8	2.0	2.4	2.8	3.4	4.0	4.7	5.6	6.5	7.7
20	2.0	2.2	2.7	3.2	3.9	4.7	5.6	6.7	8.1	9.6
25	2.1	2.7	3.4	4.3	5.4	6.8	8.6	10.8	13.6	17.0

1. Choose from the first column the approximate number of years until your retirement.
2. Choose an estimated annual rate of inflation. The rate of inflation cannot be predicted accurately and will vary from year to year.
3. Find the inflation factor corresponding to the number of years until your retirement and the estimated annual inflation rate. (Example: 10 years to retirement combined with a 4 percent estimated annual inflation rate yields a 1.5 inflation factor.)
4. Multiply the inflation factor by your estimated retirement income and your estimated retirement expenses. (Example: $6,000 × 1.5 = $9,000.)

Total annual inflated retirement income: $_____.

Total annual inflated retirement expenses: $_____.

SOURCES: The above figures are from a compound interest table showing the effective yield of lump-sum investments after inflation that appeared in Charles D. Hodgman, ed., *Mathematical Tables from the Handbook of Chemistry and Physics* (Cleveland: Chemical Rubber Publishing, 1959); *Citicorp Consumer Views*, July 1985, pp. 2–3, © Citicorp, 1985; *Financial Planning Tables*, A. G. Edwards, August 1991.

PLANNING YOUR RETIREMENT INCOME

Once you have determined your approximate future expenses, you must evaluate the sources and amounts of your retirement income. Possible sources of income for many retirees are public pension plans, employer pension plans, and personal retirement plans. (See Exhibit 14–8 on page 418.)

■ OBJECTIVE 5 ■

Determine your planned retirement income.

PUBLIC PENSIONS

Public pensions have existed since 1927 and were initially paid only to those over the age of 70. Federal programs are the major source of public retirement pensions, but most provinces and the territories also provide income supplements for residents in financial need.

Canada's retirement income system has three levels; the Old Age Security (OAS) provides the first level, or foundation. If you meet certain residence requirements, you'll be entitled to a modest monthly pension once you reach the age of 65; The Canada Pension Plan (CPP), or Quebec Pension Plan (QPP), is the second level of the system. It provides you with a monthly retirement pension as early as 60, if you have paid into it. Also available is the Guaranteed

415

Income Supplement (GIS) and Spouse's allowance (SPA). Public pensions are not intended to meet all your financial needs in retirement. Rather, they provide a modest base for you to build upon with additional, private savings. The third level of the retirement income system consists of private pensions and savings.

The various types of public pensions were and are tied to either residency requirements or income requirements, and could be contributory or non-contributory.

CANADA/QUEBEC PENSION PLAN (CPP/QPP)

The CPP dates to 1966, when the federal government started the program as a mandatory defined benefit indexed pension plan for all Canadians (besides residents of Quebec, who have a similar plan called the Quebec Pension Plan [QPP]). There are three kinds of Canada Pension Plan benefits: disability benefits (which include pensions for disabled contributors and benefits for their dependent children), a retirement pension, and survivor benefits (which include the death benefit, the surviving spouse's pension, and the children's benefit).

CPP CONTRIBUTIONS The contribution you are required to make is based on your salary. If you are self-employed, it is based on your net business income (after expenses). You do not contribute on any other source of income, such as investment earnings. If during a year, you contributed too much or earned less than a set minimum amount, you will receive a refund of contributions at income tax time. You pay contributions only on your annual earnings between the minimum and a set maximum level (these are called your "pensionable" earnings). Currently, the minimum level is frozen at $3,500. The maximum level is adjusted each January, based on increases in the average wage.

Your required annual contribution to the CPP or QPP is calculated by multiplying your pensionable earnings by the contribution rate, outlined by year since 2000 in Exhibit 14-6. If you earned a $45,000 salary in 2005, for example, your CPP contribution would be $1,795.86, calculated as 4.95 percent of $36,280 ($39,780 − $3,500). The $39,780 is called the year's maximum pensionable earnings. This means that there exists a limit on the amount of your pensionable earnings that count to calculate your CPP contribution. If you were self-employed, you would have been asked to pay double the amount—because employee CPP contributions are matched by the employer, and your payment would need to represent both employee and employer. This means that the maximum self-employed contribution you could be required to pay into the CPP in 2005 would be $3,591.72—that is, 9.9 percent of $39,780 − $3,500.

BENEFITS Both CPP and QPP benefits are payable at age 65, whether you continue to work or not. You can also start to receive your benefits as early as age 60 or as late as age 70. If you do so, however, the amount you receive will be reduced or increased by 0.5 percent for each month earlier or later than the month of your 65th birthday. The full CPP benefit is paid only when you retire at age 65. The full CPP benefit is based on 25 percent of your average monthly pensionable earnings adjusted for increases in each year's maximum pensionable earnings.

There are two clauses in the CPP/QPP regulations that favour a better benefit for you. The *dropout clause* allows you to leave the lowest 15 percent of your monthly contributions during your working years out of your calculations of contribution rates. The *child-rearing clause* allows up to seven years per child of not contributing. The overall objective of these clauses is to minimize the effect on your CPP benefits of financially adverse life events.

Year	Employee/Employer Rate %	Combined/Self-employed Rate %
2000	3.9	7.8
2001	4.3	8.6
2002	4.7	9.4
2003	4.95	9.9
2004	4.95	9.9
2005	4.95	9.9
2006	4.95	9.9

Exhibit 14–6
Canada Pension Plan Contribution Rates

Review Exhibit 14–7 for the types of benefits available through the CPP, the average monthly benefit in 2004, and the maximum monthly benefit for 2005. You should also note that a portion of your CPP benefits can be assigned to your spouse or common-law partner, provided that he or she is at least 60 years old. This may give your family a tax advantage if your spouse is not in a position to receive CPP benefits.

OLD AGE SECURITY (OAS)

This public pension benefit was introduced in the Old Age Security Act, which came into effect in 1952. It is indexed to inflation on a quarterly basis. If you are over the age of 65 and have been a resident of Canada for at least 40 years since age 18, you qualify for full OAS benefits. With a minimum of 10 years of residency, you will receive 1/40 of the full benefit for each year you were a resident of Canada between the ages of 18 and 65.

This benefit is taxed and will be *clawed back* at a rate of 15 cents for each dollar once your net income (in 2005) exceeds $60,806. By the time your net income is $98,547, the entire OAS received will have to be repaid to the federal government.

GUARANTEED INCOME SUPPLEMENT (GIS)

Also introduced in the OAS Act of 1952, this pension is payable to low-income OAS recipients who are 65 and older. The amount you receive depends on your marital status as well as your income. As of 2002, the

Type of benefit	Average monthly benefit (October 2004)	Maximum monthly benefit (2005)
Disability benefit	$749.08	$1010.23
Retirement pension (at age 65)	$456.92	$828.75
Survivors benefit (under age 65)	$336.68	$462.42
Survivors benefit (age 65 and over)	$274.27	$497.25
Children of disabled contributors benefit	$192.68	$195.96
Children of deceased contributors benefit	$192.68	$195.96
Combined survivors & retirement benefit (pension at age 65)	$622.03	$828.75
Combined survivors & disability benefit	$889.59	$1010.23
Death benefit (max lumpsum)	$2,219.07	$2,500.00

SOURCE: www.sdc.gc.ca/en/isp/pub/factsheets/rates.shtml.

Exhibit 14–7
Canada Pension Plan Payment Rates January–December 2005

Canada Pension Plan rates are adjusted every January if there are increases in the cost of living as measured by the Consumer Price Index.

maximum monthly supplement for single individuals with no income was $562.93. For each $24 dollars of annual income reported by the individual, the monthly benefit is reduced by $1 ($12 per year). Thus, earned income essentially reduces benefits by 50 percent. This is not a tax, but rather an adjustment to benefits reported upon filing taxes. (Note: OAS benefits are not included as income for determining reductions to the GIS benefits.) This benefit is not taxed.

SURVIVOR ALLOWANCE   Yet another pension introduced in the OAS Act of 1952 was the spouse's allowance, newly termed the *survivor allowance*. These benefits are payable to widows, widowers, and the spouses of OAS beneficiaries who are between 60 and 65 years old.

EMPLOYER PENSION PLANS

Another possible source of retirement income is the pension plan your company offers. With employer plans, your employer contributes to your retirement benefits, and sometimes you contribute, too. These plans are termed to be either *contributory* or *noncontributory*. Pension plans held by employers for their employees were formally called a *Registered Pension Plan*, or RPP.

Since private pension plans vary, you should find out (1) when you become eligible for pension benefits, and (2) what benefits you will be entitled to. Most employer plans are defined-contribution or defined-benefit plans.

defined benefit pension plan A plan that specifies the benefits the employee will receive at the normal retirement age.

DEFINED BENEFIT PENSION PLAN   In a **defined benefit pension plan**, the plan document specifies the benefits promised to the employee at the normal retirement age. The plan itself does not specify how much the employer must contribute annually. The plan's actuary determines the annual employer contribution required so that the plan fund will be sufficient to pay the promised benefits as each participant retires. If the fund is inadequate, the employer must make additional contributions. Because of their actuarial aspects, defined-benefit plans tend to be more complicated and more expensive to administer than defined-contribution plans. It is generally the employer's responsibility to ensure that sufficient funds are available to pay your pension when you retire. The employer assumes the risk of investing all contributions wisely to guarantee the future value of your pension.

Companies nationwide are switching their retirement plans to defined contributions from defined benefits. "Paternalistic employers are dying fast—if they're not already dead," says an actuary with an international consulting firm. The result is that "the shift to defined contributions has forced employees to take more responsibility for retirement. They have discretion as to how to invest the money and must make substantive decisions about their own financial futures."[2]

DEFINED CONTRIBUTION PENSION PLAN   Over the last two decades, the defined-contribution plan has continued to grow rapidly, while the number of defined benefit

Exhibit 14–8

Sources of Retirement Income

SOURCE: Ho & Robinson, *Personal Financial Planning* Third Edition (Captus Press, 2000, page 383).

Pensions	Non-Pension Savings
Old Age Security (OAS)	Registered Retirement Savings Plan (RRSP)
Guaranteed Income Supplement (GIS)	Deferred Profit Sharing Plan (DPSP)
Canada Pension Plan (CPP)	House (if you trade down)
Employer's Registered Pension Plan (RPP)	Vacation property (if you will sell)
	Tax shelters
	Reverse mortgage
	Unsheltered savings
	Locked-in funds

[2] Carol Kleinman, "Firms Shifting Retirement Planning, Risk to Workers," *Chicago Tribune*, January 19, 1992, sec. 8, p. 1.

plans has generally dropped. A **defined contribution pension plan** has an individual account for each employee; therefore, these plans are sometimes called *money purchase pension plans*. The plan document describes the amount the employee and/or employer will contribute, but it does not promise any particular benefit. When a plan participant retires or otherwise becomes eligible for benefits, the benefit is the total amount in the participant's account, including past investment earnings on amounts put into the account.

What happens to your benefits under an employer pension plan if you change jobs? One of the most important aspects of such plans is vesting. **Vesting** is your right to at least a portion of the benefits you have accrued given the employer's contributions to a pension plan, even if you leave the company before you retire. Typically, you become vested when you complete two years of continuous service with a participating employer, unless your employer established a vesting period of less than two years. If you leave your employer before your benefits are vested, you are entitled to a refund of your contributions, plus interest.

DEFERRED PROFIT SHARING PLAN (DPSP)   Although not a registered pension plan governed by federal pension legislation, a DPSP is considered by some to be a company pension plan. A DPSP is a form of retirement saving set up for contributions from the employer only; these are tax-deductible for the company. The contribution is based on the company's net income according to an agreed-upon formula, and you will not be taxed on the DPSP holdings until you withdraw them.

One issue to consider with registered pension plans and DPSPs is that all contributions made to a defined contribution plan and deferred profit sharing plan, or deemed to have been made in the case of a defined benefit plan, reduce an individual's RRSP contribution room. Furthermore, while the employee's portion of the contribution to registered pension plans of both types (DCPP and DBPP) generates a non-refundable tax credit, the employer's contribution to a DPSP does not. As a result, the employee will not be able to make as large an RRSP contribution as otherwise might have been possible, but will not have any compensating tax credit.

GROUP REGISTERED RETIREMENT SAVINGS PLAN   This type of plan is an RRSP set up for a particular company's employees. The advantage this plan may have over a regular RPP relates to liquidity. Group RRSPs are the property of the employees, so they can take money out if they are in financial need (despite disincentives set up by the company to discourage this). Additionally, participation in a group RRSP by an employee may lower payroll tax withholding. The principal disadvantage to a group RRSP is that it may provide a smaller return than would a company pension plan.

PLAN PORTABILITY   At one time, employees who changed jobs could not take their pension credits with them. Recent legislation enforcing *pension portability*, the right to transfer pension credits from one employer to another, changed that. Now, workers with vesting rights have three different options when they change jobs. They can leave their pension credits with their former employer and receive a pension on retirement, transfer their credits to their new employer if that firm's policy permits it, or transfer their benefits to a locked-in RRSP. In cases where the employee has not met the criteria allowing them vesting rights, changing companies will signify a total loss of their pension credits.

Use the checklist in Exhibit 14–9 on the next page to help you determine what your pension plan provides and requires.

PERSONAL RETIREMENT PLANS

In addition to the retirement plans offered by public pension plans and employer pension plans, many individuals have set up personal retirement plans.

The most popular personal retirement plan is an RRSP.

defined contribution pension plan   Also called a "money purchase pension plan," this plan specifies the contribution from the employee and/or employer but does not guarantee the pension benefit you will receive.

vesting   An employee's right to at least a portion of the benefits accrued under an employer pension plan, even if the employee leaves the company before retiring.

Exhibit 14–9   Know Your Pension Plan Checklist

A. Plan Type Checklist

My plan is a:
☐ *Defined-benefit plan*
☐ *Defined-contribution plan*

B. Contributions Checklist

My pension plan is financed by:
☐ Employer contributions only.
☐ Employer and employee contributions.
☐ Union dues and assessments.
I contribute to my pension plan at the rate of
$_____ per I month I week I hour or
_____ percent of my compensation.

C. Vesting Checklist

My plan provides vesting after _____ years.
I need _____ more years of service to be fully
vested.

D. Credited Service Checklist

I will have a year of service under my pension plan:
☐ If I work _____ hours in a 12-consecutive-month
   period.
☐ If I meet other requirements (specify).
The plan year (12-month period for which plan
records are kept) ends on _____ of each year.
I will be credited for work performed:
☐ Before I became a participant in the plan.
☐ After the plan's normal retirement age.
As of now, _____ [date],
I have earned _____ years of service
toward my pension.

E. Retirement Benefit Checklist

I may begin to receive full normal retirement
benefits at age _____.
Working beyond the normal retirement age ☐ will
☐ will not increase the pension paid to me when
   I retire.
I may retire at age _____ if I have completed
_____ years of service. Apart from the age
requirement, I need _____ more years of service
to be eligible for early retirement benefits.
The amount of my normal retirement benefit is
computed as follows: _____
The amount of my early retirement benefit is
computed as follows: _____
My retirement benefit will be:
☐ Paid monthly for life.
☐ Paid to me in a lump sum.
☐ Adjusted to the cost of living.
☐ Paid to my survivor in the event of my death
   (see "Survivors' Benefit Checklist" below).

F. Disability Benefit Checklist

My plan ☐ does ☐ does not provide disability benefits.
My plan defines the term *disability* as follows: _____
_____
To be eligible for disability retirement benefits, I must
be _____ years old and must have _____ years of service.
A determination as to whether my condition meets
my plan's definition of disability is made by:
☐ A doctor chosen by me.
☐ A doctor designated by the plan administrator.
☐ Other.
I must send my application for disability retirement
benefits to _____ within _____ months
after I stop working.
If I qualify for disability benefits, I will continue to
receive benefits:
☐ For life, if I remain disabled.
☐ Until I return to my former job.
☐ Other.

G. Survivors' Benefit Checklist

My pension plan ☐ provides ☐ does not provide a
joint and survivor option or a similar provision for
death benefits.
My spouse and I ☐ have ☐ have not rejected in
writing the joint and survivor option.
Electing the joint and survivor option will reduce
my pension benefit to _____.
My survivor will receive _____ per month
for life if the following conditions are met (specify):
_____
_____.

H. Plan Termination Checklist

My benefits ☐ are ☐ are not insured.

I. Benefit Application Checklist

My employer ☐ will ☐ will not automatically
submit my pension application for me.
I must apply for my pension benefits ☐ on a special
form that I get from _____ within _____
months ☐ before ☐ after ☐ retire.
My application for pension benefits should be sent to
_____.
I must furnish the following documents when
applying for my pension benefits: _____.
If my application for pension benefits is denied, I may
appeal in writing to _____ within _____ days.

J. Suspension of Benefits Checklist

☐ I am covered by a single-employer plan or by a
   plan involving more than one employer.
☐ I am covered by a multi-employer plan.

SOURCE: Based on *Know Your Pension Plan* (Washington, DC: U.S. Department of Labor, 1992), pp. 5–10.

WHAT IS AN RRSP? An **RRSP** is an investment vehicle that allows you to shelter your savings from income taxes. Despite the common misconceptions, it is not a specific type of investment but a way to shelter your money in one or more of a variety of investment vehicles.

Legally, an RRSP is a trust, an arrangement in which certain property is given by a settlor to a trustee, an independent third party, who holds the property on behalf of the beneficiary (or beneficiaries) who will receive income and/or capital from the trust. As contributor to the plan you are the settlor, and more often than not the trustee is a bank, though it can also be a trust company, a brokerage firm, or a life insurance company. You are the beneficiary, unless you have designated the plan as a spousal RRSP, in which case your spouse is the beneficiary.

Perhaps the result of aggressive promotion in the personal finance industry, another common misconception about RRSPs is that everyone should have one. This is not correct. The principal motive behind RRSPs should be to allow you to defer taxation. The idea is to defer your income taxes to a time when your marginal rate of taxation will be less. Exhibit 14–10 on the next page shows the power of tax-deferred compounding of earnings. If your financial circumstances are already such that you pay little or no income tax, you likely don't need an RRSP or its restrictions—Canada's federal *Income Tax Act* allows you to register only certain specified investments as RRSPs. Other restrictions include contribution limits and early withdrawal penalties. These are discussed below.

Eligible Investments You can choose to register a number of investments, in combination or individually. Qualified investments include savings accounts, cash, Canada Savings Bonds and treasury bills, term deposits and GICs, corporate bonds (including stripped bonds), stocks, eligible mutual funds, and real estate. Qualified investments can be divided into three categories.

The first of the categories is *guaranteed funds*, such as savings accounts, term deposits, and GICs. These funds ensure the return of your principal plus a guaranteed rate of return, and are available from most financial institutions.

A second category of RRSP investments is *mutual funds*. These have no guarantee regarding rate of return or safety of your principal and are available from most financial institutions including investment dealers and life insurance companies. Mutual fund investments include equity funds, bond funds, balanced funds, and money market funds.

Finally, *life insurance and life annuity products*, sold by life insurance companies, may also qualify as RRSP investments. Be aware, however, that tying your life insurance to your RRSP may not be a sound financial plan, as doing so might require fixed annual payments that limit your annual contribution and your freedom to move your funds within the RRSP.

Types of RRSPs The most commonly held RRSP, known as a "regular" RRSP, is the type that most Canadians have. A regular RRSP draws on the two first categories of investments only. They are a popular choice because fees are minimal and your investments require minimal management by you, but the return on investment is lower, given that your funds are invested in principally low-risk, low-return investments.

The second main type of RRSP, a self-directed RRSP, allows you greater scope and permits you to invest in all categories. Available from most financial institutions, including investment dealers, this type of RRSP allows you to invest in cash, treasury bills, bonds (including CSBs), mortgages, mutual funds, and stocks. The fees are higher than for regular RRSPs, and you need to pay closer attention, but many people find that the investment return and other advantages outweigh the disadvantages engendered by price and effort.

Another type of registered pension plan is a spousal RRSP, which is also available to common-law couples and same-sex couples. With this plan, you contribute to an RRSP in which your spouse is named as the beneficiary. This can be especially useful in cases where one spouse does not participate in the labour market, such as when young children must be cared for. Note that your contribution reduces your allowable contribution to your own plan, and you may not transfer funds from your own RRSP to your spouse's except in conditions where one spouse dies or under court order following a break-up. Further, if your spouse withdraws the

Registered Retirement Savings Plan (RRSP) An investment vehicle that allows you to shelter your savings from income taxes.

Exhibit 14–10   Tackling the Trade-offs (Saving Now versus Saving Later)

SAVER: ABE				SAVER: BEN			
Age	Years	Contributions	Year-End Value	Age	Years	Contributions	Year-End Value
25	1	$2,000	$ 2,188	25	1	$ 0	$ 0
26	2	2,000	4,580	26	2	0	0
27	3	2,000	7,198	27	3	0	0
28	4	2,000	10,061	28	4	0	0
29	5	2,000	13,192	29	5	0	0
30	6	2,000	16,617	30	6	0	0
31	7	2,000	20,363	31	7	0	0
32	8	2,000	24,461	32	8	0	0
33	9	2,000	28,944	33	9	0	0
34	10	2,000	33,846	34	10	0	0
35	11	0	40,494	35	11	2,000	2,188
36	12	0	37,021	36	12	2,000	4,580
37	13	0	44,293	37	13	2,000	7,198
38	14	0	48,448	38	14	2,000	10,061
39	15	0	52,992	39	15	2,000	13,192
40	16	0	57,963	40	16	2,000	16,617
41	17	0	63,401	41	17	2,000	20,363
42	18	0	69,348	42	18	2,000	24,461
43	19	0	75,854	43	19	2,000	28,944
44	20	0	82,969	44	20	2,000	33,846
45	21	0	90,752	45	21	2,000	39,209
46	22	0	99,265	46	22	2,000	45,075
47	23	0	108,577	47	23	2,000	51,490
48	24	0	118,763	48	24	2,000	58,508
49	25	0	129,903	49	25	2,000	66,184
50	26	0	142,089	50	26	2,000	74,580
51	27	0	155,418	51	27	2,000	83,764
52	28	0	169,997	52	28	2,000	93,809
53	29	0	185,944	53	29	2,000	104,797
54	30	0	203,387	54	30	2,000	116,815
55	31	0	222,466	55	31	2,000	129,961
56	32	0	243,335	56	32	2,000	144,340
57	33	0	266,162	57	33	2,000	160,068
58	34	0	291,129	58	34	2,000	177,271
59	35	0	318,439	59	35	2,000	196,088
60	36	0	348,311	60	36	2,000	216,670
61	37	0	380,985	61	37	2,000	239,182
62	38	0	416,724	62	38	2,000	263,807
63	39	0	455,816	63	39	2,000	290,741
64	40	0	498,574	64	40	2,000	320,202
65	41	0	545,344	65	41	2,000	352,427
		$20,000				$62,000	

Value at retirement*			$545,344	Value at retirement*			$352,427
Less total contributions			$ 20,000	Less total contributions			$ 62,000
Net earnings			$525,344	Net earnings			$290,427

*The table assumes a 9-percent fixed rate of return, compounded monthly, and no fluctuation of the principal. Distributions from an RRSP are subject to ordinary income taxes when withdrawn and may be subject to other limitations under RRSP rules.
SOURCE: *The Franklin Investor* (San Mateo, CA: Franklin Distributors, Inc., January 1989).

www.mcgrawhill.ca/college/kapoor

funds sooner than two years plus the amount of time remaining in the year you make your contribution, the full amount of the funds will be taxed as though it were in your hands.

RRSP funds can also be used for a down payment on your first home under the Home Buyers' Plan. If you qualify as a first-time buyer you are allowed to withdraw up to $20,000 as a loan from your RRSP to buy or build a home, without counting the withdrawal as income. You must then repay the loan, without interest, over the next 15 years.

Generally, you will have to repay an amount to your RRSPs each year until you have repaid the entire amount you withdrew. If you do not repay the amount due for a year, it will be included in your income for that year.

RRSP funds can also be used to finance full-time training or education for you or your spouse or common-law partner under The Lifelong Learning Plan (LLP). LLP lets you withdraw up to $10,000 a year. You have to repay these withdrawals to your RRSPs over a period of no more than 10 years. Any amount that you do not repay when it is due will be included in your income for the year it was due. See how the Dlins used their RRSP in the Financial Planning for Life's Situations feature on the next page.

Contribution Limits If you have earned income (salary, wages, royalties, business income, rental income, or alimony) in a given year, you can contribute to your RRSP, but the amount allowable is subject to a maximum set by the government.

The amount of your maximum annual contribution depends on whether you also participate in an RPP, which has the effect of reducing your allowable contribution by a pension adjustment calculated by your employer and by the Canada Customs and Revenue Agency. The result of that calculation is sent to you late in each year and will differ for defined benefit plans and defined contribution plans.

If you don't participate in an RPP, you can contribute up to 18 percent of your earned income or the stated maximum, whichever is less. The maximum was $15,500 in 2004, $16,500 in 2005, and will rise to $22,000 in 2010 (as proposed in the 2005 federal budget). Having invested the maximum, your earnings would have to be $86,111 in 2004, $91,667 in 2005, and $122,222 in 2010.

There are also other rules to consider. You are allowed to exceed your limit by $2,000 without incurring a penalty, but beyond this amount, you will be fined 1 percent per month. Further, in the event that you are unable to make your full contribution to the plan, you are allowed to "carry forward" the full amount of unpaid contribution to a later year. This means that if you for any reason have a year in which savings are minimal, you will be able to make up for your contribution shortfall by investing more in a year when you can put more aside.

OPTIONS WHEN YOU DEREGISTER AN RRSP Your RRSP must be deregistered by the end of the year of your 69th birthday. At that point, you will have six choices as to what to do with your funds. The options available are to withdraw the funds and pay the income tax, purchase a single-payment life annuity, purchase a fixed-term annuity, set up a Registered Retirement Income Fund (RRIF), set up a Life Income Fund (LIF), or set up a segregated fund. Each option is discussed below.

Full Withdrawal The least favourable option when you deregister your RRSP is to simply withdraw the funds and pay the income tax on them, as doing so will negate the whole purpose of using this tax minimization tool. It is likely that your accumulated funds will be large enough to draw the highest marginal tax rate if you accept them as a lump sum. At the time of withdrawal, the financial institution is required to apply a withholding tax calculated as a percentage of the sum withdrawn. For example, withdraw less than $5,000 and there is a 10 percent withholding tax (outside Quebec); withdraw $5,001 to $15,000 and there is a 20 percent withholding tax; withdraw $15,001 plus and there is a 30 percent withholding tax. The full withdrawal must be added to your taxable income and the withholding tax is entered as the tax already paid. Any additional taxes due are determined the following April when you file your

By Camilla Cornell,
IE:Money

For 29-year-old Rich Dlin, contributing to an RRSP was, he says, "part of my socialization. It's something you just do." Since he graduated from university with a joint math and teaching degree in 1999, and married Marla Nadler-Dlin, 28, the couple has managed to save an average of $5,000 a year between them—even without the benefit of a financial planner to lay down the law.

That money has given them options that aren't available to others in their age bracket. Instead of spending money on rent, the couple took advantage of the federal government's New Home Buyers' Plan to roll their RRSP money into a down payment on a condominium in 2000, without having to pay a tax penalty.

By the time their son Jonah was born two years later, the Dlins were able to trade the condo for a house. And, when Marla opted to give up her job as an accounts manager with a mid-sized company in favour of self-employment last year, they had enough money in RRSPs to provide a cushion should things not work out.

While retirement may be in the distant future for those under 35, Lenore Davis, a registered financial planner and senior partner with Dixon, Davis & Co. in Victoria,

B.C., points out that having some assets can have implications for the present as well—as Rich and Marla's experience shows. "If you've got an asset base, you've got the freedom to pick and choose your jobs and your lifestyle," says Davis. "The people who don't have options are the people who have nothing to fall back on."

In addition, the couple is getting all the conventional benefits of an RRSP: namely, the investments are tax deductible, while the earnings accumulate tax free until you take them out, ostensibly at retirement—at which time, your income level and tax rate are both going to be lower. Rich, a self-employed computer consultant in the 26-percent tax bracket, figures it out this way: "If I contribute $100, that reduces my taxable income by $100, which reduces how much tax I'm going to pay by $26. That's $26 in my account, rather than Revenue Canada's." He admits he and Marla puzzled over whether to opt out of RRSP contributions for a few years and focus on paying down their mortgage. But they came to the conclusion that if they put money into an RRSP, they could use the tax refund to pay down their mortgage, getting maximum bang for their buck.

SOURCE: www.slam.ca/IEMoneyFeb99/ie_rrsps35. html.

income tax return. If, by chance, the withholding tax exceeds the tax bill generated by the withdrawal, you will receive a tax refund at the time of filing your annual return.

Annuities Annuities are an investment that usually pays a fixed level of payments on a regular basis (usually monthly or annually) for either a specified amount of time or until the death of the holder. They are meant to provide retirement income in much the same way as a salary provides regular income. If the annuity is bought with funds from a registered plan, then the purchase of the annuity is tax free, but the entire amount of each annuity payment is taxed. There are two main types of annuities: life annuities and fixed-term period annuities.

Following is a list of advantages and disadvantages that annuities have over other retirement income options:

Advantages
- Payment can continue until death, if it is a life annuity
- Level payments may suit your income needs better
- Simplicity—not having to worry about investments or withdrawals
- No heavy record-keeping requirements
- A legitimate tax shelter
- No investment limits
- Tax-free transfers between annuity companies

Disadvantages
- Less control over investments
- Less control over payout of income

- No protection from inflation, unless it is indexed
- No opportunity for retirement income to grow
- No opportunity for tax deferral
- Can't take out a lump sum for major purchases, unless cashable
- No protection for spouse, unless joint or a guaranteed minimum payout is specified
- No estate planning benefits, unless joint or a guaranteed minimum payout is specified

Make sure you take into consideration such fees as commission, underwriting, fund management, and penalties, when choosing your annuity provider.

Life Annuities If you purchase a single-payment life annuity, then the full amount of your RRSP funds will be transferred directly to the life insurance company from which you bought the annuity. The company will then convert those funds into a lifetime income payable to you, and your marginal rate of taxation will be based on your annual income rather than the whole of your funds. At any time, you have the option to cancel the annuity and take the commuted value of the remaining payments. Having done so, you can then either remove the funds from the tax shelter and pay the tax, or you can roll the funds over into an RRIF, discussed below. It must be noted that when the holder dies, there will be no payment to the beneficiary or estate if the guaranteed minimum number of payments has been made.

Fixed-Term Annuities Fixed-term annuities are available from both life insurance companies and trust companies. As with the life annuity above, this method allows you to convert your RRSP funds into income. The principal difference is that the benefit paid and cost of this type of annuity is not based upon your life expectancy, or on the pooling of your funds with those of others. Instead, your funds are simply converted into an income stream to be paid out for a fixed term. In the event that you die prior to the end of the term, the remaining unpaid funds will be paid to your estate or beneficiary, and your monthly income is based on the amount of your purchase, the term, and the current interest rates. As with the life annuity, you have the option to cancel at any time and either pay the taxes on the commuted value or roll it over to an RRIF.

Registered Retirement Income Funds (RRIFs) An RRIF is similar to a self-directed RRSP in that you can make your own investment decisions if you choose. Alternatively, you may also set one up so that little management is required. In either case, the Canada Customs and Revenue Agency will require that you withdraw a minimum amount from the plan until you reach the age of 71. The minimum withdrawal amount starts at 4.76 percent of the total value of the RRIF at age 69 and increases incrementally to 20 percent by age 94. You can adjust the amount and the frequency of the payments you receive. Monthly, quarterly, semi-annual, or annual payments are all options, as are lump-sum withdrawals. For example, if you have a RRIF worth $250, 000 and are aged 65 on January 1, in that year you will be required to withdraw at least $11, 900 (4.76 percent of $250,000) and will be accordingly taxed on that amount. Exhibit 14–11 on the next page shows a sample RRIF contract.

Life Income Funds (LIFs) Upon terminating your membership in your company RPP, or when you have transferred funds from a locked-in RRSP, you may elect to purchase an LIF. This income fund is available in all provinces, and the minimum deposit you must make to start one is $10,000. Similar to an RRIF, with an LIF you must withdraw a minimum amount every year, and the tax treatment is the same, but with this plan you are also subject to a maximum annual withdrawal amount based on interest rates and available investment returns. The balance of the funds in your LIF must be used to purchase a life annuity before December 31 of the year you turn 80. If you die before the end of the LIF term, the amount remaining in the fund will go to your designated beneficiary.

Segregated Funds Similar to mutual funds, but sold exclusively through life insurance companies, a segregated fund is essentially the purchase of units representing a share in a pool

Exhibit 14–11

RRIF Minimum
Withdrawal
Amounts

SOURCE:
www.canadian
moneysaver.ca

Age	Percentage	Age	Percentage
69	4.76	81	8.99
70	5.00	82	9.27
71	7.38	83	9.58
72	7.48	84	9.93
73	7.59	85	1.33
74	7.71	86	10.79
75	7.85	87	11.33
76	7.99	88	11.96
77	8.15	89	12.71
78	8.33	90	13.62
79	8.53	91	14.73
80	8.75	92	16.12
		93	17.92
		94	20.00
		95	20.00

of assets supervised by a fund manager. The term "segregated" refers to the fact that the money in these funds is kept separate from the company's other assets. The principal advantages that segregated funds have over mutual funds are (1) that when you die, your fund's assets go directly to your beneficiary rather than to your estate, and (2) that a percentage of your capital is guaranteed no matter how poorly the fund performs. The percentage is generally around 75 percent but can go as high as 100 percent, in which case your only concern would be the depreciation of your money due to inflation.

WILL YOU HAVE ENOUGH MONEY DURING RETIREMENT?

Now that you have reviewed all the possible sources of your retirement income, estimate what your annual retirement income will be. Don't forget to inflate incomes or investments that increase with the cost of living (such as CPP benefits) to what they will be when you retire. (Use the inflation factor table in the Financial Planning Calculations box on page 415.) Remember, inflation is a major uncontrollable variable for retirees.

Now, compare your total estimated retirement income with your total inflated retirement expenses. If your estimated income exceeds your estimated expenses and a large portion of your planned income will automatically increase with the cost of living during your retirement, you are in good shape. (You should evaluate your plans every few years between now and retirement to be sure your planned income is still adequate to meet your planned expenses.)

If, however, your planned retirement income is less than your estimated retirement expenses, now is the time to take action to increase your retirement income. Also, if a large portion of your retirement income is fixed and will not increase with inflation, you should make plans for a much larger retirement income to meet your rising expenses during retirement.

CONCEPT CHECK 14–5

1. What are possible sources of income for retirees?
2. How do defined-contribution plans differ from defined-benefit plans?
3. What options do you have for deregistering your retirement investments?

Miss White is 34 years old and is employed as a Senior Sales Representative for a small technology company in Montreal. Her gross annual salary is $30,000, and she has 31 years left to retirement. Miss White recently came into a $10,000 inheritance left to her by her grandmother. Should Miss White use the $10,000 to pay down her mortgage or contribute it to an RRSP? There are many factors to consider before we can make our decision. We are assuming the following:

- Marginal tax rate of approximately: 26%[1]
- RRSP annual compound rate: 8%[2]
- Whether or not she has achieved maximum contribution to her RRSP for current or previous years: No
- Amortization period: 25 years
- Frequency of payments: Monthly
- Mortgage term: Fixed rate 10 year closed at 8.15%[3], in the first year of payment.
- Down payment: $10,000 (High ratio mortgage)
- Mortgage amount: $79,000
- Total value of house and property: $89,000
- Prepayment penalties on mortgage: None, unless exceeding the 10–20% of the remaining capital.[4]

We are assuming that because of her young age, she will have plenty of time and money to pay off her mortgage and contribute to her RRSP. Given this factor, we are leaning towards the option of placing the $10,000 in her RRSP. In addition, we know that an RRSP contribution will reduce her taxable income and will most likely give her a tax refund, which she can then apply as a mortgage payment. Those closer to retirement may be tempted to pay down their mortgage and rightfully own their house sooner.

Miss White has placed a $10,000 down payment on her home and has foregone any contributions toward an RRSP. However, she can go back seven years and make payments of up to 18 percent or $13,500 (the lower dollar amount of the two options) of her income toward this RRSP. Therefore, she will be able to contribute $10,800 for the past two tax years (18% × $30,000 = $5,400, then $5,400 × 2 = $10,800). This guarantees that the option to contribute to her RRSP is open.

Financial advisers recommend that you pay down your mortgage in the earlier stages of its life span. Miss White is in the first year of mortgage payments; approximately 85 percent of her payment is still going towards the interest. Gaining equity in your home sounds like an attractive offer. Laws favour home ownership. "Once you build equity in your home, you'll never again pay the high non-deductible interest expense charged on credit cards, car loans, and other consumer debts. As a homeowner, you can obtain a low interest rate home equity loan (tax-deductible, no less) to cover your essential borrowing needs."[5]

The following numerical example evaluates the differences between applying a one-time lump sum against the principal of a mortgage versus an RRSP and the likely outcomes of both situations.

Scenario	Years to Pay off Mortgage	Mortgage Savings	Extra RRSP Savings	Total Benefit
#1: Apply lump sum to mortgage	17.8	$43,670	N/A	$43,670
#2: Invest lump sum in RRSP + apply tax savings to the next mortgage payment	22.7	$17,135	$70,143	$87,278

It is clear from our calculations, if she chose scenario #2, not only would Miss White reduce the life of her mortgage, but she would be able to build a nest egg. The total benefit in scenario 2 exceeds scenario 1 by an amazing amount of $43,608.

In conclusion, "Choosing between putting more money into your RRSP or paying down your mortgage involves a lot of serious number crunching, and the results depend on your mortgage rate, how many years you have left before your mortgage is paid off, as well as the return on your RRSP. Because of all the variables, some of which are hard to nail down, a good compromise is to maximize your RRSP contributions and to take the tax refund that the contributions earns you and put it down against your mortgage."[6] In other words, we are going to have our cake and eat it, too!

BIBLIOGRAPHY

1. www.hrblock.ca. From this site, we discovered how to determine the marginal tax rate, given our annual salary, and we used the Mortgage Calculator.
2. www.scotiabank.com/invest—RRSP rate of return.
3. www.bmo.com/mortgage—Terms of mortgage.
4. *Buying and Selling a Home for Canadians for Dummies*, by Tony Ioannou, Moira Bayne, Wendy Yano. CDG Books Canada Inc. Toronto, Ontario, 2000.
5. *106 Common Mistakes Home Owner's Make and How to Avoid Them*, 3rd Edition. by Gary W. Eldred PhD., published by John Wiley & Sons Inc. New York, 2002.
6. *Personal Finance for Canadians for Dummies*, 3rd Edition, by Eric Tyson, Tony Martin. CDG Books Canada Inc. Toronto, Ontario, 2001.

SOURCE: Assignment by Alexandra Fuoco and Christina Fuoco for the Introductory Personal Finance Course Comm499F JMSB, Concordia University, Fall 2001.

LIVING ON YOUR RETIREMENT INCOME

■ OBJECTIVE 6 ▮

Develop a balanced budget based on your retirement income.

As you planned retirement, you estimated a budget or spending plan, but you may find your actual expenses at retirement are higher than anticipated.

The first step in stretching your retirement income is to make sure you are receiving all of the income to which you are entitled. Examine the possible sources of retirement income mentioned earlier to see whether you could qualify for more programs or additional benefits. What assets or valuables could you use as a cash or income source?

To stay within your income, you may also need to make some changes in your spending plans. For example, you can use your skills and time instead of your money. There are probably many things you can do yourself instead of paying someone else to do them. Take advantage of free and low-cost recreation, such as walks, picnics, public parks, lectures, museums, libraries, art galleries, art fairs, gardening, and church and club programs.

TAX ADVANTAGES

Be sure to take full advantage of all the tax savings and benefits available to retirees. For more information, contact Human Resources and Development Canada (HRDC; www.hrsdc-gc.ca/en/home.shtml). The HRDC provides a number of guides and publications available to help you understand your available options.

WORKING DURING RETIREMENT

You may want to work part time or start a new part-time career after you retire. Work can provide you with a greater sense of usefulness, involvement, and self-worth and may be the ideal way to add to your retirement income. You may want to pursue a personal interest or hobby, or you can contact your provincial or local agency on aging for information about employment opportunities for retirees.

Exhibit 14–12   Dipping into Your Nest Egg

Starting Amount of Nest Egg	You Can Reduce Your Nest Egg to Zero by Withdrawing This Much Each Month for the Stated Number of Years...					Or You Can Withdraw This Much Each Month and Leave Your Nest Egg Intact
	10 Years	15 Years	20 Years	25 Years	30 Years	
$ 10,000	$ 107	$ 81	$ 68	$ 61	$ 56	$ 46
15,000	161	121	102	91	84	69
20,000	215	162	136	121	112	92
25,000	269	202	170	152	140	115
30,000	322	243	204	182	168	138
40,000	430	323	272	243	224	184
50,000	537	404	340	304	281	230
60,000	645	485	408	364	337	276
80,000	859	647	544	486	449	368
100,000	1,074	808	680	607	561	460

Note: Based on an interest rate of 5.5 percent per year, compounded quarterly.
SOURCE: Select Committee on Aging, U.S. House of Representatives.

Over 50 percent of recent retirees want to continue working part time or even full time after retirement, and only a small percentage are worried about outliving their financial resources. There is a rich talent pool of Canadians in the 55 to 75 age range, over 50 percent of whom are retired—and many of them are interested in continued employment. These individuals, with their proven skills and abilities, provide a flexible, cost-effective resource that can sustain our productivity gains and economic growth. What drives many of them is the desire to remain productively engaged in life.

If you decide to work part time after you retire, you should be aware of how your earnings will affect your public pension income. As long as you do not earn more than the annually exempt amount, your payments will not be affected. But if you earn more than the annual exempt amount, your payments will be reduced. Check with your Human Resources and Development Canada office for the latest information.

INVESTING FOR RETIREMENT

The guaranteed-income part of your retirement fund consists of money paid into lower-yield, very safe investments. To offset inflation, your retirement assets must earn enough to keep up with, and even exceed, the rate of inflation.

DIPPING INTO YOUR NEST EGG

When should you draw on your savings? The answer depends on your financial circumstances, your age, and how much you want to leave to your heirs. Your savings may be large enough to

Exhibit 14–13   Major Sources of Retirement Income: Advantages and Disadvantages

Source	Advantages	Disadvantages
Public Pension Plans		
In planning	Forced savings	Increasing economic pressure on the system
	Portable from job to job	as population ages
	Cost shared with employer	
At retirement	Inflation-adjusted survivorship rights	Minimum retirement age specified
		Earned income may partially offset benefits
Employee Pension Plans		
In planning	Forced savings	May not be portable
	Cost shared or fully covered by employer	No control over how funds are managed
At retirement	Survivorship rights	Cost-of-living increases may not be provided on a regular basis
Individual Saving and Investing (including housing, LIF, and RRSP plans)		
In planning	Current tax savings (e.g., RRSPs)	Current needs compete with future needs
	Easily incorporated into family (i.e., housing)	Penalty for early withdrawal (RRSPs and LIF)
	Portable	
	Control over management of funds	
At retirement	Inflation resistant	Some sources taxable
	Can usually use as much of the funds as you wish, when you wish (within certain requirements)	Mandatory minimum withdrawal restrictions (RRIF and LIF)
Post-retirement Employment		
In planning	Special earning skills can be used as they are developed	Technology and skills needed to keep up may change rapidly
At retirement	Inflation resistant	Ill health can mean loss of this income source

As you approach retirement, assess your financial condition using the following checklist.

Don't wait too long, or you will miss one or more opportunities to maximize your future financial independence.

	Yes	No
1. Do you talk regularly and frankly to family members about finances and agree on your goals and the lifestyle you will prefer as you get older?	☐	☐
2. Do you know what your sources of income will be after retirement, how much to expect from each source, and when?	☐	☐
3. Do you save according to your plan, shifting from growth-producing to safe, income-producing investments?	☐	☐
4. Do you have your own credit history?	☐	☐
5. Do you have a current will or a living trust?	☐	☐
6. Do you know where you plan to live in retirement?	☐	☐
7. Do you anticipate the tax consequences of your retirement plans and of passing assets on to your heirs?	☐	☐
8. Do your children or other responsible family members know where your important documents are and whom to contact if questions arise?	☐	☐
9. Do you have legal documents, such as a living will or a power of attorney, specifying your instructions in the event of your death or incapacitating illness?	☐	☐

SOURCE: Adapted from *Staying Independent*, American Express Consumer Affairs Office and IDS Financial Services Inc.

Visit the Web site
See the Post-Test under Chapter 14 on the online learning centre at www.mcgrawhill.ca/ college/kapoor.

allow you to live comfortably on the interest alone. Or you may need to make regular withdrawals to help finance your retirement. Dipping into savings isn't wrong, but you must do so with caution.

How long would your savings last if you withdrew monthly income? If you have $10,000 in savings that earns 5.5 percent interest, compounded quarterly, you could take out $68 every month for 20 years before reducing this nest egg to zero. If you have $40,000, you could collect $224 every month for 30 years before exhausting your nest egg. For different possibilities, see Exhibit 14–12 on page 428.

Exhibit 14–13 on the previous page summarizes major sources of retirement income and their advantages and disadvantages. Finally, use the Financial Planning for Life's Situations box above to assess your financial condition as you approach retirement.

CONCEPT CHECK 14–6

1. What is the first step in stretching your retirement income?
2. How should you invest to obtain retirement income?

SUMMARY OF OBJECTIVES

Objective 1
Recognize the importance of retirement planning.
Retirement planning is important because you will probably spend many years in retirement; public pensions and a private pension may be insufficient to cover the cost of living; and inflation may erode the purchasing power of your retirement savings. Many young people are reluctant to think about retirement, but they should start retirement planning now, before they reach age 40.

Objective 2
Analyze your current assets and liabilities for retirement.
Analyze your current assets (everything you own) and your current liabilities (everything you owe). The difference between your assets and your liabilities is your net worth. Review your assets to ensure they are sufficient for retirement.

Objective 3
Estimate your retirement spending needs.
Since the spending patterns of retirees change, it is impossible to predict the exact amount of money you will need in retirement. However, you can estimate your expenses. Some of those expenses will increase; others will decrease. The expenses that are likely to be lower or eliminated are work-related expenses, clothing, housing expenses, federal income taxes, and commuting expenses.

Objective 4
Identify your retirement housing needs.
Where you live in retirement can influence your financial needs. You are the only one who can determine the location and housing that are best for you. Would you like to live in your present home or move to a new location? Consider the social aspects of moving.

Objective 5
Determine your planned retirement income.
Estimate your retirement expenses and adjust those expenses for inflation using the appropriate inflation factor. Your possible sources of income during retirement include the CPP, other public pension plans, employer pension plans, and personal retirement plans.

Objective 6
Develop a balanced budget based on your retirement income.
Compare your total estimated retirement income with your total inflated retirement expenses. If your income approximates your expenses, you are in good shape; if not, determine additional income needs and sources.

KEY TERMS

defined benefit pension plan 418
defined contribution pension plan 419

Registered Retirement Savings Plan (RRSP) 421

reverse annuity mortgage (RAM) 408
vesting 419

FINANCIAL PLANNING PROBLEMS

1. *Preparing a Net Worth Statement.* Prepare your net worth statement using the guidelines presented in Exhibit 14–3. (Obj. 2)

2. *Comparing Spending Patterns during Retirement.* How will your spending patterns change during your retirement years? Compare your spending patterns with those shown in Exhibit 14–4. (Obj. 3)

3. Jean and Dan Sladek both work. Each earns a salary of $30,000, but only Jean is a member of a registered pension plan. Both she and her employer contribute 2 percent of her gross salary to a defined contribution pension plan. Dan has

$15,000 of unused contribution room carried forward since 1991. Calculate the maximum RRSP contribution that each can make. (Obj. 5)

4. *Calculating Net Pay and Spendable Income.* Assume your gross pay per pay period is $2,000 and you are in the 26-percent tax bracket (ignore provincial tax). Calculate your net pay and spendable income in the following situations: (Obj. 5)

   a. You save $200 per pay period after paying income tax on $2,000.

   b. You save $200 per pay period in an RPP.

5. *Calculating Monthly Withdrawals.* You have $50,000 in your retirement fund that is earning 5.5 percent per year, compounded quarterly. How many dollars in withdrawals per month would reduce this nest egg to zero in 20 years? How many dollars per month can you withdraw for as long as you live and still leave this nest egg intact? (Obj. 6)

FINANCIAL PLANNING ACTIVITIES

1. *Conducting Interviews.* Survey friends, relatives, and other people to get their views on retirement planning. Prepare a written report of your findings. (Obj. 1)

2. *Obtaining Information about Reverse Mortgages.* Obtain consumer information about reverse mortgages in the Royal Bank's *Your Money Matters*, available in all Royal Bank branches or online at www.royalbank.com. Evaluate the information. How might a reverse mortgage help you or a member of your family? (Obj. 2)

3. *Determining Expenses during Retirement.* Read newspaper or magazine articles to determine what expenses are likely to increase and decrease during retirement. How might this information affect your retirement-planning decisions? (Obj. 3)

4. *Evaluating Retirement Housing Options.* Which type of housing will best meet your retirement needs? Is such housing available in your community? Make a checklist of the advantages and disadvantages of your housing choice. (Obj. 4)

5. *Balancing a Retirement Budget.* Outline the steps you must take to live on your retirement income and balance your retirement budget. (Obj. 6)

CREATING A FINANCIAL PLAN

Planning for Retirement

Long-term financial security is a common goal of most people. Retirement planning should consider both personal decisions (location, housing, activities) and financial factors (investments, pensions, living expenses).

Web Sites for Retirement Planning

- Revenue Canada, at **www.ccra-adrc.gc.ca**, provides important tax-related retirement information through its Forms and Publications link.
- RetireWeb, at **www.retireweb.com**, provides information on retirement planning and activities. A great site, it also provides annuity, life expectancy, RRIF, and other calculators.
- The Canadian Association for Retired People, at **www.carp.ca**, is a non-profit organization dedicated to 50+ lifestyles.
- Cannex, at **www.cannex.com**, is an online financial rate site providing up-to-date rates for annuities, GICs, RRSPs, mortgages, and other financial products. It is a great site to get information on the current market.
- Benefits Canada, at **www.benefitscanada.com**, is a magazine that claims to provide the most current pension and investment information available in Canada.

- Seniors Canada On-line, at **http://www.seniors.gc.ca/**, provides single-window access to Web-based information and services that are relevant to seniors 55+, their families, caregivers, and supporting service organizations.
- Human Resources Development Canada (HRDC), **http://www.hrdc-drhc.gc.ca/menu/seniors.shtml**, provides detailed information for seniors on retirement issues.

(Note: Addresses and content of Web Sites change, and new sites are created daily. Use search engines to update and locate Web sites for your current financial planning needs.)

Short-Term Financial Planning Activities

1. Identify personal and financial retirement needs for various stages of your life.
2. Compare the benefits and costs of an RRSP, an RPP, and other pension plans.

Long-Term Financial Planning Activities

1. Research costs and benefits of various housing alternatives.
2. Estimate future retirement income needs and identify appropriate investments to meet those needs.
3. Develop a plan for expanding personal interests and increasing contributions to retirement accounts.

LIFE SITUATION CASE

To Be Young, Thrifty, and in the Black: The Importance of Starting Early

Ann Farrell, a 28-year-old hydrogeologist, is one of the lucky ones. As a college senior in 1991, Farrell attended a seminar on investing early for retirement. "I remembered the figures if you started saving when you were young," she says. Indeed, the payoff is huge. Through compounding, 25-year-olds who invest $2,000 a year and stop at 34 will earn $142,000 more by the time they are 65 than someone who begins investing $2,000 at 35 and contributes $2,000 each year for the next 30 years.

Farrell already has $22,000 in her RRSP. That's a nice start compared with most of her peers. Research has found that nearly 70 percent of adults ages 22 to 32 have saved less than $10,000 for retirement.

When Farrell was a new employee in 1991 at an environmental consulting firm, she was barred for a year from the company's pension plan. Once eligible, she committed 8 percent of her paycheque in the two most aggressive stock funds offered (retirement growth and asset manager). The company matched 50 percent of her pre-tax contributions, up to 5 percent of her $28,000 salary.

Of course, it helped that her expenses were low. After graduation, Farrell—with only $500 to her name—moved back in with her parents, who charged her $200 a month for rent. She also travelled three out of every four weeks on work. "There is nowhere to spend money on the road," she claims. Still, she had to repay a $10,000 school loan and a $4,000 car loan. She also wanted to build an emergency fund. Once she began making headway on these goals, Farrell moved to her own place and gradually increased her pre-tax contribution to 10 percent. Last year, she upped it to 13 percent. The government allows employees to make a pre-tax contribution of up to $13,500 a year. Farrell is currently chipping in about $5,000 a year.

Oddly, the lack of growth in environmental consulting has worked to Farrell's benefit. While most Gen-Xers find themselves job hopping every two years or so to get ahead, Farrell stayed put because there wasn't much movement in her industry. So, she will become fully vested in her RPP this October, after five years in the plan.

Farrell has done a lot right, but she has a long road ahead of her. When she makes her next move—she may leave her company and go to business school—she needs to recognize the potholes that exist when protecting her retirement assets. For instance, if she decides to roll over her RPP, she'll have to examine all of the investment options and rollover requirements. If she doesn't, she could lose her head start on retirement savings.

Questions

1. What did Ann Farrell learn when she attended a seminar on retirement?
2. How much money did Farrell originally commit to her company pension plan? In what funds did she invest her money?
3. What is the maximum contribution Farrell can make to her RRSP?
4. After how long and when did Farrell become fully vested in her RPP?

SOURCE: Adapted from Toddi Guttner, "To Be Young, Thrifty, and in the Black," *Business Week*, July 21, 1997, p. 76.

15

Estate Planning

A PLAN FOR THE ENDGAME

Harry Frank talked to his lawyer about drafting a living will, but never completed one. Then, in 1995, he suffered severe brain damage in an automobile accident and spent three years in a persistent vegetative state. Last year, after his wife moved him to a nursing home to be close to his parents, she requested that his feeding tube be removed. Other family members objected. The device eventually was withdrawn, and Frank died—but only after an agonizing legal battle that tore his family apart.

Imagine suffering a stroke or being left in a coma as a result of an auto accident. Would you want to be kept on life support, fed through a tube, or given pain-controlling drugs, even if they hastened your death? You have the right to make these choices. You'll need two documents, called *advanced directives:* a living will that tells doctors and hospitals how you want to be cared for should you become terminally ill, and a health-care proxy who designates an advocate who can make sure your wishes are honoured.

Living wills do not give a hospital the right to "pull the plug" without consent of a patient's legal representative. If you want doctors to exhaust every effort to keep you alive, no matter what, you can also request that in a living will. You can say: "I don't want anything done," or you can say: "I want absolutely everything." Lawyers say it is important to be as specific as possible. If you want morphine or other pain medication in your last days, even if it is addictive or makes you drowsy, say so. If you want life support turned off if you are near death, write that down, too. Whatever its contents, a living will is one legal document that should not be kept in your safety deposit box. Give copies to your lawyer, your doctor, and your adult children, and take one to the hospital on your next visit.

Putting your wishes in writing does not guarantee that a hospital will honour them, however. To make sure it does, you'll need to appoint a legal representative, usually a relative or friend, who can handle your health-care decisions if you cannot. You make this choice by executing a designation of health-care proxy, health-care surrogate, or medical power of attorney. You might want to make your spouse your representative. But think about giving backup power to an adult child if you are not sure your spouse could handle such difficult decisions at a time of great stress.

QUESTIONS

1 How can you protect your wishes and your peace of mind with a living will?

2 Would you want to be kept on life support? Why, or why not?

3 In your opinion, who should have the right to make life-and-death decisions?

4 Should you keep your living will in a safety deposit box? Why, or why not?

LEARNING OBJECTIVES

1 Analyze the personal aspects of estate planning.

2 Assess the legal aspects of estate planning.

3 Distinguish among formats of wills.

4 Appraise various types of trusts and estates.

WHY ESTATE PLANNING?

Your **estate** consists of everything you own. While you work, your objective is to accumulate funds for your future and for your dependants. As you grow older, your point of view will change. The emphasis in your financial planning will shift from accumulating assets to distributing them wisely. Your hard-earned wealth should go to those whom you wish to support and not to the various taxation agencies.

Contrary to widely held notions, estate planning, which includes wills and trusts, is useful not just to rich and elderly people. Trusts can be used for purposes other than tax advantages, such as choosing a guardian for children and avoiding family fights over personal belongings. Furthermore, most people can afford the expense of using them.

This chapter discusses a subject most people would rather avoid: death—your own or that of your spouse. Many people give little or no thought to setting their personal and financial affairs in order.

As you learned in Chapter 14, most people today live longer than those of previous generations and have ample time to think about and plan for the future. Yet, a large percentage of people do little or nothing to provide for those who will survive them.

Planning for your family's financial security in the event of your death or the death of your spouse is not easy. Therefore, the objective of this chapter is to help you initiate discussions about questions you should ask before that happens. Does your spouse, for instance, know what all of the family's resources and debts are? Does your family have enough insurance protection?

The question of whether your family can cope financially without your or your spouse's income and support is a difficult one. This chapter can't provide all of the answers, but it supplies a basis for sound estate planning for you and your family.

WHAT IS ESTATE PLANNING?

Estate planning is a definite plan for the administration and disposition of one's property during one's lifetime and at one's death. Thus, it involves both handling your property while you are alive and dealing with what happens to that property after your death.

Estate planning is an essential part of retirement planning and an integral part of financial planning. It has two components. The first consists of building your estate through savings, investments, and insurance. The second involves transferring your estate, at your death, in the manner you have specified. As this chapter explains, an estate plan is usually implemented by a will and one or more trust agreements.

Nearly every adult engages in financial decision making and must keep important records. Whatever your status—single or married, male or female, taxi driver or corporate executive—you must make financial decisions that are important to you. Those decisions may be even more important to others in your family. Knowledge in certain areas and good recordkeeping can simplify those decisions.

At first, planning for financial security and estate planning may seem complicated. Although many money matters require legal and technical advice, if you and your spouse learn the necessary skills, you will find yourselves managing your money affairs more efficiently and wisely.

■ **OBJECTIVE 1** ■

Analyze the personal aspects of estate planning.

estate Everything one owns.

Visit the Web site
See the Post Test under Chapter 15 on the online learning centre at www.mcgrawhill.ca/college/kapoor.

estate planning
A definite plan for the administration and disposition of one's property during one's lifetime and at one's death.

Begin by answering the questionnaire in the Financial Planning for Life's Situations box on the next page to see how much you and your family know about your own money affairs. You and your family should be able to answer some of these questions. The questions can be bewildering if the subjects are unfamiliar to you, but after reading this chapter, you'll be able to answer most of them.

PROVINCIAL FAMILY LAW

Provincial family law can have a significant impact on your estate planning. Getting married, for example, will usually void a will made prior to the wedding. Equally, divorce and separation might also affect the validity of part or all of a will.

Provincial family law might also impact your capacity to order the disposition of your estate. In effect, you must provide for the support of your spouse, dependent children, and other family members who can prove personal financial needs that have normally been met by you. If inadequate provisions are made, your will can be contested and declared invalid. The court will order the estate to make provision for dependants according to the law of the province. Family law also stipulates similar support in the event of a marital breakdown. Notice, however, that these laws do not oblige the deceased to provide for family members who were not being financially supported at the time of death.

The particular nature and scope of the laws vary from province to province, although the motive behind these laws is always the same. The idea is to protect those who have traditionally needed to depend on you and to ensure a just distribution of your estate. While provincial family law differs significantly across Canada and can be very complex, in the event that a marriage terminates through death or divorce, most legislation provides for the equal division between spouses of *family assets* acquired during the marriage. Exceptions are often made for gifts, inheritances, lottery winnings, and insurance settlements received during the marriage, and any property brought into the marriage, with the exception of the matrimonial home. Even the definition of family assets that may be subject to division can differ from province to province. Quebec, for example, has a much more restrictive definition than other provinces, covering only the family's residences, furnishings, motor vehicles, and pension benefits acquired during the course of the marriage. It should be noted that most provinces do not yet recognize common-law unions for purposes of determining matrimonial rights.

Regardless of your familial situation, you should take the necessary steps to ensure that you clearly make your desires known regarding your estate. While these instructions might be constrained somewhat by your provincial laws, the alternative is to have your will declared invalid, die *intestate* (without a will), and have the whole of your estate distributed through an insensitive and not always apt legal system.

THE OPPORTUNITY COST OF RATIONALIZING

Daily living often gets in the way of thinking about death. You mean to organize things that others need to know in case you die, but you haven't done this yet. One of your rationalizations may be that you are not sure what information you need to provide.

Think about the outcome of your delay. Your beneficiary will meet people who offer specific types of assistance—morticians, clergy, lawyers, insurance agents, clerks of federal government agencies, and so on. These people will probably be strangers—sympathetic, courteous, and helpful, but disinterested. Also, your bereaved beneficiary may find it difficult to reveal confidences to them. Today, however, the information survivors need is as close as the Internet. Visit the Canadian Financial Publishing Group's Web site at www.cfpg.com/common/ estate/index.htm for a comprehensive review of estate planning, as well as to link to its informative article "What to Do When a Family Member Dies."

DID YOU KNOW ?

Forty percent of adults age 50 and older do not have a will.

SOURCE: www.metlife.com AARP Program Development and services, 4/00

Do you and your family members know the answers to the following questions?

1. Where are your previous years' income tax returns?
2. Where is your safety deposit box located? Where is the key to it kept?
3. What kinds and amounts of life insurance protection do you have?
4. Can you locate your insurance policies—life, health, property, casualty, and auto?
5. Who are the beneficiaries and contingent beneficiaries of your life insurance policies?
6. Do you and your spouse have current wills? Who drafted them? Where are they kept?
7. Do you have a separate record of the important papers you keep in your safety deposit box? Where is this record located?
8. Do you have a record of your spouse's and children's social insurance numbers?
9. Where is your marriage certificate and the birth certificates of all members of your family?
10. Do you know the name and address of your life insurance agent?
11. Do you know the principal financial resources and liabilities of your estate?
12. Are you knowledgeable about simple, daily, and compound interest rates? About retirement funds and property ownership?
13. Have you given any thought to funerals and burial arrangements?
14. What papers and records will be important to other people when you die?
15. Do you understand the functions of a bank trust department and the meaning of joint ownership?

SOURCE: *Planning with Your Beneficiaries* (Washington, DC: American Council of Life Insurance, Education, and Community Services, n.d.), p. 2.

The moral is to plan your estate while you are in good health and think through the provisions carefully. Last-minute "death-bed" estate planning may fail to carry out your wishes. Many Canadians are considering pre-planned funeral arrangements as part of their estate plan. Pre-planned funeral arrangements allow for family input, minimize the chances of additional costs, and ensure that your wishes are followed without burdening family members.

CONCEPT CHECK 15–1

1. If you needed information about estate planning, would you go to the library or the Internet? Why?
2. Why is estate planning an important component of financial planning?
3. Why is estate planning important for single as well as married individuals?

LEGAL ASPECTS OF ESTATE PLANNING

When death occurs, proof of claims must be produced or the claims will not be processed. If no thought was given to gathering the necessary documents beforehand (with a sufficient number of copies), a period of financial hardship may follow until proof is obtained. If needed documentation cannot be located, irretrievable loss of funds may occur. Your heirs may experience emotionally painful delays until their rights have been established.

Important papers include the following:

[1] Birth certificates—yours, your spouse's, and your children's.
[2] Marriage certificates—always important, but especially important if you or your spouse were married previously—and divorce papers.

■ OBJECTIVE 2

Assess the legal aspects of estate planning.

[3] Legal name changes—judgment of court documents pertaining to any legal changes in the names that appear on birth certificates (especially important to protect the adopted children of a previous marriage or children who have been adopted through adoption agencies).

[4] Military service records—or any other official statement of your military service details, if appropriate.

Here is a list of additional important documents:

- Government benefit documents.
- Veteran documents.
- Insurance policies.
- Transfer records of joint bank accounts.
- Safety deposit box records.
- Registration of automobiles.
- Title to stock and bond certificates.

You should have several copies of certain documents, because when you submit a claim the accompanying proof often becomes a permanent part of the claim file and is not returned. Remember too that in some circumstances, children may be required to furnish proof of their parents' birth, marriage, or divorce.

WILLS

will The legal declaration of a person's mind as to the disposition of his or her property after death.

One of the most vital documents every adult should have is a written will. A **will** is the legal declaration of a person's mind as to the disposition of his or her property after death. Thus, a will is a way to transfer your property according to your wishes after you die (see Exhibit 15–1).

Whether you prepare a will before you die or neglect to take that sensible step, you still have a will. If you fail to prepare your own will, the province in which you legally reside steps in and controls the distribution of your estate without regard for wishes you may have had but failed to define in legal form. Thus, if you die **intestate**—without a valid will—the province's law of descent and distribution becomes your copy of the will. See Exhibit 15-2 on page 440 for the distribution of property in Ontario when a person dies intestate.

intestate Without a valid will.

THE EFFECT OF MARRIAGE OR DIVORCE ON YOUR WILL As mentioned above, changes to your marital status can affect the validity of your will. Even if does not, you may personally wish to make changes related to the changing role of a partner in your life. In the case of divorce, for example, the issue of ownership of familial debts and assets is often heatedly debated, and you should ensure that your will respects whatever agreement you come to.

If you marry after you have made a will, the will is revoked automatically (except in Quebec) unless certain conditions are met. For example, marriage does not revoke a will if

Visit the Web site See Personal Financial Planning worksheets under Chapter 15 on the online learning centre at www.mcgrawhill.ca/ college/kapoor.

- The will indicates an intent that it not be revoked by a subsequent marriage.
- The will was drafted under circumstances indicating that it was in contemplation of marriage.

Because your existing will's legal status may be uncertain, you are better off drawing a new will to fit your new circumstances.

COST OF A WILL Legal fees for drafting a will vary with the complexities of your estate and family situation. A standard will costs $300 and up, not including a living will or power of attorney. The price varies from place to place, but generally the cost of writing a will is less than that for writing a living trust (to be discussed later in the chapter). Look for an attorney experienced in drafting wills and in estate planning.

Exhibit 15–1   What's in a Will

A will requires careful planning to ensure all aspects are covered. The chart below outlining the contents of a basic will clearly demonstrates this point.

Common Clause	Purpose of the Clause
Identification and Revocation Clause	Identifies you and your residence. Declares that this is your last will which revokes all prior wills.
Appointment of Executor(s)	Designates the individual or institution you appoint as your executor. May also designate alternative and successor executors if your original executor cannot act. The clause may provide for the payment of compensation to the executor for their services.
Payment of Debts	Directs your executor to pay all debts, such as mortgages, loans, and funeral and estate administration expenses.
Payment of Taxes and Fees	Authorizes your executor to pay income tax or probate fees that may be due.
Specific Bequests	Outlines the distribution of specific personal property, such as furniture, jewellery, cars. May also refer to your RRSPs, RRIFs, and pensions.
Legacies	Directs specific cash amounts to be paid.
Residual Estates	Outlines the distribution of your remaining property after all the specific bequests have been made.
Trusts	Sets out the terms of any trust created by your will.
Power Clauses	Enables your executor to exercise various powers in the management of your estate without the approval of the court.
Life Interest Clause	Used when you want to leave someone the income or the enjoyment of the asset, rather than the asset itself. Upon the life tenant's death, the asset would pass on to another beneficiary.
Encroachment Clause	Used in a trust when you want the trustee to be able to give the life tenant or a capital beneficiary additional funds for special circumstances or needs.
Common Disaster Clause	Outlines the distribution of your assets if an intended beneficiary dies at the same time as you.
Survival Clause	States that a beneficiary must survive you for a set period of time (often 30 days) before he or she can benefit from your estate.
Guardian Appointment	Names the individual(s) who would be appointed guardian of your minor children.
Testimonium and Attestation Clauses	These clauses are found at the end of your will. They ensure the legal requirements for a validly executed will are met.

SOURCE: Ho and Robinson, *Personal Financial Planning*, Third Edition (Captus Press, 2000, page 426).

CONCEPT CHECK 15–2

1. What are the legal aspects of estate planning?
2. What is a will? Why is it an important estate planning tool?
3. How does marriage or divorce affect a will?

Exhibit 15–2

Distribution of property when a person dies intestate (without a will)

Dies Leaving	Distribution
Spouse and no children	All to spouse
Children only	All to children, *per stirpes**
Spouse and one child	$200,000 to spouse, rest split equally, *per stirpes*
Spouse and children	First $200,000 to spouse; 1/3 remainder to spouse, and 2/3 to children, *per stirpes*
Spouse and relatives	All to spouse
No spouse or child	Closest next of kin according to table of consanguinity

* *per stirpes* means that if the entitled person is deceased, his or her share of the inheritances will go to his or her children, equally.
SOURCE: Carr, Stevenson & Mackay, Barristers & Solicitors, www.csmlaw.com/estates.htm

TYPES AND FORMATS OF WILLS

■ **OBJECTIVE 3** ▎

Distinguish among formats of wills.

holographic will
A handwritten will.

formal will A will that is usually prepared with an attorney's assistance.

beneficiary A person who has been named to receive property under a will.

notarial will A will made in the presence of a notary and at least one witness, and that does not require probate. Available only in Quebec.

probate The legal procedure of proving a valid or invalid will.

There are three types of legal wills. A **holographic will** is a handwritten will that you prepare yourself. It should be written, dated, and signed entirely in your handwriting; no printed or typed information should be on its pages. Some provinces, however, may not recognize a holographic will.

A **formal will** is usually prepared with an attorney's assistance. It may be either typed or on a pre-printed form. You must sign the will and acknowledge it as your will in the presence of two witnesses, neither of whom is a **beneficiary** (a person you have named to receive property under the will). The witnesses must then sign the will in your presence.

A **notarial will**, available only in Quebec, is typed and signed in the presence of the notary and at least one witness. The notary keeps the original will and can issue a certified copy to the heirs once proof of death has been established. A notarized will is considered a legal deed and, as such, the will does not need to be probated (see later discussion).

WRITING YOUR WILL

The way to transfer your property according to your wishes is to write a will specifying those wishes. Joint ownership is no substitute for a will. Although jointly owned property passes directly to the joint owner and may be appropriate for some assets, such as your home, only a will allows you to distribute your property as a whole exactly as you wish. Select a person who will follow your instructions (your *executor*). By naming your own executor, you will eliminate the need for a court-appointed administrator, prevent unnecessary delay in the distribution of your property, and minimize settlement costs. See the Financial Planning for Life's Situations feature on the next page for guidance on important aspects of making a will.

An executor will have many important tasks. One of these is to obtain probate from court. **Probate** is the legal procedure of proving a valid or invalid will. It is the process by which an executor manages and distributes your property after you die according to your will's provisions. A probate court generally validates wills and makes sure debts are paid. You should avoid probate because it is expensive, lengthy, and public. As you'll read later, a living trust avoids probate and is less expensive, quicker, and more private.

SELECTING AN EXECUTOR Select an executor, referred to as a liquidator in Quebec and a trustee in Ontario, who is both willing and able to carry out the complicated tasks associated with executing a will. These tasks are preparing an inventory of assets, collecting any money due, paying off any debts, preparing and filing all income and estate tax returns, liqui-

1. Work closely with your spouse as you prepare your will. Seek professional help so that your family objectives can be met, regardless of who dies first.

2. Write your will to conform with your current wishes. When your circumstances change (for example, when you retire or move to another province), review your will and, if appropriate, write a new one.

3. Do not choose a beneficiary as a witness. If such a person is called on to validate your will, he or she may not be able to collect an inheritance.

4. If you are remarrying, consider signing a pre-nuptial agreement to protect your children. If you sign such an agreement before the wedding, you and your intended spouse can legally agree that neither of you will make any claim on the other's estate. The agreement can be revoked later, if you both agree.

5. Consider using percentages, rather than dollar amounts, when you divide your estate. For example, if you leave $15,000 to a friend and the rest to your spouse, your spouse will suffer if your estate shrinks to $17,000.

6. Both you and your spouse should have a will, and those wills should be separate documents.

7. Be flexible. Don't insist that your heirs keep stock or run a cattle ranch. If you do so, they may suffer if economic conditions change.

8. Sign the original copy of your will and keep it in a safe place; keep an unsigned copy at home for reference.

9. Alter your will by preparing a new will or adding a codicil. Don't change beneficiaries by writing on the will itself; this may invalidate the will.

10. Select an executor who is both willing and able to carry out the complicated tasks associated with the job.

---

dating and re-investing other assets to pay off debts and provide income for your family while the estate is being administered, distributing the estate, and making a final accounting to your beneficiaries and to the probate court.

Your executor can be a family member, a friend, an attorney, an accountant, or the trust department of a bank. Exhibit 15–3 on the next page summarizes typical duties of an executor.

SELECTING A GUARDIAN In addition to disposing of your estate, your will should name a guardian and/or trustee to care for minor children if both parents die at the same time, such as in an automobile accident or a plane crash. A **guardian** is a person who assumes the responsibilities of providing the children with personal care and of managing the estate for them. A **trustee**, on the other hand, is a person or an institution that holds or generally manages property for the benefit of someone else under a trust agreement.

You should take great care in selecting a guardian for your children. You want a guardian whose philosophy on raising children is similar to yours and who is willing to accept the responsibility.

Through your will, you may want to provide funds to raise your children. You could, for instance, leave a lump sum for an addition to the guardian's house and establish monthly payments to cover your children's living expenses.

The guardian of the minor's estate manages the property you leave behind for your children. This guardian can be a person or the trust department of a financial institution, such as a bank. Property that you place in trust for your children can be managed by the trustee, rather than by the guardian of the minor's estate.

guardian A person who assumes responsibility for providing children with personal care and managing the deceased's estate for them.

trustee A person or an institution that holds or manages property for the benefit of someone else under a trust agreement.

ALTERING OR REWRITING YOUR WILL

You should review your will if you move to a different province; if you have sold property mentioned in the will; if the size and composition of your estate have changed; if you have married, divorced, or remarried; or if potential heirs have died or been born.

Exhibit 15–3

Major
Responsibilities
of an Executor

The complexity of the
estates determines the
duties to be performed
and the sequence.
Certain provincial
statutes may vary
these duties.

SOURCE: Adapted
from Ho and Robinson,
*Personal Financial
Planning*, Third Edition,
(Captus Press, 2000,
pages 431 and 432).

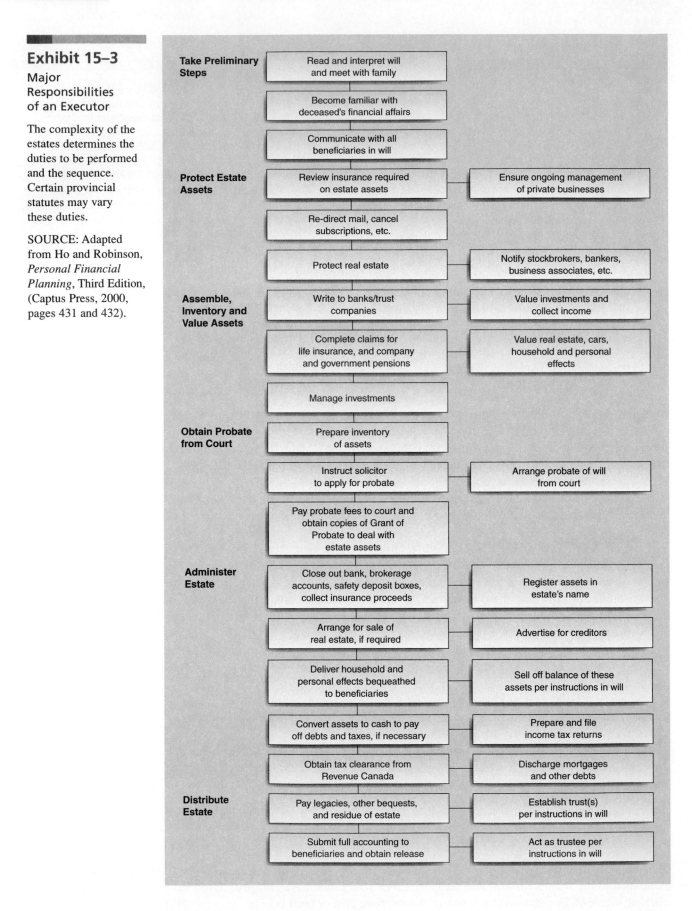

Take Preliminary Steps

- Read and interpret will and meet with family
- Become familiar with deceased's financial affairs
- Communicate with all beneficiaries in will

Protect Estate Assets

- Review insurance required on estate assets — Ensure ongoing management of private businesses
- Re-direct mail, cancel subscriptions, etc.
- Protect real estate — Notify stockbrokers, bankers, business associates, etc.

Assemble, Inventory and Value Assets

- Write to banks/trust companies — Value investments and collect income
- Complete claims for life insurance, and company and government pensions — Value real estate, cars, household and personal effects
- Manage investments

Obtain Probate from Court

- Prepare inventory of assets
- Instruct solicitor to apply for probate — Arrange probate of will from court
- Pay probate fees to court and obtain copies of Grant of Probate to deal with estate assets

Administer Estate

- Close out bank, brokerage accounts, safety deposit boxes, collect insurance proceeds — Register assets in estate's name
- Arrange for sale of real estate, if required — Advertise for creditors
- Deliver household and personal effects bequeathed to beneficiaries — Sell off balance of these assets per instructions in will
- Convert assets to cash to pay off debts and taxes, if necessary — Prepare and file income tax returns
- Obtain tax clearance from Revenue Canada — Discharge mortgages and other debts

Distribute Estate

- Pay legacies, other bequests, and residue of estate — Establish trust(s) per instructions in will
- Submit full accounting to beneficiaries and obtain release — Act as trustee per instructions in will

Don't make any changes on the face of your will. Additions, deletions, or erasures on a will that has been signed and witnessed can invalidate the will.

If only a few changes are needed in your will, adding a codicil may be the best choice. A **codicil** is a document that explains, adds, or deletes provisions in your existing will. It identifies the will being amended and confirms the unchanged sections of the will. To be valid, it must conform to the legal requirements for a will.

If you wish to make major changes in your will or if you have already added a codicil, preparing a new will is preferable to adding a new codicil. In the new will, include a clause revoking all earlier wills and codicils.

If you are rewriting a will because of a remarriage, consider drafting a **pre-nuptial agreement**. This is a documentary agreement between spouses before marriage. In such agreements, one or both parties often waive a right to receive property under the other's will or under provincial law. Be sure to consult an attorney in drafting a pre-nuptial agreement.

Wills have existed for thousands of years; the oldest known will was written by the Egyptian pharaoh Uah in 2448 b.c. Recently, a new type of will, called a *living will*, has emerged.

codicil A document that modifies provisions in an existing will.

pre-nuptial agreement A documentary agreement between spouses before marriage.

A LIVING WILL

A **living will** provides for your wishes to be followed if you become so physically or mentally disabled that you are unable to act on your own behalf. A living will is not a substitute for a traditional will. It enables an individual, while well, to express the intention that life be allowed to end if he or she becomes terminally ill. Exhibit 15–4 on the next page is an example of a typical living will.

To ensure the effectiveness of a living will, discuss your intention of preparing such a will with the people closest to you. You should also discuss this with your family doctor. Sign and date your document before two witnesses. Witnessing shows that you signed of your own free will.

Give copies of your living will to those closest to you, and have your family doctor place a copy in your medical file. Keep the original document readily accessible, and look it over periodically—preferably once a year—to be sure your wishes have remained unchanged. To verify your intent, redate and initial each subsequent endorsement.

Working through end-of-life issues is difficult, but it can help avoid forcing your family to make a decision in a hospital waiting room—or worse, having your last wishes ignored.

A living will can become a problem. A once-healthy person may have a change of heart and prefer to remain alive even as death seems imminent. Living wills call for careful thought, but they do provide you with a choice as to the manner of your death.

living will A document that enables an individual, while well, to express the intention that life be allowed to end (i.e., no extraordinary medical measures or life support equipment be used) if he or she becomes terminally ill.

power of attorney A legal document authorizing someone to act on one's behalf.

POWER OF ATTORNEY

Related to the concept of a living will is a **power of attorney**. A power of attorney is a legal document authorizing someone to act on your behalf. At some point in your life, you may become ill or incapacitated. You may then wish to have someone attend to your needs and your personal affairs. You can assign a power of attorney to anyone you choose.

The person you name can be given limited power or a great deal of power. The power given can be special—to carry out certain acts or transactions, or it can be general—to act completely for you. A conventional power of attorney is automatically revoked in a case of legal incapacity.

DID YOU KNOW ?

Only certain provinces—Alberta, British Columbia, Manitoba, Newfoundland, Ontario, Prince Edward Island, and Saskatchewan—have laws making health-care directives binding. Quebec and Nova Scotia permit health-care proxies but not living wills or advance health-care directives; however, court decisions suggest that living wills may be legally enforceable even in those provinces that do not have legislation authorizing them.

SOURCE: www.professionalreferrals.ca/article-113.html

Exhibit 15–4

A Living Will: Example

SOURCE: *Don't Wait until Tomorrow* (Hartford, CT: Aetna Life and Casualty Company, n.d.), p. 11.

Living Will Declaration

Declaration made this _____ day of _____ (month, year)

I, _____, being of sound mind, willfully and voluntarily make known my desire that my dying shall not be artificially prolonged under the circumstances set forth below, do hereby declare

If at any time I should have an incurable injury, disease, or illness regarded as a terminal condition by my physician and if my physician has determined that the application of life-sustaining procedures would serve only to artificially prolong the dying process and that my death will occur whether or not life-sustaining procedures are utilized, I direct that such procedures be withheld or withdrawn and that I be permitted to die with only the administration of medication or the performance of any medical procedure deemed necessary to provide me with comfort care.

In the absence of my ability to give directions regarding the use of such life-sustaining procedures, it is my intention that this declaration shall be honoured by my family and physician as the final expression of my legal right to refuse medical or surgical treatment and accept the consequences from such refusal.

I understand the full import of this declaration, and I am emotionally and mentally competent to make this declaration.

Signed _____

City and Province of Residence _____

The declarant has been personally known to me, and I believe him or her to be of sound mind.

Witness _____

Witness _____

LETTER OF LAST INSTRUCTION

In addition to your will, you should prepare a *letter of last instruction*. This document, though not legally enforceable, can provide your heirs with important information. It should contain the details of your funeral arrangements. It should also contain the names of the people who are to be notified of your death and the locations of your bank accounts, safety deposit box, and other important items.

CONCEPT CHECK 15–3

1. What are the three formats of wills?
2. What are the steps in writing your will?
3. What is a power of attorney?
4. What is a letter of last instruction?

TYPES OF TRUSTS AND ESTATES

A trust is a property arrangement in which the **settlor** sets up a trust by gifting property (the *subject* of the trust) that is legally owned and managed by a *trustee* according to the terms of the trust deed for the benefit of someone else, referred to as the *beneficiary*.

It is a good idea to discuss with your attorney the possibility of establishing a trust as a means of managing your estate. Basically, a **trust** is a legal arrangement through which a trustee holds your assets for your benefit or that of your beneficiaries. "Trusts today are used for everything from protecting assets from creditors to managing property for young children or disabled elders,"[1] according to one tax attorney.

TYPES OF TRUSTS

There are two types of personal trusts: a living, or inter vivos, trust and a testamentary trust. A trust established for the sole benefit of your spouse is referred to as a spousal trust. It can take either of the two forms just mentioned.

LIVING OR INTER VIVOS TRUST A **living trust**, or *inter vivos trust*, is a property management arrangement set up during the settlor's lifetime. Assets are deemed to be transferred to the trust at their fair market value unless the trust is for the sole benefit of the spouse, in which case they are deemed to have been transferred at the settlor's adjusted cost base.

Living trusts can provide many advantages.

[1] The settlor can retain control of how assets transferred to the trust are to be managed and how the income and capital of the trust are to be distributed to the beneficiaries.

[2] Assets transferred to the trust no longer form part of the settlor's estate and so are not subject to probate; nor are they deemed to have been sold upon the settlor's death.

[3] If the trust is *irrevocable*, the assets transferred to the trust cannot be seized by the settlor's creditors.

[4] A trust can be established to manage property for the benefit of disabled individuals, seniors, or minors. If the trust is established for a disabled individual, the *preferred beneficiary election* may permit income earned and held in trust for the beneficiary to be taxed at the beneficiary's lower rate.

Most of the disadvantages of a living trust centre around their tax treatment. Unless the trust is established for the sole benefit of a spouse, assets are deemed to be transferred to the trust at their fair market value, an assumption that may trigger an immediate taxable capital gain. Any income not distributed by the trust is taxed at the highest personal marginal tax rate, and income distributed from the trust to minors or a spouse remains subject to the attribution rules discussed in Chapter 3. Capital losses incurred through the disposition of assets held in trust cannot be allocated to beneficiary, but must be used to offset capital gains generated within the trust. Finally, the assets of non-spousal inter vivos trusts are deemed to be sold every 21 years, likely triggering a capital gain.

TESTAMENTARY TRUST A **testamentary trust** is established by your will and becomes effective upon your death. Such a trust can be valuable if your beneficiaries are inexperienced in financial matters and it might be beneficial to limit access to assets until a later date. A testamentary trust also provides the benefits of asset management and financial bookkeeping. Additional benefits include the following.

[1] Assets are protected from the beneficiary's creditors.

■ OBJECTIVE 4 ■

Appraise various types of trusts and estates.

settlor The creator of a trust; also called the grantor.

trust A legal arrangement through which one's assets are held by a trustee.

living trust A trust that is created and provides benefits during the settlor's lifetime.

testamentary trust A trust established by the creator's will that becomes effective upon his or her death.

---

[1] Lynn Asinof, "Trust Funds Are Just for the Rich? Think Again," *The Wall Street Journal*, January 9, 1995, pp. C1, C10.

Waiting too long can be very costly, say the pros. Too often people either don't want to think about death and incompetency or they do not have enough information to make informed decisions. Then a problem occurs, and by then many valuable planning opportunities have been lost. Anyone with a home, savings, or minor children should consult an experienced estate planning attorney.

The term *estate planning* generally refers to the legal issues involved in planning for death, incompetency, and reducing or avoiding estate taxes. The process for settling a deceased person's affairs is called *probate*. Probate is a court process with two primary goals: (1) to make sure all debts are paid, and (2) to distribute property to the proper recipients. A will is a set of your instructions to a probate court judge for settling your affairs. A will allows you to avoid some of the more expensive aspects of probate. If you have minor children, a will is an absolute necessity for naming guardians, who will raise your children if you and your spouse are deceased. If you don't have a will, your province will give you a will by statute. This is called *intestate probate*. Intestate probate usually takes much longer and is more expensive. Everyone should at least have a will or risk leaving the families with a lot of unnecessary cost and aggravation.

Planning for incompetency may be even more important than planning for death. What will happen if, because of age or illness, you are unable to make decisions for yourself? Everyone should have durable powers of attorney for health care and property management. A *durable power of attorney* is a document that authorizes the person you choose to make decisions for you if you cannot make decisions for yourself. A *living will* is a statement of intent that you do not want your life to be artificially prolonged by a life support system.

A *living trust* is a modern approach to solving many of the problems of basic estate planning. A properly established living trust avoids probate and guardianship and may reduce or eliminate estate taxes. When you create a living trust, you establish a new legal "person" that becomes the owner of your property. You do not give up any control of your affairs. Typically, you are the trustee (the manager of your property) and the beneficiary (the person entitled to the property). During your lifetime, there will be no effect on your day-to-day affairs. However, upon your death, because your trust—not you—is the legal owner of your property, there is no need for probate. Your designated successor trustee, typically your spouse or children, takes control of the trust and distributes your property according to your wishes without the cost and time of probate. If you become incompetent, a trust will empower your successor trustees to manage your affairs for you without the need for guardianship. A living trust can also be an invaluable tool to reduce or avoid estate taxes.

---

[2] Inheritances are not subject to division upon the breakdown of a marriage unless one spouse has chosen to share, or commingle, them with the other. A testamentary trust can prevent the beneficiary from commingling assets with a spouse.

[3] Income earned in a testamentary trust is taxed at progressive tax rates, although the trust does not benefit from personal tax credits. As long as income is payable to the beneficiaries, the executor of the trust can file an election to have the income taxed in the hands of the trust at the lower personal tax rates. This can significantly reduce the tax burden if beneficiaries are in the highest marginal tax bracket.

SPOUSAL TRUST Subject to certain conditions, you can create a trust for your spouse (or common-law spouse). The principal conditions are that (1) all of the income of the trust must be paid to the spouse during the spouse's lifetime, and (2) that none of the capital can be distributed to anyone else during your spouse's lifetime. This trust can actually be classified as either an *inter vivos* trust or a *testamentary* trust. The condition that the surviving spouse cannot remarry would nullify the trust. Assets can be transferred to a spousal trust at their adjusted cost base, thus avoiding capital gains. However, unlike non-spousal trusts, the assets are deemed to have been disposed of at their fair market value once the beneficiary spouse dies. Non-spousal trusts can transfer assets from the trust to the beneficiaries at their adjusted cost base, thus deferring any capital gain until the beneficiary sells the asset. Spousal trusts are not subject to the 21-year disposition rule and can be used if

[1] The beneficiary spouse needs guidance in financial management.

[2] The deceased wishes to provide for the surviving spouse in a second marriage, but wishes to pass assets to children from a first marriage.

[3] The deceased wishes to avoid double probate of assets (once in the hands of the deceased, and a second time upon the death of the surviving spouse who has received the assets outright).

ESTATES

Your *estate* is everything you own. It includes all of your property—tangible and intangible, however acquired or owned, whether inside or outside the country. It may include jointly owned property, life insurance, and employee benefits. Thus, an important step in estate planning is taking inventory of everything you own, such as

[1] Cash, chequing accounts, savings accounts, GICs, and money market funds.

[2] Stocks, bonds (including provincial and Canada Savings Bonds), mutual funds, commodity futures, and tax shelters.

[3] Life insurance, employee benefits, and annuities.

[4] Your home and any other real estate, land and buildings, furniture, and fixtures.

[5] Farms, grain, livestock, machinery, and equipment.

[6] Proprietorship, partnership, and close corporation interests.

[7] Notes, accounts, and claims receivable.

[8] Interests in trusts and powers of appointment.

[9] Antiques, works of art, collectibles, cars, boats, planes, personal effects, and everything else.

ESTATE ASSETS NOT DISTRIBUTED BY A WILL

By law, there are two situations in which your assets will go directly to a beneficiary, independently of your will. The first is one in which your assets, such as life insurance, annuities, and RRSPs, already have a named beneficiary. Unless your beneficiary has pre-deceased you, these assets will be transferred directly without being subject to the process or expense of probate. In cases where the beneficiary has pre-deceased you, then the values will be transferred to your estate.

The second situation occurs when you have assets held in *joint tenancy*, which confers the right of survivorship. Note that this is not the same as *tenancy in common*, where the assets are owned in undivided shares. For example, if a couple owns a home in joint tenancy, then the ownership of that home will pass in its entirety to the spouse upon death of the other spouse. However, if the same couple owns their home as *tenants in common*, where the tenants have the right to dispose of their interest in the joint property at death, there is no automatic right of survivorship and one-half of the value of the home will count into the deceased spouse's estate.

LIFE INSURANCE AND EMPLOYEE BENEFITS

Life insurance proceeds are free of income tax and excluded from probate. Assignment of ownership to your beneficiary or a trust removes a life insurance policy from your estate. Death benefits from qualified pension plans are excluded from your estate, unless they are payable to it.

DID YOU KNOW ?

Without an estate plan, the government may get up to 55 percent of your assets.

SOURCE: www.metlife.com AARP Program Development and Services, 4/00.

The old saying that "there are only two certainties in life—death and taxes" holds true even at death. There is no escaping it, but there are ways to lessen the burden of this unanticipated beneficiary, called the government. While there are no true "estate taxes" in Canada, three potential taxes or pseudo-taxes may be incurred at death:

- Income tax due to the deemed disposition rules
- Provincial probate taxes
- U.S. Estate Tax on your U.S. assets

DEEMED DISPOSITION

In the year of death, a final (terminal) tax return must be filed by the estate's executor/liquidator that includes all income earned by the deceased up to the date of death. Also, included in income at death is the net capital gain recognized under the deemed disposition rules. The deemed disposition rules of the Income Tax Act treat all capital property owned by the deceased as if it was sold immediately prior to death. Thus, all unrecognized capital gains and losses are triggered at that point with the net capital gain (gains less losses) included in income. The Income Tax Act does contain provisions to defer the tax owing under the deemed disposition rules if the asset is left to a surviving spouse or to a special trust for a spouse (spousal trust) created by the deceased's will. This provision allows the spouse or the spousal trust to take ownership of the asset at the deceased's original cost. Hence, no tax is payable until either the spouse or the spousal trust sells the asset or until the surviving spouse dies. The tax is then payable on the basis of the asset's increase in value at that point in time.

RRSPS AND RRIFS

In addition to the potentially significant tax liability from recognized capital gains, it is also necessary to deregister (i.e., collapse) any registered assets, such as RRSPs or RRIFs, at the point of death. The full value of the RRSP or RRIF must be included on the deceased's final (terminal) tax return. There are exceptions to this deregistration requirement if the RRSP or RRIF is left to the surviving spouse, a common law spouse, and, in some cases, to a surviving child or grandchild. An RRSP or RRIF can be transferred tax free to a surviving spouse's own plan. Similar treatment is accorded the transfer of RRSP or RRIF assets to a mentally or physically infirm child or grandchild. If the RRSP or RRIF is left to a dependent child or grandchild under the age of 18, the registered funds must be used to purchase a term certain annuity with a term not exceeding the child's eighteenth year. This choice is available even if there is a surviving spouse.

PROBATE TAXES

Upon death, the executor of your estate will typically be required to file for probate with the provincial court. The estate's executor must submit to the court the original will and an inventory of the deceased's assets. Upon acceptance of these documents by the court, letters (called "certificate of appointment of estate trustee with a will" in Ontario) are issued. This document serves to verify that the submitted will is a valid document and confirms the appointment of your executor. With the executor's submission to the court, he/she must also pay a probate tax. This tax is based on the total value of the assets that flow through the will. The rate charged varies between provinces with some provinces having a maximum fee. In situations where the estate is extremely simple and does not require any involvement with a third party, such as a financial institution, the will may not need to be probated. As well, probate taxes can be reduced by using previously discussed strategies, such as the naming of beneficiaries, Joint Tenancy with Right of Survivorship agreements, and the use of living trusts.

U.S. ESTATE TAX

In addition to the taxes payable in Canada, you may also be subject to a tax bill from the U.S. Government. Canadians who own U.S.-sourced assets, such as real estate, corporate stocks and certain bonds, and government debt are required to pay U.S. Estate Tax based on the market value of their U.S. assets at the time of death. For more information on U.S. Estate Tax, the Royal Bank of Canada offers a publication entitled, *Tax Implications of Investing in the United States*.

SOURCE: RBC Investments - Education Centre, www.rbcinvestments.com/ep_taxes.html

CHARITABLE DONATIONS You can structure charitable gifts both during your lifetime and in your will to further your estate planning goals and make the most of available tax credits. There are a number of ways in which gifts of capital or property can be made with significant tax benefits. One example of this would be if you elected to make a charitable gift through your will. In this case, your taxable income in the year of your death would be reduced by the tax credit for charitable donations. The gift could be up to 100 percent of your net income in the year of death, and excess can be carried back to the preceding year. If a similar gift was made during your lifetime, the gift could not exceed a maximum of 75 percent of your net income, and any excess would have to be carried forward for up to five years.

If you sit down with a qualified adviser and carefully map out a gifting strategy for your estate, it is possible to both fulfill your philanthropic desires and have your estate receive favourable tax treatment as well.

SETTLING YOUR ESTATE

If you have had a will drawn, you are *testate* in the eyes of the law, and an executor (named in your will) will carry out your wishes in due time. If you have not named an executor, the probate court (the court that supervises the distribution of estates) will appoint an administrator to carry out the instructions in your will.

PROBATE AND ADMINISTRATION COSTS Your estate administration costs will include fees for attorneys, accountants, appraisers, executors or administrators and trustees, court costs, bonding and surety costs, and miscellaneous expenses. These administration costs may run to 3 to 5 percent of your estate, depending on its size and complexity. While the percentage usually decreases as the size of the estate increases, it may be increased by additional complicating factors, such as handling a business interest. Inversely to administration costs, probate costs tend to rise with the size of the estate. The exact costs, payable to the court, are paid out of the proceeds of your estate and are set by the court.

If you don't have a will, you become *intestate* at your death. In that case, your estate is put under the control of a court-appointed administrator for distribution according to the laws of the province in which you reside.

Although the very process of estate planning is a trying one as it forces you to think about emotionally charged issues, such as what you leave behind and to whom, a will may be its most important feature. Remember the old adage that the act of not deciding is a decision in itself.

As we discuss earlier in this chapter, if you don't make a will or use some other legal method to transfer your property when you die, provincial law will determine what happens to your property. This process is called "intestate succession." Your property will be distributed to your spouse and children or, if you have neither, to the closest next of kin according to a statutory formula (usually in this order: parents; if neither is surviving, siblings; if none, nieces/nephews; if none, other next of kin). If no relatives can be found to inherit your property, it all goes to the government.

CONCEPT CHECK 15-4

1. Differentiate among the types of trusts.
2. What is included in an estate?
3. What are the two types of joint ownership?

SUMMARY OF OBJECTIVES

Objective 1
Analyze the personal aspects of estate planning.
Estate planning is an essential part of retirement planning and an integral part of financial planning. The first part of estate planning consists of building your estate; the second part consists of transferring your estate, at your death, in the manner you have specified. The personal aspects of estate planning depend on whether you are single or married. If you are married, your estate planning involves the interests of at least two people, and more if there are children. Never having been married does not eliminate the need to organize your financial affairs.

Objective 2
Assess the legal aspects of estate planning.
In the event of death, proof of claims must be produced or the claims will not be processed. Among the papers needed are birth certificates, marriage certificates, legal name changes, and military service records. Every adult should have a written will, which is the legal declaration of a person's wishes as to the disposition of his or her property after death. Thus, a will is a way to transfer your property according to your wishes after you die.

Objective 3
Distinguish among formats of wills.
The three formats for wills are holographic, formal, and notarial. A holographic will is handwritten and requires no witness but is a poor choice for most people and some provinces will not recognize it. A formal will is a typed document signed by you and witnessed by two individuals who must not be beneficiaries or the spouses of beneficiaries. A lawyer is usually employed to draft a formal will. A notarial will, available only in Quebec, is typed and signed in the presence of the notary and at least one witness. The notary keeps the original will and can issue a certified copy to the heirs once proof of death has been established.

Objective 4
Appraise various types of trusts and estates.
Establishing a trust can be an excellent way to manage your estate. Popular forms of trusts include living trusts, spousal trusts, and testamentary trusts. An attorney's help is needed to establish a trust.

KEY TERMS

beneficiary 440
codicil 443
estate 435
estate planning 435
formal will 440
guardian 441
holographic will 440

intestate 438
living trust 445
living will 443
notarial will 440
power of attorney 443
pre-nuptial agreement 443

probate 440
settlor 445
testamentary trust 445
trust 445
trustee 441
will 438

FINANCIAL PLANNING ACTIVITIES

1. *Preparing a Written Record of Personal Information.* Prepare a written record of personal information that would be helpful to you and your heirs. Make sure to include the location of family records, your military service file, and other important papers; medical records; bank accounts; charge accounts; the location of your safety deposit box; Canada Savings Bonds; stocks, bonds, and other securities; property owned; life insurance; annuities; and government benefits information. (Obj. 1)

2. *Developing Long-Term Estate Planning Goals.* Develop a list of specific long-term estate planning goals with your family. Discuss how those goals could be achieved even if you or your spouse died unexpectedly. (Obj. 1)

3. *Drafting a Simple Will.* Draft your will, using Exhibit 15–1 as a guideline. Who will you appoint as a trustee or guardian for your minor children? Why? (Obj. 2)

4. *Comparing Costs of Preparing a Will.* Contact several lawyers in your area to find out how much they would charge to prepare your simple will. Are their fees about the same? (Obj. 3)

5. *Using the Internet to Obtain Information about Wills.* Visit Metropolitan Life Insurance Company's Web page at www. lifeadvice.com. Using this information, prepare a report on the following: (a) Who needs a will? (b) What are the elements of a will (naming a guardian, naming an executor, preparing a will, updating a will, estate taxes, where to keep your will, living will, etc.)? (c) How is this report helpful in preparing your own will?

6. *Preparing the Letter of Last Instructions.* Prepare your own letter of last instructions. (Obj. 3)

7. *Determining Criteria in Choosing a Guardian.* Make a list of the criteria you will use in deciding who will be the guardian of your minor children if you and your spouse die at the same time. (Obj. 3)

8. *Establishing a Trust.* Discuss with your attorney the possibility of establishing a trust as a means of managing your estate. (Obj. 4)

CREATING A FINANCIAL PLAN

Developing an Estate Plan

Most people do not think they have enough assets to do estate planning. However, the planned transfer of resources with the use of a will, trusts, and other legal vehicles is a necessary phase of your total financial plan.

Web Sites for Estate Planning

- Learn what's involved in developing an estate plan and how to take advantage of all your options at the TD Canada Trust site, **www.tdcanadatrust.com**.
- The Canadian Financial Publishing Group, at **www.cfpg. com**, has articles on wills, probate, taxation, and other estate planning issues.
- The Royal Bank, at **www.royalbank.com**, has information on estate planning as part of its *Your Money Matters* series of guides.
- The Law Society of Upper Canada, at **www.lsuc.on.ca**, offers a guide for Ontario residents with regard to probating a will.

- The College Institute Educators' Association (CIEA) of BC, at **www.ciea.bc.ca**, has a great retirement guide called "Planning for the Rest of Your Life."

(Note: Addresses and content of Web sites change, and new sites are created daily. Use search engines to update and locate Web sites for your current financial planning needs.)

Short-Term Financial Planning Activities

1. Investigate the cost of a will. Decide on the type of will and provisions appropriate for your life situation.
2. Using the Canada Customs and Revenue Agency and other Web sites, identify recent estate tax law changes that may affect your financial planning decisions.
3. Compare the benefits and costs of different trusts that might be appropriate for your life situation.

Long-Term Financial Planning Activities

1. Develop a plan for actions to be taken related to estate planning.
2. Identify saving and investing decisions that would minimize future estate taxes.

LIFE SITUATION CASE

Don't Let Your Windfall Blow Away

Warren, a married entrepreneur who owns a successful promotions business, doesn't yet have kids, but he is already making plans. Last December, Warren received an unexpected inheritance of $1.4 million, after taxes, from his late grandfather. Instead of buying a Porsche or a new home, he did the right thing by his family-to-be and invested it all. "Warren is extremely fastidious," says Lesley Sommers, his financial planner.

Warren did what smart people do with sudden wealth: They decide not to blow it. A 1997 survey found that 59 percent of 1,000 respondents who received cash payouts of $20,000 or more had sought professional advice. An equal number had invested every dime. When Warren got his windfall, Sommers invested all but $100,000. Warren says, "She taught me that this [windfall] should not change where I eat or go on vaca-

tion." So, if you win the lottery, don't blow it on houses, cars, vacations, and luxury items. Instead, pay off high-interest credit card and other debts that offer no tax deductions. Then, find a financial adviser. This professional can help you find a competent estate planner and create an investment plan.

Questions

1. What did Warren do with his $1.4 million inheritance?
2. What do smart people do with sudden wealth?

SOURCE: Adapted from Joan Oleck, "Don't Let Your Windfall Blow Away," *Business Week On-line*, December 1999, p. 116. Reprinted from the March 1, 1999 issue of *Business Week* by special permission. © 1999 McGraw-Hill Companies, Inc.

PLANNING FOR TOMORROW

Life Situation
Pamela, 48; Isaac, 50; children, ages 21, 19, and 16

Financial Goals

- Replenish savings and investments used for college costs
- Plan for retirement in about 15 years
- Consider estate planning activities

Financial Data

Monthly income	$ 5,700
Living expenses	4,600
Assets	242,500
Liabilities	69,100

With two children in college, the Mortimers once again find their life situation changing. Compared with five years ago, their total assets have decreased from $262,700 to $242,500 due to college expenses. The Mortimers' oldest child will graduate next year, but the youngest will enter university in a couple of years. Therefore, the drain on the family's finances will continue.

The family's finances are adequate, but both Pamela and Isaac are beginning to worry about retirement. Over the years, Isaac has taken advantage of different career opportunities. Today, his annual salary, $68,400, is higher than it has ever been. But his employment changes have resulted in a smaller pension fund than would be available had he remained with the same organization. The current value of his pension plan is just over $115,000. The investment program he and Pamela started almost 10 years ago is growing and is now worth about $62,000. But they still worry whether they will have enough money to finance their retirement dreams when Isaac retires in 15 years. According to Isaac, "If I retired today, we couldn't maintain our current lifestyle. In fact, we couldn't even exist."

Questions

1. How would you rate the Mortimers' financial condition at this stage in their lives?
2. Given that Pamela is 48 and Isaac is 50, what should be their major priorities as they continue planning for retirement?
3. What types of estate planning, if any, should the Mortimers consider at this time?

The Time Value of Money: Future Value and Present Value Computations

"If I deposit $10,000 today, how much will I have for a down payment on a house in five years?"

"Will $2,000 saved a year give me enough money when I retire?"

"How much must I save today to have enough for my children's college education?"

As introduced in Chapter 1 and used to measure financial opportunity costs in other chapters, the *time value of money*, more commonly referred to as *interest*, is the cost of money that is borrowed or lent. Interest can be compared to rent, the cost of using an apartment or other item. The time value of money is based on the fact that a dollar received today is worth more than a dollar that will be received one year from today because the dollar received today can be saved or invested and will be worth more than a dollar a year from today. Similarly, a dollar that will be received one year from today is currently worth less than a dollar today.

The time value of money has two major components: future value and present value. *Future value* computations, which are also referred to as *compounding*, yield the amount to which a current sum will increase based on a certain interest rate and period of time. *Present value*, which is calculated through a process called *discounting*, is the current value of a future sum based on a certain interest rate and period of time.

In future value problems, you are given an amount to save or invest and you calculate the amount that will be available at some future date. With present value problems, you are given the amount that will be available at some future date and you calculate the current value of that amount. Both future value and present value computations are based on basic interest rate calculations.

FUTURE VALUE OF A SINGLE AMOUNT

The future value of an amount consists of the original amount plus compound interest. This calculation involves the following elements:

$$FV = \text{Future value}$$
$$PV = \text{Present value}$$
$$i = \text{Interest rate}$$
$$n = \text{Number of time periods}$$

The formula for the future value of a single amount is

$$FV = PV(1 + i)^n$$

EXAMPLE A

The future value of $100 at 10 percent after three years is $133.10. This amount is calculated as follows:

$$\$133.10 = \$1.00 (1 + 0.10)^3$$

Future value tables are available to help you determine compounded interest amounts (see Exhibit A–1 on page 461). Looking at Exhibit A–1 for 10 percent and three years, you can see that $100 would be worth $133.10 at that time. For other amounts, multiply the table factor by the original amount.

This may be viewed as follows:

	Future value (rounded)	$100		$110		$121		$FV = \$133.10$
			Interest		Interest		Interest	
	After year	0	$10	1	$11	2	$12	3

Using a financial calculator (BAII Plus Texas Instrument), you would solve the problem as shown below:

*Remember always clear the time value of money function before any calculation by pressing [2ND] [CLRTVM]. The examples that follow assume that interest is compounded once per period. Therefore, we must set the number of compounding periods per year in the BAII calculator to one. To do this, press in turn the [2ND] button (yellow), the [I/Y] button (for the P/Y function shown above it), the number 1, the [ENTER] button, the [2ND] button again, and finally the [CPT] button (for the quit function above it).

[2ND]	[CLRTVM]
3	[N]
10	[I/Y]
100	[PV]
0	[PMT] (Optional, if registers are cleared)
[CPT]	[FV]

The solution of −$133.10 is displayed. Remember from Chapter 1 that the BAII Plus displays the present value solution with a + and the future value solution with a − because it assumes one is an inflow and the other an outflow.

EXAMPLE B

If your savings of $400 earn 12 percent, compounded *monthly*, over a year and a half, use the table factor for 1 percent for 18 time periods. The future value of this amount is $478.40, calculated as follows:

$$\$478.40 = \$400 (1.196)$$

Using a financial calculator (BAII Plus Texas Instrument):

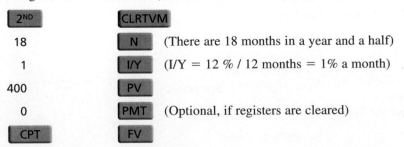

[2ND]	[CLRTVM]	
18	[N]	(There are 18 months in a year and a half)
1	[I/Y]	(I/Y = 12 % / 12 months = 1% a month)
400	[PV]	
0	[PMT]	(Optional, if registers are cleared)
[CPT]	[FV]	

The solution of −$478.46 is displayed.

Sample Problem 1 What is the future value of $800 at 8 percent after six years?

Sample Problem 2 How much would you have in savings if you kept $200 on deposit for eight years at 8 percent, compounded *semi-annually*?

FUTURE VALUE OF A SERIES OF EQUAL AMOUNTS (AN ANNUITY)

Future value may also be calculated for a situation in which regular additions are made to savings. The following formula is used to compute the future value annuity factor:

$$FV = \frac{[(1 + i)^n - 1]}{i}$$

This formula assumes that (1) each deposit is for the same amount, (2) the interest rate is the same for each time period, and (3) the deposits are made at the end of each time period.

EXAMPLE C

The future value of three $100 deposits made at the end of the next three years, earning 10 percent interest, is $331. This is calculated as follows:

$$\$331 = \$100 \times \frac{[(1 + 0.10)^3 - 1]}{0.10}$$

This may be viewed as follows:

Future value (rounded)	Deposit $100 Interest 0	$100 Deposit $100 Interest	$210 Deposit $100 Interest	FV = $331
After year 0	1	$10 2	$21 3	

Using Exhibit A–2 on page 462, you can find this same amount for 10 percent for three time periods. To use the table for other amounts, multiply the table factors by the annual deposit.

Using a financial calculator (BAII Plus Texas Instrument):

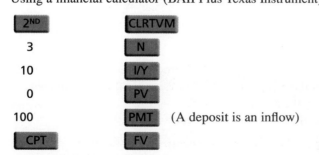

2ND	CLRTVM
3	N
10	I/Y
0	PV
100	PMT (A deposit is an inflow)
CPT	FV

The solution of −$331 is displayed.

EXAMPLE D

If you plan to deposit $40 a year for 10 years, earning 8 percent compounded annually, use the table factor for 8 percent for 10 time periods. The future value of this amount is $579.48, calculated as follows:

$$\$579.48 = \$40(14.487)$$

Using a financial calculator (BAII Plus Texas Instrument):

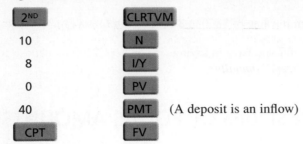

2ND	CLRTVM
10	N
8	I/Y
0	PV
40	PMT (A deposit is an inflow)
CPT	FV

The solution of −$579.46 is displayed.

Sample Problem 3 What is the future value of an annual deposit of $230 earning 6 percent for 15 years?

Sample Problem 4 What amount would you have in a retirement account if you made annual deposits of $375 for 25 years earning 12 percent, compounded annually?

PRESENT VALUE OF A SINGLE AMOUNT

If you want to know how much you need to deposit now to receive a certain amount in the future, use the following formula:

$$PV = \frac{1}{(1 + i)^n}$$

EXAMPLE E

The present value of $100 to be received three years from now based on a 10 percent interest rate is $75. This amount is calculated as follows:

$$\$75 = \frac{\$100}{(1 + 0.10)^3}$$

This may be viewed as follows:

Present value (rounded)	$75		$83		$91		$100
		Deposit (interest) $7.5		Deposit (interest) $8.25		Deposit (interest) $9.05	
After year	0		1		2		3

Present value tables are available to assist you in this process (see Exhibit A–3 on page 463). Note that $1 at 10 percent for three years has a present value of $0.75. For amounts other than $1, multiply the table factor by the amount involved.

Using a financial calculator (BAII Plus Texas Instrument):

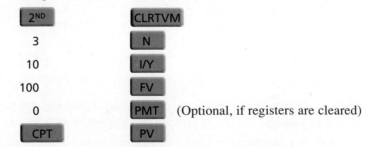

2ND	CLRTVM
3	N
10	I/Y
100	FV
0	PMT (Optional, if registers are cleared)
CPT	PV

The solution of $75 is displayed.

EXAMPLE F

If you want to have $300 seven years from now and your savings earn 10 percent, compounded *semi-annually*, use the table factor for 5 percent for 14 time periods. In this situation, the present value is $151.50, calculated as follows:

$$\$151.50 = \$300(0.505)$$

Using a financial calculator (BAII Plus Texas Instrument):

2ND	CLRTVM	
14	N	(7 years × 2 periods per year (semi-annually) = 14 periods)
5	I/Y	(I/Y = 10 % / 2 periods (semi-annually) = 5% a period)
300	FV	
0	PMT	(Optional, if registers are cleared)
CPT	PV	

The solution of $151.52 is displayed.

Sample Problem 5 What is the present value of $2,200 earning 15 percent for eight years?

Sample Problem 6 To have $6,000 for a child's education in 10 years, what amount should a parent deposit in a savings account that earns 12 percent, compounded *quarterly*?

PRESENT VALUE OF A SERIES OF EQUAL AMOUNTS (AN ANNUITY)

The final time value of money situation allows you to receive an amount at the end of each time period for a certain number of periods. The following formula is one to compute the present value annuity factor:

$$PV = \frac{1 - \dfrac{1}{(1 + i)^n}}{i}$$

EXAMPLE G

The present value of a $100 withdrawal at the end of the next three years would be $2.49, calculated as follows:

$$\$2.49 = \$100 = \left[\frac{1 - \dfrac{1}{(1 + 0.10)^3}}{0.10} \right]$$

This may be viewed as follows:

Present value (rounded)	$249		$174		$91		$0
	Withdrawal – $100		Withdrawal – $100		Withdrawal – $100	
	Interest + $25		Interest + $17		Interest + $9	
After year	0		1		2		3

This same amount appears in Exhibit A–4 on page 464 for 10 percent and three time periods. To use the table for other situations, multiply the table factor by the amount to be withdrawn each year.

Using a financial calculator (BAII Plus Texas Instrument):

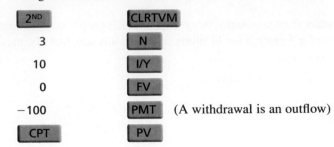

2ND	CLRTVM
3	N
10	I/Y
0	FV
−100	PMT (A withdrawal is an outflow)
CPT	PV

The solution of $2.49 is displayed.

EXAMPLE H

If you wish to withdraw $100 at the end of each year for 10 years from an account that earns 14 percent, compounded annually, what amount must you deposit now? Use the table factor for 14 percent for 10 time periods. In this situation, the present value is $521.60, calculated as follows:

$$\$521.60 = \$100(5.216)$$

Using a financial calculator (BAII Plus Texas Instrument):

2ND	CLRTVM
10	N
14	I/Y
0	PV
−100	PMT (A withdrawal is an outflow)
CPT	PV

The solution of $521.61 is displayed.

Sample Problem 7 What is the present value of a withdrawal of $200 at the end of each year for 14 years with an interest rate of 7 percent?

Sample Problem 8 How much would you have to deposit now to be able to withdraw $650 at the end of each year for 20 years from an account that earns 11 percent?

USING PRESENT VALUE TO DETERMINE LOAN PAYMENTS

Present value tables can also be used to determine amortized payments for a loan as follows:

$$\frac{\text{Amount borrowed}}{\text{Present value of a series table factor (Exhibit A–4)}} = \text{Loan payment}$$

EXAMPLE I

If you borrow $1,000 with a 6 percent interest rate to be repaid in three equal payments at the end of the next three years, the payments will be $374.11. This is calculated as follows:

$$\frac{\$1,000}{2.673} = \$374.11$$

Using a financial calculator (BAII Plus Texas Instrument):

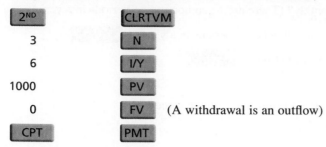

2ND	CLRTVM
3	N
6	I/Y
1000	PV
0	FV	(A withdrawal is an outflow)
CPT	PMT

The solution of $374.11 is displayed.

Sample Problem 9 What would be the annual payment amount for a $20,000, 10-year loan at 7 percent?

ANSWERS TO SAMPLE PROBLEMS

[1] $800(1.587) = $1,269.60. (Use Exhibit A–1, 8%, 6 periods.)
[2] $200(1.873) = $374.60. (Use Exhibit A–1, 4%, 16 periods.)
[3] $230(23.276) = $5,353.48. (Use Exhibit A–2, 6%, 15 periods.)
[4] $375(133.33) = $49,998.75. (Use Exhibit A–2, 12%, 25 periods.)
[5] $2,200(0.327) = $719.40. (Use Exhibit A–3, 15%, 8 periods.)
[6] $6,000(0.307) = $1,842. (Use Exhibit A–3, 3%, 40 periods.)
[7] $200(8.745) = $1,749. (Use Exhibit A–4, 7%, 14 periods.)
[8] $650(7.963) = $5,175.95. (Use Exhibit A–4, 11%, 20 periods.)
[9] $20,000/7.024 = $2,847.38. (Use Exhibit A–4, 7%, 10 periods.)

Calculator Solutions

[1] Calculator : 2nd CLRTVM; 6 N; 8 I/Y; 800 PV; CPT FV; Solution $1,269.50
[2] Calculator : 2nd CLRTVM; 16 N; 4 I/Y; 200 PV; CPT FV; Solution $374.60
[3] Calculator : 2nd CLRTVM; 15 N; 6 I/Y; 230 PMT; CPT FV; Solution $5353.47
[4] Calculator : 2nd CLRTVM; 25 N; 12 I/Y; 375 PMT; CPT FV; Solution $50,000.20
[5] Calculator : 2nd CLRTVM; 8 N; 15 I/Y; 2,200 FV; CPT PV; Solution $719.18
[6] Calculator : 2nd CLRTVM; 40 N; 3 I/Y; 6,000 FV; CPT PV; Solution $1839.34
[7] Calculator : 2nd CLRTVM; 14 N; 7 I/Y; 200 PMT; CPT PV; Solution $1749.09
[8] Calculator : 2nd CLRTVM; 20 N; 11 I/Y; 650 PMT; CPT PV; Solution $5176.16
[9] Calculator : 2nd CLRTVM; 10 N; 7 I/Y; 20,000 PV; CPT PMT; Solution $2,847.55

CALCULATING THE EFFECTIVE ANNUAL RATE (EAR) USING A FINANCIAL CALCULATOR (BAII PLUS TEXAS INSTRUMENT)

The formula for calculating the effective annual rate is as follows:

$$EAR = [(1 + APR/m)^m] - 1$$

Example from Chapter 4 (page 115): How much is your nominal EAR on a $100 loan at 12 percent yearly, compounded monthly? (There are 12 compounding periods in a year.)

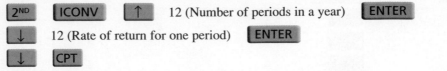

2ND   ICONV   ↑   12 (Number of periods in a year)   ENTER

↓   12 (Rate of return for one period)   ENTER

↓   CPT

The effective rate of 12.68 percent is displayed on the screen.

EXAMPLE J

Assume your bank offers a 10-percent interest rate that is compounded every three months, while a competitor offers 10 percent compounded on a monthly basis. Which one offers a higher effective rate?

BANK (10% compounded every 3 months = 4 periods)

2ND   ICONV   ↑   4   ENTER

↓   10   ENTER

↓   CPT

The effective rate is 10.38 percent.

COMPETITOR (10% compounded weekly = 52 periods)

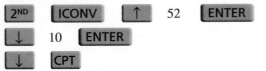

2ND   ICONV   ↑   52   ENTER

↓   10   ENTER

↓   CPT

The effective rate is 10.51 percent.

As you can see, the competitor offers a higher return than your bank.

Exhibit A–1   Future Value (Compounded Sum) of $1 after a Given Number of Time Periods $FV = PV(1 + i)^n$

Period	1%	2%	3%	4%	5%	6%	7%	8%	9%	10%	11%
1	1.010	1.020	1.030	1.040	1.050	1.060	1.070	1.080	1.090	1.100	1.110
2	1.020	1.040	1.061	1.082	1.103	1.124	1.145	1.166	1.188	1.210	1.232
3	1.030	1.061	1.093	1.125	1.158	1.191	1.225	1.260	1.295	1.331	1.368
4	1.041	1.082	1.126	1.170	1.216	1.262	1.311	1.360	1.412	1.464	1.518
5	1.051	1.104	1.159	1.217	1.276	1.338	1.403	1.469	1.539	1.611	1.685
6	1.062	1.126	1.194	1.265	1.340	1.419	1.501	1.587	1.677	1.772	1.870
7	1.072	1.149	1.230	1.316	1.407	1.504	1.606	1.714	1.828	1.949	2.076
8	1.083	1.172	1.267	1.369	1.477	1.594	1.718	1.851	1.993	2.144	2.305
9	1.094	1.195	1.305	1.423	1.551	1.689	1.838	1.999	2.172	2.358	2.558
10	1.105	1.219	1.344	1.480	1.629	1.791	1.967	2.159	2.367	2.594	2.839
11	1.116	1.243	1.384	1.539	1.710	1.898	2.105	2.332	2.580	2.853	3.152
12	1.127	1.268	1.426	1.601	1.796	2.012	2.252	2.518	2.813	3.138	3.498
13	1.138	1.294	1.469	1.665	1.886	2.133	2.410	2.720	3.066	3.452	3.883
14	1.149	1.319	1.513	1.732	1.980	2.261	2.579	2.937	3.342	3.797	4.310
15	1.161	1.346	1.558	1.801	2.079	2.397	2.759	3.172	3.642	4.177	4.785
16	1.173	1.373	1.605	1.873	2.183	2.540	2.952	3.426	3.970	4.595	5.311
17	1.184	1.400	1.653	1.948	2.292	2.693	3.159	3.700	4.328	5.054	5.895
18	1.196	1.428	1.702	2.026	2.407	2.854	3.380	3.996	4.717	5.560	6.544
19	1.208	1.457	1.754	2.107	2.527	3.026	3.617	4.316	5.142	6.116	7.263
20	1.220	1.486	1.806	2.191	2.653	3.207	3.870	4.661	5.604	6.727	8.062
25	1.282	1.641	2.094	2.666	3.386	4.292	5.427	6.848	8.623	10.835	13.585
30	1.348	1.811	2.427	3.243	4.322	5.743	7.612	10.063	13.268	17.449	22.892
40	1.489	2.208	3.262	4.801	7.040	10.286	14.974	21.725	31.409	45.259	65.001
50	1.645	2.692	4.384	7.107	11.467	18.420	29.457	46.902	74.358	117.390	184.570

Exhibit A–1   (Concluded)

Period	12%	13%	14%	15%	16%	17%	18%	19%	20%	25%	30%
1	1.120	1.130	1.140	1.150	1.160	1.170	1.180	1.190	1.200	1.250	1.300
2	1.254	1.277	1.300	1.323	1.346	1.369	1.392	1.416	1.440	1.563	1.690
3	1.405	1.443	1.482	1.521	1.561	1.602	1.643	1.685	1.728	1.953	2.197
4	1.574	1.630	1.689	1.749	1.811	1.874	1.939	2.005	2.074	2.441	2.856
5	1.762	1.842	1.925	2.011	2.100	2.192	2.288	2.386	2.488	3.052	3.713
6	1.974	2.082	2.195	2.313	2.436	2.565	2.700	2.840	2.986	3.815	4.827
7	2.211	2.353	2.502	2.660	2.826	3.001	3.185	3.379	3.583	4.768	6.276
8	2.476	2.658	2.853	3.059	3.278	3.511	3.759	4.021	4.300	5.960	8.157
9	2.773	3.004	3.252	3.518	3.803	4.108	4.435	4.785	5.160	7.451	10.604
10	3.106	3.395	3.707	4.046	4.411	4.807	5.234	5.696	6.192	9.313	13.786
11	3.479	3.836	4.226	4.652	5.117	5.624	6.176	6.777	7.430	11.642	17.922
12	3.896	4.335	4.818	5.350	5.936	6.580	7.288	8.064	8.916	14.552	23.298
13	4.363	4.898	5.492	6.153	6.886	7.699	8.599	9.596	10.699	18.190	30.288
14	4.887	5.535	6.261	7.076	7.988	9.007	10.147	11.420	12.839	22.737	39.374
15	5.474	6.254	7.138	8.137	9.266	10.539	11.974	13.590	15.407	28.422	51.186
16	6.130	7.067	8.137	9.358	10.748	12.330	14.129	16.172	18.488	35.527	66.542
17	6.866	7.986	9.276	10.761	12.468	14.426	16.672	19.244	22.186	44.409	86.504
18	7.690	9.024	10.575	12.375	14.463	16.879	19.673	22.091	26.623	55.511	112.460
19	8.613	10.197	12.056	14.232	16.777	19.748	23.214	27.252	31.948	69.389	146.190
20	9.646	11.523	13.743	16.367	19.461	23.106	27.393	32.429	38.338	86.736	190.050
25	17.000	21.231	26.462	32.919	40.874	50.658	62.669	77.388	95.396	264.700	705.640
30	29.960	39.116	50.950	66.212	85.850	111.070	143.370	184.680	237.380	807.790	2,620.000
40	93.051	132.780	188.880	267.860	378.720	533.870	750.380	1,051.700	1,469.800	7,523.200	36,119.000
50	289.000	450.740	700.230	1,083.700	1,670.700	2,566.200	3,927.400	5,988.900	9,100.400	70,065.000	497,929.000

Exhibit A-2   Future Value (Compounded Sum) of $1 Paid in at the End of Each Period for a Given Number of Time Periods (an Annuity) $FV = \dfrac{(1 + i)^n - 1}{i}$

Period	1%	2%	3%	4%	5%	6%	7%	8%	9%	10%	11%
1	1.000	1.000	1.000	1.000	1.000	1.000	1.000	1.000	1.000	1.000	1.000
2	2.010	2.020	2.030	2.040	2.050	2.060	2.070	2.080	2.090	2.100	2.110
3	3.030	3.060	3.091	3.122	3.153	3.184	3.215	3.246	3.278	3.310	3.342
4	4.060	4.122	4.184	4.246	4.310	4.375	4.440	4.506	4.573	4.641	4.710
5	5.101	5.204	5.309	5.416	5.526	5.637	5.751	5.867	5.985	6.105	6.228
6	6.152	6.308	6.468	6.633	6.802	6.975	7.153	7.336	7.523	7.716	7.913
7	7.214	7.434	7.662	7.898	8.142	8.394	8.654	8.923	9.200	9.487	9.783
8	8.286	8.583	8.892	9.214	9.549	9.897	10.260	10.637	11.028	11.436	11.859
9	9.369	9.755	10.159	10.583	11.027	11.491	11.978	12.488	13.021	13.579	14.164
10	10.462	10.950	11.464	12.006	12.578	13.181	13.816	14.487	15.193	15.937	16.722
11	11.567	12.169	12.808	13.486	14.207	14.972	15.784	16.645	17.560	18.531	19.561
12	12.683	13.412	14.192	15.026	15.917	16.870	17.888	18.977	20.141	21.384	22.713
13	13.809	14.680	15.618	16.627	17.713	18.882	20.141	21.495	22.953	24.523	26.212
14	14.947	15.974	17.086	18.292	19.599	21.015	22.550	24.215	26.019	27.975	30.095
15	16.097	17.293	18.599	20.024	21.579	23.276	25.129	27.152	29.361	31.772	34.405
16	17.258	18.639	20.157	21.825	23.657	25.673	27.888	30.324	33.003	35.950	39.190
17	18.430	20.012	21.762	23.698	25.840	20.213	30.840	33.750	36.974	40.545	44.501
18	19.615	21.412	23.414	25.645	28.132	30.906	33.999	37.450	41.301	45.599	50.396
19	20.811	22.841	25.117	27.671	30.539	33.760	37.379	41.446	46.018	51.159	56.939
20	22.019	24.297	26.870	29.778	33.066	36.786	40.995	45.762	51.160	57.275	64.203
25	28.243	32.030	36.459	41.646	47.727	54.865	63.249	73.106	84.701	98.347	114.410
30	34.785	40.588	47.575	56.085	66.439	79.058	94.461	113.280	136.310	164.490	199.020
40	48.886	60.402	75.401	95.026	120.800	154.760	199.640	259.060	337.890	442.590	581.830
50	64.463	84.579	112.800	152.670	209.350	290.340	406.530	573.770	815.080	1,163.900	1,668.800

Exhibit A-2   (Concluded)

Period	12%	13%	14%	15%	16%	17%	18%	19%	20%	25%	30%
1	1.000	1.000	1.000	1.000	1.000	1.000	1.000	1.000	1.000	1.000	1.000
2	2.120	2.130	2.140	2.150	2.160	2.170	2.180	2.190	2.200	2.250	2.300
3	3.374	3.407	3.440	3.473	3.506	3.539	3.572	3.606	3.640	3.813	3.990
4	4.779	4.850	4.921	4.993	5.066	5.141	5.215	5.291	5.368	5.766	6.187
5	6.353	6.480	6.610	6.742	6.877	7.014	7.154	7.297	7.442	8.207	9.043
6	8.115	8.323	8.536	8.754	8.977	9.207	9.442	9.683	9.930	11.259	12.756
7	10.089	10.405	10.730	11.067	11.414	11.772	12.142	12.523	12.916	15.073	17.583
8	12.300	12.757	13.233	13.727	14.240	14.773	15.327	15.902	16.499	19.842	23.858
9	14.776	15.416	16.085	16.786	17.519	18.285	19.086	19.923	20.799	25.802	32.015
10	17.549	18.420	19.337	20.304	21.321	22.393	23.521	24.701	25.959	33.253	42.619
11	20.655	21.814	23.045	24.349	25.733	27.200	28.755	30.404	32.150	42.566	56.405
12	24.133	25.650	27.271	29.002	30.850	32.824	34.931	37.180	39.581	54.208	74.327
13	28.029	29.985	32.089	34.352	36.786	39.404	42.219	45.244	48.497	68.760	97.625
14	32.393	34.883	37.581	40.505	43.672	47.103	50.818	54.841	59.196	86.949	127.910
15	37.280	40.417	43.842	47.580	51.660	56.110	60.965	66.261	72.035	109.690	167.290
16	42.753	46.672	50.980	55.717	60.925	66.649	72.939	79.850	87.442	138.110	218.470
17	48.884	53.739	59.118	65.075	71.673	78.979	87.068	96.022	105.930	173.640	285.010
18	55.750	61.725	68.394	75.836	84.141	93.406	103.740	115.270	128.120	218.050	371.520
19	63.440	70.749	78.969	88.212	98.603	110.290	123.410	138.170	154.740	273.560	483.970
20	72.052	80.947	91.025	102.440	115.380	130.030	146.630	165.420	186.690	342.950	630.170
25	133.330	155.620	181.870	212.790	249.210	292.110	342.600	402.040	471.980	1,054.800	2,348.800
30	241.330	293.200	356.790	434.750	530.310	647.440	790.950	966.700	1,181.900	3,227.200	8,730.000
40	767.090	1,013.700	1,342.000	1,779.100	2,360.800	3,134.500	4,163.210	5,529.800	7,343.900	30,089.000	120,393.000
50	2,400.000	3,459.500	4,994.500	7,217.700	10,436.000	15,090.000	21,813.000	31,515.000	45,497.000	80,256.000	165,976.000

Exhibit A–3 Present Value of $1 to Be Received at the End of a Given Number of Time Periods $PV = \dfrac{1}{(1+i)^n}$

Period	1%	2%	3%	4%	5%	6%	7%	8%	9%	10%	11%	12%
1	0.990	0.980	0.971	0.962	0.952	0.943	0.935	0.926	0.917	0.909	0.901	0.893
2	0.980	0.961	0.943	0.925	0.907	0.890	0.873	0.857	0.842	0.826	0.812	0.797
3	0.971	0.942	0.915	0.889	0.864	0.840	0.816	0.794	0.772	0.751	0.731	0.712
4	0.961	0.924	0.885	0.855	0.823	0.792	0.763	0.735	0.708	0.683	0.659	0.636
5	0.951	0.906	0.863	0.822	0.784	0.747	0.713	0.681	0.650	0.621	0.593	0.567
6	0.942	0.888	0.837	0.790	0.746	0.705	0.666	0.630	0.596	0.564	0.535	0.507
7	0.933	0.871	0.813	0.760	0.711	0.665	0.623	0.583	0.547	0.513	0.482	0.452
8	0.923	0.853	0.789	0.731	0.677	0.627	0.582	0.540	0.502	0.467	0.434	0.404
9	0.914	0.837	0.766	0.703	0.645	0.592	0.544	0.500	0.460	0.424	0.391	0.361
10	0.905	0.820	0.744	0.676	0.614	0.558	0.508	0.463	0.422	0.386	0.352	0.322
11	0.896	0.804	0.722	0.650	0.585	0.527	0.475	0.429	0.388	0.350	0.317	0.287
12	0.887	0.788	0.701	0.625	0.557	0.497	0.444	0.397	0.356	0.319	0.286	0.257
13	0.879	0.773	0.681	0.601	0.530	0.469	0.415	0.368	0.326	0.290	0.258	0.229
14	0.870	0.758	0.661	0.577	0.505	0.442	0.388	0.340	0.299	0.263	0.232	0.205
15	0.861	0.743	0.642	0.555	0.481	0.417	0.362	0.315	0.275	0.239	0.209	0.183
16	0.853	0.728	0.623	0.534	0.458	0.394	0.339	0.292	0.252	0.218	0.188	0.163
17	0.844	0.714	0.605	0.513	0.436	0.371	0.317	0.270	0.231	0.198	0.170	0.146
18	0.836	0.700	0.587	0.494	0.416	0.350	0.296	0.250	0.212	0.180	0.153	0.130
19	0.828	0.686	0.570	0.475	0.396	0.331	0.277	0.232	0.194	0.164	0.138	0.116
20	0.820	0.673	0.554	0.456	0.377	0.312	0.258	0.215	0.178	0.149	0.124	0.104
25	0.780	0.610	0.478	0.375	0.295	0.233	0.184	0.146	0.116	0.092	0.074	0.059
30	0.742	0.552	0.412	0.308	0.231	0.174	0.131	0.099	0.075	0.057	0.044	0.033
40	0.672	0.453	0.307	0.208	0.142	0.097	0.067	0.046	0.032	0.022	0.015	0.011
50	0.608	0.372	0.228	0.141	0.087	0.054	0.034	0.021	0.013	0.009	0.005	0.003

Exhibit A–3 (Concluded)

Period	13%	14%	15%	16%	17%	18%	19%	20%	25%	30%	35%	40%	50%
1	0.885	0.877	0.870	0.862	0.855	0.847	0.840	0.833	0.800	0.769	0.741	0.714	0.667
2	0.783	0.769	0.756	0.743	0.731	0.718	0.706	0.694	0.640	0.592	0.549	0.510	0.444
3	0.693	0.675	0.658	0.641	0.624	0.609	0.593	0.579	0.512	0.455	0.406	0.364	0.296
4	0.613	0.592	0.572	0.552	0.534	0.515	0.499	0.482	0.410	0.350	0.301	0.260	0.198
5	0.543	0.519	0.497	0.476	0.456	0.437	0.419	0.402	0.320	0.269	0.223	0.186	0.132
6	0.480	0.456	0.432	0.410	0.390	0.370	0.352	0.335	0.262	0.207	0.165	0.133	0.088
7	0.425	0.400	0.376	0.354	0.333	0.314	0.296	0.279	0.210	0.159	0.122	0.095	0.059
8	0.376	0.351	0.327	0.305	0.285	0.266	0.249	0.233	0.168	0.123	0.091	0.068	0.039
9	0.333	0.300	0.284	0.263	0.243	0.225	0.209	0.194	0.134	0.094	0.067	0.048	0.026
10	0.295	0.270	0.247	0.227	0.208	0.191	0.176	0.162	0.107	0.073	0.050	0.035	0.017
11	0.261	0.237	0.215	0.195	0.178	0.162	0.148	0.135	0.086	0.056	0.037	0.025	0.012
12	0.231	0.208	0.187	0.168	0.152	0.137	0.124	0.112	0.069	0.043	0.027	0.018	0.008
13	0.204	0.182	0.163	0.145	0.130	0.116	0.104	0.093	0.055	0.033	0.020	0.013	0.005
14	0.181	0.160	0.141	0.125	0.111	0.099	0.088	0.078	0.044	0.025	0.015	0.009	0.003
15	0.160	0.140	0.123	0.108	0.095	0.084	0.074	0.065	0.035	0.020	0.011	0.006	0.002
16	0.141	0.123	0.107	0.093	0.081	0.071	0.062	0.054	0.028	0.015	0.008	0.005	0.002
17	0.125	0.108	0.093	0.080	0.069	0.060	0.052	0.045	0.023	0.012	0.006	0.003	0.001
18	0.111	0.095	0.081	0.069	0.059	0.051	0.044	0.038	0.018	0.009	0.005	0.002	0.001
19	0.098	0.083	0.070	0.060	0.051	0.043	0.037	0.031	0.014	0.007	0.003	0.002	0
20	0.087	0.073	0.061	0.051	0.043	0.037	0.031	0.026	0.012	0.005	0.002	0.001	0
25	0.047	0.038	0.030	0.024	0.020	0.016	0.013	0.010	0.004	0.001	0.001	0	0
30	0.026	0.020	0.015	0.012	0.009	0.007	0.005	0.004	0.001	0	0	0	0
40	0.008	0.005	0.004	0.003	0.002	0.001	0.001	0.001	0	0	0	0	0
50	0.002	0.001	0.001	0.001	0	0	0	0	0	0	0	0	0

Exhibit A–4   Present Value of $1 Received at the End of Each Period for a Given Number of Time Periods (an Annuity)

$$PV = \frac{1 - \dfrac{1}{(1 + i)^n}}{i}$$

Period	1%	2%	3%	4%	5%	6%	7%	8%	9%	10%	11%	12%
1	0.990	0.980	0.971	0.962	0.952	0.943	0.935	0.926	0.917	0.909	0.901	0.893
2	1.970	1.942	1.913	1.886	1.859	1.833	1.808	1.783	1.759	1.736	1.713	1.690
3	2.941	2.884	2.829	2.775	2.723	2.673	2.624	2.577	2.531	2.487	2.444	2.402
4	3.902	3.808	3.717	3.630	3.546	3.465	3.387	3.312	3.240	3.170	3.102	3.037
5	4.853	4.713	4.580	4.452	4.329	4.212	4.100	3.993	3.890	3.791	3.696	3.605
6	5.795	5.601	5.417	5.242	5.076	4.917	4.767	4.623	4.486	4.355	4.231	4.111
7	6.728	6.472	6.230	6.002	5.786	5.582	5.389	5.206	5.033	4.868	4.712	4.564
8	7.652	7.325	7.020	6.733	6.463	6.210	5.971	5.747	5.535	5.335	5.146	4.968
9	8.566	8.162	7.786	7.435	7.108	6.802	6.515	6.247	5.995	5.759	5.537	5.328
10	9.471	8.983	8.530	8.111	7.722	7.360	7.024	6.710	6.418	6.145	5.889	5.650
11	10.368	9.787	9.253	8.760	8.306	7.887	7.499	7.139	6.805	6.495	6.207	5.938
12	11.255	10.575	9.954	9.385	8.863	8.384	7.943	7.536	7.161	6.814	6.492	6.194
13	12.134	11.348	10.635	9.986	9.394	8.853	8.358	7.904	7.487	7.103	6.750	6.424
14	13.004	12.106	11.296	10.563	9.899	9.295	8.745	8.244	7.786	7.367	6.982	6.628
15	13.865	12.849	11.939	11.118	10.380	9.712	9.108	8.559	8.061	7.606	7.191	6.811
16	14.718	13.578	12.561	11.652	10.838	10.106	9.447	8.851	8.313	7.824	7.379	6.974
17	15.562	14.292	13.166	12.166	11.274	10.477	9.763	9.122	8.544	8.022	7.549	7.102
18	16.398	14.992	13.754	12.659	11.690	10.828	10.059	9.372	8.756	8.201	7.702	7.250
19	17.226	15.678	14.324	13.134	12.085	11.158	10.336	9.604	8.950	8.365	7.839	7.366
20	18.046	16.351	14.877	13.590	12.462	11.470	10.594	9.818	9.129	8.514	7.963	7.469
25	22.023	19.523	17.413	15.622	14.094	12.783	11.654	10.675	9.823	9.077	8.422	7.843
30	25.808	22.396	19.600	17.292	15.372	13.765	12.409	11.258	10.274	9.427	8.694	8.055
40	32.835	27.355	23.115	19.793	17.159	15.046	13.332	11.925	10.757	9.779	8.951	8.244
50	39.196	31.424	25.730	21.482	18.256	15.762	13.801	12.233	10.962	9.915	9.042	8.304

Exhibit A–4   (Concluded)

Period	13%	14%	15%	16%	17%	18%	19%	20%	25%	30%	35%	40%	50%
1	0.885	0.877	0.870	0.862	0.855	0.847	0.840	0.833	0.800	0.769	0.741	0.714	0.667
2	1.668	1.647	1.626	1.605	1.585	1.566	1.547	1.528	1.440	1.361	1.289	1.224	1.111
3	2.361	2.322	2.283	2.246	2.210	2.174	2.140	2.106	1.952	1.816	1.696	1.589	1.407
4	2.974	2.914	2.855	2.798	2.743	2.690	2.639	2.589	2.362	2.166	1.997	1.849	1.605
5	3.517	3.433	3.352	3.274	3.199	3.127	3.058	2.991	2.689	2.436	2.220	2.035	1.737
6	3.998	3.889	3.784	3.685	3.589	3.498	3.410	3.326	2.951	2.643	2.385	2.168	1.824
7	4.423	4.288	4.160	4.039	3.922	3.812	3.706	3.605	3.161	2.802	2.508	2.263	1.883
8	4.799	4.639	4.487	4.344	4.207	4.078	3.954	3.837	3.329	2.925	2.598	2.331	1.922
9	5.132	4.946	4.772	4.607	4.451	4.303	4.163	4.031	3.463	3.019	2.665	2.379	1.948
10	5.426	5.216	5.019	4.833	4.659	4.494	4.339	4.192	3.571	3.092	2.715	2.414	1.965
11	5.687	5.453	5.234	5.029	4.836	4.656	4.486	4.327	3.656	3.147	2.752	2.438	1.977
12	5.918	5.660	5.421	5.197	4.988	4.793	4.611	4.439	3.725	3.190	2.779	2.456	1.985
13	6.122	5.842	5.583	5.342	5.118	4.910	4.715	4.533	3.780	3.223	2.799	2.469	1.990
14	6.302	6.002	5.724	5.468	5.229	5.008	4.802	4.611	3.824	3.249	2.814	2.478	1.993
15	6.462	6.142	5.847	5.575	5.324	5.092	4.876	4.675	3.859	3.268	2.825	2.484	1.995
16	6.604	6.265	5.954	5.668	5.405	5.162	4.938	4.730	3.887	3.283	2.834	2.489	1.997
17	6.729	6.373	6.047	5.749	5.475	5.222	4.988	4.775	3.910	3.295	2.840	2.492	1.998
18	6.840	6.467	6.128	5.818	5.534	5.273	5.033	4.812	3.928	3.304	2.844	2.494	1.999
19	6.938	6.550	6.198	5.877	5.584	5.316	5.070	4.843	3.942	3.311	2.848	2.496	1.999
20	7.025	6.623	6.259	5.929	5.628	5.353	5.101	4.870	3.954	3.316	2.850	2.497	1.999
25	7.330	6.873	6.464	6.097	5.766	5.467	5.195	4.948	3.985	3.329	2.856	2.499	2.000
30	7.496	7.003	6.566	6.177	5.829	5.517	5.235	4.979	3.995	3.332	2.857	2.500	2.000
40	7.634	7.105	6.642	6.233	5.871	5.548	5.258	4.997	3.999	3.333	2.857	2.500	2.000
50	7.675	7.133	6.661	6.246	5.880	5.554	5.262	4.999	4.000	3.333	2.857	2.500	2.000

GLOSSARY

accident benefits Automobile insurance that covers medical expenses for people injured in one's car. 232

account executive A licensed individual who buys or sells securities for clients; also called a *stockbroker*. 333

actual cash value (ACV) A claim settlement method in which the insured receives payment based on the current replacement cost of a damaged or lost item, less depreciation. 230

adjusted balance method The assessment of finance charges after payments made during the billing period have been subtracted. 168

adult life cycle The stages in the family situation and financial needs of an adult. 9

all risk A policy in which any event that causes loss or damage to the insured property is covered unless it is specifically excluded. 227

amortization The reduction of a loan balance through payments made over a period of time. 199

annual percentage rate (APR) The yearly interest rate quoted by a financial institution on a loan. The APR may be compounded more frequently than once a year, in which case the effective annual rate on the loan will be higher than the APR. 163

annual shareholder return A stock's annual dividend and increase in value divided by its beginning-of-year stock price. 328

appraisal An estimate of the current value of a property. 205

assets Cash and other property with a monetary value. 39

automated teller machine (ATM) A computer terminal used to conduct banking transactions. 105

average daily balance method A method of computing finance charges that uses a weighted average of the account balance throughout the current billing period. 168

average tax rate Total tax due divided by total income. 66

bankruptcy A set of federal laws that allow you to either restructure your debts or remove certain debts. 21

bear market Occurs when investors are pessimistic about a nation's economy and sell their stocks. 327

bearer bond A bond that is not registered in the investor's name. 355

beneficiary A person designated to receive something, such as life insurance proceeds, from the insured. 254

beneficiary A person who has been named to receive property under a will. 440

beta An index that compares the risk associated with a specific stock issue with the risk of the stock market in general. 329

blue-chip stock A safe investment that generally attracts conservative investors. 321

bodily injury liability Coverage for the risk of financial loss due to legal expenses, medical costs, lost wages, and other expenses associated with injuries caused by an automobile accident for which the insured was responsible. 232

bond indenture A legal document that details all the conditions relating to a bond issue. 349

budget A specific plan for spending income. 46

budget deficit The amount by which actual spending exceeds planned spending. 50

budget surplus The amount by which actual spending is less than planned spending. 50

budget variance The difference between the amount budgeted and the actual amount received or spent. 49

bull market Occurs when investors are optimistic about a nation's economy and buy stocks. 327

call feature A feature that allows the corporation to call in or buy outstanding bonds from current bondholders before the maturity date. 351

callable preferred stocks Stocks that a corporation may exchange, at its option, for a specified amount of money. 318

capacity The borrower's financial ability to meet credit obligations. 151

capital The borrower's assets or net worth. 151

capital gain distributions The payments made to a fund's shareholders that result from the sale of securities in the fund's portfolio. 392

capital gains yield A stock's increase in value divided by its beginning-of-year stock price. 328

capitalization The total amount of securities—stocks and bonds—issued by a corporation. 322

cash flow The actual inflow and outflow of cash during a given time period. 41

cash flow statement A financial statement that summarizes cash receipts and payments for a given period. 41

cash value The amount received after giving up a life insurance policy. 250

character The borrower's attitude toward credit obligations. 151

chartered bank A financial institution that offers a full range of financial services to individuals, businesses, and government agencies. 109

churning The excessive buying and selling of securities to generate commissions. 333

closed-end credit One-time loans that the borrower pays back in a specified period of time with a predetermined payment schedule. 133

closed-end fund A mutual fund whose shares are issued by an investment company only when the fund is originally set up. 378

closing costs Fees and charges paid when a real estate transaction is completed; also called settlement costs. 201

co-insurance clause A policy provision that requires a homeowner to pay for part of the losses if the property is not insured for the specified percentage of the replacement value. 229

co-operative housing A type of subsidized housing in which half the units have geared-to-income rental prices. 192

co-payment A provision under which the insured pays a flat dollar amount each time a covered medical service is received after the deductible has been met. 270

codicil A document that modifies provisions in an existing will. 443

collateral A valuable asset that is pledged to ensure loan payments. 152

collision Automobile insurance that pays for damage to the insured's car when it is involved in an accident. 233

compounding A process that calculates interest based on previously earned interest. 17

comprehensive physical damage Automobile insurance that covers financial loss from damage to a vehicle caused by a risk other than a collision, such as fire, theft, glass breakage, hail, or vandalism. 233

conditions The general economic conditions that can affect a borrower's ability to repay a loan. 152

condominium An individually owned housing unit in a building with several such units. 192

consumer credit The use of credit for personal needs (except a home mortgage). 130

consumer proposal A maximum five-year plan for paying creditors all or a portion of a debt owed. 176

contingent deferred sales load A 1- to 6-percent charge that shareholders pay when they withdraw their investment from a mutual fund. 380

convertible bond A bond that can be exchanged, at the owner's option, for a specified number of shares of the corporation's common stocks. 351

corporate bond A corporation's written pledge to repay a specified amount of money, along with interest. 291, 348

credit An arrangement to receive cash, goods, or services now and pay for them in the future. 130

credit bureau A reporting agency that assembles credit and other information about consumers. 144

credit insurance Any type of insurance that ensures repayment of a loan in the event the borrower is unable to repay it. 170

credit limit The dollar amount, which may or may not be borrowed, that a lender makes available to a borrower. 134

credit reporting legislation
Fair Credit Reporting Act—Applicable in British Columbia, Ontario, Nova Scotia, and Prince Edward Island
Credit Reporting Agencies Act—Applicable in Saskatchewan and Newfoundland
Personal Investigations Act—Applicable in Manitoba
Consumer Protection Act—Applicable in Quebec 148

credit union/*caisse populaire* A user-owned, nonprofit co-operative financial institution that is organized for the benefit of its members. 109

cumulative preferred stocks Stocks with unpaid dividends that accumulate and must be paid before any cash dividend is paid to common shareholders. 320

current liabilities Debts that must be paid within a short time, usually less than a year. 41

current yield Determined by dividing the dollar amount of annual interest from an investment by its current market value. 366

cyclical stock A stock that follows the business cycle of advances and declines in the economy. 321

debenture A bond that is backed only by the reputation of the issuing corporation. 350

deductions Expenses that can be deducted from total income, such as child care expenses, union dues, disability support payments, investment counselling fees, and certain employment-related expenses. 64

deed or title A document that transfers ownership of property from one party to another. 203

defensive stock A stock that remains stable during declines in the economy. 321

defined benefit pension plan A plan that specifies the benefits the employee will receive at the normal retirement age. 418

defined contribution pension plan Also called a "money purchase pension plan," this plan specifies the contribution from the employee and/or employer but does not guarantee the pension benefit you will receive. 419

depreciated value A reduction in the value of an object, based upon its age and the percent it has decreased each year. 224

direct investment plan A plan that allows shareholders to purchase stocks directly from a corporation without having to use an account executive or a brokerage firm. 338

disability income insurance Provides payments to replace income when an insured person is unable to work. 263

discretionary income Money left over after paying for housing, food, and other necessities. 43

discretionary order An order to buy or sell a security that lets the account executive decide when to execute the transaction and at what price. 334

diversification The process of spreading your assets among several types of investments to lessen risk. 294

diversification Investment technique that involves combining many assets in a portfolio to reduce its risk. 337

dividend A distribution of money, stocks, or other property that a corporation pays to shareholders. 290

dividend reinvestment plan A plan that allows current shareholders the option to reinvest or use their cash dividends to purchase stocks of the corporation. 338

dividend yield A stock's annual dividend divided by its beginning-of-year stock price. If the dividend is divided by the end-of-year stock price, it is referred to as its *trailing* dividend yield. 328

dollar cost averaging A long-term technique used by investors who purchase an equal dollar amount of the same stocks at equal intervals. 337

double indemnity A benefit under which the company pays twice the face value of the policy if the insured's death results from an accident. 255

driver classification A category based on the driver's age, gender, marital status, driving record, and driving habits; used to determine automobile insurance rates. 235

earnings per share (EPS) A corporation's after-tax earnings divided by the number of outstanding shares of common stocks. 329

economics The study of how wealth is created and distributed. 11

effective annual rate (EAR) A formula that calculates the effective return, taking compounding into account.

$$\text{EAR} = \left(1 + \frac{k}{m}\right)^m - 1$$

m = number of compounding periods in a year
k = rate of return quoted for a year. 115

emergency fund An amount of money you can obtain quickly in case of immediate need. 280

employment income Remuneration received for personal effort. 62

equity capital Money that a business obtains from its owners. 290

escrow account Money, usually deposited with the lending institution, for the payment of property taxes and homeowner's insurance. 203

estate Everything one owns. 435

estate planning A definite plan for the administration and disposition of one's property during one's lifetime and at one's death. 435

excise tax A tax imposed on specific goods and services, such as gasoline, cigarettes, alcoholic beverages, tires, and air travel. 60

face value The dollar amount the bondholder will receive at the bond's maturity. 348

family of funds A group of mutual funds managed by one investment company. 385

financial plan A formalized report that summarizes your current financial situation, analyzes your financial needs, and recommends future financial activities. 23

formal will A will that is usually prepared with an attorney's assistance. 440

future value The amount to which current savings will increase based on a certain interest rate and a certain time period; typically involves compounding. 17

government bond The written pledge of a government or a municipality to repay a specified sum of money, along with interest. 291

growth stock A stock issued by a corporation that has the potential to earn profits above the average profits of all firms in the economy. 321

Guaranteed Investment Certificates (GICs) Term deposits made for a longer period, usually from one to five years. 114

guardian A person who assumes responsibility for providing children with personal care and managing the deceased's estate for them. 441

hazard A factor that increases the likelihood of loss through some peril. 215

high-risk pool Consists of people who are unable to obtain automobile insurance due to poor driving or accident records and must obtain coverage at high rates. 236

holographic will A handwritten will. 440

home equity line of credit A personal line of credit based on the current market value of your home less the amount still owed on the mortgage. 138

homeowner's insurance Coverage for a place of residence and its associated financial risks. 223

household inventory A list or other documentation of personal belongings, with purchase dates and cost information. 224

income Inflow of cash to an individual or a household. 42

income dividends The earnings a fund pays to shareholders after it has deducted expenses from its dividend and interest income. 392

income stock A stock that pays higher-than-average dividends. 321

incontestability clause A provision stating that the insurer cannot dispute the validity of a policy after a specified period. 254

index A statistical measure of the changes in a portfolio of stocks representing a portion of the overall market. 313

inflation A rise in the general level of prices. 13

initial public offering (IPO) Occurs when a corporation sells stock to the general public for the first time. 331

insolvency The inability to pay debts when they are due because liabilities far exceed the value of assets. 41

insurance Protection against possible financial loss. 215

insurance company A risk-sharing firm that assumes financial responsibility for losses that may result from an insured risk. 215

insured A person covered by an insurance policy. 215

insurer An insurance company. 215

interest A periodic charge for the use of credit. 134

interest-adjusted index A method of evaluating the cost of life insurance by taking into account the time value of money. 257

intestate Without a valid will. 438

investment bank A financial firm that assists corporations in raising funds, usually by helping to sell new security issues. 331

investment company A firm that, for a management fee, invests the pooled funds of small investors in securities appropriate to its stated investment objectives. 378

investment income Income from property, including income in the form of interest, dividends, and rents net of expenses. 62

junk bond A type of bond that offers a very high return but is very risky as the bond is nearing or currently in default. 365

large-cap stock A stock issued by a large corporation that has a large amount of stocks outstanding and a large amount of capitalization. 322

lease A legal document that defines the conditions of a rental agreement. 189

liabilities Amounts owed to others. 40

liability Legal responsibility for the financial cost of another person's losses or injuries. 222

limit order A request to buy or sell stock at a specified price. 334

liquidity The ability to readily convert financial resources into cash without a loss in value. 21

liquidity The ability to buy or sell an investment quickly without substantially affecting the investment's value. 289

liquid assets Cash and items of value that can easily be converted to cash. 39

living trust A trust that is created and provides benefits during the settlor's lifetime. 445

living will A document that enables an individual, while well, to express the intention that life be allowed to end (i.e., no extraordinary medical measures or life support equipment be used) if he or she becomes terminally ill. 443

load fund A mutual fund in which investors pay a commission (as high as 8.5 percent) every time they purchase or sell shares. 379

long-term care (LTC) Provides day-in, day-out care for long-term illness or disability. 268

long-term liabilities Debts that are not required to be paid in full until more than a year from now. 41

Managed Asset Program (MAP) A program allowing an investor to invest in portfolios grouping together many different mutual funds. 385

manufactured home A housing unit that is fully or partially assembed in a factory before being moved to the living site. 192

margin A speculative technique whereby an investor borrows part of the money needed to buy a particular stock. 338

marginal tax rate The rate of tax paid on the next dollar of taxable income. 65

market order A request to buy or sell stocks at the current market value. 334

market timer An individual who helps investors decide when to switch their investments from one fund to another fund, usually within the same family of funds. 386

maturity date For a corporate bond, the date on which the corporation is to repay the borrowed money. 348

money management Day-to-day financial activities necessary to manage current personal economic resources while working toward long-term financial security. 36

money market fund A savings–investment plan offered by investment companies, with earnings based on investments in various short-term financial instruments. 109

mortgage A long-term loan on a specific piece of property, such as a home or other real estate. 193

mortgage bond A corporate bond secured by various assets of the issuing firm. 350

mutual fund An investment alternative chosen by people who pool their money to buy stocks, bonds, and other securities selected by professional managers employed by an investment company. 292

mutual fund An investment chosen by people who pool their money to buy stocks, bonds, and other financial securities selected by professional managers who work for an investment company. 376

named perils A policy in which only those perils that are specifically listed will be covered should a loss occur. 227

NASDAQ (pronounced "nazzdack") An electronic marketplace for over 6,000 stocks. 332

negligence Failure to take ordinary or reasonable care in a situation. 222

net asset value (NAV) The current market value of the securities contained in the mutual fund's portfolio minus the mutual fund's liabilities divided by the number of shares outstanding. 379

net business income Net income from an activity that is carried out for profit, after expenses have been deducted. 62

net income Total income reduced by certain deductions, such as contributions to an RRSP or RPP. 63

net worth The difference between total assets and total liabilities. 41

no-fault insurance An automobile insurance program in which drivers involved in accidents collect medical expenses, lost wages, and related injury costs from their own insurance companies. 233

no-load fund A mutual fund in which the individual investor pays no sales charge. 380

nonforfeiture clause A provision that allows the insured not to forfeit all accrued benefits. 254

nonparticipating policy Life insurance that does not provide policy dividends. 250

nonprofit housing Rental housing owned by a community group, religious group, or nonprofit organization to provide affordable housing. 192

notarial will A will made in the presence of a notary and at least one witness, and that does not require probate. Available only in Quebec. 440

odd lot Fewer than 100 shares of a particular stock. 335

open-end credit A line of credit in which loans are made on a continuous basis and the borrower is billed periodically for at least partial payment. 133

open-end fund A mutual fund whose shares are issued and redeemed by the investment company at the request of investors. 379

opportunity cost What a person gives up by making a choice. 5

option The right to buy or sell stocks at a predetermined price during a specified period of time. 341

over-the-counter (OTC) market A network of dealers who buy and sell the stocks of corporations that are not listed on a securities exchange. 332

overdraft protection An automatic loan made to chequing account customers to cover the amount of cheques written in excess of the available balance in the account. 119

participating policy Life insurance that provides policy dividends. 250

penny stock A stock that typically sells for less than $1 per share. 322

peril The cause of a possible loss. 215

personal articles endorsement Additional property insurance to cover the damage or loss of a specific item of high value. 224

personal balance sheet A financial statement that reports what an individual or a family owns and owes; also called a *net worth statement*. 39

personal financial planning The process of managing your money to achieve personal economic satisfaction. 3

personal line of credit A prearranged loan from a bank for a maximum specified amount. 134

policy A written contract for insurance. 215

policyholder A person who owns an insurance policy. 215

power of attorney A legal document authorizing someone to act on one's behalf. 443

pre-emptive right The right of current shareholders to purchase any new stocks the corporation issues before it is offered to the general public. 316

pre-nuptial agreement A documentary agreement between spouses before marriage. 443

premium The amount of money a policyholder is charged for an insurance policy. 215

present value The current value for a future amount based on a certain interest rate and a certain time period; also referred to as discounting. 17

previous balance method A method of computing finance charges that gives no credit for payments made during the billing period. 168

price–earnings (P/E) ratio The price of a share of stock divided by the corporation's earnings per share of stocks outstanding over the last 12 months. 329

primary market A market in which an investor purchases financial securities, via an investment bank or other representative, from the issuer of those securities. 331

probate The legal procedure of proving a valid or invalid will. 440

property damage Insurance that covers damage to another's property, as by an automobile accident. 233

proxy A legal form that lists the issues to be decided at a shareholders' meeting and requests that shareholders transfer their voting rights to some individual or individuals 315

pure risk A risk in which there is only a chance of loss; also called *insurable risk*. 216

rate cap A limit on the increases and decreases in the interest rate charged on an adjustable-rate mortgage. 200

rate of return The percentage of increase in the value of savings as a result of interest earned; also called *yield*. 115

rating territory The place of residence used to determine a person's automobile insurance premium. 235

record date The date on which a shareholder must be registered on the corporation's books in order to receive dividend payments. 316

refinancing The process of obtaining a new mortgage on a home to get a lower interest rate. 201

registered bond A bond that is registered in the owner's name by the issuing company. 355

registered coupon bond A bond that is registered for principal only, and not for interest. 355

Registered Retirement Savings Plan (RRSP) An investment vehicle that allows you to shelter your savings from income taxes. 421

reinvestment plan A service provided by an investment company in which shareholder income dividends and capital gain distributions are automatically reinvested to purchase additional shares of the fund. 395

replacement value A claim settlement method in which the insured receives the full cost of repairing or replacing a damaged or lost item. 230

reverse annuity mortgage (RAM) A loan based on the equity in a home that provides elderly homeowners with tax-free income and is paid back with interest when the home is sold or the homeowner dies. 408

rider An addition of coverage to a standard insurance policy. 226

rider A document attached to a policy that modifies its coverage. 255

risk Chance or uncertainty of loss; may also mean "the insured." 215

round lot One hundred shares or multiples of 100 shares of a particular stock. 335

safety deposit box A private storage area at a financial institution with maximum security for valuables. 37

secondary market A market for existing financial securities that are currently traded among investors. 331

securities exchange A marketplace where member brokers who represent investors meet to buy and sell securities. 332

segregated fund An investment alternative in the form of an annuity that is similar to a mutual fund but that is less risky as it provides a certain degree of insurance to the investor. 292

self-insurance The process of establishing a monetary fund to cover the cost of a loss. 216

selling short Selling stocks that have been borrowed from a brokerage firm and must be replaced at a later date. 340

serial bonds Bonds of a single issue that mature on different dates. 352

settlor The creator of a trust; also called the grantor. 445

simple interest Interest computed on the principal, excluding previously earned interest. 16

sinking fund A fund to which annual or semi-annual deposits are made for the purpose of redeeming a bond issue. 352

small-cap stock A stock issued by a company that has a capitalization of $150 million or less. 322

speculative investment A high-risk investment made in the hope of earning a relatively large profit in a short time. 284

speculative risk A risk in which there is a chance of either loss or gain. 216

stock split A procedure in which the shares of common stocks owned by existing shareholders are divided into a larger number of shares. 317

stop order An order to sell a particular stock at the next available opportunity after its market price reaches a specified amount. 334

strict liability A situation in which a person is held responsible for intentional or unintentional actions. 222

subordinated debenture An unsecured bond that gives bondholders a claim secondary to that of other designated bondholders with respect to both interest payments and assets. 351

suicide clause A provision stating that if the insured dies by suicide during the first two years the policy is in force, the death benefit will equal the amount of the premium paid. 255

take-home pay Earnings after deductions for taxes and other items; also called *disposable income*. 43

tax audit A detailed examination of your tax return by the Canada Revenue Agency. 89

tax credit An amount subtracted directly from the amount of taxes owing. 68

tax evasion The use of illegal actions to reduce one's taxes. 79

tax planning The use of legitimate methods to reduce one's taxes. 79

taxable capital gains Net gains from the sale of capital assets such as stocks, bonds, and real estate. One-half of net capital gains are taxable. 62

taxable income The net amount of income, after allowable deductions, on which income tax is computed. 62

term deposits A deposit that is made for a specified term in exchange for a higher rate of return. Can be redeemed before maturity by earning a reduced rate of interest (paying a penalty). 113

term insurance Life insurance protection for a specified period of time;

sometimes called *temporary life insurance*. 246

testamentary trust A trust established by the creator's will that becomes effective upon his or her death. 445

time value of money Increases in an amount of money as a result of interest earned. 16

title insurance Insurance that, during the mortgage term, protects the owner or the lender against financial loss resulting from future defects in the title and from other unforeseen property claims not excluded by the policy. 201

trust A legal agreement that provides for the management and control of assets by one party for the benefit of another. 104

trust A legal arrangement through which one's assets are held by a trustee. 445

trustee A financially independent firm that acts as the bondholders' representative. 349

trustee A person or an institution that holds or manages property for the benefit of someone else under a trust agreement. 441

umbrella policy Supplementary personal liability coverage; also called a *personal catastrophe policy*. 225

uninsured motorist coverage Automobile insurance coverage for the cost of injuries to a person and members of his or her family caused by a driver with inadequate insurance or by a hit-and-run driver. 233

universal life A permanent life insurance policy that combines term insurance and investment elements. 251

values Ideas and principles that a person considers correct, desirable, and important. 4

variable-rate mortgage (VRM) A home loan with an interest rate that can change during the mortgage term due to changes in market interest rates; also called a *flexible-rate mortgage*. 200

vesting An employee's right to at least a portion of the benefits accrued under an employer pension plan, even if the employee leaves the company before retiring. 419

vicarious liability A situation in which a person is held legally responsible for the actions of another person. 222

voluntary medical payments Home insurance that pays the cost of minor accidental injuries on one's property. 226

whole life policy An insurance plan in which the policyholder pays a specified premium each year for as long as he or she lives; also called a *straight life policy*, a *cash-value life policy*, or an *ordinary life policy*. 248

will The legal declaration of a person's mind as to the disposition of his or her property after death. 438

yield The rate of return earned by an investor who holds a bond for a stated period of time. 366

yield to maturity A yield calculation that takes into account the relationships among a bond's maturity value, the time to maturity, the current price, and the dollar amount of interest. 368

zero-coupon bond A bond that is sold at a price far below its face value, makes no annual or semiannual interest payments, and is redeemed for its face value at maturity. 355

zoning laws Restrictions on how the property in an area can be used. 196

INDEX